MIGHTY REAL
An Anthology of African American Same Gender Loving Writing

Edited by
R. Bryant Smith & Darius Omar Williams

Effusses/Sangha Publishing

Mighty Real: An Anthology of African American Same Gender Loving Writing

Copyright © 2010 by R. Bryant Smith and Darius Omar Williams

Individual selections copyright © by their respective author(s)

Published by
Effusses/Sangha Publishing

All rights reserved. No part of this book may be reproduced or transmitted in any form or by any means without permission in writing from the publisher, except in the case of reviews.

10 9 8 7 6 5 4 3 2 1

First edition

Front Cover Photo Image Malaysia Andrews Ravore © 2010
Cover Design Concept by The Moon Poet © 2010
R. Bryant Smith editor photo copyright © 2010 by Star Studios
Darius Omar Williams editor photo copyright © 2010 by Darius Omar Williams

Printed in the United States of America

ISBN: 978-0-557-78068-6

Acknowledgements

I am eternally grateful to my dear friend Minister Norman Van Collins, Sr. who reminded me not to ever surrender to the violence of spiritual elitism and internalized oppression. I am forever indebted to the poignant force and spiritual magnitude of my illustrious co-editor R. Bryant Smith. I extend heartfelt thanks to Phillip B. Williams, L. Lamar Wilson and Joseph Lindsey, for their constant encouragement and strength during those languid hours when I felt dejected, defeated and discouraged, 'my brothers you spoke and I stood up'. Special thanks to Larry Duplechan for instilling in me the power of spoken truth both lyrical and spiritual. To Tim'm T. West, brotherman, you are a literary gem and your spirit is "easy, easy like sun day morning". Finally, to every writer in this book who lent their literary leers to the preceding hundreds of pages, I humbly say thank you. From my heart, muscle and core, I say thank you.

~ Darius Omar Williams ~

It is with my most grateful and esteemed gratitude that I offer a simple yet much needed word of appreciation to everyone who made this book become a reality. I extend a heartfelt thank you to my co-editor, my brother, my bristah, Darius Omar Williams, who dared dream and even in the midst of an amazing feat helped to steer this project to its completion! To Charles Michael Smith, Larry Duplechan, Charles W. Harvey, and Stanley Bennett Clay, I thank you for being humble mentors still steadfast in your convictions. I shall forever hold you gentlemen in the highest esteem in which you are so very deserving. To my brother in the struggle, Gregory McNeal, one day they shall know! To Mystalic Writing and Vince Wilson, just watching you young men develop has been a tonic to my soul. To the many friends we have met along this journey, thank you for your support, kind words, and genuine concern. To those who weren't so impressed with our efforts and felt the need to attempt to be a stumbling block, thank you too. Last, but not least, to every writer, artist, attorney, friend or foe who submitted to this great work, however large or small, whether accepted or rejected, always know that the buck never stops here! It was simply at this place and at this moment in time, our Creator found it necessary that our paths cross and that has made all the difference. Hence, I bid you all God's speed as I offer you this my most humble and sincere thank you!

~ R. Bryant Smith ~

TABLE OF CONTENTS

Acknowledgements	*Darius Omar Williams*	iii
Acknowledgements	*R. Bryant Smith*	iii
Introduction	*Darius Omar Williams*	ix

POETRY

We So Fierce	*Darius Omar Williams*	3
why I love black men	*Tim'm T. West*	4
Did Not See You Coming	*Marvin K. White*	6
Beauty	*Lucy Shumpert*	8
Attraction	*Rickey Laurentiis*	11
The Cucumber	*Charles W. Harvey*	12
Tattoo	*Reginald Harris*	13
8 ways of looking at pussy	*Letta Neely*	14
Singer, sing	*Letta Neely*	16
Warning	*C.C. Carter*	17
april 16th	*Keelyn Bradley*	21
Not On My Watch	*Poet On Watch*	22
Mind Reading	*Reginald Harris*	27
two love scenes	*Keelyn Bradley*	28
Rapture	*Darius Omar Williams*	30
Next Time	*Reginald Harris*	31
Temptation	*Phillip B. Williams*	32
Dream #6	*Letta Neely*	33
Our Road of Perdition	*Mystical Writings*	35
Flight of the Black Crow	*Gregory McNeal*	36
Church of Abraham	*Rickey Laurentiis*	37
Question and Answer	*Alan Miller*	38
Everything But People	*Charles W. Harvey*	39
Ghazal for Emmet Till	*Rickey Laurentiis*	41
The Fan	*Charles W. Harvey*	42
Over Me	*Travis Montez*	44
Four to Seven Hundred Fourteen	*Uriah Bell*	49
Bench Marks	*Marvin K. White*	52
Sissy	*Vince Wilson*	53
gawd and alluh hus sistahs	*Letta Neely*	54
Full	*Rickey Laurentiis*	56
Ascension	*Darius Omar Williams*	57
For the chil'ren	*Uriah Bell*	59
The First Sign	*Marvin K. White*	61
Computer Love	*Mystalic Writing*	62
even on sun days	*Tim'm T. West*	64
For Those Newly Diagnosed	*Uriah Bell*	66
Scattered Thoughts	*LaCelle White*	68
We are our own heroes	*Alan Miller*	69

Brown Eyes and Unavailable	*Travis Montez*	71
protected	*Tim'm T. West*	74
blksestina	*Letta Neely*	78
Before Iraq Comes…	*Travis Montez*	80
Teenage Drag Queen	*Shane Allison*	84
Blessed Assurance	*Darius Omar Williams*	86
I'm a Woman (I'm a Backbone)	*Djola Branner*	87
Souliloquy	*Vince Wilson*	89
Press On	*R. Bryant Smith*	90
Kin Folks	*Shane Allison*	93
What I Should Have	*L. Lamar Wilson*	95
Breaking the Skin	*Shane Allison*	96
Sudda	*Travis Montez*	102
Hypocrisy	*Charles W. Harvey*	105
Summertime	*Djola Branner*	106
breaking silence	*Keelyn Bradley*	109
A Good Name Shines…	*Darius Omar Williams*	111
Breathing Words	*Clay Turner*	113
Surrender	*Mystalic Writing*	114
Clipped Wings Shall Fly	*C. C. Carter*	115
Ostinato	*Vince Wilson*	119
Love is	*Jonathan Thomason*	121

SHORT STORIES

Captain Swing	*Larry Duplechan*	127
Pussy Was My Drug Dealer	*Laurinda D. Brown*	138
Puficia N' Da Hood	*Donald Peebles*	145
Kevin	*Christopher David*	152
Wounded Gardens	*Doug Cooper Spencer*	161
Church	*G. Winston James*	170
Conviction	*L. Michael Gipson*	184
Alphabet Soup	*Charles W. Harvey*	204
Father to Son	*Stewart Shaw*	206
For All We Know	*R. Bryant Smith*	212
Another Direction	*Richard Peacock*	241
Open Doors	*Larry Wilson*	252
A Short Trip	*Reginald Harris*	274
Let It Go	*Durrell Owens*	279
Blessed & Highly Favored	*R. Bryant Smith*	297
It Will Rain	*Senoj Divad*	309
The Worm	*Taylor Siluwe*	326
Memoir of a Black Gay…	*Cornelius Jones*	340
Blue Light 'Til Dawn	*Darius Omar Williams*	346

ESSAYS & SERMONS

The Arsenal of Hatred Have No Place Here	*Doug Cooper Spencer*	359
A Letter to Jerry	*Buster Spiller*	361
Another 100 People	*L. Michael Gipson*	363
Why "Don't Ask, Don't Tell" Can't Wait	*Alan Miller*	366
Trick or Treat	*MacArthur Flournoy*	369
The Objectification of the Online Gay…	*Badilisho*	372
The New Renaissance	*Doug Cooper Spencer*	375
Liberation Theology: Affirms All Who…	*Buster Spiller*	376
Don't Get Distracted by the Haters	*W. Jeffrey Campbell*	379
A Case of Understanding Gay Love &…	*Tommie V. McNeil*	381
Freedom to Marry	*C.C. Carter*	384
Well It's Official…	*Badilisho*	388
After Equality, then What?	*Doug Cooper Spencer*	390
Not Another Drop	*W. Jeffrey Campbell*	392
I'm Gay, But Hold On, Let Me Explain	*Doug Cooper Spencer*	402
I'm Coming Out and Netting In	*Benjamin L. Reynolds*	404
The Right to Fully Be Who We Are	*John-Martin Green*	408
The Face of Fear	*Doug Cooper Spencer*	416
Three Talking Points You Need To Know	*Max Smith*	419
Positively	*Timothy Hampton*	424
The Unspeakable	*Tommie V. McNeil*	435
Yesterdays & Tomorrows	*H.L. Sudler*	438
Let The Healing Begin	*The Literary Masturbator*	443

INTERVIEWS

Charles Michael Smith	*Editor, Freelance Journalist, Book Reviewer*	449
Larry Duplechan	*Author*	454
Charles W. Harvey	*Writer, Novelist, Poet*	462
Stanley Bennett Clay	*Actor, Novelist, Playwright, Filmmaker, Publisher*	467
Gregory McNeal	*Art Photographer, Photo Journalist, Activist*	475
Dwayne Jenkins	*HIV/AIDS Educator, LGBT Activist*	480
Bobby Blake	*Author, Porn Star, Film Maker, Producer*	486
Sanford E. Gaylord	*Creative Activist/Actor*	491
Justin B. Terry - Smith	*Activist/Writer/Journalist*	495
Malaysia Andrews Ravore	*Sketch Artist/Seamstress/Female Illusionist*	500
Lisa C. Moore	*Publisher*	507
Steven G. Fullwood	*Archivist, Publisher*	512

PLAYS

Lo She Comes	*Renita L. Martin*	521
Cruising In the Name of Love	*Charles W. Harvey*	609
blue's song	*Keelyn Bradley*	617
Chocolate Cocoa…	*Darius Omar Williams*	641
Permissions	Contributors	715
Biographies	Contributors	717
About the Editors	Editors	723

Introduction:
A Continuum of the Real

We must begin to identify what a black gay sensibility is ; identify its esthetic qualities and components; identify specific constructions and uses of language suitable for the task of presenting our experiences in the context of literature; and then determine how this sensibility and esthetic relates to and differs from African American literature as a whole.[1]

—**Essex Hemphill**, Brother to Brother: New Writings by Black Gay Men

We have christened the name of this anthology *Mighty Real*, as a nod to the 70's disco classic hit of the same title: feverishly mediated by urba-disco diva Sylvester, in which he roars in an impassioned falsetto voice, "you make me feel mighty real."[2] The celebratory rhythm and communal resistance of Sylvester's song, encapsulates the diverse representation of marginalized voices in the African-American Same Gender Loving community. Consequently, as a nod rather than a tribute to Sylvester, this collection echoes his brashness, his whimsy, his spirit of particularized difference: the reality that black/gay/lesbian/bisexual/transgender experiences cannot be fixed, weighed down and reduced to one monolithic representation of black sexuality. The subsequent poems, short stories, essays, sermons, interviews and plays all resonate with images, metaphors, theology, African cosmology, spirituality and myth, which ultimately speak the subjectivity of the marginalized "other" into existence in a manner that both affirms and continues the legacy of past anthologized voices that have also sought to centralize the socio-political ideology of anti-heteronormative discourse. Thus, through a violent act of *mighty realness*, we simper-impose the conversation of identity against geographical space and time, while leaning heavily on past history in an effort to further the continuum of post-modern subjectivities in the 21st century.

Sixty voices emerge out of a shifting prism of visions, desires, blood memory, dreams; a syntactical landscape of cultural and sexual diversity beyond the confines of theory weaving and academe; and also a dramatic re-definition of colonial westernized aesthetics; contested conventions underscored in a plethora of canons. We invoke the genealogy of colored sexuality from a wide array of Diasporas: African, Caribbean, Creole, Biracial and even the Southern Black Diaspora (gay and lesbian southerners who also posit a non-monolithic lens in response to the violence of homogeneity). bell hooks expresses in her book *All About*

Love: New Visions, "Our confusion about what we mean when we use the word 'love' is the source in our difficulty in loving. If our society had a commonly held understanding of the meaning of love, the act of love would not be so mystifying."[3] The disconnect of love as well as the dislocation of love is the liminal space from which this book begins. Metaphorically speaking, each writer assembled in *Mighty Real*, unassumingly places their hands against the tainted window of frayed existence, truncating their fragmented words in jazz-like breathes, pinky fingered and black, contouring the unoccupied spaces of definition, with elbows rubbing away extraneous/deflecting perspectives in an attempt to narrow the divide on our journey toward transformation.

In an increasing paradox of absolutist, essentialist, singular experience, a multiplicity of writing styles, political commentaries, blogs, self-published books and anti-colonialist artists continue to emerge. Joseph Beam maintained, in a summation of his purposed life, it is through activism rather than passivism from which our own realities need to be created. As writers, we shouldn't have to pass through institutionalized structures of power in order to get to wherever we are going or wherever *we think* we are going as a matter of fact. In actuality and practicality, we don't have to. Although some literary aspirants choose to wield at the 'powers that be' to no avail, Beam affirms, "as African Americans, we do not bequeath dazzling financial portfolios. We pass from generation to generation our tenacity."[4] Unlike Beam's era, the financial conditions for many blacks have shifted dramatically over the past twenty years. However, his question of collective responsibility and accountability is still rather rich. Beam emphatically asks, "What is it are we passing along to our cousin from North Carolina, the boy down the block, our nephew who is a year old, or our sons who may follow us in this life?"[5] Beam situates the notion of passing around the typology/desire for responsible interactions among same gender loving people of color both on and off the page. So, instead of the pondering of financial stability for any of us, I pose a larger question: Who is doing the speaking as it relates to the cultural transmission of sexual experience? The short answer: an inter-mixture of colored voices from numerous backgrounds and degrees of positionality/sexuality: gay, bi, trans or straight. Also, how should the conversation transmit itself to a diverse audience? Via collective dialogue versus selective dialogue. This is a conversation that shouldn't be limited by the territorial terrain of politically and academically astute discourse, rather one with an accessibility and an accountability for all socio-economic classes.

So, does *Mighty Real* foreground the need for an expanded sexual discourse? To a certain degree, yes, but not in an idealized sense of completeness or totality. The practical function of discourse in this particular book, in all its vernacular language, traditional language, experimental language as well as the gaps in between, allows varying viewpoints and ideologies to enter the syntactical landscape of cultural and sexual diversity with pieces of bark simultaneously stripped from the hollow log of our inhumanity. *Pieces of bark, not all of the bark.*

In addition to its reclamation of/to the past, what also distinguishes *Mighty Real* from previous same gender loving anthologies, is its assemblage of poetry, short fiction, sermons, essays, interviews and plays within the contents of one book. Invoking Alain Locke's purported classic, *The New Negro: Voices of the Harlem Renaissance*, as a duende to the "mighty" and a precursor to the "real", *Mighty Real* situates itself, not as the definitive text on black SGLBT cultural imagination, but offers a continued advancement in an on-going conversation, the infantile beginnings of what is already constructing itself as The Mighty Real Movement. Just as Zora Neal Hurston, Langston Hughes and Wallace Thurman co-founded the "quarterly" magazine *FIRE!*, editors R. Bryant Smith and Darius Omar Williams radically position *Mighty Real* as a landmark document of previously silenced black multi-genders and multi-sexualities that have yet to be historicized. This is the orientated position from which this anthology functions: the metaphorical transcendence of real, an anti-fractal structure of polemical same gender loving discourse that implodes onto itself the devastating violence of internalized homophobia. Both Mighty Real, *the anthology* as well as Mighty Real, *the movement*, necessitates what Charles Michael Smith brings up in *Fighting Words: Personal Essays by Black Gay Men*, "to use words, language, as a weapon against despair, self-loathing and loneliness."[6] *Mighty Real* adds new stitching to Smith's woven metaphorical thread using notions of realness and for realness as an intermediate concept, an ambitious reaching out toward underrepresented sub-cultures within the layered dimensions of same gender loving identity. The tension and contestation between the actuality of realness and the activation of realness is the philosophical threshold where *Mighty Real* resides.

In the tradition of *Brother to Brother*, *In the Life* and *SHADE, Mighty Real* aims to shift the paradigm yet again in its mapping out of both academic and non-academic writers, its inclusion of gays, lesbians, bisexual and transgender people of color in one book. At the heart of this collection, is the overlapping/interdependent presence of believers and non-believers, crack-heads, prostitutes, beauty shop owners, preachers, thugs, effeminate drag-queens, butch lesbians and b-boys who all have a place at the table in

Mighty Real. Referring back to bell hooks's infectious insights on committed love, we assert the need for real conversations on love in this discombobulated new millennium, and so begins the new shift.

The Spirit of Inclusion/Affirming Love

Mighty Real also privileges the late Bishop Walter Hawkins's love centered, spiritually inclusive, same gender loving affirming theology. A libratory site of heteronormative resistance, the intermixture of sexualities manifested epically at Love Center Church, where Sylvester James was ironically a member. Bishop Hawkins, the first black forefather in the struggle for spiritual and sexual liberation, strategically overthrew the oppressive homophobia of black church rhetoric. In the safe domain of his revolutionary, sexually diverse sanctuary, black Christian worship took on new meaning at what is now Oakland, California's 10400 International Boulevard. The church that upheld the ideals of Christ during the turbulent 1970's, the church that eulogized Sylvester in December 1988, was the same church that rearranged preconceived notions of God's universe at the expense of being ostracized, demonized and disowned by the majority of black clergyman and neighboring parishioners. Horace L. Griffin in his award winning book *Their Own Receive Them Not: African American Lesbians and Gays in Black Churches* echoes Hawkins's black church politics as he assaults oppressive homophobia on all fronts claiming that "despite the rich history of using the bible to oppose oppression, black church leaders have ironically not taken a similar approach on sexual oppression and oppressive religious and societal actions against black women, lesbian and heterosexual, and gay men. Instead, blacks often internalize this country's racist sexual depictions of a black sexuality that is out of control and in need of salvation by Christianity."[7] The time is long overdue for the "anger management God" in hate based religion to be re-examined fully as Bishop Carlton Pearson contends.[8] Emerging out of this re-examination of a slave-based institution, is the hope for progress beyond fixed definitions of our spiritual lives. Using the continuum of "the real" as a mediator between destructive discourse and productive discourse, this anthology privileges compounded, complex, multi-layered subjectivities to keep us from collapsing on the flat periphery of disempowered cultural difference.

Dispelling Oppressive Myths about Same Gender Loving Blackness

Even more necessary, is a closer look into the implicit relationship between a symbolic reckoning of blackness versus a dialectical one, in these interchangeable literary tropes of recognition, power and resistance. In turn, different modes of temporality and history signify on the real. To put it quite bluntly, mighty realness is not autonomous by any means. Divided into five sections: poetry, short fiction, essays/sermons, interviews and plays, these narratives linguistically and structurally dispel any notion of an absolutist colored sexuality while also ungirding the literary limits of a previously encoded heterosexist blackness. The impact of these abrupt collisions and permutations constitute the immediate hope and practical basis for *Mighty Real*.

Darius Omar Williams
October 2010
Columbus, OH

NOTES

1. Essex Hemphill, "Introduction," *Brother to Brother: New Writing by Black Gay Men* eds. Essex Hemphill and Joseph Beam (Boston: Alyson Publications, 1991), p. xxvii

2. James Wirrick and Sylvester James, "You Make Me Feel (Mighty Real)," rec. 1977, Sylvester: The Original Hits, Fantasy Records, 1989.

3. bell hooks, *All About Love: New Visions* (New York: William Morrow, 2000), p. 3.

4. Joseph Beam , "Making Ourselves from Scratch,", *Brother to Brother: New Writing by Black Gay Men*, eds. Essex Hemphill and Joseph Beam (Boston: Alyson Publications, 1991), p. 262.

5. Beam, *Brother to Brother*, p. 262.

6. Charles Michael Smith, "Introduction: A Multiplicity of Witness," *Fighting Words: Personal Essays by Black Gay Men*, ed. Charles Michael Smith (New York: Avon Books, 1999), p. 3.

7. Horace L. Griffin, *Their Own Receive Them Not: African American Lesbians and Gays in Black Churches* (Ohio: The Pilgrim Press, 2006), p. 56.

8. Bishop Carlton Pearson responds to allegations of sexual misconduct lodged against his friend Bishop Eddie Long of New Birth Missionary Baptist Church in a September 2010 CNN interview where he articulates the shift in his spiritual theology called "The Gospel of Inclusion".

Poetry

Poetry

We So Fierce
after Gwendolyn Brooks
Darius Omar Williams

THE ALL-MALE PRANCING J-SETTES.
EIGHT AT CLUB CITY LIGHTS.

We so fierce. We
Talk pierce. We

Throw shade. We
Sever Trade. We

Strut at Balls. We
Vogue ya'll. We

Walk long. We
Dance strong.

why I love black men
Tim'm T. West

because I believe in blood memory
see him best
in the dark
the cacophony of chains
a lullaby
sense the desperation of being lost
at sea
floating
stacked next to
on top of
beside him
felt him dying
tasted him crying
prayed he would live to see me
in light again

because there was a time
the only way I knew I was living
was his breath on my flesh
this salt, this depth, this passion
a testimony
that we would only survive
if strong
a test of resilience
different ships, same boat
time bending forward
beyond middle passages
still gripping his hand
for dear life
until his skin began
to feel like mine

Mighty Real

because he has seen me
hung
Mandingo
Strange fruit
gun shots, hunting dogs
Faggots
Because salt is a texture
with grit like Africa
and I am black
and sometimes blue
and choose to love a black man
because I can... remember

Did Not See You Coming
Marvin K. White

I could not say that there was any of me in you. Could not say to your father, my brother, "He belongs to me." Could not lay claim to the gold chained to child rearing. You come quick. Hot and steeping, bump raised on my tongue. Weatherman got it wrong. Got me linened up on this off-season's wettest today. I am loving you like that. Out of thin air like that. *The Hair Clippers that Wore Flip-Flops. The Styrofoam Cup that Wanted to be Called Visine. The Tennis Shoe that Learned HTML. The Bottled Water that had Two Mommies. The Ink Pen that Took Vitamins. The Desk that Learned to Drive. The Baby Oil that Won the Spelling Bee.* It is not my job to interpret birthmarks, shoe sizes, the color of ears, athletic scholarship possibilities. Amongst the names we have married and changed into- Draughn, Sherrill, Ford, Thomas, Bonner, Kelly, White, Jackson, a sissy or a bulldagger has not been allowed to be a mystic in this family for centuries. So I watched you all, particularly you, boy man, rough and tumble through your adolescences. Could not live through you. Could not sideline coach or backstage mother you. Could not make appearances amongst your friends at graduation or birthday because I am "that" uncle and never wanted to make you storytellers. Force you into the exiles of brave and boldfaced lies like me. My two yolk egg surely some sign. *The Battery that Drank Grappa. The Glove that Invented Cheese. The Cowry that Went to Culinary School. The Birthmark that Wanted to be a Light Socket. The Garbage Can that Shed its Skin. The Font that Went to Nursing School. The Door Knob that Spoke Senegalese.* I could not have expected you. My head is in the oven baking when you knock. Did not know that the taunt that I "Switched like a girl." meant something they did not want me to know. Meant that a child could turn something on inside of you. Could light you up. Could. *The String that Ate Ice Cream. The Planet that Became a Masseur. The Key that Cried Oil of Olay. The Paragraph that Lost its Wallet. The Stripe that Couldn't Swim. The Wheat Germ that Learned to Double-Dutch. The Apple that Went to The Oscars.* There is in me a child that still remembers The doll dangerous and snatched from my hands as if she was leading me from my mother's side in the grocery store to pet puppies in the back of her van. There is in me a child getting lost in and inhabiting stories unimagined for boys like me who love boys like me who thought that it was wrong to think that there is in this family another like me. I have suspended belief before to feel love out of "I can't promise you nothin's" and "You lucky's we even let you around" and one stimulus check all that it takes to fire the canon that explodes us and myth and manhood. All Makes sense finally. Shame and GPS-less sperm. You. Here now. My happy ending. *The Fox that Farted Cheese. The Stereo Speakers that Decided to be a Better Listener. The Window that Decided to Learn Opera. The Shoe that Insisted on Equal Protection Under the Law. The Mosquito that put in an Application at the Post Office. The Towel that Read "The Power of Now". The Walnut that Thought it Wanted to Be a Sprinkler. The Poem that Finally Learned to Line Dance.*

Beauty
Lucy Shumpert

I see beauty as it is-
A process of definition.
Its start is sometimes in turmoil,
Angry, bitter, rumbling explosions
causing violent eruptions and spewing
forth fiery waves of pain.
And in that fire, that chaos, there is HOPE.

I see beauty as it is-
A process by definition.
From that cooling bed of burnt destruction
opposites pass, attract and mesh
causing a form new and beingless,
sightless with purpose and goals.
And in that purpose, there is POSSIBILITY.

I see beauty as it is-
A process in definition.
Yet small but vibrantly starting
to be and move, recognize and walk.
Taking shaking, tentative minor steps,
glowing with a beauty enhanced by its
newness and innocence.
And in that newness, there is LIFE.

I see beauty as it is-
A process with definition.
Pulling, pressing, impressing,

showing off and learning, sucking
up knowledge and discarding fear,
to explore life even when falling.
To laugh haughtily at shadows and unseen
friends, that are really angels.
Former playmates too close to say goodbye.
And in their closeness, there is SADNESS.

I see beauty as it is-
A process to definition.
As angels leave, replaced by
tangibles, steadies, rudiments, exercises,
to impress, attract and bring relief
and release, to comfort, calm, cajole or caress-
in this other plane, this place . . .the heart
broken and mended and broken and mended
and broken and mended and broken and
healed.
And in this healing, there is ACCEPTANCE.

I see beauty as it is-
A process recognizing definition.
New becomes old and steady.
Pep is useful yet not required.
The days come more from ritual than expectation.
For God has been constant, will be.
Has counted days and hairs and cattle and hills and joy,
and exchanged biceps for bulges-
where black, brown and even blond make gray.
And tight, taut, tone sags
And the fight with gravity is conceded.

Given up for another promise of newness.
A new day, some movement.
And even if the mind's eye wants
to still see small and vibrant in the mirror,
the mind and the soul see, smile, accept the truth,
which is the promise of newness.
When the promise is forgotten,
lost or has to be seen with glasses
or magnifiers and the right angle and light . . .
And in that promise, there is FAITH.

I see beauty as it is-
A process releasing definition.
Affixing to hope, consolation, prayer, repentance,
gathering, giving, sharing, leaving love
by releasing piety and haughtiness and accepting
the coming newness.
Looking in fact for former playmates, angels
too far away to define, but close enough to feel.
Sensing, hearing, expecting transportation.
Waiting for the day when the process is complete.
I see beauty as it is- LIFE.

Attraction
Rickey Laurentiis

By luck, I found the vines: wild, un-

tampered, unless you call the wind

a kind of tamper, each leaf turned in it,

attracted, sometimes they struggle only,

sometimes they snap. But how, I thought,

these vines keep them in tact, or try to,

reaching this way, that, up city stuff,

cold and resolved not to feel, and moving

to the end where—who wouldn't say they

wave like little, modest hands?

                                                    In another man—

this man who is always you—I found them twisting

his darkhandsome face, along his eyes, out of.

Will I reach them? I was terrified. *Will they hold?*

The Cucumber
Charles Harvey

I'm pretty cool
In my hunter green
Versace Tux
The life of the party.

While the lettuce
and sprouts wilt
and the tomato festers
bloody
I perk up the salad.

I don't mind shedding
my skin
and getting mashed up
for face creams or soaps.
Slice me and I go humbly
into the bags under your eyes.

But gay men trouble me the most
grasping me hard in the middle
as if I'm jack-off material.
And on their lazy Sundays
introducing me to meet their
assholes.

Tattoo
Reginald Harris

You move across

my sky

whisper

with the tongue's

embrace

then burst

leaving

seed   blossoms   morning

rain

your name

bejeweled

to echo

across

my

chest

8 ways of looking at pussy
letta neely

    1.
enter here and find your home
your bathwater run already
the sun setting in the distance
heat on the horizon of your clit

    2.
swollen pussy
all laid out and relaxed,
says to everyone in the room
"I have been to mecca and back
and it ain't nuthin compared to what you
done did"

    3.
when you're wet and waiting
I could be lost six
universes away without a map
and sniff my way home

    4.
baby, baby, hold still
my dreads are underneath
your thigh

    5.
with those three brwn fingers inside,
you impregnate me with desire
I grow wide and wild
my water breaks,
this dam gives and we are tossing on the rapids
tossing on the rapids
overturning canoes,
water races out and over your arm
warm cum shoots out
races up your
arm, you put
your mouth
over this geyser

6.
I love like the ocean at first light
the waves coming in to meet the edges
of earth; rushing up and back like tiny orgasms
high tide the explosion
of you
on my
tongue

7.
my teeth on your nipple tastes sweet
I clench harder bite down on sensations
like acupuncture—I feel energy rising
connecting from
one hand/nearly elbow deep in your pussy
one hand over your mouth
your sister and my boy cousin
so close they can smell but
they snore instead. you giggle
I bite harder   taste past skin
you giggle again.

8.
venus flytrap
eats me alive
everytime

Singer, sing
letta neely

she reach
her voice
round the clitoris and the soul
of every alive
thing in the room including the holy
ghost
n sho nuff
it become a meeting
house

the minute she open her
mouth n sound
sashay into air
molecules
step
aside n
bear witness

Warning
C.C. Carter

lipstick and lace make me suspect
to women who say,
"women like me
set the feminist movement back
100 years."
They watch from hard chairs
through blank stares
try to judge what they see
like
I once did strippers
who teased men
and some women
with revealed flesh
I try to cover -
Until I saw, she
was me who magnified
all my insecurities
and I was not embarrassed
for her
but for me
who could not dance free
from blind barriers and opaque obstacles
prescribed at birth
when a doctor pronounced my sex
confined my potential
to a check box
with low ceilings and brick walls
squared off from flying -
I see my sistahs
stare at me
a life size Barbie
would be -
Flashing curve and breasts
adorned lips and neck
thinking
"She needs to stop this
is what we fought hard
not to be!"
but,

we interrupt this poem with a special announcement,
An unidentified black female
has infiltrated the system
and all
We Repeat
ALL
national security defenses are at risk

Cause this is a warning warning warning!!!
there's a person passing as woman
warning warning
passing as straight
warning
passing as fake
passing
passing
passing
The way my lighter than yellow
great great mother
passed
sun kissed field workers
quick fast
on her way to the big house
passing
turned noses
snubbed shoulders
judgmental stares
cause she was the chosen one
for the good life
for the nigga wife
who hid a kitchen knife
in sweet potato pies
weaved escaped routes in quilts
then helped twenty to freedom -
Saying prayers on her back
massa riding her front
cause one more sistah
don't need to be
a victim of
this
is a warning
to my militant marys
toting hand guns and grenades

downgrading sistahs
whose weapons
are BA's or MA's
some with Ph.d degrees -
Working in corporate capitalists
man-decision making companies
for the key to the office -
While you're protesting
on the outside
she's lobbying for your rights
on the inside
passing
the key out the window
for you to come through
this
front door
is a warning
for sistahs who preach too much
about war and revolution
then suck their teeth at those
who don't lock their hair
which sometimes
has locked you out
of power positions
where you could have
helped another
worked with a brother
schooled a single mother
yet, you say I'm a sale out
cause I won't be real -
this
is a warning
for if ever
there came a time
when you really walked your talked
made the bed you laid
then this
barbie pin-up
would gladly let the hair
grow from my roots
long under my arms
thick between my legs
hide

amazon sistahs in my bush
and while checking role call
from the guest house
I pass
right by to the white house -
Don't get checked at customs
they think I've been trained well-
go in my office
pop off acrylic nails
load them into an ak 47
break my pumps
boomerang them
past
the man
all the way to the klu klux klan -
Take off my Anne Klein suit
string up my combat boots
strip down like my sistahs in nightclubs
to lace underwear
revealing floor plans
of security codes -
Stand naked
raise my arms
release the funk of fumes
that's worse than agent orange -
Take the extra key
unlock the fence
and we my sistahs will
rage war together -
Oh yes
this
is a warning
it takes a lot of women
to form an army -
It takes all kinds
to win
this
revolution

april 16th
Keelyn Bradley

even as we perform
our ritual of spit and cum
as we mirror each other's loneliness
tangled and belligerent
dancing in desperate love acts
i contemplate another casualty
in your arms   stay hard not to remember
the many men
who have tried to love you
while grinding apologies from your thighs

the morning after
you leave   my bed stained
with turmoil and tears
i murmur prayers
to the ghost of your image
blues of past dawns
shatter my sleep to dust
i stumble through the city
like a crippled wingless creature
naming all the men you've conquered
lighting a candle
at every monument
where we kissed
beneath countless descriptions of the moon
to heal sorrow
men of war forget

whenever you touch
another would be lover
whenever you fill another
trembling vacancy
with your slick emptiness
or press your cruel lips to paradise
i want you to remember
yourself brooding over deformities
in my body   spilling eulogies
over my grave
as you would
a dead lover

Not On My Watch
From The Texas Heat Series
Poet On Watch

INT LOFT: It's a cold winter evening of art, dancing and dinner that whines down in Girl's downtown Chicago loft studio apartment. There's the scent of wood chips, sage and sex burning in the fireplace as P.O.W. and Girl's causal, complicated but loving relationship develops some boundaries.

NOT ON MY WATCH

Will we not lay here next to each other/
exposed/ emotions/ bare/ ass /naked
your body/

<u>**P.O.W**</u>
(you hear kissing sounds in the back round)

"I have to get off your beautiful black behind"

<u>**Girl**</u>
(pulling P.O.W. back in the bed)

"oh baby, come on, you are so good"

<u>**P.O.W**</u>
(clearing her head)

"It's been a long night and I got to go"

Levitating

From the not so fitted cotton/ gray/ flannel/ sheets/
Soft/ Wet/ Warm and, and
grimy from the nights love oil
and you calling my name/

Girl
(pulling P.O.W. back in the bed)

"oh baby, come on, you are so good"

While AYE/ listened for the heartbeat
of your wisdom between your legs
while sipping on your inspiration

P.O.W
(clearing her head again)

"It's been a long night and I got to go. This is not helping either one of us."

Girl
(pulling P.O.W. back in the bed while unbuttoning her shirt)

"Yeah, Yeah I know"

NOT ON MY WATCH

Will I hunger in the darkness
Pant like wolves do/ WONDER,
But not caring/ who hears the screams
THE MOANS
The Ahhhhh SHIT, Uh/
MAMA,
Daddy kind of ass slaps

P.O.W.
(a little firmer, while Girl kisses on her body)

"I am not helping you make any decisions by us doing this."

Girl
(P.O.W. is back in Girl's bed and Girl has P.O.W.'s shirt)
"What decisions? Come on baby.. This again, why now why not tomorrow when we both can talk."

Me on top/ on bottom
STRAPPED/ STRAPPED,

To the headboard
STRAPPED/ STRAPPED

To the footboard
STRAPPED/ STRAPPED
Candle wax, drippings, drips, drippings
all down your ass crack/

P.O.W.
(is a little firmer, while Girl kisses on her body)

"You know what I'm talkin' about **(P.O.W. gets out the bed)**
now you got jokes, alright, gimme my shirt, thank you"
Where are my keys?

Girl
(Girl leans back on bed pillows)
"Between my legs"

my eyes ignore the salt/ sting/ stare
YOU / WATCH ME EVER SO CLOSELY
wiping down the windows that tell the stories

Girl
(Girl lean's back on bed pillows holding the keys out in front)
"Between my legs"

NOT ON MY WATCH

Will you hold back the WHISPERS
Those that seep between streams of consciousness

WHISPERS
Those that seep between streams of orgasms

WHISPERS

Those that seep between streams of confessions
While your lips just sang the gospel in the next pew

P.O.W.
(shakes her head and starts to laugh)
Come on' give me my keys.

(Girl hands keys over)
Where is my cell phone

NOT ON MY WATCH

Will we play games with each other like little girls do,
On seesaws of emotions and merry go rounds of drama

Girl
(Girl puts on robe)
"You don't have to be mean"

CAUSE, BABY/
WE BOTH KNOW WHAT THIS IS
and it is what it is/ so / let's be ok with it

NOT ON MY WATCH

P.O.W.
(has on jacket and head towards the door)
"I am not, really I'm not"

Will I/ Can I / Ignore this tunnel like vision
Block out all outside influences
Lock us into the heat of this passion
HIDE AWAY THE KEY FOR TOMORROW
So/ We can stay present for each other today

Girl
(is walking towards the door also)
"What the fuck.. You are really leavng"

P.O.W.
(Girl stops and holds the door for P.O.W.)
Come to a decision, cause/ I just did.

NOT ON MY WATCH
Will you not tell me you love me

EXT LOFT: GIRL slams the door. P.O.W stands on top of the stairs. A well kept bag lady crosses her path with her shopping cart of things. P.O.W. snuggles up in her jacket one more time before hitting the cold and the long walk to the train. It's a winter evening of art, dancing and dinner that whines down in Girl's downtown Chicago loft studio apartment. A causal but loving relationship develops some boundaries.

Bag Lady

*"You take care of that heart child. It's a good thing.
trust It's a good thing."*

P.O.W.
(P.O.W. looks back over her shoulder)
OK ..

Mind Reading
Reginald Harris

Giovanni used to tell me, "When you have a man's cock in your mouth, you can often tell what he's thinking." Maybe he was right, because Angie said, "Go ahead and fantasize about him if you like. Then come back to me."
-- Richard C. Zimler, "Learning How to Love"

Darkened rooms and car seats,

nameless faces,

backyards swatting flies in Summer's heat

dreams and days, and petty tribulations

fall away. Eyes roll, breathing quickens, shallows,

shudders, slows -- a moon-drunk tide

rushing out to sea.

The hand behind the neck is to focus vision

make Memory's run clearer, faster,

flash cards through the past:

one word, one phrase, one letter,

One --

Final flicker of the tongue is encyclopedic

causing sight to blur as each word spills

out, trembling,

gushing like the ocean's swift return.

two love scenes
Keelyn Bradley

scene 1: the first time
you say 'i miss you. and i don't miss people' (like it's a crime)
a legacy of martyred flowers
across the guarded space between us
        a carnal shrine
you decipher
scribbled faces of stickmen
Basquiat's enigma nailed to the wall
(we are miles and miles apart)
an equinox of nameless art
and broken masses
an obstinate shadow
haunting the hallway of my apartment
[directions: wade back and forth
hurting sounds wishing sounds]
as we fuck
our hearts out
in a saturnine land
deprived of metamorphosis
exalt other worlds
undo the lies we've suffered

scene 2: no longer prisoners of our tools
i say 'i believe in the intangible origin of clouds
        and the marvelous sincerity of rainbows' (as if it were an
obsession)
tattooed on my body
to avoid reliving tragedy
Frankenstein men digest
in esoteric fields
(while we dream loving revolutions)
by a river crawling with fossils
and perennial beginnings
bleed sunlight
cicatrices dedicated to spring
[directions: mouth innervision
        missing planets missing movements]

as we fuck
our hearts out
jerk haiku
in stagnant water   scry dna
obscenities gnawing us into delicacy
dismantle the machinery that digs our graves

Rapture
Darius Omar Williams

The Liberia-ness
of your smile—my

pillowed breath—
I am twisted

biopoetically by your
cocklebur of a rhyme.

Cyclones and sun-made
trumpets —your super-bad

mamma jamma locs

Uptight-alright-outta-sight

brother. You are all
chap-stick, breath-mint

and hair. The goodnight
lyric I become in the

Diaspora of your sea.
You have dittied me

into muse. Antennaed me
like a retro tee-vee set.

I am your chinless
blue skirt of a man

albatrossed inside the
sigh of a locust scented box

an all black people sitcom.

Next Time
Reginald Harris

I will climb your tree

trunk legs   Place their thickness on

my shoulders

                                  and swing

                                     for Stevie G.

Temptation
Phillip B. Williams

I am your
Will-o-wisp
Siren song to
self destruction

I am steam licking
lipgloss from your mouth
singeing nimble hairs
from the base of your chin

I am
an uncaught whisper
gossip slipped like
drug into drink

I am vertigo
prostrate dreams
flipped nightmarish

I am clawing in
shadowy room corners
Boogie-man dick
tapping your arm

I am stampeding soldiers
The snapped tendon
of slain Achilles
His skeleton brothing
my bath water

Dream #6
letta neely

we were
forced to make fire
our enemy
hands
feet
tied
our flesh burning off bone
was the last smell
we were always
plotting even in
our silence
did you not see freedom
in our eyes,
I heard fire sing "this is not my choice"
as our skin went up in smoke

        I heard the limb resisting the insistent
        pull of gravity, I heard henry defy death
        his last breath was freedom   then
        the sound of men's fingers rummaging in his mouth
        snatching teeth and tongue for souvenirs, heirlooms
        to document former wealth. I heard henry's ear
        ripped away and tucked into a pocket
        his body hit the ground and they rushed
                to
                        cut
pieces   of rope
                                from
           round
                his neck
          to save
          to reminder
          to document

I watched the children at the picnic
awed at the slowness with which reluctant fire
eats skin.   amazed at a rope's power to
suspend and swing a grown man
in mid air;   I watched them count the
minutes
the wind holds and cradles
screams

I saw them repulse at their parent's
grinning unfazed by the wind's howling.

I heard adults laughing
telling their children not to turn
                                    their
                                    faces

              I remember before:
the earth was strands of music
and color waving inseparable aloneness we were drum and
continental shelf, others were drum and volcano,
drum and coral reef, drum and cumulus cloud and chant
we stomped our feet drum and island,
we waved our arms through wind archipelago, isthmus
drum and river and swamp, rainforest drum
we were all stepdancing fancy
drawing in the dirt with our bare feet

              it was the foul stench of greed that
              crept between marrow and muscle
              amoeba and crest of wave; that makes
              us snatch our own tongues from each
              other's mouths;
              sever our feet from ankles.

              tell the children not to turn
              away from this
              and the
              smell
              of our burning flesh

Paaie van ondergang (Our Road of Perdition)
Mystalic Writing

She is a celestial aphrodisiac
With satin soft skin
Brought to, in the womb of the elements
Passing through inter-dimensional transgressions
Every boundary another lesson
And she has come to you bearing blessings

Her eyes light of brimstone
As she dances to the howls of African wolves
Painting the skies of her mood
She'll brood and stir
Slowly ingesting your thoughts
As her touch paves streets of black tar
And gold chips as they unfurl, raining ambrosia
As if the heavens had last night's case of drunken nausea
Glory will spill upon this land
And all she will ask is for you to take her hand

Fingers of a silk mass
She looked as though she should have
Been captured by stained glass
So that all could look upon the beauty of black
Carbon atoms twist and yawn between her thighs
Stretching at every chance
Shimmering at every on looker's glance
They also dance
In the impurities of life
They produce the blackness of our very substance
And on parallel cords they are the creators of our hoards
Our many black men and women
Divided by any light to be shown or given
And they become distant from the mother of
Their very existence

Thus I petition a return from our roads of perdition...

Flight of the Black Crow
Greg McNeal

Prepare your heart
For what I have seen:
Things to not talk about
New and obscene.
I've seen old things die young
And new things die mean.
The story has been re-written
Or so I am told.
Wounds that won't heal
And leaders so cold.
Suicidal children
And angels whose spirits are torn.
Men who are above it all
On their mountain tops sit
Their dedication and priorities to God
So obviously split.
Oh the things I have seen
As I soar through the sky:
A generation lost
And covering the lie;
Cities baptized by fear
Than by water
Misleading its children
Like lambs to the slaughter.
I've seen locust feed
Leaving fields bare dry
Still more moisture left in the field
Than your humanity's eye.
Wisdom sold out for stupidity and prize
Voices of hope cry out -
Their actions denied!
As I fly through the sky
And perch where I may
I see my black brothers
Themselves they do slay -
Praying to God
To one day take the pain away
Never realizing
Within you He hid the way.
Stop dying right now!
Live to fly another day!

Church of Abraham
Rickey Laurentiis

The men are pregnant.
Their eyes slide like lightning
at the women: *How?*
they ask, *Did you do this to me?*
But the women's faces won't
yield. They're cardboard.
Now all the women are gone.
Because they don't call
themselves wo-men anymore.

*

Some men claim the trees
have slammed against their
swollen bellies. Some men
swallow weeds. Some men
start a church to decide
the proper way to sacrifice
one's first born: the little
alien buried inside—.
Will any child survive?

*

Here's a man couched
in his tub, eyes on the body
rounding out his body.
Where are my feet? He mews.
My knees? He can't even see
that special member crooked
in-between—that hooks
like a leech. But, then again,
he no longer wants to.

Question and Answer
Alan Miller

Question:
Aren't you afraid
of being attacked
out here late at night
looking like that?

Answer:
No, honey,
I put that pussy
in my purse
and come out
fighting like a man.

Everything but People
Charles W. Harvey

Just you Larry and me walkin down these diamond streets
Don't know what town this is. Don't know the name of no place
just know we sixty years old and smellin like a hundred days
of bathin in piss and *MD2020*...
Look at us Larry, pants open
dick all out swingin and swingin
white girl clutching her purse as we pass—

Say "sistah don't you think you ought to be
clutching your pusseeeeeeeeee....? Can't you see
we in no condition to snatch anything from you?"

She say she goin to call a cop.
Shit man, I got Bull Conner's phone number
etched in my head by one hundred billy clubs one summer in '63
I take off my hat in deference to her. She screams
at the hills and valleys of knots in my skull.
Shit, man, after Bull Conner, I couldn't even remember
the address of NYU ...*wonder if Dizzy still comin to play for the BSU?*
Better shake my head before I remember too much

And look a here, Larry, look a here, niggas dressin up store window dummies.
One got on an NYU sweat-shirt. Niggas gettin good jobs these days.
I remember when no niggas was allowed to dress a white dummy
or sit on a park bench. Other day I sat
on a bench in front of the Big Baptist Church
and the elder said the bench was for decoration only.
I asked if I could sit there if I put on my red Christmas sweater?
Now I like Bus Stations. This old grip I carry is always packed
so I fit right in until the police begin to suspect
the *Number Nine* I'm waitin on ain't never comin in.
What bus did we catch, Larry, to go to Birmingham? A Scenic Cruiser?
Larry you was so silly cryin cause you couldn't
sit in the upper deck with the white girls like me. Well I was light

in them days. I'm mud and blood colored now.
You know Larry, you should have lived instead of giving in
to their billy clubs. Yeah, it's true we didn't give in to some stuff
we didn't shake our dicks at each other like they wanted,
didn't sign our names as Mr. Niggers
but I only left teeth and one kidney at their altar. But you Larry
gave them bastards your life. Your Mother fuckin life!
You! Going back to Poughkepsie where you was from,
 in the baggage belly of a Greyhound Scenic Cruiser--
Your dead eyes staring straight up into white girl's twats
Larry, Larry, Larry, Lord I ought to burn down this Bus Station.
Make me wanna holla, the way they use my... Alabama God damn!
I wish they would let us back in Sears
but ever since that time with me and the claw hammer attackin
cans of *Sears Best* paint I ain't been allowed nowhere but
bus stations, jail, and Ben Taub.
Larry did you know that Ben Taub used to be a man
and he turned himself into a hospital?
I wish I could do that, be Eddie Jefferson the man
then be Eddie Jefferson the Hardware store or Eddie Jefferson the planet.
Yeah that's it I ain't gonna stop at being no hardware store.
everything can live on my planet too
dogs, elephants, ants, cats, the duckbill platypus,
everything but people. Look what people did to us Larry,
so everything but people.

Ghazal for Emmett Till
Rickey Laurentiis

Quiet now your tongue You're in this cotton land
Oaks swing long limbs of men on this cotton land

You come with song stuck under your heels like heat
The moist pinprick of flesh Jazz of this tin land

You come with language of the sharp-jawed breath
Snow How it pops beneath the eyelids within land

You come They won't have your sin Your cocked fedora
Can't mask your grin much longer on this olden land

You come They will have your skin Your mettle
Your sole will leave the firmness of this whitened land

Quiet now your tongue You're spilling in the river's hand
Oaks cloud the sinking of your finger in this cotton land

The Fan
Charles W. Harvey

A majority of Emmett Till's family members said Thursday that they object to plans by the Justice Department to exhume his body in order to find clues to solve his brutal murder 50 years ago. . . . Till was 14-years-old when he left his home on Chicago's South Side to visit relatives in Mississippi on Aug. 21, 1955. His mother advised him about how to behave when interacting with white people because race relations there were a lot different than in Chicago. On August 24, Till and his cousin, Curtis Jones, went into the small town of Money, and stopped at Bryant's Grocery store to buy some candy. Some local boys dared Till to speak to Carolyn Bryant, the white store clerk. He allegedly whistled at the woman when he left the store. Four days later, Till's body was discovered in the Tallahatchie River, weighed down by a cotton gin fan tied around Till's neck with barbed wire. Two men, storeowner Roy Bryant and his half-brother, J. W. Milam, were charged and acquitted of the murder. They bragged about the crime three months later in a Look magazine article.
  -- Karen E. Pride, Chicago Defender May 6, 2005

What y'all aim to find by

digging up his old bones?

Old old bones, old and innocent bones

Why y'all want to disturb him?

He ain't with his bones.

He down here in the muck with me

and ain't nobody trying to dig my rusty ass up.

His Mama, bless her heart, she got the bones

and that head that looked like a bad cabbage.

Thousands seen it in Chicago. Millions through *Jet*.

Where was my picture? I suffered.

I used to gleam prissy and howl

now mud bugs nest in my teeth.

I kept the good stuff off that boy—his spirit, his soul, his spleen
caressed it out of his naked body
The real Emmett sometimes he runs up the road to Money
gooses that white gal between her legs—boy still gots
that spunk in him.
Then he runs back to me for shelter.
Carolyn wakes up, rubs her thigh
goes back to sleep. 1955 was a long time ago
She wants to rest. I want to rest, and even Emmett.
You got the pictures. You won't forget
Every now and agin some black boy still gets
drugged behind a car, still gets strung up in a tree
or the roof rafters of a county jail
They still make fans like me
heavy enough to drown boyish devilment.

Over Me
Travis Montez

he wrote
number one gay nigger
across his son's skull
because he thought
that was my name

he wrote
number one gay nigger
across his son's skull
because he thought
that was my name

and he wrote
my name
across his son's skull
because
i loved him

number one gay nigger
and i loved the son
when the father
couldn't stand
Black Americans or faggots
couldn't stand Black Americans
with their loud music
their tacky gold chains
their disrespectful baggy pants
and he wasn't about to let his son
be no faggot
over no
number one gay nigger
like me
see
he had traded
one star for fifty
just so his son
could be a man
and
a number one gay nigger
would ruin that dream,

would make that move
from one island with palm trees
to another island with skyscrapers
useless

and he couldn't stand
Black Americans or faggots
couldn't stand Black Americans
or their music
that crying-wailing-dying black people music
that sounded like sin

he couldn't stand their music

except for that one song
that stevie wonder song
that:
over time
I've been building my castle of love
just for two
although you
never knew
that you were my reason

he liked that one song
about love and trying
about losing and finding
because he thought
it was about him
but at the end of the day
he still wrote
number one gay nigger
across his son's skull
just to keep him
from saying my name
and the ironic thing
is just like that song,
over heart
i had painfully turned every stone
just to find
that sometimes
fathers love Leviticus
more than they love their own sons

45

like Isaac on the altar
like Jesus on the cross
sons stand forsaken
bleeding for sins
they can't name

number one gay nigger
and
he sacrificed his son
just so
he wouldn't love
no
number one gay nigger
no faggot black american
with music in the dark
no
number one gay nigger
like me

over dreams
i thought things
would be easy
believing stevie
when he said
true love just needs a chance
but we never had a chance
because one Sunday morning
while the son was sleeping
the father was thinking
about all the nasty things
we must've been doing
the night before

one Sunday morning
while the son was sleeping
the father was thinking
about all the places
i must have touched his son
with my dirty nigga-faggot hands
and all his dreams
seemed deferred

he had cashed in
one star for fifty
just so his son could be a man,
he traded islands
he traded puerto rico for manhattan
he traded islands and sand castles
for el barrio and manhood
but his son
wouldn't be a man
if i could touch him
like that
in the dark
if i could touch him
with my music
if i could touch him
with my heart

so, one Sunday morning
while the son was sleeping
the father took his breath away
he took that life away

and when the father was done
there was no son
only a body torn to pieces
flesh removed from bone
because he had been looking
for the little thing
that made his son a faggot
and when he could not find it
and there was only the skull
when there was nothing left but the skull

he wrote his reason across it,
he addressed it to me,
he wrote
he scratched
he carved
number one gay nigger
across his son's skull

because he thought
that was my name

he killed his son
over sex with a man
over sex with a
number one gay nigger

he killed his son
over islands traded
over sand castles given away
over what people might say
over machismo bullshit

he killed his son

over time
over love
over a number one gay nigger
over me

Four to Seven Hundred Fourteen
Uriah Bell

I didn't know what normal was
But
I knew when I heard that
Number – FOUR
It was not normal, or good.
I wish I could've
Counted the tears
That streamed from
My eyes as easily as
They'd been counted.
Four.
I stared blankly – hearing nothing
More of the death sentence.
Should I begin my
Goodbyes?
Would I even have enough
Time to say
What I wanted to say
To who I needed
To say it to?
I felt limp. Lifeless.
It was time to say
Goodbye.
Four.
That had to be wrong.
No one could be
Alive with just
Four.
Denial.
I wasn't alive at all.
October 2002
The 19th day to be
Exact. FOUR.
I wasn't fit to live.
FOUR.
I'm not a
Quitter.
No way.
But how?

FOUR.
I found a support
In friends
Family,
even co-workers.
I reached to God.
HE reached back.
I found my will.
Somewhere deep
In my heart, and in
God's presence,
I found my will to live.
This, like the streets of Detroit
And the addicts
I'd been surrounded with
Would
Not
Take
Me.
I'm too damned
Evil
To succumb
So easily.
FOUR IS NOT ENOUGH.
Normal is 600+.
Normal.
I've never wanted
To be normal.
No one could
Define normal
To me.
Societies acceptance?
Is that normal?
600+ is normal.
Today I am 714.
Never so proud to be "normal"
Or to
Wear
A number.
I'm an individual, but
I embrace 714.
I've lost so many.
We all have.

I almost lost
Myself.
No.
Not normal.
Better than.
Four
To
Seven hundred
Fourteen.

Thank

You

Jesus.

Bench Marks
Marvin K. White

Then it was shirt or skin. Then it was my skinny against theirs. Then it was the confusion of my body to their assigned roles. Then it was not concentrating on the ball or the net or the score or the game because I could not take my eyes off of them and couldn't look at them, both. Then it was them, all scars and young muscle. Then it was them yelling things that made each other jump higher, push back, run faster, fight. Then it was me crying inside at this boy's noise. Then it was me looking at my body and pushing it back, running fast from it, fighting. Then it was me singing the national anthem to thousands. Then it was me at the top of the cheerleader's pyramid. Then it was me, the only one of us, not to make the team. Then it was me making that ball mean more than it should of. Then it was me knowing that all boys knew how to dribble, knew how to charge, how to do a layup, how to dream about dunking. Then it was me not touching the rim and on the rim at the same time. Then it was me putting my shirt back on. Then it was me knowing these boys would never, should never see me half-naked again. Then it was me having my downcast eyes or absolute wonder misinterpreted. Then it was me knowing it was all true what they were saying. Then it was me bench and sidelined for my entire adolescence. Then it was me safe distanced from my brothers reputations. Then it was me safe distanced from my sister's space as the only girl. Then it was me not looking at myself again until I was 18. Then it was me shirtless and skinless for men like and unlike them. Then it was too late.

Sissy
Vince Wilson

lil punk
actin just like Ma
him wanna be loved too
and keep warm through winter times
and save a few extra pieces of candy for rough times
too sweet
sweeter than the day is long
crying at the drop of a dime
swishy and soft
backside much too big to be overlooked
too elegant
an odd piece of furniture in a room full of second hand artifacts
hidden in the back room when company come by
him sad
listenin to Preacha talk about hellfire that will surely burn him
and Uncle talk about life that will surely scold him

watch them eyes, Boy
Don't linger too long in my face
Mind your manners and mannerisms
Make like a real man
And don't tell nobody what happened in that back room

lil punk
just want to be loved
to be enough
and stay in the shade during summer times
with long lonely nights creeping up like long shadows at dusk

button up for the cold world

gawd and alluh huh sistahs
letta neely

on dat great gittin up mornin'
gawd and alluh huh sistahs
wuz weaving theyselves a fine Tuesday
some fixin breakfast for each other
and some still in bed ringin in da mornin' slowly/softly

one sistah said to another, "it's so much light in heah, we
need some shade"
"ummmmmm hmmmmm," they all went, even the sistahs
who wuz lovin said, "ummmmmm hmmmmm" and got off
              the clouds
   to join the circle that wuz forming

the sistahs all gathered round each other into a circle and
began callin
colors into the sky
          chantin
               "sunloveshe i found a place to lay my head
earth deep resonant
     blackness empowering soulful blackness a
     happyblacksong pulled
        from blackness
            to blackness beautifulpowerful
                  comfortingglovingblackness"

and one tall sistah started spinning round
      with her dreads flying round her and circles of
    green and blue   purple and blue
    wuz trailing round her with gawd and alluh
huh sistahs shoutin
        and clappin

"it's you my sistah, it's you, you bettah go on girl wit yo bad self,
it's you girl,
    go sistaaah, go, go sistaaaaah go, sistah go"
  and that tall ebony sistah raised her hands through the
sky and stretched her feets in the dirt till they became roots and
    she say
      "sunloveme i found a place to lay my head
earth deep resonant
    blackness empowering soulful blackness a

    happyblacksong pulled
            from blackness
                to blackness beautifulpowerful
                      comfortinglovingblackness"

            and don't ya'll know soon it wuz
      nightfall and alluh a sudden there wuz this
      sound of crickets and
      waves reachin
      all the way up to them clouds where gawd and
alluh huh sistahs
            wuz braidin and twistin each other's hair
            and makin up songs
for the second day we didn't git to read about in no
            bible neither

Full
Rickey Laurentiis

We made a crank, a clear
cry of rock against metal,

and the scent of six lit
bodies, their heads

low inside their caving chests.
When you curved into that first

heavy punch and cleaved
the white of my spine, I couldn't

know the spicy charm of it,
how you would arch my back

into the sad shape of a moon,
or how the grain

of your tackle was dear lord—
enough.

Ascension
Darius Omar Williams

they dance
legs
brown skin
veins bulge
shorts skintight
dip baby dip
legs
tattooed, shaven
bending or kicking
flying
below a flashing neon light

they vogue
picasso van gogh
watson themed paintings
come alive
as miss ross begs
to take them higher
she rallies for everybody
to extend their arms and
reach out
reach out
reach out
and
touch
greasy palms
touch
stubby cheeks
touch
synthetic wigs
touch
real hair
touch
a tear
touch

they say hey baby
hey sister
hey girl
hey miss charles
hey hey hey
dark corners
become meeting spots
for best friends   enemies   lovers
lips smoke blunt
flash teeth
grow old

they discuss recent deaths
the bud light mystery
of a misty eye forever
plays the role of Kodak camera
in motion

they discuss honey miss thang
working that dress
then dance
for miss e.t.
for miss blade
for miss cornelius
for miss dana
for miss krystal
for miss john

they all clap and say work bitch
while miss telmon walks
hoping
praying he can run
the last mile
toward all of their tomorrows
cause iron wrought souls
need some lifting up
and they know
yes they definitely know
their
lips
need
kissing

For the chil'ren
Uriah Bell

I have to give it up
for the ball kids. The ones
who live vicariously through
excitement of the crowds.
The ones who work for,
and make, and beg for,
borrow and steal labels
just for the night.
The ones whose juices flow
at the drop of a beat, tada, tuh, ta, ta ,ta.

The queens of shade, a defense mechanism
that only the kids know.
the ones that walk for
fresh face, and
butch queen.
Next to the runway can I see?
Fem/queen/versus/butch/queen,
and let's not forget
Realness,
body, and
HOUSE.

The chil'ren who beat their faces
create new styles.
Give it their all.
the house mothers and gay fathers,
the ones who find family after
family refused to accept them.
The kids who go into the world
so cruel and un-accepting, and
insist on being true to self.

This is for the chil'ren.
My sistas, and brothas.
walk your categories,
give it to 'em in vogue,
in dance, in shade
in style.
You
Betta
Work!

The First Sign
Marvin K. White

The children were gathered around the velvet rope, holding not only hands but also breaths. The gyros that spun them, perfectly teetering on it their points. For points. No one toppled in the sway of this sea of sissies. It has been days and outfits. Some even dared to be seen twice in theirs. They waited. No one would, no one could enter until they knew that a new DJ was named. It has been days since the death of the last turntablist. A world stuck in a groove is different than a world working its way out of a scratch. No one could dance, could get their life, could twirl, could fall out, could offer legs and arms and extensions and by extension, extensions. Holding on to a tune is harder than holding on to hope. If it wasn't for...wait. As if the choreographer pointed to God and said "and one..."we all held our breaths. A thousand of us baited. Waited. Pink smoke! It was pink smoke floating like incense ghosts over us. He has ascended! He is named! We can dance again! Our backs snapped into place. We lined up like perfect pearls in the knit. Entered. Was entered. Remembered. Was remembered. Swerved and served notice to dancestors that we have not forgotten the ancient ways. We go way back. Go sway back. Dance. Throw shoulders to the throne. Offer the tambourine of our assess. Drum our feet. Our feet drum. Our bodies, our cries. Our bodies, our prayers. Our bodies, our thanks. We live out this sacrifice. Leave it all there. We altarpieces. We altar peaces. We altar. We.

Computer Love
Mystalic Writing

He works best in the dark with a cigarette lit and a can of Nestea®

Blood shot eyes reread the screen over and over again

His body hunched as if he were chained to the computer desk

Scouring the sites lookin for him

Looking for that one person, that might catch his eye for the night

Him, that dude, that ole head, that young bull, that nigga

That man that's going to make his fantasies come true

The one that's going to come through with no questions or hang-ups

From adam to Black Gay Chat he's on and off never leaving the seat

Interludes of porn interrupt his search concurrently

So even if he was to find him, he wouldn't be any good

All his goods lay at the seat of the chair sprinkled here and there

He is in love

He's having a computer affair

Where else could you find cheap clips of sex

To externalize your deepest desires

And at the same time match you with 52 men in your area

Rarely leaving the seat and if so it's a bathroom interruption

And he tries to keep those to a minimum so he doesn't eat at night

He doesn't sleep at night

This is his life this is what is right

"Are you up" Appears on the screen

Instant messenger signals his message

Never hesitant he replies

"What are you getting into tonight?"

"Dunno" Appears very quickly on the screen

And he quickly types

"Well how about getting into me"

Door bell rings

He grabs a towel wraps it around his waste

Walks to the door

Enter his nightly fling

Not a word said

Words can only break the concentration

Straight to the bed

A lil nipple suck

Some quick head

And they began to fuck

Not a word, not even a grunt

Hastily the man gets dressed after the discharge of his internal love

And our friend our beloved computer hustler

He gets up and goes back to his throne

So he can find the next victim to bring home

Funny though through all the typing

And loving he has done

He still finds himself alone

Still he loves no one

even on sun days
Tim'm T. West

I am rich with touch
urgent for the sensuality of now
will not deny the way my eyes
make the world naked
today
fleshly, softer
tempting our sweat

this hunger
is a call from God
desire, a ritual
parallel to prayer
and these lips that whisper
to Jesus
are full of kiss

these songs of praise
began
with my tongue em bodied
em beded, en joy
so touch me
the deepest, most neglected parts
surrender
making art of sacrifice

this is my body
broken
taste its wounds
dance to my heart
still beating
place your ear
where it drums
jazz-lick til I laugh
like an angel or a star
fall into me
like tears do

cuz we know God in this
and this is how we know God
perfect
sweet
passionate
and because making love
is gospel
even on sun days

For Those Newly Diagnosed
Uriah Bell

That moment you're called into the office
Will undoubtedly be the most numb you'll
Ever feel.
You'll experience feelings of questioning
And denial, but
Ultimately accept that it's reality.
The numbness will surpass that
First love lost,
When you were sure you couldn't go on.
The news will unquestionably come at a time
when you're on top of the world.
Overloaded by fear and doubt, and all hope is gone.
No matter what your past is
You'll wonder for days; who.
And after all the tears have collected
You'll accept its truth.
To those newly diagnosed
Is to hold tight to faith.
This is no death sentence, but
Merely a wakeup call.
An obstacle; Gods way
Of putting you through the fire, only
For you to emerge as pure and priceless
as gold.
The most important thing to learn, is
That you are not dying, merely living
In a new light.
Suddenly the sky's blue means more.
Being awakened by the birds singing
is no longer annoying, but a blessing.
The snickers and whispers of others
are grains of salt, washed away by your rebirth.
Instantly, positive becomes positive
And your world is reversed.
When you first hear those words,
And you have no idea where to go,
Who to tell,
What to do,
This is your second chance.
This is your new opportunity

Mighty Real

To right the wrongs,
get closer to God and yourself.
Listen to the birds songs, and
your heart.
This is your chance to
Forgive, as you've been forgiven.
This is your moment
To take control of
Your life.
When you first hear
That diagnosis, use it
As your permission slip, an
All access pass to live.

Scattered Thoughts
LaCelle White

I mean…some clubs be chargin' like $10 to walk through the door
only to have me look at all the showcased, top shelved liquor on their top shelf
yet I still have to point to the cheap, bottom shelf
after I finally fight through the tsunami to order our drinks
I go for the $2.00 draft
cuz you want a drink and so do I
but you don't have money and what I have is low
I mean…I just wanna take you to a bar where we walk in hand in hand
and get handed a menu
we order whatever our heart's desire
while we desire each other
I just once wanna take you to the mall
put that high-tech surround sound stereo system we saw at Sears on my credit card
but I ain't got good credit so the card is out of the question
and the money I have left after bills is bullshit
so instead we end up at the riverwalk
walking for free…soul to soul
we talk about our dreams and our aspirations and expectations of ourselves and the world
and of love
I love that we can enjoy nature and it be just as fulfilling as buying that high-tech surround sound stereo system
I mean..my ex always said I "need to make a concerted effort to be clear in your thoughts and words"
which brings me back to what I initially wanted to vent about…
the clubs that charge $10 just to walk through the door
I mean…I wish my ex and I could still walk hand and hand through the club door and fight hurricane Katrina at the bar
but she dumped me.

We are our own heroes
(for the BBLAM Brothers Reading, 10/20/09)
Alan Miller

We are the murderer's row of poets,

the four horsemen of the apocalypse

and their four-legged friends

galloping across the field, leaving

gardens of plenty in our wake.

We are the creature gatherers for the ark

each blowing a horn of plenty,

the clucking mothers of new cookbooks,

the architects of spiritual skyscrapers,

the inventors of vaccines against homophobia

and hatred, the wet nurses of a new way,

baring our bountiful black bosoms

and our bouncing black asses

in hostile towers and corners.

(We are not the red-headed Rapunzels,

locked away, or repentant Hesters branded

with scarlet letters in the forest).

We are ridiculous and careless

and humble and absurd and prideful

and scandalous and new. We are nurturers

and fools and Cadillac and wise and wasteful,

solemn and sweet. We are rotten to the core,

and cured, sweet to the taste and twisted.

We are evil and good, welcome
and shut-in. We are shocked and shocking
and shameless. We are getting older
and wiser.

We are the keepers, the caretakers,
of mothers and memories,
the keepers of fathers and fables,
the man and woman in union.
We are the ones families turn to in crisis
and we are Isis and Rebecca and Deborah
and Sarah and Rachel, the men of faith
and the infidels. We are Daniel, David and Isaac.
We are Samson and Moses.

We are the bloody sacrifice
and we are the bloody hands,
the makers of dollar-store gumbo and gourmet goulash,
the librarians of love, the superheroes of funk
and sweet and cold, and we have enough anger
to last through several global warmings.
We are the beaters of earth and planters of seed,
the mamas and the papas for future generations.
We are law-makers and law-breakers,
the justices and the judged.

 We are our own myth, our own truth, our own window
reflecting a newnew oldnew world.
Tonight, tonight, we will sing our own songs.

Brown Eyes and Unavailable
Travis Montez

1.
he will never read this
he will never unfold these pages
and read
breathe
feel
these words
and know what I know

he will never see
the him that I see
have always seen

not even now

words spoken
to the music of heartbeats
said out loud
lived
but still
he will never hear this

he will never hear:

the first day I saw you
really saw you
I thought
you have kind eyes
brown kissing green
a gold in certain sunlight
like
my grandmother's
and
I have
a particular love
for the way
your laughter
spills out
covers everything around you
like a child's fingerpaint

messy and genuine
sweet

you are sweet
like Sunday mornings
in spring
and simple love notes
that say
"just thinking about you"

and sometimes
I stare at you
so I can remember
every bit of you
when you are not around

2.
maybe this
is not loving him
as much
as it
is hating myself

3.
he will never hear this
he will never see this or me
even
with eyes
like my grandmother's
to his senses
i am something
else
another country
language
an unfamiliar dance

and even with simple words
like
try me
get to know me
see me

he does not understand
there is no chorus or harmony
not here
not between us

friends
both mine and his
say
I am foolish
to want
someone so intent on not being had
they say,
I am great and I can do better
but no one
no friends
have a clue
or a map
as to where
I can find
better

and they don't get
that when I close my eyes
and just listen
I hear him
like the ocean

4.
he will never read this
after words spoken
pressed against heartbeats

still

I am not what he is looking for
I am not what he sees

my mother would say
sweetie, you can't have the ocean

5.
love something
you can have

protected
Tim'm T. West

remind yourself
they are raindrops
heavy
not the sound of him
coming
again
you are not
the blur between 3 and 4
mom and dad didn't leave you here
with him
again
you will breathe easy this time
pillows hold breath
and Jesus loves you
little one

remind yourself
you are 37
can protect yourself
choose the breath beside you
choose who comes to you
with you
on you
if at all
choose the knight
that will protect
from the nightmares

it is the sound
of your heart beating
loud
or rain
not footsteps
anymore
this is Houston
not Dallas
Texas is hot all over
your sweat
is from that
not a panic attack
like 16
thinkin' the pain
could end
if life did
asking Jesus to save you
or forgive
the courage to take a life
tainted
for desiring to be
protected

there is a single tear
for feeling left alone
again
unprotected
remember
you are not a crier
you are a man, no longer a boy
are strong
can kick ass, if needed
sharp knuckles, strong grip,
learned how to box early
knock niggas out
do death grips, find the weak points
for protection

you are 37
strong(er)
can bench press, rap, and basketball
have gotten over fragility
remember
you are loved today
there are angels around you
who'd protect if they knew
you get afraid
sometimes
at 37
they will not run away
like disciples
at crucifix time
think you are too intense
for bearing truth
the way God has called you to
will stay and protect
when truth gets thick
like tonight

and you are older
and life can smile
like Jesus to a child

if you make it so
hug the pillows tighter
remember
they are big heavy raindrops
and it is the fan blowing
not breath
heavy
some preacher man
telling you to trust God
and breaking your flesh
and spirit
hours after
3 or 4

go back to sleep
write the poem as therapy
about being the real man
you promised to always be
a manly man
a protected protector
by baritone and glare
by swagger and swole
cuz therapists simply make you
feel it all over again
and you have prayed to Jesus
to make you forget

but tonight
the dark feels lonely
and you'd give anything
to be held
right
to cry
not for hurting
but because
there are arms
that can make you forget
you were ever 3 or 4
left with a man
of God
to be protected

blksestina

for nirmalani ngozi abiaka
letta neely

Adenenye's sleep was filled with heavy rain and dirt
slipping through cracks in the ceiling from mountain
while an elder sat in the rainforest twisting magic
in her locks, and songs which would not be called music
here rose from her inclining ants and goddesses to dance
like blues in the flame of fire

With hot colors swirling down the mountain she met fire
She walked outside barefooted, her toes mingling with cool dirt
Adenenye felt the plum colored elder call her to dance
She saw the sunrise and followed her up the mountain
There, she saw a goddess playing djembe to the elder's music
Adenenye dove headfirst into the waves of magic

Coming through the song, she became magic
Laughter flowing through her entire body, she was on fire
inside and everything—the water, her footsteps, the stones—had
       its own music
The rhythms all ancient as dirt
She stood watching a goddess sift dreams through her earth
       brown hands over an edge of mountain
Dreams dusting over like snowflakes made her want to dance

Adenenye became the wind when she started to dance
She also conjured ghosts and spirits with her swaying side-to-side
       magic
It was an old-fashioned revival up there on the mountain
Cuz Adenenye had waded through fire and found dirt
underneath her pores that tasted like music

She found she could make music
Just by exhaling—making her nasal hairs dance
Just by drawing a circle with her toe in the dirt
The goddesses knew Adenenye's magic
They had long ago walked through the dreaming fire
Into the mountain

Heavy dreams and dirt fell from the mountain
while an elder with skin like red clay plucked music
into her locks with songs that burned blue like fire
and Adenenye opened her eyes in slumber to dance
and pour from her own hands magic
black and deep as dirt

Adenenye awoke to dirt underneath her tongue and stones in her
bed from a mountain
of magic piled up inside her and the music
dripping from her eyes was the ocean she had danced through to
meet fire

Before Iraq Comes/A First-Love Poem
for billy
Travis Montez

[one]
if I had ever written him a love poem it would have gone like this:

you found me
in the middle of things
falling apart
or maybe just becoming
what they were always meant to be

back then/i was thick glasses.
dark skin. good grades.
and feminine.

back then/junior high school boys
with cracking voices
and absent fathers
used me to test
the shadow
of their new manhood

back then/i was sissie.oreo.faggot
invisible
and all my things   were falling apart
when you found me
in gym class   too ashamed to undress
in the locker room
in front of normal boys
because i believed my skin burned
with the unwanted fingerprints
of the night time things
that happened to me

back then/ you were track-football-wrestling star
light skinned. masculine. popular. envied.
and you found me   there
trying to be invisible
looking down at the locker room floor
trying not to see or be seen

and you said my name
in front of your friends
you said   Travis
and smiled at me
called me friend.brother.same-as-you

you looked at my body
and didn't see fingerprints
burned flesh or the night time things
instead, you asked me if I worked out
and said i had the natural build of an athlete
just like you…

that was the first time I fell in love with you

the second time came
when you told me
that your white mother
never taught you
how to comb your black hair
and you asked me to show you

and i fell in love with you again
when you passed me a note
in fourth period science class
telling me that your brother
had done to you
the same night time things
my cousin did to me
so, you understood
my need to be invisible

and my fear of locker rooms
you understood the tears
and the dreams of blood and fire
you promised that the world
wouldn't stay like that
you promised that it was more
than junior high school boys
and night time things

you convinced me
that the blood and fire would
set with the sun one day
you convinced me   that despite the tears
i wasn't really falling apart
just becoming
what i was truly meant to be

[two]
he leaves for Iraq
just after the new year
and in one way
it makes sense
because he has always
protected me
from things
larger than myself

but in another way
i cannot get my mind
around the idea
that i may lose him
to something i cannot fight
or touch or name
even in poetry…

i have always had him
since i was 12 years old
for 14 years now
he has been my billy

it was my love for him
that made me realize

that only the love of a man
could make me complete

it was my love for him
that made me step
into myself

he is not gay
we have never been lovers
but we have always been
unconditional and real

and i have always had him
the day after being raped
the day after being dumped
the day after graduating from law school
the day after nothing at all
his shoulder has always had a place
for me to cry/laugh/rest/be
whatever i needed to be…

so i put this
in the wind
in the universe
in the hands of god

keep him safe
because i am not done yet
i still need him
to be my unconditional and real place
and i must promise him
that life will not always be   war
and that i will be here
the day after suicide bombs
the day after injured civilians
the day after anything larger than himself
or even nothing at all

keep him safe

we are not done yet…

Teenage Drag Queen
Shane Allison

I walk into the bathroom of homecoming queens,
The glass stalls of cheerleading squads
To strip to my underwear.
Stretch my cock, tucking it between teenage thighs
Spray myself with Estee Lauder perfume
Pull out the lipstick I stole from Mama's purse

Stare into the medicine cabinet mirror pursing
My lips to veil them redder than those of a queen.
The high school fills with the scent of Estee Lauder perfume
As I prance down hallway squads
Of butch boys who tease and taunt, grabbing at my stocking thighs.
Teachers in wide-eyed disbelief can't believe what I'm wearing.

I have balls of steel to wear
These heels and come to school with a purse
Beneath my arms. Greeted with angry eyes for showing a little thigh
And having the gall to walk down these high school halls like I'm the queen
Of England. *Oh my God,* says a squad
Of girls in the bathroom, with their bottles of perfume.

They gawk with their made-up, perfumed
Faces. Tease their hair as I pull out the underwear
That rides up my ass when suddenly a squad
Of bullies with outbursts of curse words rushes in and grabs my purse

pinning me to the wall of a nearby stall like the faggot teen queen
I am with my dick taped high to my thighs.
Fucking faggot! One of them yells as he knees me in the thigh
And holds me by the neck in a bathroom that reeks of perfume
From a gang of promising prom queens.
He asks, *so you like to wear girl's underwear?*
He rummages through my purse
As the squad

Of girls from the cheerleading squad
Struggle in pulling the brutes off. I knee a thug in the nuts with my
bruised thigh.

He drops my purse,
Breaking the bottle of perfume.
I kick him in the face with the heels I'm wearing
Before the principal, Mrs. Queen

Storms through the squad of bullies
And girls with their pretty faces and perfumed
Bosoms with borrowed purses hanging off their shoulders
Wearing thigh-high stockings.

Blessed Assurance
Darius Omar Williams

he sashay shantay in a dress on the outskirts of town
the stank aroma of worn out pussy. his aged smile,
like murmurs and edicts and the misery of cracked feet,
he insists on smiling at everybody. his hateful self:
the old tasteless burden of bloodstained underwear.
his blood stained breath. his hair, honey yes.
one of those refashioned rihanna-styled wigs
accessorized with beyonce-ass-shaking-devotion.
shit, bitch i can't be late
church going god fearing sistah
he smell like blue tropical wind
is baby you better learn it well. i remember him.
when he was the choir director at my church.
those fixin-to-go-somewhere hands.
how they told the sopranos, tenors and altos
to repeat the second verse. today he turned forty-two.
is a bitter drag-queen, a whispered epitaph.
he became she. made new melody up. sanctified?
baby, he soniafied. comes correct. comes dressed to the nine.
sanctified? baby, he soniafied.
creasing us with wings as he unrumbles earth. miss thing serves.
make a ho over yonder scream
like how the chil'ren do in paris is burning.
he mother. mother of a ruthless house.
ruthless as a sissy with no teeth.
he walks. yes. he walks. i declare. he walks
until his feet start to hurt, until he nears a sorrowful spot,
the spot where all the streetlights done blown out.
a police car pulls up, traces of dried up cum on his leg.
serious sirens blare—an unfriendly reminder of how trade
dicked him down raw as ever—just snuck up in his shit: a stern/heavy
hello. i ain't scared of no damn police, he recites like poetry to himself.
violent like slave owners and torture. he sees no faces just lights. this
incipient road of contradiction in which his flowered head splits apart.
mercy to jesus mixed with rhythms of gun shells. gun shells grinding
against his wig and *faggot nigger bitch, don't move!*

I'm a Woman (I'm a Backbone)
for Chaka Khan
Djola Branner

i believed all the lyrics you sang
like/*thangs have been going wrong
long enough to know/everything
is right*

and *I'm a Woman (I'm a Backbone)*

were real/cause
you were always laughing
like a chorus of exotic bird
or crying like a fork in the Nile

and i wish you had cried
more often Chaka
cause then
you wouldn't have been snorting
and shooting
(who knows?)
and smoking so much
and maybe i could say right now
i don't feel betrayed.

we made love some Saturdays
when mama thought
i was singing to pass the time
and keep from cleaning house

      your voice moved into mine
like the sun moves into dawn
defined the tone
the pitch
   the rise
      and fall
         and the end result
was always live

somebody say Chaka
and my name was uttered
in the same breath
bernardandChakaandChakaandbernard

and friends heard me screaming
your name at concerts
        shouting/ SING IT GIRL!
and yeah baby
           ooow
                get down
                      and crawling
all over chairs
to get within view of your nubian eyes
but never touching you
(though i could have once)
cause i would have known
you were flesh
and blood
and not a backbone
or a sweet thang
or any other words your songs
described you as.

you were just trying to make it
     like the rest of us
laughing when we could find time
and trying to keep from crying

and i wish you had cried
more often Chaka
cause then
you wouldn't have been snorting
and shooting
(who knows?)
and smoking so much
and maybe i could say right now
i don't feel betrayed
and that i had not betrayed you
believing you were a backbone/
and not

a woman.

Souliloquy (A Septet of Haiku)
Vince Wilson

I'd better go now
It's so late that it's early
A new sun listens
Two nappy head men
shining in the afterglow
of forbidden touch
forming silhouettes
indivisible, sticky.
Should have gone by now:
the whole world hates us
taught us to hate each other
but we're Black rebels,
a pair of confused
and unlucky refugees
two homeless spirits
so i'll stay a while,
meditate in/be-side you,
and forget the world
as we, once again—
one again—patch the jagged
fragments of our lives

Press On
R. Bryant Smith

Press on, stunt worker.
You doer of iniquity!
Oh, how you turn me on
With that silver tongue
That speaks such sweet melodious rapture...
All words befitting royalty.
All lies!
No truth in them at all!

But you're good, stunt worker!
You are good enough
To make me work
Three full time jobs
And two part time jobs on the side
When I look into those bedroom eyes;
When I look at those sensual lips;
Those masculine features;
Those manly ways;
That would allow me to take you home
To meet the entire family...
And that body that no one else
But a magnificent God could have created....
Um, um, um
Hallelujah!
Thank You, Jesus!
If you are a chip off of the old block
Then let me see the damned block!

I know your type!
And you know mine!
And you know what to say,
How to say it,
And when to say it!
Press on!
Press on!
Press on, stunt worker!

I can't stand the sight of you
Because you are an appetizer,
A full course meal,

And a dessert on the side,
Washed down with a 1920 glass of Chablis.

But you're no good, stunt worker!
You know this!

But I fool myself
And play along with the game
Thinking that somehow
I can be heroic...
The Saint of all saints!
The one who saves you
From the error of your ways,
And perhaps I can
If you take your lips off my neck.
Your hands off my waist,
Your crotch off my butt,
Your smell,
Oh, that smell...
Your earthen chemistry
Born out of Africa
Beat down for generations
Of sweat
Tears
Pain
Camouflaged with the sweet mix
Of myrrh,
Sandalwood,
And precious spices.

And I sin
When I think about what we can do
With clothes on -
With clothes partially on -
With clothes partially off -
With no clothes on at all!
Um, um, um
Have mercy!
Have mercy!
Have mercy!
You are so fine, stunt worker,
And you present all the qualities before me
That I desire in my mate!

You play havoc
On my senses
But not on my good judgment!
Press on, stunt worker!

Yeah, I've been down that road before!
I can't save you
Until I save me!

Don't look so sad
Because I picked your tea
And penetrated through your mask.
You know, the one you wear so well!
But if I don't stop now
I'll hate you tomorrow
And to hate you tomorrow
Is to hate myself!
And to hate myself
Is to hate God!

Press on!
Press on!
Press on, stunt worker!

Everything that my God made was good!
And so I am!
And so are you!
Press on!

I can love you in friendship!
I can love you in brotherhood!
I can love you in genuine camaraderie.
But there will be NO
One night stand
One week stand
One month stand
One year stand
For you, stunt worker,
Press on!

Kin Folks
Shane Allison

The face of Aunt Norris
when she saw me hanging
flyers for a gay poetry group on a bulletin board.
The face of Uncle Weed
when he got the word from Aunt Norris
that I might be queer.
My face when he asked,
drunk off his ass, if I suck dick.
The face of Aunt Earline finding out the news from Uncle Weed,
who found out from Aunt Norris,
that the nephew who loves her jelly cake
more than life, likes men the way women do.
The face Auntee Alice made when it was whispered in her ear
by her daughter, my cousin, Chrissy,
that her nephew, the son of one of her brother's, is a punk.
The faces of cousin Melvet and cousin Toni,
who used to give me free chicken at Popeye's
and all the burgers I could eat from Burger King,
that the cousin she never sees is a fag.
The face of the twins, Kee-Kee and Kenny,
finding out from cousin Sean in a game of gin rummy,
about the rumor that the 'ham' of the family,
is a faggot.
The wrinkles of Auntee Mable's face stretched,
her husband's mouth, dropped open, when they got wind
of the latest familial scandal that their nephew,
the cousin to her daughters,
Tameka, Monique and Kim,
the second cousin to their children,
plays for the pink team.
The face of Leisha getting the call in Virginia.
The face of Duane hearing of it in Wakulla.

The faces of Ebony and J.R. putting two and two
Together after figuring out exactly which cousin, and being
none other than shocked beyond belief that I kiss and lie with men.
The face of my uncle they call 'Chicken Man,'
the brother to sisters, the brother to brothers,
the father to son and daughters, and the ex-husband to
the ex-wife in Woodville,
hearing that I am an all out abomination,
a sinner, a sodomite.

What I Should Have Told The Homeless Man In Cleveland Who Mistook Me for Mary's Son
L. Lamar Wilson

Jesus, Jesus, Jesus ... By the time I hear it,
I have passed the beggar by three long strides,
sashaying in my low-rise jeans like Tudda taught
me accenting the hips Mama brought me. I am bound
to bask in an estrogen sea at the House of Blues.
I think he's talking to you, my friends tell me. Instantly,
I am wailing during midweek prayer meeting,
the church mothers' cries lifting my petitions. *O Lord,
I want to be like you. O Lord, I want to know your heart. O Lord,
I want Your thoughts to be mine. None but the righteous shall
see God*, they moaned on those hot summer nights,
their Savior some no count man who ran off & left
them, making me want him all the more. Who knew
I'd find him here, prostrate, before me? How sweet
the sound now, this fallen soldier's plea for penance
on this corner of Euclid Avenue, his insanity my salvation.
I am born again. Our heads crane, mouths agape,
both begging for communion. I cradle his grimy palms
& whisper words only he & I hear. Then I rise, put my arms
around my stunned women friends & make our way
to hear Floetry's love letters. But what I should have told
the homeless man in Cleveland who mistook me
for Mary's son is: I am not the man you seek. I turn water
into ice. I will never forsake my mother, will never
follow their Father's edicts. I will kiss a man tonight,
but they would not call it holy. He will flay my flesh
with the tip of his tongue, & we will dance, then ooze
with the guilt I welcome, earnestly, on my knees.

Breaking the Skin
Shane Allison

This is a sad poem.
This is a bitter poem.
I'm a crazy goddamned poet with a lot of shit on my mind.
I am a gay, black male.
I like penises. I'm a top. I am 28. I am shy.
I am not your stereotypical gay man.
I prefer white men.
I like red heads best. Brunettes.
I like black men too. I'm just picky about them.
My pride doesn't come on a tee shirt or a bumper sticker.
I don't have a boyfriend.
The right guy hasn't come along yet.
I'm waiting for him to fall into my lap.
I like gay-situated films.
I like gay-situated books.
I am promiscuous damn it. I admire virgins for their devotion.
I took an HIV test in 1995. It came back negative.
I don't go out much. I drink on occasion.
I don't go to bars.
I like to cruise public toilets for my sex.
I don't think that's disgusting so fuck you.
Fuck you man!
My favorite food is steak.
My favorite color is Black.
I don't have a favorite actor. I have many favorite TV shows.
I watch a great deal of television. I eat a lot.
Everybody's always asking,
"How old were you when you knew you were gay?"
I was six when I first kissed a boy.
They pretend to be surprised, but I don't think they ever believe me.
His name was Tony. He had curly hair and soft, fat lips.
We would sneak off in the bathroom with yellow tile
and he would sprinkle me with kisses.
His breath was darling.
 We had to stop 'cause
our teacher was getting curious.
Ira Miller poured milk in my face.
He kicked my ass using karate.
His brother was nice and took me to his mom's house
when I burned my hand on the cap of my grandma's stove.

I was hungry trying to cook wieners.
Karen told me not to touch anything. She went to the mall.
I hated being left alone.
There was this one boy.
His name was Von and he lived up the street from me.
We went to the same school together.
He was in a grade higher.
We would run off like lovers giving
each other blowjobs in the woods on an old,
dirty mattress that smelled of piss.
I knew how to suck dick even then.
He shot baby semen in a pile of dead leaves.
Von would call me every afternoon.
He was obsessed.
I was the only gay boy he knew.
He liked to have fun.
His cock would rub against the pink roof of my mouth.
I used to hear stories about him
on the school bus about how he would invite boys over to spend the night
and spill cocoa butter lotion in the bed while they were asleep.
Then they would wake up the next morning feeling wet.
Von would say, "You came in the bed."
Everyone knew he liked boys.
He has orange hair now and is wanted for grand theft auto.
Greg, the only white boy on our street liked acting black.
I pinched his butt one morning as he was getting on the bus.
He told everybody about it. I didn't care.
I was a grade school slut at Woodville Elementary.
I sucked Melvin Blake off in the bathroom across from Mrs. Gerrell's class.
I'm gonna write a poem about him next.
I often wonder if he's married with children
and sneaks off into the sheet of night to get his dick blown through
the glory holes of bus stop bathrooms.
I discovered masturbation at 12.
I used to jerk off sitting on the floor of Tillie's bedroom.
I kissed my cousin Darrin on the lips once while he was asleep.
I showed my cousin Mario my dick in the bathroom of my grandma's bedroom.
He pretended to be surprised by the size of it.
We call him Bobee.
He has a girlfriend. I hear she's not pretty.

When I gave Junior a blowjob,
he was the same age I was when I kissed Tony
with the thick-set lips and curly hair.
I hated Orange Avenue Apartments.
 Did I mention Daniel Stuart?
He had bucked teeth and bad B.O.
He sucked me off in the royal blue bathroom
in the seventh grade wing after lunch.
We had Sloppy Joes that day I think.
He gave the best head until he met a girl named Debbie.
After that, he wouldn't go down on any more black boys
in royal blue-colored bathrooms.
I was asked by a guy to go take some pictures
of my dick and bring them to school.
I think he was joking. Or was he?
Eldridge James thought he caught me
 jacking off in the bathroom.
He used to wipe boogers on my shirt.
He didn't see a thing, but spread it around
the whole school anyway.
I went to Nims Middle School and hated it.
All the boys wanted to fight me instead of wanting to fuck me.
They picked at my red, leather All-stars.
I remember the burgundy corduroy jeans I wore in a fight with Ron Allen.
He was so cute, but a real asshole.
I had a crush on my 9th grade gym teacher.
His name was Jim Teter.
He had a perky butt.
He could've been gay. I wish he was. I really do.
I lost 10 pounds that year.
Thanks coach.
I used to wear an extra pair of shorts
under my sweats so people in class wouldn't
know that I had a hard-on.
I hated Rickards High.
I was obsessed over Ben Hood.
I used to stick letters in the windshield wipers of his car.
I knew where he worked. I had his home phone number.
I used to call him and he would angrily ask, "Who the hell is this?"
I got over him after he graduated.
They use to call me a fag in Woodshop.
They used to throw textbooks at me in World History.
I carried my dad's rusty hunting knife to school.

The school sheriff almost caught me red-handed.
I wanted to stab Cleveland Richardson for calling me a fag.
His brother was a talented singer.
He killed himself over a girl.
Beticia Johnson made straight A's.
I thought I liked her once in middle school.
She got pregnant.
She shot herself in the front seat of her car over a boy.
A white girl lied and said I walked out of the bathroom
with my cock hanging out of my zipper.
That's what the principal said she said.
She lied.

I had a crush on Eric, a substitute teacher in American History.
I had a crush on Francisco Ortiz.
He was the only Latino at our school.
I used to call his house and hang up.
He was a very talented artist.
I had a thing for Mr. Collier.
He had a jerri-curl and was originally from Miami.
Deep down he was gay. He denied it.
I use to look at guy's dicks at the urinals at *Parkway 5 Theatres*.
Robert Brummerhop made the cutest usher.
He used to be on the swim team.
I heard he really let himself go and is living in Texas.
I watched him through the door of the bathroom stall.
He saw me and said nothing. I got scared and left. He looked at me
as I sat in the lobby.
Heard his brother Ben is a real whore.
I saw him at Club Park Avenue wearing daisy duke shorts.
I got arrested at 17 for showing an undercover cop my prick.
He had blond hair and blue eyes.
I didn't know he was a cop undercover.
My folks were supposed to wait outside the mall for me.
I was there to put fliers in people's windshields about my dad's
new storage building business.
That was the year acid wash jeans were in style.
They handcuffed me like the criminal I was.
A lesbian cop interrogated me in a white room. She asked,
"What if he had have given you a blowjob?"
They released me to my parents.
 I told them I was a victim of racism.
My dad thought it was bullshit.

He talked to me about sex.
He thinks gay men are freaks.
I went to juvenile court.
I had 3 months probation and 75 hrs of community service
working at the animal shelter.
They killed cats and dogs if they were not adopted by a certain date.
I had to see a counselor to talk about my lewd and lascivious act.
My dad went with me.
The psychologist asked me in front of my dad,
 if my parents had ever sexually abused me.
I was as mean as a snake to him.
He thought it was because he was white.
He had me shipped off like a slave to a Dr. Dana Dennard.
He has an office in the back room of a bookstore he owns.
It is called, *Amen-Ras Books*.
It smells like incense.
I had to tell him all the dirty details.
He grimaced as I mentioned the words, *penis and stall*.
"You should think about dating girls," he said.
This was his psychological advice to me.
This was his cure for my being homosexual.
I think he thought that black men were not supposed to be gay.
I think he thought it was a "white thing."
I told him what he wanted to hear, that I was getting better and there
was this one girl who...
My mama found him attractive,
but I thought he was an ugly, hideous monster.
I got arrested again at 25 in Tom Brown Park.
He was a black dude in plain clothes.
He asked me to pull down my pants and sit on the rocks.
I did what he said.
A guy in a red shirt caught us.
"Don't even try to run," he said.
I was taken away in an Oldsmobile to a spot where the real cops hung
out.
I sat in a backseat for 3 hrs. I just wanted to go home.
They were catching guys like me in butterfly nets.
I was taken off to jail.
They made me take off my shoes and empty out the contents of my wallet
on a table.
I called my then friend Lynda to come bail me out.
She had no money.
Marc wasn't home.

I ran out of friends.
Didn't want to call my parents again but I did anyway.
I lied and told them I was stopped for speeding.
They called a bails bondsman and he discovered the hidden truth.
They released me on pre-trial release.
I called back and told them they didn't need to bail me out.
They had to come pick me up. My truck was still at the park.
The drive home was a hanging at high noon.
I had to go to court where I got six months probation.
Paid court fees out the ass.
My mother said she would rather be dead then for me to be gay.
I told Lynda what happened.
I told Doug and Marc what happened.
Locked myself away and wrote poems about the experience.
I wanted to kill myself.
I hate this town.

Sudda
Travis Montez

sometimes
i have to remind myself
that your name
is andrea
i have never
called you that
out loud or in my head
you have always been
sudda
my big sudda
as in sister to a toddler's tongue

so,
sudda,
i cannot know
what it took
for you
at 13 and 14 and 15
between double dutch and crushes
to hide
from a precocious
little brother
that we were poor
or hungry or had not
i could not
have known then
the lioness
you were
or the shadows
you gave your youth
to keep from under my bed

you gave your girlhood
for my freedom
to play and do homework and dream
on them days
mama worked a double shift
or was in love
with some man
who was not in love
with us

on them days
we had to stay
with granny
or friends
in beds not our own
but any day
that ended
with you
rocking me to sleep
was good and perfect

girl

these days
i'm a man
a lawyer
for boys
taught to think themselves
hungry and poor and
having not...

i bring to the table
a lion
all my own
but,
often wonder
how different
their lives
would be
if they'd been blessed
with a sister
a lioness
in pigtails
sassy with double dutch
willing to be hungry
and scared but brave
so that i could be warm
and sure and free

how different their lives would be
if they had a sister
a big sudda
like mine

Hypocrisy
Charles W. Harvey

A misguided soul said to me,
"AIDS cures fags."
I whispered softly into his ear
with my flickering tongue,
"You've been misinformed, My Sweetness,
AIDS cures hypocrisy.
It brought to light all of your afflictions.
I've seen you circling the weed choked corners
picking from the crop of tattered boys
in the fields littered with pieces of red glass
and oxtail bones. I peeped you
on your knees in the dark underbelly of
'STUDZ 24 HOURS' and you were not praying
to one god, but to three gods who towered over you
with pants twisted around slender ankles as
their future generations oozed down your chin.
On Blue Monday, me and the sun caught you
tipping out the wounded red side door
of the Men's Health Clinic.
Your dark shades did not obscure my eyes
or the sparkling iridescent pills in your glass vessels.
Now you're cruising cemeteries
looking for a resting place.
Had you told yourself the truth at twenty,
you would not be dying from hypocrisy at thirty.

Summertime
for Amanda Hughes
Djola Branner

i couldn't lieve my eyes
but there she was
at the meeting
a Market and Post
      bout noon
singing *Summertime*

clicking her tongue
tween her teeth
and her upper
palate/
the same sound
i'd always considered unique
      considered something
that would make her famous

so i could say/
i member when Amanda sang
me a bad-ass ballad at the QT
      kept me from sulking
cause i was sitting
in some low-down bar
on Polk Street
fighting off old men and melancholy
on my 22nd birthday

and i didn't have a dollar to tip her.

i had to blink three times
      to ensure i was seeing correctly
but there she was
at the meeting
a Market and Post
      bout noon
singing *Summertime*

like she used to do at Ivey's
in Oakland
      where i was sposed to be waitering
stead a watching Amanda
wrap my favorite lyrics
round the bar stools
and the middle-class niggas
sitting on em

who didn't even tip her.

voice crawled all up inside ya
      high notes
like/long nails scatching
a dusty chalkboard
      low notes clamoring
tween the dust and the nylon fibers
in a carpet/

the girl was bad!

so i couldn't lieve my eyes
but there she was
at the meeting
a Market and Post
      bout noon
singing *Summertime*

clicking that tongue
tween her teeth
and her upper
palate/
the same sound
i'd always considered unique
      considered something
that would make her famous

so i wanted to run up to her
say hey!
member me/and
where you been for two years
      and what you doing working
street corners

       wit yo face all broke/
don't you know you bad
and don't all these stuck-up
       white folks in threepiecesuits
and fuckmepumps
know it?

       and i would put a dollar
in the hat
you got laying on the sidewalk
but i still ain't got one

it's *Summertime*/but
       the fish *ain't* jumping

but i didn't speak

i pulled out my last food stamp/
put it in the hat
and slunk on away.

breaking silence
for Essex Hemphill
Keelyn Bradley

"but when we are silent
we are still afraid

So it is better to speak
remembering
we were never meant to survive."

        Audre Lorde
        "A Litany For Survival," *The Black Unicorn*

we struggle to speak
eager tongues beat
with hungry words
rites buried

in the dark
we hear no pulse
strange patience moves us
slurred gestures
embrace us

nakedness our only defense
our hardness aches with torrents
forgive and forget me nots
in the dark

we stand
sound of walking over tracks
in our ears
tonight goes on forever
even the stars are showing signs of age

we stand
chanting guerilla poems
all lips and open arms
chanting brother father lover son
at stonewalls and chain-link fences

quiet welcomes us
we are shadows to stillness
secrets of the city
street light remembrance
countersigns of love

we struggle to speak
thousand and one details of discomfort
being freak fairy faggot
holding death in our bellies for too long
tender flesh blooms obituaries in our hands

A Good Name Shines in the Dark
Darius Omar Williams

for those in fab wigs
for those with faces beat
for those in stiletto boots
for those with corn rowed hair
for those with six pack abs
for those with goddess hips
for those with six figures
and those who are still trying to
figure themselves out
we need to chant the month
of June forever lifted in our hands
we need to heal our veins pulse
we need to dance on dry earth
raining oceans on our tongues

may we fight for the destruction of wars
may we scream for the effacement of lies
may we stitch vintage Motown on our sanctimonious lips
may we always plant our love under another brother's skin
may we honor this house we are in

i wish us disco balls rolling courage off our chests
i wish us plum filled nights of yellow poetry in the dark
i wish us new flags not rainbow ones
i wish us tender hugs and confident arms
i wish us gold lungs and toe-tapping songs
i wish us *A Love Supreme* bulging beautiful brown necks
i wish us cocktails down the sink
i wish us dignified throats
i wish us Aretha soul like 'ride sally ride' and life life life life life

on the east coast and the west
at the office at the gym at the club …
at the church   black men   on the campus
on the corner on the screen on the stage
preserve yourself
i said preserve yourself
preserve say it preserve
our art   our private parts
preserve preserve

for those bombarded by contradicting images of themselves
for those bamboozled challenged insulted disrupted
fists planted against baby brown faces
you mother-fucking faggot punk
dick sucker man you ain't shit nigger
mother-fucking punk   mother-fucking
punk mother-fucking punk

for those disillusioned by the holy ghost of their fears
who read and snap their fingers
while dancing until dawn and partying with their tears
who wait wait wait wait
for affirmations self proclamations
the graduate school of brother love
of lift every voice and sing
for all the experiences
the shared experiences
of teddy pendergrass and turn off the lights
and wait wait wait for love

for those who fight to build bridges
bridges made of copper and steel and
hair and fingernails and dress
pageants balls *paris is burning*
shade homo-thug trade-boy bitch
calling all same gender loving brothers
calling all same gender loving brothers
come and be blessed by the fire of this poem
come and share in the strength and possibility of this poem
calling all same gender loving brothers
calling all same gender loving brothers
calling all same gender loving brothers

Breathing Words
Clay Turner

Take your wings and expectations
Fly upon me
Take me the sacred
Just beyond the paper enriched plains
Lying in the distance, still
Waiting
Breathing thoughts
Togetherness
Amidst extreme silence
Seeing words
Touching sounds
Hearing expressions
Re-writing ourselves
Becoming second wind
Moving like energy
Procreating harmony
Chasing atmosphere
Yearning to become
To become spoken
To become heard
To become a voice
To become ingested like oxygen
Yearning to breathe as one
Living forever in imagery

Surrender
Mystalic Writings

If I surrendered today would this pain...go away?
If I lay down my shield and sheath my sword
Would you comfort me in reward?

Hold my hand in yours as I cry
And lie my head to your shoulder
While I die

For I am but a broken child

I reach and there is no one their
Only the echo's of silent air

If I surrendered today

Would the battle be displaced
Am I but the disgrace straining in your stoic face
Does it hurt to see me left

I am lost
In a world of desire passion and lust
Lost amongst the voices of them
And not the voices of us

My truth is resilient
It will not bend or break
But it cannot breathe in
Darkness
And I cannot stay

So I ask again

If I surrendered today can you take my pain away

Clipped Wings Still Fly
C.C. Carter

My world was blue sky and white clouds
engine hums and pretty bright smiles
My first time on a plane
I knew I was meant to fly
But daddy said I couldn't be a flight attendant
He didn't raise me to be a high priced waitress
I didn't question the 34 out of 52 weeks
he spent in the hands of crest bright teeth
from the girls serving coffee, tea,
and the comfort of safety

He didn't understand that I really lived in the air
needed to soar, desired the difference of
taste
smell
skin
life

My house was filled with family night TV
watching TMC old movies
memorizing lines from Betty, Bogie, Sammy and Sydney
It was soul train and band stand amateur hour
the bop, the twist, the stroll
off beat bodies on rhythm
It was impromptu concerts of
Ain't No Mountain High Enough
lyric harmonies
My brother and me – two young versions
of Marvin and Tammy
Alto and tenor flat renditions of
parents reunited with Peaches and Herb
It was weekend community play house
Broadway productions of revelations by Ailey
So when I told my daddy I wanted to act
and my mother that I knew how to dance
and the teacher's said I was a natural
They said, "What kind of career is that?
We will not support a going nowhere desire."

I didn't question
the 500 albums or more of Coltrane
Hendrix, Temptations, Gladys and Pips
or the collection of black and white prints by
Parks of Billie, Myles or James
or the thousand dollars they spent on
ballet, modern, african dance classes
The two-hour on Saturday's nine to eleven
piano lessons
a clarinet which earned me first chair in band
so that they could brag to their friends
how they had raised a well-rounded cultured child

My mind was inner torment
that my 8th grade teacher confirmed as brilliance
but my grandmother validated as art
Reciting poetry secretly
to show me that I was normal
Every weekend a new verse of Wheatley
another poem by McKay
another writer like myself   herself
Tormented by voices who wrote words on paper
in books
in collections
in masterpieces
So when she died I asked for her diaries
Family told me that she lied on linen
that they were filled with unrequited dreams
and what "Did I want them for?"
I did not question the library collection
in our basement of dust covered 1st edition books
leaves of grass, raisin in the sun, don quixote, simple stories
Masterpieces by writers with unfulfilled dreams
and great imagination
I did not offer them the untold story
of a woman whose life
was no crystal stair
but who too was america
and whose dreams were deferred
because of era
because of color
because of gender
because of sacrifice

for the family who called her a dreamer

My ambition was to write
so I told my parents that I would
forgo theatre
go to college
but major in English
Become a poet holding fast to a part of my dream
like Langston
still rising like Maya
ego tripping with Nikki
all the while wearing a mask
and flapping caged wings
like Dunbar
They said a degree in anything
other than the arts was better
but take two classes in education to be safe
cause writers don't make money till they're old
and nobody remembers them till they're dead
I did not question
how the use of words
bought furniture
lobster dinners
mercedes
and a four bedroom
three level house into my life
from a father who made his living on words
Sunday morning sermons
that caused people to tithe more than they intended
join the church when they were just visiting
shout when all they meant to say was "Amen"
Or from a mother whose gift of language
motivated young minds
cultivated new teachers
developed school policies
and ultimately made
her the diva of educational reform

My life is about words now
so I told my parents
I am a poet
I am an actress
I am an artist

I am respected
I am well-known
I do get paid
to live in the air
plane to place
They said, "How come you can't write about nothing
but something we aren't?
We're proud of you
but we still cannot brag."
They have never questioned
how Gwendolyn Brooks
endorsed her name on a check
declared me the best of my time
or why colt matter that
Oye rules my sun sign
and Oshun my rising
I am an air child
embraced by all things artistically woman
My destiny is not my choice
but my birth right
I am their daughter
but I am their opposite
air to their earth
art to their stability
writer to their speech
out to their inhibitions
I am now
what they could not be then
proof
that a bird with clipped wings
still
can
fly

Ostinato
Vince Wilson

I, too, sing, America.
I sing America

I sing Blackness, America
A conglomerated and ambiguous Blackness in perfect three-part harmony
these songs:
of retribution and of pain;
of solace;
and all the mysterious things that seemed to have just dropped in the ocean,
and the people who jumped out of cargo ships find them—and never came back;
of the people who could not escape to be free in Liberia
of those of us who cannot be free today

My vibrato is wide enough for enslaved hostages to escape through.
And they do escape through it
Every song I sing reclaims lost souls and takes me closer to Home
And I slap my
sunshine, cinnamon, amber, coffee, midnight
hands together to maintain tempo
hands that have come from Hands that worked by sun dawn moon candle - light
and in darkness
My hands sing vivacity when I bring them together

Can't hear the chains jingle
Sounds like freedom blowing through empty space
When my soul vibrates to the beat, I laugh
Nothing's funny
I laugh at Life so that when Life looks,
It doesn't have a chance to laugh at me first
My song is the only joy that exists in the world.

When I'm sound-years away, my song will just be reaching your
unwilling ears, America
and you'll be sad
You'll miss the
Spirit
that I imbued
and the plain emptiness that I offered. My hues while I was dying,
waiting for the new day to turn. And you will then know that
I sang America, too, America.

Love is
Jonathan "Jona Bryant" Thomason

Love is you.
You are love.
And when I hate you it's because the love I have for you has excelled love's boundaries.
If I could define love there would be no diction,
verbiage,
pronunciation,
subliminal terminologies
and no articulation.
just pictures.
Pictures of you angry.
Pictures of you happy.
Pictures of you sad.
Pictures of your smile.
Pictures of you sleep.
Pictures of you awake.
Pictures of you crying.
Pictures of you because love is you.

If I could define love there would be no diction,
verbiage,
pronunciation,
subliminal terminologies,
and no articulation.
Just sounds.
The sound of your voice.
The sound of your laugh.
The sound of your boldness.
The sound of you humble.
The sound of you breathing.
The sound.
Just the sound of you.
Love is you.

Love is memories when you're gone.
Love is calling another by your name.
Love is spiteful behavior if that's what brings you back.
Love is hanging up when there is no good in my mouth.
Love is seeing what's not there.
Love is not seeing what's in your face.

Love is blind.
Love is colorless and uncompromising.
Love is compromising when the compromise makes us closer.
Love is you.
You are love.

Love is jealousy when you admire a man more handsome than me.
Love is confidence that you can never see a man as being more handsome than me.

Love postpones anger.
Love defies logic.
Love is the only logic.
Love is humbly arrogant.
Love is you.
You are love.

Love is sleepless nights when I don't hear you.
Love is loneliness when I don't feel you.
Love is the echo of your voice when you depart.
Love is the comfort even when I can't feel you.
Love is the ruler of the unruly.
Love is you.
You are my love.

Love is you.
You are my love.
My love is yours.
Your love is mine.
Our love is strong and emotional.
It is untimely and unpredictable.
Love is trying with you what I wouldn't try with the other.
Love is doing for me what you wouldn't do for another.
Love is loving past the past.
Love is loving into our future.
Love is hating anything that isn't love.
Love is the way your lips taste and feel.
Love is praying for you before each meal.

Love is you.
You are love.
You are my love.
My love is in you.

My love is yours, and yours mine.
Love restricts and confines.
Love runs wild and freely.
Love restricts our freedom to the confinements of each other's hearts.

Love is.
Love is.
Love is
…you.
Love is me.
Love is we even when there is no us.
Love is you.

Short Stories

Captain Swing
Excerpt from Chapter Five
Larry Duplechan

1990. Johnnie Ray Rousseau is a 34-year-old black gay man; a semi-pro jazz vocalist living in his native Los Angeles. He's still in mourning for his life partner, Keith, over a year after Keith's death in an automobile accident; he's in therapy; and he's currently in St. Charles, the tiny Southwest Louisiana town where both his parents were born. Johnnie's estranged father, Lance, is dying of pancreatic cancer, and has summoned Johnnie to his bedside. At least, so claimed Johnnie's Aunt Lucille. Upon his arrival in Louisiana, Johnnie discovers that his father had never asked for him: it was a sweet, well-meaning lie on his aunt's part; but a lie, nonetheless. Having been tersely dismissed by his father, Johnnie (called by his baby name, Junie, by this Louisiana kinfolk), has decided to head back home. Complicating an already complicated situation is the presence of Johnnie's beautiful 18-year-old cousin, Nigel.

I was safe between the headphones, flat on my back on the too-soft double bed in the too-warm backroom, my arm across my eyes and a smile beginning to soften the corners of my mouth as Billie sang "Swing, Brother, Swing" directly into my head. It was the gentle but insistent swing of the Count Basie Band (1937-vintage), live from the Savoy Ballroom (stompin' at the Savoy, indeed) and the raspy, world-worn alto of Lady herself, managing to cool my overheated brain in a way the swamp cooler sweating and roaring above me could not begin to cool my moist, prickly skin. Lady didn't always sing the blues. When the mood struck her, she could swing like sixty. And nothing short of a shot of Cuervo or a gram or two of tryptophan – not yoga breathing, not visualization, not deep, focused meditation in which I surround myself in white light and reaffirm my position as a beloved child of the Universe – pushes the saw-toothed man-eating hellhounds of emotion away from my throat like Lady Day swingin' on the Walkman.

I asked Dennis once why a man born all but simultaneously with rock and roll should, in the midst of his life's most emotionally harrowing episode to date, find refuge, solace, succor in the sound of music performed and recorded some twenty and more years before. Why not the music of my own childhood and increasingly remote youth, but the music of my parents' childhoods? Why Basie and Billie and the Ellas – Ella Fitzgerald, Ella Johnson of the Buddy (her big brother) Johnson

Band and Ella Mae "the Cow-Cow Boogie Girl" Morse? Why not the Beatles, the Supremes, Freddie and the goddamn Dreamers?

Dennis shrugged, did his patent-pending inscrutable look, and said, "What difference does it make, as long as it makes you feel better?"

For this I'm paying $150 a fifty-minute hour. Well, the thirty percent my medical insurance doesn't cover, anyway.

At the touch on my arm, I cried out "Hah! and jackknifed up in bed, victim of the unavoidable startle so common to the headphone addict. Nigel stood at the side of my bed, his brow crimped, his lips attempting a smile. "Sorry," Nigel said, not entirely audible over Billie and one solidly swingin' horn section. I pulled the phones from my ears in time to hear Nigel say, "You wanna go for a ride?"

Giving the matter absolutely no thought, I shrugged and said, "Sure."

"Me and Junie goin' for a ride," Nigel called out to no one in particular, and did not await a reply as he preceded me through the front door.

I sighed one of my all-too-frequent audible sighs as Nigel started the car and the air conditioning kicked in, the first blasts of air musty-smelling but oh, so cool. I sighed for the feel of my moist shirt going cool against my skin, puckering my nipples, sighed for this sweet respite from 85 degrees and 80-some-odd percent humidity in a car with childhood memories tucked into the creases of the upholstery like lost nickels and dimes and Al Jarreau on the tape deck pulling and twisting notes like handfuls of Play-Doh. I closed my eyes, raised my arms, and grabbed the headrest behind my ears, enjoying the cool air in my armpits. "Where are we going?" I asked finally.

"Does it matter?" countered Nigel.

"Nah," I said, leaning back into the cool. After an elongated moment, just to make something resembling conversation, I said, "You know, you really shouldn't drink raw eggs."

"Shot who?"

"Athena tells me you've been sucking raw eggs. Which is the best way we know of to get yourself a nice dose of salmonella poisoning. Which could kill you." I waited a moment for a reply, then opened my eyes and looked toward Nigel.

"Don't go," Nigel said, looking directly ahead.

"What?"

"Don't go," he replied. "Stay."

A little smile pushed at the corners of my mouth. I didn't know what Nigel was getting to, but something about the deadly earnest look on my cousin's face made me smile. "Why not?" I asked.

Nigel braked for a stoplight. I wasn't sure if I'd already seen the strip mall out the passenger window or if it looked exactly like one I'd already seen. "Well," Nigel said. "You're already here."

"No arguing that one," I agreed.

Nigel didn't crack a smile. "And I do realize your daddy has totally dissed you and you're stung. But just because he acted like an asshole don't mean he might not chill out some if you try again, right? I mean, you might as well finish what you came for, right? Besides," he added as the light went green and he hit the gas, "you go back to L.A. tomorrow, you go home to what?"

So much for my smile. The kid had a point. "Anything else?" I asked.

"I don't want you to go," Nigel said, his voice rising at the end of the sentence so it almost sounded like a question.

"Oh?" I said, my voice a bit squeaky, my heart doing a funky little drum roll.

"We're here," Nigel said, pulling the car over in front of a small wood-frame house (probably the same vintage as Aunt Lucille's house, though not even half the size) in dire need of paint. I followed Nigel to the front door, which Nigel opened as if he lived there, and inside.

Momentarily blinded by the abrupt change of light upon entering the dimly lit house, I paused just inside the doorway to allow my eyes to adjust inside somebody's rather cluttered, eclectically furnished living room. A 19-inch portable television sat atop an old wooden wire spool in one corner, its screen dark, facing a big, rambling sectional sofa whose color and pattern when new would have been difficult to discern. A Magnavox console stereo, all but identical to the one my parents had owned when David and I were little, stood against one wall, filling the room with the sound of the Stax house band and Rufus Thomas's cement mixer of a voice singing, *"I'll show you how to Walk the Dog."*

I didn't notice the two old men seated at the collapsible card table just to one side of the front door until one of them startled me by nearly shouting, in that peculiar overcompensating volume of the hard-of-hearing, "How you doin', Nigel?" When I looked, a very old, very black man in a faded, rather threadbare long sleeve shirt and nondescript pants, smiled a toothless smile in our direction.

"Just fine, Mr. Freen," Nigel said, raising his voice several decibels higher than normal. "Evening, Mr. Fitty," Nigel added for the benefit of the other old man. He was light skinned enough to pass for white (though presumably not), painfully thin, and bent like a question mark over the checkerboard on the table, his gnarled, veiny hands flat against the tabletop. "Evening, Nigel!"

"How's the game?" Nigel said, leaning toward the table.

"This old niggah cheatin'," Mr. Fitty said, still not moving his eyes from the board. "Gots to watch him every minute, yeah."

"Now you know I ain't never cheated, you ugly ol' Cajun," countered the still-smiling Mr. Freen.

"Y'all, this my cousin Junie," Nigel said, touching my shoulder lightly with his fingers. "My Uncle L.J.'s son."

"Naw, it ain't," Mr. Fitty finally looked up from the checkerboard. "Not dis here growed-up man here." He held out a knotty hand and offered a smile which included very few teeth. "You better come on over here; shake your Uncle Fitty's hand."

I did as I was told. The old man's grip was surprisingly strong; his skin dry and crisp as parchment. "Boy, I been known you since you wasn't nothin' but your mama wantin' some vanilla ice cream and some sardines." He laughed a wheezy *heh-heh-heh*. "Don't remember me?" he said, still holding my hand. I shook my head no. "Been a long time," the old man said, releasing my hand. "Long time, Freen," he yelled as if his friend were across the street instead of across a card table, "Freen, this here L.J.'s boy."

"I heard," Mr. Freen said with an exaggerated expression of exasperation. "I can hear, y'old high yella muthafucka." He grinned that dark crevice of a grin again and held out a dark, straight-fingered hand. I accepted it, and Mr. Freen clasped his other hand around mine and held it tightly. His hands felt cool and padded, like a brand new chair. "Pleasure to meet you, young man," he said. "Yo' family sho' do make some nice-looking mens," he added, winking an eye.

"Thank you, sir," I said, stifling a laugh.

"You watch out for that black sumbitch," Fitty said, his eyes back on the checkerboard. "He like 'em young."

"Damn right," Freen said, looking up and speaking directly to me. Tugging on my hand, he brought my face over and down, closer to his own. "Lemme tell you somethin', baby," he said, his oddly sweet-smelling cologne filling my nostrils. "You ain't had none yet 'til you had it from a man wid no teef." And he laughed a long high note, before finally relinquishing my hand. I looked toward Nigel, who refused to meet my eyes.

"Where Anna Lee at?" Nigel asked the table at large.

Fitty replied, "She out in the back, getting some meat out the deep freeze."

"No, she ain't," said a high-pitched wind chime of a voice. I turned to see the owner of the voice walking toward me on tiny white-sneakered feet, every inch of five-foot-two, wearing light blue overalls and a man's white t-shirt, a smile dimpling a round face the color of baking chocolate, a full key ring attached to her overalls jingling like sleigh bells as she walked. "Nigel," she said in that incredible baby-doll voice, "this your new yaya?" I couldn't help smiling.

"Anna Lee," Nigel said, "This is my cousin, Junie. Johnnie Ray Rousseau."

"The singer?" Anna Lee cocked her head, a Medusa like headful of dreadlocks corralled in a brightly colored scarf. "My pleasure," she said, holding her right hand up and out toward me. Her handshake was like that of a small but energetic man. "I have your album in my collection," she said.

"You sent Muh two copies," Nigel said, "and I absconded with one and gave it to Anna Lee."

"And I play it often," she added.

"Really?" I said, a smile spreading across my face.

"Sugar, Anna Lee don't never bullshit about good music," she said, reaching up to pat me on the cheek, as if I were a very large child. From the stereo, Rufus Thomas had given way to Mahalia Jackson ripping through "When the Saint Go Marching In." "Child, you can really blow. You still singing?"

Just the tiniest little schmertz. "Not recently, I said.

"Shame," said Anna Lee, then shrugged her small shoulders. "Well, welcome to my little home," Anna Lee said. I searched her smooth brown face for some clue as to her age, but she could have been thirty, or forty, or sixty. "Y'all hungry?" she asked.

"Not really, thank you," I said, although it was high time I'd had something to eat.

"Got some good-ass gumbo in the kitchen," she said in a singsong like Glinda the Good Witch getting funky.

"Could we have the guest room for a while, Anna Lee?" Nigel asked.

"Child!" She shot Nigel a look. "With your cousin?"

Nigel smiled sheepishly. "We just need to talk in private."

"If you say so," she said with another little shrug. "Go 'head, ain't nobody back there. Just put the sign out. After you finish you come back out here and have some of this good gumbo, hear me?"

"And just who, may I ask, is this Anna Lee person?" I asked, following Nigel down a narrow hall covered on both sides with ancient framed photographs, portraits of black, brown, and café-au-lait people staring blank-eyed through a disconcerted Johnnie Ray Rousseau and into eternity.

"Anna Lee's a friend of mine," Nigel said as he pushed open one of three doors on the right side of the hall. "She used to be my favorite high school English teacher. Now she's my friend. I do odd jobs around the house for her sometimes. Come on," he said, and I followed him into a small bedroom. Nigel moved a "Do Not Disturb" card (obviously removed from some hotel somewhere) from the inside doorknob to the outside and shut the door behind us.

My immediate assessment of the room was that it seemed outwardly clean, if sparsely furnished – there was a chenille-covered double bed, a plain blond-wood bureau with a mirror – rather like a room in a Motel 6. I stood just inside the doorway, trembling slightly with confusion and a vague sexual excitement. Nigel untied and kicked off his high top Converse basketball shoes (not those big, puffy, hundred-plus-dollar things kids were wearing in L.A. but the old fashioned kind I remember having worn as a child, and which my most recent piano accompanist like to wear in mismatched colors – red on the right foot, white on the left). Nigel plopped down and sat cross-legged near the head of the bed.

"This is a much better sit than the chair," Nigel said.

I didn't budge from where I stood. I could feel my heart beating up in my throat. "Cousin Nigel," I said slowly and carefully, "what exactly is going on here?"

Nigel grinned his bad-boy grin and said, "I didn't lie to Anna Lee. I brought you here 'cause I want to talk to you in private." He shrugged. "Okay?"

None too sure how okay this whole situation was, I nonetheless said, "Okay," and joined Nigel on the bed. Pulling off my shoes, looking down at my Nike's instead of at my cousin, I said (not quite a question), "So, you're gay."

"Truth to tell," Nigel said, "I've always preferred… 'enchanted.'" He grinned that grin of his.

"Shit," I said, drawing the word out over three long syllables.

"Shit?" said Nigel through a little laugh. "What you mean, shit?"

I opened my mouth to speak, but no sound came. What could I say? I was sitting Indian-style on a bed in some stranger's guest room on the outskirts of Nowhere, Louisiana, with my beautiful eighteen-year-old cousin, and the feeling was decidedly strange. Not the least of my problems was the fact that Nigel, having announced his gayness, was suddenly rendered even more attractive in my eyes than before. Never one of those gay men who lust after heterosexuals, I found the possibility of mutual sexual attraction considerably more seductive than the possibility of rejection, disgust, and bodily injury.

Whether it was the recent knowledge of my cousin's sexuality or something about the light in the room in which we sat (supplied by one inelegant fifties-vintage overhead light fixture and the last dregs of sunlight filtered through the dime-store window curtains), I found myself suddenly more cognizant than before of the voluptuous lump of my cousin's Adam's apple, the particular fullness of his florid lower lip, the cords of muscle in his forearms. The skin of Nigel's upper chest, exposed by the tank top he wore, dark brown and glossy as the belly of a chocolate Easter bunny, gave the impression that, should I have chosen to bite into my cousin, the boy might prove to be crème-filled. If Aunt Lucille smelled edible, Nigel looked it.

"Does your mother know?" I asked finally, my mouth having gone a bit dry.

Nigel said, "Yeah. We don't talk about it, but she knows." He laughed a little snort of a laugh. "I think she blames herself, for raising me in a house with just women in it. I don't believe in blame, me."

I shook my head slowly and said, "Blessed Mother of Us All." In my head, questions pushed ahead of other questions like teenagers in a movie line. Was there gay life out here in Bumfuck, Louisiana? Did Nigel have a steady boyfriend? Why the hell wasn't the boy hopping the first plane, bus, or boxcar out of this hick town?

Nigel beat me to the punch. "That why things so fucked-up between you and your daddy? Because you're gay?"

Pain like a cast-iron elbow pressing hard into my belly. "Yeah," I admitted through a tight jaw. One thing and another, I had managed to forget, however briefly, my reason for coming to Louisiana in the first place. To fly to the deathbed of the father who didn't want me, who'd told me to get out, go home. My throat constricted and my eyes burned from the residue of a lifetime's paternally inflicted hurt, and from the impotent frustration with the way the old man could still inflict that hurt, still bring tears. "You know," I began, then thought better of it and said, "Never mind." Why go into all that shit? I considered my handkerchief, then wiped at the moistened corners of my eyes with the heel of my hand instead.

"What?" Nigel said, leaning in a little.

I sighed a long one. Did I really want to cover this kind of overly traveled territory here, now, and with Nigel, he of the severe haircut and the impossible long, curling eyelashes? Well, maybe some of it.

"The fact is, he never liked me," I said. "My father. Maybe he loved me, for like five minutes, when I was a baby. But he never liked me. I was never his idea of firstborn son." I made a little face. "Of course, I was never any man's idea of a firstborn son. Except maybe Harvey Fierstein."

"Were you girlish?" Nigel asked, leaning back against the headboard, cupping his hands behind his head.

"Oh, child," I said, averting my eyes from Nigel's biceps and armpits, "I was wildly effeminate. Rather play with a Barbie doll than a Tonka truck. Couldn't throw a ball to save my neck. Still can't. Couldn't fight. Still can't. Cried a lot. I haven't changed much." A little laugh.

I pushed myself farther up onto the bed and leaned against the floral-papered wall. Across the room, atop the dresser sat my double on the looking-glass bed. I spoke to my mirror self rather than toward Nigel. "You know what he used to call me sometimes? Trixie. Like if he caught me playing with my cousin Camille's dolls, he'd say, 'Get away from there, Trixie.'" I waited out the little schmertz.

"Then David came along, and suddenly Dad had a real boy for a son. David, as they used to say, was 'all boy.' Do people still say that? 'All boy'?" I continued without waiting for an answer. "David ran and jumped and got dirty and played Little League ball and all that shit. So, after David came along, Dad ignored me for the most part. There are worse things, I guess." I closed my eyes, bounced the back of my head against the wall, just hard enough to feel it.

"But it wasn't 'til David was killed that Dad really started to hate me. From the moment we learned David was dead, I could see it in Dad's eyes that —" I felt the tears coming, but I breathed them back, blinked them back. "That if one of his sons had to be blown away in a drive-by shooting in front a fast food restaurant, then it damn well should have been me." I opened my eyes and finally turned to Nigel, who sat against the headboard, arms across his chest. "I don't think he's ever going to forgive me for being the one who lived."

"You don't really believe that," Nigel said softly.

I barked a mirthless, *Ha!* "You obviously don't know my father," I said.

"So what are you doing here?" Nigel asked. "Why come all this way to see him?"

"He's my father," I said, not the least sure, even as I said it, why a chance genetic fact, a mere toss of Nature's dice, shoulder braid a seemingly unbreakable cord stretching over hundreds of miles and over a dozen or more years; nowhere near sure exactly what I was doing here. "He's dying," I added. I felt my lips tremble and I blinked rapidly, trying to keep the tears back.

Nigel extended his arms toward me and said, "C'mere." I leaned away from Nigel's hands, an involuntary move, almost a reflex. "I was just going to hug you," Nigel said, lowering his arms. "Isn't that what y'all do in L.A.? Sit in hot tubs, drink Chardonnay wine, and hug each other all the time?"

"I'm sorry," I said. "It's just –" How to say this?

"Just what?" Nigel crossed his arms tightly across his chest.

I studied the backs of my hands for a moment. "I'm not sure it's such a good idea for me to have that kind of physical contact… with you." I didn't look at Nigel until I'd finished the sentence.

"Zat a fact?" Nigel said, cocking his close-cropped head to one side.

"Look," I said. "I'm attracted to you, okay? I mean, physically attracted to you."

The smile returned to Nigel's face. "Then we've come to the right place, Captain," he said, slapping the bed beside him.

"No!" I said, surprising myself with my own vehemence.

"Yo, Cap," Nigel said, holding up a protecting palm, "Maybe I'm not understanding something here. So bear with me, if you will. You just said you're attracted to me. And I'm telling you right now, I'm stone attracted to you. So what seems to be the problem?"

"The problem?" The boy must be joking, I held up an index finger. "You're my cousin." Another finger. "You're just a kid, for cryin' out loud. And –" three fingers. "Your mother would grind my balls for boudin if she even dreamed I'd laid a hand on you." I thumped my head against the wall again. "'What's the problem,' he says."

"You serious with that shit?" Nigel said.

"Of course I'm serious," I said.

Nigel shook his head, rolling his eyes heavenforward. "Fine," he said. "Really. Not like I need to force myself on nobody. But lemme tell you something," He held up a finger. "My mamma ain't got nothin' to do with this." Two fingers. "Cousin don't mean shit. Not like one of us was a woman or something and we was gonna make feeble-minded little black babies. And –" Nigel wagged three fingers in the air. "I ain't no kid. I'm old enough to drink, vote, and march my black ass off to war. And I'm grown enough to know what I want. Which just might be more than I can say for other people in this room." He punctuated this last with a head nod and a pointed look, then settled back against the headboard, arms crossed.

I looked at Nigel. I looked at my mirrored self. I felt more than a little silly. All the kid had ever offered was a hug. "Is that hug still available?" I said.

"I don't know," Nigel replied. "I'm not sure it would be such a good idea for us to maintain such close physical proximity. We might turn to salt or something."

"Oh, shut up and hold me," I said, scooting myself backward between Nigel's outstretched legs, against my cousin's hard, flat front and into his arms.

After a moment, Nigel said, "Can I ask you something?"

"Sure." Anything, I thought, just keep hugging.

"Why don't you sing anymore?"

I waited out the tiny pinprick pain in the center of my chest near my heart, then said, "It's just not there anymore. When Keith –" A bigger pain, a penknife. "It's just not there anymore," I repeated, hoping Nigel would let it drop.

Nigel rubbed my chest with his palm in a little slow circle. "I see," he said, and nuzzled the back of my head.

And his beard is tickling the nape of my neck.

"Keith!" I'm giggling like a kid on the upswing of a seesaw. "Baby, you're tickling me."

We're sitting on the beach in Venice, in the summertime, on the blanket we bought in Puerto Vallarta in the spring. I'm cross-legged and just a bit hunched forward; Keith is wrapped around my back like a big, warm cloak, his skin hot and sticky against my own, his muscular arms around my shoulders, his hands stroking up and down my forearms. Keith's legs, thick and covered with sun-bleached fuzz, form a fence around mine, his feet resting sole-to-sole in front of mine.

I'm holding one of Keith's big feet in each of my hands and massaging the deep arches with my thumbs as we lean into one another, laughing and cuddling, oblivious to the dozens of people around us.

And he's kissing my ear. And making me cry.

Crying.

"That's okay, baby," Nigel said, folding his long, sinewy arms around me and holding me close against him.

"I'm sorry," I blubbered, tears and snot falling freely from my face, since I couldn't reach my handkerchief from my present position.

We sat for maybe half an hour more, not talking, just sitting and hugging. After a while, after the crying stopped, after I'd wiped my face and caught my breath, after I'd steadied myself against my cousin. I could feel the hot lump of Nigel's hard-on hot against my tailbone, and my own dick straining against the confines of my Levi's.

Aunt Lucille was at the stove, stirring a great pot of seafood-smelling something (okra gumbo with shrimp was my immediate guess) when I followed Nigel through the front door. She turned and said, "Junie."

I stopped. "Ma'am?"

Aunt Lucille tap-tapped her spoon on the rim of the pot and set it on the stovetop. Wiping her hands on a dishtowel, she came to the kitchen door. "Junie," she said, an attempt of a smile on her lips, "you still angry with your old aunt Lucille?"

I shook my head. "No."

Aunt Lucille's face split into a smile. "Bless your heart," she said, gathering me into her arms in a surprisingly forceful hug. "I do hate to see you go so soon," she said, letting me go.

"I've changed my mind," I said. "I'm going to stay around for a while. Might as well finished what I started."

Aunt Lucille smiled a fresh smile, swept me into another hug, and said, "Bless your heart. Bless your little heart."

Pussy Was My Drug Dealer
Laurinda D. Brown

Pussy was my drug dealer. I gave her everything: my money, my job, my car, my life, my friends, my husband and even my kid. She didn't care what I had to do to get her paid. Just make sure she got her money. For a dinner date, I got a bump-n-grind in the stall of the ladies' room at a five star restaurant. For a trip to the club, I got all the Coronas and nachos with extra jalapenos I wanted. Then we'd end up in the passenger side of her car or some seedy hotel because she was too ashamed to take me back to her house. For a night out dancing, I may have, on very rare occasions, gotten to sleep over because all night long we would've been closer than close inhaling one another's pheromones while they mixed with the smell of sweat and wet snatch. The sex was so intense I once found myself on my back hanging off the side of the bed in a handstand while my shit pulsated to the beats of Bootsy Collins' "I'd Rather Be With You." The lava lamps oozed red and blue paraffin in pints of mineral oil, up and down, encased in glass cylinders. Every blob, big and small, was reminiscent of the separation of me from those things dearest to my heart. All because of pussy. As the blood rushed to my head, I steadied myself to keep from falling. I felt her tongue sting my clit followed by a gentle nick on its tip with her teeth. My lactating nipples, the size of black grapes, were like dripping faucets running toward my chin. The sensation was erotic, hypnotic for me as the heroin gave me a high while she examined every inch of me inserting her pink and white speckled needle inside me. I lifted myself to the center of the bed and met her lips with mine. Blunt blazing, she inserted the butt of it inside her and inhaled. Her eyes rolling in the back of her head until the whites showed, I was mesmerized. It didn't matter if she came from the east, west, north or south side of town. I gave her anything, and she took everything. Pussy was my drug dealer.

I sat in the driveway of my modest four bedroom home with my panties in my purse. I hadn't brushed my teeth, and my hair was still mashed down on top from where I had been on my head most of the night. I didn't have any sleep in my eyes because there was never a point where we had actually closed our eyes for more than a couple of minutes at a time. My chest, chin and lips were sticky from the milk, and my breasts were full. We never shared breakfast together; I was to be gone before dawn…before the neighbors got up, before the newspaper came, and before the birds got a chance to take over chirping from the crickets. There were never any good-byes but never any promises for tomorrow. It wasn't that big of a deal because all she had to do was light my crack pipe, and I'd come running even if I were needed somewhere else. With all of the windows cracked for fresh air, I reeked of pussy – the seducing concoction that got me hooked in the first place.

The undeniable smell of bacon and homemade biscuits seeped into the car as the sun peeped above the roof of the house. The porch light went off. He knew I was home. My cell phone vibrated. I looked inside to see which of my phones it was. I had two: one for her and one for home. "*R u going 2 stay in the car all morning? Breakfast is ready,*" it read. I didn't hate Jarred. At least I didn't think I did. Most women pray for a husband who will cater to them, love and honor them, cook and clean for them, and keep them. A man who changed diapers and did 2 a.m. feedings; a man who wanted his wife in five inch heels and massaged her feet when they were tired from extreme elevation all day; a man who paid to have the lawn manicured; a man who took the kids to the park while she went to the spa; a man who shopped for her; a man who worshipped her. Well, I did hate Jarred. He gave me all those things, and I deserved none of it.

We'd been married three years. No long courtship or anything like that. We were introduced by a mutual friend and hit it off quickly. In less than four months, we got married. We honeymooned in Cap Jaluca, and, from there, we hopped on a plane to Switzerland. He was an IT consultant making ninety grand a year and promised me I'd never want for anything. And I never have. Our son, Danny, is eight months old. I had an easy pregnancy. He was the spitting image of his father, and sometimes I found it hard to look at him. I played with him and gave him the best love and affection I could. I nursed him to try to bond with him, but, just as my love was for his father, I was empty. Is it wrong to hate someone so much for loving you?

"Good morning, baby," Jarred said as he stirred cheese into the grits bubbling on the stove. I had lied again to get out of the house. "How's your cousin doing? I know that ER gets crazy. I tried to call up there, but I couldn't get through. Why didn't you answer your cell?" Dazed, I opened the refrigerator and pulled out the orange juice. He knew I loved Simply Orange with Pineapple in it, so he always kept it stocked for me. The glasses were in the cabinet by where he stood, and I couldn't risk him getting a whiff of my scent. I took out the juice and sat it on the counter. The first thing Jarred did every morning was unload the dishwasher. Maybe three feet from him, I made my way to the dishwasher praying he'd forgotten this one time. I'd heard his question about my cell phone but ignored it. I laid my phone on the counter next to where I'd placed the orange juice. He was fervently stirring the grits to keep them from getting lumps and sticking to the pot. I walked over to where Danny was joyfully sitting in his high chair and kissed him on the forehead. I couldn't pick him up...not right now. When Jarred jotted to the refrigerator to get the milk, I took the opportunity to move in the direction of the dishwasher. "You know, it's empty, honey," he said, scrambling to get back to the stove. "Why don't you go on and take your shower. I'll bring your juice to you."

"Okay."

By the time I got to the bedroom, I was completely naked having stopped by the laundry room to toss my outfit in the wash. I flung my purse to the bed and darted to the shower. Jarred had created a sanctuary for me in our bathroom. He rarely used it, opting to use the one in the guest room closest to the master bedroom. The shower was made of black marble and had six body sprays. I turned the water on but stood in the threshold of the shower door contemplating whether I wanted to cleanse my body. Deep down, I didn't want to. The longer it stayed with me the longer my fix lasted. Of course, if I didn't, I was sure to get caught. I stepped in the shower and let the force of each spray massage me. With alternating force, the water penetrated a place within me that I didn't want touched. That place I had saved for her. I reached for my shower gel and squeezed a small portion into the palm of my hands. Delicately, I lathered my legs and arms but stopped short of going between my legs and across my breasts which were on the verge of exploding. I felt it fair enough to rinse heavily and take my chances.

When I stepped out of the shower, a small glass of orange juice was waiting for me on the sink. I drank it in one gulp and then stopped to brush my teeth. Standing in the mirror, I stared at myself and noticed track marks along my neck and beneath my navel. I didn't panic. I didn't flinch. As I was pulling my toothbrush from the holder, Jarred appeared in the mirror with Danny in his arms. "I know you haven't had a chance to release this morning. Can you feed him real quick?"

The baby was fussy and obviously hungry. "Yeah, I'm so sorry, pumpkin," I whispered gently as I took him from his father's arms. Teary-eyed, Danny reached for me and clung to my chest almost instantly. He nestled against it and began sucking on my skin as if he were looking for satisfaction.

"Wow," Jarred laughed. "He's never done that before. L'il man must be hungry."

Fighting Danny away from my chin, I replied, "Seems like it. Did you feed him last night?"

Shocked, he responded, "What kind of question is that, Felicia?"

"I mean, I'm sayin', Jarred. Look at him."

Noticeably annoyed with me and my question, Jarred said, "I gave him the last of the milk you left around one this morning. You don't want me giving him regular milk, so I've been giving him juice in his sippy cup until right before you got home."

"Come on, stop, Danny," I ordered firmly. I wasn't going to hit him, but I wanted to. I was tired and only wanted to go to bed.

"Look, if you don't want to nurse him, then just pump the milk, and I'll feed him."

Still tussling with the baby, I said reluctantly, "No, it's fine. Give me a few minutes."

"Once you get finished, you want to come have breakfast with me? I made your favorites." Sitting down to breakfast with him always made me feel uneasy. I felt like I was in the hot seat. It was kinda like telling your child you were going to beat his ass and make him wait until you were ready. You'd walk by his ass day long as he sat there naked, anticipating that first lick. It could be a leather strap, a switch, a flip-flop, or a straight backhand. You always braced yourself for impact. That's how I felt being alone with Jarred.

"Let me finish with him, and I'll come down. Okay?"

There were many secrets I kept from husband, but the main one was hard for anyone with good morals to digest. The first time I nursed Danny I didn't like the feeling I got. It wasn't that special time they talk about in the parenting classes and magazines, nor was it the time when I was able to look into my son's eyes and let him absorb my face into his memory. I wanted him to forget my face because I was getting pleasure from him being on me. So, that was the first and last time I fed Danny like that. I insisted on pumping the milk. I'd walked out last night without releasing. I needed to feed my baby. Cradling him in the comfort of the left pocket of my naked body, I sat on the side of the tub and guided my son's head to my left breast. He latched on with his eyes rolling in the back of his head until whites showed. I was satisfying him. I looked away. Tears streaming from my eyes as I spread my legs, I took my right hand and opened my lips. With my other nipple streaming milk down my stomach, onto my thigh, and to the floor, I leaned back, exposing my clit for my pleasure. He, my infant son, was satisfying me. The drug dealer had taught me how to survive whenever she wasn't around.

After lying Danny down, I got dressed and went to the kitchen. Jarred poured me a cup of coffee and gave me the hazelnut creamer. He prepared my plate with eggs, bacon, and biscuits and then gave me a separate bowl full of grits. Jarred fixed his plate and sat across from me. He blessed the food and began eating. I wasn't hungry.

"You never told me how your cousin was doing," he said as he poured sugar over his grits.

"She's fine."

"That's good," he answered as he took his first spoonful. "Now, which cousin is this?"

And there it starts. "What?"

"What cousin is this that you went to see last night?"

"Oh," sighing heavily, I lied, "My cousin, Tisha, on my dad's side of the family. You've never met her. She's my dad's sister's child." I nervously began separating my eggs into tiny portions.

"Aw," he said snapping a piece of bacon between his lips. "I thought you told me your dad was an only child?"

Here this niggah goes. I was getting agitated with him because he knew he had already caught me in a lie. A couple, actually. "What exactly is it you want to know, Jarred? I'm not interested in bantering with you this morning."

"No need to be like that. I was just trying to make conversation with you." Having only eaten a morsel of food, I slid my chair from underneath the table and dumped my food in the garbage. "You're not going to eat?"

"Obviously not," I said calmly as I rinsed my plate and placed it in the dishwasher. "I'm going to take a nap." I returned to the table to get my coffee and poured it down the drain. As I headed toward the door, I reached for my cell phone.

Jarred, sitting there slopping his last biscuit in molasses, said, "Oh, yeah, yeah. Um, while you were in the shower, your phone rang."

I looked at the screen and didn't see where I'd had any missed calls. "Did you answer it because I don't see any missed calls?"

Wiping his mouth with the sleeve of his shirt and pulling a toothpick from the holder in the center of the table, he said, "No, not that one. The one in your purse. What's going on, Felicia? You're leaving the house almost every night of the week. You don't spend any time with me or Danny as a family. You don't answer your cell when you're out. You're lying to me every chance you get, and then while I was coming through the bedroom to bring you your juice I hear this vibrating in your purse. I open it and find a cell phone with a pair of your dirty panties wrapped around it. I scrolled through the contacts, and all I see are numbers of women. So, I'm asking you is there something you want to talk about?" Jarred tossed the phone on the table.

Coming clean would set me free. "I can't do this anymore," I admitted. I pulled my chair back to the table and rested my hands in my lap. With my head hung low, I confessed to him, "I don't love you, and I want out of this marriage. I want my freedom."

"Freedom? You act like I'm holding you hostage or something."

"I'm not saying that."

Jarred, always mild-mannered, calmly sat staring at me and was taken by how nonchalant I was. "I don't see how you can sit here and tell me you can't do this anymore. I give you everything, Felicia. I do everything, Felicia. Hell, I do for you and Danny before I have a chance to wipe and wash my own ass, and what about him? We have an eight month old son that needs both his parents."

The expression on my face was blank. "I haven't decided what I want to do about him."

"What the hell?" If he were that type of man, Jarred would have killed me right then. "I can't believe you're saying this crap to me. Who is it, Felicia? Who is he? What is it he does for you that I'm not? I'll change whatever it is."

"It's not that simple, Jarred."

He got up from his chair and began pacing. "It's not that simple? How can you say that? We've got a home, a life, a family." He paused and turned to me, "Please don't tell me you're in love with him." The cell phone began vibrating.

My emotions were frozen. Jarred pulled up a chair and came close to me, close enough to snuggle his head against mine. I could feel his breath as he began kissing my forehead and then my temples. I pulled away from him. "Jarred, stop." My eyes focused on the blinking screen of my phone. I thought maybe after going to voicemail that the ringing would stop, but it didn't.

Jarred looked at me and saw my discomfort with not being to answer the phone. "You want to get it, don't you? Look at you. You've broken into a damn sweat for this niggah you letting call my house." My palms were sweating, and the moisture between my thighs was causing my pajama pants to stick to my skin. I slid my hands underneath my thighs to keep me from getting to the phone in front of him. "Answer the phone," he finally resigned.

The buzzing phone stopped. "Jarred, I'm not happy. Why can't you hear me when I say that?"

With his head in hands, he said softly, "Because you've never said it before now."

"I shouldn't have to say it. You can freaking see it. You just choose to ignore it."

The vibrating started again. This time he snatched it. "Hello? Hello? Seems like you got a whimp. Ain't even man enough to speak when he hears another voice pick up your phone."

"Jarred, leave it alone and give it to me."

"No, I won't. Hello! Hello!" he kept yelling.

"Shhhh, you're going wake up the baby."

"What the hell do you care? Hello!" he started again, but this time someone responded.

"Um, may I speak to Felicia?"

Startled to hear a woman's voice, Jarred's anger quickly turned to embarrassment. "I'm sorry. Here she is," he said as he handed me the phone. The red light on the baby monitor starting blinking. Seconds later, Danny's broken sleep summoned Jarred. I watched him, defeated, leave the room.

Pussy was my drug dealer. I met her at the corner with my life in a nickel bag. She got out the car and walked over to where I was standing against the light post. I got a contact high just from being in her presence. I was uplifted, shape-shifted into the ranks of Frank Lucas. I didn't need the Range Rover, the four bedroom house, the black marble bathroom, the hot breakfasts, or the foot massages to have it all. I left the kid, the man, and the dog to be with Pussy, my drug dealer.

PUFICIA N' DA HOOD
Donald Peebles Jr.

Puficia Coleman crossed the intersection of Waltham Street and 106th Avenue in South Jamaica, New York when he noticed three young girls staring dead at him from across the street. He was already used to the stares in his drug-infested, crime-ridden, and hooker heaven neighborhood. He knew he was looked upon as an outsider. He was gay and proud of it. He wasn't trying to perpetuate by living life on the down-low like many of his African-American, Caribbean, and Latino neighbors and fellow residents.

He constantly got into verbal battles with bitter straight African-American and Caribbean women in the 99-cent stores. They always commented on his "faggot ways", how funny and fruity he was, and his desire to become a full-fledged woman. He saw what they all attempted to do, so he ended each bullshit confrontation by letting them know how they ought to take their sexual frustrations with their boyfriends and husbands instead of arguing with him. As they went on with their madness, he definitely read them by suggesting they take their typical straight angry Black woman attitude out of his orbit. When that didn't work, then he told them to go and fuck themselves. He hated going to the 24-hour laundromat on Sutphin Boulevard right off Liberty Avenue for the simple reason it was bound for the Jamaican customers to start shit with him. The Jamaican men referred to him as a batty bwoy yet they were always the undercover ones checking him out. The Jamaican women were incensed when they couldn't get away with calling him a chi-chi man so they had to cry like whiny wenches to their posse of rude bwoys and gals so they could attack him. He held his own, letting them know they weren't going to beat and kill him for being a proud African-American gay bitch in America. He wasn't going to turn up like many unfortunate gays, lesbians, bisexuals, and transgenders who were beaten, attacked, raped, stoned, lynched, and murdered by the citizens and the police all over their country. Once they heard what he knew, they backed off him and went on about their business. He wasn't having that bullshit at all.

He just knew he looked good with his honey blond curly Afro, dark deep-set eyebrows, brown eyes, broad nose, thick pink-brown lips, and medium dark brown skin. He stood at 5'9" and weighed 185 pounds of lean body mass and muscle build. His two-hour cardio and circuit-training workouts at Bally's from Monday to Friday nights definitely paid off. He even prided himself on possessing a big fierce badookadunk, which made the down-low African-American, Caribbean, and Latino men go crazy. He loved walking through the hood most of the time in his skin-tight blue jeans, black spandex, Daisy Dukes, or cootchie cutters to show the men his delicious-looking ass. He fantasized about being hip-hop's first gay video vixen, shaking his ass in front of the rappers' faces. He wanted his badookadunk to grace the covers of *KING, SMOOTH, SWEETS, AS-IS ASSETS MAGAZINE, TITANIUM GIRLZ, BLACK MEN MAGAZINE, SKIN TONES, SMOOTH GIRL, STRAIGHT STUNTIN*, and *SHOW* as hip-hop's first openly Black gay urban bitch diva. He had a massive list of rappers whom he wanted to slay his badookadunk, such as L.L. Cool J., Ghostface Killah, Jadakiss, Bun B., David Banner, DMX, Timbaland, Gravy, and Lloyd Banks. He knew personally the number of rappers who loved getting their dicks into the apple bottoms, badookadunks, big booties, and onions, whether their owners were women or men. He knew they didn't mind slipping and sliding into his badookadunk.

    He always loved and embraced hip-hop ever since he was a little boy. He danced to the Sugar Hill Gang's "Rapper's Delight", Kurtis Blow's "The Breaks", and Grandmaster Flash and the Furious Five's "The Message" on the record player in the living room. Whenever he played with his friends at the Norelli-Hargreaves Playground across the street from his grandparents' house on 142nd Street, he would convince them to sneak into the other side, where the older kids and adults danced to the latest hip-hop hits at the park jams. He enjoyed watching "New York Hot Tracks", "Friday Night Videos" and "Soul Train" on the weekends. His fascination with hip-hop increased after hearing the gossip about the musical rivalry between Roxanne Shante and The Real Roxanne. He came home after school to watch "Video Music Box" on Channel 31. He was amazed by Salt-N-Pepa and M.C. Lyte. He danced secretly to Salt-N-Pepa's hit "Push It" every night at 9:30 when he was supposed to have been in the bed. By the time he graduated from junior high, his interest in the male rappers waned as he began watching "Rap City" and The Jukebox Network (The Box) to check out the female rappers. He became a die-hard fan of Queen Latifah, J.J. Fad, B.W.P. (Bytches With Problems), Oaktown's 3.5.7, Nikki D., M.C. Trouble, Miss Melodie, and Monie Love. He took a hiatus from watching "It's Showtime at the Apollo" to jam to "Pump It Up!" with Dee Barnes. By the time he reached high school, he developed crushes on various male rappers. He bought issues of *RIGHT ON!, YO!,* and *YSB* just to jerk off to images of Candyman, King Sun, Positive K., and D-Nice. He finger-fucked himself when he watched the muscular guys in Grand Daddy I.U.'s music video "Something New" and the steppers in Chubb Rock's music video "Just the Two of Us". By the time he entered college, he lost his virginity to the tune of The Fugees' "Ready or Not". Years later, he couldn't believe the massive collection of rap/hip-hop CDs he had stacked in his numerous CD cases. He had milk crates of his favorite magazines such as *VIBE, XXL, HIP-HOP WEEKLY, DON DIVA MAGAZINE, F.E.D.S., THE SOURCE, and URBAN LINK*. His extensive homothug porn collection was up and poppin' on top of his DVD player. Tiger Tyson, Jason Tiya, Ty Malone, Supreme, Breion Diamond, and the Chocolate Cream/BC Production actors were his popular Black and Latino sights to watch, admire, and jerk off to. He even possessed Snoop Dogg's porn productions of "Snoop Dogg's Doggystyle" and "Snoop Dogg's Hustlaz: Diary of a Pimp", Ice-T's porn production of "Pimpin' 101: The XXX Guide to Workin' A Ho" and celebrity sex tapes with R. Kelly, Treach, Ray J. and Kim Kardashian, and Karrine Steffans (Superhead). Many people always believed how he couldn't be into hip-hop. They figured since he was a Black gay bitch in the hood, he would've been so far removed from hip-hop and ventured more into the genres of house, disco, dance, trance, or electronica music. Well, he was a hip-hop head and would be till the day he left Earth.

He enjoyed the hot gossip in the hip-hop industry, especially if a certain rapper was rumored to be living life on the down-low. He used to listen to "The Wendy Williams Experience" from 2 to 6 PM on 107.5 WBLS daily to hear who Wendy referred to when she asked "How U' Doin'?" He and his other gay friends and associates traded lists of alleged down-low rappers like their lives depended on it. Since he worked at a hip-hop magazine called *BIG BALLAZ*, he had the exclusive experience of sampling many of the alleged down-low rappers via casual sexual encounters, booty call sessions, quickies, threesomes, orgies, and gang bangs. The magazine was unaware about him keeping journal volumes of intimate nights with this or that rapper from the East Coast, the West Coast, or the Dirty South. He felt his exploits could rival that of his homegirl, Karrine Steffans (Superhead), whom he admired for telling it all in her New York Times best-selling *CONFESSIONS OF A VIDEO VIXEN*. Unlike her, he didn't plan on publishing his sexual experiences. Although he worked at a hip-hop magazine, he wasn't a mover or shaker. He was just a receptionist on one of the main executive floors, where the hip-hop artists, the recording industry execs, the label figure heads, and public relations representatives conducted interviews with the magazine. In order for them to see whoever they had to see, they had to sign in with him. Since many of them were public figures who had girlfriends, fiancées, wives, wifeys, chickenheads, hoes, sidepieces, jump-offs, and groupies, the ones on the down-low had to be discreet but he already knew what time it was. He played the game 100 percent well. He understood there were no strings attached with those down-low rappers. Once they slipped him their business cards with their cell numbers on the back, it was definitely on and poppin'. Of course, he swore not to spill the beans to Wendy Williams, Jamie Foster Brown, Sandra Rose, Necole Bitchie, Janine Morrow, and other Black gossip personalities about his sexual flings with the down-low rappers. Otherwise, he knew everything in life had consequences and snitches got stitches. He wasn't trying to get shot and killed execution-style by drug dealers, gang members, the Mob, or goons, who wouldn't mind dumping a Black gay bitch into the East River. He knew the risks which would've came to him had he rattled out those down-low rappers he got fucked by. He had no choice but to remain quiet and take their secrets to his grave.

Don't hate me because I'm beautiful, he thought to himself as the stares of three teen-aged girls struck him as if he was a circus freak.

"I don't know if that's a man or a woman," one of the girls said to the other two.

Tired of people fucking with him, he flung his hands on his hips and threw visual darts at the girl, who was dark-skinned and fourteen-years-old. "By the way, Half-Pint, I am a BLACK GAY HOOD BITCH!" he confirmed with shade.

Looking dazed and confused, the girl sought her eldest sister, a brown-skinned, seventeen-year-old girl, for backup since she wasn't prepared for Puficia's comeback attack. "She wasn't even talking about you," the eldest sister said, playing herself royally.

"Yes, she was talking about me but that's okay because I'm going to live my life how I see fit. First of all, she shouldn't be so concerned with whether I'm a man or a woman. Second, she's a child who needs to stop getting all up in my Kool-Aid because I'm not the one. Third, instead of y'all hating on me, y'all need to be taught some etiquette, manners, charm, and poise. Better yet, your Mama ought to teach y'all class, grace, and style instead of grooming y'all into the future South Road hoes of tomorrow," he snapped, cutting them to shreds without giving a fuck if they were teen-aged girls.

"Don't be talkin' about our Mama like that, you ..."

"You what?" he asked, crossing his arms together. "Just fuckin' say FAGGOT since you think you're grown and shit. I'm entitled to my Freedom of Speech as an American, so I can say what the fuck I want. If I want to talk shit about your Mama, then there's nothing you are going to do about it," he said with a Cheshire Cat grin.

"You don't know who you're messin' with when it comes to dealing with our Mama."

"Oh no, you black Mary Ingalls! You don't know who the fuck you're messing with. I'm not some weak-ass faggot who gets fucked over. I'm a Black gay hood bitch who decides who I fuck over. I'm a shady bitch cunt from way back. The phyne-ass drug czars, kingpins, and dealers be all up my badookadunk and they give me every fuckin' thing I want. If I want to get rid of sugar baby bitches like you, all I have to do is tell one of my gentlemen friends that Baby Boy is being messed with. Once their dicks hit my G-spot, they confirm that my orders go through with no returns guaranteed. I'm 100 percent sure you know now I'm not the motherfuckin' one. If y'all still don't know, then your blood will be on my hands," he threatened.

The three sisters simply looked at each other. They had no choice but to remain silent. They quickly got the hint, knowing they weren't going to mess with him anymore.

"I see we understand each other. Anyway, I got places to go and people to see," he said, walking up the concrete porch steps to the rooming house where he lived. He turned back to face the three sisters. "I got one last thing to say. Y'all can eat my wet pussy."

The three sisters looked at each other in amazement with their "No the fuck he didn't" double-Dutch sistagirl gazes before running into their own apartment.

He nodded his head as he inserted his key into the main entrance's lock. "What a bunch of candy ass clits!" he laughed, turning the knob open, walking inside, and closing the door behind him. As soon as he opened the door to the third floor of the rooming house, someone knocked on the door violently hard. "Fuck!"

He walked back downstairs to answer the door. When he opened it, he noticed a dark-skinned woman with her arms crossed and a pissed look on her face. She had brown locks, a pear-shaped face, brown eyes, broad nose, thick brown lips, and stood at a medium-sized stature. She wore a sweater with the Rastafarian colors of red, yellow, and green, skin-tight blue jeans, and a pair of brown Timberland boots. *Oh shit*, he thought to himself, recognizing her as the ghetto-acting mother of those three Miss Grownies who lived across the street. "Hi! How can I help you?" he wondered, not wanting any drama.

"My girls told me you were talking mad shit about me and you threatened them. I don't know you but you're not going to be doing shit to my girls over my dead body. I thought we could be nice and friendly to each other, but I see I can't be neighborly with a snotty faggot like you," she remarked with fury.

"Excuse me, but what the fuck did you call me?" he wondered, quite taken aback by her emergence as a spitfire.

"I called you a faggot because that's what the fuck you are. I noticed how shady you've been towards me ever since you moved around here. You can never be me or have what I have. I don't know why all of you are so jealous of women. I guess this is why you made up in your mind to hate me because I am a woman. Well, you are not a woman and you can never be one."

He nodded his head in disbelief. *Oh hell nah, Miss Ghetto Rasta is not going to come all up in my face and think she can flex*, he thought to himself. "Listen, Miss Ghetto Rasta! I'm proud to be an African-American gay man so I know who and what I am. You have lots of nerve coming up here from the islands, talking shit about me wanting to be a woman. You don't fuckin' know me, Miss Ghetto Rasta! Personally, I don't have a reason to be jealous of a ragamuffin who thinks she is saying something. Before you come up in my face trying to dis me, you ought to start getting up in the mornings to wash, scrub, clean, and dry your nasty, fishy, and yeast-infested snatch of yours. A real woman does not leave her home smelling like a ghetto fish market. Real men are not going to put up with a bitch who thinks she is Sleeping Beauty. Oh please, Miss Ghetto Rasta! In your own unique case, you are so pathetic hoeing your life away every day until your knight in shining armor comes home. You talk about me wanting to be a woman? I am so glad I'm gay because I feel sorry for bitter straight women like yourself who think y'all got it all together with your Cinderella lives and Prince Charming hopes. Oh please, Miss Ghetto Rasta!" he said, giving her one of his gay reads.

"Excuse me, but my name is Rasheeda, not Miss Ghetto Rasta! Get it right!" she snapped.

"Whatever, Miss Ghetto Rasta! Can you do me a favor? Please stay out of my motherfuckin' face while your daughters are on their way in becoming the future South Road hoes of tomorrow. I'm not going to allow your presence affect my weekend. I got more important people to focus on than on some insignificant bitter bitch. I hope when your baby daddy is released from prison, he could return and put your mealy mouth ass on the next plane back to where the fuck you came from. I am the main Black gay bitch diva up in this hood and there's no room for a wannabe," he rebutted, rolling his eyes and twirling his neck.

"I want you to know I'm not going to let you get any of my men for yourself."

"You are really bugged-out for real. I don't want your men. Oh please, you are so fuckin' tacky because not all gay people want to sleep with straight people. Plus, your men are not my type at all. First of all, I'm only attracted to hood brothas. Second, they must be built like football players because I like all my men big, huge, chunky, stocky, meaty, husky, cock-diesel, stacked, and muscular. Third, my name is Puficia Coleman, not Kim Porter. I never wait for a man on the sidelines while he shows off what he thinks is his trophy piece to other insecure men who silently covet what he has. Having said all of this, I hope you know you can have your men because no one wants them but you," he said with shade.

By the time Rasheeda was going to put her two cents in, Puficia's cell phone rang in his Hegwear-designed rainbow handbag.

"Look, I got to go now to answer my phone so this conversation is over," he said, his hands holding tight on the knob to close the door.

Rasheeda quickly tightened her grip onto the side of the door before her fingers had a chance to get smashed. "I don't give a shit if your cell phone is ringing, but you're going to hear me out, you faggot bumberclot. I want you to know pussy doesn't rule me. I am not Miss Ghetto Rasta. My name is Rasheeda Richburg. I am a proud African-American and West Indian woman," she proclaimed.

Puficia got pissed when his phone stopped ringing and his call went straight to voice mail. "See what you made me do, Rasheeda? You made me miss that call. It could've been important unlike this moment," he snarled.

She rolled her eyes and placed her hands on her hips. "This conversation may not be important to you but this is not over, Puficia," she warned, storming back across the street to her home and slamming her door.

"I'm an independent Black gay bitch in the hood. I am happy and confident of myself. I get fucked by the phyne-ass Black macks and Latino papis the world has to offer. Whenever I want something from them, I get it. I wear the finest designer fashions in style. I get monthly manicures and pedicures. I get my hair dyed the first of the month. I work at a hip-hop magazine. I get invited to all of the trendy hip-hop parties. I have what it takes so I don't feel bad for being a Black gay bitch in the hood," he snapped.

Puficia Coleman was a Black gay bitch who sought money, power, and respect by employing his sexual wiles on the big ballas, gangstas, drug kingpins, street corner entrepreneurs, hard-core rappers, young-and-full-of-cum athletes, and other brothas who were heavily invested in the hood of South Jamaica, Queens. He was determined to become the first Black gay bitch to make it in the hood so he could proudly tell all the haters to shut the fuck up, lie on all fours, and eat his wet pussy.

Kevin
Christopher David

IF THERE'S ONE THING I HATE it's a bitch telling me how to handle my fucking relationship! *Who the fuck does Jared think he is?* He acts like I'm one of them young bitches out there running around trying to keep a man! I know how to keep my man—*okay!* I've got one, does he? Hell no! Yet he's gonna tell me how to handle my damn' relationship?! Friend to friend, does that make any sense? You know what, as a matter of fact keep your opinion, because it doesn't matter! The point is he should learn to mind his business and so should the *rest* of you bitches out there trying to judge me!

I don't have a problem with my man meeting new people, never have and I never will. Just as long as I know what's going on. In no way am I the jealous type but the girls are fierce nowadays! Honey they will steal your man right from under your nose! You'll be sitting around thinking, *"oh they're just friends"*, and behind your back they're justa humpin' and a fuckin'!

How do I know? Honey 'cause I've played that scene one too many times before.

I remember back in L.A. I had this one ole' fine piece of trade! *Whew!* Girl she was TDH! Tall Dark & Handsome! And had dick for days chile! I mean a big ole' chocolate thang! We use to get down and nasty any and every chance we got—and it didn't matter where, just as long as we didn't get caught. Chile just thinking about that man and all that dick is making me hot!

I met him one day while shopping at the Beverly Center. I walked into Crate n' Barrel to buy some candles with my friend Hector when I noticed this vision of manliness strolling my way. He had on a charcoal gray velour sweat suit with white Nike tennis shoes. First I noticed the b-boy walk, then the face—but honey as my eyes traced the curves of his body I noticed the imprint of the dick that would forever change my life! He wasn't wearing underwear so his meat was just a swinging back and forth, and forth and back! I almost had a heart attack and died right then and there! I couldn't help but stare! *But* when our eyes met he gave me the nastiest look like, *"what the fuck you looking at faggot!"*

I paid it because honey first of all I don't look like no faggot! I may cut up with you girls and talk this way but out in the streets I know how to represent—*okay?* So don't get it twisted! Second of all I work out faithfully! I got body *downnnnnn*! If she would've even *thought* about stepping to me with some bullshit I would've beat that bitch with a bat!

Anyway chile like I was saying, she screwed her face up like she was crazy so I just looked at her like, *"what, got a problem?"* He pretended not to notice my defensive stance, paid for his shit, and left the store. Hector and I purchased the candles and continued about our shopping spree. About an hour later we were walking through the parking lot when I saw Trade be-bopping to his car. He stopped, turned, smiled, and then kept walking. I looked at Hector like, what the fuck was that about? He shook his head and brushed it off. So again, I paid it.

Honey as I was preparing to pull my Nissan out of my parking spot a *fierce* black convertible BMW 528i with sixteen-inch chrome rims pulled up and blocked my exit. Annoyed, I blew the horn to let whoever it was know I was trying to leave. But they didn't move, so I blew the horn again, yet still, no response. Pissed, I put the car in park, jumped out, and stormed to the car. Quite to my surprise it was Trade.

"What took you so long?" He asked in a comfortable masculine voice.

"What?" I frowned annoyed by his directness. "What are you talking about? Could you just back up so I could get the hell out of here!"

"First of all niggah take it down a notch ah-ight!" He demanded.

Honey, my pussy got moist! He was a man! A real man! A man's man, and he wasn't taking no shit!

"Now..." he continued. "I saw you checkin' me out back there in the store...what was that about?"

I swallowed hard as I began to take note of his position. He was sitting with his left hand on the steering wheel; the right one however, was between his thighs holding something. I couldn't tell if it was a gun or a knife or what, but I knew it something. Many a girl had been bashed for cruising the wrong trade so right then and there I decided not to take any more chances. I was outta there.

"I don't know what you're talking about man..." I said backing up from the car, my heart beating a mile a minute. "But right now all I want to do is get out of this space. I don't want any problems."

He laughed revealing his pearly whites. "Chill man...I ain't gonna' do nothin' to you. I just wanted to know if you're feelin' me that's all."

The tone of his voice changed drastically causing me to laugh quietly to myself. Trade was cruising *me*!

"I guess you can say that." I smiled suddenly feeling my confidence return.

"I thought so." He asserted. "So listen, let me get the digits so I can hit you up lata."

I looked back at Herman, and winked. "Sure, you got a pen?"

"Yeah right here, what is it?" He said revealing the hidden object. After taking the number he smiled and said, "I'll call you tonight", then sped off.

True to his word he called at exactly 1:57 am. I had just drifted off to sleep and was in the middle of one of my recurring dreams with Morris Chestnut when the telephone rang.

"Hello?" I yawned into the phone.

"What's up niggah?" The voice boomed. "You sleep?"

Shocked that he had actually called I sat up in the bed. "Nah, not at all."

"Good, you up for company?"

"Now?" I asked surveying my apartment. It was a mess. Clothes, dishes and CD's were everywhere.

"Yeah now! Why? You got somebody else over there?"

"Nah, it's just that," I paused searching for the clock, "its 2:00 in the morning!"

"So what! It's Saturday night!"

"Well...I don't know—I mean—"

And then I thought about it—fuck principles! So what if I just met him! This man was fine, and he called at two o'clock in the morning to spend time with me. And here I was about to kick his ass to the curb—a fine one at that. What if he never called again? This could be a once in a lifetime opportunity to sample some *real* trade and here I was about to let *pride* stand in the way?! Besides what was the worst he could do? Kill me?

"As a matter of fact yes," I said suddenly, "I do want company. Let me give you directions."

A half-hour later Trade rattled the door. I finished the last of my cleaning, sprayed on some cologne and rushed to the door. Standing in my doorway he looked better than I remembered; taller and definitely sexier. His tank top and see through basket-ball nylons only added to the effect. He smiled as he walked in.

"What's up?" He said in his now familiar velvety voice.

"Nothing," I smiled, "just waiting on your ass."

"Cool, cool. You got a nice place here." He said taking in my studio.

"Thanks. Can I get you want something to drink?"

He paused. "Yeah what you got?"

"What you want?"

"Some Maddog."

"Some who?" I shrieked.

He laughed. "Some Maddog? You know the malt liquor?"

I shook my head. "Look I have some Vodka one of my boys left by here if you want some of that, but I know I don't have any Maddog."

He laughed. "That's cool. I'll take it"

We sat on the couch and talked for about an hour and a half. During which time, I learned a lot about him. His name was Hakeem Johnson, he was twenty-four and lived in Compton with his girlfriend. He had two kids by his ex-girl, a daughter She'kira, four, and a son, Ja'keel, two. He loved his kids and did everything possible to ensure unlike his childhood they'd never want for a thing.

He loved music, specifically hip-hop and talked extensively about his collection of Too-Short, Ice Cube, and Easy-E CDs. One day he hoped to manage his own rap group, and to ensure his future plans he was taking night classes at *El Camino Community College* in Business Management.

His favorite pastimes were playing basketball with his peeps from around the way as well as spending that much needed quality time with his kids.

The more he talked the more I learned, and the more interesting he became. He was smarter than he led others to believe which he felt gave him an advantage. His reasoning, if people think you're stupid then they're prone to explain things in detail. The more they explained, the more he learned, and thus, the smarter he became. I thought it was bullshit, but hey if it worked for him, it worked for him.

After the fourth drink he leaned over and kissed me. For the next few moments, I allowed his tongue to explore my mouth. Confused I stopped him.

"What about your girlfriend?"

"What about her?" He asked kissing me gently on my neck causing every hair on my body to tingle.

"Aren't you in a committed relationship?"

He stopped abruptly and stared deep into my eyes. "Look I love my girl ah-ight. And ain't nobody gonna take her place. But at the same time you offer me something she can't."

"And what's that?" I asked curious.

"This." He said grabbing my dick. "She can't give me what you can give me." With that he leaned over and let his tongue explore my mouth once more.

And then it happened, and from that moment on I knew there was no turning back.

He began by gently massaging the shaft of my dick, and with each pull he coaxed it to grow larger and larger. I moaned in excitement as I thought of how I met this man—this beautiful, beautiful masculine man. A part of me knew it was wrong to mess around with him, but then the other part of me longed for the pleasure I knew only his strong muscular body could provide.

Within moments we were both stripped and grinding on the carpet, pre-cumming like crazy. He broke loose and took to kissing my body starting with my lips, then slowly making his way down my neck, then my chest, pausing long enough to pay extra special attention to my nipples. His lips, thick, full and sensuous created sensations I never knew my body could feel. As they made their way down my stomach I anticipated their arrival on my dick. With the grace of an angel, and the determination of a pro, he took my piece in hand and gently guided it into his warm mouth. The feel of his tongue on my dick sent my hormones rocketing. Trade knew how to suck some dick! He caressed and held it as if it were a long lost friend; one he missed dearly. Feeling myself nearing climax, I pushed him away.

"Whatcha you do that for?" He asked disappointed.

I smiled. "I'm not ready to cum yet."

"So what you want?" He asked seductively. "Some ass?"

Honey can I tell you something? There is nothing like a trade *down*—thugged out—masculine ass—motherfucker, asking you if you, want some ass! Especially one as phine as Trade! My dick throbbed at the thought of pumping his tight ass. He felt it, grabbed his shorts, pulled out a condom and a small tube of lube and proceeded to fit my piece into the rubber. Once done he turned over on his belly and added, "Handle your business daddy!"

Honey I proceeded to wear Trades' ass out! I had him climbing the walls, screaming all types of obscenities at me! Motherfucker this, motherfucker that—you name it he yelled it! The sight of this man doggy-style clawing my carpet in erotic excitement nearly caused me to nut. But before I did, I pulled out. He wasn't getting off quite that easy.

"What the fuck you do that for?!" He yelled annoyed I had fucked up his ride.

I smiled. "I'm not ready to cum."

"What? Why?"

"Because, fucking you like that has made me hot. I want you to hit this." I said tapping my ass.

He smiled retrieved another condom, and squeezed, let me reemphasize that, *squeezed* his fat dick into a magnum condom. Then he laid on the floor, and began stroking it, as I readied my ass with lube.

I mounted him cautiously, then slowly—very slowly—slid down his massive dick. With only one third of it inside me I felt both pain and pleasure I had never experienced before. He moved to slide the rest in but I jerked, letting him know, not so fast girl, mother can only take but so much at a time! A few minutes later, the fucking began.

Honey, I thought I knew how to fuck! I thought I knew how to smack it up, flip it and rub it down! But that man, with that dick, wore-my-ass-out! He had my legs crossed, bent and pinned in positions I never thought they could do! My body trembled with pleasure with each stroke. We hit about eight different positions before I demanded he take it out! He obliged, removed the condom, and laid next to me. Within minutes we both jerked our dicks to climax, shooting warm cum all over each other's body.

We dated for a year and a half, and the sex just got better and better. During that time, I met his two children, his ex-girl friend, and his live in girlfriend. I was even the best man in his wedding. His wife thought I was crying out of happiness for them. If she only knew I was crying because I was living a lie and so too was the man I loved.

When the priest bellowed, *"Is there anyone present that knows of any reason why these two should not be joined together in holy matrimony, let them speak now, or forever hold their peace..."* I wanted to scream out to the top of my lungs *noooooooooo!* But knew I couldn't. Hakeem watched me with knowing eyes. I had promised him the night before I wouldn't say anything when that part of the ceremony came. Through tears I expressed how I felt about him. I told him how difficult it would be for me to stand next to him and watch him dedicate his life—our life—to another. I told him I could no longer go on with this charade. That I could not keep pretending and hiding my feelings from him and the world. I explained to him how every kiss, every touch, every moment spent with him had been recorded in my heart, and that the pain of loss, was causing it to break. I told him how it pained me to lie to his children, to his mother, to his fiancé! I wasn't ashamed to tell the world that I loved him, but he was! He was ashamed of our life and, our love—but I wasn't.

Regrettably I agreed to honor his day. But in my heart I knew that, that night was the last night we'd spend in the dark sneaking around. It was time for a change.

I dated him when he had a girlfriend. I accepted that. But I refused to date him with a wife. My father ran around on my mother for years and I saw the pain in her eyes whenever he came home with the scent of another on his breath. I watched as she hung her head in shame every time someone informed her of his misdeeds. And I watched in horror as he denied her claims time and time again. I watched as she cried, and he laughed.

So there was no way in hell I was going to continue participating in this secret rendezvous' if he chose marriage. Enough was enough. I wasn't going to hurt his wife the way my father hurt my mother. I told him, but he didn't believe me. That is until I stood to give the Best Man toast at his wedding. All eyes were on me as I spoke.

"Today we're here to honor a beautiful couple, Hakeem and Sharese Johnson, on their decision to become one in holy matrimony." The words pained me as they parted my lips. *How could he do this to me? How could he choose her over me?* Emotionally distraught I continued, "Many people today don't seem to understand the importance of marriage or the symbol for which it represents, and that disappoints me; because marriage is an important step in a couple's relationship. It announces to the world that they have found *the one*. The one that makes all their dreams come true. The one that finally completes them."

"Marriage is a way of saying: I could possibly love you always. It is a way of saying: you are my best friend and I *choose* to spend the rest of my days with you; come what may through it all, you can always count on me."

"That is why Hakeem and Sharese stood before us today. To announce to all of us that their love is a mighty love, and nothing, and I do mean nothing will pull them under. Nothing will stand in their way—simply because, nothing else matters. At least not when you have love."

"I commend them for taking such a courageous stand because it says something about them, and, about their love."

I paused and wiped the steady stream of tears flowing down my face. "Hakeem and Sharese I honor you and I love you, and I hope you two have many loving years ahead of you. I wish you love, and I wish you happiness in the years to come. And," I paused grabbing Hakeem's attention, "I will miss you both."

Hakeem stared at me with tearful eyes. Both he and Sharese were crying uncontrollably. She because of my description of their love, and he, because he knew what the words meant.

"This is both congratulations and goodbye. Tonight I will be leaving Los Angeles and moving to New York but, not to worry, I will carry you both in my heart. So," I said raising my glass, "congratulations and much happiness for your future."

I sipped then placed my drink on the table and left. Hakeem rushed after me and caught me in the lobby. Hugging me tightly he whispered, "Why baby why?"

"Because it's time for me to move on; you've found the one that brings you happiness, the one that completes you. It's time for me to do the same."

"But you can't leave me Kevin! You can't!" He said hysterically embracing me tighter. "What am I supposed to do without you?!"

"Love that beautiful woman you just married in there, that's what."

We stood there quietly for a long while holding onto the moment, afraid to let it pass. "I love you Kevin," he cried into my flesh, "and I always will."

"I know you do baby, I know you do. Now, get back in there with your wife, before everyone thinks we ran off together."

We both laughed.

"Yeah you're right. I'd better go." He said releasing me slowly. He wiped his face and stared deep into my eyes. "I'm gonna miss you boy...I am. Promise you won't forget about me once you get to New York."

"I promise."

"And promise me you'll keep in touch."

"I promise."

"Cause I don't wanna have to come to New York and kick some niggahs ass if he tries to keep you away from me!"

"There won't be a need for that Hakeem. Because I will always carry a special place in my heart just for you man, just for you."

That was the last time I saw him. It's been eight years. I still think about him from time to time and I wonder how he's doing. I wonder if he's still as fine as he was the day I first saw him in that gray velour sweat suit. And yes, I wonder whether or not Sharese ever really learned the truth about us. You see because to her, we were *"just friends"* but to each other we were much, much more.

Wounded Gardens
Doug Cooper Spencer

The grass by the bus station had turned brown. It had Calvin arranged the last cans on the shelf. He knew by day's end they would be knocked over once again by his co-workers just so they could mess with his head but for now he did what he could do. He looked at his watch; it was a little more than an hour and forty-five minutes before he got off work.

"I don't know why you lookin' at your watch. It ain't like you got shit to do." It was Broderick, one of the ringleaders. The other workers laughed.

"You don't know what I got goin' on," Calvin snapped as he turned away from the hecklers.

"Probably one 'a them gay hotlines," Broderick scoffed as the laughter turned into howls.

Five o'clock. Calvin zipped up his jacket and tucked his hands deep into his pockets as he walked across the lot to the bus stop. He always hid his hands. He sat on the bench and clasped his hands between his legs and raised his face to feel the last warm rays of the late autumn sun before it lowered itself beyond the trees.

His co-workers tore out of the lot and sped past him. No one looked his way. If only the bus would get there before the sun was gone and the chill set in. He leaned forward and looked down the road. There were only a few buses that came to their town so he knew he had a while to wait; but that would all end once he got his car out of the shop. The last car drove out of the lot.

Just as the sun started to disappear, the bus came up the road. 'Finally,' he whispered as if this was an unexpected event. After all, the bus came the same time every day. He got on the bus and paid his fare. He looked for a seat near the front so he wouldn't have to walk past the curious eyes of the riders as they dissected him, probably making up tales in their heads about what he did when he was out of their sight. There were no seats at the front of the bus so he began to search for a seat that was empty or at least one that held an unconcerned rider. There was only one. An elderly woman sat with a bag. She smiled at him and let him slide in beside her. He put his hands back in his jacket pockets and looked out the window as the bus headed down the road.

By the time he got home it was dark. The few street lamps that dotted his street stopped just before they got to his house as if the town had suddenly run out of money two homes down from the one in which he lived, but at least the porch light was on as the only friend that greeted him each night. He opened the mailbox; more bills and advertisements.

Unlocking the door, he turned on the light in the living room. It was good to be home away from the smart ass remarks and the mocking stares he endured during the day. After all the years you'd think either they would have gotten used to him or at least he would have grown thicker skin, but neither had happened so he simply endured.

He put the bills in the drawer of his desk that sat near the window and crumpled up the advertisements then hung up his jacket and fixed himself something to eat. Turning on the TV, he sat down in the living room and ate his dinner. Every once in a while he looked over at the desk. It was covered with papers stacked neatly in small piles and beside each pile were envelopes. He would be sending out his story once again this weekend, then wait for the rejections to come.

It was a Friday night without his car so he had no way of going up to Breckfield which was the nearest town with a black gay bar. Even though the ride was a two and a half hour drive, just being around people who didn't gawk at him was worth it. At 'Mama's' he could dance, talk and laugh with people who knew him. After the bar closed he would sleep over at a friend's house instead of making the long drive back. He didn't go often but when the people of Roosevelt got on his last nerve he would jump in his car and head up there. Other than that he spent his weekends in the house and visiting his parents. He had no real friends in Roosevelt.

It was late, and after having dozed off twice while watching a movie, he decided to go to bed. Later, he was awakened by a knock at the door. He looked at the clock by his bed. Three fifty-two. He got up and walked down the hall to the living room, looked out the window then opened the door.

"You sleep already?" Broderick leaned against the door jamb.

"Yeah."

"It's Friday, man."

Calvin stepped aside as Broderick came in trailing a smell of alcohol as he passed.

"You want somethin' to eat?" Calvin asked.

"Yeah. Whatcha got?"

"I got some cold cuts."

"Nah." Broderick shook his head. "Make me some eggs and bacon."

"I don't feel like cookin'."

"Man, just do it."

After Broderick mauled his way through the food, he got up and walked down the hall towards Calvin's bedroom. Calvin turned off the lights and followed him. He undressed and climbed back in bed and watched Broderick as he stumbled out his of shorts and fell back onto the bed.

"Gimme some head."

Calvin moved down, his face sliding along Broderick's stomach and began to take care of him. Soon Broderick was on top of him moving inside him calling him 'baby' and telling him how good it is.

Calvin held onto him. He felt safe under Broderick's weight and with the powerful thrusts, he knew Broderick needed him.

In a moment Broderick was done. Grabbing Calvin in his arms and calling him 'ooh baby', it was over and he pulled out and fell asleep. Calvin turned on the TV in the bedroom and continued watching the movie he had been watching earlier. At five thirty, just before the sun rose and the neighbors began to stir, he woke Broderick and walked him to the front door.

"A'ight," Broderick said.

"Okay."

"You still writin' stories?" Broderick glanced over at the desk.

"Yeah."

"Oh. A'ight. I'll catch you later."

"Okay."

Calvin shut the door and went to bed.

The garden was brown year round. Calvin stood in back of the house and looked at the dark, ragged shoots that leaned forth from the crumbling soil. He used to grow things there. He'd gotten permission from ol'man Aiken to let him plant a garden out back.

There was a time the garden was green, a deep verdant of collards and mustard with shocks of orange carrots and yellow bell peppers. Once all of Roosevelt was that same green, but now, little by little, patches of brown were collecting as if to form its own community of death.

Some people said the residents of Roosevelt had lost their African roots, that they had forgotten the earth and now the earth was forgetting them, but Calvin didn't believe that. He saw the tankers that came in from out of town and left empty. He figured that had something to do with it and that became the story of his novel.

Looking out over the fields that lay beyond the small brick and wood frame houses the memories came back; he and Kerry used to stroll through the fields imagining they were movie stars. They would take turns playing the role of the starlet and then they would relax in the shade of the large tree beside the brook that ran along the southern edge of town.

Now the brook was gone and all that was left was a gray scar along the earth where the brook once flowed. Even Kerry was gone. He had told Calvin Roosevelt had nothing to offer and that if he wanted to be abused, he'd rather have it done in a city he liked.

Calvin understood what Kerry meant, but he had no plans of ever leaving Roosevelt. It wasn't that he was endeared to the little community; it was simply the only place he knew well.

That last evening together they sat under the tree by the brook and talked for hours.

"Let's leave together," Kerry said.

Calvin had shaken his head. "Nah, I can't."

"How come? Ain't nothing gonna happen here. It's just a town full of ignorant black folks."

"Somethin' might happen. They might change."

"Boy you sound crazy. People been sayin' nasty things to us all our lives."

"Times change though. It might change here too."

"Well I ain't got time to wait. I'm outta here."

Kerry moved away to Atlanta. They kept in touch for a while but over time the correspondences died away. Calvin prayed that Kerry hadn't done the same.

He had told Kerry that times would change, but change was always slow to make it to Roosevelt. Ever since the 1.2 square miles were allotted for the black folks in order to keep them near the factories, but out of nearby Campton, the citizens of Roosevelt had worked hard to make their town the model of progress. But that progress didn't include welcoming men who liked men, or women who liked women; they said it worked against the advancement of black people to be that way.

So while some 'sweet' men and 'bullin'' women moved away, others stayed on and solemnly made do with what was expected of them. But Calvin, on the other hand, was something else. He had no way of hiding who he was; it was that walk he tried to correct, and that voice he tried to change, they were parts of him that just wouldn't go away. Even his hands; they were long and thin. His father hated them. When Calvin was a boy his father would smack him on the head whenever Calvin's wrists 'went soft'. Some of the citizens of Roosevelt wondered in that case why Calvin wouldn't just hurry up and leave town. But he stayed on, inviting the ire of the residents of Roosevelt.

The rest of the weekend went as any weekend would without a car. Calvin visited his parents for Sunday dinner where he fought with his father who said his jeans were too tight, and he tried to infuse happiness into his mother's eyes which had gone dim from years of trying to change him. By Sunday night he was done.

He walked home from his parents' house that night. As he came to the corner of Ward and Hempler, he heard a car coming up behind him. It slowed a bit and went around the block. He recognized the car. It belonged to Big Bug.

'Shit', he thought to himself. He knew Big Bug would circle the block to see if anyone was looking and come back.

A second time around, Big Bug slowed alongside him.

"'ey."

Calvin didn't answer.

"Nigga you hear me talkin' to you."

"What?"

"Why don't you let me come over?"

"No."

"How come?"

"'Cause I don't wanna be bothered."

Without another word, Big Bug drove off.

Calvin knew it wasn't over. He didn't want to be with Big Bug because he liked to make Calvin get on his knees while he did it to him from behind. Calvin didn't like that because it didn't make him feel wanted. Stepping up his stride, Calvin tried to make it to his house before the car circled again, but it was too late. Big Bug had returned.

"You don't get in this car, I'mma git out and whup yo' ass."

Calvin continued to walk.

They were now in a darkened part of the block and Big Bug pulled the car in front of him, blocking Calvin's path. He opened the car door and started to get out.

"Nigga you think I'm playin'?"

Standing in the darkness, Calvin felt his stomach knot. Slowly he went around and got in.

That night he undressed to take a shower. He pulled off his shorts and threw them in the trash can in the bathroom. The blood had soaked through. He looked into his jeans and only a light pink was there. He put the jeans in the laundry hamper and climbed into the shower.

The letter came that Thursday. Thursday night he took out the mail and went through it. Mostly bills and advertisements as usual, but tonight there was something different. The envelope had the name: Balfore Productions and was followed by a flowing logo in the top left corner. Calvin slit open the envelope and unfolded the letter. It was from a Randal Balfore.

Dear Mr. Preston,

As President of Balfore Productions...

Calvin stood stone still. It was happening. A company called Balfore Productions wanted the option to buy his story. It was happening, yet he had been unprepared for it. The letter allowed Calvin time to 'discuss it further with his attorney', but shit, he didn't have one.

He waited a day and a half so as not to look too needy then he sent his reply. Within a month the check came along with an agreement to give him screen credit, but they refused to offer him a percentage of the box.

The next day at work went as usual: the cans on the shelves had been scrambled, his cart had been hidden, and his co-workers made disparaging remarks to him; but now Calvin didn't care. He straightened the cans, and hummed while doing it.

"What the fuck you always singin' about?" One of his male co-workers asked. He stood with Broderick and a young lady and they all frowned as they demanded an answer.

"Yeah, he's always singin' an' shit," the young lady said.

"I'm workin'. What does it look like?"

One of the managers called his name and demanded to know why he left his cart in the middle of the store. His co-workers began to laugh. Calvin told him he didn't put it there, but that he would move it for the third time that day, hoping his boss would gain a clue about what was really going on. He figured he did, but Calvin knew he was at his disposal.

That Friday night, Broderick came over as usual. As he sat in the kitchen and ate, Calvin pulled up a chair. "I sold my story."

Broderick raised his head from his plate and looked at him. "You did?"

"Yeah," Calvin grinned, shaking his head.

"That's alright. What now? They gonna pay you?"

"Already got the check."

"How much?"

"Don't tell anybody."

"I ain't man. Shit. How much?"

"Thirty thousand."

Broderick dropped his fork. "Fuck! You fulla shit."

Calvin shook his head. "Here's the receipt." He pulled it out of his pocket and slid it across the table.

Broderick looked at it and his mouth dropped. "Damn..." he whispered. "So whatcha gonna do with it?"

"I don't know."

"You cashed it yet? Is it good?"

"Hell yeah."

"So whatcha gonna do?"

"I don't know yet."

Broderick held Calvin in his arms that night. They lay in bed and talked about what to do with the money. They talked about Calvin getting his car out of the shop, and Broderick getting a 60" flat screen and sound system. He said he would also need some tires for his car soon. Then he kissed Calvin and cradled him as he made love to him, slow, long and sweet. Then they slept with Calvin's head on Broderick's chest until it was time for Broderick to go.

"I'm proud of you man," Broderick said as he stood in the living room. He looked over at the desk, and nodded his head. "Yeah," he whispered before kissing Calvin and leaving.

After he left Calvin watched Broderick walk to his car. That body, that walk... he smiled and went back to bed.

His mother's eyes lighted for the first time in many years when Calvin told her. She was happy to see something good happen to her son. She had all but given up on him ever becoming a man, but with a mother's love she held onto hope that something or someone good would come his way. It was the least she could pray for. Maybe this was that something. She wasn't sure, but it was something nonetheless. When he told his father, his father looked confused. He didn't see how it would help him become a man, but he acknowledged his pride anyway. He did grin though when Calvin bought him the same TV he had bought Broderick.

As the weeks went on, Calvin got his car out of the shop, but instead of going to Breckfield, he and Broderick would go up to Carlisle for the weekend and spend their time partying, shopping and making love before coming back to Roosevelt Sunday night in time to get up for work Monday morning. Even at work, Broderick cooled on harassing him though the others didn't. But Calvin didn't care because he was beginning to feel unlike himself. He was becoming aware of things that were outside of whom he was and the effect he now had on those things.

One night, after he had gotten in from work he looked at his bank statement and saw how much of the money he had gone through. There was still a nice amount, but suddenly he realized how fleeting it could all be.

That Friday he pulled Broderick to the side so the other employees wouldn't see them and told him they shouldn't go out of town for the weekend. Broderick asked why and Calvin told him the money was going too fast. Broderick told him that was what money did and all he had to do was write another story. Calvin said they could talk about it that night. And that night they did. They argued most of the time and Broderick closed down, only getting his dick sucked, getting some ass and leaving. The next weekend Calvin took them out of town again.

This time they rented a car and stayed in the best hotel they could afford, ate at the best restaurant they could afford and partied and made love all weekend long. They even took that Monday off so they could spend an extra day in Carlisle.

That Monday night after they came back, Broderick pulled up a block from where he stayed so no one might see him with Calvin.

"That was a nice time, baby', he said, as he rubbed Calvin's thigh."

Calvin grinned. "Yeah. Thanks."

Broderick looked around to see if anyone was looking then leaned over and gave Calvin a kiss. "I'll see you."

"Okay."

Calvin watched Broderick hurry out the car and gather up his bags then rush down the street and disappear into his building. It was a chilly autumn night under a deep starry sky. Inside the car the stereo was playing. A soft song came on. Calvin smiled as he thought of his mother and his father. Finally he slid behind the wheel, turned the car around and headed away from Roosevelt; far, far from Roosevelt under the stars and the nighttime sky.

CHURCH
G. Winston James

Eerie. That's what it was. Eerie walking into that Church after all those years. It was like hearing myself say, "Why do I gotta go to Church, momma?" all over again. It was like hoping that it wasn't first Sunday this Sunday—since those services tended to be too long—and praying that if I had to be there that at least the Gospel Choir would be singing. I felt, walking in from the bright light of the summer morning and into the calm dim of the chapel, that I was stepping into the past. The past of a family and friends and a Jersey town I'd left long ago for a bigger life that could contain my young boy grown-up dreams.

But that Sunday was not what those Sundays of yesterday were. I'd come back carrying my lived dreams folded into small compartments in my mind. It wasn't hopes for tomorrow moving me anymore, but the realities of the past propelling me. My life. The stirring in my belly, the tickling in my throat told me that I was going to make some noise in the Church that day. Maybe make a few people angry. Perhaps force some to feel at least a little regret. Some small fraction of what I'd come to know. I was going to sing a bitter song of my own from the heart. Whether I knew the words fully in my mind or not.

It was all Black people. Black women mostly. Dressed to the teeth. I'd almost forgotten what it meant to go to a Black Baptist Church. This was the place where the well-to-do and the can-hardlies mingled and shook hands with equal pretense. It was beautiful to see, even when I was a child. Though I never could stand those old women pinching my cheeks and mussing my hair. The Church was a venue where you could witness the Black family defining itself: the faithful wife, the obedient young children, the disappearing older children and the often-absent husband. Every Sunday was an experience, though each was painfully similar to the one before it. I'd chosen to leave it all behind for various reasons, but mostly because I thought that too much of anything just couldn't be good for you. I'd stayed away because I'd continued to believe I was right.

But there I was coming back. Following behind my momma, as she ushered my young niece and nephew to their seats in the sanctuary. Besides wondering how my momma would react to what I was planning to do, all I could think of as I walked was how the years apart seem to slip away when you come face to face with something you were accustomed to. Some of the backs of the heads were the same that day as they were fifteen years ago. Albeit a bit greyer. The stained glass windows were just as stained and no more or less allegorical than they had been when the pastor had interpreted them for us years before.

It was Sunday all right. Memories of more innocent, happier times captured my thoughts as I walked down the aisle. Those reminiscences, as with the realities of my life, pressured me to carry myself away from my family. To sit on a wooden pew apart from them. At least for a little while.

Having become quite the loner over the years, I didn't resist the urge to isolate myself. I left my momma, as I normally did in Church when I was young—though back then I would have gone to sit with my friends—to find a seat in which I could be more or less sequestered. I needed to attend to the considerations I'd conveyed into Church with me that day. My niece and nephew put up a bit of a fuss, infatuated as they'd become with me as this almost mythical uncle who had only recently become real. I reassured them, though, that I'd come and sit with them later, even though I wondered—at four and seven—how much they'd understand about what was going to happen.

I didn't dwell on those disquieting thoughts. I sat where I used to sit, talk, giggle and doze off with my childhood friends. I decided that I'd simply review our old conversations in my head as I waited for the right moment, and hope that none of the congregation noticed as my lips mimed the past.

"Good morning, son!" I felt a hand on my shoulder. "We ain't seen you in such a long time."

"I know," I said, as I stood up to greet her. "I've been away, Sister Bailey." I recognized her immediately. She smelled strongly of perfume. The same perfume as years before. A scent applied by hands that had never known the meaning of "enough."

"Well, you welcome back," she said. She lightly pinched my cheek, then patted my face and looked at me with her head slightly tilted to the side, her white handkerchief dangling from her palm. Her dentured smile was so genuine that I wanted to hug her up just like I had my momma when I'd first arrived at home. The wrinkles in her face and her deep set eyes made me think of gentleness and grandmommas, even though I never knew mine. "Such a handsome boy," she added. "You enjoy the service. O.K." She smiled broadly. "The Lord's got a message for us all."

"I will, sister," I said, remembering all the sermons I'd slept through when my friends weren't there to keep me company. "I'm sure the Lord does."

I looked at Sister Bailey for another moment and imagined her with her mouth agape and wrecked after I finished saying all I wanted to later during the service. I knew there was some rule in hostage taking about not becoming personal with your victims. But what I'd come to do was personal. There was no way around it. I tried to tune my affection for Sister Bailey out, but couldn't. The birds in my belly fluttered their wings. Waited.

I continued watching Sister Bailey as she took her seat three rows ahead of me. Against my better judgment, I thought about who she was. About how old she was, and how old she had always been. I decided then, in fairness, to give the Church some due—it did have a way of giving certain people the whatall to keep going on.

It was third Sunday, I believed. I picked up my bulletin and quickly flipped through it just to check. Sure enough it was. I skimmed and read what I'd been hoping to find. Whether the idea of tradition was reassuring or not didn't matter. Whether "tradition" was just another word for "stagnation" or not was besides the point. It was third Sunday—still the Sunday the Gospel Choir would be singing.

I had always preferred the Gospel Choir to the Chancel or Youth Choirs. It wouldn't so much make a difference what the Reverend had to say in his sermon, as long as I could feel that gospel music mixing with the marrow of my bones. I'd never been able to resist that deep, soulful, foot-stomping, Church-shaking singing. The way it fed and energized people. Brought even the sleeping and dejected back to life.

Oh yes. I could remember Almetra singing "One Day at A Time, Sweet Jesus." I recalled how Sunday after Sunday it would move me to tears. Singing. Singing. And I could see Grace, born to a name that defined her and guided her to open her mouth in the service of her Lord. She sang. Yes, she did. "God Is." It was "God Is" every time she stood up in front of the choir. Every time she gospeled "He promised to lead me, never to leave me. He's never ever come short of His word," she was joined by the chorus and...well...by the Holy Spirit as it worked on even the least holy of the holies in the congregation.

Yes, this was Church! I was still as conflicted about the institution as I had ever been. I'd always wanted to believe in some essential way that God existed and dwelled in this place, but in the end Church consistently seemed like a duty I had to perform for my parents and the watchful eyes of others. Sermons resembled lessons taught in detention. Prayers were only moments ripe for meditation. Gospel music was the only thing that gave the idea of God light and consequence in my life. To see and feel the radiance of this music, of the Gospel Choir, and its effect on the congregation, had always made me feel a part of something mysterious and grand. Surrounded by others who were weak, but made strong under this seeming breath of God.

But even the most holy of them in the congregation were hypocrites. No matter how many times their Lord bent them low, and made them holler "Save me Jesus! Save me, my God. I'm a sinner," I could still see the flames of self-righteousness licking at their heels. I always thought that I must have been the only one that God didn't give shoes, because I felt the fire. So I'd walked slowly—so as not to stoke the flame—away.

I was lost in recollection—moving through sheer force of habit during the processional hymn—so I sort of missed the ushers walking, white gloved, down the center aisle—the way they fanned out as the preachers climbed those short steps to the altar. We had all sat down again before I actually came to. Then there he was. Reverend Rollins up in the pulpit.

He had never been a fiery preacher—though at times he'd tried, but he was, according to my parents, a well-respected man in the Baptist community and in the city. In his way, he sort of resembled Martin Luther King. It was in the roundness of the face, I think, and the little mustache. I'd always thought that perhaps one person too many had spoken of that resemblance, and that had left the right Reverend feeling that he could do nothing less than try to achieve more than he was actually able to dream. His sermons had all begun long ago to end with extraneous, unconnected, Jesse Jackson-like "Keep hope alive" refrains. I sometimes wondered if he knew where he was and exactly to whom and about what he was preaching.

I looked away from him and scanned the congregation. Wondering how these people's lives had been. Why they never left. Why they married whom they did. We were more than half-way into the service before I admitted to myself that I really wasn't there. I was doing more wondering and surmising about irrelevant things than I was doing participating. Even as I came to that realization, I wondered whether all the "uh-hum"s and the "yes"s from the congregation weren't actually these other people inadvertently affirming aloud conclusions they'd come to in their own private, pointless wonderings. Speaking responses to questions they had silently been thinking.

Then I started asking myself if maybe Church wasn't mainly about this: bouncing your own ideas about life, love and religion off the walls and the ceiling of the chapel in hopes that maybe one or two of them would spring back and hit you squarely in the face, and maybe make you moan, or even better, holler.

When the Deaconess called for the welcome of visitors and announcements, she brought me back to the pertinent present. Reminded me that I had come into Church that day for a purpose that had little to do, I thought, with understanding the motivations of members of the congregation. I'd come to tell my Church family something troubling about themselves and about me that I'd been holding onto for much too long. I was afraid, though, that my musings had begun to make me weak and hesitant about accomplishing what I'd set out to do.

As Deaconess Jones stood up in front of the pulpit, I recollected the time when the Pastor had stood by my side in that same spot and had asked the Church whether they would second and ratify the motion from the Deacon Board to allow me to become a member of the Church.

He'd said, "All in favor say 'Aye'." I'd bowed my head for fear that he would be answered with a chorus of nays, but he wasn't. I was put on that path that led to baptism in the cool waters in the pool up high at the back of the chapel, above the altar.

He'd asked me softly, "Are you ready?" as he led me into the water. I was dressed in a white robe. He crossed my arms over my chest. Supplicant and feeling blessed. He'd stood behind me with his right palm in the crease of my back. Then he whispered "Hold your breath," into my ear before tipping me backwards and immersing me in the sacred water. I was too young to put my finger on the feeling then, but in hindsight I am amazed how sensual the faith I had in him was in that instant. How close the trust I placed in his hands came to desire, and that faulty thing I later came to call "love."

I'd held my breath. But not long enough. When he dipped me into the water, I'd suddenly felt that his strong arms mightn't be enough to hold me and keep me from drowning in the knee-deep water. I let go and the holy water filled my nostrils and stung my eyes. He lifted me snorting and gagging to my feet before the congregation. They chanted "Amen" and I breathed. Relieved. Confused. Reborn.

"Are there any visitors?" Deaconess Jones asked. "If so, please stand and state your name."

I rose to my feet. Away so long. Now as a visitor in my own home. I turned to glance at my momma, knowing she'd be feeling proud that I seemed to be part of a Church family again. Her Church family. But perhaps I should not have looked at her—beaming as she was—in that moment.

"Good morning, Calvary," I said. "My name is Langston Ambrose, and I am a member of this Church, though I've been away a long time."

"Well, welcome home," she said. "It's good to see you. All grown up." She smiled.

"Thank you, Sister Jones. I'm very glad to be back." The anticipation in my throat became frenzied. I fought back the words hidden in my voice, even as those words battled new ones that had arisen since I'd walked into the Church, seen Sister Bailey and looked back at my momma. It was not the time. Yet. Truth be told, in the presence of such warmth, I'd become unsure of my purpose and even the reason for my plan.

I was about to take my seat when Reverend Rollins rose to his feet in the pulpit and went to the podium. He dropped his pastorly demeanor for a moment and said "Langston Ambrose, come here," as he motioned with his arm. Then he said, "Praise the Lord that the lamb never stray far from the fold."

He was, as always, predictable. This was what I'd expected when I plotted this protest out in my mind. To be called to the podium and asked to account for all the years of my absence. I went smiling. I shook his hand, felt his still steely grip, and wondered again what he might be trying to prove with it.

"It's been a long time," he smiled, still holding my right hand and gripping my right shoulder with his left hand.

"Yes. It has." I replied.

"Now did you graduate already?" he asked.

I sort of chuckled then, hoping that he would remember all the years that had passed, so that I wouldn't have to embarrass him. But he didn't recall, so I said, chortling, "Yeah, Pastor Rollins. More than ten years ago. I'm in my thirties now."

"More than ten years! Thirties!" he exclaimed, grabbing my shoulders as though I were a runaway child that had only just returned home. "Time," he said. "Our young ones are growing up. Praise the Lord." He held me out from him, as if appraising a young son, then asked, "Now you went to that school in…"

"New York," I finished for him. "New York University."

"Amen," came the response from the congregation. For a black man to go to college, let alone graduate was still a reason for celebration.

"What'd you get your degree in, Langston?"

"I earned a Bachelor's degree in Latin American Studies," I said.

"Well, amen. And what have you been doing?"

"A lot of things, Reverend Rollins," I said smiling, knowing—uncomfortably—that he and the rest actually cared. "I worked for a few years here and there doing international relief work with people like Save the Children and CARE before setting off to travel on my own. I've, uhmm, even written some books—"

"Praise the Lord." he interrupted. "We've got an author. Heh heh," he laughed. "What kind of books?"

"Books of poetry, a collection of short stories, and a novel," I said. I felt as if I were divulging childhood secrets. There I was testifying from the pulpit about my writing when no one in my family had ever seen any of my work. I'd been writing and being published for a long time, yet it still seemed like such a private act, the fruit of which I shared with particular people at particular times. My parents never could understand why I never showed my writing to them, but I had my reasons. Aside from some of the obvious ones, ever since I was a child, I never really thought they appreciated the things I did that were art, especially when my particular art tended to be so revealing.

"When are we gonna see these books?" the Reverend asked. "You're gonna give us some copies to put in the Church library, aren't you?"

"Sure," I laughed. "I hadn't thought about it," I lied. The fact of the matter was that I knew it would be a long time before there was room on Calvary's shelves for my books. But standing up there, looking at all those proud faces, to my surprise I thought "*Just maybe.*"

"So where have you been that you couldn't come to Church every once in awhile?"

"Well, I've been a lot of places. I've lived in Venezuela, Brazil, Angola, Mozambique, Switzerland and England." I took a deep breath. "I don't stay put much." A few people in the congregation simultaneously "uhmm"ed.

"Well, no, you don't," the Reverend answered. "You're a man of the world, huh?" He patted my shoulder.

"I guess."

"So how long you gonna be with us? You back to stay?"

"Yes. I'll be living here for awhile."

"That's good. So we'll see more of you then?"

"I think so."

"What made you decide to come home, Mr. World Traveler?" Reverend Rollins asked. "You seen it all or you just back for a change?"

"A change? Well, not really, Reverend Rollins," I said. I hesitated a moment. The time was fast approaching. I took a deep breath to still myself. Then opened my mouth to begin to give sky to the wings that had been beating in the pit of my stomach. "No, I've got a reason. You see, I'm not doing all that well."

Pastor Rollins looked confused. He waited while I struggled.

"Actually—to tell you the truth," I continued, turning the crank on the floodgates separating my heart from my voice. "I'm…well…I'm dying, Reverend Rollins. I wanted to come home to die. Ain't no use in dying someplace where only a few people even know your whole name."

In that moment, I tried to recall if I'd ever heard such silence in that Church. Tried to remember if I'd ever stood this close to a man and not heard him breathe. For awhile I was trapped in the vacuum I'd created. The fact that had emboldened me to come back into that Church in the first place was now suffocating me.

"I've got a kind of cancer," I sighed. "It's eating me up inside. That's why I came home. And in a way that's sort of why I came to Church, Reverend Rollins—hoping that you would call me up here. Because I've got a few things to say."

"That's all right," Sister Bailey crooned. "Tell us."

I looked to Reverend Rollins and he nodded his assent to let me continue. Strangely, I wondered then about the structure of the Church. I couldn't quite figure out where the hierarchy started after the Trinity. Right then I thought that it just had to be the old women of the Church and the deaconesses who sat most close to God.

But what would Sister Bailey have said if my cancer had been showing all over my face, instead of on my legs and increasingly tied up in my intestines? She probably wouldn't even have dared to touch me, I bet. But there was no point in thinking about it. I realized it was unfair to hypothesize about a woman—or any of them—the particulars of whose lives, I less than barely knew. I couldn't discern the adulterer from the diabetic, or the child molester from the nurse or repentant whore. I decided at that moment simply to take Sister Bailey at her "That's all right," and each of them at their word.

"I've only lived a short time," I began.

I couldn't bring myself to look over towards my momma again. Though I'd already told her about my illness, I didn't have a clear idea of how she was going to react there in public. In her Church home. When I'd arranged this scheme, even before returning to my parents' house, I'd told myself that I didn't care if she became offended or hurt by what I was going to do and say. From the moment I saw her at her front door, though, I'd begun to lose that resolve. In fact, to wonder what on Earth I'd been thinking.

"But as you've all heard," I continued. "I've lived a full life. I'm not afraid to die."

"The Lord is thy shepherd," someone shouted. "Amen. Amen."

"I don't want to die. Don't get me wrong, Reverend Rollins. I feel like there's still so much to do. So much more to see. But it doesn't do any good to complain, does it?" I tried to laugh. To lighten the mood. "But one thing I've lived with for as long as I can remember has been weighing on me lately. It's about the Church, and I've just got to get it out."

"What is it son?" asked Sister Bailey. She was standing in her place. I thought to myself how beautiful her spirit was and how just then she was the Church for me. I'd imagined her earlier as one of my many hostages that Sunday, but I began to wonder which of us was really the other's captive. Which one of us had the power to set the other free.

I had so many things to get off my chest and out into the air that I almost didn't know where to begin. I was bitter inside and angry at so many institutions, people and myself. I'd come into the Church upset and dying. With kerosene in my thoughts and with matches. I'd wanted to set the whole damned place afire. But as I stood there in front of Sister Bailey, Reverend Rollins and my momma, despite myself, I fully reconsidered.

Finally in their presence again, I remembered—truly recalled—where I was and who all were listening. I looked around at the people I knew and those I didn't. Though I had demonized this place when I was most depressed—unprotected, down on dirtied knees or prostrate far too often in other activities than in prayer—I was actually in my Church home again. I had to admit since the moment I'd entered I'd felt no enmity there.

I accepted that none of these people, including my family, knew the totality of me. During the pregnant pause I'd created I pondered and recognized that fact was perhaps more my fault than theirs. Face after face I looked and realized that I'd judged myself before any of them. I'd never challenged them. I'd left rather than risk rejection, open myself, or attempt to share.

As a self-proclaimed activist I was ashamed of myself as I stood there with my mouth open, tongue drying, no longer ready to be radical. To act up. To fight back against the Church that I'd felt had shunned me. The problem was that it took my return to realize that this particular Church never had.

It was not fear of their reactions that gave me pause, but fairness and belated acknowledgment of the major part I myself had played in my becoming an outcast. I realized that the congregation I was looking at held little blame for what I had become and done and suffered.

In the presence of God and those witnesses, I decided to let most of my sleeping dogs lie right where they'd grown so fat over the years. I was embarrassed to have come so close to reading them all for filth only to have faltered. I figured, though, that there wouldn't be any use in logging a case about spiritual abuse if none of the people present had played a part in the crimes of which I'd originally wanted them to stand accused.

Instead of all the provocative statements I could have made, I said, "It's my love for children, Church." My voice was much less strident than I'd stolen into Church intending. I felt somewhat off topic, but decided to make a more constructive, yet still important and relevant, point, considering that I still had the pulpit. My years of international service had made me quite the impromptu speaker, and I still felt that there were useful things of which these people could be convinced.

"I've never had any children," I continued, "so I've never had the chance to raise any, but I love them just the same. I see too many of them wasting their lives being angry the wrong way. Being rebellious in a pitiful way. Like they've got a different kind of cancer eating them up inside."

"I know it," someone said.

"We've got to teach them, Reverend Rollins. We've got to teach them what it means to live. Dying isn't hard. I can tell you that. Hell, I've been doing it for a long time. But, now, living. That's another question."

"Yes. Uh hum."

"Reverend Rollins, promise me that when you tell the Church that they won't know the minute nor the hour, that you let them know that it's not just for God. When you're staring death in the face, you've got to come to terms with yourself and your own life before you ever set eyes on God. Tell them that it's all right to go out there and fall and get hurt. God made bones to heal. Tell them that the world is a big place and that there's somewhere out there where they'll be happy, and that they shouldn't stop looking until they find it. Or they shouldn't stop struggling 'til they build it."

I looked over at Pastor Rollins, and was suddenly ashamed for making him "Johnny-on-the-spot" this way. His face said in a thousand ways that this was not what he'd planned for this Sunday's service.

"I'm sorry," I said. "I guess I'm just being selfish, taking up all this time."

"No. You're not," Reverend Rollins said. "You're saying what you feel like saying. Who am I to say that it's not the Lord speaking through you. I prepared a sermon. It's true. But maybe so did He." Then he turned to the congregation. "Can I hear amen?"

"Amen."

"Can I hear a hallelujah?" he asked.

"Hallelujah!" they yelled. "Hallelujah."

"Thank you, Calvary," I said, feeling both weak and inspired. The kerosene I'd brought into Church had set the inside of my chest on fire. "I've seen so much death in my life—you just don't know, Calvary! Children starving, senseless wars, stupid drugs…AIDS." My pulse faltered. I paused to take a breath. "People just dying all over the place. So young. I've stood by too many bedsides. Listened to too many stories about what they would've done and what they wish they could do. There can't be much worse, Reverend Rollins, than to realize when you're just about to die, that you haven't really lived. So tell them to live."

"God grants them the gift of life," Reverend Rollins said. "It's not for any man to tell God's children how to live."

"I'm sure," I said, as I recalled how many times Reverend Rollins had done just that in his sermons, though I'd never quite felt singled out. "But He also gives them other gifts and talents that they can choose to use productively or not," I continued. "I'm just asking you to tell them to really use this one. The gift of life." I smiled. "It's probably the most important of all."

He looked at me for a moment. Sizing me up, it seemed. Then he said. "Of course, I'll tell them." I guessed he'd decided that he didn't want a public debate. At least not with a man who'd just told his congregation that he was dying.

"Now are you really o.k.? For now?" he asked, as he stood to my left with his right hand on my shoulder. He was completely unaware of the accusations of narrow-mindedness and abuse I'd once been prepared to hurl across the sanctuary at him. "If not, you've got the whole Church family to help you," he offered. "Never forget: you're always in the hands of God."

"Yes, I know," I replied. "And I'm thankful. Yeah, I'll be o.k.," I said, as my eyes caught my momma's. Across rows of distance she held me with them, and a whole 'nother truth began rising in my chest. "I've just got one regret," I said. "One that's bigger than all the others." I was almost speaking directly to my momma. As I thought about what I was about to say, a lump formed in my throat. I stood there in silence, wondering, as I had about the other things I'd been on the verge of saying, if this was the place to do this.

"What is it, Langston?" the pastor asked.

"I just—" I stopped to fight back a sob.

"That's all right," someone said. "Take your time."

"Well it's something I guess I never outgrew. I saw my mother... That beautiful woman over there." I pointed to my momma. "I saw her cry once. She'd told me to hurry back from playing outside, and I'd said something like 'Ah, ma' before I went out. When I got back she gathered my brother and one of my sisters and me around her. She lowered her head, then she said softly, 'Do you all hate me too?' Then she cried. One of my sisters had told her she hated her because she corrected her about something. I've felt since that day that maybe if I had said something like 'Of course, mom. I'll be back' maybe she wouldn't have had to cry. I promised myself then that I would never hurt my momma again. I never wanted to see her cry again, Reverend Rollins. Never."

I took a few deep breaths as the tears started rolling down my cheeks. "And now I'm gonna die. And my momma's gonna cry." I couldn't hold back the grief. "She's gonna cry. Cry again because of me." I started to sob.

"Jesus. Jesus," various people whispered. "Mercy."

Then I looked up again to see her. My momma. Someone was holding her, trying to console her. But she was struggling against them. Fighting to get up, even as my niece and nephew slept on. She cried, "That's my son. That's my baby." She bolted from her pew and carried all her seventy years running to the front of the chapel. The whole way she was screaming and shaking, "That's my son! Oh, my God, that's my baby. Jesus! Jesus! Can't no AIDS just take my baby! Not just like that, Lord Jesus. I love him too much!"

Before she reached me, I fell to my knees as the congregation lit up with the Holy Spirit. I was so full. So full of regret. So full of love. I don't know what I did. I think I rocked back and forth on my knees. Moaning. Reverend Rollins knelt down beside me and put his palm on the top of my head. I heard him praying "Life." That one word. "Life."

As my momma made her way screaming, two women and some man jumped up from their seats and fell in the aisles, convulsing as Reverend Rollins prayed and I cried. They were just shaking and kicking. Some people were hollering, "Praise God!" And others were just wailing.

I heard Sister Bailey try to start up a chorus of "Swing Low Sweet Chariot," but her "coming forth to carry me home," was drowned out by all the bawling. Then as my momma grabbed me up in her arms and pulled me against her breasts, I got lost in my childhood. I couldn't say anything but "Momma, Momma, Momma" over and over again.

While she cradled me, I dreamed that a sweet soprano voice floated from the back of the chapel, from in front of the doors. It cut through the hysteria that had settled on the congregation. The voice sang, "One day at a time, sweet Jesus. That's all I'm asking of you."

I whispered "Almetra" because in my dream I saw her. She'd just walked into the chapel. Singing. Singing. Her voice seemed to attract the Holy Spirit like a magnet. It lifted the holiness from the congregation and carried it like clouds on her every note. Then the Gospel Choir rose up behind me to accompany her.

When my sobs woke me from my dream, the choir was up. They were singing a verse of "Hush, Somebody's Calling My Name." The music gave the congregation some focus again. As we all recovered and softly sobbed together, Reverend Rollins asked that we stand and pray. We did. Then he asked the choir to render another selection.

As the choir prepared, my mother and I started for our seats. I felt so humiliated and contrite. Not because I'd cried in front of a whole bunch of people, but because my momma had loved me enough to declare my affliction when I had been too reluctant, too conservative...too ashamed...to do it. I still had so much to learn from her. While we walked, I looked around at the chapel, and thought to myself, "This is Church." I felt my momma's arm around my waist, and knew, "This is family." I cried my tears, and witnessed, "This is love."

Then I turned around and looked at the altar. I wondered teary-eyed, those three truths notwithstanding, whether there actually was a

God. That's when I saw Grace stepping out from her place in the choir. I thought "God Is." But when she began, she was singing something different. It was "Better Than Blessed." She sang and I thought, "Well goddamn, what a Black woman can do to a song!"

She sang, "I've got God, the Father above me. I've got his Son Jesus Christ walking beside me. I've got the Holy Spirit within me. And I've got all of God's Angels all around me. And I know I'm blessed. Better than blessed. Thank you, Lord."

I thought then that she was singing about more than God. Walking with my momma, and crying with my niece and nephew, I knew that she was singing about family. She was singing about the Church family. The Black family. Even in its weaknesses, it was stronger than all tribulation. Even I could have been stronger than I knew.

Grace was singing, "I complained that I had no shoes, then I saw a man with no feet to use. And I know I'm blessed. Better than blessed. Thank you, Lord."

I realized that that's just what I was trying to say when I was up at the podium. Realizing how slight most of our limitations really are. Especially once we've given up on anger and resentment. Then I found myself wishing that I could believe in more than just gospel music. I wanted to believe in God because of how good that burning in my heartfelt at that moment. So I thought about the verses Grace used to sing. I remembered "God is the joy and the strength of my life." And I wondered if maybe God wasn't whatever made you truly happy in life. Then I looked up at the ceiling of the chapel. I threw my question to the exposed wooden beams. As Grace was singing, "I am blessed" one more time, my question bounced off the ceiling, fell down and slapped me to the floor. And I cried, "I'm gay! Praise God! Hallelujah!"

The congregation fell silent. Reverend Rollins looked at me across the sanctuary, took off his glasses and said, "Langston, God knew you before you were born. We've known you ever since."

I closed my eyes. My momma held my hand. I heard one member of the congregation then another say, "Amen!"

Conviction
L. Michael Gipson

They tell me it says that I'm going to hell. They tell me it says that I'm an abomination, whatever that word means. I don't always understand words like abomination, sometimes they too big for me. It's sitting on Sister Shaw's desk next to the skinny white book that Sister Shaw uses to give us our weekly worship and lesson. But I'm smart enough to know that all the white book does is repeat what's in the big black book. Looking at its big black cover I can't help but shake a little bit, probably just the devil climbing up my back anyhow. They say I got the Devil in me, or at least some of the Devil's demons. Maybe that's why I get scared or feel funny whenever I look at it. Maybe it's the Devil's demons in me making me so scared of that black book.

I don't know why it scares me, since I like the way it looks. The cover is so shiny, and the pages are so skinny and light. The sides of the pages look like they were dipped in gold, even the two words on the front cover is made of gold. It's probably the prettiest book I ever seen to not have any pictures. In fact, I think that it's the only book in our house that don't have no pictures in it.

It's funny to me that something that looks that pretty got so much to say about my ugly self. I don't understand why it has anything to say about me at all. How does that thing even know who I am? Momma says it knows me and the preacher says it knows me and since I seen my name in it before. I reckon that it does know who I am. I can't say for sure I know that it knows me. I guess I kinda just take folks word for it, even though my Daddy always says that a man shouldn't take anybody's word for anything. He says that a man should know or find out what he needs to know for himself.

But I don't have much choice but to take folks word for it, since I don't always understand what I read too good. It's not like I ain't tried to know what's in that book for my own self. I tried to read what it had to say about me when I was about eight or nine, after Momma showed me that my name, Ezra, was in it. I wanted to read my own story, instead of listening to the Reverend or my Momma tells me what it had to say about me. So, to see what else it had to say about me, I picked it up and tried to read the letters, but I didn't understand but a few of the words. Every year, for the past five or six years, I try to read those words again since Daddy says a real man don't ever quit and every year I get encouraged 'cause I understand a few more of the book's words. But I'm almost fifteen now and I still don't know my story, much less other folk's stories.

I even tried to pronounce the letters by the syllables like my tutor in special ed is always trying to teach me to do, but it was so many words that I had to try and pronounce the syllables for, that I got frustrated and gave up.

My tutor gets mad at me when I get frustrated. She says it's why I'm always givin' up on stuff. She the one who always get my Daddy riled up into preaching to me about quitters. I don't ever bother to tell my tutor that I don't understand what frustrated means when she asks me if I feel that way, I don't know from frustrated all I know is that I feels tired. I don't care what her and Daddy say, after six years of trying to understand what that book got to say about me, I gets tired of trying. The only reason I keep trying to read that book in the first place is to find out why everybody keeps telling me that the book says I'm a bad person. People say to me if I don't read the book, God gone send me to hell. I don't understand why that book got to say so much against me, since I ain't never done nothing to nobody who had a hand in writing that book. I wasn't even thought about when them 'postles or disciples or whatevah was writing that book, so I can't figure how them peoples know me. So, what they know about me?

Me and my play cousin, Joseph, is waiting in the Sunday school room for the pastor to send us out to the prayer warriors of the church. They say that what they caught us doing is so sinful that they gots to lay hands on us. They say a lot of other things that I'm not trying to think about right now. I'd rather sit here by this window and try to catch me a breeze, since they got it so hot up in here. It's so hot in here I already feel like they got me in hell, 'stead of it being where I'm going. Joseph over there, sweating his good shirt out, sitting all the way across the room from me, like he scared of me or something. In between getting up to get him some water from the fountain, he rocking and crying in the corner of that long bench, looking crazy as a betsy bug.

I can't stand to look at him. When I do look at him, I cut my eyes at him, but he don't see me. At least he tries to act like he ain't paying me no mind. I do know that he gone make me get up and punch him in his chest if he don't stop making all that noise. My Daddy would say that a man ain't got no business crying like that, and looking at Joe right now I gotta agree. Besides, I don't understand why he crying so much for now. We both done already got our whippings for messing with each other. We got caught and we got beat. I cried when my Daddy beat me but there ain't no reason to cry about it now. What's done is done.

But I know I'm being stubborn, trying to act like I don't get how bad things really is for us right now. I reckon Joe crying like that cause both our Mommas is real mad and our Daddies keep going back and forth between being real quiet and getting real loud. But they been mad at us before and being that we always getting into trouble they probably gone be mad at us again. I don't know what to do about them being mad, but I know crying ain't going to help it none.

To tell you the truth, I'm sick of crying. I feel like I cried enough when they was beating me with that extension cord. As far as I'm concerned, they can't do no worse to me than that. The marks on my legs still sting. I look around the room for something that might make them feel better. But all I see in this room is colorful pictures talking about Jesus' life, the chalkboard behind Sister Shaw's desk, that there's the little white water fountain with the funny tasting water, and our old rickety benches. Joseph gets up to get him some more water from that little white fountain, he better watch it before he burst from all that nasty water he drinking.

I cut my eyes at him again and start looking at the picture of Jesus up on that cross, all cut up and bleeding from the stakes in his hands and feet and the thorns on his head, just looking at all them cuts make me wish I had some ointment or something to rub on my legs. I lift my shorts up my legs for the third time today, to see the purple and red marks crisscrossing my legs like railroad tracks. Like if I look at them they gone hurt less. I know it sounds silly, but them marks do hurt a little less every time I look at them since looking at them makes me mad. The madder I get, the less it hurts.

I'll tell you another thing, the madder I get the less scared I feel about why Joseph and I are sitting up in this hot room waiting on them grown folks to get it together. Maybe that's another reason I ain't crying and carryin' on like Joseph over there. I'm too mad to cry. Every time I think about the beatings I keep getting and the reason I'm in trouble this time, I get mad at that book. I know I ain't supposed to think evil thoughts like these, but I can't help it. Guess that's the devil itching after my soul again. But I know if it wasn't for that book, I wouldn't keep getting so many whippings! Seems like lately that's all my parents do is whup me. *Spare the rod and spoil the child*, well that's one scripture that book say that my Momma and Daddy follow to the letter. I ain't never known what it is to be spoiled and it seems to me that I'm always feeling plenty of my Momma's rod. But believe me when I say it's better to feel hers than my Daddy's, him being so heavy-handed and all. I been trying to tell Momma and Daddy that at fourteen and a half years old, I'm too old for whippings. I tell them that by being almost able to kiss fifteen, I'm almost grown. But they don't ever want to hear what I gotta say. They tell me that I ain't never going to be too grown to get a whipping. I wonder if the Good Book tells them that too.

"You know we going to hell for what we did." Joseph says, sniffling. His yellow face is all red and puffy from crying. Ain't said two words to me since the Reverend brought us up in here for counselin', and the first thing he want to do is doom me to a lake of fire, ain't that nigga got some nerve?

"No, we ain't stupid. Reverend Lee says all we gots to do is repent," I say feeling a little mean spirited. "You need to clean all that wax out yo' ears, and then you'd have heard the man say that to you, while you talking all that mess."

"If all we had to do was repent, then I can repent from right here. I repented after we was finished messing around anyway. I always repent after we mess around. Naw, what we did gonna take more than just us repenting. If that was all we had to do then they wouldn't be taking us out in front of the whole congregation to lay hands on us in front of everybody we know," Joseph says shaking his head in assurance. "Uh, uh I know what we did going to take more than repenting."

I think about what Joseph had to say about everybody seeing the Pastor and them old prayer warriors laying hands on us, and I suddenly feel sick in my stomach. All this time I just been thinking about my parents and the people from the church knowing about what me and Joseph did. I ain't even start thinking about all the kids from school who was sitting out in them pews waiting to hear why Joseph and me was in trouble. Now what we did was not only going to be all around the church, but it was going to be all around the school too. I pray that they don't tell them people the reason why our parents asked the church to lay hands on us. Please, Lord, don't let them kids find out why we in trouble! Please Lawd!

"I don't care what you say, Joseph! You may think you know better than me, since you always reading the Bible and stuff. But I know you don't know better than the Reverend, Mr. Know It All, and the Reverend say that to save our souls all we had to do was repent. And since we both already did that I don't know why you over there carryin' on like you deaf or something. We gone be all right with God. You need to be worried about what them kids gone say about us tomorrow at school," I say, but I sound like I know more than what I really know. A part of me wonder, whether or not Joseph did know something more than me about all of this. Maybe we wasn't going to be alright with God. If all we had to do was repent then why was we in here waiting on Reverend Lee and the deacons to take us to the prayer warriors? Why was we waiting on my Daddy?

I look at the door of the Sunday school room and I start feeling a little scared again. I start wondering when they going to come get us. Would it be after testimony? After the choir sang? During sermon? I prayed that they didn't lay hands on us during pastor's sermon. Anybody the pastor and the prayer warriors laid hands on during sermon always got embarrassed the worst. Then they would tell the kids at school what we did for sure.

"It's all your fault, I wouldn't have even let you do those things to me unless you hadn't told me it was going to feel so good. Reverend Lee is right about you, you got a demon in you!" He screams.

Joe making me want to sock him again, he better quit yelling at me like that. I get tired of people yelling at me, like I ain't got good ears.

"If I gots one in me, then you gots one too! I didn't hear you complainin' when I was doing it to you. And you definitely ain't had nothing to say when you was doing stuff to me. 'sides, you was the one that was always trying to rub your booty all up against me when you spent the night at my house, so don't try to act like it's all my fault," I shout back at him.

I remember where I am and get quiet. I know we ain't suppose to talk about sex and stuff like that in church, much less boy sex. I know the Lord can hear me, they say that the Good Book say that he can hear all things. I wonder if he heard Joseph when Joseph was calling out his name while we was doing it on that old mattress in my attic. I can't help but be a little bit more scared for Joseph than I am for myself, at least I didn't take the Lord's name in vain.

"If you say we got to do more than repent, what else you think it is we gots to do?" I ask more quiet-like.

"Well, I don't know. I hadn't really thought about it. I guess we got to promise never to do it again." Joseph says uncurling his legs from underneath his arms to look at me. I'm glad that he at least stopped crying.

"But, we both promised when my Daddy was giving us whippings. Why we got to promise again?" I ask. My Daddy said to me after he beat us with that extension cord that Joseph and me had committed the worst sin a black man could ever commit against his family and against God. I wonder why the Good Book don't say it's a sin for white boys to do what Joseph and I done. I bet good money if we was white we wouldn't have gotten beat, either. Seem to me that white boys get to do everything fun, and that us black boys always get beat if we try to do the same thing. Why the Good Book say stuff different for them than for us?

Joseph thinks about what I said about them making us promise again, 'fore he speaks. "I guess they want us to promise again so they know that it counted, and we wasn't just sayin' it. I mean, anybody liable to say anything when they gettin' beat. They probably want to see if we mean what we say."

"But we both know that if we don't say we promise again that means we just gonna get another whipping, so ain't we basically promising the same thing the same way?" I ask confused.

"Don't ask me. I don't know," he says dropping his peanut head between his knees and covering it up with his chubby little arms. I guess he don't feel like talking about it no more. I turn to look out the window to see the sun hitting all the different colored cars parked around our church making even the dirtiest of them cars shine. I can't wait till the next six months is over so I'll be old enough to get my learners and can start driving. After I get my license, maybe Joseph and me can just drive away from here, where nobody will bother us about what we did. I start thinking about if a place like that even exist, where we could go and what it'd be like for us not to talk about demons and sin no more.

" Ezra?"

"Yeah?" I say turning back to him.

"Did you mean it when you promised not to do it again?" he asks me while staring at the ground. At first I get mad 'cause I don't know why he wanna be asking me about that now. But then I think about it and I want to smile. I know I shouldn't want to smile 'cause Daddy say that the Good Book say that pride is one of the worst sins, probably second on the list after messing around with boys. And right now I'm feeling real prideful, so I bite the inside of my jaw to keep from smiling. I'm in enough trouble with God without needing to make it any worse.

"Yeah, I guess," I say after I finally get myself to stop smiling. "Why you ask?"

"'cause if you keep your promise, then I'll be able to keep my promise too, since you the only person I ever wanted to do that with. I ain't never want to do that with anybody else but you, so now I ain't gotta worry about doing it again," he says looking up at me with those pretty gray eyes.

"For reals?" I ask. Him saying that makes me feel real funny inside, almost like I'm happy but I'm scared to be happy 'cause I know that my Daddy wouldn't like me being happy about something like that.

But Daddy don't know how thick and soft Joseph feel in my hand. Daddy don't know see how pretty Joseph's face is for a boy with a peanut head. And here pretty boy Joe is saying that he only wants to do "it" with a skinny, rusty butt black boy like me. I mean I know what he said shouldn't matter when we in trouble and all, but hearing Joseph say all that about me makes me feel good, real good. It makes me want to hug him again, like I used to hug him in the attic. I start feeling sad cause I don't know if we ever going to be able to hug in the attic ever again. I don't know if my Daddy will even let Joseph come over to our house anymore, since I heard him tell my Momma that he blame Joseph for what we did. He say its cause Joe's grandmamma was white, and her white blood done made Joe go that way.

"Yeah, I mean I know if you won't try to do it to me no more, then I ain't gone do it with nobody else," Joseph says to me.

"What if I can't keep my promise?" I ask under my breath. His eyes get real big and he starts crying again.

"But, you promised! You gotta keep your promise to your Daddy, Ez. And if not your Daddy, you at least got to keep your promise to God! If you don't keep your promise then you didn't mean it when you repented. Pastor always says that repenting don't mean nothing if you gone to commit the sin again. You ain't even 'pose to think about sinning again. Yeah, demon, I bet you sitting in here wanting to do it again, ain't cha?!" Joseph starts shaking his head again when I don't say nothin' back to him.

"See, I told you that you got a demon in you. Now you gone see to it that we both go straight to hell!"

I can feel myself getting mad again. I don't want to keep my promise to my Momma, or my Daddy, or to God. I like touching Joseph's soft, yellow skin. I like the way he squirm and move about underneath me when I'm in him. I like the way he feels on the inside. And the way I feel when he say my name and he looking up at me with his gray eyes. We ain't even gotta be messing around, and I feel good when we together. He more than just my play cousin, Joe's my best friend too. I ain't never want to touch no girl the way I want to touch him. And I ain't never had no girl make me feel like Joseph makes me feel.

But everyone keeps telling me that the Bible says this and the Bible says that. Everyone keeps trying to tell me that what I feel is wrong. I don't know; it's all just confusing me. I guess that's the demon inside me trying to confuse me. Pastor always telling me that the Good Book says that the flesh will lie to you and that the Devil is a lie, I guess that means that I'm a bad saint for listening. Maybe Joseph is right, and we both gone end up in hell cause of me. 'Cause I ain't strong enough not to listen. 'Cause lately all I wanna do is listen to Joe.

Joseph still balled up in that corner, wrinkling up his clothes, and crying. I look at the door a good long time, because I want to get up and give Joseph a hug so he'll stop crying, but I know if the saints walk in and see me touching Joseph there'll be hell to pay. Suddenly, Joseph jumps off that hard wooden bench and gets on his knees and starts praying. His booty is sitting on the heels of his good Buster Brown dress shoes. The heels of his Busters are digging into the back of his blue dress pants. Looking at his blue booty makes me remember what it feels like to be inside him and I feel my Johnson starting to get hard. I feel like God is watching me, I don't want to disrespect God by getting no hard-on in church.

So, I look back out the window and begin singing a Latin Church song I learned in the school chorus, until I feel my hard-on go away. I had to teach myself that trick after my teacher made me stand up in my special ed classes and I got caught standing at attention making all the kids laugh at me. Standing there listening to them laugh I got so embarrassed that I tried to come up with some way to help me control my Johnson. That Latin song just popped in my head and I kept repeating the lyrics over and over, concentrating real hard until my hard on disappeared. I get hard-ons all the time these days, most of the times I don't even be thinking about messing around and I get them. I wonder if the demon inside me keeps my Johnson hard, or if other boys get these hard-ons all the time too? I get scared to look at theirs to see, 'cause I don't want the boys at school to think that I'm that way. I wish I could ask somebody other than, Joseph, somebody who ain't got the same demon I got.

Joseph knows why I'm singing my Latin song, 'cause I told him how I got my Johnson to keep from getting hard. But he act like he don't hear me. He tries to whisper his prayer, but the room is so small that I can still hear everything he got to say in between his sniffling.

"Lord, please take these unholy desires away from me. And please forgive me for my sins and fornications-sniff- Lord, I try to obey your will, but my mind is weak and the flesh is strong. It's so strong. Please give me the strength to do your will, so that I can ignore the demons inside of me that make me sin against you. Sniff! Oh, Lord, please take these demons from me so I can be whole again. Give me the will to fight; give me the strength to keep my promise to you. Give Ezra the strength to keep his promise to you too. Oh, Lord, so that we can both do your will. Sniff! Lord, please forgive us both for all our sins and please have mercy on our souls. Amen."

After Joe finish praying, he gets up to get him some more nasty water from that fountain. He drinks that water in big gulps like he is dying ah thirst or something. I don't care how hot I get in this here room. I ain't drinking none of that nasty water. After he finished gulping that mess down, he gets back on his knees and pray some more.

I watch him rocking and praying and praying and rocking and feel myself envying him for always being so sure. I don't ever feel sure about anything, not about who I am, what I like, where I want to be. I don't ever feel sure about nothing. Joseph always carries himself like he always so sure about his beliefs and feelings. I wonder if it's because I'm too dumb or just too much of a sinner to ever feel the same way he feels. I wonder if I could read what he reads in the Good Book would I be able to feel like he feels. If I could learn as much about God as he learned about God from them scriptures would I believe like he believes?

Joseph reads his scriptures every night before he goes to bed. I know 'cause even at my house he would read those scriptures before going to bed with me. But then I think about how reading all those scriptures didn't stop him from messing around with me, so maybe just reading them scriptures ain't enough. Maybe reading the Good Book just make you feel sure that you're a bad person for doing what you do. I don't know what to believe. I feel like I don't know anything anymore.

All I know is that I don't feel like he feels about what we did. I know that I should feel that way because everybody who loves me and everybody I love says that I should. I'm scared that if I don't feel the way that everybody says I'm suppose to feel, the way that Joseph feels, that means that something is wrong with me. When I think about some of the things that we did to each other in the attic, then I think that something must be wrong with me 'cause other boys don't do to each other what Joseph and I did. Do they? I don't think other boys even know how. I'm not even sure how we knew how to do some of the things that we did to each other, except for the names we heard the boys at school call each other when they gets mad with each other. Them words they use is what my tutor calls action words or verbs. Daddy told us that white people taught us how to do what Joe and I did to each other. But I don't see how since don't no white people live around us or go to our school. When I say that to him, he just shoot me a look and say that I must have got that white boy demon from watching faggots on TV. I knew not to say anything else to him about it, but I know that in our Christian home we ain't never been allowed to watch no TV shows with nothing like that on it, so I don't know what he talkin' about. Sometime my Daddy just be talkin'. He don't know where I got it from and I don't know neither. My

Momma say that Daddy don't like to talk about what he don't know, but I ain't seen that.

I look at the big black book sitting on the Sunday school teacher's desk with its gold edges and letters and I feel ashamed. Maybe I don't feel like everybody say I'm suppose to feel cause I don't ever seem to understand what everybody else understands. I wonder if my not understanding like everybody else, even my not being able to read like normal people read is a demon too. I wish the saints could lay hands on me so I didn't have to go to special education classes and feel and understand like everybody else. I'm just not sure that I want them to lay hands on me to stop liking Joseph. A part of me likes liking Joe.

I look back at Joseph and look at him and look at him until I can't stand it no more. I get up and walk over to him, and kneel down next to him. I wrap my arms around him and I hide my face in his shoulder. I can feel his body trembling beneath my hands as he cries and rocks and prays. He don't push me away though, and that make me feel glad. He even move closer to me when we hear the choir singing and shouting as the white floor beneath our knees shake from the congregation stomping its feet. I can hear Preston, the Minister of Music, playing the organ keys until them keys are moaning behind Sister Shelby's hollerin' voice as she leads the church into worship. I hear tambourines ringing and the church member's clapping hands smack so hard it sounds like its thundering in the church. And for the first time I can remember, I am afraid of its sound, the sound of the church coming to get me and Joseph. I hug him tighter and close my eyes against the noise. I press my cheek against Joseph's soft skin, and—on account of me stayin' up all night worrying—I accidentally fall asleep.

Sometime later, the door to the little Sunday School room flys opens. I feel Joseph shove me to the ground and watch him with the sleep still in my eyes as he jumps up in surprise. His shove lays me flat on my back as two of the ushers and one of the deacon's angrily lean over my body. All three of them look real mad, standing tall as oaks over us.

"What are ya'll doing in here?" Brother Johnson asks me, causing me to remember my mother's scream after she flung open the attic door to see Joseph laying underneath me on that old, bare mattress. She saw my face come from behind his neck. She saw that his shirt was off and both our jeans were wrapped around our ankles. When I saw her face, I stopped moving between Joseph's legs, scared to death, and not really knowing what I should do. And still she asked us in the same voice that the usher was asking me.

"What are ya'll doing in here?!" She say it in a voice that told me that she already knew what we was doin, but couldn't believe what we was doing.

"Nothing" I quickly say to her. I think I say this too quickly. I think to myself that I sound guilty to my own ears. I didn't know why I sound so guilty when I say it this time to the usher, since I know that the only thing I was doing was hugging Joseph and trying to sleep.

"The blood of Jesus!" the deacon curses at us "THE BLOOD Of JESUS AGAINST YOU! Even in the church the devil gots ya'll fornicatin'! Wait till I tell Pastor, what goes on here today!"

"It wasn't like that ya'll! Joseph tell them it wasn't like that!" I beg. I look to Joseph to back me up, but he is quiet and bawling with his head bowed. Ignoring him, I try to get them to see that we wasn't doing nothin' wrong.

"I swear to God, it wasn't like that! We ain't do nothin'."

"Liar! Blasphemer! The blood of Jesus against you!" the deacon shouts, bending down into my face. I wipe the spit that accidentally flew out of his mouth off my face and try to keep from crying. I don't even know why I try and I really don't know why I'm surprised since adults don't ever listen to me. I'm hot and tired and sweating and I just don't care anymore. I let out one long breath and give up. Let them believe what they want to believe. I could understand why Joseph didn't back me up, he smarter than me. Joseph already know'd there weren't no point arguing with adults that don't think you have anything honest to say. At least, I hope that's why he didn't back me up. I look back at him, huddled in the corner.

"I really hopes," I say to myself.

"Come on both of you!" the ushers say while pulling me up from the ground. They march us out of the room, down a wood paneled hallway covered with bulletin boards filled with announcements and pictures of church revivals and socials. The hallway is lit by bright bulbs dangling from light fixtures in the ceiling that remind me of this jail movie I once saw of this prisoner walking down death row to the electric chair. As I try to think about how the movie ended, I slow down my walk a little bit, since I ain't exactly in a hurry to see the kids from school watch me fry. One of the ushers' push me into Joseph, trying to get me to hurry up just like the cops did to that prisoner in the movie. I want to get an attitude about it, but in the heat I can feel my anger quit on me again and the fear settle in my chest as the bright lights of the sanctuary hits me on my head and the eyes of the whole congregation fall on Joe and me.

Before we walked into the sanctuary the only thing I can hear in the room is the handmade fans swaying back and forth trying to fight the July heat, but the second we walk in front of the pulpit, the sanctuary fills up with the buzz of all the folks' whisperings. From the sounds of all that whispering, I can see that Reverend Lee done already clued them in on what me and Joe up here for.

I think about what they must be saying under their breath and suddenly I begins to feel a little sick to my stomach. I bite my bottom lip and push back on them bad nerves trying to do me in.

Looking at all the people's faces in this heat, I feel like I can't breathe, so I try to do what they taught us in choir practice and look over the heads of the people to the back wall of the church. That way I don't have to see their faces judging me, and they don't have to know that I ain't being judged.

I can feel the sweat dripping off my face and down the collar of my shirt when I hear the Reverend Lee's scratchy voice begin to speak. I close my eyes to keep from crying as he calls me and Joseph that word I don't like. I don't want my Daddy to see me cry in this room in front of all of these people, he disappointed in me enough as it is and I don't wanna make it worse. Without opening my eyes, I know my Daddy sitting to the left of Reverend Lee in his preacher's robe, looking down on me in judgment. I'm usually sitting behind him, sitting with the choir and admiring him from the rafters. Today, I gets to be the one who gets watched, but I know there ain't no admiration on nobody's face.

"In the Old Testament, Leviticus 20:13 reads: If a man lies with a man as with a woman, both of them have committed an abomination; they shall be put to death, their blood is upon them. Leviticus 18:22 says that you shall not lie with a man as with a woman, it is an abomination. Now, that's scripture. But the boys before you are not men. They are children. Children who have turned from God and have been corrupted by the evils of this world; children who have been possessed by the demons of Satan," the Pastor says before taking one his long pauses.

I can't see Pastor's face, since he got us facing the congregation. Since I don't wanna feel them folks eyes on me, I try to imagine in my head what Pastor is doing between his sermon breaks. Usually, Mother Sheldon give Pastor some water for him to sip in between his breaks or Pastor busies hisself wiping up all that sweat pouring out of his fat face and under his thick neck with one of the handkerchiefs sitting in the pulpit. His face always swell up like a beach ball when he preach, and his voice goes back and forth from being real loud and hoarse to real soft and hoarse. Reverend Lee always sounds to me like he needs him some cough syrup. I try to concentrate on the funny pictures in my head of what I think he doing, so I don't have to hear what more he gots to say about me.

"Now I know some of you are saying to yourself as you look at these boys. Pastor, I know them two boys, you says, them is good boys raised by fine, upstanding, righteous Christian families. You may even say to me, Reverend Lee, one of them boys, Ezra, is the son of your right hand, the youngest son of one of the most spiritually gifted pastors of this church! That the other, Joseph, is the grandson of one of oldest deacons in the history of this church! You might even say to me that children raised on the knee of God, reared and loved under the watchful eye of saints, don't just turn from God and his word. Not children like these, not good boys like these! You shout in disbelief!!! 'Cause if these children can't do God's will, then what about my child? If the sons of pastors and deacons are lying with one another as they would with women, committing acts of fornication and homosexuality, then what hope is there for my child?! What hope is there for children who are not sitting in the church like these boys! Children who don't read the Bible, who don't sit in Sunday school, prayer meetings, revivals, and Bible studies three, four, five days out of the week! If the Devil can get to children like these, then what hope is there for our children when the sons of righteous men are secretly wallowing in sin!!! And let there be no question these boys have sinned!! These boys have willfully, knowingly sinned before God!!" The Reverend shouts while pointing his finger at Joseph and me. Joseph is standing next to me bawling with his head bowed and I try to keep looking over the paper fans at that back wall, I keep trying not to cry. I know my Daddy don't want me to shame him no more by crying. I dig my fingernails into my palms to help stifle myself.

"But, I want you to look at these two children and see not the children of ministers and deacons. I want you to look at these two children and know that the Devil is real! That the Devil is alive and well in the houses of the Lord and if you don't keep your house in order, if you don't lean on God's everlasting arm and pray for protection, pray for mercy, pray for wisdom!!! Then the Devil is going to take advantage of whatever weakness you got in your home and in your heart!! A house not in order, a house not abiding by God's will is an invitation for the Devil to come into your life. Saints, I'm telling you that the Devil will be in your home with your wives and your husbands while you spending too much time at work, the Devil will be in your finances when you ain't tithing, and as the Lord has revealed to us today, a house not in order will even be an invitation for the Devil to teach your children the wicked ways of the world, the wages of sin, when you too busy to spend time with them!! I tell you that if you don't get your house in order, the Devil will turn your children into liars, cheaters, backstabbers, fornicators, adulterers, or worst of all homosexuals!! First Corinthians 6:9 says that the effeminate and the abusers of themselves with mankind shall not enter the Kingdom of Heaven!! Church, I'm a living witness today that the Devil will even use your children to destroy the houses of the Lord!!" Reverend Lee breaks and I can hear over the mike his handkerchief travelin' over his Moon Pie face.

"But, never fear church! The Devil ain't goin' win here today, cause this church is a righteous church. This church believes in God and his word. The saints in this church are about taking care of the business of delivering souls to Christ. Ain't none among you who ain't done battle with Satan and claimed the victory. Satan get thee behind cause the Lord said victory! Victory! Say it with me saint's, VICTORY! VICTORY! Shall Be Mine! This church is gone get its house in order today! We gone root out Satan and his evil spirits!"

Joseph falls to his knees next to me and begins to cry and pray like he did in the Sunday school room. Three, then four of the church's prayer warriors fall down beside Joe, pushing me out of the way, until they're all around him. They all start whispering prayers on top of each other as they lay hands on his head and body, with one or two of them shouting "Halleluiahs!" and "Have Mercy Jesus!!!" I stumble away from them and I look back at my Daddy. He's looking at Joseph with a look of hate so strong that I fall to my knees in surprise and fear. I ain't never, never, ever seen my Daddy look at anybody, but white folks, the way he lookin' at Joseph. I know from that look that Joseph ain't gone never be welcome in our house again. Then my Daddy turns and looks at me, but the look in his eyes is the same look he had for Joe, and I begin to tremble.

"When Reverend Jacobs came to me about his son, his heart was heavy. For saints, he thought that he had kept his house in order. Reverend Jacobs has raised his son, Ezra, to know God, to worship God, to love God. And still Ezra sinned, but I tell you that all among us have sinned. Others in the church, people in this very church—Hallelujah—that Reverend Jacobs had confided in had advised him to keep Ezra and Joseph's sin a secret. They told Reverend Jacobs that his son's sin would be seen in the eyes of this congregation as a reflection of him as a father and a pastor! See saints, Reverend Jacobs knew that some of ya'll was going to question whether or not you wanted to follow a pastor who cannot keep Satan out of his own home, a reverend who had not kept his house in order according to the word of God. But Reverend Jacobs knew in his heart that in all secrets lie the work of the Devil, Reverend Jacobs loves this church too much to allow Satan to get an invitation into the hearts and minds of the children of this church, through the Satanic demon in these children. God had revealed to Reverend Jacobs—through the Devil's work with Ezra—that he had been negligent in his duties as a father and a husband; that he was in violation of God's divine order. You see Reverend Jacobs had become too busy, and had like many of us men do, and let the women in our homes take up the slack. Reverend Jacobs had begun to let his wife serve as the head of his household while he was busy doing the work he was called to do in his father's house. You see saints, Reverend Jacobs house, like many of the houses in this church, was not in order!! Reverend Jacobs thought his house was in order because he was doing the Lord's work, but in Reverend Jacobs experience we see a testimony, a lesson from God, of what happens when God's divine order is not heeded as a man's highest calling. Reverend Jacobs wanted you all to see what can happen when you allow the Devil an invitation into our homes. Get your houses in order saints! Get them in order! Women, let your men be the men God intended them to be, and stop following the ways of the world by trying to be the man of your house! Let me say it again for those of you who didn't understand me clearly. Sistahs! Stop trying to be the men in your household, that ain't yo' job. You can see the result when the will of the lord is defied," Pastor says motioning toward Joseph and me.

    I look at my Momma after Pastor say those things about us and I see her sitting in the pew looking real stiff like in her yellow hat and suit. Behind the veil on her hat, I can see the tears sliding down her cheek, but she don't look sad. She got her lips pressed together so that they looks real thin, like a white woman. She looking real mad, I reckon she mad about the way Pastor talking about her in front of everybody. Maybe God getting her back today for all the times I hear her and the other sisters in the church talking about the other women in the church. Seem like I done heard everything about everybody up in the church from the doorway of my Momma's kitchen. From Usher Parker's husband cheating on her with the sisters of the church to Mother Adam's gambling problem, I done heard it all. I guess now I done give them church women something to talk about her fo'. I wasn't trying to hurt her; I didn't expect her to get called out like that. I feel bad about that, cause I know my Momma don't like to be gossiped about. She always saying that Christians shouldn't gossip. Looking at the pain in her face, I guess now I can see why. She know she ain't gone be treated like a first lady of the church no more, not after what Pastor done said in here this afternoon.

    "Saints, you are a living witness to what happens to your children when they do not witness God's Divine order in the home. Yes, these boys have sinned, but they have asked to be delivered from their sins! They have begged to be delivered from the homosexual demons that are consuming their souls. They have asked for God's forgiveness and his mercy!"

I open my eyes and turn around to look at Reverend Lee, because I cannot believe the words that have just come outta his mouth. I cannot believe that my pastor just lied to the whole congregation. He lied! I never told nobody that I wanted to be delivered from nothing including no homosexwhatever. I don't even know if I am *that*. I just know that I like being with Joseph, that I love being his best friend and him being my play cousin. I don't understand why the pastor would lie on me like that. Why the pastor would commit a sin about something like that? Why would he lie over a sinner like me?

"Saints, cover yourself with the blood of Jesus!" Pastor orders after he hears that Joseph's cries are turning into screams. The members of the church open their hands and move them back and forth over their heads and repeat " the blood of Jesus, the blood of Jesus, the blood of Jesus" over and over to ward off the demons coming from Joseph's deliverance.

The prayer warriors' prayers start getting louder and it seems like the whole church is shouting and rebuking Joseph.

" I rebuke you spirit in the name of Jesus…"

"…in the name of Jesus…"

"…Loose that spirit, Oh, Lord…"

"I demand that you loose that child, Satan, in the name of Jesus!!!"

" Hallelujah!!"

"Glory! Glooooorrrrrrraaaaaaaaaaaaaaahhhhhhhhhhh!!"

I look at Joseph through the powerful, hiding hands of the prayer warriors on what my grandmother calls the wailing floor and I see Joseph scream a loud piercing scream right before he sticks his fingers down his throat. His head is bowed and the others are too busy praying and shouting to see what I see. Real easily, Joseph starts to throw up clear liquid with chunks of what looks like eggs. But Joseph hates eggs; they always make him throw up. I look at the clear vomit sliding down his shirt onto the floor and I remember all that water he drank. He throws up some more in between crying and screaming, just like we had both seen tons of people do on this floor during their deliverance from the Devil's evil spirits. Only they didn't have to stick they fingers down their throat to make the demons come out, at least I never thought they did.

Then it hits me! Joseph is faking! Joseph knew what the pastor and 'em expected, and he was giving the saints what they wanted. Joseph, who read the scripture every night and who could quote scripture better than any girl in church, was faking deliverance. As I gets to thinking about it, I can see that Joseph planned on faking the whole time. My head starts spinning and I feel weak, 'cause I don't know what to believe anymore. I don't know what to do anymore.

Why is the pastor lying? And my Daddy watching him lie and ain't saying nothing about the lying? Why is Joseph faking if he really believes that he got a demon inside of him? Does he want to keep his demon? Does he even believe that he got ah demon?!

Then Joseph screams a real high-pitched scream that sounded like one of them F sharps he was always showing off and hitting in choir. And the Pastor shouts, "SHE'S out of his body! Saints get on your knees and pray! Children plead the blood, so that you cannot receive Satan's unholy spirit! THE BLOOD OF JESUS AGAINST YOU DEMON! I rebuke you in the name of Jesus! The blood of Jesus against you! This child has been saved, delivered from his sins! Delivered from her, delivered from hell!!" Pastor shouted "Hallelujah! Thank you, God!"

I look at the Pastor and wonder why the demon gotta be a "her"? And how he know the demon is a "she"? I start believing that maybe Joseph ain't the only one faking, that maybe Reverend Lee is faking too! I ain't never been no sissified boy, so I know that I ain't got no "her" or "she" in me. I ain't feel like no she when I was holding Joseph or when I was inside of him! So, how is my demon a she? None of this makes any sense to me.

"Now, what about your sins, saints? How many of you are inviting Satan to your home by not having your house in order? Get your house in order! As the Pastor of this church I'm going to start right here and right now to get my house in order, and I'm gone start with Reverend Jacob's child. Reverend Jacobs come down here, so we can lay hands on Ezra. We getting the Devil out of this church today. Hallelujah! Yes, Lawd!"

I look at Joseph—and I mean really look at him—as the saints in the church lift him up. And I see the vomit on his shirt and the tear stains on his face and his wrinkled clothes. I look at him and think about all the times that we played video games and softball and wrestled and did roundhouses and cartwheels on old mattresses in the field. I think about our late night talks and secret late night trips to the fridge and even our nights fornicatin' in the attic. Then I think about what Joe did, I think about him faking it and how that don't fit with what he say, and my Momma and how her attitude and gossip don't fit with what she say the Bible say, and my Daddy and how his sayings about white folks don't always fit with what he say God say, and even my Pastor and how his lying goes against everything he taught me about being a Christian. And I can't believe what they got to say about me. I can't believe that they can truthfully tell me what's in that Good Book, no mo' either. I know I gotta listen to what my heart tells me, nah. And it tells me I ain't gots nobody's demon. It tells me there ain't nothin' wrong with how I feel about Joseph. It says there ain't nothin' wrong with love, and I know that I love Joseph.

And so I say it to them in that room with the eyes of the church pressin' against my back. I say loud enough for everybody to hear me.

"I love him!"

My Daddy stops dead in front of me, with Reverend Lee at his side.

"What you jus' say tah me, boy?" Daddy whispers. His face looks like he done just seen my dead granddaddy walk clean across this sanctuary.

"I said I love him. It can't be a sin, 'cause I love him." And I do love Joe, I knew the second I saw him standing there looking a mess that I loved him, in spite of himself.

My Daddy slaps me down in front of the church and I can feel the taste of blood fill my mouth. I look up at him from the wailing floor with tears in my eyes.

"You goin' repent, boy, and we gone get you delivered from that demon. Ezra! I ain't goin have no sinnin' faggots in my house. Or in the Lawd's house." He says in his Mississippi drawl.

"Daddy, I need you to hear me, please, Daddy," I fight the tears I want to wipe from my eyes cause I want my Daddy to see me stand up as the man he taught me how to be. A man who stands up for what he knows is the truth and don't take nobody else's word for it. A man that don't quit or give up on what he knows is right just 'cause he gets frustrated or 'cause it gets too hard. I want him to see that I'm the man he raised me to be.

"I love Joseph, and you told me where there is love there is no hate. Where there is love there is no sin. Cause God is love. That's what you always told me, Daddy. God is love, and I love God. And I love Joe," I say.

"You ain't my child, you belong to the Devil!" my Daddy says spitting these words at me. "Either you get delivered from your wretchedness, these white folk afflictions, or I ain't gots no son named, Ezra. Ya' hear me? Do as I say or I ain't gots no son named, Ezra! Nah, either do as I say this minute boy or so help me..." He raises his hand high over his head, looking down on me as if I was less than the bait we uses to fish. As if I was less than the dirt beneath his feet.

"What you sayin' to me, Daddy?" I ask, not wanting to understand him.

"You gone obey me or you gone find your grown, sinnin' self anotha place to live, boy."

"That ain't Christlike, Daddy! What you saying to me ain't in love. It ain't no Christ love in that! Is what you sayin to me…is your kind of love in that Bible too?" I ask as I stands up on shaky legs, with my lips trembling and my voice cracking and my chest aching. I stands up and I looks at my Daddy for the first time. The room is filled with noise, but me and my Daddy are still.

"Reverend Jacobs you know that the Devil is a liar and manipulator of words, don't you listen to the demon in that child talk to you like that. Rebuke him in the name of Jesus! You make that child get delivered, nah!" Reverend Lee hisses to my Daddy while looking at me. My Daddy stands there looking at me dumbfounded.

Ignoring my Daddy, Reverend Lee waves to the prayer warriors to come and get me. They grab at me and I begin kicking and screaming as my Daddy just stands there watching me. I scramble off the floor, kicking one of the deacons in the mouth and slappin' the hands of the prayer warriors off me as they reach for me. I get up and run past my brothers and sisters in Christ, their hands waving back and forth over their heads as they chant the "Blood of Jesus" against me. I look back at my Momma who is still sitting stiff with her back to me. And I ask my brothers and sisters in Christ "Don't ya'll know love no more? How can ya'll say my lovin' him is a sin, when ya'll was the ones who taught me that God is love. I can't get why ya'll can't see nothing,' but sin no more. Why can't ya'll see love?" But I could tell from the horror on their faces that they ain't wanna see and they ain't wanna hear nothin' else from no child. And so I ran out of my father's house, away from their sin, so I could love. My Daddy didn't know it, but I did get delivered, delivered to God's love.

But the once bright, blue sky had filled with black clouds from an approaching storm. And as I ran past the parked church cars down the dark, uncertain road, I kept shouting for all who could hear me "God is love, and he loves me. God is love and he loves me," I shouted it until I could believe it, 'cause now God's love was the only love I knew for sure I had. The only one I had to protect me from all the dark, scary walk ahead. Amen.

Alphabet Soup
Charles W. Harvey

He was a cute yellow haired boy, about three years old. Blue eyes as big as marbles. He sat punching at a floppy dog shaped purse until the soup his Mother ordered for him arrived. It must have been his birthday. His sparkling red and blue pointed hat was the brightest thing in the Holiday Hotel's dim dining room. After his Mother cooled the soup with a few whooshes from her lips, he took a few sloppy sips and put his spoon down.

"Don't you like alphabet soup, Honey?" she asked. He shook his head first side to side, then up and down. His Mother hunched her shoulders and turned to the rest of the clan seated at the table. He picked up his spoon, stirred a bit and started making noises at the soup.

"Bu...bu...bu," went his round pink mouth. "Bu...bu...bu..."

I guess there were more B's in the bowl than A's, Z's, D's or M's. I like M's myself. "Mmmmm." I can "Mmmmmm" all day long especially when my nerves are worked up. But my little friend got stuck on his B's.

"Bu, bu, bu. Bu, bu bu," he chanted. His Mother turned and looked at him as if he was the Christ child. Right away she picked up on his scholarly intentions and encouraged him.

"Beeeee," she said in a sing song motherly way. "Beeeee. You want to tell Mommy all the words that begin with Beeeee?"

And so he recited, "Bu, bu, bu...bull. Bu, bu, bu...Bill. Bu, bu...bear. Bu, bu.. Bill. Bu, bu... ball. Bu, bu.." He stopped and looked at me. "Bu, bu, bu..black.

I smiled at him. The rest of the clan sat around the table looking like folks caught in the bathroom examining their private parts. They appeared to be nice people; tweed jacketed, wool sweatered, and blue jeaned. The men wore loafers and the women flats. The Mother looked startled at me as if I had suddenly appeared out of nowhere. I nodded and smiled back to be reassuring that all was well in the state of race relations. She gave a faint smile back.

I looked out the window at the Hotel's pool that was as blue as the pot of Faultless Starch my Mother boiled on her stove for dipping her pillow cases and my Father's shirts. I saw out of the corner of my eye someone lean over and whisper something to the boy's Mother. She glanced at me and snatched her purse from the table. I sighed. My Mother's broad back filled the window next to me as she hung my

Father's shirts on the line. In the sun they shimmered aquamarine and white until they dried stiff as plastic.

An urgent matter in the Hotel's lobby needed the attention of the boy's parents. The rest of the family soon took their attention from him, leaving him to be with his soup and me. I smiled at him and quietly mouthed "Bu,bu, bu beee…" at him. Over and over I went, "Bu, bu, bu, beee…" until he mimicked back. He was ready for lesson two.

"Bi iii biii…iii…" like the beginning of itch as if from a mosquito bite. "Biii Biii iiitch" He furrowed his little yellow brow and slightly shook his head no. I smiled and nodded yes. I whispered a quiet but dramatic "Surprise Mommy." The little boy stared at me with his brow in a knot. I wondered what kind of words he had heard his father use.

Children I believe, have a seventh sense about dangerous words and dangerous deeds. Something told him that I was leading him down a bad path. Just as good sense told me red Easter egg dye in my Mother's pan of starch holding my father's boiled white shirts would not please her. But children don't always have the capacity to resist. Can't see the domino effects of their actions beyond immediate gratification or curiosity satiation. Those shirts stayed red forever. Every once in a while she would come across one and hold it up to my face and shake her head—even after I turned thirty. I've never dyed eggs again. As I spied Mom and Dad coming back into the restaurant I quickly repeated the lesson to my little friend. "Bi iii itch." He smiled.

His parents plopped into their chairs all red and flustered. They explained that their neighbor had called and said the cleaning lady had locked herself out of the house.

"That Millie is always doing something," the Mother said.

The boy, glad to see his parents, was eager to continue his alphabet lesson. He tugged at his Mother's sleeve until she smiled at him. I quickly and quietly paid my check. But I lingered near some plastic ferns pretending to be interested in the wispy lifelike leaves.

"And so what other B words can you tell Mommy?" There was a moment of silence. The boy stared in the empty space that had held my body. He began slowly.

"Bi, bii, biii…Bitch!"

All heads turned toward him. His little hat wobbled before I heard him cry out like a hurt cat. I blew dust from the plastic fern and stepped into the hotel's swarming lobby. "Victory for Millie too," I said to myself.

FATHER TO SON
Stewart Shaw

You watch the boy as he stands inside the sheltering nave of trees; smell his fear; musk, loamy and dank. The park is dark, hollow and echoes with ghostly, angel sounding voices. Two blocks away he has left his breath behind, severed it with the closing of a front door. Two blocks away he has left his youth. You can smell this man-child.

He shivers and you watch as he eases down to his knees, pine trees all around breathing for and with him; their scent clean and pure and life affirming. He has left his old life behind, two blocks away.

****

SON

"Shoot!"

I can remember hearing her disclaim, an air of dismissal and contempt standing at attention in her mouth, her words all mocking and stuff, as she, my older sister Candace, calmly and showing all of her crooked front teeth, just flatly blurted out,

"...he dances the way all them gay guys dance."

She sat there at the end of my parent's bed expecting me to comment. Like hell girl, I thought to myself, I'd be dead and in a heterosexual hell before I justified a homophobic statement like that.

"Look how he throws his hands all around like some spastic disco chicken with its tight ass on fire."

I waited for the derision flavored "humph" to fall from out of her mouth like rotten teeth that would stink up the room, making me gag and cover my nose. Lord knows the stuff that she was saying was stank-butt funny, hilarious no less, but just not in the way that she intended. The sense of familial camaraderie she tried to foster between us, died the minute her mouth opened and those words popped out. But...

Like always, I tumbled back inside of my hurt, smiled, turned around and quietly, behind her back, mumbled *forget you girl*, softly to myself, as she continued to flay and rip me apart with her statements.

The words, *she don't have a clue*, Miss-I-ain't-got-a-thing-against-gays, reverberated through my echoing mind as I continued to watch the images that washed vacantly across the television screen, trying my best to ignore my sister.

Light from the TV flickered throughout the darkened bedroom, music and Candace's harsh, cackling laughter, filled the spaces between my silence; a quietness that my sister didn't even know that she had created. I sat there beside her on the sloping end of the bed and thought just how totally wack it was that people could actually and honestly mistake a lack of malice for caring.

"Well," my sister (whom, regardless of her attitudes, I still loved almost more than anyone else in my life), would always say when the subject of "Them Folks" came up, "at least I don't hate them people. They're human too. Carl at work is the biggest sissy there is, and we hang all the time." She and my father would laugh out loud, while my mother would in a quiet, though conspiratorial way, smile politely while looking anxiously in my direction.

Her words "they're human, they're human," would always make me mad, and I would think to myself, "thanks for at least giving us that." Yet, I would say nothing, just letting the bullshit pile up higher and higher till I felt that I would suffocate from it all. My sister would always give her opinion of gays in the same tone of voice she reserved for speaking about rapists and child molesters.

"...mm, mm, mm. But, I don't hate them."

I didn't want to be a "them" and wasn't yet ready to come out as a sissy, punk, queer or fag to my family, so I took the madness. I kept silent, taking the verbal abuse, even after my father called me "faggot" that first time.

I was sitting at the kitchen table sipping on a cup of Red Zinger tea, talking to mama and that sister girl of mine, just doodling around the edges of a fierce poem that I had written earlier that morning. I had just recited it out loud like I was Mos Def on the mic, or Lawrence Fishburne in Hamlet or something. Mama smiled like she always did, praised the poem to high heaven, saying over and over again how good it was. Sis laughed when I stumbled over the words in my haste to get it out, but I could tell that she was gigging on it though. I didn't know that pops was in the room, so when he cleared his throat, I jumped.

"What you doing boy? Real men don't write poetry."

His words were meant to be cautionary or something, kind of like that dumb ass old country song, "Mamas don't let your babies grow up to be cowboys." Instead if my father were writing the lyrics they would sound more like "mamas don't let your babies grow up to be faggots and punks." Whatever, he always did believe that mama coddled and babied me too much. "Baby," he would always say to her, "don't keep doing things for that grown-tail boy, he gonna grow up to be soft and a punk."

 So, anyway, that morning in the kitchen, he stepped up to the table his long, thick fingers with their nicotine stained nails, taking hold of my poem twirling it around and around in circles on the little four cornered, yellow and green splotched Formica topped table. Looking around, trying his best to make it look like he was speaking to no one in particular, *yeah right*, he loudly interjected, "Only girls, people who are fifty-one-fifty, and faggots write poetry. Not real men." He looked over at me as he spit out the word "faggot." His face contorted, eyes glaring wide open, and his mouth twitched, looking all nasty and hateful. Coughing loudly once then twice, he moved over to the sink, spit then poured his coffee down the drain and left the room.

 But, I was fifteen, just... I was scared of my own sexuality, and still in love with him, and the idea of father and son bonding; the idea of protector and protected. So once again I let the stank go, not wanting to dirty my new shoes in it not ready or willing to confront his statement and thus myself. But two years later when he stormed into my bedroom without knocking, screaming at me to take "take that faggy-stank-butt calendar" off of the inside of my closet door, where it had been hanging in relative obscurity for the past eleven months, or he'd personally remove it, and then kick my faggot ass up and down Bonar street, then right out of his house, I had enough. Right then and there, my heart racing like horses charging down the straight-away, I knew it was time for me to be a man, and get my move on. So I packed my stuff, making sure to take with me my "faggy-stank-butt" calendar; twelve fine brothas all nicely clad in next to nothing, and got on with myself.

 At that moment I knew that I might have been a faggot, but I was damned sure I wasn't gonna be his, or any other fools, whipping boy; if I had to be a faggot, I was gonna be my own. I was still not sure what it was gonna mean to be my own person, to live for me, but it was time. Besides, the minute that pops tried to lay a hand on me, I would've kicked the crap out of his dusty black ass like he was my child. This six foot four, one hundred and ninety six pound, muscled, don't-ask, don't-tell, chocolate-drop, dreadlocked faggot-butt brotha, would've tried to make sure that pops never again called me, or nobody else a "faggot."

So, I stepped. Went out into the world carrying only a gym bag with a couple pairs of boxer briefs, a few pairs of pants, three shirts, deodorant, toothpaste and brush, an extra pair of shoes, fifty hard-earned dollars, and nowhere to go.

You know, all of my life I heard from my pops, the neighbors in the hood, from friends and even my gay uncle, who's so under and on the DL he could kiss his own ass, "that black men aren't gay. It's a white thang, a white man's disease." I always wanted to pimp slap my uncle when he would say stuff like that; scream at him for not being more of a man and standing up to my father, his older brother and rightly claiming who he was.

I would stare at myself wondering "what the hell am I, if not black and gay?" For that point, what were my frightened uncle, and all those other brothas and sistahs, that I saw nightly hanging out at the gay clubs doing? Were they performing some sort of strange, sexual masquerade? My father and all them folks were perpetrating, acting as if gay black folks were just confused, or got this way from some airborne virus transmitted to them by their white next door neighbor, or that skinny white dude that sat down next to them early one morning while riding the BART train to work.

So, I found myself and left- left his house, his presence and my childhood behind. I, I still couldn't get over it though. My pops, my own flesh and blood, the man who professed to love and care for me, called me a "faggot." Then and there he relinquished his hold on me and the spell of love cast between father and son was broken. I remember hearing my pops yelling "Go on, go on boy, go ..." as I stepped on out onto the front porch, out into the world, right into the dark and chilly night. Then the door slammed and he was gone.

****

FATHER

" ...take your funny self on outta here!"

I can feel my voice tumbling from my mouth like dusty and jagged stones down a steep hill. I can't catch my breath as I scream, and I want to stop, but the heat keeps rising, and I keep picturing him, my son, my own flesh and blood bent over some bathroom stall letting some pervert abuse him over and over again, and him moaning with pleasure. So, so, I keep screaming and ranting like some mad man.

"You ain't no son of mine, ain't, ain't nobody in my family that way." I can feel my breath as it explodes from my mouth, coming out in choppy spurts watering the air in front of my face, feel the sweat trailing my face, sliding down my front, I sense my chest rising and falling, my pulse racing and hair standing on end all over my body. I am electric and can't turn off. I watch my wife as she stands off to the left staring towards the front door and alternatively in my direction. She looks at me as if I am a stranger to her, some crazy man from the nuthouse or out of the pages of one of those true crime magazines she reads. Her eyes widen with fear or loathing, her mouth parts and trembles. In slow motion I watch as she stands in the middle of the living room floor, staring, afraid to approach or take her eyes off of me; her mouth trembling with pain and anger yet refusing to cry out. Somewhere close by I know my daughter stands passively watching. Her stance gapped and wide, eyes wide resembling mine, arms crossed soaking it all in.

"Boy, boy, you, you bettah ask the good lord for forgiveness and ask him to save your sick and damned soul 'fore it's too late." My ears listen as I shout out and call upon a god I aint talked to or even thought all that much about since I was a child. I hear myself call out "Lord, Lord," over and over again; louder and louder till my voice breaks and the tears my wife refuses exit, course down my heated face like race horses, wetting my cheeks and soaking my fingers that wipe the wet away and then continue to claw the air in front of my face.

I try to recall some old church song, any old song my mama used to sing while getting ready for church early Sunday mornings, but nothing comes to mind. So I just keep speaking the name of my savior over and over again, "Lord, Lord, Lord", and all the while my mind is filled with him, my son, that faggot. So I stare. I see the front door with the silver filigreed, ornate handle that I had been planning on replacing as soon as time permitted. I see the door, frozen in space, hard wood scratched and dinged, not sure when he opened it or if he closed it behind. Not sure if it slammed with anger or was gently eased shut with the grace of a child coming home late from a date or sneaking out in the middle of the night, shoes in hand and living on the mind. My mind won't playback the moment he left to hear if he cursed me or smiled my way before he kissed his mama on her cheek and told her he'd see her later. All my ears hear is a terrible, animal-like wailing sound, a car horn somewhere blaring, a pair of lungs forcing air roughly out and grasping for it again, and the bubbling of snot as it expands from my nostrils in bubbly breaths.

    Chimes like church bells ring in the wind somewhere and I lay here on the couch dehydrating like a fiend, foaming at the mouth, my wife, the boy's mother and guardian angel, she mumbles to herself while looking down at me on the couch. "It's cold out there tonight; I hope he has his heavy coat."

She whispers something to me in Morse Code, her breath harsh and hot on my skin. Something about love. Something about love not always being a lot, but sometimes it's all we have. Something about family. She keeps repeating something about my son, something about that faggot.

    "… he loves you fool man. He loves you."

For All We Know
R. Bryant Smith

Just before every dusk there is the day. Just before every dawn there is the dark. For every yesterday there is a today. For every today there is a tomorrow. For every illusion there is a reality. For every condemnation there is a justification. For every storm there is an unclouded day. For every mountain there is a valley. For every sadness there is happiness. For every wrong there is a right. For every hatred there is a love. For every friend there is a foe. For every hello there is a farewell... for all we know.

A tear fell from Myron's eye as he turned the pages of an old and worn photo album marked 1990-1991. Myron's tear came as he viewed the beauty of the moment on the faces of the countless people captured in laughter or unexpected poses or "beat" poses. *So many gorgeous black men! Young! Fine! Beautiful! Such a wonderful variety! Short! Tall! Stocky! Thin! Dark skinned! Light skinned! Bald headed! Heads full of hair! A creation that only God could create!* As Myron began to organize his year 2000 photo album, he noticed that so many of the faces that were present in 1990 had disappeared from the album of life. The only thing left to commemorate these lives were a final photograph and an obituary placed in a future photo album to mark the life of one of God's beautiful creations. And yet the world seemed to continue on with or without these great people and it seemed as if all had forgotten just what lives had been lead deep down in the rural South.

Myron flipped to a page that made the tears flow abundantly as he glanced at it. The photo bore the last time his crew hung out together. Tears flowed down his face like running streams as his mind flowed back to that great evening that had changed the course of his life forever...

The year was 2000 - The New Millennium.

Myron had come home to attend the funeral of a classmate who had lived in his home town of Holiday Crossing, TN which was located in the middle of nowhere and shared absolutely no modern conveniences the normal world had to offer. There was not much of anything in Holiday Crossing except the downtown area which consisted of Town Hall, The Post Office, Planters Union Bank, First Baptist Church, First United Methodist Church, and Cumberland Presbyterian Church. There were two gas stations in town and one grocery store. Everything closed at five o'clock except during the holiday season when everything closed at six o'clock. Myron hated everything about Holiday Crossing. For the century to be so close to an end, the town was still as segregated as it could be. African-Americans still lived predominantly on one side of town across the railroad tracks behind town square. Whites lived on the opposite side of town behind the bank.

African-Americans still worshipped at St. John Baptist Church, St. Paul C.M.E. Church, St. James Cumberland Presbyterian Church, or St. Mark Church of God In Christ. None of these buildings were huge cathedrals either. St. John was the largest of the four congregations and only during major funerals would the sanctuary be filled to the capacity of holding 150 people. Generally that was room only for the family and choir. But if the Methodist or Presbyterians got haughty, people would pack a funeral out at their little churches that could hold no more than 65 - 70 people. This only meant that chairs would have to be placed in the most inconspicuous places inside and outside of the church to seat the people. The Saints at St. Mark would always host a five or six hour funeral where they would literally shout their dead on into heaven or somewhere. But, this was Holiday Crossing and funerals were a major social gathering for its African-American community. Everyone had to see who would scream the loudest to prove undying love for the deceased or who was "put away" the grandest or the cheapest. New clothes had to be bought and best behaviors, out of respect to the "grieving family," had to be put on. Often Myron felt as if he did not know the deceased by the end of the funeral. Proclamations and accolades of: "He/she was so nice and kind" in reference to the deceased could get so extreme sometimes until a known sinner would instantly become a saint if the right people organized his/her funeral... in Holiday Crossing. Such was the case with Robert Wyatt.

Myron Williams, Kevin Franklin, Gussie Miller, and Robert Wyatt had all grown up in Holiday Crossing. Upon graduation, all four of them left to begin a new life elsewhere. Myron was accepted into Lane College in Jackson, Tennessee. Kevin joined the United States of America Army. Gussie moved to Memphis, Tennessee and landed the best paying job he had ever seen in his lifetime... a C.N.A. position at Molly Grove Nursing Facility. Robert enrolled into college first at Tennessee State University in Nashville, Tennessee, then Fisk University in Nashville, Tennessee, then Tugaloo College in Tugaloo, Mississippi and then he moved to Jackson, Mississippi to enroll in Jackson State University where he finally got a degree in something in which no one in his immediate group knew. And the group became family on a chilly night when they all so happened to be in The Apartment Club in Memphis, Tennessee at the same time.

"Guhl, whacha durin' in heah?" Myron heard someone yell as he turned in the direction of the loud yet strikingly familiar voice.

"I knew that had to be somebody from Holiday Crossing talking that damn flat and country and loud," Myron laughed as he hugged Gussie.

"Yeah, honey," Gussie laughed which made his body jiggle slightly. "I'm representin' tonight, hurney."

"Representing what?" Myron asked. If Gussie was anything like he was in high school, he was still a barrel of fun and a barrel of pranks.

"Representin' all de country ho's in de house," Gussie chuckled as he gulped down a huge swallow of beer.

"When you heard from Kevin?" Myron asked slyly.

"Stop fishin', bitch," Gussie chuckled. "If you wanna know somethin' jurst ask, guhl."

"Well is he gay?"

"Is you momma black, bitch?" Gussie laughed.

Myron was almost floored and yet he was not surprised. He knew that there was something different yet quite familiar about Kevin in high school that he could not quite put his hand on. Now Myron could admit that he had a crush on Kevin way back when; however, after attending Lane College that infatuation quickly ended.

Before Myron's thoughts could continue to reflect on Kevin, Robert walked past Gussie and him.

"I know dis bitch ain't gonna walk past me and not speak," Gussie gurgled and tapped Robert on the shoulder before Robert could get far out of arms distance.

"Yes," Robert said as he turned slowly around and revealed a slight smirk on his face.

"Bitch, I know you ain't gonna walk by nobody and not speak," Gussie said so loud until it seemed as if everything in the entire club stopped.

"I, I,I.." Robert stuttered.

"I hell, bitch," Gussie wailed. "You from Holiday Crossin' just like we iz and..."

"Damn, Gussie, it ain't that important," Myron whispered in an attempt to save Robert from this nominal *reading* he was about to endure from Gussie. The one thing about Gussie that Myron had always liked was the fact that he would talk much trash to people and if they got offended he would be the first to *"pass the first lick"* in a brawl and the last to pass the last lick in a brawl. He enjoyed a fight more than he enjoyed an argument. Sensible people didn't argue with him.

"Actually, I didn't see you all, Gussie," Robert said.

Gussie stepped back from Robert and took a long look at him.

"Child, what the hell is wrong with you?" Gussie said.

Myron was amazed. How could Gussie possibly know something was wrong with Robert and none of them had seen one another in at least two to three years?

"Man problems," Robert whispered as his head bowed slightly.

"Guhl, come heah," Gussie said as he grabbed Robert's arm. "You come on too, Myron! Both ya'll need to heah dis what I got to tell ya."

Gussie pushed his way through the crowd as Robert and Myron followed him. When Gussie reached the back of the club where a little lounge and television area was, he sat down on one of the old sofas with such a plop until dust gushed into the air.

"Yeah, I know I got a big ass," Gussie chuckled. "Now sit down heah. Both of ya! If ya can finda clean spot any damn where!"

Myron and Robert complied and sat on the dusty opaque colored sofa. The sofa had once been white or beige but time had worn the color completely.

Just as Gussie opened his mouth to speak Kevin walked into the little room.

"Is this a Holiday Crossing party that I wasn't invited to?" Kevin smiled as he entered.

"You'll fuck up a wet dream, tramp," Gussie grunted as he turned his head away from Kevin.

"What are you doing here?" Myron laughed as he jumped up to hug Kevin.

"Shit, the same thang you doing here," Kevin laughed as he hugged Myron. "Checking out the scenery!"

"Who give a shit about dis dilapidated shit in heah?" Gussie grumbled. "I was talkin' befoe you brought you ass in heah prancin'."

"Oh, I'm sorry," Kevin giggled. "Please continue."

"Den sit yo ass down," Gussie said as he turned and looked directly at Robert. "So what the hell is eatin' you?"

"Oh, I'm just recently out of a relationship and I just miss him so," Robert said softly.

"You in a big ass club wid a hundahd or mo men and you worried 'bout de one?" Gussie asked. "I know I didn't go to no college and perhaps dis shit is over my head but I don't understand dis."

"I love him, Gussie," Robert said as tears began to well in his eyes.

"Does he love you?" Gussie asked seriously.

"I don't know," Robert said. "All I know is that we had an apartment together in Jackson, Mississippi and the next thing I knew he just didn't come home for several nights."

"Child, he gone," Gussie said. "But I don't understand why in de hell you is pining over dis mothafucka when you got everything it takes to get who you want up in heah. Look at ya..."

Gussie was indeed true. Robert was a tall slightly muscular built man with a models look in every sense of the word. He was typically gorgeous for the day and era. He was always impeccably dressed and smelled of the scent of any new designer cologne. Myron, on the other hand, was short, somewhat stocky, and high yellow. He was well proportioned for his height. His asset was his "high ass" and thick legs. Kevin was average height. He was dark and muscular built as well. Being in the military had defined his once bony physique into a remarkable sight to behold. Gussie was cocoa brown, over weight yet had a beautiful face that accompanied a raunchy mouth. Gussie was Gussie! He did not have a problem with his weight and was quick to tell a person: *"Child, I can have yo man if I want him."* And if Gussie desired someone else's man, he would do just that... he would have the guy. He went by a strict philosophy: *"My weight ain't a problem to me why should it be a problem to you? Either you want me or you don't!"*

"But I don't feel like going through the motions," Robert complained. "I've been out for five years now..."

"What?" Myron yelled.

"Really," Kevin crooned.

"Get over it bitches," Gussie snorted. "Just because ya'll are late bloomers don't mean everybody else has been at home bakin' tea cakes and cookin' biscuits."

"Well, shit we've only been out of school for four years," Kevin said. "Hell, I've been in and out of the army so fast until my head swam."

"Ha'muhsy," Gussie grunted. "De army! Child I would have gone stone crazy up in dere. Two places I don't never wanna be is in de military or in jail. I just wouldn't be able to control myself."

"What would you do in jail, Gussie?" Myron asked a bit shocked.

"It would be my fuck fest of de century, honey," Gussie laughed. "There is some fine men in jail, guhl. You bettah ask somebody."

"I guess," Kevin laughed.

"But somethin' else is botherin' you, Robert," Gussie said as he gulped down another swallow of beer. "It is written all over yo face!"

"Ya'll can't tell nobody," Robert said as he looked around the room to make certain there was no one in ear shot of what he was about to reveal.

Gussie looked around the room with wide eyes.

"Guhl," Gussie finally said. "Who de hell know us in heah?"

"Let's make a pact," Myron said and extended his hand to the remainder of the group. "Since we are all from Holiday Crossing from now on we'll look out for each other."

"Bet," Kevin said as he placed his hand atop of Myron's followed by Robert and finally Gussie.

"O.K.," Gussie said. "Now what de hell is goin on?"

"I think he is on drugs, ya'll," Robert said as tears began to stream down his face.

"Well if he on drugs, guhl, he did yo crazy ass a favor by leavin'" Gussie said and turned away from Robert.

"How do you know this, Robert?" Myron asked attempting to block out the remark made by Gussie.

"Well," Robert began. "At first I began to miss money and shit. Soon, my VCR came up missing and then my stereo..."

"And he still had an ass left?" Gussie questioned as a look of sincere honesty appeared on his face.

"What do you mean, Gussie?" Kevin asked seriously.

"That motha fucka wouldn't be takin my shit I done worked hard for to de damned dope house and still have an ass left. Ya'll know I would have cut him from ass hole to appetite and thought nothin' about it."

"He told me that something was wrong with them and he had taken them to get them fixed," Robert said. "And after about a month I asked him about it and then he came up with a million excuses. Then he started losing weight and his skin started looking crazy and then he lost his job and..."

"Guhl, he wasn't workin and you sittin heah cryin because de some-a-bitch is gone?" Gussie roared in a loud but contagiously jolly laugh. "Guhl, was he dickin you down dat damned good?"

Everyone's eyes became as large as saucers as a silence fell over the group.

"Say no damn mo!" Gussie said as he took another gulp of beer. "I will say dis, though. Control de damn dick and don't let de dick control you!"

"You mean to tell me, Gussie, that ain't nobody ever dicked you down before to where you gave up everything to be with him as much as possible?" Kevin asked.

"Hell yeah," Gussie laughed. "But I have something dat I love bettah dan a fat ass dick."

A silence again fell over the group again. The group perched up to hear what Gussie was about to say. For Gussie to be taken advantage of by a man had to be a very interesting story that the three of them wanted to hear desperately. Gussie was known wherever he went to not take shit from anybody and to hear him say that a man had taken advantage of him was unbelievable.

"And what is that?" Myron asked.

"My damned money, guhl," Gussie said. "I like knowin dat my bills is paid and I'm takin my fat ass to de hair dresser every week and takin my fat ass out to eat at least three times a week. So, yeah, I love to get dicked down but I be damned if I let a dick control me, honey. A fuckin crack head will say every damned thang there is to say that is right in order to weaken you but fuck dat, guhl. I happen to like my fat ass bettah dan bull shit."

"Well, we see you are comfortable with your weight," Myron said sarcastically.

"Hell, yeah, guhl," Gussie said sternly. "If I don't love me, how in de fuck you thank somebody else is gonna love me? Since I learned how to love myself I can honestly say I don't have a problem findin a niggah to keep my toes curled. I told ya'll I had a niggah who took me through where I was buyin his ass every damn thang just in order to be in a relationship. But one day, I came home and de some-a-bitch had cleaned me out of every damn thang."

"Child, no," Kevin groaned. "What did you do?"

"I found dat motha fucka and when I got through workin on his ass he didn't need to go to no damn drug rehabilitation center to get rehabilitated. Every time dat some-a-bitch hit a fuckin pipe he will remember dat ass whippin Gussie put on him."

"You go, bitch!" Myron laughed.

"So, when did you realize that he was on drugs?" Kevin asked Robert.

"Strange men kept coming over to the house at all times of day and night and..." Robert said as tears began to pour down his face.

"What happened, Robert?" Myron said as he put his arm around Robert in order to attempt to console his friend.

"I lost my lease and now I'm out in the fuckin streets and I don't want to go back to Holiday Crossing," Robert said as he cried on Myron's shoulder.

"Guhl, is dat all?" Gussie said as he stood up. "Child, you can stay wid me if you wanna."

"Are you sure, Gussie?" Kevin asked, astonished of this generous gesture from Gussie.

"I said it didn't I?" Gussie said as he began to walk out of the room. "Hell, we said we was gonna help one another. It ain't murch but it's mine. Talk with me befo I leave here tonight. I see some trade I need to beat downright quick."

Gussie left and found his trade.

Robert moved in with Gussie only to discover that Gussie was living rather well in a four bedroom townhouse in Mid-town Memphis. Yes, Gussie was, by all means, a hick from the sticks but the one thing Gussie learned at a young age was how to conserve money in order to obtain the tangible things in life that he wanted. Yes, he was a C.N.A. at a nursing home but Gussie had learned how to live small before he lived large. For the first few years he lived in a one bedroom apartment with nothing more than a bed and a few items inside it. When he had saved the amount of money required to move up, he did just that. After negotiating in only a way that Gussie could, he talked the new owner of the condo down from the original asking price to a price that Gussie felt was reasonable. Gussie then moved up into the condo and slowly decorated it in the manner in which he wanted. Gussie had a good heart and always wanted to make his home a safe haven for *"the children."*

As time would have it, circumstances brought Myron and Kevin to Mid-town as well and Holiday Crossing, Tennessee now lived together in a condo in Memphis, Tennessee.

The first year living with Gussie was wonderful. Four people now occupied the townhouse. The rent was split four ways. Everyone bought furniture for his own bedroom while Gussie furnished the remainder of the condo with rather exquisite Queen Anne furniture. They all rotated cooking and everyone cooked on Saturday evening for Sunday dinner.

Deeply religious, everyone in the group still attended church every Sunday according to his own faith. Hence, Robert was always the first home from church being he was C.M.E. Kevin followed him shortly being Cumberland Presbyterian. Myron followed Kevin being Baptist and Gussie was always the last to come home on Sunday afternoon from church. Gussie was Church of God In Christ and let the entire house know as much.

"Child, ya'll should've come wit me dis moanin," he would often say. "Dat choir, dat choir, dat choir! Whew dem bitches sho sang today."

"Ours did too," Robert laughed.

"Don't nobody wanna hear dat hymn book shit," Gussie would chuckle as he entered the kitchen to begin his normal Sunday litany of putting the rolls in the oven to bake immediately before Robert, Myron, and Kevin could finish putting the dishes they had cooked or baked on the eating table.

"I go to church to hear the word," Myron teased.

"It ain't helpin you none," Gussie laughed.

"Sho' ain't," Robert laughed. "I heard you last night."

"What happened last night?" Kevin asked as he placed a pineapple upside down cake strategically on the table.

"I read my Sunday School Lesson and had prayer service with a friend," Myron laughed.

"Child, you had more than prayer service in there as loud as you were hollering," Robert laughed.

"That Guhl was just learnin the new version of *Sendin' Up My Timber*," Gussie laughed as he opened the oven door to remove the hot rolls.

"It was more like *On Jordan's Stormy Banks I Stand*," Kevin laughed as he finished placing the silverware on the table that now held smothered chicken in gravy, green beans, corn-on-the-cob, macaroni and cheese, yams in cinnamon sauce, potato salad, black eyed peas, and the pineapple upside down cake.. "Ya'll bitches were so loud in there last night until you scared my trade piece off."

Myron blushed.

"Were we really that loud?"

"I don't know I was at work," Gussie chuckled as he placed the rolls into a bread basket and then onto the eating table.

"I was all right until I started hearing the damn thud on the walls," Robert laughed. "That's when I decided to go on to the club."

"Damn, guhl," Gussie said as he looked up at Myron. "What de hell was ya'll doin?"

"Child, it sounded like they were trying to rearrange the furniture in there," Kevin laughed. "Thump... bump... thump... holler... holler.. holler... bump... thump... thump!"

"We weren't that loud!" Myron protested.

"The hell ya'll weren't," Robert insisted. "I came out into the living room to check the front door on several times thinking that somebody was knocking until finally I said this shit here is too much for me and like I said earlier, I put my glad rags on and got the hell out of here."

"I ain't saying a word," Myron grinned.

"Um hum," Gussie said. "Myron got dicked down last night and tryin to be cute about it. Did you repent on de altar this moanin', guhl?"

"Hell, no!" Myron laughed. "I plan to have some more of that tonight. Ain't no used in me lying to God about it. So wasn't no used in telling God I am sorry about it when He certainly knows that I was not."

"And wit dat," Gussie said. "Let's say grace."

They all bowed their heads and Gussie lead them into grace. Then, the meal began.

"Child did you all hear about Glover Holly getting killed last week in Holiday Crossing?" Kevin asked as the various dishes were passed from hand to hand.

"No, child," Gussie yelled as if he were in a state of shock. "When?"

"They tell me that Red Bone killed him," Kevin reported.

"Red Bone?" Myron asked knowing that Red Bone was his third

cousin twice removed just as Gussie was his second cousin once removed and Robert was his first cousin twice removed. Kevin's people had married into his family as well.

"It was over dope, child," Robert commented. "You know that shit has all but taken over Holiday Crossing now. They got to fighting at The Burning Spear over a rock and Red Bone killed him."

"Lawd, ham muhsy," Gussie wailed. "Oh, Glover was a fine ass niggah, child. Lawd, ham muhsy!"

"Child, is that all you can think about?" Myron asked. "He was one of our classmates."

"I don't give a damn," Gussie wailed. "He show was a fine as mane!"

The others thought about it for a minute and had to agree. Glover was a fine man. Tall, thick lips, rough looking, but had a smile that could penetrate the soul of the devil.

"Yes, he was, girl," Robert sighed. "Well, are you all going to the big event then?"

"Child, I wouldn't miss it for the world," Kevin laughed. "I've already bought a new black suit. Now I have somewhere to wear it."

"Where is it gonna be held?" Myron asked knowing that funerals were a big celebration in Holiday Crossing.

"At your home church, child," Robert laughed. "You know you all are the only ones who can hold a funeral as big as his is gonna be. Plus Cuttin' Clara Mae done already got on the phone calling all over the world telling us when, where, who, and what time."

"Well, I ain't buyin nothin new," Gussie said. "I got a closet full of shit dat ain't been worn yet so Glover will just have to get an old outfit. Plus it'll be too damn hot up in der for me any way. I never did like funerals at St. John. Child, I can see Miss Annie Bell already. If nobody else is a ursher at St. John, that woman sho know she is de ursher board dere."

"Leave Miss Annie Bell alone," Myron laughed. "Child, she is gonna get you seated fifteen to a pew where you can't turn or nothing. And if you holler, that box of Kleenex is in your face so fast until it almost scares you."

"Child, don't forget Cuttin' Emma," Robert laughed. "She's gonna read forty-five resolutions and fifty-five sympathy cards."

"Ooo, child," Myron laughed. "Or Uncle Bud's thirty minutes

remarks. He gets to talking and forgets who he is talking about and then remembers who he's talking about and by the time he is finished everybody else is scared to get up and say anything about the dearly departed."

"Naw, child," Gussie laughed. "The one I hate is Daddy Poppa who always got to sang all one hundred verses to "Dis May Be My Last Time" at everybody's funeral."

Everyone laughed as they thought about Daddy Poppa. A little thin man who always wore his hair slicked back and died jet black. Daddy Poppa still wore his thick eye glasses from the 1950's but was always dressed in a 1970's three piece suit. He was, by his own standards, *sharp* at this point. No one told him differently either. In order to make certain you knew that he could sing, he would always place himself on program whether it was a regular afternoon program, a revival service, a watch meet service, a sunrise service or a funeral. Daddy Poppa was always going to sing *This May Be My Last Time* and it was always going to be every verse that he knew.

On that chilly February afternoon in 1994, Gussie, Myron, Kevin, and Robert traveled back to their origin of Holiday Crossing to attend the funeral service of one of their classmates. Just as predicted, St. John Baptist Church was full to its capacity for the funeral. Fortunately, Miss Annie Bell squeezed the four of them onto the next to the last pew in the back of the church.

"Child, if I fart everybody is gonna know it," Gussie whispered.

"Child if you fart, this pew is going to break with all fifteen of us," Robert laughed. 'If you move the wrong way it is going to affect us all so be as still as you can."

The funeral was conducted in the regular manner of Holiday Crossing funerals. The choir had to sing the saddest songs which made everybody cry and scream out. Myron often wondered if the people were crying because of the deceased or because the songs were so sad and pitiful until you had to cry if you had a portion of a heart. Miss Annie Bell strolled around the church in her white uniform with her usher badge pinned neatly on her left lapel. She passed boxes of Kleenex and fans that had the face of Martin Luther King, Junior or Jesus Christ on one side and the local funeral director's insignia on the opposite side to various ushers on their post. The ushers in turn passed the tissue and fans to the crying mourners. Cousin Emma read her resolutions and sympathy cards while Uncle Bud gave his remarks. As normal, he forgot who he was talking about, remembered, and forgot again. Daddy Poppa sang *This May Be My Last Time* and Reverend Dr. B.B. Jean preached the people through with his old "Baptist" hum.

"I ain't preachin' to the dead but to ya'll who is livin'," he opened.

"Child, he can preach all day to the corpse and he won't hear him no way," Robert whispered.

"Amen, saint," Gussie giggled.

Finally, the services ended. Gussie, Myron, Robert, and Kevin went to their respective homes and decided to meet at the town tavern with everyone else before they went back home to Memphis.

The Burning Spear was a pinnacle of black society in Holiday Crossing just as the churches were. Although preachers often preached about the ills of The Burning Spear, the church members were the patrons who kept it open. Deacon Rufus Light best summed it up when he told his pastor: *"Ain't no used in tellin' dese folk not to go to de Spear, Reburn. De same amount o'money de men folk is spendin' in De Spear is de same amount o'money dey wives is spendin' at the chuch house. Now I don't see how nobody is huttin'. Let de folk have sometin' to come to de altar and repent fur on Sunday moanin'. You act like dey got a whole lot to do around heah. And jurst like you said in yo sermon last week. It rains on de jurst as well so as de unjurst. Well, preacha, it rains on de Spear jurst like it rains on de chuch house. Jurst keep preachin' and mindin' de business of de chuch and let Bang Bang mind de business of de Spear."*

And that was that!

Gussie, Robert, Myron, and Kevin all met up at The Burning Spear to pay their normal tribute to straight clubs for the year. The Burning Spear was no city club in any shape, form, or fashion but it was sufficient enough for the inhabitants of Holiday Crossing. An old brick building painted white sat in an open field that had gravel around it for parking. From afar, it looked like a cozy place to party. For Holiday Crossing's African-American community, it was this and more. Inside the building there was a bar with a Pabst Blue Ribbon mirror hanging behind it. The establishment had a beer license but no liquor license. Nevertheless, if a person wanted something a little stronger than a beer or a cooler, he/she could always go to the back room and buy a 1/2 pint of gin or whiskey for five dollars. There were two pool tables that sat in a corner for the normal group of men who played pool. On one corner of the building was a juke box that still played old Blues hits such as *The Thrill Is Gone, Misty Blue, I Forgot To Remember To Forget About You, The Night Time Is The Right Time To Be With The One You Love,* or *Tonight Is The Night.* Fats was the local DJ. The DJ booth was a small table that sat in front of a makeshift dance floor that could hold no more than thirty people at a time which normally constituted a shoulder to shoulder, foot to foot, behind to behind, jam packed dance floor. Every now and then the crowd would dance so hard until a record would scratch and he would yell out: "All right you mothafuckas, don't stomp too damn hard up in heah or you gonna have to pay for this damn record!"

Gussie, Robert, Myron, and Kevin sifted through the crowd and luckily found a table to sit at for the evening. As always, everyone packed The Burning Spear out after a funeral. Everyone would be there except the old or the devoutly religious. Gussie always enjoyed himself at The Burning Spear and before the group knew it, he had gone to talk to this person or that person or to dance with the crowd when *The Electric Slide* was played. Robert realized that he had to use the restroom and had to literally push his way to get to it. When he finally made it past the pool table and to the little room with the wooden door on it, he opened it and the normal smell of urine, beer, and marijuana hit him.

"That's all right," he said as he closed the door and walked outside.

"Whazzup, Robert?" he heard as he walked outside of the tavern.

"Nothing, much, whazzup?" Robert said as he continued to walk behind the building to find a semi-private area to relieve himself.

Just as he began to release, someone touched him on his shoulder which scared him so bad until he urinated on the man's shoe.

"Damn," the man said. "I didn't mean to scare you."

Robert laughed slightly.

"I didn't mean to pee on your shoe either, man," Robert giggled.

"So, what's really up?" the man said. "I haven't seen you in a while."

Robert looked into the man's face. Damn, he was fine as hell. He wore a black leather trench coat that was unzipped just enough to reveal the thick gold chain around his thick neck.

"I live in Memphis now," Robert said softly becoming a little nervous but turned on as well. Lawrence Packard was always considered the ladies man of Holiday Crossing. Robert had heard about how many women would fight over him just for one night in bed with him. He was all of that and a king sized bag of chips too.

"Maybe I can come down and visit you one day," Lawrence grinned a curious but wide grin that revealed his gold canines. Robert's heart almost melted just at the sight of this fine ass man in front of him.

"Maybe you can," Robert said provocatively.

Lawrence stepped forward releasing his trench coat open and revealing his huge body and huge masculinity as well. Robert took another look at this man who now revealed what he liked the most in an African-American man. Thick bow legs on a tall man!

"Can you handle it, baby?" Lawrence jeered and flashed the most gorgeous set of eyes on Robert.

"The question is," Robert whispered wickedly. "Can you handle it?"

Lawrence took Robert's hand and placed it into his crotch area to reveal his hard-on.

Robert's heart stopped again.

"Lawrence," someone yelled from the other side of the building.

Instantly, Lawrence walked away and Robert walked away.

At different times, they entered the club. The entire night, Robert felt Lawrence's eyes on his every move; hence, he sat in his seat at the table with loud mouthed Gussie, the seemingly bored to death Myron and the very talkative Kevin.

"Child, what the hell is wrong with you, Myron?" Kevin finally asked.

"I'm ready to go home," Myron said. "I'm fine with the straight club scene and all but I don't feel like myself here anymore. Plus, I miss my honey."

"What ever," Gussie laughed as he poured himself a glass of beer. "I enjoy de hell out of dese country fuckas every time I come down heah."

"That's because you are one of them," Myron said shortly.

"And you is too, bitch!" Gussie said as he glared with resentment at Myron, stood up, and mingled further with the people of Holiday Crossing.

When finally, the party began to break up and people began to leave, Gussie came back to the group and asked if they were ready to go back to Memphis. Myron jumped straight up and headed for the car without being asked a second time. Kevin quickly finished his beer and walked with Gussie toward the car. Robert walked back to the bathroom only to be followed this time by Lawrence. When Robert entered the bathroom, Lawrence forced his way in and leaned against the door whereas no else could enter.

"Can't nobody know about this," Lawrence said as he allowed Robert to fondle his manhood.

"Know about what?" Robert teased.

"Stay here tonight and I'll take you back to Memphis tomorrow," Lawrence urged.

"What's in it for me?" Robert teased.

Lawrence simply wiggled his hips.

Gussie, Myron, and Kevin traveled back to Memphis alone on that chilly February evening.

"I hope Robert knows what he's doing," Kevin said. "You know I don't do trade too quickly."

"I think he feels that he can convert Lawrence into something that Lawrence isn't," Myron interjected.

"He's a lowdown motha fucka," Gussie rattled. "Robert's playin a dangerous game fuckin' wid him."

Myron and Kevin looked at one another and then at Gussie.

"What in the hell are you talking about, Gussie?" Myron asked.

"Child, Robert can fuck off wid Lawrence provided he keep his mouf shut but if he go around talkin' Lawrence will beat de hell out of him."

"I'm so sick of these type men until I could scream," Myron said. "Gay but homophobic."

"Dem type men don't wanna be gay but can't help sleepin wid gay folk," Gussie said sternly.

"Well, we'll see," Kevin said. "All I know is that I don't want nobody from Holiday Crossing. Plus, ya'll know that I always have liked a queeny type of man that was comfortable with himself."

"Child, jurst don't brang no mo of dem hos home like dat last crazy bitch you brought home," Gussie teased.

"What's wrong with Arlington?" Kevin asked defensively.

"What's wrong with Arlington?" Myron perched. "That pretentious bitch, child, please!"

"He is not pretentious," Kevin defended. "He was just raised in a very cultured society."

"Culture my ass," Gussie roared. "Dat bitch is from Orange

Mound and got out of de hood and forgot where she came from."

"Arlington is not from Orange Mound," Kevin defended.

"De hell you preach," Gussie wailed. "I know too many people from over der and all of dem know dat crazy guhl. Why is you so damned defensive about huh anyway?"

"Well," Kevin said softly. "We are actually getting ready to get an apartment together but I really didn't know how to tell you guys."

"It's a got damn mistake but it show is yo mistake," Gussie blazed.

"I love him," Kevin whispered.

"That trophy piece, money grumbin, dressed up ho?" Gussie yelled.

"How dare you talk about my baby, you fat-assed, loud mouthed, lonely, controlling, wanna-be-grand, country-assed, bitch?" Kevin spat the words so quickly with such poisonous venom until silence fell over the car.

Tears flowed down Gussie's eyes like rushing rivers on a stormy afternoon.

No one dared say another word as they traveled the remainder of the way to Memphis. The radio played an old cut by Roberta Flack and Donnie Hathaway that made tears flow from everyone's eyes... *For All We Know!*

When they entered the condo, Gussie traveled straight into his bedroom, closed the door behind him and locked it. Kevin did not even go into the condo but jumped into his car and drove, so everyone assumed, to Arlington's apartment in Raleigh. Myron went into his room and called his new romantic endeavor.

On the following day, Kevin moved completely out without saying a word to anyone in the house. Robert did not come home. Myron and Gussie passed one another in the dining room and Myron could not go on in this manner.

"Sit down, child," Myron said.

"If dat motha fucka wanna go, let his ass," Gussie said as tears began to stream down his face. "All I ever tried to do was be a friend to him and mark my words, Arlington don't give a fuck about his silly ass."

"Well, Gussie," Myron said as he reached into the refrigerator and retrieved a bottle of wine, poured two glasses, and sat down adjacent

Gussie. "Love has no barriers and if it is true then it has to be unconditional. If you love Kevin as you say you do, respect his choice of who he wants to be with."

"I jurst don't wanna see his ass get hurt by dat crazy bitch," Gussie said as he gulped down the entire glass of wine. "Kevin is a sweet man and I'm so sick of seeing dese bitches destroy our good men until I can't help myself."

"If you love him, Gussie, you have to let him make his own mistakes and be there to pick up the pieces," Myron comforted. "That's what friendship is all about."

"Well, at least I know what he really feels about me," Gussie said as he began to pour a second glass of wine. To his amazement, Myron retrieved the wine and glass from him.

"Let's talk about you and this now," Myron said as he looked into Gussie's sad eyes.

"It ain't nothin', guhl," Gussie said in shame.

"The hell it ain't," Myron said softly. "Everywhere we go, you have to drink your share and everybody else's share. What is the real deal, honey?"

"I drink to forget," Gussie said as tears began to fill his eyes.

"Forget what?" Myron said as he looked deep into his friend's face for answers. "You can advise everybody else with some damn good advice and you are trying to forget… I don't understand."

"I'm trying to forget that I'm fat, I'm controllin', and I'm loud mouthed," Gussie cried. "These are my only weapons against bein' called fat and ugly."

"But you are still loved, Gussie," Myron said attempting to break through whatever this new issue was that had presented itself before the group. Gussie was the strength of the group and to see him falter almost destroyed Myron's belief in him.

"Yeah," Gussie laughed. "I'm loved but for what reasons? I am dating a niggah right now dat is fine as all outdoors but I don't feel beautiful around him simply because he tells me dat so damned murch."

"You need help, guhl," Myron laughed.

"I'm used to bein' in control, Myron," Gussie laughed. "It scares the hell out of me when other people are in control. Thomas is everything I ever wanted in a man and he has even asked to move in with us but I'm scared as hell."

"You don't think Ben scares me, Gussie?" Myron laughed. "All of my life I wanted a big dick man who could sex me up and treat me like a queen."

"Well," Gussie sniggled. "He obviously does dat."

"He wants more but I just want the sex right now," Myron confessed. "Until he can get in touch with himself, I cannot see us being an item but the sex has almost got me hooked."

Gussie laughed for the first time in two days. Myron always loved to hear Gussie laugh because it was always a deep throaty laugh from within that could not be identified with hypocrisy in the least. It was as genuine as Gussie was. Yes, Gussie had his faults as everyone does but he was Myron's constant reminder that a person could become whomever they wished. Within the gay community, Gussie was a well known gay rights activist. His loud mouth and country cursing provided many luxuries for many gay men in the South. Yet he was often unheralded for his works. Never was there a gay person in the area who could be turned out of their homes that Gussie would not make room for them in his own. Gussie had a sense of family and always wanted the chilren' as he called them to feel as if they had a safe haven in his home.

"Jurst be careful, child," Gussie finally managed to say. "Too murch shit is happenin' to us. Don't become a statistic."

"Child, please," Myron laughed. "Yeah, it is rough fucking but it is still protected fucking."

Again Gussie laughed his hearty laugh.

"I always knew dat if dere was one person in dis house who had sense it was you," Gussie laughed. "Dem otha guhls keep me in prayer all de damn time."

"When will I meet the new fella?" Myron asked.

"Hell, he back der sleep right now," Gussie laughed.

"You better work Mother," Myron laughed and noticed that Gussie lit up when called *Mother*.

"Child, you like being a mother, don't you?" Myron asked.

"I raised all my damned sistahs and brothas, if you recall," Gussie said. "No, I didn't get as murch education as de rest of dem but I always made sho' dey got dier's and dat's all dat matters to me."

This time it was Myron who wiped tears away.

After four days, Robert finally came home.

"Guhl, where in de hell have you been?" Gussie asked as Robert pranced into the living room.

"With Lawrence," Robert giggled like some school girl. "He is so magnificent."

"You jurst watch yo mouf around him," Gussie warned. "I mean it, Robert."

"Oh, he won't hurt a flea," Robert said as he gazed into the air. "He is such a gentleman."

"He a got damn dope dealah," Gussie grumbled as he walked into the kitchen followed by Robert.

Robert stopped dead in his tracks as he entered the kitchen.

Before him stood the tallest, darkest, most handsome, bald headed man he had ever seen in his life. To make matters worse, the man, had on nothing but a towel and flip flops as he walked about the kitchen with a glass of orange juice.

"Thomas, this is our other roommate, Robert," Gussie said looking up at Thomas with such adoration until only a fool would not realize that Gussie was truly in love with Thomas.

"Hey, whazzup, man," Thomas said as he extended his hand to Robert.

"Well, it's nice to meet you," Robert said never noticing Gussie's dreamy gaze upon Thomas.

Myron walked into the kitchen.

"Damn, boy," Myron grumbled. "Don't you ever put on any clothes?"

"I just got out of the shower, Myron, thank you," Thomas laughed.

"I won't be home for the rest of the week," Myron announced. "Ben and I are going to Hot Springs, Arkansas to spend a little time together."

"Don't come home pregnant," Thomas teased.

"Child, if I could, I sure would," Myron teased. "Just don't you get my Gussie pregnant."

Robert froze in his tracks. He felt as if someone had just dashed a glass of ice water into his face.

"I'm headed back to Holiday Crossing this weekend too," Robert announced. "Lawrence and I are going to paint the town a few new shades."

"You are watchin' yo mouth, ain't cha?" Gussie inquired.

"I haven't told nobody but Sherry Ann about Lawrence and my affair," Robert confessed.

The room stood still!

Everyone knew that Gussie was about to explode.

"Have you done lost yo motha fuckin' mind?" Gussie yelled. "I told you to keep yo damn mouf shut about Lawrence for yo own damn good!"

"Sherry Ann ain't gonna say nothin'," Robert said calmly attempting to diffuse the situation.

"That gossipin' bitch," Gussie said as he slid into a chair at the dining room table. "Lawd ham muhsy! The mo I try to teach yo dumb ass the dumber I get."

"What are you saying?" Robert asked trying to avert his eyes from Thomas who, like Lawrence, was bow legged, tall, dark, muscular, and fine as hell.

"Nothing," Thomas said which more or less ended the conversation. Myron looked at Thomas and the expression on his face as he looked at Gussie.

"I'm outta here," Myron said as he walked out of the kitchen and into his bedroom shutting the door behind him as he began to pack for his trip.

Robert went into his bedroom and began to pack for his trip.

Gussie and Thomas went into their bedroom. Gussie turned the stereo on in his bedroom and put in his Roberta Flack and Donnie Hathaway cassette tape. And on this night, as Donnie and Roberta sang in sweet rapport the sweet chords of *For All We Know*, Gussie fell deeply in love with Thomas as he sang in tune with Donnie. Thomas held out his hand and drew Gussie close to him. *This may only be a dream*, stuck in Gussie's mind as Thomas made hot, passionate love to him. For the first time in his life, Gussie felt complete. For the first time in his life Gussie felt as if he had a hero in another person. For the first time in Gussie's life, he could exhale. *This may only be a dream...* remained in his mind throughout the night and well into the wee hours of the morning as Thomas slept snugly beside him.

The Burning Spear,
Holiday Crossing, Tennessee - Winter 1994

Robert drove up onto the gravel drive of the Burning Spear and pulled beside Lawrence's fully loaded Cadillac. He stepped out of his car as a storm began to approach. Lightening began to flash and the wind began to howl. A chill ran over his body.

As he walked into the tavern, the normal crowd was there. Those old men who hung around the bar telling everything from the latest gossip to the latest lie - anything to pass the time as they drank quart after quart of beer. There was no DJ on this night but the juke box played song after song. Betty Wright was now singing "Tonight Is The Night" which only gave way to many of the patrons in the back of the club to yell and testify to the lyrics. Lawrence was playing a game of pool with a group of his cronies. Robert noticed that Lawrence did not acknowledge his presence when he walked up to the table.

"Hey, Lawrence, whazzup?" Robert asked coyly.

"I need to talk to you after this game," Lawrence said which pretty much ended what little dialogue there could have been between the two of them.

Robert noticed how Lawrence's partners looked at him in disgust which made him feel a bit uncomfortable.

Because he was beginning to feel uneasy for the first time ever in Holiday Crossing, he decided to calm his nerves by ordering a drink. He walked to the bar and ordered a *Bud* and drank it slowly until Lawrence signaled that he was ready to talk by pointing toward the door. This meant it was pretty serious and was to be discussed outside.

As Robert walked outside he noticed a strange look on Sherry Ann's face as she passed him on her way into the club.

Lawrence soon came out of the club and the rain began to pour down upon the earth.

"Get in my car," Lawrence said as he quickly stepped into his car and unlocked the door for Robert.

Robert stepped into the car as Lawrence cranked it and blasted the music.

"We need to go for a ride," Lawrence said as he sped out of the parking lot and through the town of Holiday Crossing.

Robert remained quiet.

Finally, after driving for what seemed an eternity, Lawrence pulled into an old and unfamiliar grove that was far off of the main highway. He turned the music down and then faced Robert.

"What's wrong?" Robert asked.

"I told you when we first met to keep it on the down low, didn't I?" Lawrence said monotonously without in as much as a flinch of his facial muscles.

"I haven't told nobody about us, Lawrence..." Robert began.

"Then why did Sherry Ann ask me about you as well as all of her sisters and cousins and half of Holiday Crossing?"

Robert was speechless.

"You'll never fuck me over like this again," Lawrence said as he swung at Robert.

Robert could not move as he watched in disbelief as the first of many blows came at him from out of nowhere.

When he finally caught his breath, he reached for the door, and attempted to get out of the car. He noticed a shiny object in Lawrence's hand and did not want to become a new statistic. He could not get the door open as he felt a stinging sensation on his side. Too afraid to look down or up or anywhere except the door handle which would afford him an escape, he pulled with all of his might on the door handle until something in his mind triggered: "Unlock the car door!"

In two seconds he was out of the car and running with Lawrence fast on his heels. He did not know where in the hell he was running but the only thing he knew was that he did not want to die in the middle of nowhere.

Lawrence over powered him chasing him like a lion seeking its prey. Upon catching Robert, Lawrence began to stab him and then beat him until he lost consciousness.

Union Townhouses, Memphis, Tennessee

The doorbell rang continuously as if a maniac was at the other end of it.

Gussie, Myron, and Thomas scrambled in their night gear, attempted to get out of their beds, out of their bedrooms, down the hall, through the living room, and to the front door in order to see who in the hell could be ringing the doorbell at five o'clock in the morning as if no one had to go to work on a Tuesday.

"What in de hell do you want at dis time of moanin'?" Gussie yelled as he flung the door open wide.

"Robert is in the hospital at Methodist Central," Kevin said.

"What in de hell is you talkin' about?" Gussie questioned as he pulled Kevin into the room.

"He is in the hospital," Kevin said.

"Was he in a car wreck?" Myron said as he pulled his house coat closer together for comfort and security.

"Somebody found him on Dead Man's Curve about ten miles outside of Holiday Crossing last night and I just got the news," Kevin said.

"What in de hell was he doin' out dere?" Gussie asked.

"Somebody had beat him unmercifully and left him for dead," Kevin said. "My mother said he ain't recognizable."

Silence fell on the group.

"I told him 'bout dat motha fucka," Gussie finally managed to scream. "Got damn it!"

Myron stood in disbelief at what he was hearing.

"Nobody wants to listen to me," Gussie raged. "I don't know shit about folk."

"What the hell are you talking about, Gussie?" Kevin asked as he walked into the living room and sat down.

Thomas turned a light on and the remainder of the group sat down as well.

"He got his ass kicked by dat trade boy like I told him he would if he went around Holiday Crossing runnin his damn mouf," Gussie said. "I told him dat just because trade wanna fuck don't mean dey wanna even think 'bout no relationship especially wid no man."

"I can't even imagine it," Myron said. "You mean to say that you think Lawrence beat Robert up? I thought they were an item?"

"What's this about Robert and Lawrence?" Kevin asked.

"Robert has been seeing Lawrence from Holiday Crossing," Thomas commented.

"Drug dealer Lawrence?" Kevin asked.

"Dat's da motha fucka," Gussie grumbled. "I told Robert to watch out for dat no count bastard."

"Hell, if he was fuckin Lawrence he is lucky to be alive," Kevin said. "You all know Lawrence was crazy as hell in school! What makes Robert think he is any different now?"

"He tryin to reform some got damn body and just because trade fucks you don't mean dey wanna be a reformed punk," Gussie yelled at the top of his voice. "I'm so damn sick of dis shit until I could scream!"

"So sick of what, Gussie?" Thomas asked genuinely.

"Some-a-bitches fuckin off wit gay men by night and by day dey claim dey fuckin straight," Gussie roared. "Den when de shit comes out dey wanna go and fuck up de person dey thank told de shit when if dey didn't want nobody to find out dey never should've been fuckin' no man in de first damn place."

"Well, it is a person's right to his own privacy," Kevin said calmly.

"You have lost yo damned mind, too," Gussie roared.

"I beg to differ, Gussie," Myron said. "You warned Robert about Lawrence and what danger he might be in but he was the one who went and told Sherry Ann his business when who he was fucking was nobody's business except his own."

"Child, he did not tell Sherry Ann he was fucking around with Lawrence, I know," Kevin asked.

"Yes he did," Gussie grumbled.

"Hell, he might as well have published the shit in the damn *Commercial Appeal*, then," Kevin snickered. "That bitch can't hold water."

"It still does not give Lawrence the right to do what he did to Robert," Thomas said.

"In Holiday Crossing it does," Kevin said. "They could fuck for years if nobody knew about it but if the shit gets across town then there is chaos in Holiday Crossing."

"Child, Ma Bell will be ranging off de hook before noon today," Gussie grumbled. "By one o'clock de whole damn town'll know what happened."

"Shit, I go out of town for a weekend and all hell breaks loose," Myron attempted to jest.

Methodist Central Hospital, Memphis, TN

Gussie, Thomas, Myron, and Kevin walked into the room where Robert was. Tears welled in Myron's eyes as he looked at the condition his friend was in. Bandages were wrapped around his entire body. His arm was in a cast. Both of his eyes were blackened. His lips were swollen as if he had been stung by a thousand hornets. The once beautiful man was no longer beautiful as he lay in the hospital bed.

"Hey, honey, how yo durin'?" Gussie asked as he leaned over the bed to speak directly to Robert whose eyes began to fill with tears.

"We brought you something, guhl," Myron teased as he placed a large teddy bear in the bed with Robert.

Robert looked directly at Gussie.

"You told me," Roberts whispered. "It took five cracked ribs and a fractured bone in my arm plus fifteen stab wounds for me to listen."

"No, child," Gussie chuckled. "He didn't do enough. He should've hit yo ass in the head to wake you up."

"Gussie!" Myron chastised.

"Naw, fuck dat," Gussie grumbled. "I ain't gonna baby him. Dis here is bullshit and he never had to even go down dis road."

"Well," Kevin said tartly. "Such as it is, he is down this road and he is feeling bad enough without your help, Gussie."

"How is Arlington?" Gussie asked tartly.

"I wouldn't know," Kevin said softly.

"And why not? Don't tell me Ms. Beautiful is on safari or something?" Myron teased.

"Shit! Arlington left me for somebody with more money and more culture," Kevin laughed. "And if you say a word Gussie I'm kicking your ass today."

"I ain't sayin' shit except when is you movin' yo ugly ass back in?" Gussie laughed which made Robert laugh and then cry out in pain.

"He moved his shit in last night," Thomas chuckled. "Didn't you hear him?"

"Hell, naw," Gussie laughed. "Dat really got by me. I murst be slippin'."

"You *murst* be," Kevin laughed as he hugged Gussie.

Rehabilitation

Gussie, Myron, Kevin, and Thomas took turns nursing Robert back to good health. This was a painful process for Robert because he hated listening to Gussie complain and cuss every day over the same thing. *"Watch trade, guhl... dey ain't no damn good, guhl... leave 'em alone, guhl..."* Robert almost went crazy just listening to him daily. Sadly enough, Robert was relieved when Gussie's schedule changed at the nursing home and rather than working first shift, Gussie was moved to third shift, which meant that he was too tired to fool with Robert upon arriving home from work. When Gussie did wake up, Robert made certain that he was asleep.

Thomas became instrumental in helping to nurse Robert back to good health and spirits in so many ways.

"What in de hell is going on in my motha fuckin' house?" Gussie screamed as he opened Robert's bedroom door one evening. Gussie was supposed to work but realized after he got to work that it was his day off so he came back home.

Robert and Thomas jumped out of the bed and scrambled to put on clothes.

Myron and Kevin ran into the room because they had been startled out of their sleep by the ugliness in Gussie's voice.

"Wait a minute, Gussie, we can explain," Thomas said as he tripped as his underwear hung on his foot rather than sliding up his leg. He regained his footing but managed to get his underwear only around his ankles when Myron and Kevin entered the room.

"Oh, my God," Kevin said as he looked in disbelief at the sight before him. Thomas was completely nude and sported a hefty ten inches on soft, not to mention a fine tight body, a nice round bubble butt, and bow legs to ice the cake.

"I can't take no mo of dis shit," Gussie said as he reached for Thomas who began to run around the room like a retreating Zulu warrior. As Gussie swung at him and then at Robert, Thomas managed to pull his underwear up and stand beside a hemmed up Robert beside a nearby dresser.

"Child, I can't either," Myron said. "I'm outta here for good. I'll be gone by morning!"

Gussie stopped in mid track.

"What?"

"I am leaving," Myron said. "I can't take the chaos anymore. I'm moving into my own place by myself."

"Well," Kevin began. "To be honest, it's been real but Arlington and I are getting back together so I'm leaving too."

"Thomas and I are moving out too," Robert confessed.

"Actually, Robert," Thomas said. "When I leave here in the morning, I'm leaving by myself just like I came."

Gussie looked around the room in disbelief at what was actually occurring.

"So dat's how yo bitches is gonna do me?" Gussie said as tears welled up into his eyes. "When I needs you, you leave?"

No one said a word.

Slowly everyone left the room except Gussie who just stared out of the window.

We Come And We Go

Six years had passed since the group had lived together. Gussie never spoke to anyone who had lived in the Condo again. Thomas left and was never heard from again. Kevin and Arlington bought a two story home in Bartlett, Tennessee. Myron dated Ben on and off for all of the six years until Ben finally begged him for a committed relationship.

"What's your definition of a committed relationship?" Myron asked him.

"I don't know," Ben laughed. "I guess something like what your friend Kevin and Arlington have."

Myron never spoke to Ben again.

Robert moved back to Jackson, Mississippi.

He was murdered in February of the year 2000.

Gussie, Myron, and Kevin all attended Robert's funeral in Holiday Crossing, Tennessee. They sat on totally opposite sides of the packed out St. John Baptist Church. After the funeral, they spoke to everyone accept one another.

To their amazement, they had all parked beside one another in the small parking lot of the church. They all glanced at one another. Myron's lips parted slightly. His heart screamed to say something yet the words did not come. The tears that watered Kevin's eyes would not fall as he looked at the group. Gussie squared his shoulders, gazed at Kevin and Myron and opened his car door.

Upon getting into his car, Gussie heard someone singing:

I'll hold out my hand...

Gussie noticed a tall man dressed in black walking toward his car.

But my heart will be in it...

Tears began to stream down Gussie's face as he closed the car door.

For all we know...

Myron recognized the familiar spirit of the man. He was tall, handsome, bow legged. This man, in whom Myron attempted to recognized, sported dread locks. He perplexed Myron by all accounts because Myron knew he knew the man but could not figure out who the man was.

This may only be a dream... the man sang.

Gussie cried as he looked up to see the only man who had ever sung this song to him. It was the only man that Gussie had ever fallen in love. It was once upon a time when he was fifty pounds heavier and he did not have a social title within several social organizations behind his name. When he had loved himself more because he thought he knew himself only to discover that he really did not know himself at all.

So love me, love me tonight ...

Kevin grabbed Arlington's shoulder softly. For the first time ever, tears streamed down Arlington's face. He knew who the man was. This man was the missing piece of the puzzle that Kevin never spoke of but cried out in his sleep at night over. He loved his old friends from Holiday Crossing but did not know how to bring them back together after so many years.

Tomorrow may never come... he sang so beautifully.

Gussie looked at the man and then at the group as tears flowed from his face.

He watched as the man inched within ear shot of his barely opened car window.

The group seemed to hold their breath as they watched Thomas attempt to reach Gussie on his own behalf and on theirs.

"For all we know," Gussie managed to mutter as he cranked his car up and pulled off into the sunset.

Another Direction
Richard Peacock

Everybody needs a friend. Damian too.

For Damian, it was Carlos.

He and Carlos had become friends through employment. At a call center in the 941. Bradenton, to be exact. They first met at work. Before Damian quit. The customers calling, the constant demands they made: invariably, every one of them wanted their Internet service back on now, immediately, this minute, right away! The nerve-racking customers were too much for Damian.

"I can't believe you're still there," Damian said as he slid his thumb against the neck of the beer bottle in his hand.

Carlos, hilariously giggling and marijuana-drunk, brought his head back to rest on the back section of the sofa where he was sitting. It wasn't that Damian's bitterly expressed memory of the call center was all that funny or amusing—no: Carlos would have laughed at anything Damian had said—could've been anything. His giggling caused Damian to do same in the chair in which Damian sat. A mint-green sofa and chair, both the same color. Carlos and Damian, the two of them in the darkened living area of Carlos's apartment. A dimly lit floor lamp and the blades of a ceiling fan circling above them. Carlos raised his head from its resting place before he spoke: "So, you passed me over for him? Alexander, the Jamaican truck driver. You got something against Puerto Rican boys?"

Leave it to Carlos to bring it up: Damian never did want to have a romantic relationship with him. As usual, it was fronted as some kind of joke, some suggestion from Carlos that he wasn't to be taken too seriously. Damian couldn't always tell just how strong Carlos's feelings were for him, no. He knew enough to know that whenever Carlos brought it up, those feelings were real in some way. Damian never flat-out told Carlos that he didn't like him like that. Just wouldn't tell him. Damian's strategy was to keep quiet. You know, he'd become reserved when Carlos started talking about it; sometimes, he'd put on his own front, put on a closed-lip smile—like he was doing now.

Carlos was the first real friend he made after he moved to the 941 from Bartow, which is in the 863. Carlos had come to the 941 a few months earlier, from Orlando, the 407 area. Truth be told, Carlos was his only friend, really. It was hard making friends. A hard time for Damian. Who do you trust? Who can you trust? Who? Damian decided to trust Carlos. Not his own family. Talk to Pastor Jackson, they said. God doesn't want you to be gay, Damian; that's what *you* say you are.

Alexander, the Jamaican Carlos had brought up, he had become Damian's regular lover after that night in the laundromat when the two met, when they exchanged cell numbers. Outside of that, he didn't know what to make of it. After months, for several months now, he knew that he more than liked Alexander. More than liked him, Damian thought as he continued to massage the neck of his beer bottle with his thumb.

"He still works there?" Carlos asked, somewhat sobered.

"No, he quit doing that laundromat work a long time ago," Damian said. "He was just doing it for a little extra money."

"So, that's how the fishing trips started?" said Carlos. "He asked you for your number; you gave it. And right, you didn't know it was leading to something else? When you call his house, his wife answers the phone and she thinks, 'That's the fishing buddy.'" Carlos laughed louder than he had before, his tongue and his teeth out; his face, a chubby boy's face with chubby-boy cheeks.

Damian wasn't sure if he should continue to laugh along with him.

***

Damian, Little Alex, and him. The three of them were at the pier that day.

Little Alex swung his arms and fists wildly while his father's outstretched arm and hand held the five-year-old in place, at the boy's head. Son and father at play while the three waited for fish to bite. Three fishing rods, two for adults, Damian and Alexander; and one fishing pole for a kid, that one for Little Alex. All three poles rested against the pier's wooden railing. "Stop windmilling," the father said to his son. "You swing like a girl. You're leaving yourself open to get punched." Alexander and Damian sat on upended buckets the two of them brought. Little Alex's arms were tiring, his arms slowing down like wide swim strokes, each arm dragging to make it around. Alexander grabbed his son, pulled him in by his small arms, the son flying into his daddy's chest, where father and son hugged each other in laughter. A very warm breeze. A very warm sun. Sun rays that sparkled on the calm water below. A cap on Alexander's head. Smiling, Damian remembered the last time he and Alexander embraced each other. At Damian's place, in Damian's bedroom: he and Alexander hugged and kissed in a room faintly illuminated by a movie on a television that went unwatched. Alexander had on the same cap, too.

A pelican landed on the pier walkway and sauntered past, waddling on its webbed feet. Little Alex, enraptured, chased the bird in spite of his father's objections: "Alex, boy, leave it alone. Did you hear me?" And there was Damian: "Alex, come back." Little Alex didn't go far. First daddy, then Damian. Voices of authority. Little Alex turned around and came back. His father thumped him on his forehead. "Oww!" the boy said, wincing too late. The father put Little Alex in a soft headlock that caused the boy's shirt to rise, caused the boy's belly button to be exposed; that caused him to laugh even more as he wrestled with his daddy. And there was a gull that distracted Damian momentarily. Damian's eyes came back to his lover and Little Alex. "Let's take a break," the father said and released his son, who spun himself around, into Damian, at whom he smiled when he stopped in place. Smiling Little Alex, with his two missing front teeth. "My mummy's pregnant," Little Alex said and Damian said, "She is?" The little boy nodded his head happily. Damian looked at Alexander for confirmation, for the truth.

"What did I tell you, Alex?" the father said and pushed his son in the head with his pointer finger. The boy's head tilted, snapped sideways when struck. "You don't go around telling everybody that."

"But I told Mr. Damian," Little Alex said. His eyes welled. The boy was bewildered.

"Don't—cry out here and see what I do to you, boy," Alexander said to his son with a hiss and a brow of his furrowing.

Damian pulled Little Alex toward him and wrapped his arm around the boy's body while Little Alex cried silently, his head away from his father, burrowed into Damian's shirt. "Alex," Damian said, "it's okay. Don't worry, Alex. I'm not gonna tell nobody." From his pocket, out of his wallet, Damian pulled out a couple of dollars. "What about a snow cone?" Did Little Alex want a snow cone? The boy nodded faintly. Little Alex looked at his father, such fear. "It's okay," Damian said. He patted Little Alex on his head. "Your daddy doesn't mind. Go to the man at that booth and get us a couple of snow cones. Alex, you want one . . ."

"No," the father said. "He might've used a corn sweetener and I'm allergic to it."

Two snow cones were ordered then. The boy trotted away happily, uplifted by Damian and his father's approval.

Damian said, "When were you gonna tell me?"

Alexander got up from his bucket and walked toward his fishing pole. He unlocked the release, began winding in the line, his hand circling repeatedly. "Is that how you're going to teach your son when you have one?" Alexander said. "Give him a snow cone when he cries?"

"How many months along is Michelle? . . . You weren't gonna tell me, were you?"

Alexander turned the handle faster. "Don't do that again. Alex is my son."

"Fuck you!" Damian said, low, heavy, watchful—wary of making the other people at the pier onlookers. It didn't help that Damian's naturally slanted eyes already made him look vigilant. Damian stood up, he turned his bucket right side up, he stomped toward his own fishing pole, and he started winding in the line once his fishing pole was in his hand. He was less than a foot apart from Alexander. He and Alexander were about the same height. He and Alexander, both men were what you would call thin.

"I thought you would be able to figure it out," Alexander said. All of his line had been brought back in, its hook in view. The bait, a soggy, untouched shrimp was still there. Alexander spoke only loud enough for the two of them to hear. Calm and even. "We came to the pier in separate cars today. We usually come to the pier in one car, yours or mine, and we go back to your apartment. I brought Alex with me. I didn't want to make you mad—I never knew you would get mad like this."

Damian disassembled his pole in angry silence.

"You going to see your dope head friend now?" Alexander said, still just loud enough for Damian to hear. More of a statement than a question.

As much as Damian wanted to ignore Alexander's comment about Carlos—as much as he wanted to block it out—he couldn't. Yet, he continued to disassemble his pole without speaking. When he finished, he grabbed his bucket by its handle, pole also in hand, and stomped off toward his car, passing Little Alex, who was returning, a snow cone in each hand; Little Alex, who said uneasily, "You leaving us?" Little Alex, whose smile began dissolving.

**

Carlos was stirring chili, pot lid in his hands, pepper-scented steam going up in his face. "There's too much dick out there in the world to worry about him. Forget that bitch," he said and put the lid back on the pot and looked over to Damian. Not to just to see if Damian was listening, but also to see if Damian was still in that dream space, thinking about Alexander. Him.

Damian heard Carlos from where he sat at the dining room table, heard him while he was in that dream space and he woke out of it, the pepper scent now in his nose. "I could never buy him food," Damian said. "He was allergic to, to . . . to everything, almost. Couldn't eat chili or spaghetti because he was allergic to tomatoes. Got crazy if a bug was flying around, panicked. He said a bee sting could kill him."

"Maybe he was allergic to you?" said Carlos.

It wasn't funny to Damian. He glared at Carlos—he was supposed to be his friend, was supposed to understand. Staring at Carlos, Damian blinked once, his long eyelashes folding in and opening out like the wings of a perching insect.

"Just kidding." Carlos said. And then, satisfied that the chili was doing what it needed to do on the stove, Carlos walked over to Damian. He sat next to him. "You ain't never had a boyfriend before him?"

"No," Damian said.

Carlos raised his two, finger-splayed hands up toward his chest and stopped them before they got there. He had to think a minute, for a moment, before he spoke. He thought about it, and Carlos brought his finger-splayed hands down to the kitchen table, both hands descending slowly, graceful like bird feet landing. Carlos said, "I'm just gonna tell you this. You ain't stupid. You knew that bitch was married. It ain't like he never told you. To me, he got it a lot worse than you."

Damian stared at Carlos. He turned his head toward the side. As if he were waiting for or expecting someone else to chime in.

"After we eat this chili, I got this shit I bought from this Mexican; we can smoke it if you want?" Carlos said, the early stage of a smile on his face.

Damian said no.

The two of them ate the chili while at the table. Chili poured over rice. Orange juice for Carlos and water for Damian. As was their habit, they began to talk about their time together, when they both worked at the call center. Damian wondered why Carlos refused to ask for a promotion, to be a supervisor for one of the call center teams. The other people who were team supervisors were getting paid more, yet Carlos had more experience, had been on the job longer than they had. Carlos didn't want to be a supervisor to anyone—"Those other bitches can have that." It was enough to manage his own life, he said, let alone having to worry about somebody else's.

"And why do you care?" Carlos said. "It's not like you still work there." Carlos changed the subject. "You still working at that hotel?" he asked.

Damian said yes.

How Damian could do it, Carlos couldn't see. All those long hours every day. No benefits, not even what Carlos thought of as being the super-crappy-might-as-well-be-worthless benefits from the call center. A call center would definitely pay more. Carlos said, "You working six days a week and they're taking out FICA taxes, too."

"They don't take out taxes," said Damian, spurring a surprise on Carlos's face. "They pay us in cash, the two of us who work on the grounds and maintenance crew, me and Pierre. They think I'm Haitian like him. Pierre knows but he don't say nothing, and I ain't said nothing. Pierre's looking for a new job."

"Seems like Pierre's a smart man," Carlos said. "You should be following him."

Damian had no intention of making the hotel job permanent. "It's just me. It's not like I got a wife and kids to go home to."

One of Carlos's eyebrows raised itself.

As Damian was about to leave, as he was about to walk through the door, he and Carlos hugged, embraced each other as if their hugs in the past had never meant as much.

"Don't worry so much," Carlos said. He pinched Damian near the zipper on Damian's pants, where he thought Damian's dick lay underneath. "You've never invited me for dinner at your place . . . How many times have you invited me to visit? Three times. Just three." Carlos targeted his eyes at Damian's. A sheepish look came on Damian's face. Then, from Carlos, something in jest, maybe: "You know, none of this would've ever happened if me and you would've just hooked up like I wanted—but, no, you wanted a Jamaican boy. Looks like me and you are both single now, brothaman" Carlos offered the drugs again. "You sure you don't want to party?"

Damian said no.

The two hugged once more and gave each other a good-bye peck.

***

There was some occasional sex after Alexander. Guys Damian met at a club or bar. The one-nighters when Damian went out on the weekend. Sometimes in Sarasota. Sometimes as far away as St. Petersburg (727) and Tampa (813). If he were single for the rest of his life, that would be fine, Damian thought while he sat clipping his toenails on the sofa in his apartment. Carlos was right. *Forget that bitch!* Why worry or wonder? Damian cut one of his toenails too far down, distracted, thinking about *him*. Good thing he didn't cut any skin! When the last toenail was clipped, he went to the bathroom.

Standing naked in front of the bathroom mirror, looking, looking, Damian became increasingly aware of his imperfections. A chiseled set of abs, the six-pack he had once naturally had, was faint, almost not there; at least he wanted to believe it was faint, a little perceptible, maybe. If he didn't watch it—if he didn't take care—he would end up like Carlos. Like Carlos and all those other fat people. Damian thought his dick was sort of big. Not as big as what other guys had. But Bigger than Carlos's—for sure. "My eyes are too small," he thought aloud as he studied his mirrored reflection. Damian folded in his eyelids, blurred his vision to see less of himself; instead, he saw others in the distortion he made. A flurry of faces: his family, the mother and brother he very rarely talked to since he moved away from Bartow. Faces and bodies: sex partners of the recent and distant past, the memorable ones, each one in a pose that was erotic. Damian's dick stiffened, went up, up, up, up. He stopped squinting his eyelids, and when he did, he saw himself again.

***

Carlos complained while he fiddled with the radio knobs and buttons inside the car he and Damian rented. Too many country music radio stations! Too many when he touched scan; too many when he pushed seek. Carlos, irritated, sat up in his seat on the passenger side. "I knew I should've brought my cds with me," he grumbled.

"That gay shit," said Damian.

"Oh," Carlos said, "I forgot you don't like it." Sarcastic. Carlos then turned to look at the endless stretch of orange trees outside his window. The sun, all around, its brightness could be seen; its intense heat couldn't be felt because the car was air conditioned well inside. Carlos began tapping on the window. "I should've drove," he said. "We would've been there by now."

Carlos's teeth: they were yellower now, it seemed, and more sooty gray in spots. Maybe black even, some of them. I hadn't noticed them before—or had I? Damian thought as he looked over at Carlos. Carlos had lost weight, too; yet he still had those chubby-boy cheeks.

Throughout the trip, from time to time, the two of them argued about the best route to take to Fort Lauderdale. Carlos wanted to take I-4 and then the turnpike. That's what he did when he lived in Orlando. Orlando, I-4, and then the turnpike. Damian felt the back roads would be best to take—State Road 70 to Highway 27, ride through the counties below Polk County. "I'm from Polk County. I know the area," Damian said when they were loading their duffle bags into the car. And, he added, to save money, to avoid a toll, they could go through Highlands County. 70, 27 and then through Highlands: no toll at all.

"Let's just take the turnpike, you cheap bastard!" a snarling Carlos said now that the two of them were on their way. "No more of this country backwoods shit. I want to see people. I'm driving on the way back, bitch!"

"Your period on?" Damian almost regretted saying it. But still, Carlos was getting on his nerves. He didn't want to get in an argument. When Carlos got mad—and he was hard to calm down—he'd get loud. To argue back with him when he got like that was to run into a wind that was blowing against you no matter which way you turned (and, if he was high or drunk, it was worse).

They were traveling to Fort Lauderdale (the 954) to get away for the weekend. Spur of the moment thing. Carlos's idea. The two hadn't been together or seen each other for at least a month. ("Bitch, why you ain't called me?" Carlos said once in a cell phone message about how he and Damian had gotten out of touch. "Trying get rid of me like you got rid of him? Is that what you trying to do? Or what, the boy from little ol'Bartow found another friend, finally?") Carlos was going to take Damian to some wild place. A place he wouldn't believe. "Ain't nothing like this place in the 813 or 727, where you've been before, the gay clubs there," Carlos once said. "When you get there, you'll see. You even might go in another direction. The boys down there, you'll see, they'll make you forget that you even knew or met that bitch Alexander."

"Ain't nobody said nothing about no Alexander," Damian retorted.

"Bitch, don't." Carlos said. "Don't. I can see right through them eyes and them long eyelashes you got. I've been knowing you too long. That's why you ain't been by to see me like you used to. You ain't over him."

Several times before, Carlos had been to places like the one in Fort Lauderdale that he and Damian were going to—"It's a 'men's club'" Carlos nervously giggled during an explanation. Sometimes, Carlos would go with a travel buddy, some smoking buddy (like Enrique or Marcus), a guy unlike Damian who'd be willing to "party" with Carlos when Damian would not; most times, he'd go alone. "To save money, I used to go straight from the club and drive more than three hours to get back home," he said to Damian. "I stopped doing that shit after, when I was by myself, I woke up while driving and saw I was headed straight for the little building on the turnpike where they take your toll money. After that, I was like, fuck that, I'm staying my ass in a hotel."

They got to Fort Lauderdale just before nightfall. Carlos directed Damian through the streets of the city. After they went through a stop light, he directed Damian to turn into a parking lot of an adult store.

"Carlos!" Damian yelled. "I know me and you ain't been on the road for more than three hours to come to no bookstore. Tell me this ain't happening, Carlos."

"Calm down, bitch, and park the car," Carlos said. Damian did. Carlos went inside the store and came back shortly with a plastic black bag whose contents Damian couldn't make out, the items being so small and it being night now. Plus, the light in the parking lot was so dim.

"What did you buy?" Damian said.

Carlos pulled out two small bottles and Damian thought it might've been pills. "No," Carlos said. "Poppers. For later."

Damian didn't want any. Wouldn't use it. Poppers, the chemical smell, would give him a headache.

Later, at the place—The Pile Driver, it was called—he and Carlos paid twenty dollars each to get in. That's what it cost for a one-time membership, the man behind the window said after he checked Carlos and Damian's photo I.D.

White guys. Blacks. Latinos. The old and the young. Damian asked, "How did you find out about this place?" And Carlos said, "Internet."

The Pile Driver was dark inside, lit enough to make out a body a few feet away. There were private rooms inside. Private rooms that could get darker if the occupants of the rooms wanted it that way. Each room had a switch inside it that could adjust the brightness or darkness—could make a room totally dark if that was what somebody wanted. And there was throbbing music. Electronica. Loud and throbbing.

Carlos and Damian circled, walked to and from the same spots again and again. There were eyes that eagerly looked to get attention. There were eyes that got attention and then looked away when the attention didn't suit the person on whom the attention was brought. Two men walked away from a corner, one following the other into a private room where a door shut behind them.

"You should take off your shirt," Carlos said as he and Damian walked by the back wall again. "You have a nice body." Carlos and Damian, the two of them again looking at the men around them, the men who watched Carlos and Damian pass.

Damian hadn't spoken much since they arrived, his eyes staying constantly in motion. To him, a new place. Exciting and worrisome, both. Wherever Carlos went, Damian followed. The Pile Driver didn't appear to be large on the outside, but its inside seemed spacious: so, so many rooms; so many corridors. Even in spots where Carlos and Damian would return to again in the walking trips they made, those places, those spots seemed different each time, something else Damian didn't see before, like another room and its opened door.

There were many shirtless men. Some almost shirtless, the buttons on their shirts all undone. Some in underwear. Some, no clothes at all. And these men, some of them bounced and danced in place where they stood.

Carlos stopped and so did Damian. Near a corner that led to a back way. The two of them stood against the wall with other men. "That guy over there," Carlos said, "he's been checking you out."

True: the man, a beautiful silhouette in the distance, had been. Was.

"Go over to him," Carlos said. "You know you want to."

Damian and the silhouette man finished. In the room they darkened, locked and made private for themselves, they had been considerate of each other, each doing something to ensure that the other would come: caressing, kissing, licking, sucking; but each of them agreed there would be no ass fucking. Damian came first and then the silhouette man. No disappointment for either. And the electronica, the music even could be heard in their closed-door room.

Damian pulled up his pants and turned the knob to adjust the dim lighting, making the room brighter. The man was dark-brown and bald and clearly uncircumcised. Bushy eyebrows—the man he had just had sex with was beautiful in every way, Damian thought. The silhouette man pulled up his pants. The tattoo on his right shoulder? Damian asked.

"Oh," the man stopped tying his sneaker. "That's my son Cory." His daughter's young face was tattooed on his other shoulder like her brother's, the man showed. "I want my children to always be with me."

"Are you married?" Damian asked.

The man gave a swift no and pushed his arms through his T-shirt. He had been divorced for about eight years now. "You think I'd be doing this if I were married?" This was his first visit, he said.

"Mine too," added Damian.

The man patted Damian on the butt as he unlocked the door. "I got to go. Take care."

With his shirt in his hand, Damian went to search for Carlos. He was ready to go, too. In one sweeping flashback, he could remember everything he did with Alexander; he remembered everything Alexander ever said.

You going to see your dope head friend now?

When Damian got around the corner, a group of five to six guys were hovering and crowding at a peep hole. Each one maneuvering. Some bumping into one another. Each man moving to get his chance to look through the hole in the door. "Man, he's giving it to him," one of them said. Damian made his way over, his own curiosity piqued. A man in the front felt Damian hovering next to him. "You want a look?" the man in front said and moved aside so Damian could see. Damian saw: Carlos—bent over, getting fucked. There was a wafting smell, too: it was the poppers.

He couldn't argue with Carlos. Carlos was too out of it to know what Damian was saying. What he had said. Carlos smelled like burnt cloth. He sat in the chair in their hotel room while he wiped at his face and eyes with both of his hands, on and off, in a paranoid manner. Damian had never seen Carlos like this. It was more than the poppers—and it couldn't be marijuana!—that much Damian knew. He sat on the hotel bed watching Carlos. Afraid Carlos would hurt himself. The digital clock by the lamp said 5:47 a.m. Checkout was at eleven. There was no way Damian was going to sleep.

***

I'm driving on the way back, bitch! There were two four packs of Red Bull next to Damian. Carlos stared intensely in the passenger seat, ahead. He had stopped wiping at his face a few hours ago, but the drugs were still affecting him although less than before. Damian wished the turnpike had been built in the part of Highlands County the two of them were now driving through: that way, he wouldn't worry as much about the bubba cops who would certainly stop him for the speeding he was doing; that way, he could drive faster—the speed limit on the turnpike was much faster.

Carlos rotated his head slowly in Damian's direction. "What's up, boo?" Carlos said. Carlos smiled. Tooth decay. Missing. Clearly, some of Carlos's teeth were missing. Yes: it was clear.

***

Damian dropped Carlos off at his apartment before he took the car back to the car rental place. The lady behind the counter at the car rental place, she didn't ask if Damian was Carlos. She gave him the receipt after he gave her the key. Now, if he could only stay awake long enough to get himself home.

That Sunday, Damian dreamed a strategy while he slept at home all day. He was mad at Carlos but sad too. He dreamed about Alexander.

Alexander.

Carlos.

Open Doors
Larry Wilson, Jr.
(Dapharoah69, the King of Erotica)

My name was Marvin Frank Leander.

I was a 29 year old Jamaican/Haitian who was originally from Plantation, Florida but found a new home further down south, in Perrine, Florida when I was five years old.

I had to roll my car windows down, because I was hot in the T shirt, leather coat and black slacks.

I thought back to that time, a time I was lost, confused and damaged. Damaged from watching the elders I loved live haphazardly, and my own feelings of inferiority.

Present day I was very guarded, an extremely private person who has been through a lot in life.

I have an education, of course, getting a degree in business from Morehouse, a degree in Psychology from Florida International University and getting a Masters from the University of Miami and never putting it to use.

I been out of school for so long I forgot what I got my Master's in. How pathetic, I know.

But if I'm not using it then why bother.

I was sitting in my car, on my cell phone, calling someone about a business matter. Something I read in a letter from a new friend propelled me to press the numbers.

But it took an act of confirmation for me to actually go through with it.

I loved music, played Dominoes with the boys, watched sports and once a week I did one other thing.

I went to the graveyard to pay homage to Bill.

My ex boyfriend.

My Moms Jackie moved from Plantation when I was five and called herself setting up shop in the Rainbow City Projects in Perrine, helping out my GrandMa Lily, who was six feet two inches tall, had an attitude out of this world and a sick view on life. She was never the mushy type, so I grew up rough and tough, and was taught to tuck my feelings so far in my brain my subconscious ate it for dinner.

Perspective changed for me when Mom moved away. I had to leave all my little friends on the block, and even though I was five at the time, I had friends who were about ten, eleven and twelve. I would never see them again.

I learned then that I should never get attached to people. Because they would one day be ripped from your life and you will be forced to live with it, whether you wanted to or not.

I had a rough life, yes. I listened to my Grandma's blues music, watched her get drunk with young men about twenty-six years old and then retire to her room having unprotected sex with each one of them.

There went my crash course in commitment and giving your body to that one special person you loved.

And this morphed into my soul. I didn't learn to let go grudges and I never learned to turn the other cheek.

"We Are the World" was never my theme and "Self-destruction" was never my favorite music video.

Growing up in Rainbow City Projects, I had to fight every day. I went from a soft talking young man to being environmentally shaped in the laws of the ghetto. I got tired of being jumped on because I was the new face in the neighborhood so I started carrying tree branches that was damn near bigger than me to R.R. Moton Elementary School.

Being eighty pounds proved to be an advantage because it allowed me to stick and move when I fought.

When I got the reputation as the Stick Bandit, Niggahs pulled away from me.

Miraculously, they started trying to be my buddy. I didn't need buddies. But I wound up with them anyway since I didn't have siblings and Mom and Grandma were too wrapped in their sex life (and scheming dumb ass men for their money) to remember I was alive and needed to be properly clothed and fed, so I was always a loner.

The streets molded me into the vicious boxer I would become, eventually knocking niggahs out with one shot.

The Laws of the Ghetto were as follows. Dream little and think even smaller.

If your Daddy wasn't in your life you told people your mother was your father.

You said he was doing life without parole if he was a crack head or if you never met him. Wasn't a lie.

If you were a boy you played a sport. Tennis and soccer need not apply.

Little Debbie Snack Cakes were our favorite desserts.

You had to touch a girl on the ass and run. You had to kiss a girl before you turned twelve and your boys had to be present.

If not we told everybody you were a faggot and disowned you as a friend.

You lied on your dick just to make your value raise fifty-eight percent.

You had to watch porno tapes to learn how to fuck a woman.

Lose your virginity before you turned 17. If she got pregnant you up and left her ass and you denied the child. Out of the tons of men in my 'Hood, I could count on one hand how many men actually raised their kids (and I wouldn't count past the first three fingers).

Nine times outta ten it wouldn't be your kid anyway because she let eight other Niggahs have playing time on her home court.

You begged for five dollars when you were broke and if you couldn't get it that way you found a soft little Niggah who didn't have any friends and you whipped his ass and you took it.

If that failed you collected empty cans around Perrine and you took it to the Can Place by Marlin Road and S.W. 107th Street for some loot.

They paid by the weight so you put sand in select cans so you get paid a little more.

You never admitted that to anyone because then people would assume your parents were on welfare, even though five out of seven mothers were being assisted by the government.

You found at least two peers and formed a little clique.

To determine who the Leader was, you pulled your dicks out and the Niggah with the biggest pole was the big kahuna and the Niggah with the smallest pole was the runner, the do-boy and the gofer.

He stole from the stores and brought the Leader the merchandise to be distributed amongst the crew.

You didn't invite others in your circle and you didn't trust a new face.

If your boy didn't have money you gave him some.

If he spent it on a girl or gave it to anybody else you whipped his ass and made him get it back.

You couldn't publicly cry or show emotions. If you did you were automatically out the crew. Men weren't supposed to cry; at least that's what they told me. Crying was a sign of weakness.

If a new kid moved into the Hood you fought his dumb ass to see how much heart he had.

And if all three crew members wanted a new member he had to be initiated. I would line an open space with marbles—about ten feet in length.

He had to keep his chest out and shoulders straight and walk the line while we stomped his ass.

He couldn't cry, whimper or make a sound. Real thugs were born not made. No bitches in the crew.

If he successfully walked the line we spit on each other's hands and we piled them atop each other.

You ate at a friend's house everyday so your Mama could save the little food she did have. You tore open that government peanut butter and you put government cheese on those cheap hamburgers.

You ditched Kix cereal and told Mom to get King Vitamin cereal with her WIC coupons.

When Halloween came around you made a costume because half of our parents could barely pay the rent let alone afford expensive characters we saw on TV.

You waited until trick or treating was almost over and you started running by kids and snatching their bags.

The older people didn't set the example of what an American should be and half of them still cried over their forty acres and a mule the government would never give them. I learned then to never whine for your money. You went out and took what was yours. This made me hostile.

I didn't have positive images in my home. The only image I did look up to was a white man with blonde hair and blue eyes. He was named Jesus. I wished he was my Dad.

I saw the television movies TV stations only played on Easter and learned that when you prayed to Jesus and asked for it he gave it to you. I prayed for a better family and steady food flow in our home.

He never sent it.

And even when I'd gone to church some people (always the adults) didn't take it seriously so I didn't. It was funny to me.

When I got smacked for laughing at them speaking in tongues (sounding like drunken Chinese sailors) I was very upset when the older men could fuck the older Sisters of the congregation and slap booty cheeks.

Hypocrites.

And this turned me off from church early on so when I turned twelve I never set foot in one again. It had gotten so bad I took down the Jesus picture and burned it in the back yard. Prayer was baloney and I hated baloney.

Mama had a very good professional career that brought her ends. She ran numbers (the ghetto Lottery) from the living room and, well, my GrandMa, who I loved dearly, coached her and showed her how it was done.

We all lived together. When I turned thirteen we moved out of Rainbow City and into a little three bedroom house across the street from it with a broken down Cadillac sitting on four cinder block.

I remember I discovered masturbation in that broken down car. I used to jack off every day after school in peace, because Mom and Grandma were never home and I loved the humidity of the heat, sweat trickling all over me, down my hole and all on my face while I thought about all the men that turned me on.

I never told my friend I wanted to sleep with guys, because they were too busy watching me kiss girls and slap their asses and run.

After a while masturbation lost its flair and I somewhat never thought about being with men ever again.

The biggest blotch mark in my life was that I didn't have good role models. My folks didn't even graduate high school or get G.E.D's. But they knew those streets like I learned those books. Somebody had to be the book worm in the family.

Most young black men in Dade County had it rough. Most of us didn't know our fathers and the ones who did sometimes told me it wasn't worth the learning experience.

My father, for instance, was too busy making a name for himself in the streets. He was a thug. He smashed windows, robbed tourists and set up stings against other cats that came from other states selling their drugs.

Daddy drove nice whips, whipped a Niggah's ass if they didn't pay what they weighed and fucked the Hoes.

In my eyes that spelled H-E-R-O. But of course, at the time, I thought this was how a black man expanded his Corporate American Chops.

When it came to women I wasn't home schooled. Mama didn't teach me about the birds and the bees and Grandma threw me a condom when I was thirteen years old, locked me in the room with a nineteen year old paid Ho named "Meagan Rodriguez" from Little Havana and told me through the door, "You *fuck* her good! You fuck her better than your Grand Papi, rest his soul, fucked me. I had your Mama from a fifteen minute sex throw down that was more of a pity party!"

She didn't know that I'd finally decided to sleep with another dude, but as great as it felt I felt disgusted with myself and tried not to think about it again, even though me and him fucked about four times after that.

The first time was in the abandoned car in the yard. We were playing hide and seek with our friends, and we hid in the car and locked the door.

The windows were tinted and you couldn't see the inside of the car from the outside.

But we could see them walking past it, looking behind the house for us, and eventually going inside my crib.

It was hot in the car and my boy looked at me, we were both sweating and could hardly breathe.

"I'm getting out, 'cause I can't catch my breath," he said and he leaned over to me and said, "Let me help you, I been waiting a year to do this," and he pulled out my dick and started giving me head for the first time in my life.

I instantly loved it.

Pushing that to the back of my mind, grandma punched the door and I jumped in front of the lady, who was gorgeous.

I didn't want to sleep with this strange girl, but grandma said I didn't have a choice.

She bit her nail and crossed her legs and was swinging side to side. My dick was so hard it felt like God put rocks in my testicles.

"You better not fall in love with the pussy either. I don't want my grandson turning out to be a dick-in-the-ass faggot like my oldest son Gilbert and if I don't hear the headboard knocking the walls and the cops showing up at the door saying someone called because there's a disturbance from your home then I will get that switch and show you how you beat ass."

How did I tell Grandma that I am gay? That I always wanted to sleep with men, that I was attracted to my friends?

That me and a friend in my crew named Bill already gave each other head and he let me fuck him and I loved it, the warmth on my growth that filled me up inside.

How did I tell her? I was still in denial myself.

How did I tell her the sweet taste of his sweat on my tongue when I was digging him out in his Mama's bed drove me bananas, sucking on his neck, dying for his heat. His rising passion? How did I tell her I came inside him and he reached back and pulled me deeper inside him, becoming my secret fantasy? Being everything I never knew existed?

With that in mind I looked at the Spanish hooker, shaking her trembling hand, trying to hide my unease and nervousness and she said, sucking her teeth "I'm not here to become *friends*. She paid me good so pull it out, let me suck it, put it in me and hurry up and get your nut and let me go."

I looked at the condom. I didn't have a clue how to put it on because I didn't wear one with Bill.

Part of me felt like I was betraying Bill, even though we weren't an item, but when you gave your body to someone something emotional attaches you to the person;

Rolling her catty eyes, Meagan took it and ripped it open, held the tip and told me to pull it out. I was a little shy but I did and her eyes were wide, licking her lips. "Aye aye, I likes what I see, Papi."

"No shit?" I asked, my pants falling down my legs.

I grabbed my dick and rolled the condom half way down my shaft. I felt the electricity when she touched it. My heart pounded and my breathing quickened.

I can never tell Bill. He'll hate me. I told him my dick would always be his, and that his booty was mine.

And I'm going back on my word. But if I didn't fuck this girl Grandma will think I'm gay, and I can't lose my family.

So I'll be Casper the Friendly Ghost till I'm grown.

I couldn't believe it was about to happen, my first female encounter.

With Bill I was eager, clumsy, nervous and vulnerable.

With this bitch I was uptight, hesitant and reluctant.

Meagan lay on my bed, pushing my books on the floor. She spread those gorgeous legs and she had the prettiest pussy I had ever seen, even though that was the first one I ever lain eyes on in person.

Thinking about Bill's soft, sexy body I compared her vagina to his chocolate rosebud, how beautiful it looked, remembering how I pushed his legs back and tasted him and he shivered, tears running down his face and I reached up, ran my fingers over his gorgeous eyes and wiped his tears on his anus and I tasted perfection.

I didn't have the same desire with Meagan.

She spread the walls and she put her legs in the air, those high heels looking tempting.

"What are you waiting on?"

I was trembling as I approached the bed. "What do I do?"

"Get on your knees and eat the pussy. All men do it. I'll show you."

I didn't know if I wanted to eat where women pissed from. Was it even clean?

Yet thinking about Bill, I never thought of eating him out as a nasty thing.

Because I'm in love with him.

I didn't love this cunt.

And Mama said women bled and cramped once a month. My lips didn't want to participate.

I got on my knees and slowly put my face down there. She smelled so good. I let down my guard. She took my head and shoved it up her gash. The wetness on my nose, I started licking wildly and she said. "Oh Papi." And said something in Spanish.

I held her thighs and went to town; happy pussy was in my face, after finally admitting it to myself.

My boys would say I was the man, but I could never tell Bill.

Bill and I even got a tattoo. A small one, so the boys didn't get suspicious. It was behind my ear, of two hearts with a sword through it. And "Boys forever" underneath.

I loved the tat.

I looked up at her and she had tears falling from her eyes. She loved my performance. This boosted my confidence.

"Papi give me the Pinga! Now!"

OK. She didn't have to tell me twice. I got between her legs and I pushed them back, sliding up inside the most warm, soft place on earth.

My mouth wide with surprise, she gazed at me like she loved me. Each inch of my dick swallowed her insides with a satisfying gulp. She was wetter than Bill, and definitely a lot hotter.

But my heart was with Bill. I loved him.

I'll just sleep with women on the side and never tell him. Yea. That'll work!

She held my booty cheeks while I slowly grinded in her. She slapped my booty and she grinned.

"Yea, *get* it, Papi! Pull it all the way out and put it all the way in. Yeahhhh! *Like that, Papi!* Damn, you're so *big*, Papi. Mami gotta cum already!"

I felt her throbbing on my shaft, a rush of wetness all over me. I felt like a big man so I went crazy, going side to side, getting lost in it. Every time I moved she jerked and begged me to punish her.

"Be my police man and APB this pussy!"

I couldn't go any further because I felt a burning in my loins I still didn't understand.

Felt like I had to take a piss. It felt so good I pumped faster, my rhythm sloppy and full of jerks.

"Oh, shit!"

I had to pee. Or so I thought, I was so inexperienced.

I pulled out and white liquid spurted from my dick and all over her face, lips and tits. I couldn't believe this feeling. I had a smile on my face, my dick tingling with sensation.

I noticed the condom was hanging from her walls, but I didn't worry too much about it.

"Damn Papi you shot a load!" She wiped it up and sucked it from her fingers. For some reason this made me get harder.

I didn't have another condom and I wanted seconds so I slid back up in the pussy and had the Ho limping by the time we were through.

When we came out of the bedroom I was dressed and her blouse and skirt was on backward.

Grandma was smoking trees, brushing her wig with a stocking cap over her bald head.

Her dentures sat in liquid solution on the kitchen table. Crack was cut up on the table, sectioned off with plastic bags.

Mama pretended to comb her hair and my nasty-looking Uncle Fat Fat was pleased.

"At least wash your pussy!" GrandMa told her.

Embarrassed, Meagan tugged on her thrifty shop-inspired blouse and smiled coyly. "I'll wait until I get home. I'm ready to go so will you take me like you promised?"

Mama was laughing and GrandMa said, "You're catching the bus. I'll tell you how to get there!" She handed Meagan some twenties and she counted them, frowning.

"It's not all here."

Grandma put on her wig and slid into her house slippers. She looked into her eyes and said, "Yes it is. Forty dollars."

"When you picked me up from Little Havana, you told me a hundred."

"Well, the other sixty went in the gas tank. Sorry. Now go shower."

She walked past Meagan, who was steaming, and opened the hall closet. She pulled out a douche bottle and a bar of soap and handed it to her.

She dropped it on the floor and tried to get feisty.

"I want my money."

Meagan pulled out her mace and GrandMa pulled her small .22 from her bra and aimed it at her.

Defeated, Meagan squatted down and picked up the douche and the soap. "I'll take that shower now." She fidgeted towards the bathroom.

My mouth ajar, I stood there in complete silence. I learned about guns from GrandMa. When someone didn't do what you say you whipped it out and put it in a bitch face for respect. Duly noted.

"Did I ask you to walk off, Meagan?"

She paused at the closed door. She didn't look back. "No." Her legs drummed together.

"Towels are in the hall closet. Never mind the roaches. They are my security guards. When you fuck you wash your ass in here."

GrandMa glared at me and Mama was grinning. She nodded her head like she was proud of me. "And you shower with her. Go in there and wash her back. You show my Grandson how to bathe a woman. I wanna hear some slipping in sliding while ya'll take it to the house."

GrandMa was slapping palms with Mama, stomping her feet. She pulled on the weed and handed it to Mama, who was piling numbers on top of each other.

Against my will we showered together. She wept the entire time, and I felt sorry for her. Part of me was angry I cheated on Bill, and went back on my word but the other part of me knew my Grandma was trying to show me how to be a man, since my Daddy wasn't doing it and this shit was wrong on all levels. But what could I do? She was my guardian, and my own Mama supported it.

I held her and let her cry on my shoulder. I would never see her again. I didn't wash her back nor did I want to. I did want it again so I turned her around and hit the pussy one more time, making her cum before she got dressed, crawled outta the bathroom window and had never run so fast in her life.

And that was my abrupt introduction to life dealing with women.

I loved them but I hated them.

I turned off the shower and dried off. I looked up in the mirror and I jumped out of my skin. Bill was standing behind me. And he wasn't a happy camper.

He was staring at me and I avoided is eyes, wrapping the towel around me.

I truly didn't know what to say.

"So you slept with a Spanish whore."

"No, Bill. I didn't."

"Liar," he said, getting in my face. "So you're telling me she hopped out the bathroom window practicing to be a firefighter."

I looked at him, and touched his cheek and he pushed me into the wall.

"Bill, my grandma and family is out there."

He lowered his voice. "I hate you, Niggah. I thought you were different. I thought you cared about me."

"I love you." I said, feeling so damn helpless.

"I'm asking you again. Did you sleep with her?"

"No," I lied. I couldn't force myself to tell him the truth.

"I saw you, Marvin. I was standing at your bedroom window the entire time." He ripped a card in my face and threw it at me. "I came to bring you a Friendship card, to tell you that you were special to me, for us losing our virginities together and you go off and fuck some tramp bitch behind my back."

I hugged him and he was trying to push me off him and I fell to my knees and he kicked me and I was pissed and angrily jumped up and pushed him so hard he fell backwards, reaching out for me and my heart plummeted into my stomach when he crashed through the window.

"BILL!"

A huge chuck of glass fell on his neck before he could get it up.

"BILL NOOOOO!"

My Grandma shot the door off the hinges and Mama was panicking, rushing past me.

"What happened to Bill?"

I shut down, fell to my knees.

Frantic and not knowing what to do, Grandma was trying to hug me and Mama tried to pull the glass from Bill's neck.

Uncle Fat Fat was telling us to lie, that we were going to come up with a story and stick to it, no matter what.

I didn't want grandma touching and in my heart I hated her.

She made me fuck that girl and caused all this. It was her damn fault and I will never talk to her again!

He took his last breath with his eyes on me.

I died inside.

Short Stories

******

The next couple years proved to be life changing and were filled with emotional withdrawal, mental walls and privacy. I shut everybody out, and when I graduated high school I didn't tell my family. I gave them a later date, and said that was my graduation day so when I got my diploma, I was on my way on a full scholarship to Morehouse and would never look back.

I cried for Bill every night. He consumed me, and the guilt killed me inside.

It killed me to lie to the police and said he was trying to rob us and I pushed him when he tried to flee and he crashed through the window.

My family backed me up, but telling the truth would have landed me in prison and destroyed my life so sometimes doing what's right ended any chance of you (especially when you're black) having a promising future.

I stayed to myself in college, my first year proving to be the weirdest, because I had to get used to Atlanta, Georgia, a new place, and fighting off the closet homosexuals that tried to suck or fuck me.

I would never love again. If I couldn't have Bill then I would never sleep with another man and women would never get my commitment or hand in marriage.

My second year I wound up having homeboys anyway, joined a fraternity and really found out that sometimes an extended family was more reliable than a real family.

Ladies. I lived for them but I could definitely live without them.

Sluts. They made my dick hard when you got to fuck them for a McDonald's meal and a ride to the club.

And yet when you found out they screwed your homeboys you gave them fifty-five feet to get the hell away from you.

Whores. They fucked for a fee and made tricking the new form of prostitution.

Lesbians. I could be one when nature called for it. I loved pussy just as much as a lesbian did but I was still in love with Bill and still hurt in private.

Dykes. Sometimes they turned me on and often times they pissed me off.

Butches. Got on my damn nerves. I didn't like females looking like Barry White and had voices deeper than mine and mine traveled deeper than the Atlantic Ocean.

I just about summed that all up.

I say this because right now my respect for women was a little on the defunct side. I didn't dog them but I did tell them about their asses when they showed it. Women didn't know how to talk to real men like me anymore.

When you swallowed your pride and told them they were a) pretty or b) the shit and they stuck their noses in the air like they were giving microphones checks before millions.

They thought they were the Catch of the Day. They got me fucked up with those Little Dick Niggahs, those lame ass Niggahs who barely smelled pussy.

And being that I was environmentally shaped to never really give a woman respect, which played a hand in why I hardly dated them.

So a Ho gives my homeboys Mercy Pussy and their balls swelled up, weighing more than elephants. I laughed at lames like that. I had no problem slaughtering pussy in the sheets and leaving it dripping and longing when I put on my gear and was out the door, deleting their numbers from my cell phone.

So I decided to talk trash to them. I found a good job and got my own crib just to tell a bitch she wasn't welcome. And it's funny how the women who didn't give up the pussy when you didn't have a crib and a luxury car suddenly had an interest in you when your music thumped up the block and your rims shined brighter than the lights on their cell phones.

Like Rebecca. She let every thug bang the pussy and not me. I begged to fuck ole girl, she was that fine. But the real reason why I banged her was because her brother reminded me of Bill, and I was trying to get close to him, thinking if I got him it would replace what I lost.

Wouldn't happen that way because a) he wasn't gay, and b) he wasn't Bill. Bill was buried back in Miami.

Rebecca and I did smoke weed together, and as much as I rubbed her leg and eventually ate her out, she never gave me the panties.

She laughed in my face sucking her apple Blow Pop.

So I ditched her by my third year of college and upon completion of my fourth year, just before graduating, I decided to move back to Miami.

And that's how it played out. Going back home, and seeing my family for the first time since I lied about my high school graduation.

Mama started to cry when I walked through the door with my degree from Morehouse. She hung it on the wall, and cooked me a big dinner, calling over the boys I grew up with, who all had high school diplomas, but never left the ghetto.

It was a tearful ceremony, telling them why I left and why I didn't come home for the next four years.

I never told them about Bill.

I met a girl named Samantha a few weeks later, when I got a job working for the state, collecting garbage.

We were at the Sunoco Gas Station by the Villages of Naranja. Big Louis had parked the huge diesel garbage truck under some trees, for the shade, and we went to buy cool drinks on our break.

When I got out the truck I saw her giving some black man some head in his truck, and when I gawked at her, the way she swallowed it like a piece of candy, I was hard myself

When she got her money and looked up I looked away and went in the store.

Samantha had on hip-hugging shorts, a halter top and her hair swept from her face. She dressed like a Hoochie, but she was a very beautiful woman and still carried herself with confidence.

I told her she'd get more flavor if she sucked me up and she told me, "I don't suck Niggahs who take public transportation to work and collect garbage. I need a man with an auto. Making real money, and a career, not a Job."

She got offended when I told her "Then what's *your* excuse for taking public transportation, receiving public assistance and sucking dick for ten dollars a pop?"

She looked at me sideways, readjusted her tit in her little sister's halter top and tugged on a skirt that looked like her Mama's.

"Don't be telling my business in public," she said, glaring at me. She had a stink walk. She sashayed past me and up to some Niggah clad in a South Pole shirt and the jaggiest pants known to mankind.

He drove a beat-up Impala with the rustiest rims I'd ever seen.

I walked over to her because ole boy didn't run anything over here.

I got in her face and said, "You suck dick in public yet I can't talk about it? I'm a grown man. I can talk if I want to."

Ole boy tried to get jiggy with it, telling me, "Homeboy you bettah watch your mouff."

I stared him down. "Or what, you fake Blatino. I don't know why you're going around telling people you're half Columbian when you're blacker than tar and your hair is nappier than my pubic region. Are you going to shoot me?"

I pulled out my gat and held it in his face. A few Niggahs kept walking by like this was a stage play.

Or maybe because this gas station has seen more murders than the show *The Wire* B.E.T. was seriously playing out like yesterday's news.

Unperturbed, he grabbed his pocket and let me know he was down for a gun fight.

"Think about it, homeboy. I'll cap those gold teeth out your mouth and make these silver bullets permanents in your ass before you pull it out. You wanna gun fight over this Ho?"

"What the fuck. Nobody pulls a gun on Lil Bob Cat."

"What she do," I went on, "…suck you up for ten dollars? She probably did it for five because you look broker than these crack heads bumming change."

He sneered, telling old girl to step aside. I looked at her and said, "You stay your funky ass right there."

She was smiling, like she was a Hood Bitch. "Look at him, got a red rag hanging out his back pocket. Are you flaming? You a folk?"

"A what? Bitch, red is my favorite color and I'm on the clock. Don't bring up that Blood shit. We don't do that down here in Miami. All these off brand Niggahs moving here from other states bringing that bullshit down here."

"Just because you got a gun…"

I put it in her face and she swallowed those words. My GrandMa would be proud. Lil Bob Cat got in his ride and was studying me.

Something seemed off.

Short Stories

So it was me and her, in broad daylight. I was acting gangster. Well, it wasn't an act.

My daddy was known throughout Dade County as a Haitian Goon. I was a chip off the old block.

No Niggah scared me or put any "bitchassness" in my system, as Puff Daddy would say. And just because I had a degree and had just enrolled back in college at the University of Miami for my Masters didn't mean I wasn't 'Hood.

And that was the problem.

She slapped me and called me a male chauvinist. I had snapped, grabbed the Ho by the neck and shoved the gun at her.

Just when I was about to pull the trigger, a group of old men grabbed me and took them fifteen minutes to pull me off the bitch.

I thought my respect for them died then.

Females played too many games. They preached that all men are dogs B.S. but we all knew that females were just as bad (if not worse) than the fellahs.

I wasn't one to talk a lot of smack. In fact I didn't curse much. But one thing I couldn't stand was females who thought their pussies were the gold used to make my jewelry.

I used to be a good man.

I used to open doors for women when Bill was alive, because he used to say, "You're a good dude" every time I did and it made me secretly melt inside.

I used to buy Valentine's Day gifts and take them out when we were in junior high, before he was killed and being that that was a rule violation with the Crew, Bill always had my back, never telling them and I loved him for it.

I used to throw my money to women because I loved being around them. I used to steal money from Grandma and use it to make a lady smile. They could be fun and witty.

Understanding and caring yet the instant you fall in their hole of abysmally blind caresses they switched on you, pushed another man in your face and claimed they didn't lead you on.

I got tired of being the gofer boy. I was damn tired of being the Do Boy. Do it boy and I would do it because they had a big ass and a pretty smile.

Mighty Real

And now, even with a job working for the state, my wallet was more depressed than I was because sometimes women would come up with the most outlandish B.S. to get some of my paycheck.

Like Brandisha. I dated her, briefly, in college.

"My baby needs pampers."

"Well, where is the child's father?"

"Locked up. He's doing life."

"OK. What does that have to do with me?"

"Please help."

"OK. And how can I possibly do that?"

"By giving me about three hundred dollars."

"For pampers?"

"Yes. I gotta put gas in my car to get them. Gas prices are sky high. Hell in California it's already four dollars and some change so you know it's only a matter of time before those prices tear up the gas station signs here in Atlanta. Then I gotta get my hair done because I wouldn't be caught dead looking like a zombie in Wal-mart."

"I don't know about giving you no damn three hundred dollars. Maybe $20."

"You never know who you're gonna meet. Then I gotta get my nails done and buy that new finger nail polish that just came out. You don't want my nails looking frizzy when I'm handing the cashier the money. Gotta get an outfit."

"We haven't even been dating two weeks, Brandisha and you're already asking for shit."

"Well, life doesn't stop just because you date. Anyways, I have the black Baby Phat boots. I gotta get the matching skirt and halter top. Then I gotta buy the diapers. About twenty dollars a box. You know I burn gas to go to Wal-Mart."

"I can't believe I'm hearing this."

She was on a roll, as if I didn't say anything. After she was done talking I faked a stomach ache, went to my apartment and never called her again.

Now, heading back to my work truck so me and Big Louis can go, ole boy called me.

"Yo," Lil Bob Cat said.

I stood there looking straight ahead, my gun by my side.

"What?" I said, looking over my shoulder.

"Dawg," he went on, walking around me. He looked in my face, shaking his head.

"So we about to gun play after all?"

"No, man."

"Then get out my face."

He managed a smile, and this scared the hell out of me.

"Why are you smiling?" I asked.

"That tattoo behind your ear."

"What about it?"

"Man, my brother Bill had that same tattoo. Is your name Marvin?"

My heart shut down, and the tears welled in my eyes.

I dropped the gun on the ground.

"You're Bill's brother?" I asked disbelievingly. I never knew Bill had a brother But then again, I never met Bills' family.

He softened towards me, not at all the bully type that tried to talk mess to me a bit earlier over the whore. "Yea, man. We have the same dad, but different Moms."

I was shaken up, didn't expect to hear Bill's name, and he wasn't even on my mind.

"I miss him," I said, Lil Bob Cat picking up my strap and putting it in his pants.

"Police driving by, don't want them to see this now do we."

"Yea, Man," I said, walking past him. Bug Louis said, "We gotta go, bruh."

"Go without me."

"You'll be fired."

I looked at him. "I quit."

When Big Louis pulled off, I looked at Lil Bob Cat. He said, "Come to my crib. I have something to give you."

"What is it? I'm about to catch the bus home."

"I'll drive you. But first I have to give you something."

"What?"

"Just come."

"What if you're making this up?"

"I know my brother was in love with you," he whispered, looking round to make sure no one heard and my heart stopped.

"Um," I went on and he held a finger in front of his lips.

"I know you and my brother had sex together. The day before he died he told me."

Against my will, I went to Lil Bob Cat's crib.

He lived in a two story house in Cutler Landings, on Moody Drive.

He said it was his wife's house, and that she was at work. She was a paralegal.

"So why am I here?" I asked and he looked me over.

"Have a seat, Man. I'll get it."

He left the room and I sat on the couch, leaning forward, clasping my hands together.

I closed my eyes, wiping away tears. I killed his brother, but I didn't mean to. I pushed him for kicking me and unfortunately he crashed through the window and then that huge chuck of glass fell into his neck.

And he bled to death.

I have asked God over and over to forgive me. I have lost sleep and my appetite over this.

I have to live with that for the rest of my life, and I couldn't even forgive myself.

Lil Bob Cat came into the living room and handed me a folded note

It had Bill's handwriting on it.
Marvin,

I write this note a few hours after we first had sex together.

I write this note because I don't have the heart to tell you how I feel. I mean we're growing boys, right? And homosexuality was taught to us as being wrong, that God detest it.

But I fell in love with you. And it warms my heart. When I look at you I see the most perfect person in the world. I see my friend. And in some ways I see my brother. I love you as a brother, but those feelings are conflicted because I love you as a boyfriend.

The say we kissed and touched I was lifted into something I never really had experienced. We were each others' first, and I will never forget for as long as I live.

No one can ever take that away my boy. I will love you till my dying day.

I enjoy watching you open doors for the ladies and treat them all good. I secretly smile and tell myself what an incredible boy.

Despite how your Mama ignores you and how your Grandma treats you, I view you as a perfect person that will grow into a caring man.

If I ever died anytime soon, or if I died in twenty years after the date of this letter, I would want you to go on. I would want you to have a family, marry a beautiful woman and replicate yourself.

I will always love you, and I will always care. And even though your eyes will never grace this letter, I know in my heart something will probably lead you to these words.

Promise to be a good man and go to college and get a degree and leave the ghetto behind. Let the ghetto go, dawg and stop using all those Niggah words.

I used to hate when you said "Niggah." I see you as something better, greater.

Get your own life, forget your daddy. He wasn't a real man. Get a career you love (I hope you become a psychologist), and go after your dreams.

You are a great listener and an even greater friend.

If I died tonight, my dying wish would be that you go to college and be a psychiatrist. Help people overcome obstacles.

And open the door, like I so happily watch you do for the ladies.

Love you.

Bill.

I looked up from the letter, shaking where I stood. Lil Bob Cat hugged me and said, "I hope you give my brother his dying wish, because I heard you killed him."

I looked deep in his eyes and nodded.

"I would be more than happy to."

So that's how and why I got my Master's in Psychology, even though I never put it to use because it hurt me to know how Bill truly viewed me.

And I wasn't living up to the letter because I didn't have closure within myself for killing him.

I had gone out to his grave, but didn't say anything. I stood there reading over his name and when he was born, putting my hands in my pockets. I cried so hard I cracked open; I needed confirmation that he forgave me for killing him.

I silently prayed to God and told him, "If he forgives me send me a sign, something."

And nothing happened. I lowered my head, and turned away, walking towards my car and something out of the corner of my eye.

A chicken walked from behind a bush and I thought, "How cute," sarcastically.

I started to ignore it but it walked up to Bill's grave, pecked on it, looked up at me and walked off.

I smiled big.

"Thank you, Bill. Thanks for your forgiveness."

I got in my car, put on the seat belt, turned on some gospel music, and went home.

I planned on sending out some resumes to be a psychiatrist, to give my boy, the one man I ever loved, and would ever love, his dying wish.

Then I was packing up and moving out the 'Hood.

Forever.

A SHORT TRIP
Reginald Harris

The first thing he fell in love with were The Driver's lips. That was all Alan could see in the mirror anyway as he took a seat just in front of the rear exit of the bus. Occasionally the bus would lurch, or The Driver would turn his head, revealing more of his light brown-skinned face, the full dark brows over his clear, sparkling eyes, or the sides of his head, bare from his fade haircut. But eventually The Driver would move back to concentrate on the road, and the mirror would once again be filled with his lips, heavy and full, surrounded by a well-tended goatee.

I really should stop staring at him, Alan thought, looking out the window and shaking his head. Just mind my own business. He sighed. What's the matter with me, anyway? Didn't I learn anything after Wade? Those "pale" kids are just too much trouble. Something about their light skin must make them unstable. I was lucky to break up with his crazy ass without having to kill him. And now here I am looking at another "yalla boy." I must be really color struck to want to go through all that again.

Alan studied his passing neighborhood. Bungalow-style homes surrounded by perfectly kept lawns gradually gave way to more densely packed rows of houses as the bus ventured further into the city. The color of those living in the houses got progressively darker as well, changing from the still mainly white majority of Alan's increasingly mixed neighborhood to the rich browns and yellows of the new Central and Southeast Asian immigrant moving into town, finally reaching the multi-hued rainbow usually misnamed "Black" circling what was left of the business and shopping district in the actual center of town.

Alan Reynolds thought this was the perfect time to commute. All those who had to be at work the first thing in the morning were already in their places, and those on the second shift hadn't started stirring yet. Alan was glad his job in the records department of the insurance company allowed him to come in at any time before 11 rather than strictly at 9 a.m., just so long as he made those hours up at the end of the day. The schedule allowed him to sleep in a little in the morning, and get a good deal done in the early evening after his mainly female co-workers and their constant distractions were gone. It also meant that he could ride to work in the relative peace of a usually half-empty bus (Parking downtown was an expensive hassle) and steal as many glances as he wanted to at the new object of his affections.

Again Alan looked toward the front of the bus and thought he noticed The Driver's eyes on him in the mirror. They both quickly looked away. Is it me, he thought, or is there something going on between the two of us? No, he's just caught me staring. He must think there's something wrong with me or something. After all, I've been looking at him every day for almost two weeks now, ever since they changed him to this route. Two weeks and I still haven't even been decent enough to say Good Morning to him or anything. I just get on, and sit here pretending to read the paper, peeking at those gorgeous eyes, those luscious lips.

The sprinkling of passengers all lurched forward as The Driver suddenly slowed the bus mid-block, stopping to pick up an elderly Asian woman who had been caught between her door and the bus stop sign and bench on the corner. She was one of the regulars on the route, and she thanked The Driver profusely in a mix of Chinese and English after she got on. Alan nodded to her as she sat. That was nice of him he thought.

I bet he isn't even Gay. How could he be -- I would've seen him out somewhere by now. Unless he's new in town. Nah . . . I still would've seen him in a bar or club at some point. There aren't that many places for us to go in this city. He must be straight. Or else so far on the "Down Low" he'd never even want to be seen within a hundred feet of a man who might 'clock' him. Probably married, or has a girlfriend, kids. I know the women on here don't leave him alone. They peek at him, too, stealing a quick glance, grinning in his face as they put their fare into the change box -- I've seen 'em. At least that Nurse isn't on here today. She always has to sit right up there behind him, distracting him with some stupid conversation, bouncing her thick, white stockinged leg up and down as she talks and laughs. He just laughs with her to make her happy, I know. He couldn't really be interested in someone like that. She should just leave him alone. I was riding this bus before she was, I saw him first -- he's mine!

Okay, okay, okay. I need to chill. Let's see -- I've already seen as much of the paper as I can stand during breakfast. Widening city government scandal. Yet another innocent bystander killed by those goddamned crackheads. The Lakers win -- same old-same-o. I'll just read my book. Okay, here we go. Hmm... short stories, Black DC -- sounds good. I'll pick a real short one to start with.

Alan began to read. He started slowly, but soon his eyes were skimming the surface of the pages like pebbles skipping across a lake. When the ride grew rockier as the bus passed over a section of roadway being repaved, he glanced out the window at the sun-drenched morning, or flicked his eyes toward the front of the bus and the vision in the rear view mirror.

The Driver pursed his lips slightly as he made a wide turn into a narrow street that would take them to the main thoroughfare for their trip downtown, then wet them with the flick of a bright pink tongue. He slowed to a stop after the turn, waiting for the light to change and glanced up into the mirror.

Beads of sweat began to form across Alan's forehead. He adjusted his already loosened tie further down.

Just look at those damned lips, though, he thought. They're just . . . perfect! What is all this crap about Black lips being too big, anyway? It's partly true -- we do have bigger lips than those thin excuses circling white people's mouths. But what's wrong with that? Ours are full, bursting with honey nectar fit for African Gods. Thick as Mississippi mud, a fertile soil mixed with blood and dreams, out of which anything can grow, even love. Broader than the Amazon, ample enough to wrap your life around when you kiss.

What is it about a Black man's lips that always gets to me? Peeking wickedly from behind a beard, living under a short moustache like a monster ready to swallow you up, lips that roll bare while the serious rhythm of his speech flows between them, or sit, framed, a master's painting set off by a goatee like his, hanging up there in the mirror like a star leading to some promise of release.

Wow . . . am I that alone after four months without Wade that I get this worked up about some guy I don't even know? Snap out of it! Alan dropped his head into his hands and closed his eyes.

The bus made a wide left turn, and began its slow descent toward downtown. They reached the top of a hill, and the city spread out in front of them, a perfect postcard. Almost looks like a real city, Alan thought, someplace where something interesting happens every night where no one would have any trouble finding someone, either just to hang with or to try and build a life together. What a joke! There's nobody worthwhile in this town. All the men are either married, straight, or dogs. What's the point of going out, anyway, to see the same faces hear the same leftover lines? I'll never find anyone interesting here. Maybe I should just move . . .

Alan lifted his eyes to the rear view mirror. I wonder what he tastes like, he thought, watching The Driver's mouth smile and form transfer directions to a young woman getting off the bus. I bet they're wet and soft, like rain on a spring afternoon, coming down on you so fine you hardly notice that you're getting wet. You just stand under it, basking in the cool feeling and sweetness of its caress. "Sweet" -- yeah, I bet he's sweet, too, not like candy, but a fruit sweetness, a Summer peach, just off the tree, or a tangy apple in the Fall, with an edge like a quick bite to your lips. And warm and smooth too, hot chocolate, soothing and familiar, to keep you warm during those long winter nights.

Alan shook himself. Man, I need to stop this! I'm acting like a high school girl with a crush, or some silly, lovesick old Queen. It'll be my stop soon, and I'm going to have to walk out of here bent over, or holding my briefcase in front of me, if I'm not careful. Read your book, look out the window, think of something -- ANYthing -- to calm yourself down, and don't look at that mirror again! Who wants a damned bus driver anyway? I need a man with a real job, making some real money. Alan returned to his book, concentrating carefully on each word, until it slowly dissolved into unintelligibility.

Soon the bus turned into the downtown transportation loop, directly across from Alan's building. Commuters scurried to make connections to other busses or down the escalators leading to the subway below. "Metro Center," The Driver called as he pulled into his route's designated slot. Alan slipped the book into his briefcase and began gathering the rest of his things and himself for the beginning of his workday.

Alan stood, turned to leave by the exit behind him. Aww, what the hell, he thought. Give myself one last look to keep me going during the day. He turned around and headed toward the front of the bus.

Say something, his brain yelled at him as he drew closer to The Driver's uniformed back.

I can't, a small voice whined somewhere deep inside him

Sure you can. Say anything, it doesn't matter. Just don't get off again and say nothing.

I, the whine began. His palms dampened. His breathing quickened.

Oh -- what the hell! What have I got to lose anyway?

"Take care, man," Alan said, nodding to The Driver as he stepped off the bus.

"You too, bro," The Driver said.

Alan nodded and glided out into the cool sunlight smiling to himself. He breathed slowly and briefly closed his eyes, attempting to fix The Driver's voice and image in his mind before crossing the street.

The thick glass of the windshield blocked the feel of The Driver's eyes on Alan as he walked in front of him. He couldn't hear the mumbled, "See you later," as he passed, either.

Kurt sighed quietly. Oh well, he thought, starting the bus and heading into the second half of his run. At least he spoke to me this time. Maybe I'll work up the nerve to say something else to him tomorrow.

Let It Go
Durell Owens

The San Francisco Bay Bridge loomed large despite the patches of smog that threatened to cloud any chances of seeing the Transamerica building earmark the city like the Statue of Liberty. The sailboats glided like snowflakes deserted on the bay, and it was hard to imagine that each vessel carried with it the heavy weight of human cargo. A sea gull soared high above the bay its wings slicing the smoggy air, demonstrating what we had in mind, when airplanes were invented.

A gusty wind blew the smell of seaweed across the stretch of the beach, Trey's sense of smell perked up and his blood quickened. Soon the sun would set behind Mt. Tam; turn the western skies a burnt orange; light greenish blue stars would fill the night; the street and porch lights would flicker in the east bay hills like the flames of tiny white candles blowing in the wind.

Trey sat on the beach, hugged his knees and watched the high tide crash up against the shore. He was in a quandary. Why does it hurt so bad? Why had it seemed as if he'd never seen any of this before until yesterday? A day filled with a stubborn sentiment of foreboding. He'd woken up at three o'clock that morning, groggily got out of bed and trudged into the kitchen. He peered through the oak wood blinds that covered the floor to ceiling window the security light in the front yard was as bright as the moon. It seemed strange. The illumination never bothered him before, now it was annoying. Trey wished to blot it out.

He stood bare foot, in his white boxer shorts arms folded across his hairless chest in the semi dark kitchen. He was puzzled. He blamed the security light for waking him up, in reality, though it was his thoughts that cheated him out of a good night's sleep. His mind was trapped in a whirlpool. His thoughts kept spinning around a speck of undisputed truth that greeted him like an unwelcome stranger. As he turned and walked back into his bedroom, he realized that he hadn't really fallen asleep at 9:30 last night. He was in the bed but his mind kept rewinding the events over the last nine months of his life. He crawled beneath the guilt that covered his bed and looked at the digital clock; it was 3:10 in the morning. Trey decided it was useless trying to fight insomnia so he flipped the switch on the lamp setting on his nightstand, rested his head on two pillows, folded his hands across his lap and gazed up at a tiny spider frozen on the ceiling like a black dot. It would make things easier if he could just relax and think clearly.

Yesterday afternoon, he'd telephoned Anthony at this office to remind him of their date set for the weekend. The Dance Theatre of Harlem (DTH) was at the Berkeley Zellerbach Auditorium and Trey didn't want to miss them. Anthony told him he was interested but a new roommate would be moving into his apartment for a month in a half.

"Let's skip the date for this weekend. I've got to go with Mark to the airport and pick up the new roommate," Anthony announced. He twirled the telephone cord around in quick small circles.

"What about the tickets, Anthony? It's DTH's last performance. Baby, can't Mark go to the airport alone? Do you always have to hold his hand everywhere he goes? We've been waiting all year to see the dance troupe. Reconsider this time for our sake," Trey pleaded.

"No. Take a co-worker, best friend or somebody. Besides, you've seen DTH perform before. What's the big deal? I'm going to the airport. That's final," Anthony responded.

"I wanted to share the experience with you. I promise you won't be disappointed," Trey appealed his voice cracking.

"Forget it," Anthony replied and hung up the telephone.

Trey sensed trouble. He'd been dating Anthony for the past year. They met through Aaron, a mutual friend who died in Los Angeles, three months ago. Anthony moved to Los Angeles, from Argentina ten years ago, when he was twenty-two. He came to the U.S. on a tourist visa and vowed never to return home to Argentina. Anthony had no citizenship papers and worked in L.A. under a not-for-employment Social Security Number. Until he was fired after he spurned his supervisor's sexual advances and slept with the bosses' husband instead. The West Coast skies were overcast on that summer afternoon Anthony flew in to Los Angeles from Buenos Aries. He boarded a LAX airport shuttle, transferred downtown to a city bus, headed to the Immigration and Naturalization office and applied for citizenship. His only possessions were a brown tattered suitcase containing a pair of black oxford shoes, five pairs of fruit of the loom underwear, two pairs of identical black slacks, a white shirt, a transistor radio, Barbara Streisand's cassette, "Evergreen" and the entire collection of Jacqueline Suzanne's novels.

After dating Trey for a week, Anthony confessed that when he was a small boy, he'd learned to speak English by reading discarded American newspapers he found scattered in the streets and thrown into the trash cans of downtown Buenos Aries. Trey was a thirty-eight year old playwright. He had his first play, "Affirmative Action a Death Foretold," produced last year by the Berkeley Repertory Theatre to spectacular reviews. Trey was a curator of photography, literature and paintings done by blacks during the Harlem Renaissance. He also spent a fair amount of his spare time chronicling the lives of friends living in the last stages of HIV. Trey's and Anthony's first meeting was over the telephone one month after Aaron's death. Aaron had given Trey Anthony's telephone number as a matter of introduction.

Trey was being coy. He was the native son. Anthony was the immigrant. Trey figured Anthony wasn't going to sit idle by the telephone, twiddle his thumbs and wait for him to call and get acquainted so Trey decided to make the first move. He'd listened intently to Aaron tell him about Anthony during that warm Labor Day weekend they shared together. Aaron was ill and he didn't want Trey to know. He kept the conversation as objective as he possibly could. Aaron was terribly agitated over the Michael Jackson child molestation case and despondent about the death of his mother last summer.

Aaron and Trey sat in the afternoon sun out on his patio surrounded by red heart shaped geraniums and purple gladioli. Their wicker chairs faced Sliver Lake as they gulped Calistoga bottled water, listened to Billie Holiday, ate oranges, green grapes and munched on mixed nuts.

"For the last week, I've been listening to the talk shows and it's amazing how quickly white folks turned on Michael Jackson. I don't think they ever forgave him for turning so many tables with the blockbuster Thriller album. Now they call him, Wacko Jacko," Aaron offered.

"Well forty million albums is a lot of music to sale. He certainly made history and put a sizable dent into white supremacy as far as pop music is concerned. Nobody in his right mind can deny it without lying," Trey replied.

"Again, I just don't understand, though, why someone with so much wealth and fame would want to abuse a child. It just doesn't make any sense to me. I wondered if he's being set up by envy hearted white folks. All that money, surely he can have any mature man or woman he wants," Aaron said. His thick eyebrows came together in the middle of his face. He lit a cigarette. Trey winced as he watched Aaron take a deep puff off of the cigarette and exhale evenly. Billie Holiday finished singing, "Good Morning Heartache." It became quiet; all you could hear were the rustling leaves of the geraniums; the distant whirring propellers of the helicopter cops in the smoggy skies; and the faint tender cries of a baby from the apartment below.

Aaron continued, "What's so troubling about it is he's got more money than he'll ever out live. If he needs to fuck that bad, why can't he find a boyish looking hustler over on Sunset strip? Let's hope for his sake that he didn't do it and if he did may God have mercy on his soul," Trey countered.

"If it wasn't for the Michael Jackson case I'd still be mourning the death of my mother last summer. She was losing the Board and Care Home long before she died. My mother was up to her elbows in debt. I took possession of her Van. Everything else is in probate because she was superstitious about doing a living trust or leaving a will. I'll probably have to give the Van up, too. It's the only thing I have to remind me of her besides her wedding ring. You know, for the past five years she called me every day, except during the times she went to Vegas to gamble," Aaron said and chuckled.

"Why do you suppose she called you so often?"

Trey took a sip of bottled water.

"She knew she was going to die. She had stomach cancer and kept it a secret from everybody up until the day she went into a Hospice. By then, of course, it was all over. The cancer had destroyed her liver and we didn't have enough money or a suitable donor for a liver transplant," Aaron shared. He looked straight ahead at Silver Lake. Trey bent over and gently patted Aaron's bony thigh.

"I'm sorry, to hear about your mom," Trey responded.

"She'd take these little trips for one or two weeks alone. Wouldn't tell anybody where she was going. Every time she came back, though, she looked thinner. I should have known something was up when she started wearing a wig a year ago. Talking about if Lola Falana can wear a wig so could she. I'd laugh but I'd say mama, Lola is a former Las Vegas showgirl and a star. Mama would tell me, "So what, I'm a former Fresno valley-girl and a bitch," Aaron laughed.

"That's too funny," Trey said and chuckled.

"Look let's go for a drive down to Santa Monica and Venice Beach. Liven things up a bit," Aaron suggested.

"I'm game," Trey consented.

They climbed in the Van. Aaron backed it out of the drive-way of the apartment. Aaron chauffeured Trey through the bustling streets of Los Angeles. Aaron showed Trey the teeming gay community of Santa Monica; the sidewalk bistro's; the bars; the androgynous upscale queens; S

& M shops; tanned and tattooed muscle men; street hustlers; club boys; tattooed and bikini wearing roller blade skaters; and an around the clock busy stream of aging white men cruising up and down Santa Monica Boulevard in convertible BMW's for young trade. Aaron turned on the radio, let down the window and lit a cigarette. Aaron parked the Van then they headed to a sunny sidewalk café and bar called, "Quincy's." Trey and Aaron sat at a tiny round table with two high back chairs. When the waiter came over to the table they ordered Margarita's and jambalaya. Aaron picked over his food and only ate the tomatoes. He complained about having heartburn from the grapes. Before they left the restaurant, Aaron told Trey about Anthony's recent move to San Francisco from Los Angeles. To let Aaron tell it, Anthony had a ton of friends, but was having a difficult time finding employment in San Francisco. Aaron suggested that Trey look up Anthony when he got back to the bay area and make his acquaintance. Aaron borrowed a pen from the waiter, scribbled down Anthony's telephone number on the back flap of his match book, tore it off and handed it to Trey.

They drove to Venice Beach, found a park. Before they climbed out of the Van Aaron persuaded Trey to go topless. Aaron kept on his long sleeve yellow flowered silk shirt. He flirted with the muscle men that weaved through the throng of vendors, tourists, surfers and artisans littering the beach. After walking for fifteen minutes, Aaron was spent and out of breath. They sat down on a bench for a few minutes then turned back around, found the Van and headed to the apartment.

For the past year, Aaron's live-in partner, Mark who is Trey's best friend had provided Trey with the details of Aaron's illness. Aaron had AIDS. All he knew about Aaron was second hand information passed along to him by Mark. The last time Trey flew to Los Angeles on a sunny pre-Labor Day afternoon, it was Aaron instead of Mark who was waiting to greet him at the airport. Trey had met Aaron on one other occasion, during his book signing tour, over one year ago, when the couple lived in Fresno. Now, Trey was struck, though by Aaron's sharp cheek bones, deep set eyes, loosely fitting jeans and under shirt. He'd lost half of his normal weight.

Mark was visiting relatives in San Diego and wasn't expected back until Sunday. Trey felt awkward meeting Aaron because he was expecting Mark. Aaron was delighted it turned out this way because it gave him a chance to get to know something about Trey and see if they could be friends without using Mark as a crutch.

Five months after returning home from Los Angeles Trey decided to call Anthony and invite him to brunch at the Marriott at the Berkeley Marina.

"Hello, is Anthony there?"

"Speaking."

"Hi, I'm Trey a friend of Mark and Aaron. Aaron told me that you had moved to the city and that you might need some help getting situated in the Bay Area."

"Who is this?"

"Trey. Aaron's friend, he gave me your telephone number and suggested that we meet."

"You were supposed to have called me five months ago."

"Well, I've been busy working on a new play. I'm in the final stages of the work and I've been in solitude for the last five months."

"Oh. I see. I didn't mean to be so presumptuous."

"That's very L.A."

"I'm trying to rid myself of bad habits. It's not easy."

"That's obvious."

"Tell me a little something about yourself. Now I remember about Aaron telling me that you are so cute and I just love black men one hundred percent."

"So you like every black man you see?"

"That's it as long as they are black."

"Don't you have other requirements?"

"What do you mean?"

"What I mean is, I think it's very shallow to pursue a guy just because he is black. I would think you would want him to have some other redeeming qualities."

"Oh. I see your point. I like certain types."

"I'm listening."

"I can't stand black men with attitudes. As though they are God's gift, but I can deal with the others."

"Can you be more explicit?"

"I like sexy, hung, handsome and intelligent black men."

"One at a time or does it really matter?"

"I prefer them one at a time, though, to be honest, I've done my share of tricking."

"I can imagine that you have, given the fact that there are reputedly no black folks in Argentina. Did you take up your interest in black men in the back streets of L.A.?"

"Actually, I dated white guys when I first moved to L.A. but I got tired of the rituals they played. Did Aaron tell you that I fell madly in love with him?"

"That's what he said, but I want to hear about the rituals. That's a more interesting topic of conversation."

"Did you say rituals?"

"You mentioned rituals or do we have a bad connection?"

"You know the status seekers. To put it another way, it's men who will only involve themselves with someone who is credentialed, and interested in the mundane."

"I don't mean to cut you off, but did you know that Aaron is dying? Mark called me last night. Aaron's in intensive care."

"I know. I can't deal with death and dying."

"Didn't you just tell me you fell madly in love in with Aaron?"

"That has nothing to do with it."

"Wrong. It has everything in the world to do with it. Correct me if I'm amiss, but if you love someone it's an act of betrayal to turn your back on them, just because you can't deal with death."

"Mark is Aaron's lover. I'm sure he's there to console and comfort him in his last hours."

"It seems to me that your lack of concern has to do with the fact that Aaron loved Mark and not you."

"Aaron is a very complicated man. What you don't realize is that after Aaron was hospitalized, I was driving to L.A. to visit him and my engine blew up. Boom! It happened just like that."

"You could have flown to L.A. to see him."

"I still don't have a job here and no money."

"What about the tons of friends Aaron told me that you had? Surely under these dire circumstances they would have financed your trip."

"This conversation isn't going anywhere."

"It's not going anywhere, because you are being insincere, Anthony."

"I can see now we're getting off to a great start."

"Anthony, I believe in dealing head on with death. I also feel that it's cowardly to use a phobia as an excuse for a sheer lack of concern and caring. Anyway, if you are interested in hooking up, I'm usually home after six-thirty in the evening."

"Cool. I'll call you next week. I'm booked this week with job interviews."

Trey hung up the telephone feeling ambivalent about actually going out on a date with Anthony. He'd never met anyone from Argentina, let alone South America, but he was curious about him just the same. So he decided to take the plunge.

Anthony and Trey met on a Monday night in the city, at Anthony's apartment in the Castro, one week after Valentine's Day. After reading the galleys from his latest play at work he left his office and headed to Anthony's apartment. He was almost picked up by a guy who looked like former NFL running back Roger Craig, who talked him into giving him a lift to the Gift Center. Trey didn't ask the hitch hiker for his telephone number because he wasn't out to score. When he reached Anthony's apartment, he rang the buzzer and Anthony let him in. Trey was surprised to see that Anthony had blond hair, blue eyes and a thick waist. He must have forgotten that he'd told him that he was fair complexioned. Trey didn't ask Aaron how Anthony looked. He just assumed that he was an olive complexioned Hispanic type. Anthony had a sharp tiny nose and wore wire rimmed glasses. Trey was sort of taken aback at first. Anthony's accent over the telephone sounded so rich with a Spanish flavor. Trey wanted to turn back around and say he left his keys in the car then leave, but he didn't want to be rude.

He was trapped.

After a few glasses of white wine, fantasies about what it would have been like to date the Roger Craig look-a-like, conversation about his writing life, Anthony's roots in Argentina, the mesmerizing vocals from Shirley Horne's breakthrough CD, "Here's to Life" Trey broke one of his rules and went to bed with Anthony on the first date. It was lust not Trey's intention to date him steady. Anthony was unemployed and Trey felt sorry for him. Anthony had been out of work for over three months. There were no prospects. Trey broke another rule in dating someone outside of his race who was unemployed and broke. Yet Aaron had died and Anthony was Aaron's friend. Trey fooled himself into thinking that he wanted to console Anthony and felt foolishly obligated. Besides, Anthony was hospitable and had a huge collection of Nancy Wilson CD's classic feature films and panoramic views of the city from his living room window. Trey was impressed by Anthony's fondness for R&B. He seemed sweet, but underneath that sweet exterior, lurked a weasel.

On the next few dates, Anthony flirted with every black man who walked in his path. It turned Trey off and annoyed him to no end. Two months after dating him, Trey couldn't come to orgasm during sex with him. Anthony blamed the position they used. Anthony liked to "sit on it." It has never worked for Trey. He hung in there. Trey's best friend, Kelvin told him to be patient and that there may be cultural differences that are insurmountable.

Trey was bored.

After Anthony finally landed a job with the help of his roommate Mark, sometimes a week would pass and Trey still hadn't heard from him. He'd call Anthony to see if he'd been laid off from work again.

"I've been very busy, getting to work early, coming home late, and going straight to bed."

"There are telephones. I've left you messages. You've got my office, cell and home telephone numbers."

"I'll do better in the future. I promise. I don't carry all of your phone numbers in my wallet. Did I tell you that Mark is going to quit his job at the end of July, travel to Salt Lake City to visit relatives and sublet the apartment? He's a Mormon, you know."

"Very interesting, that's mighty abrupt. Who is he renting the place out to?"

"I don't know."

"That's an even more interesting answer from someone who has to get used to a new roommate for that long without the benefit of knowing about his background."

"Mark says that he is a fresh black twenty-nine year old law student, from Ohio, and will fly into the city Saturday night. We've got to pick him up at the airport at nine o'clock sharp. So I'm going to skip our date for tonight."

"Wow! I thought we were going to Cindy's house warming party in Dublin?"

"Forget it."

"Damn."

"What's your problem? After all, the guy will be living with me for the rest of the summer. The least I can do is go and greet him at the airport."

"Since Mark, arranged to have him move in can't he pick him up there without you to chaperon and co-host?"

"Trey there you go being suspicious."

"I'm really pissed, because Cindy and Laura expected us to be at their party. We've already bought the gifts."

"Well you go by yourself. I'm going to the airport with Mark so give Cindy and Laura my best regards."

Mark and Anthony picked up the new roommate at nine o'clock sharp.

"You must be Blair."

"Hi. You must be Mark. The rental agency told me who to expect. How are you?"

"Fine and this is Anthony, my roommate," Mark said.

"Hey. It's a pleasure," Blair said. He shook both of their hands.

Anthony liked Blair instantly. He was just as dark as Aaron except that he too, like Anthony wore horn rimmed glasses, and was giddy. That annoyed Anthony. Once they all arrived at the apartment, Blair and Anthony walked into the living room and peered out of the wide front room windows at the city. It was absolutely beautiful and made the odds and ends littering the living room picked up from various garage sales seem larger than life. Blair picked up his bags and Mark showed him his living quarters. Mark came back out to the living room. He stood next to Anthony.

"When Trey meets Blair, he is going to flip!" Mark said.

"I don't care. I hope that he does. I've had my fill of Trey, but Blair reminds me so much of Aaron, until it's spooky."

"Careful Antonio, American blacks don't like being called spooks. I learned that in Salt Lake City. Don't forget I'm still a non-practicing Mormon."

"To be honest, I love Trey, but I'm in love with Blair. Look stop calling me, Antonio. You know I don't go by that name anymore."

"I apologize but that is the only name I've ever known you by until you came to San Francisco. Besides, you've just met Blair. How can you say you are in love so quickly?"

"Silly boy haven't you ever heard of love at first sight? Blair appears to be very intelligent."

"Trey isn't exactly a dummy or slouch either. He's a gifted playwright. Blair is not cute. He is a little chubby and that stupid giggle. Oh well, he's probably ample even more so than Trey."

"You never know. Trey is packing, but I wouldn't be surprised if he was you know black men."

"I don't you do. I'm not into black guys. Are you going to work Blair anyway, though, Anthony?"

"Do Bears shit in park? What Trey doesn't know won't hurt him. Although I wish that he would agree to an open relationship. Then that way nobody gets hurt. You know me I've never had a piece of cheese cake or met a black man I don't like and this is no exception."

"How can you be sure that no one would get hurt in an open relationship? What if you find that you like Blair, more than you like Trey?"

"Well, as Janet Jackson says in her song, "That's the Way Love Goes."

"Do you really love Trey, Anthony?"

"I did once, when we first met. I know Trey is an up and coming playwright and has a body to die for. I just couldn't fall in love with him though. He thinks too much about writing plays. I love him like I do you as a best friend, but I'm not willing to sacrifice my soul for him. I realized I didn't love Trey when he asked to borrow one of my Betty Davis biographies."

"What did you say to him?"

"I told him, no. That's when I realized that I wasn't in love with him."

"That was mean, Anthony. Trey's a playwright and a natural book lover. If you can't loan a book to a writer who can you loan it to? Besides, I bet you haven't even read the book yourself. Good heavens you can be such a mean little bitch."

"I know I should come clean with how I really feel about Trey."

"Why do you keep him hanging on then?"

"It's out of habit and a need to punish him."

"What has he done to deserve being disciplined about?"

"I can't put my finger on it. I tried to get him to leave that Richmond ghetto, move here to the Castro and rent an apartment. In that way, we could be together more. Do you know what he said?"

"What?"

"He's lived in Richmond all of his life and his family needs him. I said what about me and my needs."

"Does he know about you?"

"Trey wouldn't care if he knew I changed my name from Antonio to Anthony. All I did was Americanize it. What's the big deal anyway?"

"What I mean is does Trey know that you don't have any citizenship papers?"

"No. That's none of his business. I hope that you keep your big fat mouth shut about it, too."

They changed the conversation and talked about the sharp increase in gas prices, trading in gas guzzlers for more fuel efficient vehicles when Blair walked into the living room. Anthony's interest was aroused when he saw Blair wearing a smoke jacket, Elizabeth Taylor's passion cologne and red boxer shorts.

"I guess that you two want to be left alone. I'm heading to my bedroom. Goodnight," Mark offered.

Anthony told Mark goodnight and he couldn't seem to take his eyes off of Blair. Anthony offered Blair a glass of wine. They sat and talked about how different the city was from Buenos Aries and Cincinnati, Ohio Blair's hometown. To Anthony's chagrin Blair set his unfinished glass of wine on the coffee-table told Anthony that he was a bit tired and jet lagged.

"I'm turning in. Goodnight, I'll see you later," Blair said.

"Is there anything I can do for you?" Anthony asked.

"I'm good. See you tomorrow."

Anthony trudged off to his bedroom disappointed that he didn't score with Blair the first time he met him the way he had with Trey. He fell asleep and had a dream he didn't want to come to an end. In the dream, Blair felt dehydrated got out of bed during the middle of the night went to the kitchen for a glass of water. He'd forgot to put on his glasses, fumbled in the dark, got Anthony's room confused with his then found himself in bed naked with his new roommate. They made love like thieves until the small hours of the next morning. Anthony woke up from the dream in a cold sweat. His sex was hard and stiff.

Next morning, Anthony still reeling about having had his advances by Blair spurned went to work in a bad mood. He took his disappointment out on Trey and refused to accept his telephone calls. Anthony cooked up a tiny plot. Since he was unable to get Blair to share his bed, he invited Trey over to spend the night and sleep with him because Blair would not. That night, when Trey came over to see Anthony he ran into Blair at the apartment, Trey found that he had some things in common with Blair. Mark had told Blair earlier that evening about Trey's work as a playwright. Blair had a draft of one his screenplays that he wanted Trey to critique for him. Blair was working on a re-make of a Streetcar Named Desire with an all black ensemble cast. Blair had Beyoncé in mind for the role of Stella. Trey suggested that The Rock may be a good choice for the role of Stanley. Trey was flattered and told Blair that when he was comfortable with showing the screenplay to him that he'd give it an objective but fair critique.

Trey made love with Anthony, that night. The lovemaking was tired. Trey knew that to try to make a life with Anthony was going to be more difficult than getting a producer to back his next play. Especially after he ran into Mark at Gold's Gym one afternoon who'd asked him for a spot on the flat bench then dropped a bomb. Mark told Trey that Anthony had been going straight from work to hang out at clubs in the city every chance he got. Now, Trey understood why Anthony's whereabouts had become increasingly hard to determine. Trey had been hard at work, fine tuning his play while editing Blair's screenplay. He took a break, lucked up and reached Anthony, at the State Farm Insurance office in Ingleside where he worked. Trey invited Anthony out to a movie.

"I'm going to take a rain check. Mark is going to make dinner tonight and he, Blair and I are going to go to the Badlands Bar afterwards."

"You mean to tell me that you won't be having leftovers again tonight?" Trey kidded.

"That's very funny."

"I'm not kidding. What about me? I'd rather spend the evening alone with you, Anthony. We don't see each other but once a week. You've got the new roommate to entertain and guest flying in from L.A. tomorrow. God knows if I'll be able to see you at all this weekend."

"Well fine. What do you want to do?"

"I want to go and see Janet Jackson, in Tyler Perry's movie, "Why Did I Get Married," at the Opera Plaza. It's received such good reviews."

"Well only if you join us for dinner tonight at my apartment first."

"It's a deal," Trey said.

Later that evening, Trey left home, drove to Anthony's office, picked him up headed to the apartment. Once they arrived at the apartment, Mark was in the kitchen. He chopped garlic, sliced bell peppers, boiled spaghetti made a ketchup-thin colored sauce. Ground beef simmered on top of the stove. Mark rinsed his hands in the sink then offered Trey a glass of white wine and some fresh fruit. Trey apprehensively drank the wine, stared out of the living room window at the lights on the Bay Bridge. He munched on the grapes as though they were sour.

Trey noticed that the table was set for four, but Blair was conspicuously absent. Trey wanted to know why Blair was not present.

"Where's Blair?" Trey asked.

"Oh. Blair told me he may be a bit late," Mark explained. A few moments later, Blair accompanied by a handsome guest walked into the dining room. He apologized for running late and introduced his guest. Trey's eyes were not playing tricks on him there was no mistake about it, Blair's guest was the same guy who hitched a ride from him to the Fashion Center a while back, the first night he met, Anthony. *Is this karma?* Trey thought.

"Everyone, this is David," Blair said.

"No problem, I'll just get another place setting," Mark said. His face flushed red from embarrassment.

"Don't bother we will not be staying for dinner. We've got reservations at Tony Roma's. Sorry for the late notice but David is just crazy about baby back ribs. Right Boo?" Blair said.

"Yes, baby and that's the God's honest truth," David said. He looked at Trey and winked.

"Well, it's at that hour we've got to get a move on," Blair said.

"It was nice meeting you guys. I'm sure we'll be seeing a lot of each other from now on," David said.

They hurried off.

Anthony had warmed up to Trey, but now he'd turned cold, distant and in what was an obvious bad mood. Anthony considered overturning the beautifully embroidered lace covered dinner table set with three lit long stem white candles, Corbel extra dry champagne graced by a bouquet of beautiful lavender gladioli. He decided not to, because he'd ruin his new beige slacks, have a huge mess to clean up and he'd still be hungry.

Trey watched Anthony's face. It became crystal clear to him as he sat for dinner that he was in the middle of something he knew as over. Anthony didn't look Trey in the eye while they ate dinner. Mark maintained an uneasy and awkward silence. All you could hear was the humming of the fish aquarium; a siren screaming outside and Anthony chew and smack his lips as though he hated food. After dinner, out of politeness, Trey asked Anthony if he still was interested in going out with him to see the Tyler Perry movie. Anthony surprised him when he accepted his invitation. Trey was hoping that he'd say no because it would give him a way out. Spare him the awkwardness of pretending to enjoy Anthony's company.

They climbed into Trey's car and headed to the theater. Once they got inside of the darkened movie theater, Trey fought back the urge to hold Anthony's hand. He decided not to reach for Anthony because he'd lost his way with him. Trey didn't feel anything now. He knew that this would be the last time they'd ever be this close again.

As they walked out of the movie theater, Anthony reached for Trey's hand. Walking hand and hand towards the car they were harassed by a group of rednecks. A truck full of young men hurled homophobic slurs at them.

"Hey, you fags going to get married!"

"We hope you AIDS infected disease carrying homos die. Die faggots die!"

Laughter came from the men in the truck that was as insidious as the venomous screech of a witch. The tires from the truck burned rubber, quickly sped away from the scene and left Anthony stunned into silence. Trey was vengeful.

"Faggots! It takes one to know one! If you are such big men, why the fuck are you running away! You ignorant, cowardly, stupid pea-brained trailer trash!" Trey yelled at the back of the truck. They watched the red tail lights of the assailants disappear into the night.

As they drove away from the theater there was a silence so complete between them until it was deafening. It was broken only when Anthony began to cry. He wished it was only this incident that had caused him grief but there was so much more to weep about. He wasn't just crying over gambling with the lives of Trey and Blair then standing to lose them both. Anthony had never grieved over Aaron's death or over the utter difficulty of living a life in the shadows as an undocumented immigrant. He'd never cried over the pile of rejected tax returns he filed over the last ten years that were stamped invalid by the government. Anthony had never shed a tear over his daily fear of deportation from a country that offered liberty and justice for all but practiced hypocrisy, racism and homophobia. It was as though a dam had been broken. Anthony's tears streamed down his face like a warm sheet of rain. Trey handed him a Kleenex. Anthony blew his nose and quickly regained his composure.

When they arrived back at Anthony's apartment, Mark and Blair could not be found. Anthony glanced over at Blair's room, trying to figure out if his bedroom door was locked. He slightly pushed the door ajar and saw Blair and David snuggled in the bed together like newlyweds. He backed away from the room as though he was trying to escape from rattlesnakes.

Trey was sweaty, so he took a shower and let the nice warm water drench his body. Trey dried himself off and went into Anthony's room, hopped upon his box spring for a mattress bed next to Anthony. He bruised his back on a protruding spring. It was out of pity rather than love that made Trey feel he wanted to have sex with Anthony. It was the last hurrah. Anthony turned to face Trey, his eyes were red and swollen. He placed both of his hands to his face. Moments before he'd cried, this time he sobbed.

"I have a stomach ache," Anthony lied.

"You had a stomach ache, the first night I met you. That didn't stop me then from fucking you. I'm not buying it."

"I went to the restroom twice while we were at the movie."

"Oh? I thought you were out in the lobby on your cell phone calling Blair to find out if he loves you more than David," Trey said.

"Is that supposed to be funny?" Anthony asked.

"If it didn't hurt so much it would be funny."

"Is that all you want to do is have sex with me?"

"I'd prefer to call it making love. That's what we used to do. Remember?"

"It's been a long time since we made love, Trey. What we do is have sex."

"It's not just sex, I make love to you. When did you start hating me, Anthony? Was it when you started fucking Blair? Or did the hatred precede his arrival?"

"You've always had an inquisitive mind so I'll just tell you the truth to make things easier. I've never made love to Blair. David beat me to the punch. Would you like for me to take you on a tour to Blair's room so you can see for yourself," he said.

"I'm a playwright Anthony, not a voyeur."

"I'm not one of your stage props either, Trey."

"I've never treated you like one, Anthony."

"I loved you, Trey."

"Not the way that I wanted you to."

"I did the best that I could."

"Your best wasn't good enough for me."

"What do you want from me?"

"I want true love Anthony, not just somebody's best efforts. This is not a basketball game."

"Can you forgive me?"

"I'll not only forgive you, I'll forget you, Anthony."

"You promise?"

"I promise."

Trey looked deep into Anthony's eyes. He tried to find something in his eyes, anything that could operate between them like a bridge to re-connect, re-build, and repair the part that was broken. Then he looked at

Anthony's lips and wondered if a kiss could spark a magical flame to burn all the hurt away. Trey's eyes fell to his own feet and that was when he knew it was best for him to leave and walk away. Anthony had handled Trey as though he were chips in a poker game only to find that when everything was said and done he had come out on the losing end. What Anthony felt now was a wave of pain that he put next to ten years of living the life of an invisible undocumented immigrant who could find "get out" and "help wanted" signs aimed at him all on the same block. He put the pain next to not being able to get health care unless he went to ER where he found himself shunned, treated as less than human, misdiagnosed and denied follow-up care. Anthony knew that Trey suffered from being black and gay. If Trey knew about my fears and what I went through would he understand and feel closer to me or would he still walk away from me? Anthony mused.

    Trey got up from the sandy beach, wiped the sand off of his jeans, found his car and headed home. He had a new play to stage, a meeting with the director, the producer, actors to audition and cast. Trey had a tour of the Curran Theater planned that evening. Trey steadied his thoughts about the last nine months of his life and tossed them to the winds of change that blew the sands across the deserted beach. Anthony was more than a notch on his memory. Trey would remember him as a lesson in what love is and what it is not supposed to be.

Blessed & Highly Favored
R. Bryant Smith

The telephone rang at the normal time... ten thirty at night.

Kevin picked up like clockwork on the third ring.

"Hello," he said in his normal nonchalant tenor.

"May I speak to Kevin," the voice asked.

"This is he speaking," Kevin chuckled. "Who else would it be, Myron?"

"Well, proper protocol suggests that you ask for the person in whom you are wishing to speak," Myron teased. "Were you busy?"

"Ah kind of," Kevin said. "Just eating."

"Well, good," Myron laughed. "I'm doing exactly the same thing so we can stay on the phone and not be insulting to one another because we are both doing the same thing."

"I guess," Kevin laughed. "So, what's up?"

"Nothing much," Myron said. "I actually just woke up and ran out to get something to eat before the restaurant closed."

Myron smiled as he listened to Kevin speak. It had been six months since he had moved to Fairhaven, Tennessee from Nashville, Tennessee. For the first time in life, he had moved away from a large city and to a small town in order to clear his mind, heart, and soul in reference to a broken relationship. In boredom one evening, he took the advice of a friend and dialed up the notorious Memphis telephone chat line to see who was on. After listening to about thirty minutes of pure sex solicitation, he was surprised to get a message from someone who was from Oak Bluff, which was a neighboring community to Fairhaven. The person seemed intriguing enough for a personal introduction. Forty-five minutes later, Myron found himself driving to Oak Bluff to meet this mysterious person in whom he had just met on the chat line.

He was slightly apprehensive because, after all, Oak Bluff was a small town and this man was a total and complete stranger. Nevertheless, he followed his intuition, put his gun in the glove compartment of the car, and drove the thirteen miles south of Fairhaven to Oak Bluff to meet this new person. No, the person was not the man he had been so in love with until he literally gave up an entire world for but the person was indeed a welcome breath of fresh air from the chaos of the previous relationship.

In order that there would be some safety precautions involved, Kevin had suggested that Myron pick him up at Oak Bluff's only service station.

Myron complied and drove out to the service station and waited for the mystery man to walk up. After waiting ten minutes in an inconspicuous location on the side of the service station, Myron noticed a tall, thin, fairly attractive man walking toward his car.

"Damn," Myron said softly. "He's kind of cute and just like he said; we are the same height and same weight."

"You must be Myron," the man said as he approached the car.

"In the flesh," Myron chuckled. "You must be Kevin?"

"That's me," Kevin said a bit awkwardly as he looked over his shoulder. "May I get into the car?"

"By all means," Myron said. "Please do."

*****

Six months later, after hours of conversation, Myron discovered a very helpful truth from this new man in his life.

"Oh, really," Kevin laughed. "So how was your day or shall I ask how was you night?"

"Shit," Myron laughed. "You know how my Saturday nights are as well as how my Sundays are."

"So, how was the club?" Kevin laughed.

"Interesting as fuck last night, believe it or not," Myron laughed.

"Oh, did you meet a new man?"

"I told you that meeting a man was not my purpose for going out," Myron laughed. "But I did see a lot of my ex friends there."

"That must have been interesting," Kevin chuckled.

"Actually not," Myron confessed. "I saw this preacher that I used to date and he had the nerve to give me shade."

"He didn't speak to you?"

"Oh, he spoke but he had an attitude problem," Myron giggled. "He is still obviously upset over the fact that we are not together and too stupid to press on rather than holding a grudge against me because we are not together."

"Why did you guys break up?"

"Well," Myron said after a slight pause in an attempt to remember why it would have been worth salvaging a relationship with the guy. "We both knew things were not working out. We just couldn't get along as partners but he could not get over the fact that he asked me out of the relationship and I accepted after two years of putting up with him."

"You guys stayed together for *two* years?"

"I am amazed every time I think about it," Myron giggled. "But, yes, we hung in there for two years. But I was miserable as hell and I know I made his life equally as miserable."

"How?"

"He complained constantly about everything, which only drove me up the wall," Myron recounted the time spent with the man. "The only thing that gets me with him is I accepted the fact that we just couldn't work things out and he never forgave me for it."

"Really," Kevin snickered.

"Yeah," Myron chuckled. "I guess the only thing that really gets me with him is the fact that he has the nerve to stand before a congregation of people and preach how they are going to hell for whatever reasons yet he holds shit in his heart against people for years at a time. God forbid if he dies with all of that on him because the same hell that he so adamantly puts everybody else in is the same hell he will be going to."

"Well," Kevin said. "I just can't get with him being in a pulpit preaching to anybody anyway. I just think it is wrong for a person to be gay and be in the pulpit."

"Well," Myron said attempting not to justify his ex. "I can't stand in the seat of God and say who can or cannot be called into the Ministry to proclaim the Gospel. Personally, I don't feel that it is worth it if you don't have your own life together."

"What does he feel about Leviticus and what it tells you?"

"Child, I can get his telephone number and let you ask him that question because I don't know," Myron chuckled.

"Naw, that's all right," Kevin laughed. "I just can't understand how people can think they are going to heaven and be gay."

Myron began to feel uncomfortable with the conversation but felt compelled to persevere through it with Kevin. So many times before they had shared their beliefs but for the first time in a while, the conversation began to settle on the altar of Myron's heart.

"We do share a difference in opinion anyway," Myron said.

"Well, I just can't get into people running around talking about it is all right to be gay when the Bible specifically tells you that it is a sin!"

"Where in the Bible has it ever stated that a man went to hell because he was gay?" Myron asked.

"It tells you in the story of Sodom and Gomorra," Kevin defended.

"Wrong," Myron said. "The story of Sodom and Gomorra tells you about how two cities were so wicked until God brought ultimate destruction on them. They were doing everything conceivable in the human imagination and God destroyed the cities but does it mean the people went to hell?"

"Yes, they went to hell," Kevin said.

"Are you sure?" Myron asked coyly.

"That's what the Bible says," Kevin laughed. "That's all I've got to say."

"Well, I'm not going to argue that point with you anyway," Myron said firmly.

"It's best not to because we believe two totally different things," Kevin said. "I don't feel that homosexuals will go to heaven ... period! That's why I feel people need to get saved."

"So, are you saying that I'm not saved because I am openly homosexual?"

"I can't sit in that seat but I don't feel that I am saved because of this and I feel that I need to be freed of this."

Myron's heart sank with sadness as he listened to his friend. He could not fathom the idea of hearing a person say they were not saved because of what they may or may not do in life.

"Well, I just cannot utter those words out of my mouth," Myron exclaimed. "I have known God as my personal Savior for far too long to sit here and denounce what I believe just because of who I am."

"Well, how can you claim salvation and never run into the Scriptures dealing with homosexuality?" Kevin asked emphatically. "It is as if you just throw Leviticus out of the door as well as First Corinthians. Both teach against the sin of homosexuality. But then, you don't feel that it is a sin, though."

"I never said that I did or did not feel homosexuality was or was not a sin," Myron defended. "I will say this however, since you brought it up, all sex outside of marriage is a sin and I do believe that."

"So, you are saying that you do believe that homosexuality is a sin?" Kevin questioned.

Myron became slightly agitated.

"I'm saying that I believe that if two people are not married when they have sex then they have sinned," Myron said as his anger began to rise somewhat. "No matter how you put it, if you are whatever and not married then you sin by not being joined to what God has for you."

"What's the deal with you?" Kevin asked. "You just cannot say it! Can you?"

"Say what?"

"Homosexuality is a sin."

"Hell, in what way do you want me to say it?" Myron said. "I just told you that I don't believe that people should have any type of sex and not be married."

"But that is not answering my question," Kevin said.

"OK," Myron said firmly. "This is what I believe. I believe that far too long people sit under these crazy assed people and listen to so much hate coming from the pulpit until people loose focus on where God wants them to be in this life. We turn into people exactly like you, no pun intended. We beat ourselves over the head with the thought of going to hell for being who we are and stop doing what God calls us to do. Do I believe homosexuals are going to hell? No. Because I don't serve a God like that but I don't bump people who feel that they are going to hell. My theory is simple. If you think you are going to hell then you are!"

"So you mean to tell me that you approve of people living that type of life style," Kevin asked.

"I'm asking this," Myron said as he sat up in his chair in order to give complete attention to Kevin. "Since when has God given mere humans the ability to send another soul to hell?"

"I'm sorry but I just can't see turning the Bible around to suit your needs and to me that's exactly what you have done," Kevin said. "I don't think any less of you but I personally feel that God is going to change me."

"Well," Myron said wryly. "I pray that He does change you but what happens if He does not? Where does your soul go then?"

"I don't know?" Kevin answered earnestly.

"So you mean to tell me that you will live a life time of praying to God to be changed or better put in your words ... saved and not spend any time glorifying Him for what He has already done in your life?"

"I'm not saying that either," Kevin said. "I just feel that homosexuality is a sin and I can't get with these preachers who are homosexuals or anything like that."

"Since when did you become God?" Myron asked.

"I'm not saying that I'm God but I know what I read in the Bible."

"Well," Myron said. "My question to you is this, how did you read the Bible?"

"What do you mean?"

"Did you read the Bible with a carnal mind or a Spiritual mind?"

"I still don't understand what you are asking me," Kevin asked attempting to understand where Myron was taking this point in his attempt to change his staunch belief in the sin of homosexuality.

"Well," Myron said. "I'll explain this to you first and then I will ask the question again. The reason I dismiss many things that are said in regard to homosexuals from the pulpit in these rural communities is because many of the preachers are so illiterate in the first place."

"Ugh, oh," Kevin laughed. "Here we go with this country preacher thing again."

"No, I'm saying this simply," Myron explained. "How can you lead God's people when you seldom preach Spiritually? You cannot preach God's word or even read God's word with a carnal mind and expect to get Spiritual results. If you read The Bible with a carnal mind, you will get carnal results every time but if you honestly pray and ask God to show you His will then He will answer you Spiritually and show you where to go every time."

"So, you are saying that many of these preachers around here in Oak Bluff don't rightly divide the Word?" Kevin laughed.

"Hell, no, they don't," Myron chuckled. "And it shows in the community."

"What do you mean?"

"If preachers were rightly dividing the Word of God, then the Word itself would draw people to it. The Word would not run people away from it."

"OK." Kevin snickered.

"So, if you are casting people out of the church under the umbrella of *'Dis is what de Word says in my opinion'* then you are misleading God's people and God ain't pleased with that shit at all."

"So you are saying that gay people should have a special seat in the church or something?" Kevin questioned earnestly.

"No, I'm saying that if the Word is truly going forth, salvation occurs in many ways. The Word can literally stop you from sleeping with a certain person but it will also alter the way you live. Since we have been in this discussion the only thing you have considered a sin was homosexuality but believe me there are far more sins than that."

"Well, I know that but this one is the only one that applies to me," Kevin laughed.

"Oh really?" Myron smirked. "So you are guilty of no other sins? You know the Bible says that you can think a sin and guess what? That thought is equivalent to a man lying down with another man."

"Well, you got me there," Kevin laughed. "What I am trying to get you to see, though, is that it is not right going around acting like it is all right to be a homosexual when it is a sin."

"What I'm trying to get you to see is that you are not God," Myron said evenly.

"I know I'm not God," Kevin laughed.

"Then what gives you the right to say that people are going to hell just because they may be gay?"

"That's what the Bible says," Kevin said.

"Oh, really," Myron said. "Find it for me."

"The Book of Leviticus tells you right there that anyone who lies down with mankind should be put to death," Kevin said.

"Leviticus also says that if a woman is on her period then she is not to be caught in the church for seven days because she is unclean," Myron said. "How much do you want to wager that there is a church full of women who still come to church on their periods?"

"Well, there is no way of knowing that, plus we live in a very different world now," Kevin said.

"That is precisely my point," Myron said. "But the only difference now is that so many people want to say that we are to live under the Law of Moses only when it benefits them. But if you are going to live under "The Law", then live completely under it and follow all of those commandments to the letter. Don't just pick out one and run with it. But remember, if you live under the Law of Moses, then you are not following Christ."

"How do you figure?" Kevin asked.

"Christ came to fulfill The Law," Myron said. "Furthermore, The Hebrews didn't want to hear what Christ had to say because he dealt with issues of humanity. No doubt, there were some gay people who followed Christ. No doubt, he saved them too. Certainly, if Mary Magdalene followed him and was converted, many unnamed people followed Him as well and were saved."

"Yeah, you have a point," Kevin laughed.

"Forgive me," Myron said. "I just can't get with this thing on just because you are gay you are going to hell when I see with my own eyes just how destructive the church has been to innocent souls and because of this many people are going to hell because the one place that should have embraced them with love didn't."

"So you are saying the church should embrace homosexuality?"

"No, I'm saying the church should embrace all hurting souls just like Christ did. Can you imagine how long it has been for some people since anyone honestly told them: 'I love you in the Spirit of Christ.'?"

"Well, you're not going to hear that around here anyway," Kevin laughed.

"While we are talking about this anyway," Myron said. "When was the last time you've been to church? You know I went this morning like I go every Sunday morning."

"It's been a while," Kevin admitted.

"Well, you need to find a church home and get in fellowship with other Christians but get in fellowship with Christ by yourself."

"I hear you," Kevin laughed. "Just don't expect me to go to one of those gay churches because I don't believe in them."

"Child, everything that is available to you may not be for you," Myron laughed. "I don't attend a gay church but I can support one because sometimes a gay church may be the only Jesus a person has. I keep telling you, God can work things out in all types of ways but the main thing is if a person's soul is together before he or she makes the great exit and transitions on to another life. Be it bad or be it good, there is no such a thing as a waiting place between here and there. You either go to heaven or you go to hell."

"Well, I still hold to my belief," Kevin said.

"And that's a good thing," Myron chuckled. "That's why I love you!"

There was silence between.

"Well, ugh, you know," Kevin began.

"Wait a minute," Myron laughed. "I love you Spiritually, child, not carnally. I love you like a brother, man! That is permissible in this lifetime you know. Regardless of what people may feel, gay people can love without thinking carnally."

Kevin laughed.

"I just didn't want to..." Kevin began.

Myron knew where the line of conversation was going. He realized that he and Myron had slept together on several occasions. He also realized that as much as it pained his heart, Kevin would never be his next lover. If Kevin had been openly gay, there would have been no better catch for Myron. Kevin was indeed everything that Myron had looked for in a man. However, Kevin had insisted on *"taking things slow"* which allowed Myron the full opportunity to mourn the passing of his previous relationship. During this season, Myron began to adjust to Kevin and the role Kevin would play in his life. Kevin was his exact opposite yet he was his exact equal. They would never agree on Spiritual versus the carnal and Myron accepted this. Myron did not believe in an unforgiving, unmerciful God of fire and brimstone. Kevin did not believe that a person could be openly gay and go to heaven. They had enjoyed wonderful nights of passion together in a world created for only themselves: A world free of humanity and the discussion of God; A world of friendship and brotherly kindness; a world of exploration - physically, mentally, and Spiritually. In many instances, both would have to *"put the brakes on"* in order to stop an infatuation or dangerous liaison.

Neither of them felt that their meeting would expound to a friendship on a level that was above the norm. Kevin told Myron to go out and date other people because Myron was used to a world of being open about one's sexuality when Kevin believed totally against it. Offended, Myron did exactly that only to realize that the game was no longer fun. Myron in return began to analyze people and situations only to discover that the rural south was indeed far behind the   remainder of the country in the struggle for gay rights; AIDS/HIV prevention and education; or getting to know the meaning behind one's existence. Hence,

Myron discovered that he not date anyone who was not his equal -- mentally, physically, and Spiritually.

Myron was satisfied with the relationship that he and Kevin had.

Kevin was satisfied with the relationship he and Myron had.

Neither Kevin nor Myron wanted to commit to a higher level of a relationship for personal reasons.

"Believe me," Myron laughed. "I feel you."

"Well," Kevin laughed. "I just didn't want you to feel that you have to be in this boyfriend-boyfriend type of relationship in order to be complete because that's not what I'm looking for."

"Hell, I know that, Kevin," Myron laughed. "I think we've been over that before. And believe me; I don't need to be in a relationship with a man in order to validate me. I've done that for far too long. It's time to grow up."

"So, you are not looking to hook up with somebody when you go out?" Kevin asked for the zillionth time.

"There is more to the world than trying to find somebody to hook up with, Kevin," Myron explained. "Yeah, I want a relationship eventually but I know that right now I'm not emotionally prepared for one. For one, I enjoy my independence and freedom. Second, I refuse to cast my pearls before the swine any more... Now I'm speaking Spiritually, you better catch on, boy."

"Yeah, I hear you," Kevin laughed.

"So, when I told you I love you," Myron said. "I want you to know just that. I don't love you sexually or physically but brotherly."

"OK," Kevin laughed. "I feel you. But you mean to tell me that you are not attracted to me in the least?"

"Well, hell yeah!" Myron chuckled. "I told you that when we met but I'm not going to get myself all spun around when you are going through this Spiritual battle with you. I really thank God that He sent you into my life when He did. I had forgotten what it was like to live in the rural south and how many brothers think and feel like you."

"Yeah, I know you think we are backward," Kevin laughed.

"Well, yeah, I do," Myron confessed. "But I feel that not everybody is backward because I truly feel that you are more educated in a lot of things than a lot of people are in this area. The only thing that worries me about this area is how sexually active these people are."

"How do you know these people are sexually active?"

"Child, any time somebody comes up to me to solicit sex and don't know me from Adam, this town is sexually active," Myron laughed.

"Who did that?"

"Some guy," Myron recounted the story. "I was at the service station down from the house and this guy flagged me down. Well, I stopped and talked with him for a minute. Then he sprung his intentions on me."

"What were they?"

"He wanted me to pay to go to bed with him."

Kevin laughed.

"I gotta here this," Kevin laughed. "What did he say?"

"He started with this old lame story about he was not a whore and that he was not gay but he liked to have sex with men," Myron said.

"OK," Kevin said. "Go on!"

"And me being me, I wanted to hear what else he was going to say before I dropped the bomb on him. So, he went on into this whole spill about he just got out of jail and was unemployed and needed some quick cash for a meal and a coat because it was getting cold."

"What did you tell him?" Kevin asked curiously.

"I told him to wait a minute and I would go get him a coat but as far as getting my coins, I don't pay for something I can get for free. Then he looked at me like I was crazy! So, I broke it down for him and told him that I don't pay for sex. Hell, I told him that I am so good until he would give me a refund plus the fact that if there was going to be any exchange of money for sex, I would be the recipient."

Kevin roared with laughter.

"Who was it?"

"Now that wouldn't be holy for me to tell you that," Myron laughed. "You know I don't drop names!"

"Well, what did he say to that?"

"He was like: *Oh, I respect that. So you saying that you get paid too?*"

Kevin roared again with laughter.

"I told him *hell yeah*," Myron chuckled. "Shit, I didn't feel like being bothered again in the future plus that Bradley Kelly syndrome hit me."

"Yeah, I heard about Bradley," Kevin said shortly.

"Well, I certainly respect him," Myron laughed. "He's not lying down for free."

"Well, did you give him the coat?"

"I surely did," Myron laughed. "I don't know where in the hell I got the coat but it was brand new but too little for me and it was cold as hell out there. So, I put a handful of condoms in the pocket."

"I'm sure he appreciated that," Kevin laughed.

"I told you, it is a mission work in everything you do," Myron laughed.

"Well, I guess so," Kevin said. "Hey, look, I've gotta go for now."

"I understand," Myron said. "You have a goodnight and a pleasant tomorrow."

"I will and you do the same."

"I will."

It Will Rain
senoj divad

Set 1

"Get yo ass up!!" I kept hearing myself say to myself. "Nigga you got too much shyt to do to be tryin to sleep in and shyt." Kelly Price's *It Will Rain* was blastin from the cd player. This was the day that I had planned to move the rest of my shyt to my new place in Jackson. Coming from Alabama, I knew the drive was gonna be slow today so I did take my time and loaded up the truck. I picked up one of my boxes and a letter slid through the bottom onto the floor. I put the box down and opened the old letter. By the way, my name is Cordeas. My friends call me Cor for short. Anyway, I began to read the letter and realized it was from the first guy who ever broke my heart. His name was Melvin. Melvin was the most popular brother in the neighborhood. When we were growing up he used to be the one everyone looked up to. This kat was 19 years old, 6'1" dark skinned with a tight body and he always liked to walk around the hood with his shirt off. Melvin had eyes like the sky during the setting of the sun and his lips looked like chocolate formed to his face. He was one of the sexiest brothers in the hood and everyone knew it. The guys, the girls the parents; everyone knew that Melvin was the man. But this letter brought back so many memories of the way I kinda fell in love and got my heart broken.

Dear Cor,

It's been a while since I have heard from you or seen you. Your moms told me you were doing well and that you had graduated from college and stuff. I hope you are doing as well as she said. I am writing this letter to tell you how much I miss you and the love we had. Remember when we were in the hood and I taught you how to play basketball. How you use to cheer me on when I was playin against the other guys from the hood? Remember when your moms use to let me take you to the parties and the Palladium? I never thought I would be lovin a lil nigga from my neighborhood and especially that it would be you. You was just supposed to be my lil buddy. I am coming to Alabama on business and I hope that I can see you while I am there. I really miss you. I have been with other guys and women too and I almost got married but I got to the altar and all I could see was your face the day that I told you it was over. I turned around and walked away from the altar and ever since I have been trying to find you. I never was good at writing long letters so I am going to end this right here. My cell number is 555-224-7642. I hope that you will call me so that we can make plans to see each other on my visit. I love you Cor.

Always,

Mel

After reading that letter, it did take me back and I want to take you back to my first time with this brother named Melvin. You see in our hood, everybody knew everybody. Melvin and his family lived right across the street from my mother, sister and I. He was like my big brother. One day my big brother turned into my first love.

It was the summer before my Senior year in high school. Mel had just come back from college for his summer break. My mom had asked me had I seen him since he had been home. I told her no and she just went on about how he came over to take me out one night but I was at my grandmother's house. I was a little disappointed because I had missed him. See you have to understand, I was the oldest child and didn't have a big brother and Mel was the closest thing to that. Anyway, I continued to talk with my mom and she told me that he said for me to come by and holla at him when I got back home. Before she could even finish I was out the door running across the street. I rung the doorbell and the door opened and to my surprise, Mel was standing there smiling.

"What's up lil brother?" he said. He opened the screen door and gave me dap and a brother hug and I replied,

"Nothing big bro. Just glad you back. I missed you man."

"Awww gone somewhere with that lil man. I know you been keeping the girls busy around here." he said with a smirk.

"You know it bro, but it wasn't the same without you dawg."

We sat for hours talking about college and the things that he had done while he was there. He told me that he had stopped playing basketball because he wanted to concentrate on his studies. I didn't think he would ever stop talking about the girls he had conquered while playing ball but finally he did. But while he was talking, I felt my dick getting hard in my pants. I was glad that I wore a long shirt and that it covered up my erection because I would have been embarrassed if he would have seen that.

It was getting late and I was getting sleepy and he called my house and I heard him ask my mother could I spend the night and I guess she said yes because he hung up the phone and told me that we was gonna watch movies and kick it tonight. So we started watching movies and I began to really fall asleep and I felt myself leaning on his arm. All of a sudden he wrapped his arm around me and laid me down in his lap and told me to go to sleep. I didn't pay any attention and just went to sleep. I slept hard but I could remember being moved in my sleep. I woke up early the next morning to find myself lying in Melvin's embrace and it felt good, honestly it did. I was still fully clothed but he was holding me like I had held girls before.

I tried releasing myself from the hold and it startled him and he just held me tighter. "Don't go." he said.

I started to feel strange, like he really wanted me to stay. So I did and we slept a little longer in each other's embrace. I got up around noon and went home and my mom and sis were up getting ready to go shopping.

"Did you have a good time with your Big Brother?"

"Yes ma'am. We watched movies all night and talked about College", I replied. "Mom, do I have to go to college?"

"Nope. All I ask is that you keep your grades up now and graduate from high school ...you know you could be Valedictorian next May when you walk?" she said with pride.

"Yeah Ma I know" I replied. "Mel just sounded like he was having so much fun so I wanna have fun like that too."

"Well baby, keep your head up and work hard and you can. Now Tina let's go!" She screamed for my sister. "I gotta get me a new outfit for the Memorial Day barbeque."

After they left, I was watching TV when I fell into a deep sleep and began to dream about Melvin. It was strange. He was touching me in places that guys had never touched me before. I was shocked because in the dream, I was enjoying it so much and I could tell by my responsiveness to Melvin. He was kissing me and touching me and the door bell rang and woke me ....

Set 2

It was around 2 o'clock and I wiped my eyes as I stumbled down the hall to answer the door.

"Who is it?" I yelled in a raspy sleep tone.

"Melvin" he answered. I slowly opened the door and saw him standing there in his usual Saturday, *"I ain't got nothing to do"* attire. He wore these basketball mesh shorts, a wife beater, long tube socks and his *Adidas* flip-flops. He thought he was "tight" in his get-up. The fact is he was!

"So you gonna let ya big brother in or not?" he laughed.

I took the chain off the door and let him in. After last night I got a little scared. I didn't know what Mel expected of me and it was really monopolizing my thoughts. We went in the living room and I turned on the television. I gave him the remote and went to the kitchen to get us something to drink. See, I knew what my big brother liked. He always liked to drink a *Nehi* Peach soda in a glass with only four ice cubes. Don't ask me why, that's just how he always had to have it.

When I returned to the couch he was watching Sports Center checkin out the highlights from last nights' sports competitions. Of course the Lakers and the Nicks were in the playoffs and if anyone liked the Lakers more than Melvin, they had to be from another planet.

"Man you and them sorry ass Lakers." I said as he turned to me with the ugliest face he could make which really wasn't possible since he was one of the most handsome brothers I had seen in my life.

"Man are you crazy?" he asked.

"Naw nigga you are." I replied after I handed him his drink. He sat the drink on the table and immediately after I sat my drink down, he tackled me to the couch.

"Man get off me." I shouted.

"Nigga fight back!" he shouted to me.

"Mel, I just woke up man and I don't feel like playing man" I whined.

"Aight." he said as he let me go. He relaxed in his seat and continued to watch TV.

"Cor?" Mel had been looking at me for a minute and I felt he was about to ask me something.

"Yeah man, wassup?"

"Did I make you feel uncomfortable last night?" he asked. For a minute there was complete silence.

"Melvin, I wasn't uncomfortable but I was nervous. You were holding me like I hold the girls and it was just strange. It felt good but it was strange."

He looked at me and smiled. I asked him why he was smiling and he replied.

"Cor, have you ever thought about me in any way except as your big brother?"

I looked at him and said "Naw nigga, I mean you like my best friend and my big brother." As I finished my statement, I remembered the dream I had just awaken from before he got to my house. "Mel, man actually before you got here, I had a dream about you." I said.

"So you gonna tell me about it man?" he seemed to get excited as I began to tell him how he was touching me and holding me in the dream. I told him how he was starting to kiss me when the doorbell rang and woke me up.

"Can I finish your dream for you Cor?" The look in his eyes was so sensual and I knew what he meant.

"Man what you talking about?" I said, in a tone becoming of a thug like I tried to be at times.

"I wanna make your dream come true Cor. I been thinking about you since I went away to school and I was hoping you wouldn't reject me when I held you in your sleep." At this point I began to feel a little weak, like I was about to give in. "Cor, I don't want you to think that I want to have sex with you. I want something real with you."

Okay, this was really confusing me. A guy wanting to have something *real* with another guy. Is that possible?

"I want you to be the person that I write letters to and the Valentine I send gifts to. I want to be the one who you look out and see on your graduation day. I wanna be more to you than just a big brother and a best friend, Cor. I want you to be mine!"

I put my head down, confused and scared, and went into deep thought. Mel lifted my head and pulled my face closer to him and began to kiss me softly on my lips. I resisted slightly but gave in because the feeling was soooooo wonderful. As soon as I began to let my eyes close, I saw the light of my mom's car pulling up to the drive way so I pushed back and got into chill mode as he moved back to the other side of the couch.

My mom had dropped my sister at one of her friends' house and couldn't get the door opened with all the bags she had from shopping. I opened the door and she was laughing at the fact that she could not even get through the door with the bags. Melvin came over to help and gave my moms a hug.

"Hey Momma" he said.

"Hey Mel, how you doin baby?" she said, sounding like someone's granny.

"I'm fine, just tryin to spend some quality time with my lil brother Cor." He replied.

"Are ya'll kids ever gonna call my baby by his name? It's Cordeaus, not **Cor!**"

Mel and I laughed and moms went off.

"Quit laughing and get these bags and close my door the air is on." she exclaimed.

We continued laughing as we carried the bags to her room. She was gonna start pulling everything out of the bags and telling us how good the deals she got were. Before she could start, Mel was already making his exit.

"Well Momma, I'm gonna go home now, we are taking my momma out to eat for her birthday." He said as he walked towards the door.

"Did she get the card and flowers we sent?" moms asked.

"Yes ma'am, they delivered them this morning and the card came in the mail yesterday. Oh by the way she's cooking and told me to ask ya'll to come over after church tomorrow." he told her.

"Well, tell her we will be there."

"Ok Ms. Hall." he replied. As I walked him to the door he turned to me and said " Please think about what I said Cor. Let me know when you are ready to let me know. I ain't rushing you. See ya later" he said and winked at me and I watched as his sexy bowlegs walked away from me yet calling me to follow. As I closed the door I heard moms yelling for me.

"Cordeaus Cortez Hall!" she screamed. "Come here boy." I entered her room and she showed me this dress she had bought. "Ain't yo momma fine?"

I laughed and she strutted in the long red and black gown she had gotten on sale at *Lilly Rubin* in the Mall. Honestly, for a 46 year old woman with a handsome son and a beautiful daughter, Moms is tight.

"Yes momma you are one foxy lady…and where you wearing that to?" I asked.

"That ain't cha business" she said in a sassy voice. "Now get out." she said as she laughed and closed the door behind me to get changed.

As I slowly walked to my bedroom, I began to think about the things that Mel and I had talked about. He made me think about my future, my relationships and whether something "real" was really possible between two guys; two guys like Mel and me.

Set 3

"Rain down on me Le le le le let it fall on meeaaee" Kirk Franklin and the Family blasted from the CD player in the living room. I was still in the bed and didn't really want to get up because I had been up all night thinking about Mel, and God and my senior year in high school and college and so many other things.

"C.C. get up now, you know I ain't gonna be late to service!" My mom was a very spiritual woman; not religious but spiritual. She was up at 6 o'clock every Sunday morning cooking breakfast and getting ready for church. I smelled the bacon and cheese eggs she was cooking this morning and decided to go ahead and get up to eat and get ready.

During church service, I looked around as I always did to see where my friends were so I could easily get to them after church. I saw Willie in the balcony and Markus was three pews in front of me. He turned around and gave me a head nod to acknowledge that he saw me. I responded likewise. The choir sang and everyone was up out of their seats. I was singing along with them and at the same time hoping no one came to sit by me so I could have some space this morning. Eleven o'clock service was always packed. As the choir finished and I was about to sit down, guess what? Someone came and sat down right beside me. To my surprise it was Melvin, his mom, dad and younger sister. We all enjoyed the rousing message from our pastor and as he began to close the service, we prayed and the choir sang *Til We Meet Again*. Another wonderful church service was over and me and my buddies fellowshipped outside when out of nowhere I got a pop on the back of my head. It was Melvin of course.

"See ya at the house man. My mom made a peach cobbler. She said it was yours but I know you gonna let me get some right?" he asked.

"Yeah man but I get first dibbs on it." I responded.

"Aight man see ya" he said as he walked with his parents to their car.

After church, I got home and took a nap before we were to go to dinner at Melvin's house. My mom woke me up when she was ready to go over. My sister came home while I was asleep and she gave me a bag with some things in it that she had gotten me from the mall. I didn't know she loved me like she did. She bought me some FUBU jeans and a silver platinum FUBU T-shirt and some White and Silver Nike sneakers. I was shocked and I couldn't stop thanking her. "I love my big brother" she said as we exited our home in transport to Mel's house. As we walked over I could see Mel looking out of his upstairs window. He made me a little nervous when he winked at me. I thought my mom and sister saw him but then realize that they were too far in front of me to see.

Melvin answered the door and took the dish from my mom's hand. She had made a banana pudding and let me tell you that bowl is gonna go home with us spotless. Melvin and his dad loved my momma's pudding. They always asked how she made it and she would never tell them. Mrs. Jackson would try to make it all the time and they would tell her that it just wasn't the same as my moms. As we proceeded into the house Mel popped me upside my head like he always does and copped a feel on my ass with a quickness that I never saw coming.

"Hey Mrs. Jackson, how are you?" I said with an excited tone.

"I'm fine baby, just fine. Happy that the Lord let me see another year. Nettie, I tell ya, your kids are growin up to be so handsome and pretty." she exclaimed while rubbing my sister's hair.

"Well, thank you, Gloria. Your heartbreaker ain't bad lookin hisself." My mom replied lookin at Melvin.

She was right too. It was something about him that just made you want him.

"Well I just hope he ain't breakin no hearts and ain't makin no babies either." she said with a smirk on her face that said a lot more than the words she had just spoken.

"For this food and fellowship we give thanks, Amen!"

If you could have heard the way Melvin spoke that prayer, you would have forgotten all about eating. I just sat there playing with my food and wondering why I was really beginning to feel the things that he had said to me the other night. Was I wrong for wanting to tell him yes? I mean he has been this close to me all this time and it would probably make us even closer if I just said yes to his proposition. What am I gonna do?

I began to make an attempt to eat the good home cookin Mrs. Jackson had prepared and I ate it all. I still couldn't stop thinking about Melvin and how he had been so patient and not hounded me about giving him an answer. After dinner, he and I washed dishes and put the food away. While doing so, he asked me had I given his question any thought. I told him that I had and his face lit up in such a way that if we turned all the lights off we wouldn't have trouble seeing anything.

"So are you gonna make me a happy bruh?" he asked with such sincerity. "I mean I just wanna go back to school knowing that besides my mom and pops, I have a reason to come home." When those words came out of his mouth I became offended slightly. Did he mean that I wasn't enough reason to come home without being his partner, lover or mate? Maybe he was just saying that it would be a more personal reason if we were an item? I don't know but it was confusing me and I just wanted to leave but something came over me.

"Mel, this is a hard decision for me to make. I mean you are like my big brother. I know you are only 3 years older but it's just that we have been this close for so long and I wouldn't want to risk that." He put down the drinking glasses that he was drying and turned completely facing me.

"I know what you mean but it won't be like that. If it doesn't work, I will always be your big brother and you will always be my lil buddy. Just give me a chance to love you like I wanna love you and show you what you mean to me, Cor." Silence was stiff in the room. I continued to wash the dishes and he just turned away in disgust. I don't wanna hurt him but what do I do. This would change my life. Was I really gay? All these things began to run through my mind and I couldn't take it. I told him that I needed to go home and I dried my hands and left. He tried to stop me and succeeded by standing in front of the door. His parents were in the den so they couldn't hear anything.

"Don't leave, Cor! Stay the night! You know it is cool with your mom and my parents if you stay here. Please for me?" I looked into his eyes and the seriousness of his words pierced me.

"Can I go get some clothes and my house key?" I said with a slight attitude. He let me out and I walked home slowly. It seemed like I was in my own world cause all I saw was lights flashing and the next thing I know it was complete darkness......

I couldn't believe I had been hit by an SUV. I must have been in such a deep train of thought about Melvin that I wasn't paying attention as I crossed the street and here I am laying up in a hospital. I hear the beeps and feel the tubes in my arms but I don't wanna open my eyes. I can't feel anything but pain. I hope I am not here alone but if I am so what. As I opened my eyes the first and only face I see is Melvin's.

"Cor, can you hear me? How you feelin?" he asked.

"What happened" I said with sleep still in the sound of my voice.

"Man you were walking across the street to go home and I heard this screeching sound and the next thing I know you were laying there stiff as a nail. It was a drunk driver in an *Explorer*. The doctor said you will be fine but they still have to run some more tests."

I looked around to see if my mother was hiding behind the curtains or something. No one else was there. "Where is my mom Melvin?" I asked with a tremble in my voice.

"She went to go call her job to tell them she wouldn't be in today. She was here all night with you and I was too." Was I really hearing this? My big brother stayed here with me while I was sleeping and hurting?

"So did they catch the guy?" I asked.

"Well, I got outside in just enough time to get the license plate number and I told the police when they arrived. They found him about two miles down the road and arrested him for attempted murder and drunk driving."

"What if I would have died? What if he had killed me with that truck?" I began to cry and the tears filled my eyes and rolled down my face.

Melvin whispered in my ear "I would have died inside" and kissed me on the cheek. I knew that when I got out of this hospital, I was gonna be his and his only. I knew that we would be together.

"Melvin, can I have a moment with my baby?" my mom had entered the room. Her face was flushed.

" Yes ma'am." he said softly as he gave her a hug and went into the waiting room with my sister.

"Baby, how you feelin?" I had never seen my mother so sad. She looked as if she had almost lost her world. "Cordeaus, you are my first born and only son. When Melvin came and told me what had happened I couldn't even speak. I ran to the street so fast that I almost ran pass you lying there." We both giggled. "I never dreamed of my only son getting hurt. You are always so careful about everything and to see you lying there helpless, not breathing; it just tore me apart." I could see the pain in my mother's eyes. I wanted to hold her but my body hurt so bad that I couldn't stand to be touched too long.

"Momma, I love you and I promise I will be more careful next time. I just had a lot on my mind." Although I couldn't tell her what it was, I knew she was there and would always be there no matter what.

"Can I see my lil brother now?" shouted Melvin.

"I know right. I haven't seen my big brother since dinner last night." My little sister chimed in.

"Hey Niki, come give ya brother some love babygirl." She came over and hugged me and I flinched and she started cryin.

"What's wrong baby girl?" I grabbed her arm.

"I thought my brother was dead. You the only brother I got and I don't know if I could have gone on without you." Her tears began to flow like the Mississippi River after a storm.

"You would have had momma and I know Mel would have been there for you just like he's been there for me. He loves you and mom just as much as he loves me. Let's not talk about that though. You know what? Today, I was gonna wear my new clothes you bought me at the mall, but it looks like I gotta wait til I get outta here." As I spoke, I saw her face brighten up and the tears subsided.

"Visiting hours are over for the morning." A nurse had come in to check my vitals and make sure I was ok. Everyone gave me a kiss on my forehead and as Melvin was leaving I grabbed his hand and whispered "YES". He knew exactly what I was speaking of and his face was spread like the smile on the Kool-Aid Man. He let the door close slowly as he looked at me until our eyes departed each other. This was the person I would fall in love with and he was a man.

After a week of tests and treatment I was finally released from the hospital. Since the doctor's couldn't reach my mom I called Melvin. He came to pick me up and was so gentle as the touch of cotton in the way he handled me. When we got to our street, before he parked the car he asked me if I wanted to go to my house or stay at his house. I told him that I would rather stay with him until my moms got home. He was happy and I could tell by the way he quickly pulled into his driveway. I asked him where his parent's cars were he said his moms car was in the garage and they had driven to Galveston for the weekend. As he helped me in the house, I sat on the couch and grabbed the phone to call my moms job. "Thank you for calling Hall & Brown LLP, this is Ms. Hall speaking."

My mom was so professional when she answered the phone. She was a successful divorce attorney and in Texas, divorce lawyers had plenty of business.

"Ma, it's C.C." I said.

"Hey baby, where are you?" She kept her cool because she was at work.

"I am at Melvin's. He came and got me after they couldn't contact you."

"I am sorry baby, I was with a client. Is Melvin takin care of you? Put him on the phone." She didn't even give me time to answer the question. "Melvin, you take care of my baby 'til I get home you hear?" She was talking to him like he was her child. "Yes ma'am. He's in good hands."

I didn't know what Mel meant by that until he hung up the phone and turned to me.

"So are you sure you wanna be mine and mine only Cor?" I did say yes didn't I?

"Melvin I said yes and that's what I meant man."

With that, Melvin helped me up off the couch and led me upstairs to his room.

He undressed me to my boxer briefs and laid me down on the bed. He undressed his self and laid there with me. He held me and caressed my body with a touch that felt like the finest of silks. As he rubbed my chest and grazed my nipples from behind, he slowly turned me over on my back and began to use his tongue to explore every part of my being. He started at the top of my forehead, softly maneuvering the tool across my face. As he reached my lips, he slid in my mouth and wrestled with my tongue. He pulled out and to each ear he went. He must have realized that my ear was one of the few spots that made me quiver because he didn't let up. His tongue searched every nook and corner of my ear. He slowly moved from my ear to my neck licking in circular motions making me tremble with every rotation.

He came back to the entrance of my mouth and licked my lips quickly before moving to my chest. He sat up and inspected my nipples and began to gently caress them as if they were delicate flowers that he wanted to protect. He then took the right one in his hand as he seductively led his eyes and mine to the left one. He began to touch the nipple with his tongue and started to lick around the nipple as it began to grow hard. Sucking the left nipple, he grabbed the right one, squeezing with force. I enjoyed the roughness because he traded back and forth; ruff with gentility. I began to moan at this point because this feeling was overwhelming. As he began to move down I could feel his hard penis on my leg. It had to be at least ten inches long and it was thick. I thought *"Damn, can I handle something that size?"* Well today was *gonna* be the day I tried.

As he continued to treat my nipples like ice cream he didn't want to waste, he rubbed my arms and lifted me up as to make room to grab my ass and grab he did. He pulled me closer to him as his tongue went up and down my stomach and torso area and on my sides and around my navel. I began to moan even louder with ecstasy. He was making me feel like I had never felt

At this point, he was making his way toward my member. He took it in his hand and began to stroke it with such care that I thought I would release from just his touch but I held back. He lowered his mouth onto the head and began to lick around it and gradually insert it into his hot waiting mouth. I instinctively grabbed his head and was running my hands over it when he deep throated me and I almost came. He continued with much patience as to say he didn't want to stop. He then moved down and took my balls in his mouth lickin and rotating them and then he did something that made me jump, but felt so good. He started to hum with my balls in his mouth. It was an amazing feeling. *Like I was vibrating from a remote source or something.* He did this for a few seconds and went on to lick lower. He lifted my legs up and spread the cheeks of my ass and began to circle my hole with his lips. The sensation was exhilarating. He then probed the hole with his tongue making an attempt to get me loose. This was hard because I had never done anything with a man and my ass was tight as 4 fat women in a YUGO. He loosened me up and inserted one finger inside me. He then stopped. He reached into a drawer near his bed, pulled out some KY Jelly and a condom. He put the condom on himself and gave me the KY to rub on my entrance. I was on my stomach and was hoping this was the best way to take what he had to give.

Mel began to play with my hole using the head of his dick. The warmth of his member warmed the entrance to my insides. He inserted the head and I moaned in pain. He was a big brother in that area.. He told me to relax and I immediately did. The sound of his voice made you relax. It was so smooth and soothing. So as he began to push in I began to push out. The muscles of my ass started to loosen up allowing him full access to what he wanted. He stoked slowly for a while and then would speed up and slow down making me feel every inch of his huge piece. He made me feel like a man and it felt good to know that he didn't want me to moan like the females he had been with.

"I want to know that if I close my eyes right now that I am making love to a man." he said with strength in his tone. SO being the man that I am I obliged. After moments of his slow, deliberate movements in and out of me the pain subsided. I wanted it faster now.

"Fuck me yo! GO faster! It feels so good." I exclaimed in breathless tones. "I think I love you Melvin." I said without hesitation. He slowed down and lowered himself to my ear and said "I love you to Cor and I want us to be together always." As he began to slow down I could feel the fluids rising up through the apparatus inside me. HE began to speed up again and started to shout "I'm coming baby, I'm coming!!!" He grabbed my waist and began to thrust with every bit of force he had. He came and I could feel the hot fluids release into the condom and his dick going limp. It was still hard enough to keep itself inside me and he seemed as if that's where he wanted it to be. He collapsed onto my back with the sweat causing our bodies to stick together. He lay on my back as we slept good sleep for hours until I moved and woke him.

"You ok, Baby?" He asked with sleep and concern in his voice.

"Yeah just hot. Can you turn the air on?" I asked.

"Of course baby, anything for you." he answered in that sexy seductive manner he was known for. I knew that this was the person for me. I wonder did he know the same thing.

"You know I leave for school next week right?" Melvin said in an unenthused tone.

"Yeah I know. So what does that mean for us?" I asked.

"Cor, I love you but I don't know when I will be able to see you again. I don't want to hurt you but I don't know if I can only be with you. I love you but when I get back to school, I know I am not going to be able to resist the females, Cor. You know I still like women."

After this, I was about to start cryin when he grabbed my head and put it to his chest and began to kiss the crown of my head.

"Don't cry baby! I will always love you but I can't hurt you knowingly." His words soothed my pain but only for a second. The tears started to roll down my cheeks as I released myself from his embrace and left the comfort of his room.

As I stepped in my front door I quickly wiped my eyes as I heard my mother calling me to the kitchen. Of course she was cooking some of her famous fried chicken and mashed potatoes.

"Cor, come taste these potatoes" she screamed. I entered the kitchen, face red from the tears and she could tell something was wrong. "Baby, are you alright?"

"I'm fine Ma." I lied and she, being my mother, could figure that out.

"What is it Cor?" she asked. As I started to tell her, the tears started flowing heavily. "Ma, Mel is leavin next week. He's going back to school and he said he doesn't know when he will see me again." She tried to comfort me and it worked. There is no touch like that from your mom.

"Baby, he will be back. You know that." She spoke with confidence. "He'll come back to see you, baby. You're his lil brother." I left it at that with ma.

Mel didn't even call or stop by to say good- bye. He was gone from me and I didn't know when or if he would be back.

I started and finished my senior year in grand style. I graduated number 7 in my class of 467 students and got accepted in the one of the best HBCU's in the country - Hampton University.

The summer after graduation, all I did was sit on my porch and wait for Mel.

He never came.

The Worm
Taylor Siluwé

"If the fish are sleep, how we gonna catch 'em?"

Buddha queried, settling down as instructed. The rocking slowed and for a moment all that was heard was the gentle splish-splash of the oars.

"They're waking up now," I said, smiling.

"And they'll want *this* for breakfast?" He grinned and pulled a huge Night crawler out of the container and I winced inwardly; it squirmed in the strange carroty light of almost-morning, as if it knew the end was near.

"Yeah, according to that guy at the tackle shop, they will." He'd even looked over his glasses and said ... *Be gentle with them up there*, which sorta creeped me out.

I rowed us out toward the middle of the Baker Lake, which sat in a crescent-shaped basin surrounded by pines in Monroe, NY. I could see Mike and Tito's summer cabin near the shoreline; the bathroom light drawing my eye like a beacon in the mist. I made a mental note to not be so careless with their electricity.

It was so serene and tranquil and quiet that my mind went blank, as if sucked dry by the void. No, not blank really - open. And I felt almost sedated. Like the time they gave me Lithium in the emergency room when I was rushed in with chest pains. The pains were fake, a minor ruse to get out of work, but I had hyperventilated so much with my performance that I felt like I really was dying.

Drenched in sweat on that 90-degree day, all I'd wanted was to get out of the tunnel for a while, chill in a nice cool hospital while enduring a relaxing battery of tests. Then I'd take the next week off (doctor's orders, of course) and luxuriate at Riis beach under my canopy with a cooler full of beer and my trusty binoculars. It seemed like a good way to end the monotony of watching traffic whiz beneath the Hudson River from my tiny booth with an air-conditioner which wasn't living up to its name. Boredom and misery made to do crazy things while waiting for a car to breakdown. So I fingered my mic and made the call, adding that I couldn't breathe for good measure.

A few minutes of dramatic breathing and blaring sirens later, I was on a squeaky gurney being wheeled down a corridor. A very *cool* corridor. An IV was put in place and then a nurse said, "This should make you feel better," and sent a hypodermic of Lithium into my vein.

BAM!

Instant bliss and serenity; like floating on a Lake at sunrise with your seven-year-old son you rarely got to see, preparing to fish with him for the very first time, and bond, and have those poignant conversations that only a father and young son can have, out in a tiny boat, alone together.

"Do worms taste like chicken?" Buddha asked, putting it close to his face as if he was gonna test my answer.

"Maybe to the fish they do. Or better, maybe they taste like bacon."

He pondered in that squinty way we shared and I saw a snapshot of myself, a little older than him, getting my first pair of glasses. Then he inexplicably squeezed it in his fist and dark juices ran over his hand. He examined it further as the poor creature thrashed in distress. I stopped rowing; water dripping from the oars - which hovered over the lake's dark surface like a dragonfly – was the only sound.

I liked bugs as a kid, but not worms. Worms were just gross no matter how you looked at it; they oozed dirt from their little worm asses and if you hacked one in half the pieces wiggled in opposite directions. They were nature's most disgusting life form, no doubt about it. Unlike some little boys, I would cry and run away if someone showed me a worm. Squeezing the juice out of one of them with my bare hand would have sent me straight into therapy. My revulsion was under control; my rational adult mind knew that worms couldn't hurt me. Still, I kept my dealings with them very limited.

But Buddha was on another level.

"No," he sniffed it, "Chicken."

"Yeah, that's probably our best bet. Everything else does." I almost joked that neither of us was ever gonna find out, but realized that Buddha was likely to shock me, yet again, by tasting the gooey mess and forcing me to the realization that my one and only was a little demented. I didn't want that epiphany so I froze a smile and ran through possible future occupations for him, ones where his special detachment might come in handy. Surgeon and serial-killer were all that came to mind.

He stuck his hand in the water and splashed it clean, sending the macerated worm to its watery grave. "Do they go to Hell?" he asked.

"*What?*"

"Worms. When they die."

Tory strikes again. She was determined to blind this boy before he ever got to see. I struggled to hold onto that picture of bliss from seconds before - that bucolic, almost Norman Rockwell-*esque* snapshot of serenity.

Tory was a "saved" co-worker who I'd instantly bonded with when I started working at the tunnel a decade ago. Exactly why is still a mystery, maybe because she was funny and I didn't know anyone else. But she clearly had a different agenda, which asserted itself after my New Year's Eve bash. "... I mean what makes you think they go to Hell, Buddha. Why not Heaven?"

"'Cause they're gross. Heaven is for good stuff."

He had a point. Who the hell would want to be in a Heaven full of all the worms ever martyred on a hook? But I took a deep breath, "Well, I don't think worms go anywhere. When they die they die. After all, they're just worms." I impaled a couple on our hooks trying to think of something else, something pleasant, and something without a moist, squiggling life-form in it.

"Momma said *you're* going," Buddha continued.

This was no secret. She'd told me more than once with a conviction that suggested she was Hell's hall monitor and could see me coming. "Your momma says a lot of things she shouldn't. Don't let her frighten you with all her stories and her Hellfire. Daddy's not going anywhere." I gave him his rod. After brief instruction, we mildly cast them into the water.

"Not even Heaven?"

I pondered barely a second, "No. Not even there."

"Why?"

"Well, to tell you the truth, I don't believe there is a Heaven ... or a Hell." When at a loss for words, sometimes it's best to spit your truth and let the chips fall wherever.

"Why?"

"You have to move it around a little, so it looks like the worm is swimming and the fish'll see it. And turn your reel some, like this—" I demonstrated, remembering how Buddha had whined when I'd suggested this fishing trip. He'd wanted to go to Six Flags instead, but I knew he was too small to enjoy all the rides. I really didn't want to get into the religion thing at sunrise on the lake, but I had no intentions of ever lying to him.

The truth hurt sometimes, but it was always best - straight-up, no chaser or bullshit.

He trailed his rod left and right, bobbing it a little here and there. He already looked more at home than I did. My fishing experience was meager; but for the snapshot of us doing it together, I'd even touch worms. And this was so much better than watching roller coasters Buddha was too short to ride anyway.

"You don't believe in nothing. That's why momma said, 'cause you don't believe in nothing."

That hypocritical bible-thumpin' bitch. My eyes narrowed as I watched him fiddling with his pole, fat cheeks reflecting the sunrise, belly peeking out from beneath his tee-shirt. He got my bad eyes and his mother's weight problem, poor kid. Since he was born, Tyler Jr. was big, clocking in at ten pounds. He was so round, I nicknamed him Buddha that very first day, already seeing the Weight Watchers meetings and expensive unused home-exercise equipment in his future. Now, it seemed, it was my duty alone to keep him from turning into a fat, nearsighted, evangelical serial killer - or surgeon.

"Do you remember the story of the three little pigs?"

"The wolf blew their house in. Except the last one 'cause he used bricks."

"Do you think there really *were* three pigs who built houses?"

He just stared and blinked.

"You ever see a pig build anything? A real pig, I mean. Not cartoon ones like Porky. I mean, like the ones we saw at the farm. Did you see any of them with a tool-belt on?"

He shook his head.

"Do you think it's even possible for them to pick up a hammer with their hooves, or turn a screwdriver?"

Buddha just scratched his head. I didn't want to talk about God on the Lake at sunrise. But somehow it seemed appropriate, or meant to be.

"The three little pigs is a fairy-tale about hard work, that's why the lazy ones who built their houses with quick cheap material get eaten. It teaches us a valuable lesson though. Can you tell me what it is?"

Buddha pondered for a barely a second, "That they shoulda prayed?"

A final cricket chirped in the distance.

Tory had been working overtime. Did she read the Bible to him over Corn Flakes? He'd clearly been getting a one-sided message from his mother — beliefs indoctrinated into her by her mother and her grandmother before that, all the way back to a time when masters whipped it into the godless heathens they'd captured and enslaved.

"No, no Buddha, it's not about God. It teaches us not to build our houses with straw. And that means not to do anything half-way, or lazily. The lesson is: hard work pays off. That's all."

"Oh," he said, as he made his worm dance in the water. With a mother hell-bent on making him a Christian warrior, I knew I had to step up to balance the scales. It was at that perfect point in early sunrise when stars were still visible in the west. I pointed to them. Buddha followed my gaze.

"Thousands of years ago, before technology and all that, when people lived in caves and whatnot, man squatted around fires and looked up at those same stars and wondered what all those lights were. He wondered about all sorts of things, watching those stars, or staring into the flames. Actually, that's what early man did best, wonder about stuff."

Buddha turned from the stars to me, "Why?"

I smiled, "Because there was no internet. He had to figure it out for himself. Early man couldn't just search 'bright lights in the sky' and get answers on his computer."

"Google."

My smile broadened. "Yeah, he couldn't do that. So men wondered and pondered until eventually some of the most talented came up with answers. Those answers were told over and over just as I'm telling you now ... because they couldn't write back then. Finally, when they could write, they wrote them down. Over time these writings were rewritten and rewritten until they were embraced by different communities and became their religion. Different writings became different religions, and thousands of years later, here we are."

He just stared back at me as the stars faded and the orange light grew. I knew I had unloaded a bit much for even his sharp mind to comprehend, but I felt good having said it. Maybe he'd remember when he needed it; another snapshot set to ignite like an ancient flashbulb. But he surprised me again.

"So it's just a *story?*" he asked.

"No. I didn't say that. I *am* saying that man needed a story, and one came to him. Whether or not God put it into his head is hotly debated. Your mother and a lot of people think it was. But a lot of other people don't. I just wanna make sure that you know there are two sides to every story, and that you should always learn both."

Pushing him hard toward agnostic thought was almost as irresponsible as programming 'The Rapture' into his mind. Almost. But she'd clearly been hammering her gospel into his young brain, where it might fester and hobble him for life; I saw no reason to hold back the flip side.

"So great-nanna's not with Jesus?" He asked, looking up at the sky again.

"Nobody knows for sure, no matter what they tell you. Everyone thinks they know, but they don't—not even me."

I felt his pain. Tory wanted him to believe he'd be snatched up to Heaven one day while riding his bicycle to be one with God and Jesus, where he and the other 'believers' would look down on the non-believers as we suffered tribulation. She said I would be one of those people destined to suffer and ultimately burn because I loved my own gender. Apparently, lonely fat women who fornicate with drunken gay men were cool. I wanted him to be suspect of stories which required suspension of common-sense. But that was my hard-fought conclusion. Buddha would come to his own one day.

A loud splash nearby rocked the boat and drizzled lake water all over us.

"What's that?!" Buddha shrieked, gazing at the disturbance in the water. A large ripple moved across the dark surface east and west before slowly disappearing. Soon the water grew still again.

"I guess … uh, that means the fish are up." I said with relative calm, but still felt unnerved. It sounded and felt like a huge boulder had fallen into the water – or had been thrown. Suddenly my mind flashed an image of Bigfoot – who, according to those obsessed with catching him, is known to throw boulders at men. This wasn't what I'd signed on for.

"My worm is gone," Buddha said, dangling his empty rod.

I plucked another from the container. It wiggled thickly between my fingers and the usual chill raced down my spine. I angled the hook and took a deep breath.

"Does that hurt the worm?"

"What? Oh, uh, I don't think so. At least I hope not." Did the worm scream on a frequency we couldn't hear? Were we the worm community's tormentors, impaling them on hooks for sport? Did they secretly fear us, or, with their minimal worm understanding, maybe even worship us? But because I hated worms and didn't care if they hurt or prayed, I impaled the little fucker, and it thrashed as if it felt every bit of that cold metal.

Buddha dangled it into the water. His eyes became lost in the sky again, "Did great-nanna believe in Heaven?"

"Yeah, she did." It's was all she really believed in. It was the place where life would finally begin, and all the pain and suffering and death which torment the living would be no more. She was so consumed with that life, she never really lived this one all that much. I'd kept my disbelief from her.

I heard a smaller splash and looked out over the Lake. A ripple appeared. Two of them actually, moving north and south in a V-formation from a central point which was coming toward the boat.

I sat up straighter – an icy sensation gripping my gut. I dropped my rod, grabbed the oars and immediately began to steer us back to shore. There shouldn't be anything remotely dangerous in Baker Lake, but whatever was making its way toward us was clearly no guppy.

"What is it?"

"It's a fish, a big angry one...."

"Cool!" Buddha said, squinting at the thing.

"Just hold on!" I put my back into it, long quick strokes that made me glad for all those hours on the rowing machine at the gym. Soon we were moving at a good clip and I kept my eyes on the ripple. It changed direction about ten degrees and picked up tremendous speed, causing more ripples to race across the water. Still I rowed, more desperately now, craning my neck as the thing past us before disappearing again. But this time we'd clearly seen a piece of it, its oily back catching the early light as it dived.

"It's the Loch Ness Monster!" Buddha chimed excitedly.

"There's no such thing," I said, almost to myself.

"Yes-*huh*. I saw it on the TV!" He sprang up and moved toward the front of the boat, his shifting weight rocking us precariously.

"Sit down!" I ordered, images of prehistoric sea creatures flashing in my mind. Still I rowed. There were no monsters, but there was certainly something very large and fast out there, something I didn't wanna meet. The moment I glanced over my shoulder toward the shoreline, we hit something and all forward motion stopped; except for me falling backward - striking my head on the edge of the boat - and Buddha stumbling on top of me.

All was white for a second as I clung to consciousness, but when my head cleared I realized that the oars were gone. I sat up wondering what we'd hit. But there was nothing, just calm water and my oars floating way out of reach already.

"What happened, Daddy?" He still clung to my chest. I wrapped an arm around and held him tightly there.

"I don't know." But I knew I had to get those oars back. So I stuck my free hand into the water and tried to move us toward them. But it was useless bordering on ridiculous; they were even further away now. I made an instant decision. "You know what, Buddha, I'm gonna get in the water and push us back. You just sit tight, okay?"

He nodded. I released him and slipped into the water, ignoring the sudden cold and images of ravenous sea creatures lurking beneath me.

"Watch out for the monster."

"There is *no* monster," I snapped, as I hung onto the back of the boat kicking my legs, inching us closer to the pier. "It's just a fish." I didn't relish talk of sea monsters with my body helpless in the water.

"Yes-*huh* ... it's right there." I yanked myself higher and looked past Buddha's pointing silhouette. The cold of the water suddenly shot to my heart.

A shiny black thing protruded five or six feet out of the water about mid-way between us and the shoreline, glistening in the orange light. At first, my mind couldn't comprehend what it was, couldn't come up with anything rational to explain it. It twisted and turned disgustingly, dripping oily seaweed and crud off its body; it rose higher as if sniffing the air for something. Then, as if sucked back down into the water, it vanished in a flash leaving barely a ripple behind.

Suddenly I knew what it was. Still, the impossibility of it wrestled with what I'd just seen with my own eyes. The shape of it, the segmented body leading up to a narrow tip: It was a worm - a monstrous worm which seemed to be searching for us. I kept kicking my legs, pushing us ever closer to the pier, fear twisting my guts, believing at any moment I was going to be sucked beneath the water by my worst nightmare. Then something bumped my leg, something large and meaty. A flurry of splashing later, I was back in the boat.

"What's wrong?"

"Quiet!" I screamed, glancing around, panting, and eyeing the still water. The serenity I'd felt was long gone, replaced by an eerie Stephen King atmosphere of unreality and impending doom. All I could think about was getting Buddha to shore.

I didn't know if the worm was actually looking for us or whether it just happened to be passing by. The only thing I had to go on were the habits of its tiny cousins, several of which I'd just impaled on hooks. A shudder of dread wracked my body, but it might have been from the cold. I sat silent for a few moments, arms wrapped around my now shivering torso, feeling lost and helpless and trying to keep my knees from knocking.

Buddha just stared. He wasn't afraid. When I was a boy, I feared all sorts of imaginary monsters — under the bed, in the closet, and the one that appeared in the basement the instant I turned off the light. As I watched him, I realized that it could be worse; I could have a hysterical child on my hands on top of everything else. Bless his calmness. He certainly didn't get his fearless gene from me.

Tory was fearless, I guess, if that means bodacious and calculating and always went for what she wanted, and then yes, she was. After the party that fateful night, she stayed to help clean. I just wanted her to go, but she insisted. I don't know what happened next, having so much champagne in my veins, but when I awoke mid-afternoon, we were naked in bed together. Our relationship got weird after that, even weirder when she informed me that she was pregnant.

It was a nightmare, not my very worst but a nightmare still. At first I didn't believe I'd actually done it. I just couldn't imagine I'd fondled her 44D's and jiggled her love-handles and managed to get an erection. I couldn't imagine that I'd lifted her thick dark thighs into the air and fucked her beneath Marky Mark's famous Calvin Klein ad which hung over my bed at the time. Maybe he had something to do with it. But vague memories began to surface, snapshots and whisperings from a night which would go down in history as the most wonderfully horrific mistake I ever made.

"Don't be scared, Daddy." Buddha said, placing a hand on my trembling knee. "Let's be real quiet, and the monster will go back to sleep."

I smiled and my teeth started to chatter. Yeah, my Buddha was a blessing, despite his mother. I'd practically had to beg for this weekend alone at the cabin. She thought fishing was too dangerous.

And where did you learn how to fish anyway, on Christopher St.? She'd asked with a vile smirk.

I looked her square in the eye — *'Instead of driving a wedge between us, you should consider him very lucky because I'm not out making a mob of half-siblings to compete with him.'*

Now, it seemed, fishing was too dangerous after all. With a giant worm, or whatever, circling beneath us somewhere, I opted to take Buddha's advice and sit quietly. I damn sure wasn't getting back in the water right away, but I knew I would have to eventually. The other option was we could both dive in and make it to shore in under a minute. Buddha could swim like a fish. When he was a baby, while Tory still clung to the hope of us becoming a "real" family (as if one drunken fuck had turned me straight), we'd take him to the beach and to pools and spent hours in the water. He could even float, which is something I could never do. I guess that extra fat gene made him buoyant.

A long time passed with no sight of the worm. Still, my knees knocked and teeth chattered. I felt myself losing further control. I had to get us back to the cabin. I envisioned sitting wrapped in a blanket by the fireplace with a snifter of brandy. But I was so cold, and I couldn't shake the thought that something slimy wanted to eat us.

Times like these made a person pray. Prayer somehow focused one's energy to that pin-point of light envisioned in the mind; what I liked to believe was akin to George Lucas' all-powerful energy field. I took deep breaths and began to silently pray ....

Please, let us make it to shore. Help me pull it together and stop thinking about my son being swallowed by a worm.

Almost immediately I felt warmer. The shaking was subsiding. My energy was rising; I looked into his eyes. "We might have to swim for it. You ready for that?"

He nodded, and immediately pulled a slightly smashed mini-Snicker Bar from his pocket, ripped off the wrapper and gobbled it down. I'd told him no candy bars this weekend. Apparently he'd smuggled one anyway and the thought of getting it wet was too much to bear.

"You got any more ...." A slight hissing sound cut off my words.

The worm had risen with disturbing stealth right next to us as if it had been there submerged all along, waiting. As it turned to me, dripping greenish sludge, I stared right into the pinched hole which served as its face. It undulated and contorted and I was frozen and unable to look away. Then it opened wide and hissed and I saw row upon row of tiny backward pointing teeth inside the hole. Still, I stared, frozen.

Another splash broke my trance. Buddha had jumped into the water. I immediately flipped in after him.

It was colder than earlier. Buddha was breast-stroking his way toward shore, pudgy arms and legs propelling him with such efficiency I felt a warm swelling in my heart. Fearless little Buddha.

Let us make it to shore. Let us make it to shore. Don't let that thing get my boy.

Or me.

I felt my strength ebbing into the water like a battery losing its charge, but I kept swimming. Buddha seemed okay; about twenty more feet and he'd be out of danger. We were almost there and I started to smile in my mind, but still, I continued with my mantra.

Let us make it to shore. Let us make it to .... Something awful and cold and strong enveloped my leg and lake and sky switched places. I could still see Buddha moving toward shore, but moving now across a dark liquid sky miraculously suspended over nothing.

But the earth hadn't moved. And as water rained down my torso over my face, I realized that I had moved, and was now suspended upside-down over the water. I looked up toward my foot and screamed so loud I got dizzy. Or maybe it was all the blood rushing to my head.

The Worm had me in its mouth, one leg all the way up to the knee. The pressure increased and it sucked me further in as I struggled and kicked with my free leg. Its mouth worked, lips inching me further and further in, working their way down over my thigh now. I even heard sounds, like the little yummy sounds Buddha made when he ate ice-cream, but more guttural mixed with moist sucking inhalations. My worst nightmare was coming true: It was eating me alive. When the pressure increased and I felt sharp pains, everything went into slow-motion: I could see Buddha swimming, as if he didn't hear my scream. The miniscule part of my brain which wasn't hysterical with fear was happy about that. He would get out of the water. But then what? He'd be alone and hear his father screaming as The Worm consumed him. I couldn't let that happen.

I reached up and dug my fingers into its liver-like flesh, clawing at it like a crazy person, yelling that it wasn't gonna take me, beating it back so furiously that it bellowed and let me go in the process. I plunged into the water again, momentarily lost in a cold explosion of bubbles and muted sounds.

In a nanosecond I was swimming after Buddha. I'd lost all sense of form and wasn't trying to breath left and right. I just aimed myself in the proper direction and swam like lightning, gulping air whenever I had to.

Please, don't let it get me. Don't let it get me.

I heard Buddha's muted voice. "Swim daddy! Faster!"

He was on the shore already; I caught a quick glimpse, gulped air and put my head down again, determined to make it back in one last burst of energy. The force was with me — I could feel it in every cell of my body — and I knew it wouldn't let me be eaten by an evolutionary hiccup disguised as a worm.

Then it swallowed my arm like an anaconda. I was out of the water again, being shaken so hard I thought my shoulder would break. Its mouth worked even more hideously now, sucking over my shoulder and onto my neck, trying to get my head in. That potentiality sent me into a panic and I screamed and clawed at the soft tissue inside its throat. It wasn't gonna swallow me alive. There was no way in Hell.

Through my panic, I could hear Buddha.

"Please God; don't let the monster eat my daddy!" He kept repeating it over and over as I ripped pieces of flesh from inside its throat, until dark blood gushed from the thing and I plunged down into the water once more. Almost too breathless to swim, miraculously, a few moments later, I was stumbling onto dry land, shivering and giddy.

Buddha hugged me, and I said, "Let's get back to the cabin." I needed to put as much distance between us and the water as possible.

"You made God angry." Buddha said, in his calm detached way.

We moved toward shelter and a warm fire and away from squiggling death. I needed heat in my bones before I could process the events, make sense of it all. Because my mind was still abuzz, still flashing snapshots of my life — a sort of delayed reaction to almost being eaten, I guess. As I looked back, expecting to see The Worm moving hungrily across dry land in pursuit, a Shakespearean quote flashed in my head:

There are more things in heaven and earth, Horatio, than are dreamt of in your philosophy. No shit.

"Or, maybe," I said, as I opened the door to safety, my sense of humor trying to return, "We *really* pissed off the worms."

Morning light was just beginning to chase the night's restful gloom from the room as Buddha rushed inside ahead of me. Three steps in — as if it had been waiting impatiently — The Worm erupted through the floor in a geyser of splinters and globules of dirt-infused slime. It seemed even larger than it had on the lake, its head bent just beneath the ceiling fan, its hideous mouth agape - emitting an oily-sounding hiss. Thrown to the ground by the ferocity of its arrival and blinded by earth and goo raining around me, I still saw Buddha teetering where an area rug had turned into a crater, trying not to fall into it. Before I could stand and do anything heroic, The Worm, to my rising horror, grabbed him by the waist and began shaking him like a shark tearing into a surfer.

"Buddha!" I shrieked and my body went cold. I sprung from the ground and lunged at The Worm ... grabbing onto it I found myself sliding downward in the dark crater. I clawed at the thing and at the moist dirty walls of the crater as it rose around me; the space got tighter and my face was pressed between the crater wall and the slimy beast — which smelled like dirt and rotting meat. Buddha's voice faded; his shrieks of *"Daddy, daddy, help me!!"* grew fainter and fainter and more pitiful. Yet I was pinned and helpless. I could do nothing. I couldn't even safe myself. As mud and water filled in around me, a nightmare I'd never dreamt was coming to claim me and my son. Neither of us would wake up from this. *Oh, God,* I prayed as I gave into the almost inevitable with water and mud rising fast past my chin, *please let this all be a dream....*

"Daddy, Daddy!" Buddha's voice, gurgling and more muffled now, but oddly closer — accompanied by a rhythmic thumping against my face, leading to the horrifying reality that he was screaming to me and struggling from inside The Worm's body.

"Dad-deeeeeee!"

Buddha's hysterics became sharper, louder, and something was bumping my shoulder. I realized my eyes had closed and forced them open again. The Worm seemed to back away a little, twisting and contorting its body with Buddha's voice still emitting from it, now clear as a bell. It bumped me again and it's segmented body turned into the blue and white stripes of one of Buddha's favorite tee-shirts.

I gulped air as if I'd been holding my breath as the cabin came into view around me. My eyes darted around looking for The Worm. Seeing no signs of it, they settled on Buddha, standing by the sofa bed.

"It's six o'clock," he looked down at me, "You said we 'd go on the lake early and I'm hungry."

In a flash I had him in my arms, unable to speak, not yet convinced it was all a dream. He squirmed away after a few shocked moments and restated his breakfast demand. I staggered out of bed and around the cabin, looking for splinters and dirt and goo. There was none. I went to the window next and stared out over the dark waters of Baker Lake, the sky not yet tinged with the orange light of the dream. I squinted, looking for a tell tale sign. Nothing. Still, I stood vigil, waiting for it to reveal itself, as if the nightmare had been a premonition. *It felt. So. Real.*

"Daddy? Are you sick?" Buddha appeared next to me.

"No, I uh ... just had a dream, that's all." I said, peeling my attention from the lake and looking into his eyes.

"About what?" His eyes sparkled with interest.

"About uh ... roller coasters. What do you say we grab some breakfast on the way to Six Flags?"

"Yes!" Buddha shrieked and jumped three feet in the air. "Yes! Yes," he continued in a sing-song voice as he ran around gathering his things. "Why are you standing there, Daddy, we gotta go!!"

I smiled and took one more glance at the lake we would never *ever* fish on, as Buddha continued his excited chatter.

"I prayed you would change your mind about fishing and it worked!"

Yeah — I thought as I headed into the bathroom with The Worm branded on my brain — *I guess maybe it did.*

~~~

pianissimo:
Memoir of a Black Gay Childhood
Cornelius Jones, Junior

In eighth grade I had three best friends, Monica, Laquoia, and Sherri-"the girls." I didn't see anything odd with having girls as best friends. We did things any normal friends would do together, from homework, to sleepovers, to skating parties, to choreographing dance routines, shopping, and talking about boys. Well, they did most of the talking; I just listened and lived vicariously through them, while on the inside I could feel my desire to tell my story about Danny.

One night "the girls" and I were over Sherri's house, our favorite place to be crazy and loose. We would always gather in what I would call the basement of Sherri's petite one-story three-bedroom home. We'd have to walk down about five stairs to get to the lower level. Every room in her house was on one level, which is why anything below the main level felt like a basement to me. It was actually called the den. The floor was covered with a plush tan carpet. A sofa rested against one wall, and a fireplace, with a brick mantelpiece above was opposite. Next to the fireplace is where I was first introduced to the Ouija board (the "satanic" board game you use to speak to dead souls). And I was totally freaked out by this whole dead spirit thing. The rumor in the neighborhood and at school was that the Ouija board was also "The Devils" game, and growing up in my town, it was a given that you don't play with "The Devil" in any form, or you will suffer some bad consequences. If it was totally a myth, that some person might have created or purely superstitious I didn't care to ask the truth. Danny was the only person I needed to talk to.

Nervously, I approached the Ouija board and carefully placed my shaking fingers on the edge of the compass, which had a plastic round window in the center, shaped like that of an eyeball. The girls were already in place and were much more relaxed than I was.

"Have y'all played this before?" I quizzed quietly.

"Yeah, last week when you didn't come over," Monica says in a very deep and stealthy voice.

Sherri's plump brown cheeks rise as her white teeth are exposed letting out a laugh.

"Come on Come on!" Laquoia demands regaining our focus.

She continues, "So Cornelius, who do you want to speak to?"

"Danny," I replied, "I need to know if he's alright."

"Ok, but I need a little more information about Danny, so I can call him specifically. Where was he from?"

"Surry County," I whispered nervously.

"How did he die?" she asked as the Ouija board mysteriously brushed from corner to corner.

"Ouija board, we need to know where Danny is? We need to know where Danny from Surry County is. Ouija board, he died in a car accident and Cornelius needs to know how he is."

There was a slight pause. Laquoia turned to me, with her eyes rolled back in her head and said, "Ouija board wants to know how you know Danny." I choked. I wanted to say he was my boyfriend.

"He was my cousin."

Danny is from Surry County, a tiny town east of Richmond, Virginia.

He's three years older than me. He has the cutest round cocoa brown face with the chubbiest cheeks that get even chubbier when his strawberry red lips part to form a smile, while exposing his sparkling white teeth, just like the models on the Colgate toothpaste box cover. We met at the Elks Beauty and Talent Competition in Atlanta, GA, last summer. Our mothers were both co-producers and co-directors of the pageant. The pageant was part of a weeklong Elks National Convention that took place every summer in a different state. Throughout the week, the girls would participate in seminars and workshops about leadership and etiquette and then compete for the crown and a scholarship at the end of the week. I guess it was very similar to The Miss America Pageant.

When we arrived in Atlanta, my brother, Buddy, and I made a dash for the hotel pool and I noticed Danny wandering down the hallway appearing lost. In a shy way he was trying to introduce himself to us. I picked up on it really quickly and began to talk to him. Minutes later he became my best friend and my brother's best friend too.

The three of us had a lot of fun, especially getting so much attention from the pretty teenage beauty contestants. There were about 10 contestants in total – brown skin, light skin, and dark skin. Some were really tall with really big silky hair and bangs that were flipped in a big curl covering their foreheads and others were about Danny and my brother's height with short black and wavy Care-Free (Jerri) curls.

There was this one girl who took a strong liking to Danny. She was sixteen years-old, light skin, very tall, with honey brown silky hair and bangs. She would always stop Danny in the hallway and comment on his chest, while holding and rubbing his chest from behind. Danny would giggle shyly, my brother would laugh while egging him on, and I would smile imagining it was me holding and rubbing his chest from behind.

I don't' know what it was, but after that, I remember Danny always going out of his way to make me feel included. He would say how crazy he thought the sixteen year-old girl was. If he and my brother would decide to explore what was outside of the hotel, he would make sure I was right by his side. Maybe he picked up on my reactions when watching the girl rub his chest. I don't know but I enjoyed being with him. .

We were inseparable that weekend, and on our last night, our mothers made sure we'd stay in touch by exchanging contact information. Wow! This meant I would see him again and again…which I did. A month later my Mom drove my brother and me down to Surry for the weekend.

♂♂

The ouija board moved back and forth as it conveyed messages from Danny to me. Choked up, not from the "satanic" myth about the ouija board, but because I felt the questions about Danny were getting deeper and deeper. There was this fear that at any second, Laquoia would turn to me and ask for another piece of information about my connection to Danny. A little panicky, I didn't want this to sabotage my friendship with "the girls."

However, I believe, "the girls" knew I was gay, because everyone in my eighth grade class blasted me for being this way: I'm walking down the hallway, one morning during a class change, and I hear a classmate, Marvette-her face plump and brown with thin arched eyebrows and furrowing facial expression, say,

"You hang out with those girls. Don't you think something is wrong with that?"

"Yeah, you must be gay."

She just stared at me with these accusatory eyes, looking disgusted. There was this weird story, about gays, circulating around the small city I grew up, in Richmond, Virginia. I remember hearing something, maybe from the kids in the schoolyard, that gay people are nasty; they put gerbils up their ass, and catch diseases. I have no idea where the kids got this information from but it was traumatizing to my ears, especially since – well, Danny. I remember thinking myself into this tunnel of fear wondering, is this gerbil thing some sort of rite of passage for officially being gay?

"Do I have to do it? Will everyone think I walk around with gerbils in my ass?"

I envisioned Marvette, thinking of the nasty things I do with boys and getting diseases from putting gerbils in my ass. I envisioned "the girls" thinking the same thing. I needed to ask Danny for help.

And now, sitting with "the girls" and the ouija board, I had my chance to communicate with the one person who was like me-Danny. However, it didn't feel right, I was afraid. I needed him here physically, in the safety of my home, where we first discovered our liking for each other.

♂♂

It's Saturday morning, June 1987.

"Saved By The Bell" has just ended, and Danny's mom just dropped him off at my house!

He's staying a whole week!

At bedtime, I insist that I get Danny a towel and wash rag, and I beg my momma to let me sleep in the same bed with Danny. "Momma, momma, Buddy can take my room. I want to sleep in the bed with Danny." My momma doesn't put up a fuss about us being too big to share a twin bed because she could see how excited I am to have Danny at our home.

We flick off the lights, hop into the bed underneath the paisley sheets, and we face each other knee to knee forehead to forehead. And then in the pitch dark I notice my young sex rising and then a soft palm, Danny's palm, brushes along my stomach, and down to my sex, which is hard like a twig. He gently squeezes it and let go of his hand. Danny's warm sweet smelling "now & later" breath fills my nostrils as he waits on my response. My heart begins melting like American cheese on wonder bread. I'm feeling safe, so I reach my hand over, feeling my way for Danny's sex. I find it and I return the favor. Wow, I'm thinking while holding his penis, "He grew up." I remember when my brother grew up earlier this year 'cause it freaked my mom out,

"Whew! Oh my God, you need a jockstrap. We need to get Buddy a jockstrap!"

Puberty paid a visit to Danny just like it did to my brother. I'm not freaked out though. Instead I have many questions for Danny. How did he know I liked him? Has he done this before? What age did he "grow up?" I don't ask the questions, but they are answered without being said. Danny looks and giggles. He senses my amazement with our connection. He giggles once more as he reaches and squeezes my penis, again. It feels so amazing to be touched by his hands, even though I haven't "grown up" yet.

We continue to explore each other by touch in the bed. We rub and rub and rub all night long and kiss each other, no tongue, just lips. I'm breathing in the sweetness of his breath and he's taking in mine. Then we take turns playing this little game of revival. He plays dead and I blow into his mouth and revive him and then I play dead and he blows into my mouth and revives me. We do this until we get tired and fall asleep hand in hand, knee to knee, and forehead to forehead.

♂♂

I was ten years old when I had my first intimate experience with Danny. So whenever we would see each other we'd sneak off alone and have our intimate moments. Most times it happened at night, when everyone was asleep, or when no one was home and we were safe.

My experience with Danny made me feel like a normal person. I didn't feel isolated when I was with him because he was just like me. However, what we did was a secret. I couldn't share this with my brother, mother, father, or "the girls." It was my secret and Danny's secret. But my hiding, covering up, became a frequent habit. Keeping my secret became a lot of who I was as I aged into my teenage and young adult years. I began to have intimacy issues as I struggled with liking myself and "liking boys."

Two years later after that first intimate experience, at the age of fifteen, Danny died in a fatal car crash. I was told that he was sitting in the front passenger's seat in a friend's car; when an incoming truck came speeding, head on, towards them. Danny freaked and tried jumping in the back seat. The paramedics found him, trapped between the front and back seat. He was the first person I knew to die so young and so suddenly, and I didn't understand why he died at such an early age. I was too young to process all of what I was feeling internally. I just knew that a part of me died with him.

The funeral took place at a rather small church in Surry County. There were about twenty rows of wooden pews, and each row was filled with family members and friends of Danny. Danny's casket rested directly below the pulpit, and was surrounded with wreaths and flower bouquets. Pinned to the casket door was his yellow football jersey. He loved playing football, I remember. As I sat in the pew I pondered the many ways of how to revive him, and how he could have saved himself. His mother, hunched into the ground, paced the floors of the church- back and forth during the eulogy. At moments she would release her hunched shoulders and pelvis from her contorted posture, throw her limp hands and arms up to the ceiling, calling to Jesus, screaming "Why!" She was suffering heavily. So was I, but very softly. He was so young.

It was time to say our final goodbyes before the Bishop closed the casket, my last goodbye. Nervous, I approached the casket. I couldn't feel my feet on the ground and my body got colder as sweat beads dripped from my underarms. And there he was. He was just as I remembered. Athletic and jovial with cocoa brown skin and chubby cheeks, strawberry red lips, and although his lips were closed, I could still see his sparkling white teeth. He was quiet, though, and stiff. One of my classmates once said, that when you die, the mortician injects you with this embalming fluid to take all of your insides away, finally putting an end to any organs that may still be working, and then after the procedure is complete, your body stiffens. Well, I stood there, for what seemed like an hour. I was frozen and could not move. It felt like I was injected with embalming fluid, because I couldn't feel my insides. Then I saw what seemed to me, a smirk from the corner of Danny's lip. I could have been imagining this, but it felt as though he was communicating to me.

"I'll see you soon one day." My mom broke me out of this trance, grabs my hand, saying,

"Come on Suga. Come on. You ok?"

I just nod, a yes, silently.

"Ma, Danny was my boyfriend," I want to say, but I can't.

I don't know how.

I don't quite understand it all.

♂♂

It was four months after Danny's death, when I called to speak to his spirit on the Ouija board. I still didn't understand it all. I left my play date with "the girls" later that evening. My mom came to pick me up. As I plopped into the front seat of our car, I turned to her and asked:

"Ma, can you take me to get a board game tomorrow?"

♂♂

An excerpt from the novel
Blue Light 'Til Dawn
Darius Omar Williams

Sparkle, Mississippi was mad sopping wet. The rain ripped through the small town with a vengeance. Determined drag-queens ventured into the night; they tarried through the storm in a melancholy rift of ownership. Their high-heeled shoes wailed a dark blues as heel after heel after twelve inch heel got stuck in the mud. They eventually went home. After losing out on cash from their regular list of johns; the ones who sought them out for a regular piece of ass. It didn't take much convincing them to go home. Drenched hair and broken heels. The rush of violent rain. Those bitches hit it. Not even the crack-head men and women with red bulging eyes who sat in the demise of The Old Sparkle Inn could convince them to stop over for a spell. The drag-queens. The dainty determined drag-queens collected their scuffed shoes and went home; the memory of overused pipes falling from their fingertips.

For five weeks straight it rained. When it finally ceased one Friday afternoon, Miss Sugar Moon Beam walked out of the cemetery gates with a loaded pistol on her hip. She had been dead for fourteen years and decided it was time to start living again. She died when she was thirty years old with a tree on top of her face (baby that's how trees in Sparkle do). They stumble to the ground and strewn themselves all over cause Queen Mother Nature got it like that. The Queen Mother do whatever the hell she want without warning or good intent like how she made Miss Sugar Moon Beam get up and walk again after all these years. The sun shone its button-eyed face the moment Sugar Moon Beam came walking through them gates leaving the imprint of death behind; her daddy somewhere in another plot probably rolling in his grave. Miss Sugar Moon Beam gathered up her face and crept out the cemetery gates; *to hell with this dead beat place.* She had holes at the bottom of her feet and the sickly streets were mad sopping wet.

Sugar Moon Beam didn't give a damn about soaking her feet in mud. From where she had come, a parcel of damp earth was the only thing she knew. Although the memorable mud made her pretty ankles purr, it took awhile for her to get used to the fierce piercing of sunrays in her eyes. Let alone disturbed afternoon folk wondering how come this black woman carrying a pistol in broad daylight. Her buck naked body reeked of life, not death—and how she celebrated herself with a gardenia in her hair rather Billie Holiday like.

"Baby right about now, I wants some pig-feet, a man and a cold bottle of beer."

Then Miss Sugar Moon Beam placed one hand on top of her breasts and almost chuckled herself back to death. "Ha, ha, ha, ha, ha! Yes ma'am!" Summer in Sparkle was a particularly perfect time to eat pickled pig-feet. Hog cheese and crackers provided just as much pleasure to the mouths of reckless kids. The ones who ran around with their shoes tied tight. So Sugar Moon Beam reminisced on just about every delicacy she could remember. Together, her light cream colored gardenia and her Walther P-38, engaged Sugar's alive again soul with gumptious effusions of attitude.

Sugar Moon Beam died two years after dialysis with no will to live and less than fifty T-cells. In fact, she came running to the tree. She had been planning to for months, shortly after she burned her clothes. Not too long after she cut off all her locks. Although Sugar's face got bashed by a tree, the HIV ("Miss Helen Ivory Valentine"), damn near killed that child long time ago. So one day Sugar whispered to the tree in her dementia driven state, "Would you hurry your ass up. Fall on me goddammit. Go ahead and fall!"

The tree took its time but it eventually fell.

"Fall on me. Fall on me. Hurry up and fall on me."

"Sugaaaaaaaar! Sugar nooooo," her mama screamed with cancer chewing on her lungs.

Sugar willed the oak tree to the ground. She had to do it.

The forgetfulness drove Sugar mad. Made her cry three times a week. Made her talk to her dead daddy's ghost. The forgetfulness. It was anything and everything. It was everything. It was drool on her mouth. It was her unbrushed teeth. It was everything. Everything. Everything. Everything.

It was the triple-bypass surgery. It was her blood soaked tongue. The voices, her vagina, her boiled over skin. The pinkness of it all. The skinny. The scag. It was everything.

Her folded up prayers. Her mushy membrane of a mouth.

It was her man. Her layaway man. How Jimmy fucked her and fucked her for weeks.

It was anything and everything.

Her detachment to rock music. Her passion for Nina Simone. It was. It was. Not enough sex. It was too much to comprehend. It was "fuck it, I'm out". It was the combination of meds. The layaway man. It was dementia that led Sugar to the tree. Good lawd she was pretty. Had some mighty fine breasts. Good lawd. Good lawd that child was pretty. Seem like she knew. Damn right she knew. Sugar knew her time was up, that it was definitely going to fall. The operose oak gave out. It landed on Sugar's head. It was anything and everything. It was spiteful. The operose oak. How Sugar knew it would eventually fall. How divine her premonition. How she constantly challenged nature. How she incensed the operose oak.

The town folk remained silent as Sugar sashayed down the road. "Maybe they soulless. Maybe they don't remember me at all," she thought. Cause didn't nobody say a word to Miss Sugar Moon Beam. Even members from the Usher Board and elders of the church looked distantly at her as if she didn't belong to anybody, least nobody they ever knew. Maybe that's why Sugar threw both of her hands in the air screaming,

"Hey ya'll. Look at me. Ain't um the shit." The men gazed and stroked their penises. The town mothers were enraged. "Hey there Mama Alice. Hey there Father Pearl."

Mama Alice stopped stitching but her lips didn't move. Father Pearl leaned against a wall on his porch. Look like he start singing or praying or something. Although Sugar cut them with her eyes like she was fixing to shoot the nearest, the baddest motherfucker; not a man, woman or child uttered a word.

"Don't none of you bitches remember me? Y'all don't remember Miss Sugar Moon Beam?"

Potently proud, she strutted through town like a horsefly chafing the air with her wings, the low steady sighing of sweet indigo. A faded Coca Cola sign stood weary in the distance and about a half mile down the road the fly folks at Bill's Bar quivered each other's spines drinking imitation moonshine. Sugar held her head up and gazed beneficently down the rusty red road. When she finally reached the entrance to Bill's Bar, she shifted her gaze toward an older fellow busily cracking pecans on a cherry wood bench.

"Is Jimmy up in there?" Sugar asked.

The man was silent.

"Hey. Hey. Don't you hear me talking to you? I asked you a question man."

"Yeah I hear you. But that's about all I'm doing. Hearing you."

"Old man. Do you know who you talking to? My name is Sugar fool. Don't make me prop this gun upside your head. Now tell me where he at? Where's Jimmy? Where he at got dammit!"

"Listen here Sugar. My name is Byrd. Mr. Cephus Byrd. My mama name me Cephus but everybody call me Da Birdman. Cause I always sit outside like this. By myself. I drinks my moonshine, eat these pecans and watch them birds. I knows when they migrate, why they migrate and how often they drop a turd. Something bout how they fly over me make an old man feel safe. Listen to what I'm telling you now. You better listen. I'm a bird watcher honey. I watch birds. I even watched you walk all the way over here wearing nothing but a flower acting crazy as a road lizard and just a waving that there gun. Look Sugar. You said yo name was Sugar, right. Let me cut to the chase and tell it to you like this, cause Da Birdman ain't gone jive you bout nothing. Absolutely nothing. I'm damn near ninety years old honey. Been surviving cancer going on ten years. Last time a man threatened me he end up shitting on hisself in a coffin. You best be careful girl else you be laid up in a box like him."

"Chile, boom! You ain't said nothing but a thing. I done already done that. Laid up in a box. Breathless. Face twisted to the side. Nose smushed in. Virus still crawling on the inside of my body. Pretty breasts gone. Just gone. Laying there. Quiet. In that ugly ass box. Bruised and broken boned. Cause of that tree. That tree. That tree. That tree. You see an old oak tree up and fell on me Mr. Bird. Bout fourteen years ago. Damn near crushed my spine to pieces. Took way my breath. The rest of my life. The part I had left. My mama seen't it all. That sweet, sweet woman. Seen't her chile scream until that oak tree fell. Oh yes she did Mr. Bird, yes she did. She seen't her only daughter die. She couldn't believe I actually done it. Talked about it for months. How I was gone call that tree down so I could die of something. Something. Something other than what Jimmy give me. The gonorrhea, the syphilis, the AIDS. That shit he give me. I had to die of something other than that. You know what I'm talking about. You got to know. You just got to know what I'm talking about Mr. Bird. You got to know cause like you say you almost ninety years old. Been fighting cancer for at least eight of them years so yeah you know what I mean. Yeah I know you know. But hey I can't complain. Just look at me now. Miss Sugar Moonbeam. Naked as I please and alive as ever. Alive as ever baby!"

"What you want with Jimmy girl?"

"Mind your own business and just tell me if he here?"

"He over there by the pool table honey. Lemme go get him for you, child. Ain't no need in you going up in there with no clothes. What's your name again dauhling?"

"My name is Sugar Mister. Miss Sugar Moon Beam."

"Now it come to me. I thought I recognize you. You Dolly's daughter aint cha'. Bless your heart. But, Sugar died long time ago honey. You can't be her. It's impossible."

"Anything's possible baby. Long as you believe. I believed I'll see my mama again after all these years. I believed my body alive and bountiful again. I believed myself back to this earth. So, it's me baby. Yes ma'am. You better believe it's me. Now get your eyes off the sky and look again."

"Mercy Jesus. Lord have mercy on my cancer ridden soul. It's you dauhling. It really is you. Don't you member me. I'm your Great Uncle Bird. Your daddy's favorite uncle, god rest his soul."

"Yes, I member you Bird. I membered you the whole time. I'm just glad, so glad you finally membered me."

"I do. I do. I really do. You was the prettiest girl in Sparkle. Hell the prettiest girl in the state. The whole state of Mississippi. Everybody kept saying, why she with Jimmy. She don't need to be with no Jimmy. Jimmy ain't no damn good. He mess around with men and women. Fuck you good as he please but don't be studying you at all. Like how he left you when you first got sick. Told you, your mama and your AIDS to go to hell. Baby, lemme tell you something. You sho' don't look sick today. You look real good Sugar. Real good."

"Why thank you Uncle Bird. Yes, I reckon I do look kinda good. Wait. Let me stop playing. Hell, I know I look good. I guess that's what a shovel of dirt will do. Besides, it wouldn't never me in that ground no how. Not really. My spirit just went a sailing just as soon as that oak tree fell. And after being gone from here so long, looking for me some answers and then finding myself again, God give me back my body just the way I like it. He swooped my spirit down in that cemetery dirt. Seem like I was descending forever. Cause of how long he swoop me down. He swoop me into the ground. I could taste the flowers Uncle Bird. Their juices, their fragrances and they roots. I tasted insects and bugs and ginger scented dirt. By the time I hit my body again, the Lord done already put my bones back together and gave me new blood. The freshest blood I done ever tasted. And my hair. Mercy to God. My hair. He grew it back longer than it was. Pretty soon I was breathing. Hallelujah I was breathing. After fourteen years I could feel my lungs moving, my teeth grinding, my heart beating in places I ain't never felt before. And that's round the time I started pushing Uncle Bird. Just pushing and pushing myself out the ground. I pushed myself out my casket, I pushed myself past my dirty wet clothes. I pushed myself past the insects, the flowers and the dirt. I pushed hard. I pushed and I pushed and I pushed. Felt like I was having a baby the way I pushed myself out that grave. By the time, I settled on top of the earth the sun was just a shining in my eyes. Shining something fierce. That's when I start laughing, laughing myself silly. I said thank you. Thank you Lord. Thank you. Then I stooped down a little and picked this pretty white gardenia off my grave. Ain't it pretty Uncle Bird. Ain't it real pretty. I stuck this gardenia in my locks and stood right on up I tell you. I bathed in a shallow pool inside the cemetery. Then I went and hocked this gun off another fella wouldn't lucky as me. I reckon he didn't want life back as bad as I did. I reckon he didn't know how to push. So, I shoveled up the rest of his grave, grabbed hold of this gun and walked straight over here to Bill's Bar. Cause I got to talk to Jimmy. See I got to Uncle Bird. I just got to talk to Jimmy."

"But what if he don't come out."

"Oh he most definitely gon come out. Else I'll go in there and get his ass. Now let's stop it with all these stories I say and go get Jimmy for me. I'll watch the birds for you, Uncle Bird. Sugar ain't going nowhere. Me and these birds made a pact, a long ago pact. We both fly. We real, real fly. We too fly for each other most days. That's how come I don't shit on them and they don't shit on me. Now go in there and get Jimmy for me chile."

"Be right back Sugar. I'll go get Jimmy. Just do like you promised me baby. Keep your eye on the birds."

"I will Uncle Bird. I promise," Sugar assured him, then waited impatiently for Jimmy—the only man she ever slept with in her life—the only man who ever fucked her in the ass. She remembered his angular face. She remembered his gorgeous dick. She remembered everything about Jimmy, his shameless desires, his lacy speech, his conniving cum dripping down the inner portion of her thigh. Her mind was growing weary from the constant memory of him. Visions of this man titty fucking her and throwing her on her back was as fiery as the holes in her feet where the blazing street burned inside her like an old iron pot. Today in Sparkle, this woman relished inside the terrible beauty of pain, her road of broken stone, the wonderful sight of blood and Sugar's feet pressing firm against the rocks. Blood traveled from her feet and flocks of birds swarmed overhead as she drank water from a nearby drinking well. She concentrated on the water, every tasteful drop, how she lapped it with her tongue, her pretty hands around a wood dipping spoon. Sugar lapped the water with her tongue. Then started humming Lena Horne. Remembering music rather than Jimmy. Cause music was a reminder of her own pleasures in life. She shifted her mind to herself rather than the firmness of his grip. Her singing and the shifting. It never dawned on her the contradiction. Her off-key blues. Her alive again self. The taste of spring water. The sinuous sight of blood. Folks gone awry on the road where she stood. But Sugar wouldn't studying they asses one bit and dared anybody to lay they filthy hands on her. As unusual as it seemed, Sugar opened her mouth to sing. She threw her head back releasing AIDS, Jimmy and her luminous death. Softly, this warrior woman sang while standing there naked as ever:

> *Bird flying high, you know how I feel*
> *Sun in the sky, you know how I feel*
> *Breeze drifting by, you know how I feel*

The barrel house timbre of Jimmy's throat interrupted her singing,

"Sugar. Is that really you? What you doing here girl?" He sounded embarrassed and mortified as if he had been reduced to nothing at the naked sight of her. Jimmy's throat rolled into a ball and trembled. His peach stone face and teeth couldn't hide the terror on his skin.

Sugar didn't laugh, she screamed. It was a howl. It was her freedom. It was her feminine declaration, "Aaaaaaahhhhhh, hey Jimmy! Hey baby! Yeah it's me! It's me! You damn right it's me!" Sugar galloped toward Jimmy, jumped high in the air and wrapped her legs around his waist. She planted kisses on his forehead, his eyebrows, his nose, his cheeks, his lips. "Oooh, Jimmy baby did you miss me? Tell me. Tell me baby. Tell me baby. Did you miss me?"

"Who the hell is this woman Bird? What the fuck this 'sposed to be, some kinda joke. Sugar been dead for fourteen years. Naw, baby you can't be Sugar. Least not my Sugar." He threw her to the ground then gazed surprisingly at the hand where she was still holding her gun.

"I was dead for fourteen years. You damn right. But I'm alive again baby," Sugar screamed.

"Fourteen years you been gone. I saw you in that casket girl. That's right. I was there. I had to be sure you was dead. So you couldn't vex me no more. So that monkey could stop riding my back. I saw all your brothers put you in the ground Sugar. I saw them. I saw them." He towered over her body and noticed the blood start seeping from her knees.

"Everybody get back. Get back. This bitch right here got AIDS. Crazy Bitch!"

"So now you wanna embarrass me Jimmy. Huh. You wanna embarrass me like that. In front of everybody. Telling these folks I got AIDS. Calling Sugar out her name. Man you must crazy. I ain't got to take this shit!" Sugar stood on both feet and inched closer toward Jimmy. She lifted both her arms and cocked the Walther P-38.

"I thought you had changed after all these years. But you still the same low-down motherfucker Jimmy," Sugar dug inside her throat and shot spit in Jimmy's face. Jimmy wiped it in a hurry, his hands rubbing violently against his cheeks.

"Don't worry. It won't hurt you dauling. I been washed in the blood of the lamb."

"You can't shoot me girl. Your heart's too soft. You love me too much."

Sugar wept, "My heart was soft for your Jimmy. Loving you was easy baby but oh how I paid the cost. I come back to say I forgive you. I forgive you for hurting me like you did."

"Fuck you bitch. You ain't got to forgive me for shit."

"Fuck me Jimmy. Fuck me? You the reason I got sick. You infected me man. Telling me you love me. Telling me I'm the only one."

Jimmy frowned. The way he did when he used to pounce his fists on Sugar, he frowned like how angry men do in Mississippi. Dick rock hard, liquor-stained breath. For a fellow as handsome as Jimmy it was unbelievable how easily he frowned. His masculinity. It smothered its pensive rage across Sugar's shining face. He chokingly cried, in spite of all the emptiness his tears held, "Please don't kill me baby. Please. I'm begging you. Please don't do it Sugar".

"This is for giving me AIDS motherfuckaaaaaaaaaaa!" Sugar pulled the trigger. She splattered Jimmy's brains against the rusty red Coca Cola sign.

When Jimmy tumbled to the ground, Sugar ran forward and pulled the trigger again. She lodged another bullet in his head, one in his stomach, then two in his chest. Payback meant everything to Sugar. But shooting Jimmy simply wasn't enough. So, Sugar knelt before his body and abruptly pulled down his pants. Sarcastically she whispered, "I ain't done yet." She laughed at him. Predaceous sounds of vindication. He looked small and insignificant on the ground. Her breath, the smell of insects and dirt, she breathed on his body hard, then ripped away his pissed stained underwear. Surprisingly, she was unmoved by the amorous sight of his dick. All twelve inches of him. She remembered the perpetual taste, his bulging five inch girth. The sight of it meant absolutely nothing to her. Even in the memory of its anaconda strength, Sugar was nauseated by its dangerous length. It took some effort on her part not to simply blow it off. Like a ship that had sailed for way too long, his body sank deep into the earth—and Sugar's gregarious gun, her uncertain grip, mangled by the groan of tortured throats.

Sugar pressed her gun's shaft against Jimmy's splendid piece of wood. As she stroked it with one hand, its awful scent cursed her and billowed through the crowd. Sugar reveled in the humiliation of him. Exhausted, angry, delighted by Jimmy's absent heat, nothing would stop her from mangling his flaccid dick. Not even the unpleasant cries of nearby women in the crowd. They screamed themselves silly for a lover gone too soon. Their dark, abundant moans could not and would not diffuse Sugar. Her determined malice intact, Sugar wept ferociously for him. Her swirling grieve rose just as sure as his rising stench.

Miss Sugar Moonbeam opened her soil-stained mouth, and wrapped her gums around Jimmy's filthy pipe, allowing her tremulous teeth to torture him, to humiliate him. Her teeth were the revenge for all her years of suffering and she fondled his nipples now and then as townsfolk stood in terror on Eastview Road. She remembered how Jimmy ate her pussy and even spelled the word GANGSTER on her ass. She yearned for his corpse's decay, the sight of maggots and blood. She chewed on him and cried as the chipped blue paint of Bill's Bar egoistically competed with the Coca Cola sign. Shooting everyone on sight would never suffice for how hungrily Sugar feasted on Jimmy. As she coursed her teeth through each vein, she remembered his smooth swagger walk, how eloquent it was; its serious edge. Biting his dead dick off would never measure up to how he tortured her life. To Sugar's delight, Jimmy was no more. His sensuous swagger gone. His violent gangster death as rude as his insidious name. In spite of how the women mourned for him, Jimmy laid motionless on the ground as rude and as heavy as their suffering. Sugar's face was covered in blood; even her pretty white gardenia endured a stain. Surely she would eventually have mercy on him, a virile particular man with thighs as masculine as ice.

She chewed his dick to pieces - completely ravished it in fact.

For Jimmy never felt a thing cause he was dead.

Sugar stood up—gracefully ascended from the dirt, for she held on to his dick with her hands—her equilibrium intact. Certainly, she thought, these bitches didn't think I was just gon leave it here. No ma'am.

It's mine for the keeping baby. Who knows. I'm might string it up with beads and then wear it round my neck. Use it as a bracelet or something. Something other than what Jimmy use it for. Something other than danger, violence or death. But however she decide to use it, the reality of his cowardice life remained. Jimmy was dead. Thank God. Sugar was one somebody who didn't give a rat's ass for all his suffering. And wherever Sugar went, she decided to carry his sable skin dick as a reminder to herself. And exactly where she went is a mystery to all. For Sugar strutted her stuff through Sparkle singing the same song over again. Sugar carried on with her voice. With a piece of Jimmy in her hands, a Walther P-38 on her hip and a contraption of a flower on her head, Sugar sang.

ESSAYS & SERMONS

The Arsenals of Hatred Have No Place Here
(In Memory of Carl Joseph Walker-Hoover)
Doug Cooper Spencer

On the day I was celebrating 55 years of living as a gay male, almost 700 miles away, the body of an eleven year old black boy swayed silently in an evening breeze, a broken neck, having taken his life because he was accused of being gay.

On April 6, Carl Joseph Walker-Hoover came home with one thought on his mind- - to end the pain of the taunts heaped upon him by his classmates. Later, when his mother went upstairs she found her son hanging lifeless at the end of a cord, a cord that was most likely longer than the short life he had led; and it was because of bullying.

Carl was not alone. Everyday many people find their lives wrapped in fear because they are psychologically, physically, or even spiritually diminished by the power of others. In its many forms it's called bullying and it is as old as human nature itself; and clearly, it reaches far from the playground. It happens in the communities in which we live, on the job and even in the pulpit. Recently, I re-posted an article about two gay men who were being bullied, though unsuccessfully, by people who wanted to destroy their business ('The Face of Fear', 2/17/09).

Unfortunately, bullying is a sad fact that we often encourage by partaking of it, or excusing it through our silence. One of the weapons Carl's classmates used to taunt him was labeling him as being gay.

There are many weapons in reach of bullies, but being gay is one of the more potent ones and it's a wise choice when one person wants to 'beat-down' another. It's a wise choice because we have allowed it to be. Our religious and cultural views imply it, and sometimes even the silence of people who would be gay allow it.

Was Carl gay? I don't know. As yet, that fact hasn't been established, or at least let out into the stream of public comment. But surely, it was homophobia that destroyed his young life. His mother states that "He wasn't really tough, he didn't look tough... so he had problems," and it is stated that he was considered gay, probably as a result of his not being tough; an erroneous perception since some very tough people are also same-gender loving, maybe some of the toughest, considering what they have had to endure. Yet the use of these weapons persist.

These weapons we hand each other are not by mistake, they are by design, and that's why they're kept in place. There are some who not only have a need to bully, but a need to oppress. To keep people they don't like in their places, if not outright destroy them.

There are too many weapons to name in this arsenal, but we know the effects when they are being used and nowadays we know how to intervene when we see bullying taking place. Did Carl's school, the New Leadership Charter School, in Springfield Massachusetts, do what it could to prevent things from spiraling out of hand? I'm not sure, we'll find out more as the story evolves. But for Carl, it is too late.

Now I'm left to ponder what I would have done if I had met him.

If I had had a chance to reach Carl, I would have shown him that, in the end, he would be fine. I would have let him know that people survive the undeserving blows of the ignorant. I would have told him that I had considered suicide when I was seventeen simply because I didn't want to be gay, and how I'm so glad I didn't. I would have helped him to understand the ignorant and to realize that their ways shouldn't define him because of the fact that they really do suffer from ignorance. I would have shown him just how wonderful my life has been as well as so many others who have stood in the face of this ignorance and that he has a chance to make it through as well.

But Carl has moved on as have so many others at the hands of people who feel it's okay to destroy lives because they are different. So here is where I bid him farewell.

You may rest now, Carl Joseph Walker-Hoover. The pain you endured is over. Finally, you are at peace. But know this, that while you rest in that accepting place, there are many who are still here who will fight in your name that others like you will not have to suffer your fate.

Be well, Carl. Rest and be well.

A Letter To Jerry
Buster Spiller

The following essay is actually a letter I wrote but never mailed to a college associate (who would join my church years later) that I ran into one day while on the bus on my way home from work. The time period was shortly after I came out as a same gender loving man and was I feeling pretty comfortable with myself, or so I thought. I don't have many regrets in my life because my experiences have defined me but I do regret not mailing this letter. In the 15 years since my coming out, I realize I still have some internal perceptions, gender assumptions, and discomfort as it relates to being a gay male. The label "gay" appears to be, or is in my mind, the antithesis of "manhood" which is a contradiction of how I live my life. So for me, reading my own "thoughts" again many years later is affirmation that I still have some self-work to do.

Brother Jerry,

Hey man, what's happening? I have to say it was good to see you again. When you boarded the bus, I was fairly certain I knew who you were, but as always, I am bad at matching names with faces. After we threw out names and places and established where our paths had crossed, the conversation took off with relative ease.

Except when you looked me in the eye and asked me if I had been delivered. *Delivered.* I stumbled over that word just as I am stumbling now to write these words. *Delivered.* It hit me so swift and so sudden that I can still feel its impact. *Delivered.*

I must say, as I indicated to you that *"yes",* I have been delivered. *Delivered from myself.* I know you were wondering *'what does he mean by that?'* I asked him if he was still punking, if he was still a homosexual, a fag, gay?!? What does he mean *'I have been delivered from myself?'*

Well Jerry, I am still trying to figure that out myself. Why did I answer you with those words? Why couldn't I just flat out tell you *'yes Jerry, I am still gay, a fag, a homosexual and will be that way until the day that I die.'*

Why couldn't I say that? Was it because I'm not as open and comfortable with my sexuality as I profess? Was it out of shame because I am traveling down the path that leads to the ministry? Was it because I felt you would have thought I was a hypocrite? Was it because I felt you would have viewed me as *'less than a man?'*

Jerry, all these questions and countless others raced through my mind as I tried to figure out my response to you. I will try to tell you honestly why I responded that way, not so much for your benefit, but for mine.

It took me close to twenty years to acknowledge to myself, as recently as six months ago, that I was indeed homosexual. It's been a painful process, but I feel that I have finally arrived at accepting this as gospel. I don't say this to receive sympathy from you or to have you view my response as a cop out.

For a long time I worked hard at hiding the truth and disguising what I was and who I was, but now is the time for me to allow the truth to rise and blossom. **I am a homosexual.** *I am a homosexual and that's ok.* God doesn't love me any less. In fact, He probably loves me more because I am able for the first time in my life to love myself.

I no longer have to exhibit certain behavior because that's what *"fags"* are expected to do. I no longer have to fill my days with endless activities to prevent myself from having to dwell on my homosexuality. And I no longer have to drink and destroy my body because I hated God for creating me in the manner He did.

I can finally for the first time in my life function in creation the way God intended. That is the purest freedom any person could ever receive and now it's mine for the taking! No more feeling that my sexuality defines me. On the contrary, I define it! It is one segment of a complex being that God named "me."

And I marvel at that! God is good all the time ... all the time God is good! Sound familiar? Yes, we repeat that at church all the time, don't we?

I'm glad we had this time to share. I hope you understand where I am coming from. If not, I pray one day you will be released from whatever bondage is holding you back and rise so you can experience the ecstasy I am currently feeling in my life. On that day, you will meet me in the sky and we will soar all over this marvelous creation.

Until that day my brother, I leave you with "peace"...

Sincerely,
Minister L.

Another 100 People
L. Michael Gipson

When Broadway lyricist and composer, Stephen Sondheim wrote his landmark 1970 musical, "Company", he penned a classic tune of longing, isolation, and the expectation of freedom. The song, "Another Hundred People", describes the flood of hopeful newcomers that fill Manhattan airports, bus terminal and of course, Grand Central Station; all desperate to leave behind lives of boredom, isolation, and repression to realize star studded dreams. These escapees of the mundane are desperate to follow their fantasy of a better, more flavorful life. The song speaks volumes to me about my own community of young, hungry transients. On any day of the week in hot urban Mecca's like DC, NYC, and Atlanta, another 100 people just got off of the bus, plane or train ready to begin a new life of sexual liberation, cultural immersion and professional opportunities. Or in the words of the more direct: boys, parties and gainful employment.

By the droves they come to these pink beacons of light, like their white San Francisco, Chelsea and Greenwich Village brethren before them in search of a unique kind of freedom. Braving higher rents, expenses, and image crafting bars set by those damned Joneses, the desire to be out and about, away from the prying eyes of that nosy Aunt Gladys and the eye-brow raising Uncle Phils, proves more enticing than a potentially lower quality of life. For others, it's the throbbing need to be among a new, different more exciting community; any community other than this "late", tired one at home. They are searching for a better life, so why should anyone have a problem with that?

At the door of clubs and bars and house parties in both the urban gay Mecca's—and ironically, in the old homestead—there awaits another set of men; those men that wait in constant anticipation for another hundred people to get off of those perpetually arriving buses, trains and planes. With drink in hand, they stare at the door in the hopes that their new man, new best friend, or new community will arrive at the door to rescue them from the tired sea of familiar faces with whom they've long since grown bored. They survey the room and see the men they've already fucked, read, argued with, ignored, dismissed, belittled and stereotyped. They see the community as a petulant child that they have already disowned in search of a new fresher, unspoiled baby. They need new toys to play with, to rescue them from their boredom. They return their attention to the door and wait for another hundred people to get off of the train.

For those getting off of the train, the possibility of becoming the bored man staring at the door seems remote. There are still new smells, new sights and new men to experience; a whole new world to learn that will easily take a year or two or maybe even three to learn and then discard. Those one to three years, before the specter of boredom and frustration enters the frame, can feel like a lifetime when one first gets off of that train. One to three years before the newbies have been swarmed over like locust over the fields, leaving nothing behind but empty shells. One to three years for them to dodge the ghost of desperate hunger and the need to look for a new train to board predictably returns. Maybe this time the ghost won't find them. Maybe then they can find contentment with a place and a community, at last. Maybe.

In our community, for some, the cycle of joyous expectation followed by crushing discontentment can be endless. The unrelenting search for a man, a people, a community other than the one you're already in seems hard wired in some of us, like some dormant genetic defect. Among black gay men, wanderlust seems a communicable epidemic more prevalent than AIDS. For hometown lovers uninfected with its malaise, the burden of incessant choral whispers insisting on the boring nature of home infects any joyous possibilities, leaving parasitic doubt in its wake. The carriers' inability to love and accept the community that is already before them is a flaw that helps neither the community nor the individual ever evolve, grow or heal.

Perhaps it is time that we stop looking at the door for another community to come and replace the current cast in our primetime drama. Despite what our desires imply, the new cast will not inherently be more talented, more beautiful, more cultured and more intelligent than the one we are already a part of. There is no evidence that proves this assumption to be true. To the contrary, the new cast is often more of the same. Should, miraculously, there be a cast change that proved to be an upgrade, it wouldn't take long before we downgraded their status and attributes in our search for flaws and through our self-loathing.

If in doubt about my assertions, check out the Internet. There you will find hundreds and even thousands of men from DC, ATL, NYC, Miami, Chicago, Charlotte and Houston searching for another hundred people over the Internet. When you engage these men about why they are trying to meet and connect with men thousands of miles away, the refrain is always the same. It usually starts with "Man, these bruthas here are… (fill in the negative connotation)." Be it friendship or relationship, men are staring at the door through the window of their computer screen, waiting for someone else to rescue them from the community from whom they've made little or no investment. They want a community readymade for them to be fabulous in, but have done little to make it so, besides show up. Sometimes, not even that.

Some clichés warrants saying: we are the community we've been waiting for. Warts, odd shapes, jacked grills, mixed education, dubious knowledge, sketchy sexual histories and various mental and physical challenges, it's all us and it's who we have. While there may always be another hundred people getting off of the train or another hundred people boarding that train to leave your city, in the long term there are no guarantees of a better community arriving at the door, just larger volumes of the same people and experiences with the same frustrating mess. How much better would we all be if we stopped looking at the door and enjoyed the party? How much looking would we all do if we decided to be fully present? To invest in the communities we live in to make it what we want instead of searching for something elusive and intangible, an Oz of caring Peter Pans with six-packs, six-figures and a Ph.D.

In Sondheim's tune, the song eventually declares that the hundred people that got off of the train just became lost souls swallowed whole by a city, a culture and a community of disconnected strangers. How much better would we be if got to know one another and learned to love one another and, consequently, ourselves? Can you hear them? Another hundred people just got off of the train and came back home.

Why "Don't Ask, Don't Tell" Can't Wait
Alan Miller

I find it less annoying than I used to when I hear someone argue that issues important to people outside their own group must wait for justice. I suppose I am getting old, because I am less angry than I used to be, and more perplexed than I ought to be. Like Martin Luther King and James Baldwin, who both addressed this tactic, I ask: What are we waiting for? Why should the unjust governmental policy "Don't Ask; Don't Tell" continue? Most people that make this kind of argument are disingenuous; they simply want to wait until the issue itself dies along with the folks who advocate for it. I don't believe that Andrew Wilde-Price* is waiting for me and supporters of change to die, but it doesn't matter because we (LGBT folks and our supporters) aren't going away.

First, he tells us that President Obama's plate is full with other issues. He means to imply that more pressing concerns (Name one: the economy, the war, health care, etc...) are simply more important than the official government policy on gay and lesbian soldiers serving in the military at this time. The problem with this argument is that the governments (and its agents) always work on more than one issue at a time. All of the Cabinet appointees and all of the czars don't stop working on their focus because there are other priorities. Even Obama has made this point. Thus, it isn't fair to ask LGBT folks to wait for a better time for our issues to be addressed. After all, when Katrina hit the Gulf, should all government agencies have turned their attentions solely to Katrina? No. Is it possible that some resources from agencies other than FEMA might direct their energies to Katrina temporarily? Yes. So, the business of government, in other words, must go on, even in crisis. Wilde-Price gives himself away when he argues later that he can't guarantee that a "new issue" might not capture the president's attention. In fact, he's hoping and wishing such an issue arises, in hopes that the opportunity for change passes. That becomes clear when he notes that President Obama's majority in both houses of Congress may be in jeopardy in the next election cycle—a pattern that usually holds in mid-term elections: the majority party usually loses seats. It happened with Bush (but not in his first term), Clinton, the Bush before that, and even under Reagan. So, the window may be closing; it's not indefinitely open.

Later, our staff writer argues that the issues of the majority (heterosexuals) supersede the rights of the minority (LGBT folks) and that, "simply put," it is reasonable to delay justice for the minority. If that logic were true, then surely there is no proper time for consideration of minority rights—at least not until all the problems of the body politic (and hence of the majority) are solved. Thus, the rights of minority groups are luxuries, where the rights of majorities are necessities. Such people underestimate the damage that a disgruntled minority can affect on overall morale, effectiveness and the body politic. (One of my friends asked, years ago, "What would happen to Black churches if gay folks left the choir? I would add, what would happen if gay folks left not just the choir---LEFT, as many of us have—but the institution most responsible for organizing our progress, from Nat Turner to Martin Luther King to Cecil Williams to Jesse Jackson to Al Sharpton? The world would be a very different place; the Black community would be a very different place; the Black church would be a very different place. It's like Douglas Turner Ward's play "Day of Absence," in which all black folks disappear from an all-Black town. In the military, the day of absence is already occurring, but no one has stopped to note the impact of the loss).

Members of the LGBT community are in fact concerned with all of the urgent issues Wilde-Price cites. After all, LGBT folks work, and thus are concerned with the economy. We are concerned about health issues and thus track the debates about health care policy. And, of course, we are concerned with the wars in Iraq and Afghanistan because we are already serving and will continue to serve whether there is a "Don't ask, don't tell" (DA/DT) policy or not.

Unfortunately, in his desire to find that elusive "middle ground" Wilde-Price, and perhaps Obama, fail to grasp that DA/DT doesn't only harm LGBT people. It harms all of us. It is simply wasteful. Of the thousands of soldiers expelled from the military, many served in positions that were hard to fill—often as translators of rare dialects and languages. (How many people are willing to banish the person who may be able to decipher a message of terror whose nuances few are capable of discerning?) In addition, all soldiers fired under DA/DT have received training that must be duplicated and given to someone else. Anyone following this issue must note the large number of stellar soldiers ejected from the military during a war, soldiers with rare skills, soldiers who did not harm the military's vaunted morale, but if one listens to their colleagues, did much to boost, encourage and perform at the highest levels. In other armies around the world, much-respected armies, LGBT serve openly and honestly in numerous capacities. Our government's policy is inefficient and costly. Unfortunately, we will never fully know the cost of our folly.

I am glad, as a Black man, to be able to say, we have been down this road before. When Truman integrated the military over 50 years ago with an Executive Order of fewer than 250 words, generals and civilians alike railed against the "social experiment" of integration, lamenting that it would hamper effectiveness, morale and send a dangerous message to ordinary citizens who could not abide racial segregation. Today this seems silly. It is equally silly to hear my Black brothers and sisters tell me anytime LGBT folks seek justice that our struggles are not parallel, that the strategies of the civil rights movement belonged solely to Black folks, that when the LGBT community avail ourselves of the same arguments and strategies, that WE are somehow denigrating these tactics, and indeed denigrating Black history. (I understand that racial justice has not yet been achieved, but I know that we know that telling justice to wait is like trying to hold back a flood with ten fingers). Yes, the issues of race and sexual orientation are different, but when one sees the same political tactics—divide and conquer, delay and wait, slander and name-calling—employed by the same institution to brunt progress, it is fair to say: Enough! We've seen this before. We can do better, and we can do better NOW!

Finally, one must acknowledge the issue of simple justice. Is it fair to deny LGBT folk the right to work for the government? Aren't we all, as citizens, entitled to the same basic rights? When do we work in the government, is it fair to cruelly take the financial benefits we have earned and to publicly humiliate us for doing what others are applauded for doing? In California, over 40 years ago, voters pushed back the Briggs Initiative which would have punished LGBT teachers and terminated educators who had given their gifts and talents freely. It is time for our federal government to stand up and say: "Don't Ask; Don't Tell" is cruel and inhumane. It is wasteful. It may in fact be endangering the security of this nation. Last but not least, this policy is unjust. Why, why, why have we waited so long to do what is right?

---

* Andrew Wilde-Price wrote the opinion article referenced in the Berkeley (CA) High School *Jacket*, the high school newspaper where Alan E. Miller teaches.

Trick or Treat?
Rev. MacArthur H. Flournoy

Demoralizing and dehumanizing treatment of our beloved community has taken on another disguise, dressed in religiosity and cloaked in self-righteousness by some self-appointed prophets. One such person has created an entire website devoted to spiritual violence under the guise of "Proclaiming the word of God." This individual has launched a vitriolic attack against clergy who practice an open and affirming ministry that welcomes all people in the practice of their faith with unconditional love. For these ministers of a radically inclusive gospel, such leaders are called heretics.

With great sadness, we have to acknowledge that this kind of reasoning is not foreign to the church. Church history tells us that many atrocities were done in the name of God. Women were brutalized, dismembered and burned at the stake under the auspices of preserving the "true church." There was a time when slavery and all its sadistic carnage were supposedly condoned by scripture – or so we were told according to the book of Philemon.

Racism has been hailed as the plan of God by some of our nation's founders, they themselves slave holders. This too was characterized as the will of God supported by scripture.

Domestic violence and child abuse have been touted as a fundamental sign of a "good Christian home" and consistent with the scripture, by men who claimed to speak on behalf of God. Those active in the women's suffrage movement were vilified and denounced as heretics.

Now, some gay, lesbian, bisexual and transgender people have been sanctioned as the new "whipping boy" that can be safely marginalized, stigmatized and tormented without fear of reprisal. In fact, in some the circles the greater the abuse of LGBT people, the more "holy and sanctified" the accusers are considered to be. This egregious and nefarious tactic is more than homophobic; it is a ploy intended to divide, detract and take hostage our communities.

In the 2004 election, political strategist crept into communities and assumed the role of puppeteer. A wedge issue was identified; in this case gay marriage, with the single intent to divide the votes in communities that would have otherwise opposed them. I am sad to say some prominent clergy fell for the trick and consequently LGBT folks were further stigmatized and disenfranchised.

It was a strategic misinformation campaign that had nothing to do with seeking to explore the meaning behind certain scriptural texts, but rather its sole purpose was to divide communities.

To our shame, some among us fell for the "trick", while yet others of us were complicit if only by our silence. We did not offer another perspective but allowed our faith to be defined by those who neither had the courage or boldness to speak truth to power, for fear of being made visible.

Bottom line: *It was a trick then – and it's a trick now!*

With less than thirteen months away from electing our nation's leadership, we must realize many critical issues are at stake; access to health care, fair housing, criminal justice disparities, economic development for our communities and finding an end to a war for which there is not visible sign of progress or end in sight.

We are witnessing the highest incidence of home foreclosures in the history of this nation; working families whose life savings have gone into buying a home, have watched their dream turn into a nightmare. Families, of every ethnicity who trusted financial institutions have learned that they have been victims of predatory lending.

I am convinced that what hangs in the balance is not what anyone thinks about whether or not we as the LGBT community know God, but the real issue is the future of our collective families, our lives, our ministries and our communities.

I would hope that if there is anything to be learned from the 2004 election it is that when any community is stigmatized or disenfranchised we all lose. There are those who would love to see LGBT community pitted against black community, black community against the Latino community and so forth. It seems to me we need to be wiser than before and not allow anyone or anything to jeopardize our solidarity. We have far more to gain standing together.

I believe all of us are called at this hour to broaden the conversation on civil rights, whether the issue is marriage equality for all people or the racist practices of a small town in Louisiana.

As to what did God say thousands of years ago to another group of people that lived in another time, I am of the opinion that we cannot afford the luxury of having another esoteric theological debate on the meaning and application of some scripture, while New Orleans lays in waste, health care remain unavailable to an overwhelming number of people, rights are denied our community, and health disparities soar among all groups of people.

Perhaps it's time to "increase our territory" as noted in the prayer of Jabez. Maybe it's time to move across the aisle in our churches, in our communities, in our state legislature, the halls of congress and build stronger alliances and coalitions that will enable us to address the plethora of complex issues that stand before us.

There is a passage of scripture that comes to mind that I think energizes our movement for those of us who would declare justice for everyone in the name of our God: "We are afflicted in every way, but not crushed; perplexed, but not driven to despair; persecuted, but not forsaken; struck down, but not destroyed; always carrying in the body the death of Jesus, so that the life of Jesus may also be made visible in our bodies."

Most importantly, we can take prayerful deliberate strategic action. All else is a trick.

The Objectification of the Online Gay, With Special Focus on adam4adam.com
Badilisho

I remember when adam4adam.com (A4A) was launched. Shortly after securing a large following, the site changed its overall format. Porn advertisements became the site's backdrop, and new rules allowed users to publicly post nude pictures. Along with this change came new fields to further define one's personal statistics. For example, "HIV status" and "dick size" were introduced as options in the creation of a personal profile. When I first saw these new options I thought to myself, *"Why does some random person need to know what I have in my pants?"* Several years later, I still feel this way. However, many of A4A's users have compromised or lessened their personal beliefs in order to blend in, remain relevant, be competitive, or simply score. Some, if not most, don't give a second thought to the objectifying nature of sites like A4A. After witnessing the gradual acceptance of the "new and improved" A4A, I knew there would be an overall shift in how members of the gay community would communicate with each other, both on and offline. The site changed from being a website for potential dating, community building, and social networking to a "hook-up site". If the original intent of the site had any sanctity associated with it, that intent escaped to the far reaches of never-never-land.

Call me old school, but I enjoyed the day when I could speak to someone online and they would actually return the greeting. There was no implied contract that we had to sleep together if the conversation was good. It was just that… conversation. As contrived as it might have been, I felt that I was a part of a community that provided me with a forum to communicate with my fellow same gender loving brothers. Now, unworthy prima donnas camp out on sites like A4A as a way of feeding their egos, fueling their low self-esteems, and/or holding out for their fantasy man to arrive. Of course he never arrives and these unrealistic dreamers become bitter, and you can read the thickness of their venom in the words of their profiles: no fats, no fems, no dark men, no, no, no. By the time they are done completing their disqualifying profiles, they have even disqualified themselves. People simply are asking for things online that they are not. Men that are 5'7 and 220 lbs are demanding that no overweight people speak to them. Men that appear to be effeminate are demanding the company of masculine thugs. Can you feel the love? Not! I feel the fantasy.

Ok, so A4A is a hook-up site. This is the truth that we are left with, and I am still an active member of this social experiment called the Internet. So I have found ways to cope with the lack of cohesiveness, humanity, and respect that is absent from sites like A4A. I am one of few A4A users that refuse to enter certain stats on my profile because I feel it is private information. If someone is interested in engaging me, whether socially or sexually, they need to put effort towards holding a conversation that will yield the information they need to determine if we are compatible. I am worth their time and I am not just another "dick size"!

At times my A4A profile has come off like a comedy sketch that pokes fun at some of the psychoses that I have witnessed in profiles. At times, my profile comes off like a diatribe, in hopes that people will become enlightened and start treating each other with respect [again]. I usually get feedback from people telling me how tired they are of online games, and agreeing with several points that I have made. However, no one is making any moves to improve our online interactions, and we surely can't wait on website administrators to be socially responsible. So this is a call to action. I am encouraging each swinging dick to put their dicks back in their pants. If your current way of engaging people is not working for you, change up your game. You don't have to fit in the box just because the box is there. If some random person wants to know your dick size, let the mother fucker take the few extra seconds to engage you.

To further drive the point home, allow me to offer up some comedy. Would you wear a T-Shirt to your family reunion that listed your sexual orientation, your sexual role, your fetishes, and/or your dick size? Typically, this is more information than what we would give to someone we met in a bar. Yet, we will type it in a "box" because the box is there. Hmmmm. This last comedic point is for the current A4A users that attempt to engage people with their face hidden but are more willing to show you their private parts: Would you walk up to someone with a brown paper bag on your head with your dick hanging out and just start talking to them? I write this in love. I hope this article will foster healing and progression. Hotep!

The New Renaissance
A Letter Celebrating "The Eyes Open Festival"
Doug Cooper Spencer

In 2008, there was a celebration of the arts in the black LGBT/SGL community. The celebration was called the 'Eyes Open Festival'. With the festival we wanted to herald in what I call The New Renaissance of black LGBT/SGL artists. The following piece is an excerpt from the Welcome Letter I wrote for the festival.

Welcome to All,

There's a renaissance taking place in the black LGBT/SGL community. It's a movement of song and dance, words and color. It bounds with the energy of Alvin Ailey, and speaks as bold as the paintings of Basquiat; yet it is grounded in the headiness of James Baldwin and Audre Lorde. This explosion of arts and letters is taking place all over the world and its roots are firmly planted in the black LGBT/SGL experience.

During my travels I witness this creative movement. I've been astounded not only by the spirit of these artists, but also by the boldness of their expression. But most of all I'm startled by the fact that these artists are often overlooked by mainstream media as well as the more parochial media; those media that suggests to represent them. Therefore, in the spirit of The Harlem Renaissance, the Eyes Open Festival was created to celebrate and foster an understanding of the arts in the black LGBT/SGL community.

The Eyes Open Festival honors the tradition of black LGBT/SGL luminaries such as Langston Hughes, Josephine Baker, James Baldwin, Johnny Mathis, and Lorraine Hansberry, all of whom have left an indelible imprint on world culture. Today that spirit lives on through contemporaries such as Alice Walker, E. Lynn Harris, Me'Shell NeDego O'cello, Rahsaan Patterson, George C. Wolfe, Tracy Chapman, Paris Barclay, and the list goes on...

I want to thank all the brave, bold, creative geniuses who have chosen to stand in the face of adversity and declare that they too have a voice and vision. And to those artists and supporters, who may not be gay, yet lend their talents to bring light to this movement, thank you so much.

Now the journey has begun.

Essays & Sermons

Liberation Theology Affirms All Who Are Oppressed, Including the LGBT Community
Buster Spiller

*This viewpoints column has been previously published in the Dallas Voice ("No comparison between Wright, McClurkin", 4/3/08) and the Windy City Times ("Liberation theology affirms all who are oppressed, including LGBT", 4/16/08)

The LGBT community shouldn't be quick to dismiss liberation theology when its own religious institutions embrace it.

The recent public airing of statements made by presidential candidate Barack Obama's former pastor, the Rev. Jeremiah Wright, opened a dormant Pandora's box surrounding the underlying racial tensions that still exist between the Black and white communities in the 21st century, as well as the continued existence of institutional racism.

With Sen. Obama's campaign bid to become the first African-American to hold our nation's highest elected office against New York Sen. Hillary Clinton, whom the mainstream gay community seems to adore, even their eyebrows were raised following a snippet of a Wright sermon that declared 'God damn America,' followed by 'Hillary Clinton ain't never been called a nigger.'

My first thought mirrored that of millions of Black Americans as it relates to our perception of how our white compatriots process the lingering effects of racism and its effects on the black community: they just don't get it. When I look at LGBT community, a microcosm of society at-large, it appears to me they take delight in what mainstream media has been successful in accomplishing: painting Rev. Wright as a racist and a bigot.

Without the backdrop of this election, which has provided a glimpse into the historical and current issues the Democratic Party has with it black constituents (widely acknowledged as the party's base) , the LGBT should be cautious about getting into this political fray since it is also an oppressed community seeking social and legal parity.

While the struggles of racial and sexual equality are indeed different there is some commonality, and a measure of respect by the LGBT community should be extended to ministers like Rev. Wright who practice liberation theology.

Despite his sometimes thought-provoking sermons, Rev. Wright is respected in white and Black religious circles. Trinity United Church of

Christ has diverse outreach ministries that are often duplicated by both white and black churches that seek to affirm all people as 'God's children.'

Trinity's outreach efforts also extend to the LGBT community and include active engagement in the fight against HIV/AIDS, with education and direct support services at a time when other mainstream Black denominations and churches were and are still unwilling to do so.

Donnie McClurkin, who is the pastor of a large congregation and a popular gospel singer, has seen his star rise in the Black gospel community with his testimony and profession of being delivered from his seemingly innate homosexuality through God, which strongly resonates in the mainstream Black religious community. Sen. Obama's inclusion of McClurkin in a campaign event before the South Carolina primary proved problematic for the LGBT community. This was based on the assessment that Obama showed poor judgment and insensitivity to the gay community, despite McClurkin's popularity with the African-American community.

For the record, leaders like myself in the Black same-gender-loving community, religious or not, do not support McClurkin's supposed 'conversion.' We prefer to side with the sentiment that he has been unable to reconcile his traumatic childhood experiences of sexual assault and rape with his authentic, spiritual self. Because his experience is similar to that of many LGBT members in our community who would rather hide within the Black church than acknowledge their sexual reality, we sympathize with him but simply don't agree with his position.

Black liberation theology, infused with acknowledgment of our healthy, sexual, God-given self, is how we choose to express who we are in a society that would rather oppress us, first, because we are black, and second, because we are proud, unapologetically LGBT!

This stance should come as no surprise to the white LGBT community because its own religious institutions also embody and practice the spirit of liberation theology in response to the oppression of the LGBT community and the rights and privileges we seek. The same holds for the Latin and feminist community, whose religious leaders have espoused the merits of liberation theology as necessary for the integration of their respective constituencies into society.

LGBT works of nonfiction have been dedicated to the study and application of liberation theology, including 'Gay/Lesbian Liberation: a biblical perspective' by George R. Edwards; 'A Place to Start: Toward an Unapologetic Gay Liberation Theology' by Micheal J. Clark; 'Know My Name: A Gay Liberation Theology' by Richard Cleaver; and 'Defying the Darkness: Gay Theology in the Shadows' by Michael J. Clark.

When I came out in 1994, I was and still am a member of United Methodist Church in Dallas whose predominately black congregation embraces black liberation theology. I intently started attending Cathedral of Hope, the world's largest LGBT church also in Dallas during that same period in an effort to affirm and merge who I was as a black gay man. The experience was wonderful, and at one point I contemplated changing my membership to Cathedral, now a member church of the United Church of Christ conference. In the end, I remained at my home church because it affirmed who I was as both a black and gay man.

So before the white LGBT community decides to join in the political fray of how racially insensitive Rev. Wright may seem in his acceptance of a theological pedagogy that affirms the history and current existence of black Americans, perhaps we need to look no further than how the religious LGBT community also seeks to validate its own existence and place in society through the same medium.

Don't Get Distracted by the Haters!
W. Jeffrey Campbell

As an African American same-gender loving man I have made a conscious decision to walk in my truth and do the work of creating safe spaces for members of my community and other marginalized communities to experience healing, education and fellowship. In this path I have at times found myself wounded by the people who I have often tried to support in their journey.

There was the time that a member of the church where I served as pastor told an associate minister that he had called me on several occasions and I would not return his call. The real truth is that he would leave me messages and then have his number changed so that I would not be able to reach him. I know, that's a great length to go to...but it's the truth.

Another time I was having lunch with co-workers and the waiter flirted with me. Someone at the table shared this incident with a leader in my congregation. This leader realized that he knew the waiter so he called the man and told him that I was interested in him and gave him my contact information. I noticed when the man called that he seemed a bit forward and I was a bit taken aback. Once I determined what was going on, I apologized to him and told him that we were a part of very childish prank. He was very understanding.

Most recently I was called in the middle of night by someone who called me a "bitch" and a "faggot" due to a matter that they really had no clue about. It had been a long time since I had heard someone call me a faggot...It was sort of like being called "nigger" by a white person.

All of these people have either benefited or can in the future benefit from the work that I along with other people in my circle perform. So, the question for me is, "Why do people not want to participate in their own healing and why do they continue to bring harm to the ones who have been gifted to heal?"

I realize that I am not alone in this struggle. There are others in ministry who are also wounded very deeply as we extend and expose ourselves to the community.

While in this place of wonder I am again reminded of Nehemiah's journey to rebuild the walls of Jerusalem. Chapter 3 of Nehemiah's story provides details on rebuilding of the wall. It reads....

1--Then Eliashib the high priest rose up with his brethren the priests and built the Sheep Gate; they consecrated it and hung its doors…

2—Next to Eliashib the men of Jericho built. And next to them Zaccur the son of Imri built.

There are 29.5 additional verses that allow us to visualize what it may have looked like as various families, leaders and groups worked diligently to rebuild the wall of the city. But, when you read chapter 3 you will notice that there are 32 verses in this chapter. So, what about the .5 verse that is missing.

I'm glad you asked! Verse 5b reads, **"But their nobles would not put their shoulders to the work of their Lord."** Wow! Amazing! I have preached this text on several occasions mostly putting the focus on that ½ verse about the nobles who would not do the work. But today, God has shown me a new lesson out of Nehemiah's journey. The lesson simply put is, **"Don't get distracted by the haters!"** The writer writes 31.5 verses spotlighting the work that the citizens of Jerusalem did in their individual and collective efforts to rebuild Jerusalem. Only ½ of a verse was given to disclose the nobles' refusal to do the work.

➢ Too often we spotlight those who will not do the work.
➢ Too often we bring to center stage those who cause us pain.
➢ Too often we focus on those who drag our names throughout the community with disparaging remarks.

Many times hurt people delight in being in the spotlight with mad-crazy behavior. Their behavior is often used to get us off track and possibly to cause us to completely abort the vision and the work.

Some tips on how to stay focused on your vision and mission:

➢ Nurture your prayer/communication relationship with God;
➢ Surround yourself with a support/accountability group;
➢ Address unhealthy behavior immediately by conversing and not confronting;
➢ Don't take it personal…most times it is not about you!

Whatever you are created, gifted and called to do in the church, community, your workplace and or your family, give the greater attention to those who are doing the work with you. Don't get distracted by the haters….

A Case For Understanding Gay Love & Marriage: The Letter
Tommie V. McNeil

My Love,

I have done a lot of thought, reading, investigation, discussions and yes, prayer and meditation with God. Prayer is talking to God. Meditation is listening to God.

Angela Davis, the noted civil rights activist from the 60's to the present said in an article, "We stigmatize people when we fail to question how deeply we're affected by racism and homophobia. It is especially important that campaigns to shift understandings of sexuality occur in the Black Church."

I cannot tell you how you should think or what to believe. What I do hope to do is to encourage looking at the issue of our sexuality from more than one viewpoint. I would not allow someone from over 2,000 years ago, with very limited skills in major surgery to operate on me. And so I find it impossible to accept a statement written by someone claiming it is the Word of God from the same Old Testament that says Slavery, the buying and selling of another human being is right, including Exodus 21st Chapter, 7th Verse which gives rules for a father on selling his own daughter into Slavery. Look it up. There are many examples such as this in the Old Testament.

My love for you is not an abomination: Leviticus 18:22. This is not a choice. Using drugs is a choice that destroys my life and my family. Selling drugs is a choice to destroy others for profit and gain, taking food out of the mouths of children. Two thousand years ago they did not know about DNA. God did and it took the mind of Man all this time to catch up with the Mind of God. They did not know about other natural factors which make a person male or female, but whether he or she is attracted to the opposite sex, same sex or both. I have seen so many people in my lifetime, who remained tortured souls, always in a battle between self and religion. I am not immoral. Certainly we both are guilty of sex with people we had no intimate love for. I am not molesting children. I am an adult who is in love with a wonderful spirit that is you, a Light that happens to be presently in a Body called a Man. I truly believe there would be fewer divorces if men and women paid more attention to the Light inside a person rather the physical. I told you before that I would love you if we were a man and a woman, two women or two men.

I get many wonderful gifts from God through the Church, but I separate the Eternal Living God of yesterday, today and forever from Religion which has so many different kinds of churches saying different things about what they think God said. I told you before, the New Testament is when Jesus came speaking only of Truth and Love. He is the Son of God and God made flesh come down to Earth to experience all that is the life of Man and die so that we may live. Very simple. He had the inside story and unlike the Old Testament, Jesus never said anything against who I, we are. If it was that important to God, that would have been the subject of "Sermon on the Mount II". No one separates me from God by telling me I am not worthy because of who I love.

What would make the Religious satisfied? If my eyes were taken out and I could not see you? Would that make me straight? What if I were given electric shock and my brain was turned to jelly? Would that make me heterosexual and worthy of their love and acceptance? No! They would have to cut out my heart, because it is not what I do that makes me who I am, but who I love. A straight man who has an accident or grows too old to physically make love to his wife would still be straight. So, if I never made love to you again in life, I would still be who I am in my heart. The American Psychiatric Association says, after much study that is not a form of insanity. The Supreme Court says it is not illegal and my Lord and Savior Jesus Christ; to believe in him and love my neighbor as I love myself.

Much is known about the human body and mind that could not have been know over 2,000 years ago, but people pick what they want to from the Bible to support their beliefs, ignoring other strange statements next to those Scriptures. Slavery and community stoning, the throwing of rocks at someone until they were dead were fine in the Old Testament but will get you lethal injection today.

Many people, even married go through life never coming even close to what we have shared. I love you and we connect on a spiritual and physical level. My, our Love is not a sin, an abomination or immoral. I am a kind, loving and giving person who is a true Christian, Christ-like, always teaching, giving and helping others to be the best they can be no matter what age, gender, sexuality or preference. Our Love is what it is and always will be, a beautiful thing that continues to encourage us to grow and be better; honest, loving and prosperous examples of what real humans are, made in the image of God's Love and not Man's religious bending of the Truth. It really got to me when you said you believe we are wrong, but I am grateful you said you are with me still, because you care and love me. I hope this letter gives you some things to think about and helps to bring you peace.

Always,

Love

Tommie

Keynote Speech, February 10, 2008
Excerpt from Lambda Legal
Freedom To Marry
C.C. Carter

On December 25, 2007 at approximately 12:05 am Christmas morning, my partner got on her knees, presented me with a cluster diamond ring and asked me to marry her. And I at 12:05 and 10 seconds lost all composure, let tears stream from my face, lost my breath like something straight out of a Harry Met Sally scene and cried my reply, "yes, yes, yes," accepted her ring and agreed to be her wife. But I didn't accept because I believe in death do us part, or the sanctity of marriage and not for the harmonious bliss that we could give each other.

On the contrary I am a feminist and I have rejected everything that could possibly have to do with normal if it meant normal was measured by the standards of the present hierarchy of majority rules.

Culturally, many African Americans reject the status quo of marriage not because they don't believe in living life with someone and setting up house and raising children. They reject it because not even four hundred years ago they were property, and marriage-the terms husband and wife was not recognized, as well as, husband, wives and children could be sold off with the next deal from a master or a jealous head mistress. And when welfare reform happened in the 20's, it was the unapologetic way in which a woman could not receive aid if her husband was in the household, not accounting for the two headed families that faced employment discrimination because of the color of their skin, ultimately making African American and immigrant families disproportionately economically disadvantaged and leaving single parent households headed by women – a battle we still face as a result of that reform even today.

As a woman I have rejected the idea of marriage ever since I learned at the age of ten from reading in my history books that women were property. Women could be sold for dowries of land, money and high positions in the family business. Even today, in other world countries women can be burned if the husband does not like the outcome of his heir.

But instead, I said "yes," at 12:05 am and 10 seconds because I love her. I love her enough to want to include her in all of the boring work that I do, and the unnoticed accomplishments that I've done, and enjoy the limited success that I have. In essence, I want to weave her into the ordinary mundane details of my daily life. And given the lack of choice of other types of recognizable traditions, and having no other across the board approval for what this is that we are trying to form; because the word husband and wife does not fit us, we are not business partners, we are more than lovers; there is no language to quite call this setting up of house that we want to begin. But I still said, "yes". Because even though "this ain't no ordinary love" we are two very ordinary people, living ordinary lives but in an extraordinary time to make some sort of a stance.

I said, "yes", because of Diana. She was my friend that all of us knew got tired of fighting to be normal and ran into a pole one night. And her partner, no, her girl, no, her wife, no … she was not privileged to have Diana's family so accepting to be called any of those things formally. So she was dismissed from the details of planning the funeral. Six us of sat in the cathedral church refusing to go up to the casket to see Diana in Shirley temple curls, long blue prom dress, white elbow length gloves, black patent leather pumps. We all knew she would have rather been dressed in an Armani men's tailored pinstripe suit, Dolce Cabana men's loafers, hair in ponytail down her back, cigar resting between middle finger and thumb and a men's onyx ring on her pinky. She was one of New York's finest lesbianas chic. We all sat excluded from being able to make comments about who our friend really was and listened to dignitaries that knew her not talk about a person that they met only occasionally, while her partner sat with us, not with the family and no acknowledgement of her own grief. I vowed right then to make sure that my partner, no, my girl, no, my hersband, my… would get that honor if it were me and so I said, "yes."

I said, "Yes", because of Carter, my son. Who not only has two moms but two step moms and normal his lifestyle is not. But neither is the life of children being raised by grandparents, or transracial parents or single parents or incarcerated parents or adoptive parents or drug addicted parents. And yet the lowest form of insult that can be said to him while playing the dozens at lunch time or on the basketball court or on a football field is "at least my mother ain't no dyke." If marriage to the love of my life makes a public stance and can give him armor on top of all the other ammunition he is going to need by just being a young black boy growing up where the odds have be scaled against him of a life expectancy of not making it to the age of 21 (whether by his choice or someone else), I said, "yes".

I said, "Yes", because too many of my friends and their partners have bi national and dual international relationships. They or their parents came here like everybody else to have a better life, to fall in love, to be who they can be with who they want to be with - the very place that purposely recruited our fore mothers and fore fathers to come to this country to work and set up house and fall in love and invest in its well fare – they are now being forced to leave.

I said, "yes," because not only do I want the recognition of being a Mrs. C.C. hyphened somebody, I also want the benefits and the legal rights that are afforded every other "married couple" not "civil unioned" couple. And how does that sound to introduce your friends and acquaintances as "civil unioned" – this is Mr and Mr Martinez and they're "civil unioned", This is Mrs and Mrs Smith and they got "civil unioned" in the MCC church down in Evanston. My sweetie just proposed "civil union" to me. What is at stake is the right to a civil marriage, which is conferred by the government and is associated with numerous legal rights. **A Civil Union** is a legal status granted by a state and it extends the same legal protections and responsibilities to same-sex couples at the state law level. A Civil Marriage comes with over 1,100 federal tax laws and range from more favorable laws such as access to a spouse's social security and pension benefits, hospital visitation and the right to make medical decisions on behalf of one's spouse. Civil Unions offer none of these protections.

I said, "yes," because if we can change the laws to protect us while we're together that means I am also protected when things fall apart. First responders will know what to do when they get a call on a domestic violence dispute – that it's not just two women or men fighting and no, it's not my roommate. That one parent cannot make a final decision to deny custody of a child to the other regardless of whose name is on the birth certificate – if I was a part of it from day one I'm going to be there through its entirety. And I want what's mine for the growth of a business, contributions to the household and your advancement in education that helped you get that promotion. No more five and ten and twenty-five year relationships that end overwhelmingly where one who has all the assets in their name gives nothing to the one that helped that to happen.

I said, "Yes," because I don't plan to retire in Chicago – I am a southern girl and it is cold more than it's hot. My civil union does not travel and is not recognized state to state. In 1996 the United States Congress passed the Defense of Marriage Act, and President Clinton signed it into law. The federal DOMA does two things: for the purposes of the federal law it defines marriage as between a man and a woman therefore denying federal recognition of same-sex marriages. It also gives states the right to recognize or deny any marriage-like relationships between persons of the same-sex. Whereas marriage is recognized by all fifty states, civil unions are only guaranteed to be recognized in the state in which they have originated.

Finally, I said, "yes," because I am a sentimentalist and a romantic – always have had dreams of walking down an aisle in a church even though I saw wedding bells, never thought through the actual marriage part. But like some girls in fairytales I dreamed of hearing a pastor say the words, "I now pronounce you …". and yet the Christian right has used this as their major tactic to scare people from voting for the marriage act. When the truth of the matter is when we talk about Marriage Equality for same-sex couples the right to a religious marriage ceremony, which is governed by communities of faith are not at stake. If gays and lesbians are legally allowed to marry, no religious institution will be forced to perform same-sex marriages, though it's important to note that a growing number of individual clergy and entire congregations have voiced their support for same-sex marriages. What is at stake is the right to a civil marriage, not to – and excuse the parallelism – but not a separate but equal nontransferable civil union.

And so on December 25, 2007, at 12:05 and ten seconds, I packed away every reason for why I never believed in a civil institution rooted in discrimination for so many people, women and other cultural ethnicities that could benefit from it. And forsaking the total idea of why people should have to marry just to receive a civil right of benefits or that many of my straight girlfriends have rejected the notion of marriage and yet find themselves in the "unfavorable position" of marrying in order to receive extra benefits or to make important decisions in the lives of the people they love. That withstanding, and without any other options of protection, but knowingly that I love her wholeheartedly, I stood on the side of minority rule, and I said, "yes."

Well It's Official...
Er'body Can Get Married In D.C.
Badilisho

I have watched the struggle for gay marriage rights from the sideline, and that's where I will continue to sit, on the sidelines. However, I feel the need to inject some points of view on the matter. I'd like to introduce a comparison between Brown versus the Board of Education of Topeka and laws that authorize gay marriage. In 1954, the courts determined, in the case of Brown vs. the Board of Education, that
"Separate educational facilities are inherently unequal"
[http://en.wikipedia.org/wiki/Brown_v._Board_of_Education].

To understand the root of this particular struggle is to know that African Americans wanted the same supportive learning environments that White American students were privileged to have. Prior to this decision, special education did not exist and there were very few "gifted" programs. After schools were racially integrated, tactical strategies were employed to draw a divide between students based on intelligence, or lack thereof. Some of the negative outcomes from this court decision is that the modern day African American student is able to graduate from high school reading at a third grade level and/or matriculate through school as a special education student without a valid attempt to switch the student to a "traditional" learning environment. Yes, tradition, quality and consideration went out the window when the Negroes "arrived".

I pose the following questions to concerned citizens and in particular, gay people: Why do gays want to be married? Do gay people want what straight people have? Do gay people think there is a better chance at a successful marriage than their straight counterparts?

I believe that gay people should have the right to get married. Every working American pays taxes to support several institutions in America, to include the institution of marriage. When some of those taxpayers are not allowed to partake in an institution that they are financially supporting, it is unconstitutional, unfair, and unbelievable. So the struggle for gay marriage is a necessary struggle, but *why do gays want to get married?* If it's for the sake of sitting with a loved one at their bedside during hospitalization, great! If it's for the sake of being the sole benefactor of a death benefit, fine! These unconstitutional technicalities can be addressed legally, but marriage does not appear to be the only answer for such matters. Based on statistics, marriage is more likely to end up in divorce. So why mess up a good thing by following the lead of your unsuccessful hetero-counterparts?

Is this about wanting what your neighbor has? Do gay people want 'straight' privileges? Ah, so this is more about authority, power, and justice. This is not about the issues of validating and supporting all couples. Some of the activists who are spearheading the struggle for gay marriage are not being clear in regard to the connection between power and privilege. If gays are treated just like their straight counterparts there will be less power for straight people. Here is the crux of the argument, and avoiding it will only yield a victory for those in power. Is there someone bold enough to say "yes, it is about wanting what your neighbor has, power, confirmation, and full citizenship"?

My hat goes off to those who immediately rushed down to the D.C. courthouse to get married. It gives the impression that you know what it takes to maintain a successful marriage. Maybe you know something that straight people don't, because over 50% of their marriages fail. In the case of marriage, straight people may have full control of the institution, but they clearly don't know what the heck they're doing. I would urge each American that considers being a part of a particular institution, to study it inside and out. Find out what has worked, what it has to offer, and what are some of the potential pitfalls. Had African Americans conducted this type of analysis in 1954, I don't think there would have been a mad dash to throw their children in the hands of people who didn't care. Consider the comparison mentioned here, conduct your own analyses, and Godspeed to each of you!

After Equality, Then What?
Doug Cooper Spencer

The National Equality March on Washington made headlines recently, and deservedly so. But I wonder how many of the people who marched on the nation's capital carried with them the true meaning of equality?

You see, there's a distinct class structure even within the gay community that defies equality. It reflects the very constructs of class that exists in the larger society. In the gay community, it's one that places the concerns of rich white gays and lesbians over others. It even engenders the same imperialistic notions we see in the larger society.

For example, there were some marchers who suggested that a conference of black LGBT writers, artists and thinkers from around the world who gathered that same week in Austin, Texas for the Fire & Ink Cotillion, change its date in order to accommodate the National Equality March, even though the Fire & Ink conference had been set long before the suggestion of the march.

To add fire to the flames, some of the marchers even declared that the refusal to change the Fire & Ink conference date is further testament of lack of support by the black LGBT community. They didn't look at the fact that we are fighting the same fight, but on different fronts; instead they continue to hold to their white-is-right notions. It's an imperialistic view that grows out of a legacy of racism. How will those marchers address this type of attitude?

Equal rights for gays and lesbians will pass legal muster sooner than some might think. It can be seen in the presence it has in conversations regarding civil rights and in the changing views of a growing number of former opponents such as the black clergy as well as members of the Republican Party.

But once equal rights for gays have been won, where does the larger LGBT community go in terms of fighting injustice? Are equal rights for same-sex couples the final challenge for the LGBT community? How far will words like freedom, equality, justice and liberty fly in the gay community once the fight for equal rights has been won? Will issues like racism, health & economic disparity, gender inequality and gender identification (i.e. trans gender orientation), just to name a few, take center stage?

Some might say it's too soon to ask such questions because the basic fight for equality hasn't been won. I disagree. There were many who marched on Washington who are well aware of their elite status; yet, there were numerous others who marched who may remain disaffected even after gay rights have been won.

    The National March on Washington was necessary. However, true advancement towards equality happens in the hearts and minds with a full awareness of what equality means. If not, all the posturing we saw that weekend in the nation's capital was half baked or even a sham.

Not Another Drop!
W. Jefferey Campbell

Mark 5:21-34

21-When Jesus had again crossed over by boat to the other side of the lake, a large crowd gathered around him while he was by the lake.

22-Then one of the synagogue rulers, named Jairus, came there. Seeing Jesus, he fell at his feet

23-And pleaded earnestly with him, "My little daughter is dying. Please come and put your hands on her so that she will be healed and live."

24-So Jesus went with him. A large crowd followed and pressed around him.

25-And a woman was there who had been subject to bleeding for twelve years.

26-She had suffered a great deal under the care of many doctors and had spent all she had, yet instead of getting better she grew worse.

27-When she heard about Jesus, she came up behind him in the crowd and touched his cloak,

28-Because she thought, "If I just touch his clothes, I will be healed."

29-Immediately her bleeding stopped and she felt in her body that she was freed from her suffering.

30-At once Jesus realized that power had gone out of him. He turned around in the crowd and asked, "Who touched my clothes?

31-"You see the people crowding against you," his disciples answered, "And yet you can ask, 'Who touched me?'"

32-But Jesus kept looking around to see who had done it.

33-Then the woman, knowing what had happened to her, came and fell at his feet and, trembling with fear, told him the whole truth.

34-He said to her, Daughter, your faith has healed you. Go in peace and be freed from your suffering."

Introduction

As we enter into this moment it is of utmost importance that you know of my personal mission to create safe spaces for the spoken and unspoken members of our African American same/both-gender loving and transgender community to dialogue, learn, pray, praise and be empowered through the voices of our past, present and future. As we begin to focus on this text it is important not that you look at your neighbor and say anything. It is important that you look into the mirror and speak to that person who is looking back at you and say, **"Not another drop!"** Think about the pain that you are experiencing now from rejection and abuse and say, **"Not another drop!"** Think about the times when you cried at night because your family didn't embrace your authentic self and say, **"Not another drop!"** Look at that person in the mirror and remember all of the times that you left a mainstream worship service where you were told one more time that you were going to hell because of your sexual orientation and say, **"Not another drop!"** I need you in this moment to remember the people who stabbed you in the back, the people who said you would never amount to anything, all the times you trusted someone who proved to be untrustworthy and left you with a broken heart and say, **"Not another drop!"** Come on, look into that mirror and see yourself and say, **"Not another drop!"**

What do we know about this woman?

We know that she has been sick for 12 years. We know that she has been bleeding for 12 years. We know that she has been to the doctor trying to get well. So, it is not as though she wants to stay sick. She wants to get well! Scripture says that she has spent EVERYTHING that she has trying to get well and yet, 12 years later, instead of getting better, she is getting worse.

We do not know her name. We do not know her family history. We do not know if she is married or has been married. We do not know if she has children. What we do know is that she has been sick for 12 years…bleeding for 12 years…in agony for 12 years…unable to get well for 12 years. Struggling for 12 years! Living in a culture that has issues with women and bleeding, for 12 years. Going to doctor after doctor after doctor, spending all her money for 12 years.

What do we know about her culture?

When we go back and do a study historical critical interpretation of Hebrew text we find that the Jewish people had some beliefs and laws about blood that often caused members of the community to be separated from family and not allowed in the temple.

The Jewish people taught and upheld a religious law that said if a woman was on her monthly cycle, she was deemed unclean and could not enter into the temple. As I look at this from my 21st century eyes I find that to be quite unsettling as I have spoken to my sisters who have expressed some of the pain, changes in the body and the mental matters that come along with menstruation. I have witnessed some of these changes and find that the house of God is the place where a woman needs to be during this cycle….for the prayers of the righteous avail much! LOL! My sisters might witness to this…during that time of the month you might say anything, do anything and pick up anything and knock anybody in the head. No, it is not a time for my sisters to be kept away from the house of God. It is a time in which you should be in the presence of God and God's people.

Brothers, you are not left out! If a man had intercourse with a woman during her period, he too was labeled unclean and cut-off from his family. Strange and unusual circumstances and laws designed by people who had limited understanding of the workings of the body. This is the time period in which this woman lived.

The Collision of Issue and Culture = Stigma and Ostracism

Now we know something about the woman. We know something about the culture and time in which she lived. Now, let's see how her issue and her culture collide. She has an issue of blood. Because of this issue we can suppose that she has been banned from the temple for the duration of the issues. She has been cut-off from her family and the community for 12 years.

In my 21st century mind I am supposing that in order for this woman to take care of her day-to-day chores, she had to pick unique times to accomplish these actions. If she needed to do her laundry she had to get up much earlier than the other women to go to the riverbed or creek bed and wash her clothes in order to avoid the other women with their stares and pointed fingers. Perhaps some days as she was returning from washing her clothes she encountered some of the other women of her community who, because of their knowledge of her condition, they would scurry to the other side of the road and hold their young children close to them and whisper, "She's unclean! Unclean! Unclean!"

It was not enough that she had to live with this matter in her body that caused her to bleed, she also had to deal with the social issue that this disease bore through her culture. She had to deal with ostracism, stigma, ugly words, pointed fingers and cold, accusing stares regarding a condition of life of which she had no control over. Can you imagine been physically weakened by this illness and then having to deal with the loneliness and isolation that her culture forced upon her?

It is beginning to sound a bit like the lives that many of our brothers and sisters who have lived with and died from AIDS have had to endure. It sounds similar to the stories that I have heard from some detailing how their family members didn't want the children eating after them once they knew they were living with HIV/AIDS. It reminds me of the stories shared with me about how ignorance caused their family members and friends to force them to eat from paper plates and drink from plastic cups that they would throw away once used. From those same mouths came words like, "I was already hurting because of the physical toll the virus was having on my body and then to have to endure these actions from my family just wounded me even more."

Even more so are the hateful actions that many of us who are same-gender loving have had to experience and continue to endure, not because we are living with HIV/AIDS, but simply because we live in a culture where many still believe that our sexual orientation is a sin, an abomination to God. So, we hear the harsh and hurting words from the pulpits, "God made Adam and Eve and Adam and Steve!" These words still today cause many same-gender loving ministers, worship leaders, deacons, pastors and singers to hide in a closet hurting, confused and miserable. We live in a world where in foreign lands and in this great United States of America, people are still brutalized and killed because of their sexual orientation. When will we be free?

Ostracism and stigma didn't just start in our culture; however it still is at the root of so much pain, depression and self-hatred that many individuals of various races, genders, sexual orientations and cultures live with today.

Let's See What Jesus is Doing!

I have found that when preparing for teaching and preaching it is always important to walk backward in the text and see what was going on prior to the scene at hand. With that in mind, let's take a turn and revisit the text and find out what Jesus is doing. Let's flip back a few chapters.

As Mark writes his gospel, he introduces Jesus to the hearer and reader through the voice of Jesus' cousin, John the Baptist...

"...After me will come one more powerful than I, the thongs of whose Sandals I am not worthy to stoop down and untie. I baptize you with water,
But he will baptize you with the Holy Spirit." (Mark 1:7-8)

This is the message that John the Baptist teaches...

What do we see Jesus doing?

> - In Mark 1:16 we see Jesus walking beside the Sea of Galilee and beginning to call his first disciples. That foundational group who will experience his ministry over the next 3 years and then after his death they will take on the task of preaching his gospel and calling the world to be believe and be saved.
> - He begins to teach in the synagogue and the people are amazed...While teaching he encounters a man who is possessed by an evil spirit. The evil spirit cries out to Jesus, "What do you want with us, Jesus of Nazareth? Have you come to destroy us? I know you are the Holy One of God." Jesus commands the evil spirit to "Be quiet" and to "Come out of him!" The evil spirit obeys.
> - Later in Mark 1, Jesus goes to Simon Peter's house and finds Peter's mother-in-law lying in bed ill with a fever. He goes to her, takes her by the hand and helps her up. Her fever leaves her and she begins to wait on the people in the house.
> - By Mark 2 many are beginning to hear about Jesus...the Teacher...the One whose voice demons obey...the one who heals the sick. The people begin to follow Jesus in a quest to be taught, to be healed and to witness his work. At Capernaum a house where Jesus is teaching is so full that 4 friends take their paralyzed friend to the top of the house, tear the roof off and lower the man into the center of the room so that Jesus can heal him.

> In Mark 4 while Jesus is down in the bottom of a boat a great storm comes that causes the waves to break over the boat, nearly causing the boat to capsize and sink. The disciples are going out of their minds in fear. Finally the bright light comes on and they say, "let's go down in the bottom of the boat and get Jesus. Master, how can you sleep when all of this is going on? Don't you care that we are about to die at the hands of this storm?" These are the same men who Jesus had called to journey with him in ministry. They had witnessed his works of healing and deliverance and yet while on the boat with him in the middle of the storm they fail to remember his power and ability and grow afraid. In response to their cries Jesus speaks peace to the winds and the waves and they obey. Have you ever been in the middle of your own storm and lost site of the fact that Jesus has control over all things? You have been in the doctor's office and gotten some distressing news and in the midst of those anxious moments your previous experience with Jesus moves you to call on his name and he speaks peace. Have you ever had some seemingly never ending mess going on at the job and just about the time you were going to cuss everybody out and walk out the door, you remember not only who you are but whose you are and you call on the name of Jesus and Jesus does an exceeding, abundant work that blows everybody's mind? Have you ever been in a relationship that was not working and was never going to work but because you thought no one else would love you or want you, you stayed in it…unhappy, unfulfilled and hungering to be loved the right way…somewhere over in the midnight of your life you remembered that Jesus said, "I will never leave you nor will I forsake you…" and in that moment you called on Jesus and Jesus spoke to your storm and the winds and the waves obeyed? If we can just talk about some real stuff today we can talk about the time when we thought we were in the relationship that was the be all, end all. But, you found yourself one day standing and witnessing something that made you sing Miss Nancy Wilson's song, "Guess Who I Saw Today"? It broke your heart! Messed up your mind! Tore up your spirit! And you had to run and find Jesus and say, "Wake up! The storms in my life are raging and no one can fix it but you! And, Jesus has a way of showing up in our most disturbing situations and working things out for our good! He will speak peace…peace…peace…peace. And when Jesus speaks peace the storms, waves or winds cannot argue…they must obey.

> We have to go one more place and observe the work of Jesus. In Mark 5 Jesus crosses the lake to the region of the Gerasenes. When he steps off the boat he encounters a man with an evil spirit who is living in the tombs. This man had become so consumed by the demon that nothing could control him. The text states that, "...he had often been chained hand and foot, but he tore the chains apart and broke the irons on his feet. No one was strong enough to subdue him. Night and day among the tombs and in the hills he would cry out and cut himself with stones." Have you ever awakened at some point in your journey and found that you were living among dead folks? Have you? Have you ever just opened your eyes, the eyes of your spirit and realized, "baby these are tombs around me? These are dead folks around here. There is no one alive here. Why am I here?" It was not my intent to park in this place, however, I see a need to linger here. Have you ever opened your eyes and said, "I see dead people! I see dead people all around me. Some I know! Some I don't. But what I do know is that I see dead people and I don't belong here!" This man is living among the dead. But, when Jesus steps into the place where this man lives, this man's circumstance is altered by the presence and the power of the Son of God. This is a celebratory moment...to understand that no matter how low my situation can be, when Jesus comes...as Sara Jordan Powell sings, "He takes the gloom...!" When Jesus stops by even the most maddening and sorrowful situation is turned from gloom to glory. Right is this moment Jesus is reaching out to bring you out of that dead situation into a place of hope, healing and harvest...all you need do is believe.

That's what Jesus is up to!

Now let's get back to the woman!

She has suffered for 12 years with this issue however; I am supposing that some kind of way she has heard about Jesus and his ability to heal. I don't know if she heard some of the women talking about Jesus' works while they were on their way to the river to wash their clothes. Maybe while she was in her house one day yearning to be able to return to temple, she heard some passers by talking about this man who had cast the demon out of the demon possessed man who had lived among the tombs. In her hearing these stories, perhaps she decided, "Well, if this man they are calling Jesus can do these things for others, surely he can do something for me."

In my own mind and spirit I believe that she looked around at the limitations that had been caused not just by disease but by the ostracism and stigmatism of her culture and community...she looked at her skin, paled by her loose of blood...she looked at her blood-soiled laundry and she declared in a weak voice, **"Not another drop!** If he can do this for others, today he will do it for me." I imagine that she forced her weak self up and wrapped a shawl around her arms and she began to creep out of her dwelling perhaps moving towards the voices of the crowd that she knew would surround such a teacher and prophet and with each step she declared, **"Not another drop!** Not one more drop!"

I suppose that as she got closer to the crowd, people began to see her and recognized her to be the woman with the issue of blood. Some were probably moved by the laws of the culture and they began to cry out, "Unclean! Unclean!"

Now, we are going to walk in our truth here. Some of us need some crowd control in our lives. We keep trying to get to Jesus but the crowd keeps messing with us and blocking our path. One crowd saying, "You ain't never gonna be nothing!" Another crowd saying, "Men don't cry!" The other crowd saying, "You deserve to have HIV cause you know God didn't create you to have sex with another man!" That other crowd, which is the crowd made up of members of our own same-gender loving community saying, "Girl, Miss Thing losing too much weight. She must have a House In Virginia!" We have crowd issues in our lives. Family crowds! Church crowds! Crowds made up of ex-lovers, current sex partners, the kids at the club! But don't give up...make your mind up that whatever it is that you are going through, you are not going to bleed one more drop!

How might this woman have dealt with her crowd? Being the fan of the stage musical and big screen production, Dreamgirls that I am, I think that this sister took on the spirit of Effie Melody White and as they tried to block her and keep her from getting to Jesus, she dropped to her knees (she had to be on the ground to touch the hem of his clothes...) and began to sing the first lines of Effie's signature song , "And I am telling you I'm not going...Ain't no way I'm going back like I came. I been suffering too long and I'm not bleeding one more drop!" She understood in that moment that her suffering had hung around far too long and this moment in time that she was living and breathing in was her window of opportunity for healing. So, she pressed her way through the crowd of haters until she was able to reach up from her crouched position and touch the hem of Jesus garment.

Scripture says that this moment for Jesus was so big that he felt the power leave his body. He asked, "Who touched me?" The disciples thought it was outlandish for Jesus to ask this question since there were so many people crowded around him. It must have been something different about her touch. It had to have been something different about her need and about the way that she came to Jesus that caused her touch to be different from all the rest.

Mark states, "Then the woman, knowing what had happened to her, came and fell at his feet and, trembling with fear, told him the whole truth." Once Jesus sees and hears her, he states, "Daughter, your faith has healed you. Go in peace and be freed from your suffering."

What's Your Issue?

Now the question to ask the person who is looking back at you from the mirror is, "What's your issue?" Are you sick and tired enough of the same stuff that you are willing to declare, **"Not another drop!"**? Your issue may be around any of the following...

- Sexuality
- Shame
- Depression
- Addiction
- Anger
- Abuse
- Incest
- Molestation
- Fear
- Internal Hatred
- Deception
- A Dual Life
- An HIV diagnosis
- An AIDS diagnosis (they are different)
- A broken relationship
- Living in singleness
- Rejection

...or any and many other things. I just pray that today you will decide that you are not going to bleed one more drop. Jesus is right in the room with you. Reach out your hand for healing and receive the power and healing of God. Today will mark the day that your bleeding stop and your victorious living begins. Declare: **Not Another Drop!**

May the Presence and Power of God be with You Always!

I'm Gay, But Hold On, Let Me Explain
Doug Cooper Spencer

Wait a minute! Do I really have to 'explain' why I'm gay? Some people seem to think so. For instance, I once heard someone talking about the fact that he is gay. The conversation becomes a bit obfuscated around the issue of homosexuality as an orientation, but during the conversation the guy seemed to have felt it necessary to explain why he is gay. It appears he took the role of the apologist.

During the conversation he says he was molested as a child and he says due to the molestation he believes who he initially might have been changed. Given the context of the conversation, was he talking about being gay?

Now I applaud the fact that this guy spoke openly about being gay, and I respect his experience but if he was speaking of his development as a person who is gay turning on the fact of having been molested, then I have a question about his response: What if he was destined to be gay regardless of the incident?

I have a friend who once told me he had been molested as a boy by a man while visiting the man's apartment and that was reason he 'became' gay. When I asked my friend why was he, a child, in that man's apartment he thought for a while, and then his eyes brightened with something he hadn't recalled: He had a crush on the man and would go over to visit him. Now, I'm sure we can all agree the man was wrong for taking advantage of my friend, then a boy, but that's not what I'm talking about here. I'm talking about the fact that all those years my friend used the molestation as an explanation of why he is gay, not having realized that he was gay all along.

Don't get me wrong, I have no intention of diminishing the act of child molestation, nor anyone's experience with it. I'm speaking of the habit some have of associating homosexuality with a history of trauma and also, to consider why some feel it necessary to explain their being gay in the first place.

In answer to the latter question first, the need for some to explain that they are gay most likely stems from the dynamic relationship between the oppressor and the oppressed- - the oppressed feels obligated to appease his or her oppressor even to the point of believing the views of the oppressor. Therefore, many homosexual persons have come to believe it's their obligation to explain themselves to heterosexuals, because, after all, it's the homosexual who is somehow wrong. It's a relationship that has been around for a long time.

Now, addressing the first matter: To summarily draw a connection between homosexuality and incidences of trauma implies that homosexuality simply has to be a symptom of a ruined spirit, but you know what? I don't buy that. Such an inference is an overstatement.

But this conversation goes deeper than it appears because, you see, by taking the apologist's point of view of having to explain one's sexual orientation, we stand to lose out on what it means to empower ourselves, to simply love ourselves for who we are, cut and dry. No explanations or apologies needed. That goes for anyone. We should all love ourselves.

And the problem doesn't stop there. By apologizing for being gay we can also potentially hand our power over to the person we're explaining ourselves to. Remember, there are those who don't want to extend unconditional acceptance to a gay lifestyle, and to give people like that an inch, well, they could end up taking a mile.

I, for one, do believe I was born gay, and no, there is no traumatic experience onto which I can hang a justification. In a story I wrote for Amazon Shorts called 'Bad Damon', I recount a particular summer in 1964 in which a boy has a crush on a man. It's a semi-autobiographical story. That summer of '64, I recall how I sought that man every day of that long, hot summer. I was gay. I was a gay boy without war wounds, plain and simple. No result of trauma, just gay.

Ironically, the trauma that did cause me to act against my nature was society's demand that I *not* be who I am. It's what led me, as a young man, to seek a lifestyle that was unnatural to me: heterosexuality. So I guess you could say I'm able to explain my *heterosexual ways because I was molested by society*.

Look, molestation is a horrible thing that should not happen to anyone. But to use that, as well as any traumatic experience, as a constant justification of one 'becoming' gay should really be scrutinized because there are victims of molestation and other forms of trauma who are not homosexual and never have been. Also, there are many same gender loving people who have never been molested.

But in the end, you know what I think? I think the fact that I'm asked to explain my existence to someone is what's really traumatic.

I'm Coming Out and Netting In[1]
Benjamin Ledell Reynolds

A Renewed Vision

(Revelation 21:3-5a)

> *And I heard a great voice out of heaven saying,*
> *Behold, the tabernacle of God is with men,*
> *And He will dwell with them,*
> *And they shall be His people, and God himself shall be with them,*
> *And be their God.[3]*
> *And God shall wipe away all tears from their eyes;*
> *And there shall be no more death, neither sorrow, nor crying,*
> *Neither shall there be any more pain:*
> *For the former things are passed away.[4]*
> *And He that sat upon the throne said,*
> *Behold I make all things new.[5a]*

God of Revelation,

Reveal to your church yet more light to illuminate the glory and the mystery of sexuality and the sensuality with which you

have blessed us to better love one another and to better love

our earth.

May our sexuality and our spirituality

teach each other,

touch each other,

love each other as soul –

the very life that is the starstuff of your cosmic image revealed

in us

as we follow your light that has entered this world.[2]

---

1 "Netting-in" is a term that I learned from a colleague, Nori Rost, who served as the Senior Pastor at the Pikes Peak Metropolitan Community Church of Colorado Springs during the same time I served in that city. The term refers to allowing others to know who one's sexual orientation, and inviting them into your world as opposed to coming out to theirs.

2 Geoffrey Duncan, *Courage to Love: Liturgies for the Lesbian, Gay, Bisexual and Transgender Community*, p180.

My coming out and netting-in story has particular significance for me because I chose to do so at the time I was serving as the Senior Pastor within the context of a Black Baptist congregation. I had arrived at a time and space in my journey in which it became crucial to share with the congregation who I [really] am. But before I could do so, I had to be transparent with the members of my family, including my parents and siblings, my former-wife and daughter, who were also members of the congregation.

I had already come out sometime before to Dr. Vincent Harding, my Professor, mentor and friend at the Iliff School of Theology. Dr. Harding was the first person with grey hair that I had ever told about my sexuality. This became important, because it was his idea and wisdom to gather a group of persons (Dr. Arthur Jones, Professor of Psychology at the University of Denver; and Rev. Reginald Fletcher, who served as the Minister to Youth at the church where I was pastor, and a very dear friend who I had also come out to some years earlier during our seminary tour) that I could be accountable to and supported by as I told my story in anticipation of the potential fallout. They also helped me to decide when I would actually tell the story. My point here is that there were stages to my coming out. In hindsight, I can see that I was testing the waters to see if it was safe for me to swim creating the emotional support that I needed whatever the fall-out would be.

During this time in my life I was quite fortunate to live and serve in the same city where my parents reside. I recall many weeks before I would come out to the congregation, I would drive to their home with the intention that this would be the moment that I would share my truth. After several attempts at this, on a Monday I arrived at my parent's residence emotionally whipped, and when my mother answered the door, she immediately detected that something heavy was on my mind. She said to me, "Tell me what is wrong!" With tears in my eyes, I sat the both of them down and thanked them for being wonderful parents and told them I was gay.

To my surprise, they were not surprised. My mother, who is oftentimes the spokesperson in these family-matter-sharing moments, said, "We have always known. We didn't talk about it, but we have always known." My father, who had all my life tried to steer me from being "a sissy", said, "Ten years ago, I may not have felt as I do today, but hell, being gay is not the worst thing that you can be." While his words may have had some negative connotations, for my father to be able to speak affirming of my sexuality at any level was absolutely astonishing and transformative.

The difficulty my parents faced was that they did not want me to come out to the church. In Dad's words, "People can be very mean, and church people are the meanest people God ever created." These words were meant to keep me safe, but also to help keep them safe from some of the losses that they experienced after I came out to the church and community; to include the loss of long-time friends and relationships.

On the evening of Friday, September 29, 2006, I would officially resign from the pastorate and come out to my church family in the same speech. I publicly thanked my parents and family for their support, and went on to applaud and appreciate the congregation for the journey, as I reminded them that I had been blessed to be a protégé of the congregation, since my preaching career had begun there when I was but fourteen years old. I recognized that they, in large part, had helped to shape me into the preacher that I am today...and certainly were responsible for giving me, through God's grace, the opportunity to share in this fellowship as Senior Pastor.

I then went on to share what I believed I had been trying to share with them for 45-years, that I was "same-gender loving." I had asked that the congregation take some time (a week) to sit with my statement before responding publicly, with the intention to reconvene a week later to listen to the congregational responses to the shared information. There were tears and sadness and feelings of betrayal; but it seemed out of the 400 plus persons that filled the room, almost everyone would take some time following the meeting to shake my hand and to embrace me as a symbol of [Christian3] support. The words spoken to me by one of the Deacons in the congregation will forever remain in my memory and becomes the bases of my Theological research. He said, "Pastor, I think everyone in here knew that you are gay, but I am mad as hell that you told us."

In terms of some critique, the communities with whom I shared my coming out story both declare that they "knew" that I was gay but did not want to hear it or talk about it. The silence of one's sexuality in the African American community is an intricate part of attempting to get at the understanding of who we are sexually. With my parents, although we do not have ongoing conversations about my coming out (they remain silent about that part of my life), but they had to move from silence to support because of what would come in terms of fallout in the congregation. In contrast, the congregation felt that they know because I

---

3 The word "Christian" is being used here to mean "formal, structural and institutional Christianity" rather than "genuine conversion or faithfulness to the truth as taught by Christ." This is the thing to do in this moment, and perhaps not a genuine expression of what we are actually feeling.

had articulated my truth to them, in the words of the Deacon, a week later and having had time to digest what was spoken to them, they "were mad as hell." Because of that madness and because they now possessed knowledge of my "un-repented sexuality," they had to do something about it. Rather than, leaving on December 31, 2006, as I proposed when I resigned which would have given me time to help the church make a smooth transition into new leadership, I was dismissed on October 31st and became completely cut-off from the life of my church family.

What remains most frustrating is that the congregation is aware of the kind of violence done to African American people during the civil rights movement and that this was justified by religious tradition: that European Americans could deny African Americans their own full civil and human rights because it was said that God's will and word says that humanity should not be co-mingled but should be segregated by race, and that the bible supports separation of races and even supported slavery. Of course, now, the congregation rejects such tenets as inappropriate. We condemn slavery, and consider it to be a great evil. And the separation of races too, we understand to be an artificial cultural invention that we will not accept. But me—they cannot accept either. I am hopeful that the rest of my life and my coming out will contribute to my communities' acceptance and understanding of being both Black and same gender loving (gay). As reflect, I have often found myself "caught in the middle" since the "two-ness" of identity (to use a term of W.E.B. DuBois) reflected in being both Black and gay is not wholly approved in either the Black or gay communities.

The Right to Fully Be Who We Are
John-Martin Green

When I was a boy, my father taught what was then known as Black History in New York City public schools. While it struck my brothers and me that this was important, it also pained us that he seemed incessantly to be rattling off dates, events and personages no matter the social context in which we found ourselves. It wasn't until many years later that I realized that my father's penchant wasn't just some sort of mild autism, but rather an ongoing effort to frame our experience in an historical context. Historical context is an invaluable tool where one would consider the possibility of social change.

It has long occurred to me that being black in America is a process of perpetual redefinition in the face of definitions that have been imposed on us. Hence, we have gone from being niggers, the first title assigned us, to identifying as colored, followed by Negro and Afro American and Black. Now, we are African American. Along those very lines, only a generation ago there was a great palaver amongst American Africans about whether we would identify as Negro or Black. Up to that point, for many of us, to be called black constituted fighting words. This was, of course, because all but a few of the synonyms for 'black' in Western dictionaries were distinctly negative including, but not limited to 'dirty' and 'evil.'

Since the Abolition Movement in the antebellum period, at the forefront of struggles for self-determination the world over have been African Americans. In recent times, on the heels of the sexual revolution and, as a result of some successes waged in the realm of Black folks' identity politics, others have joined the band wagon, most notably perhaps, White homosexuals with the Gay Liberation Movement. It would appear that the convergence of race and sexuality have brought us to a new historical moment and a new opportunity, if inevitability of yet another redefinition.

By now, the notion that the sexuality of Black men is threatening to White men is a cliché in the Black community. The concept of the black male brute or sexual animal is a projection of White men onto Black men. Most of the rapes against White women during slavery and since have been perpetrated by White men who have then projected images of what they fear in themselves onto those less powerful than themselves. To many heterosexual Black men, the sexuality of their same gender loving brothers is much more threatening than their sexuality has ever been to White men. The reason for this is not simply fear and anger for that which is unknowable to them about homosexuality, or even fear of their own latent potential for homosexuality. It is, moreover, fear and hatred which grows out of their paranoid feelings of inadequacy as Black men, a construct which they've been raised to believe is an oxymoron.

To many heterosexual Black men, homosexuality amongst Black men, or being "gay," is a White construct through which they see us as having copped out on both our manhood and our Blackness. One important reason for this is that there exist for us new archetypal memories of the way White men used us sexually when we were their property (both as objects of abuse and of pleasure,) just as they did our women.[4] It is because of this insecurity that many heterosexual brothers feel that, for Black men to be "gay," means that we are following behind and might even be looking to be further fucked by White men, and, in turn, sold out our Blackness and our manhood. In so doing, we make it hard for them and for the race (to appear as if we are free.)

The scary thing about this posture is the degree to which they are right. We are all of us selling ourselves short in this process of subscribing to an identification that has nothing to do with us. I even wonder about the extent to which we same gender loving brothers also, subconsciously believing we are failed men, refer to each other as "Miss Thing," "Bitch," and all manner of derogatory female sanctioning as we wear the mask of the misogynist, male supremacist oppressor.

Equally as fascinating and chilling to me as this portent is the possibility that same gender loving men have internalized the white supremacist and heterosexist notions that we are not men, and that this may account for the process by which many homosexually predisposed little Black boys commence an identification with the female that is so intense that the male self is subsumed. We take on the caste of the victim, (the Black woman, in this case), in order to be non-threatening to White men.

By the time a boy is four or five, he pretty well has the lay of the land in terms of sex roles; certainly if both parents are present. I know for my part, I watched my father get up each day and go out into a world which I already knew was, for that Black man, a particularly dangerous world, especially with the television news footage and sound bites that were a new window onto the world for my generation. This same man, often times, would return at the end of a long day in the trenches,

---

[4] In his essay, *Rereading Voices from the Past: Images of Homoeroticism in the Slave Narrative*, author, Charles Clifton makes an excellent case for the existence of those abuses as couched by male ex-slaves in their narratives.

embittered, enraged and hurting for all the insults to which he'd borne witness both for himself and for his people. A world in which he was regularly psychologically assaulted gauntlet style. Whether or not he was actually more traumatized than our mother, the world he traveled through and the work he was attempting to do in it appeared to be perilous and frightful fare.

Whereas, for my mother, while she also worked, as she made her way out into the big, ominous world to do her bit, somehow the world seemed to me less violent, less treacherous and one wherein there was more grace. This may have been, at least in part, because she was born of more personal grace than my father, but also, I suspect, because, as she moved through the world, she was perceived as less threatening to the people who held the upper hand in that world. To be non-threatening to the oppressor insures that we may get along better or more easily.

Could it not be that, for these associations, we same gender loving Black male youth determined subconsciously at an early age that our shared sexual identification with females made it easier to identify with females in other areas of our personalities as well? This schematizing, rooted in the Black child's perception of the imbalance of living in a white supremacist world, i.e., through Jim Crow's last hurrah, inspired a sense of racial inferiority. In addition, the internalized anti-homosexual attitudes we were being acculturated into made us feel ineffectual as the men we would become, along with the misogyny, which gave us to feel the women with whom we were identifying were inferior. It would appear that this negative confluence was the perfect spawning ground for a disposition of self abnegation.

Regarding the perception of Black male homosexuality as a copout on manhood, (particularly the 'protector' and 'family breadwinner' roles often attributed to manhood) many same gender loving men do, at least ostensibly, live easier lives. While people fail to acknowledge the extent to which same gender loving men, through different phases in our lives, are nurturers, taking care of our parents, siblings, nieces, nephews, and children, among others; the fact remains that most of us, certainly if we are unattached, don't have to be responsible for anyone but ourselves. And perhaps, in keeping with the learned behavior through which we would be non-threatening to White men (in this case, homosexual White men), many among us have taken up the identification "gay" so as to get along better or more easily in the dominant culture.

The proverbial elephant in the room is that African Americans, or more particularly African descended men, have permitted ourselves and allowed our families to be subjugated, overpowered and thoroughly used by White men. In aspiring to assimilate with, or otherwise be like

Whites and, incidentally, confirming their superiority, we have simultaneously attempted to disavow our recent history with them during which they dominated us completely as their slaves. We were their property. That is, they could, and did do to us and make us do absolutely anything that might occur to them no matter how unbelievably sick, sordid or otherwise outrageous it might have been.

It's as if we're operating out of a sort of collective amnesia – amnesia being a psychological defense mechanism – a trick of the mind, to help it stay sane. When the mind has experienced something too terrible to remember, it forgets. But we must wrest ourselves from this state of suspended animation because, as long as we do not acknowledge how thoroughly they domesticated us, they will continue to hold so much power over us. In other words, the trick, or trick bag, or conundrum, or dilemma for African Americans is that, by our not giving loud, regular and consistent voice to the way in which patriarchal, capitalist, white supremacists have dominated us most viciously, they continue to dominate us by decimating the public education system, insuring that our youth will not be armed with the information and skills they need to be competitive, thereby rendering them expendable, or, at best, merely consumers and authorizing police forces, like overseers, to target and beat us, (to death, if necessary) into submission and railroading us into these new-fangled plantations called prisons. When I think of how many among us, even in the twenty first century, still pass as heterosexual instead of identifying as same gender loving, it is not in the least surprising to me. Most of us African Americans, I submit, are still walking around passing for being fully human and as full citizens.

We have been and continue to be so consumed with shame for our fathers' having been treated as less than men, indeed as subhuman, that we have struggled mightily to either hide, like skeletons in closets and so much dirty laundry, or otherwise dismiss as having no bearing on who we are or what we have to do today, the horrific terrorism to which we have been and continue to be subject. Can you say, Sean Bell?[2] The truth is many of us are only a single generation removed from family members who were the children of slaves and only a few generations removed from family members who were slaves.

Rather than observing the very wise and powerful example of the Jews who will, at every turn, decry the atrocities that were done to them on other shores, that they should never happen again, we've busied

---

2 On April, 25th, 2008, three NYC Police Officers were acquitted of all charges in the November 2006 murder of Sean Bell, an unarmed Black man at whom they shot fifty rounds.

ourselves trying to hide our shame for what has been done to us right here, and find ourselves, for the absence of that acknowledgement, catharsis, and renegotiation, unhealed. The fact is, barely a generation ago in many parts of this country our fathers were still regarded as "boys" every day of their adult lives. Buying into the Capitalist credo that "New and Improved" matters above all else, we elect to forget that even our recent history of struggles for civil and human rights have been about our recognition as men and women. That buy-in leaves us ever played, suckered, duped, gypped and having sold ourselves out.

Well programmed, we play out all manner of neurotic, self-destructive and pathological behaviors, having become masters of self-denial and at blaming and being the victim. We dysfunctionally regard each other as 'Niggas,' and parroting notions like "Niggers ain't shit," and "Black people can't do anything together," and that we are "crabs in a barrel," effectively short circuiting forward movement and perpetuating self-defeating patterns.

Growing up in the South Bronx my best friend was Mark, the most popular boy in our neighborhood. His cousins, Kip and Benny were my nemeses from pre-pubescence straight through our adolescence. Wiry, cinnamon colored, squinty eyed Kip – only his parents and school teachers knew his real given name – who was a year older and half a head taller than I, seemed to think that his role in life was to attempt to bully me. Benny was a year younger and somewhat smaller than I. He shared with his big brother an antipathy for me that bordered on obsession. Benny's weapon of choice was his tongue and that tongue could be lethal. Benny was a master at "sounding" on people, also known as "the dozens." The boy was a put-down king. These two boys were an unceasing source of stress, duress, and just plain pain to me. If Kip wasn't shoving or taking swipes at me, trying to pick a fistfight, Benny was trying to bait me, making fun of my "huskies" sized, secondhand pants, or my astounding inability to play basketball, or the way I would sometimes slip around them, and "talk all proper." ("It's not shit, it's *manure!*" Benny insisted I once said).

Secondhand pants notwithstanding, the boys felt threatened by my being middle-class and intellectual and, by their suspicions about my sexuality and my greatest crime, being the object of Mark's love. His cousins loved him as much as I did. They were intensely jealous and determined, all the days of their lives it seemed, to punish me. By sophomore year in high school I had, for some years, been able to distract Kip from his quest to smack me around by feigning kindred machismo impulses and sparring with him. I punched and smacked him back just enough to let him know that I wasn't about to be whipped by the likes of him, chuckling all the while, as if we were just playing with each other. Then, just before any real sparks could fly, I would embrace him in a boxing hug, laughing at how silly we were being. At other times, I just pretended I was coming down with an asthma attack, which either scared him or made him feel sorry for me, I could never be sure which, but it got him to stop fucking with me.

For his part, Benny was a very unhappy child, and as far as he was concerned, someone was going to have to pay for that. Whenever marble-nosed, moon-faced Benny was in a foul mood, he masked it brilliantly in his guise as the court jester. Benny's jests were invariably at someone else's expense. As the king, Mark was rarely subjected to such abuse.

Benny's evil advances were frequently more daunting than dodging Kip's. I tell you, it was terrifying, the things this boy could think of to say about me and my mama. Sometimes I had to pull out all the stops and get downright vicious in order to save face, "…ignorant, stank-assed, peasy-headed, John's bargain store wearin', no-pussy gettin' mutha-fucka'!" But, the most harrowing part of it all was the knowledge, everyone's knowledge that, should the stakes get too high, Benny could always pull out the hole card everyone held on me, "Fagg'it!" As ugly as some of these contests got, to his credit Benny never pulled it.

The problem with the humor of "sounding" or "the dozens" is that it devalues intrinsic facets of our selves. "Faggot" like "Nigger" was conceived to debase and to dehumanize. The term, "the dozens" comes from a practice during slavery under which 'damaged' slaves – those born with birth defects or who, following failed escape attempts had had feet amputated – were sold as defective, by the dozen. As used by Black folks contemporarily, the phrase refers to the practice of droll demeaning that also has its bearings in slavery with the principles of Willie Lynch. It is widely believed that on the banks of the James River in 1712, a West Indian plantation owner named William Lynch delivered a speech to a group of Virginia slave-holders outlining a methodology for lasting slave control. In it he proposed, among other things, that differences between the enslaved Africans be magnified and used as points of contention, including: skin color or shade, hair-texture, age, intelligence, physical size, gender, domicile, etc.

Whether or not the Lynch speech took place, the differences stressed in it were regularly focused on to inspire fear, mistrust and envy, pitting the slaves ever against each other, while, at the same time encouraging love, trust and admiration of the master.⁵ And so have we been conditioned to regard ourselves, each other and white folks ever since. "Sounding," or humor which tears down or makes light of our intra-racial idiosyncrasies, is not simply hurtful in the moment, it renders virtually impossible, for all but the most resilient among us, the possibility of developing a healthy self-concept.

From this system of indoctrination, destructive and stupid notions like 'good hair,' 'high yellow,' and 'fair-skinned,' along with such admonitions as, 'Act your age, not your color,' and indeed, referring to ourselves and each other as 'nigger,' have sprung forth and remain with us as unconscious self-abnegations. In addition, we've devolved into "post-slavery" behaviors like hair straightening and weaving, skin bleaching, the donning of colored contact lenses and plastic surgery among those of us who can afford it, to affect more European visages. Mix the toxins from this conditioning with the institutionalized perception of our enslaved forefathers as non-entities, the incapacity of many of our fathers, even yet, to protect and provide for us, (as any good patriarch must,) and the continued psychological enslavement plays out in what Kip and Benny were doing; always and forever challenging the possibility of my and each other's manhood.

As a result, throughout my youth and well into adulthood, I secretly questioned my own manhood. As a means of self-definition and self-determination, because it didn't emanate from black culture, "gay" never empowered me. It was only after many years of therapy and other modes of self-reflection that I came upon the term Same Gender Loving and it felt right. It not only affirmed that I love or seek to love the object of my affection, it embodied a celebration of that inclination. Since then, I have joined in the building of a community and a movement for the self determination of homosexual Black people in two organizations, African American Advocacy, Support-Services & Survival Institute-New York (AmASSI-NY), and The Black Men's Xchange-New York (BMX-NY). Both organizations provide regular opportunities for engagement around the historical context framing our lives in ways that people experience transformation. We have to talk about it. The only way to divest all the stigmas of their capacity to shame us is by shedding light on them. We must see to it that African and African American history, including thorough readings of myriad slave narratives become a substantial part of every American child's education. We have to create safe spaces in which

---

5 In Post Traumatic Slave Syndrome, author Joy DeGruy Leary describes the historical process under which blacks were systematically conditioned to devalue ourselves and each other.

to review and review and review with each other, and then review in even more detail; and then exclaim and decry and decree in specific just what all has been done to us so that we can begin to critically examine how we come to be where we are, indeed *see* where we are. Only then can we begin to reconfigure ourselves. Rebuild ourselves as fully human with all the hideousness which has been done to us included. We have the right to be fully who we are. We have that responsibility to ourselves and to the world to be fully who we are and we must claim it.

The Face of Fear
Doug Cooper Spencer

I have a friend who is part owner of a business. The business he owns is doing so well that its success has pissed off some of his competitors; and as a result some of those competitors have decided to take action. The competition has chosen to discredit him and his business partner.

You see, both partners of this business are gay. And in an attempt to discredit them, some of their competitors are putting the word out on the street that their business is 'a fag' business. Now it's bad enough that in these days and times someone could still use the gay card to destroy someone's credibility and, as a result, their livelihood, but the fact that it's being used by black people against their own- - oppressing another, especially through fear- - reeks of hypocrisy.

From their inability to compete with these two men, some of the other businesses have resorted to what might be considered unsavory tactics to some while to others the whole matter might be brushed off as due punishment for being gay.

The two gay men are handling the assault on their character-- the inferred message that they are somehow unworthy as a result of their being gay-- in different ways. One of the partners is ready to jump ship while the other one sees the whole mess as a matter of inspiration, to go out and prove to the competition that, in spite of their being gay, they can continue to achieve success.

Looking at this incident I am proud of the partner who refuses to run and saddened by the one who seems to be losing faith. But what intrigues me more is the whole matter of faith and fear. How do we come by both and how do we use them?

On the surface we would see the two, faith and fear, as being polar opposites, one (faith) engenders 'fearlessness' while the other feeds into feelings of hopelessness and despair. But in fact both of these energies are firmly rooted in one's sense of self worth.

Of the two energies, fear is the more immediate and, as a result is more tenable. That's why it's used so often as a way to control others. It's a primal response that's wired into every animal and can switch on at the drop of a dime.

Now fear isn't a bad thing since it serves to both protect us from real harm as well as regulate our actions. Without it we would all just march into the jaws of a lion or commit heinous acts without knowledge of reprisal. However, if left unchecked fear can run rampant and cause the very harm it's supposed to protect us from.

Fear. We've all been there at one time or another and we all know of its effects, the most common two being 'flight' or 'fight'. In the instance of these gay business owners, their shady competitors are not only using their being gay as perceived leverage against them, but they are also betting the two men will throw in the towel from the fear of losing customers. One partner seems to be headed that way.

But what they are not ready for is that the other partner has chosen to fight. He says he has never advertised the fact that he is gay since he feels it should have no bearing on the business. But now, he says, he is ready to stand his ground and work his customers through the whole mess while drumming up new ones. Now that's being fearless.

Faith, on the other hand, is more complex because it isn't hotwired into our primal responses. We have to work for it. We have to make a conscious effort to reach into a higher part of ourselves and grope around for something that is not as immediately tenable as fear. However, the result is well worth the labor.

How do we get past fear to a point of faith? I believe it's best to take on the object of your fear in incremental steps and with great understanding. Taking small steps allows time to meditate on the object of your fear bit by bit until you can move beyond it. My own struggle to overcome the fear of someone knowing I was gay is an example.

From childhood through my early twenties I hid the fact that I was attracted to the same sex. Finally, the sheer exhaustion from years of hiding took its toll and I was forced to re-evaluate my situation. I came to stop spending so much time despising myself as the creature I had been led to believe I was to understanding 'Who' I was; you see, I went from a place of fear to a place of understanding. And one of the things I came to understand was that none of the people who held their weapon of fear over my head could tell me much about me. They had not walked a mile in my shoes.

So for them to make their assertions became, to me, a point of them being arrogant as well as ignorant, not only of my life but of life in general. But my acceptance of self love didn't come over night; it was through those incremental steps that I was able to achieve it.

A point about faith: *You cannot have faith if you don't love yourself.* That is probably the first step towards acquiring it. You can have hope, but you can't have faith. Knowing yourself, understanding yourself, excusing yourself and loving yourself, all these acts bring about energy and renewal. It opens us up to great potential and faith is but a part of the power gained.

Now, I know loving yourself can sometimes be a challenge when people are telling you otherwise, but what do they know? No one knows all the answers. See this and you will be able to put them and their views in perspective. Stop giving them power by agreeing with them. Only you and God know you, and none of us truly have the capacity to fully comprehend God, so let go of all the bull crap and move on to a place of love.

Someone once said that faith is letting go of expectation, to be able to throw your arms open and accept what is not known or understood. We should never accept hatred, but we should always embrace a faith that will bring about good.

I hope my friend's business partner comes to a place of fearlessness in dealing with their situation. They have my support and I wish them all the best.

Three Talking Points You Need To Know
Max Smith

In this 2010's world in which sound bites pass for news and in which online blogs often fall short of the traditional fact – checked rigors of established standards of journalism: corporate media seems bent on keeping the status quo.

What are we to do to advance the cause of improving the quality of life in our communities? We must adopt our own fact – checked talking points and use them repeatedly and confidently.

Over time Africans in America have been colored, Negro, Black and African American. Our named identity depended on our collective ability to define ourselves. Social, economic and political forces of faith and fear exerted variable pressure on our self – determination.

Same gender love has been the inborn reality of about 10% of all humans throughout history. As with racial identity, names to describe SGL people have changed over time. Two – spirited, arsenokoitai, malakoi, homosexual, lesbian, gay, bisexual, transgender, dl, LGBT and SGL all have described various non – heterosexuals. We need always to affirm ourselves, so no slurs are listed.

Oh, you have heard all on the list except arsenokoitai and malakoi? You are not alone! In the three talking points you need to know, those are words you need to know more than any others. Stay tuned!

Working 9 to 5 and the Old Testament's Genesis 9th Chapter, 25th verse presents a strange coincidence. For Genesis 9:25 was the Christian justification of slavery. "Cursed be Canaan; a slave of slaves shall he be to his brothers." (The quote is from the Revised Standard Version of the Bible.)

It was in the economic best interest of 15th through 19th Century slave traders and owners to interpret the Bible to mean that the people of Canaan, who were descendants of Noah's son Ham, were Black people. It was likewise in the economic best interest of those slave traders and slave owners to ignore the Old Testament's Ezekiel 16:49. "Behold Sodom: she and her daughters had pride, surfeit of food, and prosperous ease, but did not aid the poor and needy." (RSV)

That passage of scripture is called the Iniquity of Sodom.

In the ante – bellum era in the former Confederate States of America, "the poor and needy" were the slaves. This inconvenient truth was dealt with in two ways. To teach any slave to read and write was a serious crime, so that they were unable to read and interpret scriptures, such as Genesis and Ezekiel in the Black people's best interests. Secondly the Iniquity of Sodom was twisted to refer to the alleged homosexual gang rape by arsenokoitai (there goes that word again!) at Lot's door, in Genesis 19.

The number 69 is contemporary slang code for mutual fellatio. Strange coincidence that 1st Corinthians 6:9 is where arsenokoitai and malakoi appear. If those words look Greek to you: it is because they are of the Greek language.

In the U.S.A. in the 1870's and 1880's, decades immediately after the end of legal slavery, many African American religious denominations formed. Due to the centuries of making it a crime to teach slaves to read and to write English, much less Hebrew, Greek and other original languages of the Bible, those Christian denominations relied mainly on the English King James version of the Bible. Europeans had translated that text from Latin. The translators condoned slavery and homophobia.

Of course African Americans totally repudiated the Curse of Canaan. However, the Iniquity of Sodom, given the Victorian era's culture at slavery's legal end in the 1860's was at that time thought to have to do with a gang rape of angels visiting Lot. No one questioned why homosexuals, living nearly 2000 years after the alleged rape, should yet be held personally accountable for that incident in Genesis 19. Never mind that Genesis 18 sets up for stark contrast with the Sodom story a sterling example of the ethic of providing hospitality even to strangers.

Remove the homophobic lens from the Sodom story and understand the wickedness of Sodom to be inhospitality and failure to aid the poor and needy. Buying, selling, renting and leasing women, men and children without regard to the family ties or the spiritual feelings of slaves were the normal ways of life. Slave owners ignored the Commandment against adultery and raped Black women and girls with violence and impunity. These and many other abominable and detestable actions, in what for a while, were the Confederate States of America was like Sodom on steroids. Jefferson Davis was the worst sodomite of all times. To a Southern Baptist in the 1850's the "traditional family value" was about $2500, the retail purchase price of one African – American family of two adults and two children.

Corinth is a city in Mississippi. Corinth also is the name of a seaport city in Greece, from which the New Testament's Corinthians derives its name. When the Apostle Paul, from the town of Tarsus, Turkey went to Corinth, Greece as a citizen of the Roman Empire, did Paul fully understand Greek culture? No. Paul was there on a mission to spread Christianity.

The Roman Empire had conquered, then, had rebuilt Corinth, Greece. With wars of conquest going on back in those days fought with swords and shields, often involving hand to hand combat: many defeated soldiers were taken as prisoners of war. To subjugate and to humiliate those prisoners, their captors often would rape them. Was that male-to-male penetrative anal sex? Yes. Was that same gender love? No.

In ancient Greece an adult male mentor was expected to engage in culturally ritualized and sanctioned non – penetrative sex with his adolescent male protégé. This is call pederasty. Most Americans do not know that this practice is going on in 21st Century Afghanistan.

Because American society has no cultural ritual like that, it is sufficient to know that the power imbalance between an adult male and a young boy makes it rape. 90% of adult men who rape children rape young girls. Is that heterosexual love? No.

What did the Apostle Paul call the male soldiers who raped men and what did Paul call the pederasts who raped boys?

ARSENOKOITAI.

As ships came in to the seaport, Corinth, Greece: men in women's clothing sometimes would greet sailors. They would offer wine to the sailors, get them drunk and then talk the drunken sailors into having sex in exchange for the money they'd made selling their fish catch. This was the world's oldest profession in a society where powerless women were expected to stay home with their children.

Was that drunken exchange of male-to-male sex for money same gender love making? No.

Back in those days Apostle Paul knew of non-Christian cults in which priests would invite sinful men into their temples. The men were told to have sex with the priests and to give the temple cult priests money in order to be forgiven of their sins. What did the Apostle Paul call these temple cult priests and the men who prostituted themselves to the sailors? MALAKOI.

Tom Horner, an Episcopal priest, a graduate of Duke University School of Divinity and holder of a PhD degree from Columbia University and Union Theological Seminary published "Jonathan Loved David" in 1978. It is from that book that the above Greek translations of arsenokoitai and malakoi were taken.

Even now, more than 41 years after the Stonewall revolt of June 28, 1969 created an era of openness, greater awareness and honesty about same gender love: do African American denominations teach about arsenokoitai and malakoi? No. Why Not? The accurate information has been available to scholars who would seek it for decades. It is in the economic best interests of too many Black preachers to stir a homophobic congregation into a frenzy talking about Sodom and Gomorrah, in English only. Never mind that Ezekiel 16:49 spoke about aid for the poor and needy. Surely Black ministers know a person can be poor in spirit. Few things can make a person even poorer in spirit than to be lambasted and condemned from the pulpit. It can be even worse when same gender loving people tormented like that are in that same church's choir or at the piano.

A person who is poor in spirit due to church homophobia might seek emotional comfort in liquor bottles, at a casino or may confuse unsafe sexual activity as a way to look for love.

Perhaps, with many states reporting that 20% to 50% of adult same gender loving men are positive for HIV that there is an obvious need. The obvious need is for Christian denominations, generally, and individual church leaders to accept the new understanding that same gender loving attraction is inborn for about 10% of the human population. In God's infinite wisdom 10% of the human population also is naturally left – handed, as an inborn condition. To insist that being gay or lesbian or left – handed is a "lifestyle choice" is just wrong. Now is the time: for that kind of 19th Century understanding of same gender loving sexual orientation to be put 6 feet under.

Those who say adults always have to take personal responsibility for all decisions do not understand or do not want to know about the spiritual brokenness called emotional depression. A person who is heartless may refuse to acknowledge the ways societal racism; homophobia and economic stress can cause some people to find it difficult to make good decisions under multiple oppressive pressures such as these.

Is there a silver bullet for the persistently high rates of HIV? My personal solution, as a same gender loving man who is sexually active requires discipline. Yet it has resulted in my testing negative for HIV every year since 1989, and I'm 56 years old in 2010. I follow this self – imposed rule: no anal sex in any position, no exceptions. Are condoms 98% to 99% effective for penetrative anal sex? Yes. When trying to avoid a virus that would be with me for life, is a 1% risk acceptable? No.

Therefore we come to the 3 talking points you need to know, particularly when speaking with anyone who does not accept, acknowledge, appreciate and affirm same gender loving people.

1. The Bible was not originally written in English, and for lack of knowledge was financially abused to justify slavery.

2. 21st Century same gender loving people are not accountable for the Iniquity of Sodom. The Bible condemns the actions of arsenokoitai rape and malakoi prostitution because we are to love God and to love other people. Human acts of lovemaking ought never to be violent or cheap business transactions.

3. Becoming positive for HIV is not an inevitable result of same gender lovemaking. Intimacy can be fulfilling without the risk of penetrative anal sex. Thank You for your serious consideration of this essay. Please use the words arsenokoitai and malakoi to spark questions in conversation and to educate.

Positively
Timothy Hampton/Thunder Kellie

When I found out that I was facing a deadly disease, the destruction phase began.........

The day was Monday, October 13, 1997. I was 21 years old and home in Columbia, TN from college. At the time I was enrolled at the University of Montevallo, AL. where I was a theatre major. That day, I was out with my mother because she was on vacation that week. On our way home from shopping we stopped and picked up lunch at Back Porch BBQ. I remembered ordering a loaded baked potato and my mother ordered the rib platter. I thought to myself how the food smelt so good. After we received our food, we went home, ate and laughed at the kitchen table. We talked about many family issues. My mother is a funny lady. She has an opinion about everything. I would have to say that that is where I get my humor. As we were sitting and talking, the phone rang and I got up to answer it.

When I answered the phone, the female voice on the other end asked for a Mr. Timothy Hampton. I replied "This is Timothy". The lady on the other end said the she was from the Columbia Health Department and asked if I had taken an HIV test at the University of Montevallo, AL. during a Red Cross Blood Drive. I told her yes, I did take one. She told me that she was sorry to inform me but the test came back Positive for the virus that causes AIDS. I replied "What do you want me to do about it?" She explained that I would need to come down to the health department as soon as possible.

I asked her was she joking and she said quickly that she wasn't joking and if I didn't come down to the health department by the end of the day, she would send the police out to pick me up. At that time, all I could imagine was some people in contamination suits coming to my house. I told the lady on the other end that I would be right in. After I hung up the phone, my mother looked at me and asked me who was it on the phone. I told her that it was the Health Department and that they just said that I was HIV positive and I needed to come down there or they would send someone after me.

My mother closed up her rib platter and said "Well, let's get the hell up out of here!"

She grabbed her purse and we got into the car and drove to the Health Department. On the ride there, my mother and I didn't say anything! We rode in silence!

When we pulled into the parking lot, my mother turned off the car and at the same time we both took a deep breath. We got out of the car and went into the Health Department. I was nervous as I walked in because Columbia is a small town in Tennessee. Columbia is a place where everybody knows everybody's business.

I went to the check in counter and spoke with the lady about someone calling me and telling me to come in because I may be HIV positive. The lady gave me a blank stare and asked me to hold on. She got up from the counter and went to the back. When she came back, she had another lady with her. The lady who was with her introduced herself. She asked me to come to wait in the doctor's office. I realized that the lady that was taking me to the Doctor's office was the same woman that had called me at my house. When my mother and I reached the office, the lady asked us to take a seat, wait and the doctor would be right with us.

My mother and I sat there in silence and waited for the doctor.

In no time, this tall, young, handsome African-American male doctor came in. He introduced himself and shook our hand.

The doctor started asking several questions.

I was so anxious to know if I was HIV positive, I spoke up and asked: "So Doctor is it true? Do I have AIDS?"

He replied that he didn't know whether I had AIDS, but the test that I took at the University came back positive for HIV. I asked him what the difference was. He tried to explain to me that HIV is the virus that causes AIDS. I was so upset. I didn't want to hear what he was saying to me. I stopped him and asked what he wanted me to do about this disease. He explained that he was going to take another test and that it would take six weeks for him to know the results. The doctor told me that in the mean time, I needed to make an appointment with the HIV/AIDS clinic in Columbia.

My heart dropped when he told me this!

I felt as if everyone was going to laugh at me and treat me cruelly; like so many have treated many HIV/AIDS people. I told the doctor that I was **not** about to make an appointment to a clinic because everyone would find out about me and my business. The doctor said something to me that I still hear clearly in my heart.

He asked me: "Do you want to live?"

I told him that I did want to live but I have AIDS!

He told me that I could live with the disease; however, the choice was up to me. I guess I looked at him as if he was speaking a foreign language because he asked me if I wanted to live or die. I told him that I wanted to live! He told me to make the appointment to the clinic and *I shall live!*

The doctor started to explain that he would have to take more blood so that he could run the HIV test again to make sure of my status as well as check my T-Cell count. After the nurse took my blood, my mother and I left and went home in silence.

When we walked into the house, we sat at the kitchen table to finish the lunch that had been interrupted by the Health Department. Needless to say, we had both lost our appetite. My mother broke the silence with the question: "How do you feel?"

I knew that I had to be strong for my mother, so I told her that it was something that I would have to deal with. She also asked me about who was I going to tell about me having HIV. I told her that I was going to tell all of the family since HIV ends in DEATH. She looked a little upset when I told her that. I didn't know if she was upset because I was going to tell everyone or because I said that I was going to die. When she said that she didn't feel it best that everyone knew; I felt that she wanted it to be something that we kept to ourselves. I asked her why she didn't feel that all of the family needed to know, she responded that it was none of their business. I could understand why she felt the way that she did but I wanted to prepare for death. I didn't care about what the doctor said about living with the disease. All of the people that I knew that were HIV positive died of AIDS within the first year of having the disease.

I wondered who could I look up to that would help me through this.

After my mother's comments, I knew that I had to face this disease alone.

On this day I began the emotional roller coaster that would take me on a journey to my destiny.

I decided to tell my entire family about my HIV status.

The first person that I told was my step-father. He was a very unexpressive man. He was a man of few words yet he had a lot to say. My step-father was very supportive. At the time, my step father (who was a cancer patient and survivor) had just found out that the cancer that was in remission was back with a vengeance.

My two sisters were a little different. My younger sister, Melissa, was pregnant at the time and she decided that since it was a boy that she would name him after me. My older sister, Sonia said that she was there for me if I needed anything.

Telling my aunts, uncles and cousins were different stories as well. I told one of my uncles, Van, and he didn't have much to say about it. My other uncle, John, was not so silent. He called the house and asked my mother if he could speak with me. When I got onto the phone, he asked me what I had gotten myself into. I told him that it is not what I had gotten into, but what had gotten into me and I started laughing trying to make light of the situation. However, he did not think that is was so funny. He told me that he was disappointed and hoped that I could live with myself. After speaking with him, I could only imagine what my aunts were going to say. I have two aunts from my mothers' side of the family.

One is Iva Lee which is a really bossy lady. My other Aunt Flue Ellen is Schizophrenic and really doesn't give a damn about anything. Since I was a child, Aunt Flue Ellen would always talk to herself; so I decided not to tell her because she probably wouldn't give a damn anyway. When I told my Aunt Iva Lee, she was very supportive as was the rest of the family members that I decided to tell.

As a family, we would always eat Thanksgiving at my Uncle John's house; however with his recent comments to me; I knew that it could only end in disaster. Unfortunately, my mother insisted on me going to the dinner. My Uncle John's wife, Aunt Orleane, would have her family out to their house to celebrate Thanksgiving. When we got to the house, it was known where we would be eating. We went into the garage and there were some tables, chairs and a kerosene heater in there. We went on into the house to see where we needed to put our coats. My Aunt Orleane told us that we can leave them in the garage. My mother looked as if she wanted to punch her in the face, but I broke the stare and took my mother's coat and put them in the garage. Since my aunt's family had taken the space in the den, she told us that she had set up tables in the garage so everyone could have somewhere to sit. Unfortunately, my mother and I knew what they were really thinking. In the past, all of the grown up men would eat at the table. This year was a little different. I wasn't one of the lucky men to sit at the dining table. My family and I fixed our plates and sat in the garage. That Thanksgiving I felt like I was going to die a lonely man. No one understood the way that I felt.

I started going to the clinic and needless to say, I had to be forced by my mother. On my first visit the doctor revealed to me that my T-Cell count was 220. That is when I found out the difference between HIV and AIDS was based on a person's T-Cell count. A person that has a T-cell count of 200 or below is diagnosed with AIDS. I also understood that my viral load was very high. When someone's viral load is high the virus is out of control in the body. With that small amount of knowledge, I knew that I did not have long to live with this disease. The clinic that I was attending was experimenting on me by giving me a lot of experimental drugs. I was getting very sick from the medicine and the virus continued to be out of control in my body. The side effects from the medications were making me have diarrhea, nausea and vomiting.

Mentally I was worse!

I went through these different phases; such as, hating the person that gave it to me. I went through a mental phase of hating myself for, in my own words "being so stupid". I had to go and see a psychiatrist for the way that I was feeling. My feelings were that the disease was passed to me, so I wanted to pass it to someone else. No one took my feelings and my life seriously to warn me that they had the disease. I wanted to literally kill the person in whom I had contracted the disease from. I did not care about the consequences or other people lives. I only cared about my life... my own feelings.

I believed that I was robbed of my life!

I was in a committed, monogamous relationship with this person that I had unprotected sex with. Apparently, this person did not feel the same way. I was wondering, and still wonder today if this person knowingly infected me with this disease. I had to get over the bad feeling that I was feeling. I had this anger, resentment and hatred towards not only the person that gave me HIV, but I had hatred toward myself and others who were not HIV positive. I felt that GOD allowed this to happen to me. I needed to know how to die but no one could tell me how.

For two years, I continued to go to the clinic in Columbia and my health continued to deteriorate. Some of my health related issues were dizzy spells, Condyloma, migraines, night sweats and depression. I remember the first time I had a dizzy spell. It was the year of the cicadas. I was getting out of the car from hanging out with some friends who did not know about HIV my status, and before I knew anything, my face hit the ground. When I woke up, all I could communicate to my mother, who had ran outside to see what happened, was to get me into the house before a cicada landed on me.

Condyloma was harder to deal with. Condyloma is also known as venereal warts. It can cause the growth of flesh-colored bumps in the genital or anal region. I had them in the anal area. I needed to have two surgeries to have them removed. This was a painful process both times. The migraines and night sweats came every night before bed. My mother would usually come in and calm me until I fell asleep.

Depression hit me harder when cancer took my step father's life a year after I was diagnosed with HIV. When this happened, I knew that my mother needed male support as well as extra income in the house. I got really depressed and upset because I was too sick to work. I knew that I had to do something but I did not know what.

One day while I was at my visit to the clinic, one of the nurses that I had admired told me that she was leaving to work for the Comprehensive Care Center in Nashville, Tennessee. She told me of all the great services that they offered for HIV/AIDS clients. I was sad that she was leaving but in my mind I was planning on following her. The one lady that showed me respect during my illness and listened to my pain was leaving and I was going to follow her. I had to find out where this place was located. It had to be a great place if this nurse decided that she wanted to work there. I respected her and I felt that she respected me.

She didn't treat me disrespectfully because I was HIV positive on my way to having full blown AIDS. It felt as if she had love for me.

The next day I got the number to the Comprehensive Care Center and made an appointment. I told my mother what I was doing because I wasn't going back to the clinic in Columbia. I believed that they were killing me!

The day that I went to the CCC, I was treated with much more dignity and respect than the Columbia Clinic. They even made me feel as if I had a *chance* to live by the way that they welcomed me! Within a year of going to the CCC, my health turned around. My T-cells were increasing and my viral load was declining. So I decided to move to Nashville to be closer to the CCC and to get away from the small town mentality of Columbia.

Moving to Nashville produced some good and some bad behaviors in my life. Some of the good was that I became a special ed teacher's assistant, I had friends and a support group that knew that I was HIV positive. I was on a great med regimen that I took faithfully. I was exercising and eating healthy, also. I had my own transportation and lived in a townhouse with a cool roommate. I was attending a wonderful church that embraced my spiritual gift and they loved me completely. The pastor at the church made me feel like I had worth to my life. No matter how much responsibility I had and how physically healed I became, my mental stability was still young and immature.

I began to do all types of drugs, except for crack. Whitney Houston said that CRACK IS WACK! Cocaine and alcohol began to run my life and affect the ones around me that loved me. It was 5 years later and I had become a cocaine addict. I found myself pawning my personal items as well as household items to get more drugs. I would even write BAD checks to make sure that I had enough drugs to run me until I could get more. On the weekends, I would hit the clubs and snort cocaine in the bath room and all those who wanted to join in, could. If someone wanted to share drugs with me then I would be ready to use it. I wouldn't even ask what it was that I was ingesting into my body. I knew that taking drugs were dangerous, but taking drugs from people that I didn't know constituted me as a fool. One night all of the foolishness of taking drugs caught up with me.

Friday, April 5, 2002- Terry; my roommate, Linda; a mutual friend of ours, and I decided to hangout out at a local club called *"The Chute"*. When we got to the club, there was hardly anyone there. I told Terry and Linda that I had to use the restroom. I went into the bathroom and shared my "pack" of Cocaine with some guy with glasses. He asked if I wanted to share a pill with him or take the whole pill. I thought that I was an *"experienced"* drug user, so I took the whole pill. After I took the

Essays & Sermons

pill and shared my cocaine, I went to the bar and purchased a beer. When I came from the bathroom, Terry and Linda were standing with a friend of ours named Chris. There was another club across town that was opened and some of the other people were talking about going. Terry and Linda decided that he and Linda were going to the club with another group of people that they had met. I told Terry and Linda that I was not ready to leave and that I would meet them over at that club later on. Linda spoke up and told me to drive her jeep and meet them over there later on. I agreed and Chris said that he would hang out with me until I was ready to leave. Terry and Linda left and the pill that I had taken in the bathroom was beginning to have some weird effects on me. Things started to become a blur to me. I told Chris that I was F#@! UP!, but for me to say that at that time of night, was usual! We ended up staying at the club awhile longer. I told Chris that I was ready to leave and if he was going to leave then to come on. He wasn't ready, so I walked out of the club and got into the Jeep and put the key in the ignition.

Now, I really don't remember what happened or what I was thinking about getting into that JEEP but the end results was me driving down Wedgwood towards downtown Nashville, TN. There were times that I remembered a light and maybe even some music, but the thing that is clear, I feel asleep or passed out at the wheel. I hit the interstate column and the JEEP flipped over several times, throwing me out of it. The wreck occurred at about 12am. I was taken to Vanderbilt Hospital to the trauma unit. During the accident, my I.D fell out of the truck when it flipped over. The hospital had me listed as John Doe. I also lost my cell phone, fortunately, a homeless person picked up my phone when he heard it ringing. That is how my mother and roommate found out about the wreck. It was 10am Saturday morning and Terry started worrying when I didn't show up at the club like I was supposed to. He and Linda decided to leave the club and go home because they figured that maybe I was there. When they arrived at the house and I was not there, they felt that something was wrong. Terry knew that for me not to contact him when there was a change of plans was out of the ordinary. He also knew that I was in Linda's Jeep and I wouldn't be out gallivanting in someone else's truck. He and Linda went to bed guessing that I would be home soon.

When he woke up the next morning and I was not at the house, he knew that something bad had happened. He began to call my cell phone and the cell phone kept going to voice mail. He started calling around to all of my friends and no one had seen me. When Terry called Chris, he told Terry that the last time that he saw me was when I left the club. Chris said that when I left, I was going to meet Terry and Linda at the club.

By 9:30am I had not called or came home. Terry decided to call my mother to ask if she had talked to me. My mother told him that she had not talked to me in 2 days. He said that I was missing and my cell phone was going straight to voice mail. My mother became worried and began to call my cell phone and it went straight to voicemail. After about the 10th time, my cell phone started to ring and a man picked up the phone. She asked the man his name; he would not give it to her. She asked him what was he doing with my cell phone and where was I. He asked if she meant the man who had a wreck in a Jeep that flipped over several times. My mother began to panic and asked if the man could hold on while she a called to Terry. She made the phone call and added Terry to the phone line. When Terry got onto the phone, the man explained that the man who had the wreck in the Jeep was shaking in a puddle of blood. The ambulance came and took him away. Terry asked the man how he got the phone. The man said that he heard it ringing on the side of the street. Terry offered the man money to return the phone and also thanked him for the information. My mother hung up the phone and called my sisters and told them what she knew. Terry began to call around to the different hospitals asking for a Timothy Hampton. When he called Vanderbilt Hospital they did not have a Timothy Hampton but they had a John Doe that was brought in about the same time.

Terry called my cousin and asked him if he would go out to the hospital and see if it was me, while he met the man to get the phone and offer his gratitude. When my cousin, Rod got there he discovered that it was me. I had torn my left eyelid off, broken my jaw, fractured 4 vertebrates in my neck, dislocated my left arm, torn my rotary cuff, torn flesh out of my left arm, a concussion and several road burns. After several calls, my entire family and friends were at the hospital. The doctors explained to my mother about my injuries and severity of the injuries and accident. They told my mother that upon arrival, they had to lightly resuscitate me. I had lost allot of blood and had been in shock for awhile after the accident.

I had surgery for my injuries and was in and out of conscience on the trauma unit for 4 days. I remained in the hospital for almost two weeks. There isn't too much that I remember from being in the hospital, only small segments. Such as, my boss from the school where I taught came to visit me after I was put into a regular room. I remember a couple of friends coming to visit also. My mother and Terry never left my side. My mother would always make me get out of the hospital bed to walk around the nurses' station. She believes that walking is the way to healing when you are in the hospital. The one thing that my mother would not let me do was look into the mirror. At first I didn't understand why, but I finally figured out on the day that they released me.

When I got into the vehicle, the first thing that I'd done was pull down the sun visor to see if there was a mirror. When I looked into the mirror, I saw a patch over my left eye, my face was swollen and my jaw was a large abnormal size and shape. It hadn't dawned on me to what extinct were my injuries or what had actually happened to me. When I got home and saw all the people that had come to my house to see me, I was overwhelmed. I was confused because I didn't know that that many people cared about me. I remember all of my co-workers, church members, friends and even people from my past coming to see me. I couldn't believe that all these people loved me.

Externally I was upbeat and smiling but internally I was a mess!

I kept asking myself: "Why would these people come to see me?" I felt horrible. I was a drug addict with HIV that had a car wreck from taking drugs! If only these people knew the REAL reason behind the wreck then they wouldn't have come. I was telling lies about why I had the wreck. I said that I feel asleep at the wheel because I was "SLEEP Y" or "EXHAUSTED". My family kept telling stories about "The Night" over and over again. One particular story that my mother kept telling was that the hospital had to strap me to the bed because I kept fighting the doctors and nurses. Apparently I fought so hard that I kicked the foot board off the end of the bed. This story was told over and over again. I really wanted her to either shut up or change the subject. Needles to say, she did neither.

For the first 2 to 3 weeks, several people were over my house taking care of me, waiting on me hand and foot. However, there came the time when all of the noise of the people came to a halt. I found myself alone during the day and part of the afternoon. During that time I felt like I was going stir crazy. I wanted to get out of the house and go places, but because of my injuries I couldn't drive.

During the silent period is where I finally looked into the mirror and saw how the wreck affected my face. That is when I realized what had happened to me. I began to cry!

I realized that HIV wasn't the thing that was going to kill me. It was **me** that was going to kill me!

I knew at that moment I needed some mental and spiritual help.

I finished looking in the mirror and I began to pray for understanding and peace in my life.

I made a vow to GOD and myself that **I was going to live!**

After all these encounters in my life, I created these 5 steps to living with HIV....

1. Take Medication Regimen as Prescribed by doctor.
~Never miss a dose of your meds.

~If you miss a dose of your meds, never double up or catch up on your dose.
~If you are not suppose to consume alcohol, DON'T!
~Only take prescribed drugs.
~You have to report all side effects.
~Get past the side effects that occur, if you can.
~Never stop meds without Dr's permission.

2. Ask Questions and Get answers from your Dr. to know more about HIV
~Consult Dr. about side effects. Ask Dr. what you can do for them to subside.
~Know your T-cell count and viral load.
~Seek psychiatric help. Depression can kill you and affect HIV treatment.
~Stay current on treatment and new drugs.
~Don't believe that the Dr or anyone have the last word on your health.
~Know your body.
~Protect yourself (pos+pos) Condoms are a requirement.

3. Seek or Develop a support group
~Include people in your life and in the HIV experience. (People that care and won't judge)
~Talk to other HIV positive people about how they have coped with the disease.
~Get involved in HIV activities.

4. Get involved with an HIV friendly Faith based organizations or Church
~Seek a spiritual advisor
~Prayer20
~Daily Meditation -An ordinary person may consider meditation as a worship or prayer. But it is not so. Meditation means awareness. Whatever you do with awareness is meditation. "Watching your breath" is meditation; listening to the birds is meditation. As long as these activities are free from any other distraction to the mind, it is effective meditation. Meditation is not a technique but a way of life. Meditation means 'a cessation of the thought process' . It describes a state of consciousness, when the mind is free of scattered thoughts and various patterns . The observer (one who is doing meditation) realizes that all the activity of the mind is reduced to one.

5. Exercise, Diet and Healthy Lifestyle
~Find out what Meds work well with or against your Meds.
~Develop or Seek an Exercise Program
~Run/Walk for your health or someone else's.
~Limit consumption of alcohol.
~STOP SMOKING

~Seek a diet program.
~Seek drug treatment. Drugs can hinder the effects of Meds.
In Closing,

I have been blessed to be a blessing. I am overjoyed that GOD placed people into my life that have spoke life into me. My family, my friends, church family and My Pastor have helped me to get to this point of sharing my story. I know that my story is the story of many and I want the story to end in Victory and not defeat! I want this disease HIV to be eradicated. I have learned to live with this disease and wouldn't trade places with no one in this world. I know what my purpose is now. I thank GOD for giving me a purpose in life.

Life's lessons taught me to be a Victor and not a victim to HIV. I dream of a cure for this disease; not for me, but the millions that are in the dark and unaware of a healing.

I have sought and found my healing.

I have learned to **LIVE** with HIV and not DIE from it.

My mission now is to educate the world about living positively. Living is not easy, but it is worth it.

Timothy D. Hampton
"Thunder Kellie"

The Unspeakable
Tommie V. McNeil

I was on my way to one place but, wound up at another. I had been there at least twice before, once for brunch and another to show him my paintings. He always had a most eclectic grouping of people there. They just dropped by. His house is filled with interesting, soul provoking art and magnificent foods.

I remember stepping outside and a beautiful Black woman climbed an unseen stairway to the top of a palm tree and there she sang the most beautiful song I had ever heard. Clouds behind her swelled and soared upward with each note and shadows changed before her and rivers flowed. She wore a pale gold and white evening gown. I saw her later and asked if that was she and I cried as I remembered total beauty."

This was a dream I had a few years ago. It touched me so deeply I immediately wrote about it upon awakening. I had no idea how pertinent the message. You see it is so much like real life. We start out on the way to one place and end up at another. As children we envision one career and do something else later. We see ourselves happily married and one day that bliss evaporates. We head for one place, a healthy existence and along the way illness and disease propel us to another place.

I found out fifteen years ago I am HIV positive. I have AIDS. It is not where I was headed but it is where I ended up. I had just returned to Texas after living in Los Angeles for ten years. I immediately went into the hospital with pneumonia. Things were a lot different in May of 1989. Someone called from the hospital after I got out and said there was some good news and some bad news. The good news was that I had regular pneumonia, but I had tested positive for the HIV virus. Today this information would not be delivered over the telephone.

Love done.

Taste the wind in a butter Sun.

Touch my mind, feel my heart, hear the rush of Summer Candy.

I wish you loved me.

I remembered total beauty, that time, that existence before the news that I was ill and was going to die. How foolish all those years before to have elevated life's trivialities to monumental proportions. When life's road stretches endlessly before us and vistas of forever shine brightly before us and we feel invincible and we hear the rush of summer candy. Life, liberty and the pursuit of happiness. Nothing can touch us and all things are possible.

I fought the news. I resisted this information. Look at me, this cannot be. I do not look sick. This has to be a mistake. I was that cute little boy who went shopping and to the movies with my Mother. I was that inquisitive child who loved catching frogs, snakes and turtles. Butterflies and bees. Friends in my neighborhood and I played cowboys and Indians. I waited anxiously to see what treat my Daddy had for me when he brought groceries home on Friday nights.

Later in high scool, I was popular and one of the good kids. My friends and I never got into trouble. We did not skip school. Well, once. Senior year we took off to Houston, went to the zoo and bought Kentucky Fried Chicken. A fifteen peice bucket, six biscuits and a pint of gravy was only $3.99 in 1969. The principal laughed and knowingly let us slide when we each gave written excuses authored by each other. We were the good kids. We never got into trouble.

Chips falling.
My tears are Winter rain calling.
I smell carnival spinning golden strings called Hope.
If I soar, walk to hell, and promise to always be there.
In time you'll care.

Life goes on and it is not how long I live, but how well I live. I can go into any hospital in the world and find someone who is nt HIV positive, but will not live to see sunrise. How ungrateful of me. No one lives forever and what was I to do with whatever time I had left. "Touch my mind, feel my heart, hear the rush of summer candy. I wish you loved me." I wished I loved me and could stop fearing the loss of love of family and friends.

Oh, but I did smell carnival spinning golden strings called Hope and I decided to soar and persevere. I volunteered for a number of AIDS related activities. I became co-coordinator of a care team. Holding the hand and giving comfort to someone about to die from AIDS was very difficult. I felt like sometimes I was looking at my future. Real possibilities, after all I have what they have. I went to camp as a counselor with children ages 7-17 who were HIV positive and I saw me. I saw innocence, before the news and I remembered total beauty. Most of them had not been told. Many were too young to understand.

My family is very supportive and I have a wonderful job. I was offered a position as an HIV Street Outreach Worker and I teach HIV/AIDS education, primarily at Drug and Alcohol Abuse Treatment

Facilities. I am a Counselor Intern working toward becoming a Licensed Chemical Dependency Counselor. In time they cared. In time I cared.

> *I look East.*
> *Clouds blowing away quickly yesterday's feast.*
> *Sing life's picnic on soft green grass beside a lake without storms.*
> *Hold time tonight.*
> *Dance a hot trail across great mountains once more before dawn.*
> *Once more before Dawn.*

Oh, yes. I cried and I remembered total beauty. And I am aware that time is passing. "Clouds blowing away quickly yesterday's feast." But the Serenity Prayer states, "God grant me the serenity to accept the things I cannot change. The courage to change the things I can and the wisdom to know the difference. Yes, *"Sing life's picnic on soft green grass beside a lake without storms."*

The doctors say according to the numbers, I should be sick all the time or dead. I feel great and I am never ill. I know who is holding time and I am grateful. I embrace the opportunity to, "Dance a hot trail across great mountains once more before dawn. In 2001, I went on a cruise to Cancun and Cozumel, Mexico. I wanted to do something I had never done. I wanted to scuba dive. After 20 minutes of instruction we headed down to a depth of 25 ft. After I got down to a depth of 10 ft., I decided I would rather go back and snorkel. The idea of the only thing between me and heaven being a lip-lock on an air hose no longer was appealing, but I had done it. Once more before Dawn, I want to see something I have never seen. Once more before Dawn, I want to do something I have never done. Once more before Dawn, I want to love and be loved. Once more before Dawn, I want to give and be of service to this world.

I no longer work at that agency and I have had a career change. I have continued to work in the voluntary field of HIV/AIDS and Substance Abuse. I received the MLK Jr. Award, 2007 and was the Executive Producer of a play, "Before It Hits Home" by Cheryl L. West. It is about a family member dealing with acceptance, rejection, love and ignorance when he comes home ill from AIDS. May 2009 will mark 20 years.

Yesterdays & Tomorrows
H.L. Sudler

What have you learned from your life? And what will you take with you when you die? Will it be all the lessons you have learned, all the pain you remember? Romances, milestones, regrets, eras?

Somehow I always manage to return in my head to the events that have hallmarked my life, that have steered it into a direction unforeseen, jarring me out of complacency or a willful veil of ignorance; an existence created as if I lived on a whole other plane than the rest of the world. I turn these thoughts over like breakfast on a griddle, flipping events this way and that, examining them, but always arriving at the same unavoidable questions for which I have no absolute answer.

What have you learned from your life? What will you take with you when you die?

I ask myself these questions on my birthday, as I always ask myself these questions at what could be considered the most reflective time of year. Since that milestone arrives in December, the same month as World AIDS Day, I always have cause to remember the three men I had come to know in my life, all at the same time, dead now, dead from AIDS, dead and buried, dead from the world, dead before I even knew they had the disease, dead–it seems–even from collective memory.

Lawrence Blakely, Laurence Gray, and Bernard Little had all been friends of mine in high school–and let them be remembered here and now, in black and white, for they are all forgotten. We spent three years together laughing, joking, studying, spending together day to day calendar dates during a school year strung to create a finite lifetime of memories, growing as kids do, foraging into adulthood as if with blindfolds donned and hands outstretched. We held on to each other, relied on each other, fought and made up, not realizing the importance of our friendship, not realizing the importance of our bond–as men, as African American men, as gay African American men.

Laurence Gray was the sidekick of my girlfriend at that time. He was very short and lively with a wide infectious smile and an equally contagious laugh. His face beamed and lit up everything, but he was also a reservoir of emotion and would cry at the drop of a hat. He lived a terrible life at home, was poor and hungry and no one wanted him. He became one of my best friends, he constantly at my girlfriend's side, keeping her laughing, keeping her company. I was very dour and very serious then, as I am now, but he had the natural ability to make anyone laugh, even me.

He was partially responsible for me winning my student government campaign, handing out flyers, making up posters, and I helped him with his studies, divided my lunch with him, or gave him money to keep him fed during the day. We held a Secret Santa between us group of friends one Christmas and I remember him gifting my girlfriend a stuffed bear, white, that she adored. I remember him in a fight once, and I remember being shocked at how strong he was for a little guy, how much anger he carried with him. He was no taller than five feet, two inches. He was proud to be an Aquarius.

Bernard was a little taller—make that a lot. Taller than my five feet, seven inches. But he was lanky and not terribly good looking. If he had been given the opportunity to grow older, he might have grown into his looks, become handsome. Either way, he was a busybody. What old-timers would call 'a hoot.' He referred to himself as Millie and he would breeze through the school hallways his humble and meager lunch in a wrinkled plastic no frills supermarket bag that dangled from his wrist, his torn school bag held together by safety pins, both he and his outfits (that he wore sometimes two or three times a week) smelling stale. He had grown up disadvantaged and pushed on his grandmother. In his eyes you could tell he knew his future had limited options and that he was living for today only.

He was dedicated like a puppy dog and he gravitated toward me, we developing a strange friendship. He loved my bad boy attitude, that I was fearless, tough and direct. He was a confidant to me, even though we never discussed our common sexuality. Like me, he was a member of the school's drama club, and on breaks we would joke around and he would laugh gayly and without conscience. Everyone knew him—teachers, staff, the nerds, the jocks. Out of school he was considered a nobody, invisible. But in school he was a sort of celebrity in our high school soap opera; comic relief that reminded us that if someone like him could find laughter somewhere, in anything, that we with our teenage angst could find joy and delight somewhere as well, and in him. So we all embraced him as best we could.

Lawrence Blakely was constructed of a different cloth altogether. He and I were not all that close, but he was in each of my classes. He was tall, husky, black as newly applied tar and just as shiny. Yet, for as large as he was he walked in little tiny steps, girl-like, as if he would disturb the universe with his presence. He spoke in a small nasally voice, his eyes distorted behind unflattering bifocals. His teeth were unnaturally white, and from time to time he emitted a laughter that was deep and throaty, as if to hint at the man he would become. A week before our senior graduation, Lawrence Blakely and Laurence Gray got into a fight in the

Essays & Sermons

chemistry lab–an epic battle not unlike David and Goliath. I was the school's student government vice-president at that time and knowing this disruption could result with them both thrown out of the commencement ceremonies I came between them, which was a huge mistake. The massive Lawrence Blakely attacked me and all three of us found ourselves in the principal's office with the threat of suspension over our heads.

Then there was graduation. Then they were dead.

After we left high school, I never saw or heard from Lawrence Blakely or Laurence Gray ever again, and saw Bernard Little only once since we separated as a senior class. One day about five years after graduation as I was on my way to work in Center City Philadelphia, another friend from school (who was also black and gay) informed me that both Bernard Little and Laurence Gray were dead and had died within a week of each other. The funerals had been two and three weeks prior. A little more than a year later, this same friend would report to me Lawrence Blakely's death, and that despite the fact that he had lost weight, had shed his glasses and his timid gait and became a gym boy–having fully evolved into the butterfly he was meant to be–he too succumbed quickly to the disease. All of their families had disowned them and they suffered and died for the most part alone.

I was so burned by this, so ashamed that I had immersed myself in college life and parties, that I was spurred to do something in their memory. I would not allow these men to rest in my brain as nothing more than fading tombstones in a cemetery. I began to volunteer at local Philadelphia AIDS charities. At Action AIDS and For All Walks of Life, at MANNA and Safeguards, doing everything from selling pies to handing out condoms and literature at clubs. I attended fundraisers, volunteered at AIDS walks and LGBT Pride festivals. I served as a Buddy to people suffering from HIV and AIDS and I became a mentor for others to serve in this capacity.

The people I encountered at these organizations altered my life. They were angels, amazing one and all, each of them so different from the other, all of them bound together in grief and hope. The most admirable was Mister Jim at sixty-seven years old, who volunteered in the memory of his beloved son, and the rough and tough Jimmy O., as young and handsome as he was, was a man who never got over losing the love of his life, whose grief cloaked him like a scent, and so he volunteered courageously, tirelessly. The soldiers at these organizations conducted themselves as a secret society working diligently for people they had lost, for people they knew who were suffering with the disease, for people they did not know at all: men, women, gay, straight, transgendered, young, old, black, white, Latino, Asian, children. The hours were long and there was always so much to do, but we existed as a family unto ourselves and they welcomed me and my hands and my time without hesitation.

I was, and I am, ashamed of my ignorance—for that is the only word that aptly describes my situation. How dare I shield myself from this truth as prevalent as it was in its first two decades, that which had such impact on my community! How dare I believe that it could not affect my circle! That I was buffered; AIDS reduced down, chalked up, to a headline, a broadcast, something that people who were not like me suffered, something that people who were careless or uninformed suffered. Today I would like to think that if I had known about Lawrence and Laurence and Bernard, I would have come running in the pouring rain to stand beside them in their final hours. I did not even think to check on them after graduation, to inquire after them, my blood brothers, during this crisis that I knew was striking down lives indiscriminately.

This brings me to this still prevalent arrogance and ignorance on this topic, where the number of deaths and infections are rising still, affecting demographics worldwide—from the distant regions of South Africa, Nigeria and India to the American hotbed of HIV and AIDS: Washington, D.C. Where apprehensions on open, honest dialogue on sex and sexuality still acts as prevention from saving lives. Where despite the fact that there is so much money spent on preventative measures for other health issues, still not enough competently staffed and strategically coordinated efforts reaches the people truly in need for this issue: the financially disadvantaged, the uninsured and under-insured, the young, the undereducated.

What have you learned from your life? What will you take with you when you die?

I remember later in life a friend named Ted, whom I helped take care of up until his dying day. I remember his wispy blonde hair, his smiling eyes and broad laugh. I remember feeding him his dinner when he could no longer feed himself. I remember helping him bathe and use the bathroom and getting him in and out of bed. I remember sitting with him for long stretches in the evenings as we watched *Law & Order* (one of his favorite television programs). I remember when he had to be moved to a hospice, and the people there who were so pleasant and worked without fatigue. I remember him marrying his boyfriend from a wheelchair, and his heartbreaking dementia, and times when I thought he would not make it through another night; then finally his quiet death, like a light summer breeze that enters a room and just as effortlessly exits.

When I die I am determined to leave behind my ignorance, for Earth is the only place where it belongs. I shall leave behind my regrets as well, becoming weightless and free. What is past is passed. I shall take with me only my memories. Of loves and lovers and friends; of sunny, golden days long gone. Of the work I have done here on Earth and the people I have met. I shall also take with me the days of Lawrence and Laurence and Bernard. Of our fun together as children in the face of life's harsh realities, our laughter, our finite lifetime of memories. Of the lessons their presence gifted me. Of today and the schooling it will bring, and the learning left for tomorrow.

And tomorrow.

And tomorrow.

Let The Healing Begin
The Literary Masturbator

As I stand before you all I can't help but wonder when was the first time I did this? Not necessarily stand before this group but the first time I stood before an assembled group at church. Was it for an Easter speech? A Christmas one? Maybe it was during Vacation Bible School or BTU. I can't remember the first time, but what I can remember are the ladies who came up to me during my life and said "baby you sho' did say them words." I still think of those women and the way they made me feel. That whatever I did they were behind me 100%. They carried me through and for many years, many times, and many ways were the examples of the Christ that the church should and can strive to be.

To really let the healing begin I wanted to find out when the hurt started. It wasn't with those women. They comforted me and kept me going. It was in the sermons and the hypocrisy of the church dogma. No matter what school of thought, religion, or tribal custom I've learned at the end of the day I am a good ole fashioned church boy. A Bible drilling, Sunday School banner winning, pastor and wife's welcome giving, rummage sale having, fish dinner selling, black bottoms with white top for youth choir or junior usher board on 2nd Sunday church boy! So, the hurt started when I was told I couldn't be a part of that. When they said I couldn't inherit the Kingdom of Heaven because I was outside of God's will.

Being fascinated with the music department early on didn't help. Any church that had a good music department usually had a homosexual involved. Whether they were playing music, directing, or singing, someone if not more than one was attracted to or somehow involved with a person of the same gender. Growing up in Los Angeles and attending workshops and participating in community choirs meant coming into contact with Reverend James Cleveland, Gospel Music Workshop of America, and cornerstone Institutional Church. All of these places had people who were same sex identified but no one could truly be open or honest about it. The unspoken things were the most hurtful. I didn't get a lot of abomination message but you understood that two men together is not the way it's supposed to be. If you offset that with the ways they told you, you could be delivered; it leads to confusion and hurt. I had one experience where a friend who was apostolic told me if I got baptized in the Name of Jesus I could be delivered. I had been baptized in the Name of the Father, Son, and holy Ghost which she explained were just titles. Getting baptized in the Name of Jesus meant that I would receive the Holy Ghost, speak in tongues, and be delivered. So I went through with it. For the next couple of days every other word out of my mouth was

"Thank You, Jesus" while the other was "Hallelujah!" Then came Wednesday and I met this guy named Antoine. Well, that was the end of that. I was delivered but not from something. I was delivered to something.

The men I got involved with I didn't meet at the Catch, Brass Rail, Poppa Bear, The Edge and Wet, the park, or the bathhouse. I met them at Double Rock, Faithful Central, First Apostolic, New Mt. Pleasant, or Victory Baptist. There's a saying that was out when I was in college: "Game recognize Game." It meant whatever you were doing or whoever you claimed to be anyone who was of the same sort could recognize it. So no matter where I went or what I did, eventually the church boy in me would show up. One year in college I needed to make extra money so I became a phone sex operator. It paid well and I was good at it and I still recognize some voices to this day so don't laugh too much. What amazed me is that at least once or twice every couple of weeks after fulfilling my obligation to the customer we'd somehow end up talking about gospel music, church, choirs, ministers, Jesus, or the Bible. At the time, I couldn't figure out why it kept coming up. I had actually stopped attending church on a regular basis and not at all during football season. Of course I had issues concerning my sexuality but I also had trouble with the pretense that I saw. But nothing could keep me from connecting to that place inside where I first discovered on the back of those little cards from Sunday School where Jesus said: *"Suffer the little children, and forbid them not to come unto me: for such is the Kingdom of Heaven."* That Scripture from Matthew 19 touched me so. It hurt so much that I didn't have access to the Kingdom!

So, when did the healing begin? When did things change? I remember the exact moment and it showed me God was bigger than any religion, book, or school of thought. I was watching a live performance of the Alvin Ailey American Dance Theatre. I sat transfixed as they moved from dance to dance on the program and they got to the finale **"Revelations"** which is set to a suite of Negro spirituals. *"I've Been Buked And I Been Scorned", "Didn't My Lord Deliver Daniel", "Fix Me, Jesus", "I Want To Be Ready", "O Sinner Man"* and many others. But it is in the last movement where I found my deliverance, my healing. It starts with the lament *"The Day Is Past And Gone"* the goes into *"You Can Run For A Long Time"* and ends with the rousing *"Rocka My soul In The Bosom of Abraham."* By the last part of the ballet, the audience including myself was standing, rocking, and clapping in time to the music absorbing the energy of the dancers. It felt like a revival. I began to look at the different people and their reactions. It didn't matter what background they came from; their ethnic origin; or anything like that. They were transported to a special place. That place where God is unconditionally available to everyone.

As time passed, I began to think what kind of God would create a man like Alvin Ailey and give him the gift to create this piece of work that could touch people and then send him to hell? It didn't make sense to me! Then, I thought of others. Would God send James Cleveland to hell? The man whose music had shaped the modern gospel music industry... would he send him to hell? I personally didn't know of any church, especially any black church, no matter the size or place that didn't sing one of his songs. Then I thought of James Baldwin... there's no way God would send James Baldwin to hell. If I could just imagine what James Baldwin was like... he'd be telling the devil how to run the place.

It also came to me in music and magnificently enough just not in gospel music. The bridge to Regina Belle's **Make It Like It Was.** *Now when I compare, there's really no comparing. I just want it the way it used to be, just the thought of living without your love, makes me ask that you make it like it was.* This ministered to me at a time when I needed it desperately because in gospel music I had Angie and Debbie telling me I wasn't natural.

Thankfully, I was able to find that place where God's love is for absolutely everyone! God's love and healing is everywhere present and available unconditionally at all times. This is summed up in the 139th division of Psalms in the New Living Bible it reads:

{1} O Lord, You have looked through me and have known me
{2} You know when I sit down and when I get up. You understand my thought from far away.
{3} You look over my path and my lying down. You know all my ways very well.
{4} Even before I speak a word, O Lord, You know it all
{5} You have closed me in from behind and front. And You have laid Your hand upon me
{6} All You know is too great for me. It is too much for me to understand.
{7} Where can I go from Your spirit? Or where can I run away from where You are?
{8} If I go to Heaven, You are there! If I make my bed in the place of the dead, You are there!
{9} If I take wings of the morning or live in the farthest part of the sea,
{10} Even Your hand will lead me and Your right hand will hold me!

So this is where our healing is by knowing that we are a part of the whole that has always been. By knowing that whatever Scripture or doctrine they have tried to use to bind us is not true and with that knowledge we have to become a community. Fibers connecting one to the other:

I am a thread in the fabric of brotherhood
One of many woven together
Creating a blanket of community
A cloth of many textures
Some bold and bright
Others subtle and smooth
Some torn and frayed
Others mended from years of wear and tear
The fabric of brotherhood
Many societies have tried to rip us
Yet we remain a cover of strength and warmth
Determined to fulfill our duty as comforters from life's cold
A secure blanket for brothers who are asleep
For when they wake
They will be sewn into our quilt of consciousness
The fabric of brotherhood
Textile makers of an accord
For people of African descent in America
Which will benefit the whole of humanity
Be a healing ointment to salve our societies wounds
We are the fabric of brotherhood

This text is from a speech given to the National Body of the Unity Fellowship Church Movement National Convocation October 2005. The theme for Men's Day 2005 was "Let The Healing Begin." The text includes the poem *"The Fabric of Brotherhood."*

And We Speak

Interviews

~ Charles Michael Smith ~

Editor, Freelance Journalist, Book Reviewer

Works Published:

Fighting Words: Essays by Black Gay Men ©1999

His article about Harlem Renaissance luminary Bruce Nugent appeared in *In the Life: A Black Gay Anthology* edited by Joseph Beam ©1986, 2008

As one of the first African American SGL community members to publish works, how do you feel that your contribution has aided in the development of African American SGL Literature of today?
I wasn't the first but there were several anthologies that came out at the same time or during that period in which I wrote.

What first prompted you to publish your first work?
In 1982 or 1983, I was invited to write an article for the *New York City News*. It was an obscure newspaper and I was first introduced into writing for the gay press. At that time, I was involved in an organization (Committee of Black Gay Men). We were at a meeting and I was asked by Lonnie McGill, who then was President, to write a paper. At the time I was secretary of the group. I wrote an article and it began from there within the gay community. I was the editor of the group newsletter and that pretty much put me into the Andy Humm to write for the Gay City News of New York City. My first article was about gay Harlem and the 1920s. Since then, I have written for many newspapers across the country. At first I was a little leery but soon I overcame my fears and this actually helped my career in journalism. This is how I actually met Joseph Beam who had read one of my articles. Most of my articles were about black gay men.

What results have you seen after the publication of your first work (whether positive or negative)?
My work has been quoted in several other people's work. So, I would say that is a very good thing. The works that I have seen are pretty good and I definitely feel that to be quoted by other authors only means that people are actually reading my work. Several recent publications have mentioned my works and for that I am grateful. So, I would say that I have seen positive things over the years.

What inspired you to write the article/essay about Harlem Renaissance luminary Bruce Nugent which appeared in the 1986 classic anthology: *In the Life?*
Joe Beam wrote me a fan letter and sent it in care of the New York Native, a weekly gay paper I was wrote for at the time. Joe worked at Giovanni's Room, a gay bookstore in Philadelphia. The bookstore carried the paper there. Joe told me that the only time he read the paper was when I was in it. He asked me to write an article about Nugent, who lived in Hoboken, New Jersey. He gave me Nugent's number and I interviewed him on the phone. I used portions of the transcribed interview in the article. I tried to put Nugent's life and career within a larger context of what was happening in Harlem and elsewhere, artistically and otherwise. Up until Joe assigned the article to me I had never heard of Nugent. A year or so later, David Frechette (another black gay writer who was a part of the second Black Arts Movement, which is what I call the literary/artistic movement of black GLBT people in the 1980s) invited me to see *Before Stonewall*, in which Bruce Nugent appeared in on-camera interviews. Whenever I see the movie, I think back to the night I first saw it with Dave (now deceased) at a screening in midtown Manhattan.

What inspired you to edit and publish the anthology *Fighting Words: Essays by Gay Black Men?*
The idea for the book was suggested by Assotto Saint (aka Yves Lubin), who offered to publish it as a Galiens Press book. I would often go to his apartment and he and I would tear out potential articles for the book from *BLK* and *BGM* magazines. Assotto after awhile became too ill with AIDS to publish the book and he asked me if it was all right for him to turn the book over to Vega Press. I said yes. But Vega and I didn't get along very well and I took the book to Other Countries Press. That relationship was short term as well; I wasn't happy with the terms of the contract: $200 after the sale of 1,000 copies. I sent a book proposal to 7 publishers; 3 responded: Alyson, Avon Books, and Graywolf Press. I went with Avon because it was a major publisher and it was based in New York. From the time they acquired the book until the publication date took two years. Altogether I spent 6 years on the book.

In the age of HIV/AIDS within the African American SGL community how have we failed or progressed in combating/addressing this epidemic?
I think we could probably do a better job of educating people within the black community period. There was globalization within the white community once upon a time that advocated for people with HIV/AIDS but that did not happen to the [same] extent within our own community. Now there is just a higher rate of infection among our young black gay men. The black press and the black church were just late in getting started. So, I would say that we have not progressed very much as a result.

In knowing Essex Hemphill, Marlon Riggs, and Joseph Beam, Assotto Saint, Melvin Dixon how did your relationship with them shape you and your work?
I really didn't know Marlon Riggs. He was supposed to contribute to *Fighting Words* but became ill and passed away before publication.

I came to know Essex Hemphil after he did an article in *Essence Magazine*. I wrote to him to let him know how much I really enjoyed the article. We met on several occasions in New York and Philly. He was a member of Cinque with Larry Duckett.

Assotto Saint and I became good friends. He was one of my first interviews and then we just became very good friends over time. Assotto was the person who suggested that I do a book of black gay essays. Originally, I wanted to do an anthology. He offered to publish it. So, we talked about the project and the project really had no name. Originally the title was *Words With Fire*. I didn't really like that name. One night in bed I thought about how language is used to fight one another and *Fighting Words* became the controversial name of my work. It definitely had a double meaning.

In 1984, *New York Native Newspaper* created a gay supplement and entitled it *Harlem Rising*. *Harlem Rising* was poorly done. I asked to be a part of the second supplement and soon found myself as editor of the third supplement which was entitled: *Celebrating Ourselves*. It was the only time we had a poetry centerfold with now black gay literary giants in the *New York Native*. I believe that we all felt some sense of accomplishment but never even realized that the effort would become a legendary thing.

Honestly, however, they never really shaped my life but because we were all around one another, I managed to be inspired by them all. We were all young then and we were all talented and wanted to share our varied talents with the world. Essex and Joe were wonderful essayist and had they lived would have probably published works akin to James Baldwin. Their style was not romantic and fiction. Some writers have a problem with understanding style but once you understand what your style is, you find there is really no argument and comparison of work. Essays are essays while fiction is fiction. I love history which can be included or deleted from both. We just never realized back then that our work would have made a difference in today's world but then again, that is definitely history now.

Can you discuss any writers from the past that you personally connect with?
I personally connect with James Baldwin. Richard Wright, E.L. Doctoroh, Gordon Parks, Pete Hamill, Christopher Bram, Gloria Naylor, and Alice Walker. I am influenced by a lot of good writers but these are my favorites.

Fighting Words **is often times a controversial exploration of African American gay sexuality. If you could lend advice to our African American SGLBT youth what would you say to encourage them?**
Do not limit yourself to one genre. Be very flexible. Get acquainted with people from other backgrounds. This is how you will get a broader picture of the world and learn how to get a broader concept of the world. It takes stepping outside of your own box. Learn from all groups and discover the differences as well as the commonalities. Take that same attitude towards everything in life.

Can you elaborate on your childhood and how it shaped the person who you are today?
I was born in New York City (Manhattan). When I was 7 in 1956, we moved to Compton and L.A. for 11 years (1956-1967). I liked the California weather. I feel that it was a good idea for me to experience another part of the country. We did a lot of travel around California. We did a lot of traveling across the Mexican border. I would have never been able to do that in New York. It did interest me on how the west became settled and the history of blacks in the West. We went to Noxberry Farm which was an amusement place. They had an Indian Village and Train and locomotive that went to the mining town and there would be scenes that brought everything to life for me. Being part of all of that as a child just helped history come alive for me and this has really shaped me.

How did you come to love history so?
In growing up in California, we would take trips to downtown L.A. It made history come alive to me when we would visit Olvera Street which is pretty much where L.A. began as a Spanish village. The field trips helped to make history come alive for me. My mother also insisted that I do a lot of reading. So, I guess I became fascinated with how things got their origin and began to develop and shape the world in which we live in today.

What is the next chapter of Charles Michael Smith?
I will publish *At The Old Place* which is an anthology dealing with gay and lesbian bar culture from the early years to the present. It will be more intergenerational and not limited to the United States but will be as broad as possible in order to appeal to the masses. That's one project. Then, I was thinking about producing a radio program on the GLBT community because there is no radio program for us. I just want it to be a show that deals with all aspects of gay life. I would also love to do radio documentary. Radio documentary has become such a dying art. It is a beautiful art that is not being used effectively. I'm really into just being able to document the history of our people whereas the stories will not be forgotten. Last, I would like to do a follow up on an article that I read about two black men arrested in Kentucky in 1909 for sodomy. They were tried and then later acquitted. I wanted to get the background of the two men in anticipation of seeing if there truly is a story there. Those are a few things that will be the next chapter of Charles Michael Smith.

~ Larry Duplechan ~
Author

Works Published:

Eight Days A Week ©1985, *Blackbird* ©1986, ©2006, *Tangled Up In Blue* ©1989, *Captain Swing* ©1991, *Got 'til it's Gone* ©2008

As one of the first African American SGL community members to publish works, how do you feel that your contribution has aided in the development of African American SGL Literature of today?
I suppose that would be better answered by the following generation of black gay writers – i.e., y'all. Obviously, somebody has to "get there first", and I was at least *among* the advance guard. I do think that my second novel, *Blackbird*, being published by a major New York publishing house (St. Martin's Press) in the mid-1980s helped pave the way for other black gay writers and their work to be published by the larger houses. And at the time, my work was criticized by some black gay critics for not being "black enough" or "Afro-centric enough". But you had to have Sidney Poitier before you could have "Shaft". And I think there had to be *Blackbird* before you could have *B-Boy Blues*. James Earl Hardy (whose books are considerably more successful than mine, by the way) has acknowledged my influence; and I think all you have to do is read *B-Boy Blues* to see it.

What first prompted you to publish your first work?
Well, that's kind of a two-part answer: why did I write, and why did I write what I wrote?

I started writing after being in show business for about five years after college, as a singer. The lower echelons of show business, please note. Small clubs, little cabarets, the wedding/bar mitzvah circuit. Yes, I was The Wedding Singer back in the early 80s. But my husband grew weary of basically never seeing me. Because I always had a full-time day job, and I was out late into the night doing gigs several nights a week. So about seven years in, he gave me the choice, quit show business or quit him. And I'd been at this singing thing for five years and I was still working the same little clubs; and I figured a for-sure man was better than a maybe-singing career. So I quit show business. But I do have this need to create, express myself, show off. And I had this BA in English; so I thought, writing.

I was reading a lot of gay novels, back in the 1970s and early 80s. Back then, you could actually read all the gay novels that came out in a given year. There just wasn't that much. And the guys that were being published, certainly by the New York houses – Andrew Holleran, Edmund White, those gentlemen – they're fifteen-to-twenty years older than I am, and they were New Yorkers, and they were white. So while I found their books interesting, they weren't writing about people like me. Naturally, they were writing about people like themselves. But I really wrote in reaction to the Gordon Merrick books, *The Lord Won't Mind*, etc. Because those weren't "literary", those were pop fiction; and very popular pop fiction. And the guys in Merrick's books weren't just white, they were white supermen: tall and handsome and masculine and bisexual. And I wanted to read a fictional character who was more like me. So I created Johnnie Ray Rousseau, a fictional character who was *exactly* like me. Who's in all five of my books, and the protagonist of all but one of them.

What results have you seen after the publication of your first work (whether positive or negative)?
Wow, that's a wide-open question. I'll give this a shot and if I end up answering a different question than you thought you asked, let me know and I'll try again.

My first four books were published before the burgeoning of the Internet; so the only results I had at my disposal were book sales, reviews, and the occasional fan letter. With the advent of email, I hear from a lot more of my readers. Which I like. But my books tend to move in the neighborhood of 5,000-10,000 copies. So, not really big sales. As far as reviews, the gay press (by which I mean "The Advocate", mostly) has largely been very kind to me. The mainstream press has ignored me entirely – with the exception of *Tangled Up In Blue*, which the "Los Angeles Times" panned twice (in hard cover and in trade paper). I really pushed buttons with that one, apparently.

As I've mentioned, there were always black gay writers who thought I should be writing about black-on-black love in the black gay community. I also think there was some bitterness because I was being published, and being published by St. Martin's. And they were, maybe, doing chapbooks on a mimeograph machine.

But when you talk about "results", you have to realize, I didn't exactly set the world on fire. I got published and all; but relatively few people gave a fuck. Which is still pretty much true, I'm afraid.

How do you respond to the proliferation or explosion of recent African American SGL writing both positively and negatively?
If you've got a voice, and something to say, and you manage to get it out there – good on ya. Especially if you get somebody to *pay* you for it. And while the word "explosion" might be overstating the case a bit, there certainly are a lot more black gay voices being heard now than 25 years ago, when I first started. Which is a good thing, for all concerned. I mean, for a quick minute there, I was a sub-genre unto myself. I distinctly remember reading a review of Randall Kenen's *A Visitation of Spirits*, that referred to it as "another black gay novel of the Larry Duplechan variety". I think the fact that I'm not the only game in town anymore has done good things for my reputation as a writer. Because back in the day, every black gay man wanted me to tell *his* story, when I was just telling *my* stories. And lately, it seems that more and more people are taking a second look at my books and saying, "Well, what he did do, he did rather well." Because Corbin, and Kenen, and then E. Lynn Harris came along, and then Hardy, and so on. So nobody's looking to me to speak for the entire race anymore.

What inspired you to write the classic novel Captain Swing?
Captain Swing started when I attended a Duplechan family reunion, in the Los Angeles area, in 1990. I had sworn off writing forever, because the reviews and sales of *Tangled Up In Blue* were so abysmal. And at this reunion, I met this 16 or 17-year-old male cousin of mine, who was just gorgeous. Gorgeous. And I'm 33 years old at this point. So *Swing* really started as sort of a dirty old middle aged man fantasy about having an affair, which could be seen as an incestuous affair, with a much younger man. If memory serves me, the character of Nigel was originally not of legal age. Because I started writing that book in secret. I'd wait until my husband was asleep, sneak off to the computer and write on the sly; because I'd told him and all my friends that I was never going to write another book. He didn't know I was writing a novel until I'd finished it. So, initially, I wasn't even thinking about publication; I was writing because I had this story I had to get out. When I started thinking about getting it published, I made sure Nigel was 18. Because I figured enough people were going to get upset about Nigel and Johnnie being first cousins.

I also wanted to write a story about personal loss, because by this time I'd lost several dear friends to AIDS. But I didn't want to write about AIDS. I'd just done that in *Tangled Up*; and frankly, there were writers living with AIDS who were taking care of that issue from first-hand experience. So that's why *Swing* starts out with Johnnie mourning the accidental death of his life partner, and why I have him dealing with the imminent death of his father. My father was still alive. Still is. But I wanted to write about loss.

In addition, I also wanted to write about my parents' hometown: Mermentau, Louisiana (which is near Jennings, which is near Lake Charles). We'd visit there at least once a year when I was a kid; but I hadn't been there in years. Which is why I fictionalized the town and called it St. Charles. I knew my memories were sketchy, and I didn't want anybody pointing out my mistakes. But I wanted to memorialize my impressions of that place – the way the air smelled, the way the people spoke, the muddy dirt roads with crushed seashells instead of paving.

What is your opinion about the tension found in spirituality versus sexuality?
My goodness, that's a doctoral thesis.

Personally, I have resolved that issue pretty well. It's taken a lifetime, but there is very little dichotomy for me anymore. One of the times when I feel most in tune with the divine is when I'm having sex. The sight of a beautiful man, the sound of truly great music, and the experience of a really good fuck, are among the things that keep me believing in God.

Do you think that spirituality and sexuality coexist in terms of African American SGL Christians?
I can only tell you what I've observed.

At least up to and including my generation (and I was born in the late 1950s), most black folk were brought up in the black church. And it was the cornerstone of our lives, at least through childhood. Lou Rawls said, "You went to church, or else. And you didn't want to know what 'else' was." The church was the hub of the black community. And I think a lot of black gay men tried to fit into the black church as best they could, because it was home. So they sang in the choir, or played the piano; and maybe they even married the soprano soloist. And in that situation you either live a lie; or you come out loud and proud and hope not to get killed; or you leave. I left.

When people start talking about how tough it is to be "out" in the black community, I have nothing to say. Because I didn't come out in the black community. I came out in college, at UCLA, which was overwhelmingly white, and had a Gay Students Union as early as 1973. So I came out in the gay community – which at that time in that place, was largely white. I was the only black gay man I knew, my first year of college.

So, leaving the church meant that I was free to explore different faiths, different forms of spirituality. I was free to question the things I'd been told as a child in church. And I questioned everything. The Bible says it's wrong to be gay? Show me where. Then read that verse right on the next page, and tell me why you can eat pork chops but I can't be gay. Leaving the black church gave me the freedom to explore my own relationship to the Divine.

Can, in your opinion, African American SGL be Christians?
Of course. But you'd better be prepared to face the people who *don't* think so.

In the age of HIV/AIDS within the African American SGL community how have we failed or progressed within our community?
Unfortunately, like the largely-mythical "Gay Community", I'm not sure I believe there's any such animal as "the African American SGL Community". I think the stigma of "out" gayness within the greater black community, which spawned the "gay is a white issue" myth, has created an indeterminately large, generally faceless group of African American "men who have sex with men"; and a small, elite group which is currently terming itself "the African American SGL Community". I use the word "elite" because the desire to discuss this issue at all seems to be confined largely to educated middle-class people. I can't help wondering if the "African American SGL community" of which you speak, is largely comprised of writers. (smile)

The unusually high instance of HIV infection among black MSMs is obviously quite outside the control of the "gay community", black or white, simply because most of the men involved don't consider themselves "gay" or "SGL" (a term that, frankly, I'm still getting used to – it's a generational thing).

In knowing Essex Hemphill, Marlon Riggs, and Joseph Beam, how did your relationship with them shape you and your work?
Those gentlemen shaped me and my work not one bit. They were doing their thing and I was doing mine. Those guys were all East Coast guys. Los Angeles may as well have been Mars. And again, I got there first! So if anybody shaped anybody, I probably shaped them, if only by giving them an example of what they didn't want to be.

I never met Marlon Riggs. I watched *Tongues Untied* on PBS like everybody else, and was blown away by it. I own the DVD now, and that film still blows me away. But I never met him or had any contact with him.

Joseph Beam wrote a glowing review of *Blackbird* for "The Advocate"; and then they asked me to review *Brother to Brother* (the first of two anthologies of black gay male writing edited by Beam). And like most anthologies, it was a mixed bag; and in my review, I said it was a mixed bag. I said what I liked about it and what I didn't like about it. And Beam actually wrote a letter to "The Advocate" rebutting my review – which they published. I still think that was rather small of him. Later, he asked me to submit work for his second anthology, and then rather tersely rejected the story I submitted, claiming it wasn't up to their standards. That story, "Zazoo", was subsequently published in "Black American Literature Forum" and in *Calling the Wind: Twentieth Century African-American Short Stories*. So, you know, whatever.

I met Essex Hemphill once, in 1990, at a party at Steven Corbin's house. *Tongues Untied* had just recently aired – and of course, Essex is in that film, reciting free-verse poetry in full close-up. So he was a bona fide celebrity. And he was sort of holding court, sitting in a chair off in a corner; and people were going over there to kiss the ring, you know. And I went over to pay my respects; and he said to me, in this attitude of ostentatious condescension: "You could be doing so much for the cause." Which I think was the attitude of some of the more "Afro-centric" writers: that here I was writing these little Oreo novels and being published by St. Martin's, when their stuff was so much more worthy.

As Beam, and then Hemphill passed away, it was a sad sort of "A Chorus Line" experience for me – I felt nothing. It's always a shame for people to die young, perhaps more of a shame when those people are talented. And they were definitely talented voices, stilled too soon. But there was no personal sadness for me. They really hadn't been very kind to me.

I'm sure that's not the story you'd hoped for; but that's the story.

Interviews

Captain Swing is a lyrical often times controversial exploration of African American gay sexuality in the rural South. If you could lend advice to our African American SGLBT youth living within rural Southern American communities what would be your advice or encouragement to them?
My advice? Get out! (smile) But seriously, folks ...

My *parents* are from Louisiana. I was born in California. My parents and pretty much their whole generation got the hell out of the South as soon as they could. I mean, if you're happy where you are, stay there and be happy. Otherwise, get out. As soon as you can.

Can you elaborate on your childhood and how it shaped the person who you are today?
My childhood sucked. Period.
I was a sissy. I was small and delicate, I had a high speaking voice, and I was bad at sports. All of them. Life is tough for a sissy boy; and its double-tough for a black sissy boy. In America, being a black boy who can't shoot a basket is like being an admitted Communist. People are initially incredulous, and then they pretty much want you dead.

My father's disappointment in me was all but palpable. I didn't want to help him work on the car. I bought the *Sound of Music* soundtrack album with my allowance, and sang along really loud. And then the *Funny Girl* soundtrack album. I played the flute. The *flute*. As D.L. Hughley said, no man is proud of his son playing the flute. "The flute is the soundtrack for an ass-whippin'."

My mother was very, very supportive of me as far as my music, and my academic achievements; but even she had a threshold for just how much effeminacy she could deal with in her firstborn son. I remember asking my mother to help me thread a needle once: I was forever doing something artsy-craftsy when I apparently should have been outside throwing a ball. As she handed me the threaded needle, she pulled a lip-pursing face at me and said, "If you *must* sew – Trixie!"

My father worked for Lockheed Aircraft: he began right out of the Korean war, washing helicopters, and ended up an electronics liaison engineer (and don't ask me what that is, but I do know it paid much better than washing helicopters). Being a Lockheed brat was a lot like being a military brat – a good deal of my father's work was connected with air force bases in various parts of California. So we moved a lot. Never very far, always within California. But between kindergarten and college, I attended 13 schools. So I don't really have a "home town", and I have no real concept of "school spirit" (I went to three high schools). I grew up a perpetual outsider. Even if I had been tall, masculine, and able to shoot a basket; even if I had not known by the age of 12 that I liked boys in the way I was supposed to like girls, I would have been a perpetual outsider; because I was the perpetual new kid in town.

So, I turned to music (both listening and performing), and movies (especially musicals from the 1930s and 40s), and reading (just about anything and everything). It was my escape from the relentless dull ache that was my life. And in the case of performing, it was a way of expressing myself in a way that people seemed to admire. I was in high school when I discovered I was a good singer (see, *Blackbird*), and put down the flute. I still couldn't shoot a basket, but I could sing and make people smile, and cry, and applaud. Writing is another form of performance for me. The creative process is solitary, and it can take a year before I know if anybody's going to laugh at my jokes. But it is not coincidence that four of my five novels are in a narrative voice very like my own.

What is the next chapter of Larry Duplechan?
Gee, I don't know. The publication of *Got 'til it's Gone*, and winning Lambda Literary Award, have greatly diminished the belief that I died sometime in the 1990s. So people have been soliciting short non-fiction pieces from me for anthologies, like yours. And I've just started what might end up as my sixth novel – but don't hold your breath.

~ Charles W. Harvey ~

Writer – Novelist – Poet

Works Published:

Drifting ©1989, *When Dogs Bark* ©2000, *The Smoke Detector* published in *Backdraft* ©2009

As one of the first African American SGL community members to publish works within the Southern region of the United States, how do you feel that your contribution has aided in the development of African American SGL Literature of today?
I don't know. I hope it has told others that they have a voice, something to say, and that they should be heard.

What first prompted you to publish your first work?
I felt like I was a good writer. I thought I had a unique voice. I wanted to put myself out there. I had the youthful audacity to think others wanted to read what I had to say.

What results have you seen after the publication of your first work (whether positive or negative)?
It's nice to be recognized for something. But you can't rest on your so-called laurels. You have to keep going. The wind got knocked out of my sail, so the speak, when my mother took sick and all of my energy went into taking care of her. After she passed all of my energy went into trying to figure out my place in this lifestyle. There was some travel, seeking relationships, and a new habit consumed much of my time and resources. I didn't stay the course in my writing like I should have. But I'm back.

How do you respond to the proliferation or explosion of recent African American SGL writing both positively and negatively?
It's good. However all writer's need to make sure they go through a thorough review and rewrite process. The new technologies and publishing models out in cyberspace make it easy for anyone to be a published author. However not everyone is a good writer. Our stories are wonderful. However we have a duty to make them compelling for the reader. Reading is a form of entertainment. I can't speak for all readers, but for me, I want a sentence, phrase, or description to make me go, "wow!" When I pick up a book of poems or fiction I want to be dazzled. Also you don't just become a writer and that's it. Read, go to conferences,

to hone your craft. Sometimes that attention to craft can be lacking when the marketplace is open to everyone.

What inspired you to write your first and second work?
I thought the second one would be a more polished work. The internet was supposed to make publishing easier. I had had a great deal of praise for my story *When Dogs Bark*. It had been widely anthologized. So I said why not push something else out there.

What is your opinion about the tension found in spirituality versus sexuality?
It's a shame that such tension exists. If we do our spirituality the right way and bring God out of the sky and into our lives, we are going to be healthier in mind and body. Our sexuality should be a spiritual manifestation of something good. The idea of being connected with another human being in a moment of intimacy should be just as spiritual as it is physical. Sexuality is another way for adults to release tension within themselves and to get in a good place spiritually. That is if sexuality is done right. Most times, it's done wrong. We approach people from platform of deceit ands and power. Sexuality is sometimes used as a bargaining tool or as a way to hold power of individuals. If I buy this person this, they will do that. If I withhold this, they will do as I say. And of course the whole idea of sex is something shameful in most folks eyes. Some people still have to be in a blackened room and under the covers.

Do you think that spirituality and sexuality coexist in terms of African American SGL Christians?
Nope! It doesn't coexist easily because of the guilt. Many people believe they are engaging in a sinful act when they sleep with or have sex with the same gender.

Can, in your opinion, African American SGL be Christians?
They better be Christian, Buddhist, Islamic or what have you! What I'm saying is that no matter what you call God and whatever book you use as a guideline, your spiritual side needs to be nourished. Hopefully your teacher or leader in whatever religion you practice will be wise enough not to condemn you for your sexuality. Who you sleep with is not the problem. The problem is how we go about sleeping with people. I don't think going into back alleys, parks, and bookstores is the right way to go about having good sex. Nor is the exchange of money. If spiritual leaders go about the business of addressing the things that make us feel hurtful and guilty, many of these activities would cease. But most preachers, priests, and what have you focus on condemnation. This only drives

people deeper into the underbelly of our community and thus deeper into doing those things which are soul killing.

How do you negate or respond to the elitism found in the African American SGL community in terms of divisions created based on social status and/or approved aesthetic?
I feel guilty of buying into it sometimes. I'm growing a little more conscious and don't need to feel that I need to belong to any particular clique. Everyone has their pain and heartaches. It doesn't matter if you are the poster child of physical perfection or media darling... we are all human! I write because I need to. If what I write speaks to someone, then that's what matters! Sure there is a little bit of vanity and need for approval in this creative exercise for me. I won't lie and say it's never ever about that. But that's not the overriding reason I do what I do.

In the age of HIV/AIDS within the African American SGLBT community how have we as a community failed or progressed?
My opinion and it's only an opinion, is that people are living longer and healthier because of the advances in medicine. I think much though not all of the African American progress has occurred because the larger gay population has been at the forefront in demanding treatment and services and in establishing organizations. African American Churches seem to have recently discovered that some of their members are HIV positive or have AIDS and have only begun to have ministries to address the issue. I know there are some wonderful African-American community based organizations that are fighting the battle. I also believe there has been a lot of waste and greed when it comes to organizations and grant funds.

In what specific ways have your work changed in the past ten years?
More polished I hope. I attend workshops whenever I can. I read books on writing. I try to read as much as I can. I'm realizing it is work and not left to the whims of the muse. I'm more mature to know that when a line has to be deleted, it just has to be gone. No more trying to fit it in because it just sounds so clever. Maybe it will fit better in another story or poem or play

Can you discuss any writers from the past that you personally connect with?
I always liked Langston Hughes. He was very accessible. His word choices were simple and yet powerful. He loved to write about people of the streets and bars. He captured the spirit of the working class. Charles Bukowski does it for me too. Flannery O'Connor has influenced me. Writers who are still on the planet like the poet Ai greatly influenced me in some way. The imagery and story she presents in a poem is breathtaking. E. Annie Proulx of Brokeback Mountain fame—I'm blown away by her prose

When did you decide to write and why?
I don't know exactly how the decision process worked. I was a good reader as a kid. I remember there was some kind of poetry contest announced by my seventh grade teacher and I entered a poem about the Astronauts landing on the moon. It was a good poem, as I remember the comments. Nothing earth shattering. I was a teen in a government project and so I saw and was affected by what I saw and the people I encountered. I wasn't allowed to participate in any of the stuff going on around me, but I certainly observed it. I'm not a psychologist, so I can't articulate as to why the site of a little girl in a small overcoat crossing a vast parking lot on her way to school was such a powerful image for me and why I had to write a poem about that. I suspect I saw more than just a girl crossing a parking lot. I firmly believe all writers see more or see into things more than just the obvious. The black pride movement and all of that stuff of the late 60's and early 70's found its way into my childhood/High school musings. It was a way for me to process the stuff going on around me. Maybe If I had had any art skills I would have been a visual artist.

Discuss the themes found in *When Dogs Bark*.
Well it's a compilation of stories and poems—a one man anthology if you will. I think there are a lot of secrets in When Dogs Bark. And those secrets are being expressed. Man is at war with himself I is a general theme. I think the poem Secrets sums up the theme best: Red fire rages/way down below/in our bellies/watch us consume/ourselves with deception/Our black smoke/hides our truth. When the truth comes out, it comes out like a barking dog.

What do you want readers to know about *When Dogs Bark*?
Well the practical thing to know is that one can still order through amazon.com. The other thing is that it still resonates with people, especially young gay men.

Can you elaborate on your childhood and how it shaped the person who you are today?
I'm grateful for the childhood I had and for making it through it. I wouldn't want to repeat one minute of it though. I was an only child and there were times when playmates weren't available. After my Father died when I was seven, my Mother kept me a bit too close. There was a lot of love and sometimes a lot of anger in her. A bit of her is in the poem *God, Mother, and Country*. At around age eleven or twelve, I developed a secret friend, a white girl named "Alice" who could protect me from the bad stuff I sometimes experienced going on at home. I even pretended I looked like her until I saw myself in the mirror and saw how ridiculous I looked. Sometimes my Mother and I were two lonely individuals, and we would make up stories and give make believe names to people in the neighborhood. She once even drew a cartoon picture and sent it to someone she knew. I guess it was her way of sending them a caricature of themselves. It was funny to us as we imagined them receiving this anonymous piece of mail. Little did I know that this make believe thing was the beginning of my becoming a writer. My somewhat enigmatic upbringing has made me ambivalent, I think. I don't see the world as black and white. Sometimes good things come out of a bad experience. And sometimes evil lurks behind the façade of good. I tend to root for the underdog, even if he's done something horrible. That's why I like characters in fiction to be multi-faceted. People aren't as simple as good guys wearing white hats and vice versa. That's why my opening statement to this question sounds like a contradiction.

What is the next chapter of Charles W. Harvey?
A busy one I hope! I anticipate a chapter that goes for another 30 or 40 more years!

~ Stanley Bennett Clay ~
actor, novelist, playwright, filmmaker, publisher, producer

Companies Own(ed):

SBC Magazine (SBC Publishers) {February, 1991- July, 2001}
Clay Communications {April 1981-October 1989 }
Stanley Bennett Clay Productions {October, 1989-present}

As one of the first African American magazine owners/editors within the SGL community, how do you feel that your contribution has aided in the development of African American SGL Literature of today?

I began publishing SBC magazine in 1991, when there was virtually no Internet presence, therefore local, national, and international communication between members of the African American SGL community was very limited and the exposure of our literature was nearly non-existent. I was very frustrated that we were not being covered and/or addressed in the African American mainstream press or the white gay press, therefore it was essential to create our own press profile, written in our own voices, and expose our artist and literary figures in our pages. Although SBC was very political, my background as a novelist and artist (my first novel DIVA was published by Holloway House in 1988 and I had already produced several award-winning stage production, and had won the NAACP Best Actor Image Award) naturally caused me to give SBC a very artistic and literary slant. Novelist E. Lynn Harris and James Earl Hardy were very new on the scene back then. It was my duty to give them and others like them as much exposure as possible by reviewing their books, interviewing them, publishing various profiles on them, and keeping the community aware of their new projects and bourgeoning accomplishments. We also published new African American SGL fiction from many community writers who had never been published before and who now enjoy wonderful careers as writers. I am both humbled by and proud of the hundreds of African American SGL artist—novelists, poets, playwrights, critics, photographers, fiction writers, journalists, and graphic designers—whose works appeared in SBC during the ten years of our existence.

What first prompted you to publish *SBC Magazine*?
Once again, it was the lack of outlets for black SGL folks. I had a very heavy background in the magazine editing world. I was the Editor-In-Chief of Black Beat magazine for two years, Entertainment Editor of Sepia, American Correspondent for London's Blues and Soul, and had interviewed everyone from Michael Jackson to Jane Fonda, so I knew the power of those publications. When I realized that I didn't see me, or anyone who looked like me, in magazines like The Advocate, I knew something had to be done. My then business partner Devre Jackson and I first approached Alan Bell, publisher of BLK, a locally published magazine here in Los Angeles. We had all these grandiose ideas about upgrading BLK and taking it global. That's when Alan said that we should publish our own magazine and, with his blessings, we did. It was called Alternative. Alternative only lasted two issues because Devre and I had two very different ways of approaching publishing. Although we remained friends and respectful of each other business-wise, we went our separate ways and within months each published a new magazine. He published Alternatives (with an 's') and I created SBC.

What results have you seen after the publication of your first work (whether positive or negative)?
The best thing is that it encouraged other Black SGL entrepreneurs to create magazines. I am so proud of that. Black SGL magazines began popping up everywhere—Kick in Detroit, Clikque in Atlanta, Arise out of Oakland, Venus out of New York, several out of Chicago. Instead of what some would consider competition, it really created the opposite effect. It created such a hunger in our community that all of these publications were doing well. The most important thing about the press is that you cannot have one voice. Varying points of view must represent a community, therefore, the more viewpoints, the more publications, the better our community is served.

How do you respond to the proliferation or explosion of recent African American SGL writing both positively and negatively?
Positively, I think more voices are being heard.

Negatively, I think journalistic quality and integrity are being compromised. There are so many bloggers out there without any journalistic experience. Oftentimes the writing is very poor and facts are often thrown to the wind. Gossip writers masquerading as journalists are self-publishing everywhere with little or no legitimacy. And this is not just in the SGL community, it's happening in all communities.

What is your opinion about the tension found in spirituality versus sexuality?

Quite frankly, I think that's a discussion of apples and oranges. If spirituality is a state of intangibility, of relating to those forces that some of us call God, some of us call a Higher Power, some force that is perhaps responsible for all things, including sexuality, well there is no conflict. Now when you bring in the conceits of imperfect man, this thing called religion, then you can discuss conflict. Man will always be prejudice against something. It is a part of his imperfect nature, and the creation of organized religion is his greatest shrine to his bigotry.

Do you think that spirituality and sexuality coexist in terms of African American SGL Christians?

Absolutely. And although I consider myself a nondenominational Christian, I think the discussion of spirituality and sexuality cannot be fully explored when it is confined to one religion. Christianity has no more of a lock on spirituality than any other religion. There are many roads to the Higher Power—Muslim, Hinduism, Taoism, Buddhism, to name a few—and when we get up off of our egos and stop thinking of that Higher Power in terms of human traits like jealousy, anger, and destroying Job's life just to prove a point to Satan, or traumatizing poor Abraham by having him almost kill his son (the kind of shit humans do), then we will come to better understand that Mighty Power as so great and complex that it is beyond any human explanation.

Can, in your opinion, African American SGL be Christians?

They can be anything they want. I always believed that to be Christian is to be Christ-like; love your neighbor as yourself (which covers a lot) and love (and respect) that higher power, whatever you want to call it. I consider myself a Christian because I strive to be Christ-like, not because I go to somebody's church every Sunday, or condemn others who don't believe like me, or believe that those not in the majority or worship differently, such as homosexuals, blacks, left-handed people (once thought by so-called Christians to be demonic), Buddhist, Muslims, atheists, agnostics. I try to be a good Christian by respecting the rights of my fellow man to seek his spirituality, his kinship with the higher power in whatever way he wants, as long as it is not harmful to others. And another thing. Who's to say what Jesus Christ was really like. If indeed he was born human, made of flesh and blood, then he had all the bodily functions and urges of a human being. He obviously had to eat food for nourishment, relieve himself toilet-wise, and if he never masturbated, he obviously had involuntary ejaculations (what we call wet dreams). And who's to say what his sexual urges were? Whether he acted on his sexuality or not, it only stands to reason that something or someone got his dick hard, be it male or female. Sex is the gift that keeps on giving and unless someone has some sort of physical dysfunction, then it becomes normal and healthy to have sexual urges. I believe Jesus Christ was physically normal and healthy. It just pisses me off when organized religion demonizes sex.

How do you negate or respond to the elitism found in the African American SGL community in terms of divisions created based on social status and/or approved aesthetic?
Once again, I don't think elitism is a malady exclusive to the African American SGL community. There is the tendency for some in all communities to think of themselves as better than others. I wouldn't know how to negate that any more than I would know how to keep all thieves from stealing. How do I respond to it? It comes with the territory of imperfect man. I just strive to do my best to remain humble and respectful of others, and hope by example that I can encourage others to do the same.

In the age of HIV/AIDS within the African American SGLBT community how have we as a community failed or progressed?
I think that taking the battle wins as winning the war is a grave mistake. Once we started believing that AIDS/HIV was no longer an automatic death sentence, we started letting our guard down.

In what specific ways have your work changed in the past ten years?
I'm not as angry as I used to be. Even though I grew up in a barely middle class family, I grew up with very middle class values, and was pretty sheltered. My father reared 7 children working as a mailman and a pantry cook. We lived in a very nice 5-bedroom house in the suburban community of Del Amo Hills. We were probably the poorest family on the block, but my father struggled to give us the best. To this day I've never heard my mother utter a single curse word, and didn't hear my father curse until I was grown and he would come over to my place and we would hang out like old buddies. Now during my years of growing up my mother was very careful about the kind of people I was allowed to hang out with, and both my parents kept things like racism away from us. I attended a nearly all-white high school where I was an honor student, editor of the school newspaper, president of the chess club, and president of the Drama Club. Most of my friends were white and I actually thought I was a little white boy. Now when I became an adult and started hanging out in the real world, it was during the height of the Black Power movement, and all the black people I started hanging with made me

realize how much crap black people really were being put through. I became so angry and became a super militant; to sort of make up for all the years I missed in the trenches of racial politics. I grew a big afro, started smoking pot, refused to date any man but an African American preached a lot of hatred toward white people and the white establishment. I'll tell you, I was one badass militant queen back then. Much of what I was going through was reflected in my early writing, like I had to prove that I was as black as everybody else, if not blacker. Over the years I calmed down and allowed the pendulum of my life to settle in the middle. A lot of my writing is still very political, but I am so happy that I was able to cleanse the hatred out of my writing and my life.

Can you discuss any writers from the past that you personally connect with?

Wow, there are so many. I am a big fan of James Baldwin, especially when I was much younger and he shared much of my racial anger, which is why I was able to relate so much to "Another Country." And I really like "If Beal Street Could Talk." "Giovanni's Room" was, I think, the first gay novel that I read. And what a bold and courageous book, especially when you consider Baldwin published it back in 1956. John Updike was always one of my favorites. I loved the way he would examine Jewish angst in such poetic terms. A writer has to be more than a storyteller to me. There must be a certain 'poeticness,' a distinct lyricism about the work for me to really get into it. That's why I'm a big fan of Toni Morrison. She is absolutely my favorite writer, and because she takes so long to come out with a new book, I tend to read her books over and over and over again. I know I read "Sula" at least ten times, "Love" and "Beloved" three times each, and "The Bluest Eye" and "Song of Solomon" so many times that I've completely lost track. I must confess that her last book "A Mercy" was kind of a disappointment. Gordon Parks' autobiography "Voices in the Mirror" really got to me. It is so beautifully written that I cried from the beginning to the end. And there's nothing like sitting down and reading some Shakespeare. I have a 34-volume set of classics, everything from Aristotle to Fielding, which includes the complete works of Shakespeare, given to me in 1963 by Mr. Laraway, my Junior High School journalism teacher. To this day I'll crawl up on my sofa or in my bed, grab one of the volumes, and read until I'm blurry-eyed. What a total turn-on. And speaking of turn ons, I must confess that over the years I've read my portion of sexy trash. I remember reading Phillip Roth's "Portnoy's Complaint" when I was 15 or 16, and would get myself so worked up I would have to masturbate. Come to think of it, I jerked off to a lot of books when I was young—"Valley of the Dolls," "Tropic of Cancer," "The Carpetbaggers," Anything that had to do with sex and fucking.

When did you decide to write and why?
Since early childhood, I was an avid reader. And I was an exceptional reader. I was brought up a Jehovah's Witness and at the age of nine I was reading 5 page passages from The Bible in front of the entire congregation. By the time I was fifteen I was writing and delivering hour-long sermons during the main Sunday services. I don't remember when I wasn't writing something, either poems or short stories or plays. I remember when I was twelve I wrote this musical stage play which I directed and starred in in our living room. My parents helped me sell tickets to all of our neighbors. And it was pretty successful. We even sold popcorn. The next year we moved from Chicago to Los Angeles, in the dead of winter, February. And to drive from snowy freezing Chicago to 85-degree sunny Los Angeles was so awesome that I broke down and cried (yes, there is a bit of a drama queen in me). I began writing all these poems about how remarkably beautiful Los Angeles was. When I enrolled in my new Los Angeles junior high school, somehow the word got around about my poetry. That's when Mr. Laraway, the journalism teacher, asked me to join his class and join the school paper and yearbook staff. I became like the resident poet of the school and my poetry was published in each issue of the paper and in the yearbook. During my first year in high school (1965) I remember writing this short story in my English class. I couldn't quite understand why my teacher was so shocked, and why she let other teachers read it, and they were shocked as well. I guess it was because of the homosexual subject matter, which I didn't think was a big deal. It's funny how that none of the teachers ever mentioned anything about it to me. They would just kind of look at me funny (laughing). But seriously, writing always was and has remained a hopeless addiction for me.

Can you elaborate on your childhood and how it shaped the person who you are today?
I was extremely fortunate to have great and supportive parents; wonderful siblings; a fabulously progressive grandmother (who I later suspected was a lesbian); and some really cool uncles, aunts, and cousins. We didn't really need a lot of outside friends. My crazy family was party enough. When I was 8 or 9 my parents bought a piano so that my older sister could take lessons. When I asked my mother if I could take lessons too, she said no because I was already involved in so many activities. So I would go with my sister when she would take her lessons. The teacher would show her how to play something, and she always had trouble getting it. When we got home, I was able to play it by ear. I would then listen to records—my mother had a huge collection of classical recordings, and I would teach

myself to play simplified versions of Beethoven, Brahms, Tchaikovsky, Chopin, etc. When my mother realized how good I was getting, she simply said to me, "Now, write me an opera." To this day I'm still trying to write me mother's opera. My family always referred to me as special, but there was absolutely no jealousy. We kids were always taught that we were equal and equally loved. I cannot remember a single time when any of us were ever called out of our name by a parent or relative, well, except once, when my sister Renee, when she was about ten, called me a "motherfucker." My mother immediately washed her mouth out with soap. And there were times when my brother Brad and I (he's a year younger) would get into it, but other than that, I remember my mom always telling us, "I'm the most fortunate mother in the world because I have the best children in the world." If that's not enough to give a child confidence, I don't know what is. We were made to believe that we could accomplish anything, and that honor and goodness and kindness and charity and family were all the good things. I know that my parents always knew that I was gay, and were religiously against it, but their love for their child trumped their religious philosophy, and my sexual nature became a non-issue. My mother even made kitchen curtains for me when I moved out of the family home and into my first one-bedroom, one-bed apartment with my partner when I was twenty. Even though my father found it difficult to talk about it, my mother always discussed sex very frankly with us. She wanted to educate us about before we got out in the street and hard about in tawdry, nasty terms. She also taught us etiquette and we were constantly reading Emily Post. I know this all sounds oh so idyllic, but we did have our share of ups and downs. There was always a financial struggle growing up and sometimes my parents would get into what they would call 'debates' behind closed doors and usually over bills, but my parents thought that being parents was the best thing in the world, and they enjoyed every moment of it, and boy did we kids luck out. Because of my parents, I am the self-loving, proud black gay man that I am today, and I have been sharing what I've learned from my parents with my beautiful partner for six years now.

What is the next chapter of Stanley Bennett Clay?
Career wise? I just signed a new contract with Kensington Books. I'm collaborating with two of my dear friends, Terrance Dean ("Hiding in Hip Hop") and James Earl Hardy (the "B-Boy Blues" series) on a tribute book to our friend E. Lynn Harris. The book, entitled, "The Power of Love," will include a novella from each of us that will include Lynn as a character. Also we will each include a personal tribute to our late friend. I'm also getting ready to take my play "Armstrong's Kid" back on the road. Now

that I'm back to my acting roots, I'm really, really enjoying it all over again. Other than that, I'm going to just enjoy the grace of age. On March 18, 2010 I will turn sixty years old, and I am blessed. I got my health, got my wits, got my talents, got my career, got my looks, got no need for Viagra, and got my man. What more could a SGL brother want?

~ Gregory McNeal ~
Art Photographer, Photo Journalist, Activist

Works Published

World AIDS Conference, Dublin, South Africa – 2000

World AIDS Conference,

Exhibits:

Saturn 1999, Zero Hour 2006, Lost Legends 2000, Saturn Trilogy 1999 Among others

As one of the first African American SGL photographers within the SGLBT community, how do you feel that your contributions have aided in the development of African American SGLBT people of today?
As a whole, I feel like my images change the way that people look at black men. I wanted to create a series of positive images that showed the greatness and potential in my brothers. In so doing, I wanted the world to take notice of us and see what I saw as a valuable resource to humanity and how it can sometimes be wasted. My work would also change the way we see each other. I wanted us to recognize our own potential.

What first prompted you to create?
I saw so many negative images and stereotypes within every media circle that I wanted to change it. Further, I didn't see my own people challenging the stereotypes

What results have you seen after the publication of your first work (whether positive or negative)?
What I wanted to do was to inspire a new generation of photographers and inspire the way they shoot black men. As they have studied my work, some are shooting black males better or at least trying to take photography of black males to the next level. The second thing that I have learned in my experience after fifteen years is that people don't believe in black males anymore. I figured out that people are very threatened by my images or the strength of the images. No one wants to see positive and strong images of black men. One of the reason this fight has been so hard is that I thought people didn't believe in me and then I figured it out: it wasn't me that they don't believe in it was my subject matter. You can make a lot more money and get a lot more attention by falling into stereotypes and capitalizing on the negative images. If you follow my blue print, you'd have to up your game. It is much easier to

follow the crowd which I have seen many do. You have seen many do and you know who they are.

What is your opinion about the tension found in spirituality versus sexuality?
The door has been opened for us to tell our story and to let the world into the mystery that has been our lifestyle. The question is: Did we choose to use this opportunity to build ourselves up; to educate people; or to empower our own people to show the world what amazing and gifted people exist in that world or did we use it to play out the same old stereotypes only to end up exactly where we began. Are these media images that are being put out now helping us or hurting us? Are you just getting paid to act out the role that you used to get stereotyped as before the door was open? Living in Los Angeles, I am constantly surrounded by actors who don't act; singers who don't sing; directors who don't direct; and writers who don't write but while the door is open I suggest that you show the world your greatness and stop repeating the same mistakes. There was a time when unity among us was more important than your ego. I tell my models all of the time that a dream demands three things: hard work, sacrifice, and commitment. Many aren't willing to sacrifice a damn thing and their commitment is to their addiction, whatever that may be, which explains how we arrived here in this situation as a people in the first place.

How do you respond to the proliferation or explosion of recent African American SGLBT images both positively and negatively?
I believe that we are sexual creatures and if God made you gay (I believe that you are born gay) then He did so for a reason. It takes strength to be openly gay and live your life but are you truly living your life when there is a man on the podium who has the same weaknesses and flaws as you do who is telling you how to live your life? I think that your relationship with God should be between you and God. Being that He is all knowing, He knows your needs, faults and weaknesses. I think you should build a stronger relationship between you and God and not give the middle man so much power. Who knows what he's (the middle man) is doing behind closed doors? Many times have we seen people on the podium condemn other people only to get busted for doing the same thing?

Do you think that spirituality and sexuality can coexist in terms of SGLBT people?
Yes spirituality and sexuality can coexist. I feel that you should be equally satisfied sexually and spiritually. I don't mean being out there "whoring the streets" but I do mean trying to find someone to love you in the

manner in which you deserve to be loved. I never said that it would be easy but no one said that it would be.

How do you negate or respond to the elitism found within the African American SGLBT community in terms of divisions created based on social status and/or approved aesthetic?

People in your life, regardless of their education, wealth, or title have the power that you give them. Whatever the world sees in that person or the community sees in that person those same things are in you. You don't have to be like them in order to be a great leader or someone great in the world! I think the way that we allowed people in certain positions with labels and titles to intimidate us and make you feel as if you have less value and are unworthy. Take your power back. Check your history for many great things came from nothing. "One unfortunate thing about the gay lifestyle is that it collects trash and throws away good people."

In the age of HIV/AIDS within the African American SGLBT community, how have we as a community failed or progressed?

We never realistically looked at the situation. Our outreach campaigns became complacent. They were never strong and never really had any impact. If you look at the campaigns that came out, the tools that were used... most of them tried to fight HIV/AIDS nicely. Why would you want to play nicely with AIDS when it never played nicely with you? A lot of people who were over projects allowed their egos get in the way. It became more about them rather than making a statement. When it came to fighting AIDS in the black community and reaching black people, the campaigns were: never strong enough; never black enough; never serious enough... if you didn't take it serious, why should anyone else? A lot of people didn't see AIDS as a threat to our community because the campaigns did not and still do not show it as a threat. A lot of people who were over the campaigns were more concerned about people liking them than producing an outreach campaign that was raw; in your face; and made an impact. We never addressed the issue and now the present issue is not addressed. We are afraid to face the new vehicles that help with the spread of AIDS beginning with the internet. The internet is a new vehicle that spreads AIDS in secret. Back in the earlier history of AIDS when white men were dying, in the same manner that black men are now, they were allowed to put anything that they wanted to on billboards or campaigns. Now that it is black men, there is a very limited outlook on what goes on the outreach campaign. Hence, there are a lot of things that cannot be seen. So, here we are in 2009, about 25 years later, and we are still content to place "nice" with AIDS. I have mentioned before to several organizations: If you would launch your fight in the same manner as the AIDS virus has launched its campaign towards you, maybe you would have had an impact on this a long time ago." I've always felt that the AIDS Awareness Campaigns needs to come from the perspective of the virus itself which means simply: "What does the virus think about you?" The virus has stopped at nothing in order to achieve its goal. It never compromised. It has been ruthless, aggressive, and without heart or compassion. It didn't give a damn about what anybody else thought. Your outreach programs should be the same. There are many dragons in the black community. From black on black crime; to drugs; to racism; to AIDS. If the next generation could have seen you slay at least one of these dragons they would have learned that it was possible. For years because of our egos, complacency, and selfishness we have been so distracted and too divided as a people to even unite do that!

What/who inspired you to become a photographer?
I saw very negative images of us on television and I wanted to change that. I saw what was happening with our reputation and our image. If you keep showing the world those images, the world would believe this to be a truth. I saw a future where the world believed that you are these images and nothing more. I knew that I couldn't stop the negative images but I thought that I could create some part positive iconic art images to balance out some of the negative images. I figured that sometime in the future, someone would come back and look at black male images in America and they would find a lot of negative images. But mine would be there in order to balance it out.

In what specific ways have your work changed over the past fifteen years?
The more recent pictures have become more like short stories. In other words, they will tell a story. The first original images had a presence. The newer works tell a story.

Can you discuss any photographers that you personally connect with?
When I researched photography before I began shooting, I was looking for a certain type of photography. I wanted someone who could shoot very well and their images were iconic but told a story. If you want to be great, study the people who are great in your field. Two of my favorite photographers who are legends are Steve McCurry and Herb Ritts.

What advice would you like to give youth of today?
I would like for people to know that they are born of three elements: hard work, sacrifice, and commitment! When those three elements are used, it shows in the product.

Can you elaborate on your childhood and how it shaped the person who you are today?
That is funny. I am a lot like my childhood but I am also very different. When I was a child there were little things that I liked to do and I still do it. I still read comic books. The same things that kept me grounded as a child keeps me grounded now, I have always had a belief in something greater than me and I have always felt that I had a purpose in my life. One of the things that have changed is how I see people.

What is the next chapter of Gregory McNeil?
The next chapter of Gregory McNeil is going to be a book. It will be a memoir or an autobiography.

~ Dwayne Jenkins ~
HIV/AIDS Educator, LGBT Activist

Organizations:
Brothers United Network, Inc., Nashville Black LGBT Pride, Editor in Chief & Publisher, the BASU SOURCE Newsletter

As one of the first African American Activist in the State of Tennessee within the SGL community, how do you feel that your contribution has aided in the development of positive African American SGL life of today?

I think that my contribution within the African American Lesbian Gay Bisexual Transgender (LGBT) / Same Gender Loving (SGL) communities in the state of Tennessee over the past 15 years has helped in many ways. Since I am not a native to Nashville or the south, I know that there were many other individuals that have come before me that also aided in my overall process of being able to reach out and be well received in my work and the mission of the organizations that I am associated with.

What first prompted you to organize Brothers United?

When I first relocated to Tennessee in 1996, I immediately started to volunteer with Nashville CARES, the states' largest and oldest HIV/AIDS organization. While volunteering I was asked to take part in a focus group for Black Gay Men and through that process developed Brothers United. In the middle of us doing social events and bar outreach, a grant became available that we helped to write and I was hired on 12/1/06 on World AIDS Day to coordinate the Brothers United HIV Prevention program at CARES. A year later the Brothers United Network was incorporated and began forming chapters in Chattanooga, Memphis, Knoxville and West TN. As we grew, we also developed a youth group for the guys that were under 26 called Young Brothers United, and found a home for our Lesbian volunteers under the name of Sisters United.

What results have you seen after the organization of group (whether positive or negative)?
A majority of the history of Brothers and Sisters United and Nashville Black Pride has all been positive. As with any organization, we have experience a variety of things that weren't necessarily bad, but at the time felt negative. With only a handful of these types of situations, each has helped us grow as individuals and as an organization. One of our highest accomplishments beyond winning awards and other national, regional and community recognition, is that our name is still something that many have heard about, and trust. To date, we are still the only Black LGBT/SGL 501c3 nonprofit organization in the state of Tennessee. Other groups, houses and families have come and gone, and we are still standing and providing a host of opportunities to educate, empower and affirm LGBT folks across the country.

What is your opinion about the tension found in spirituality versus sexuality?
I think that there will always be some form of hesitation with the topic of SEX in included in any topic. I think that spirituality is very different than religion, and more easily can see the tension between sexuality and that more so than with someone who is spiritually connected to a higher power. To me, spirituality means that you are open and possibly guided by unwritten karma laws of what they perceive as right or wrong and not necessarily subscribe to heaven and hell more that theory of "what comes around, goes around." They can attend church, but again, less likely to be a regular person who can quote scriptures from the Bible and more naturally feel ashamed of their sexuality because of what they have heard from the pulpit.

Do you think that spirituality and sexuality coexist in terms of African American SGL Christians?
Unfortunately, from my observations over the years bring me to believe that there is a huge difference between the terms spirituality and Christian as far as faith is concerned. I think that sexuality finds its way into all of our life experiences in some form or another. Some of the people that I know have more difficulty balancing religion with sexuality, than being a spiritual person who is also sexual.

How do you negate or respond to the elitism found in the African American SGL community in terms of divisions created based on social status and/or approved aesthetic?
One of the good things about Nashville is that the city is really small in terms of people knowing one another. The most affluent person in some way or another has either heard of someone because of who they dated, hang around with or where they work just as easy as the everyday person who doesn't go out often and may not work or be as educated. The key factor is their sexuality; so many paths seem to cross over the years, especially with all of the internet and networking sites that allow you to become acquaintances with people without even actually meeting face to face. This in no way means that there isn't a visible divide within socioeconomics, gender, educational status, etc., because every community has it in some form or another! But in the same breath, you would be surprised how two folks can come together that are from different backgrounds and social statuses just because their paths cross at an event that doesn't necessarily have to be targeted toward LGBT/SGL community.

In the age of HIV/AIDS within the African American SGLBT community how have we as a community failed or progressed?
There is not enough time or paper for me to respond to this-for real! All kidding aside, I think that we have improved on a lot of things as far as HIV prevention and education is concerned. With that said, I also feel that we have taken a few steps back.

Can you discuss any writers from the past that you personally connect with?
Oh sure, put me on the damn spot will you...You know, one of the great things about working within the LGBT community over the past 14+ years is that I've had the honor to meet so many of our writers, entertainers, activist and community leaders. I must admit that having the opportunity to get to know many of the authors whose books line my shelves is really a blessing. Back in the day, it was nothing to pick up the phone and call James Earl Hardy, Ricc Rollins, Stanley Bennett Clay, Dwight Powell, or Michael-Christopher to name a few, and just to shoot the shit. As you may recall, when you (R. Bryant Smith) first came on the scene as a new author, our BU gatherings were really special. The connection went deeper than just having a good time together at gatherings. It was about reaching out to others to share that feeling of brotherhood. When you and I first spoke on the phone it was about your book. Once we got to know one another, and you offered to help develop a BU chapter in West TN, we were able to expand our

educational efforts to an underserved population of men which made a big difference for many. Each time we have the opportunity to get together during historic events such as FIRE & INK, we must take that time to treasure the moments and enjoy one another. I've also had the honor and privilege to meet other authors, film makers, and musicians that I've befriended over the past few years who I adore as much as the old heads- yeah I said it!

When you became involved with the organization of Brothers United, did you ever feel that it would grow in the manner in which it did?
Absolutely not! When I lived in Rochester New York, there was a social group called Brothas United and this group of Black Gay men hosted cookouts and other events like parties at clubs. When I relocated to Nashville and developed our group, I thought it was going to be very similar in that most of the events would be fun, and non educational in nature. Boy was I wrong! Even though there is definitely nothing wrong with social groups or organizations that focus on just having a good time, there was a greater need for us to be more than that in Nashville, the State, and southern region.

Can you elaborate on your childhood and how it shaped the person who you are today?
I'm a native New Yorker, born and raised in the Bronx. I am an only child who grew up in a two parent household that honestly wasn't spoiled and had to work and earn everything from a very young age. My childhood was fun and included a crazy family, and great set of friends who I am still in touch with today. I really didn't have issues with my sexuality because for the most part I was attracted to and dated girls, but also experimented with boys as well. Having had sex with men and women also gave me the opportunity to live freely without being called names. This doesn't mean that I didn't go through rough patches, but honestly growing up in New York also gave me a hell of an attitude which pretty much allowed folks to leave me the hell alone. I was loud and always ready to fight so calling me a name just wasn't worth it. Once I went away to college and realize my preference, I didn't have the baggage that others had of being accepted. I didn't have anyone religious around me to condemn who I was, and actually didn't give my friends or family a chance to treat me differently once they realized I was Gay.

As the owner of a Black Gay Pride, how does it help or hurt your mission for Brothers United Network of Tennessee, Inc.?
I don't think that being the Executive Director of a non-profit organization has hurt the organization in any way. The BU Network owns the Nashville Black Pride name and the annual celebration falls directly in line with our overall mission to affirm and empower the Black LGBT/SGL community. I truly feel that the transition was much simpler than that of other groups taking on such an undertaking because we already had a great 7 year track record that included a large mailing and email list, not to mention the trust of the community.

What was the purpose of the Brothers United Network of Tennessee, Inc. Annual Winter Retreat?
The original purpose of us hosing a retreat was to give the volunteers a chance to leave the city to regroup and prepare for the upcoming year of workshops, events and outreach activities. After the first year, people heard about the gathering and it became an annual gathering where predominately Black Gay Men would come together for a variety of reason which included the original focus, as well as other things like education, affirmation, and entertainment. We expanded the weekend from 2 days to 4 and included panel discussion, vendors, book signing and live vocal and other performances. We hosted ten consecutive, and very successful retreats from 1997-2006. After we became an official member of the International Federation of Black Prides organization and began hosting Nashville's Annual Black Pride celebration, the volunteer board decided to concentrate on the larger event, which still gave the same individuals the same chance to attend events, but instead of taking it to a state park, it would in the metropolitan area. This allowed us to grow from reaching 125 Men each December to over 3,000 Men, Women & transgender individuals in the same 3-4 day time span.

Did you find that it helped with its mission?
Hosting the retreats, as well as our Black Pride celebration definitely helps with our mission! If there is something going on in the African American LGBT/SGL community in or out of town, we are known to be the ones to disseminate the information first! We are generally able to get the same authors, acts and entertainers that the larger cities can, which allows us to stay current with what is hot in terms of films, DVDs etc.

Being in a monogamous relationship with your partner for well over ten years, in what ways could you advise young people and old people, for that matter, on how to keep the "fire" burning?
Yeah, yeah there you go with all that…LOL. From the very beginning my relationship with my partner has had great communication. As we move into our 14th year, one of the main things I can suggest to anyone in terms of keeping the fire burning is to be honest, laugh and be yourself at all times. Yes, you will have to compromise and be able to let some things go, but that happens in life regardless if you have a partner or not. The phrase "pick and choose your battles" is misleading. What the hell is there to "battle" over? I guess you can switch out that word and replace it with fight, but that is still a strong word. You will have to give and take, step up and step back, but you come from the stance of winning or losing, you may have already lost!

What is the next chapter of Dwayne Jenkins?
For the past few years I've asked the same question and really can't come up with something concrete. On a personal level I know I would like to travel more with my partner, do some home improvement, pay down some debt, ya' know, the simple things. Professionally, I think my job is getting harder and harder. We've come so far as a LGBT community, but sometimes when the rubber hits the road, it feels as though we are stuck in traffic. And I'm not talking about comfortable traffic either. Think hot, no air condition, beeping horns, late for an appointment traffic. I, like many others in any profession, have a rough time doing my job, but regardless of the lows, something always pushes its way through that reminds me why I continue do what I do.

~ Bobby Blake ~
Author, Porn Star, Film Maker, Producer

As one of the first African American pornographic actors within the SGL community, how do you feel that your contribution has aided in the development of African American SGL film making of today?
Do you mean erotic film-making? We still have very few African American directors of gay porn – Abednego is the only one I can think of right now. Bear in mind that I was a highly-bankable performer rather than a director or producer. However, simply being visible as a member of a minority within the larger society gives others permission to follow and build on what you've achieved.

What first prompted you to enter the porn industry?
Almost like a dare I gave myself. It felt like an adventure, and also it was a natural extension of erotic dancing, which was how I was mostly earning a living back then. I was encouraged to give it a shot by 80s porn-star Paul Hanson, after he saw me throwing down very publically at a gay sex club and thought I had what it took to succeed in the industry.

What results within the industry and the SGL community have you seen after the publication of your first work (whether positive or negative)?
I think my life speaks to a lot of people who struggle with their sexuality and their spirituality, so they see me as a mirror to the difficulties of their own lives, and also as someone who has succeeded as a porn performer while maintaining a strong spiritual life, so is a role model of a sort. A certain amount of negativity comes from people who want me to have the attitudes they have about what I do and how I've lived my life. Specifically they want me to express shame and regret about my involvement in the adult industry, and are angry when I do not. Also, some people wanted the book to be porn, rather than be about porn. My feeling there was, most of my movies are available on line, so you can already see what I do, so I didn't feel so much of a need to talk about that – though I do devote a good third of my book to that. There's a review on Amazon of white British pornstar Blue Blake's biography, by Jeffrey Mingo, a gay blatino academic, where he compares that book with mine, commenting on how mine is concerned with issues of race, racism, homophobia, mental health, spirituality and community, while Blue's is all about good times and sex. I had good times and I had a great deal of sex, but I wanted to talk about more than that.

What is your opinion about the tension found in spirituality versus sexuality?
In Christianity we're raised to exalt the spirit and chasten the flesh. We're told to see them as opposites. We're supposed to find sexual expression in marriage a divine blessing and sexual expression elsewhere as immoral. But straight or gay, we don't really experience desire in that way. So it's our struggle to try and live lives that are fulfilling on both the spiritual and the physical level that are pleasing to God. We all search for – or seek to let into our lives – both divine love and romantic, sexual love. The Church as an institution polices the physical, and it's no coincidence that I was least involved in the Church while I was most involved in porn. But I always prayed, and always maintained a close relationship with God.

Do you think that spirituality and sexuality coexist in terms of African American SGL Christians?
Of course. The struggle is to not see your sexuality as a burden or something that sets you apart from playing a part in the wider society. For me – and some see this as controversial – I feel my adventures in the world of porn were a testing ground that made me a more compassionate person who was later better able to do God's work as a counselor, especially of those struggling with their sexuality.

Can, in your opinion, African American SGL be Christians?
Absolutely. I was raised and have always been a Christian. My sexuality is a private matter between me and God. Christians have the right to make a decision based on personal conscience. The fact is that even the most supposedly literal readers of the Bible pay no attention to old-time strictures on eating shellfish, wearing cloth woven of two different materials and so on. So, whatever they may claim, they make choices that suit them. Having said that, I respect that they are finding their truth in Scripture – but I also want that they accept that I am finding mine.

How do you negate or respond to the elitism found in the African American SGL community in terms of divisions created based on social status and/or approved aesthetic?
Elitism is everywhere. Everywhere on the planet people value the wealthy and beautiful over the poor and homely, even if standards of beauty differ from place to place. There are no easy answers. Someone who has an athletic physique, takes care of himself, has discipline, is likely to be a dynamic lover and so on. Someone who earns a lot of money is probably hard-working, focused and so on. Those are good traits, so it's not wrong to find them attractive. Money insulates you from a certain level of racism, homophobia, health-problems and general insecurity. Of course some people who are beautiful are vacuous and mean-spirited, and some rich people are selfish and greedy – but some homely people are mean, and some poor people are grasping. Being a porn-star is a paradox, because as a sex-performer you are high-status in the SGL world, but as a sex-object you are objectified and may be devalued as a human being. Trying to treat each person you meet as a unique human being is a good start. Value the spirit of the person over his material trappings. In the SGL community there's a particular focus on a certain masculine style, and that can oppress those who don't match up to it, but on the other hand it's not like 'soft' or more feminine guys don't hook up or find love: they probably do as much as the more macho guys do. So in a way the idea that certain types of men are the only ones who get what they want is an illusion.

In the age of HIV/AIDS within the African American SGLBT community how have we as a community failed or progressed?
Not very well. The general conservatism around sex matters among African Americans doesn't help people be honest about what they do. Also our young SGL folks lack role models and inspirational older leaders and so don't value the wisdom the passing years bring – we live in a cult of youth. Ironically the vastly-improved new treatments for HIV are seen by many young people as a 'cure', and that encourages them to be careless, or not bother with safer sex techniques at all. The Black Church is often so personally judgmental of individuals that it pushes some away, and it hasn't taken the lead in this area that historically it has in other areas, such as Civil Rights.

In what specific ways have your work changed in the past ten years?
I retired from porn around eight years ago, re-engaged with the church, and now work as a counselor. In between that I ran the security team at a Memphis nightclub and have worked as a personal trainer. I also do safer-sex advocacy work. Members of my church know about my past but accept me on my own terms.

As an activist within the SGL community when did your mission begin and was there anyone that you personally connected with in order for you to become vocal?
Before I became involved with porn I was very active in several local churches, so I've always felt a sense of duty to the community in which I am living. While in porn I met a number of HIV/AIDS activists who spurred me on to do HIV-related awareness work. I was strongly influenced by the extreme prejudice of the early years of AIDS, where sufferers were rejected by their families and treated as damned souls not worthy of compassion.

If you could lend advice to our African American SGLBT youth what would be your advice or encouragement to them?
Find your own path to God, your own truth in Scripture. Carry yourself with pride and others will respect you. Don't feel pressured to adopt a more effeminate manner than is natural for you. Don't feel you need to go and live in a totally gay world – don't be afraid to live in the wider community. Don't let homophobia make you drop out of school. Don't accept a life where you are less than other people: you are not. I never recommend to anyone that he go into the adult industry.

Discuss when and why you decided to write your memoir?
I was encouraged by loved ones and people around me who knew some of my story and thought it was interesting. I got a lot of fan-mail over the years asking questions about this and that aspect of my life. It was widely-believed (wrongly) that I was married to my porn partner, Flex-Deon Blake, and it was known that I was active in the Church and ministry while also working in the adult industry. Many people wrote to me tormented by issues around their faith and sexuality. I thought the example of my life might help them.

Can you elaborate on your childhood and how it shaped the person who you are today?
It was tough. I go into detail about it in the book. My mother struggled with mental health issues; my father wasn't around. I had a wonderful and deeply religious foster-mother, but she was advanced in years. She gave me faith in myself and in God, and that never left me!

What is the next chapter of Bobby Blake?
My next chapter is to carry on living my life, share time with loved ones and family, and deepen my relationship with the Lord.

~ Sanford E. Gaylord ~
Creative Activist/Actor

Organizations:
A co-founding member of the 2007 Chicago Gay and Lesbian Hall of Fame inductee A Real Read, an African American LGBT Performance Ensemble. The ensemble toured locally and nationally, 1996-2002.

As an African American HIV/AIDS Activist, how do you feel that your contribution has aided in the development of positive African American SGL life of today?
That is a good question! I feel that I am walking in the path that others did that worked hard and paved a way for those that followed them. I hope to illuminate what might be a bumpy road for those that follow me.

My contributions have aided in the development of positive African American SGL life of today because I believe that our society needs to see positive, realistic portrayals of Black LGBT people. I think that if we want to see things change we have to be part of the change. I chose to be out as a Black Gay man that is an actor writer and creative activist living with HIV, because there were others that needed to see that you could simply be and thrive.

In the film series *Kevin's Room* describe your role.
My character's name is Jhalil Harris, Kevin's long time partner. When the series started, my character was a lawyer and by the end became a high school Civics teacher. It was an honor to show a relationship between two Black Gay men on film. There is joy and pain in any relationship and they all take work. Kevin and Jhalil were like any two people trying to make a relationship work. It just happened that they were in a relationship with each other.

What results have you seen after the production of *Kevin's Room* series (whether positive or negative)?
The results exceeded my own dreams. Artistically, it was an honor to be part of the groundbreaking series, which has garnered national, accolades for its realistic, positive portrayal of LGBT people of color and their allies. I think it seamlessly educates, entertains, and prompts the viewer to be proactive toward his or her own health and well-being - and that of their community.

What is your opinion about the tension found in spirituality versus sexuality?
I think spirituality and sexuality or sexual identities are things that can bring up tension especially when it comes to organized religion. I think that many people have been abused by organized religion and the ideologies associated with them. I think that one needs to find the peace within them and reconcile what others perceive you should do or be. Spirituality and Sexuality are components of who I am but they do not define me as a human being. We are all much more complex.

How do you negate or respond to the elitism found in the African American SGL community in terms of divisions created based on social status and/or approved aesthetic?
Humankind has evolved for centuries, some things tend to change, and others are slow in change. There will always be issues of classism and divisions until we make the change within ourselves.

In the age of HIV/AIDS within the African American SGL LGBT community, how have we as a community failed or progressed?
I think that we as a community failed initially because we didn't think we needed to be concerned. Some of us went into denial and others spewed hate and homophobia.

We had to contend with the dominant society informing us who was at risk for the disease. HIV stands for the Human Immunodeficiency Virus. It affects humans regardless of race or class. There is no country on the planet that has reported a case of HIV that can claim that they have stopped the spread, only slowed its advance on humankind.

I think we have progressed because messages finally reached African Americans but there is so much more work to do when every ten minutes someone is infected with HIV in this country. African American's make up more than half of the statistics but are about 13% of the population. One owes it to them self to take an HIV test and to know their HIV status. If you are living with HIV, know that there is life after diagnosis and you can claim and live a full life.

In what specific ways have your work changed in the past ten years?
My work has changes a lot in the last ten years. I initially focused on being an actor, writer and I feel that I have done some great work. I also have had a passion for public health and have been involved within the field of HIV/AIDS. Since the *Kevin's Room* series, I have focused more on working within public health.

Can you discuss any writers from the past that you personally connect with?
The first writer that I connected to from the past was Essex Hemphill. I feel in love with him when I was introduced to the book *"In The Life: A Black Gay Anthology."* Hemphill's poems, essays and interviews were very inspiring to me. I had the pleasure of meeting Larry Duckett who worked with Hemphill for years. One of my great moments on stage was portraying Larry in the play he wrote called *"We Heard The Night Outside,"* which was about his relationship with Hemphill personally and professionally.

When you became involved with the *Kevin's Room project*, did you ever feel that it would grow in the manner in which it did?
Kevin's Room grew beyond my expectations. I knew when we filmed the first in 2000, that it would be a cult classic. The three-part series has traveled the globe and has helped change the lives of many as well as my own. It's very humbling to me to be recognized for my work with the films and have people talk to me about how it affected their life even today.

Can you elaborate on your childhood and how it shaped the person who you are today?
I was born in North Carolina, raised in Chicago, IL. By the time I was sixteen, I acknowledged my sexual identity to my parents who weren't accepting and that resulted in my leaving home. I lived with a partner for a while and then struck out on my own.

I've always loved the arts and I've had many life experiences that have shaped the person I am today. It's a blessing to have had people in my life that saw more in me than I did when it mattered. They inspired me to continue to set goals and strive to make my dreams become realities. I learned that you could have a chosen family as well as a biological family.

Living my life openly and honestly has helped me to make it to where I am today. All of the good and bad were life lessons. Learning is forever; when there is no growth, there is no life.

What was the purpose of the *Kevin's Room series*?
The *Kevin's Room* series was an effort by the Chicago Department of Health's Office of Lesbian Gay Bisexual Transgender (LGBT) Health to address the crisis of HIV/AIDS in the African American Gay community. The first two films reinforced the message of inclusion, tolerance and collective responsibility while tackling the related issues of monogamy, sexual boundaries, and the re-emergence of STD's.

While continuing to explore many of the issues that were raised in the first two films, the third addressed new concerns reflected in headlines - violence, sexual identity, spirituality - and the ways in which a community can help shape its own future.

Did you find that it helped with its mission?
Absolutely, especially with the final installment, Kevin's Room: Together, which was presented in a "reality show format." It showed that the community can't wait for someone to come and save them. They have to come together and work with their allies to save themselves.

What is the next chapter of Sanford E. Gaylord?
I'm currently pursuing a Masters in Public Administration and plan to continue working in the field of HIV/AIDS. I've thought about writing a book for a while and plan to make that happen in the near future. With the right project, I'd love to do another film or theatre production. I've learned it's about the quality and not the quantity of your work.

~ Justin B. Terry - Smith ~
Activist/Writer/Journalist

Journalistic works published in:

Black AIDS Weekly; Gay Life Newspaper; Baltimore Outloud Newspaper, GBMNews.com; thebody.com; and *Swerv Magazine*

As an African American HIV/AIDS Activist, how do you feel that your contribution has aided in the development of positive African American SGL life of today?

One of the things that I feel my contributions have aided in the development in the African American SGL life is that I've opened up a dialog for people to talk about what experience they have been through, how HIV has affected and effected their lives. I also have given people inspiration. I get e-mails daily from people, especially young black gay men, daily. Some of these e-mails have said that they now have courage to tell their families and friends. They also know it's not the end of the world. Another angle to my contribution is that I've let people see what it's like to live with HIV/AIDS. We all know it's not pretty because there is an ugly side, a side that nobody wants to see. People, especially young people, think that if they become HIV positive that all they have to do is that a couple of pills and they will be fine. I'm trying to make them know that it's harder than that, much harder. I've made people think twice.

What first prompted you to become an activist?

I fell into activism. I was a coffee house junkie back in the 1999, because it was a great way to meet other students. Well I met a couple of student from Georgetown and Catholic University. We all collaborated and made the organization called, "SOBB" (Students Opposing Brutality in Burma). This organization raised money and sent students to Burma to expose how the government was treating its people. Three students went over and only two came back. The last student was interrogated by police, but wasn't detained for very long. When talking about my HIV Activism I started when I was hired at Us Helping Us People Into Living Inc. (UHU). UHU is a HIV/AIDS nonprofit which gives and refers services to people living with HIV/AIDS. It focuses mainly on African Americans in the Washington DC area. I worked as a Clerk and also helped pass out condoms at clubs and bars in a effort to use HIV/AIDS Prevention methods to stop new infections in the DC Area.

What first prompted you to become a writer?
I actually remember writing when I was in elementary school. I used to write stories for my assignment but I usually wrote more than I was supposed to. When the assignment called for writing one story every month I usually wrote 4 or 5. I've always enjoyed writing when I can find the time to do it. Later on I in high school I did well in writing but became distracted. I got back into it only a couple of years ago. I was e-mailed about an African American News site looking for writers. I answered with an article and the decided to make me a contributing writer. Then after that I started my own column called, "Justin's HIV Journal" when I myself was diagnosed with HIV. Presently, I write for about 6 publications.

What is your opinion about the tension found in spirituality versus sexuality?
It's sickening to me how people like Bishop Alfred Owens of Mt Calvary Church in Washington DC and stands there from the pool pit and spouts out bigotry. It's also crazier to me how there are still African American gay people that still go to that church. They should be protesting it. They are giving their money to a church that hates them and it hurts me inside to know that some of these people do not have enough self esteem to walk away and find a life affirming church. There are plenty of churches that are life affirming.

Do you think that spirituality and sexuality coexist in terms of African American SGL Christians?
Of course it does. There is no question in my mind that any African American gay person can be a Christian and sexually active. The Bible has several contradictions in it. Also a lot of people say that African American Gay men and women cannot be Christian because it says in the Bible that a man that lies with another man is an abomination, but it also says in the Bible that eating swine is an abomination. I will tell those same Christians what I tell them every time I hear that. "You take the sausage out of your mouth and I'll take the sausage out of mine.

How do you negate or respond to the elitism found in the African American SGL community in terms of divisions created based on social status and/or approved aesthetic?

I actually fell victim to it at a social gathering before my husband Philip and I were married. I noticed Philip was talking to a friend of mine and I guess my friend didn't know that we were dating. I said hello to them both and my friend snapped at me and said, "Do you know who this man is? He is a Dr." "What is your common denominator". I felt so hurt by that snobbish reaction, especially when I thought he was my friend. So I thought about my retort. I said, "Well since he is my boyfriend I think I know he's a doctor. I also know that ignorance is bliss and you must be very high right now". Then I excused myself and walk my future husband to another room.

In the age of HIV/AIDS within the African American SGLBT community how have we as a community failed or progressed?

Actually I can't really answer this question in full confidence. I was not alive to see the deaths in the 1980's. I think we have come a long way but we have so much more to go. We are failing at stopping this disease from ravaging out community. There are many programs out there that are not getting the proper funding that they need. A lot of these programs are targeted towards African Americans, without them we are up the creek without a paddle. Our community needs to stop stigmatizing HIV/AIDS and start talking about it. When it is talked about in the open people become informed and educated.

Can you discuss any writers from the past that you personally connect with?

My favorite writer is Langston Hughes. Here is my favorite poem by him. I feel it best describes me. I wish I could've met him.

This is a song for the genius child.
Sing it softly, for the song is wild.
Sing it softly as ever you can -
Lest the song get out of hand.

Nobody loves a genius child.

Can you love an eagle,
Tame or wild?
Can you love an eagle,
Wild or tame?

Can you love a monster
Of frightening name?

Nobody loves a genius child.

Kill him - and let his soul run wild.

Also in another interview I was compared to a writer Walter Rico Burrell one of his poems

"I'm forced to wear my own scarlet letter in the form of these abominable blotches...." "....a blazing visual condemnation for the entire world to see so they can pass judgment on me and become part of my perpetual penance."—Walter

By writing about this he owned his status and in a way I'm owning mine. He also talks about the stigma of HIV/AIDS in this passage, about being judged because of it. He died in 1990 after going public about having AIDS in 1989.

Can you elaborate on your childhood and how it shaped the person who you are today?
My childhood was a happy one but of course there were a lot of bumps in the road. My father and mother did a good job with me and my brother. I also have two little brothers that my mother and step-father are raising. Both of my parents taught me to be strong, but I was also very talkative and outspoken. My family named me the Sassy one. Now that I'm an adult they still call me Sassy. I love it honestly. It's who I am and I'm not changing that.

How did you and your partner deal with family, friends, and the community after you united in matrimony given the state of the nation against gay marriage?
We didn't care about what anyone said we knew we wanted to be together for the rest of our lives. My family was easy; they know how I am, when I say I'm going to do something I'm going to do it. Besides my mother told me she wanted me to marry him. He was automatically loved and accepted by my family, of course after they gave him a brief but thorough interrogation. His family was harder for me, the only reason why I thought this is because he was married before. He was married for 24 years to someone before me. I was afraid I was going to be compared to him but that never happened. His family loves me for who I am and they know about my activism and Gay Rights and HIV.

Being in a monogamous relationship with your partner whereas you actually married him, in what ways would you advise young people and old people, for that matter, on how to keep the "fire" burning?
Well let me tell you that whatever kind of relationship you have you have to keep the spark a live. I know a lot of people that have monogamous and polyandrous relationships and I say whatever works for them is good. Whether you are and older couple or younger you have to make sure you make time for your mate. Remember to take trips to place neither one of you have been before. When it comes to fire well we all have our definition of what kind of fire we need. Some of us need a spark, or torch and some need a bonfire. I recommend in bed try something new but make sure you talk about it with your mate before you do it. There is no need in coming out a surprising you mate in a sexually enticing doctor or nurse outfit when your mate is deathly afraid or doctors and nurses. As for my husband and I well we have a very flammable relationship.

What is the next chapter of Justin B. Terry-Smith?
Hmmmm Well I have a lot of projects going on right now. I've been asked to write for 3 more papers including the 3 other papers I write for now. I'm still keeping up with, "Justin's HIV Journal". I was sashed Mr Maryland Leather 2010 and so I go compete for the International title in Chicago, International Mr. Leather 2010. I also have another project projected to be completed sometime next year. My husband and I are THINKING about adopting next year but we will see. ☺

Interviews

~ Malaysia Andrews Ravore/ Purvis Lee Walker, Jr.~
Retail -Store Manager/ Sketch Artist/ Seamstress/ Female Illusionist

Accomplishments/ Official Pageant Titles:
Miss Jackson Newcomer 1999; Miss Sweetheart 2001; Miss Black Mississippi Universe 2008; Miss Dick and Jane 2009; Miss International Inc. 2009;
Organizations & Companies Owned:
Gamma Phi Alpha Fraternity
House of Andrews/ Home of Ravore

Interview conducted by Darius Omar Williams with Malaysia Andrews of Jackson, Mississippi.

Darius: I want to first start off by asking you, do you prefer to call yourself a drag queen, a female impersonator, a female illusionist or something else and why?

Malaysia: Well at different times I've been called different things depending on the occasion. A mild setting is a mild setting or whatnot, you know, or when in Rome do what the Romans do. In certain situations, of course, I am referred to as a female illusionist, female impersonator but I normally prefer drag queen because it's totally different for me. Female illusion is more laidback, not quite as dramatic as drag in my own definition and drag is what I do. It's a transition from who I am as P.J. to who I can turn into as Malaysia.

Darius: What are some of the other fundamental differences between being a drag-queen versus a female impersonator versus a female illusionist?

Malaysia: Ok, being an illusionist you want to look as much as you can like a person or a particular person in this instance being a female. A drag queen is more over the top, it's more of the gaudy jewelry, the heavy makeup, the big hair, the drastic clothes, and you know, a true definition of what it used to be.

Darius: What about female impersonator? Would that fall into the same category as an illusionist?

Malaysia: That would be the same thing as an illusionist. You want to project your image as soft, sophisticated or what we think or assume femininity is.

Darius: How did your childhood in Mississippi influence who you are today as a same gender loving black man and also as a black drag-queen?

Malaysia: Wow. Just different things. Of course in Mississippi we weren't allowed the opportunity to do certain things. Huh, being a black gay male and some Mississippians weren't used to something that's different from the norm so they kind of shunned it. Growing up in Mississippi, I of course just stayed in books and studied my visual arts and now I'm using that to actually adhere to what I do with my entertaining.

Darius: I'm glad you mentioned that you are a sketch artist and also a fashion designer. Why haven't you chosen not to capitalize on your talent as a fashion designer or as an illusionist on shows such as *Project Runway* or even *Rupaul's Drag Race*?

Malaysia: Well you know there's a time and place for everything. I am actually in the preparatory stage, excuse me, I'm getting myself prepared to audition for *Rupaul's Drag Race*. As far as *Project Runway* is concerned, my designing and sewing is more of a hobby and I firmly believe if you have a hobby and it's a passion for that hobby, you may need to leave it as a hobby instead of trying to do it every day and getting tired of it or frustrated with it and not wanting to do what God has given you a talent to do.

Darius: How has the explosion of hip-hop over the past fifteen years affected the art of drag both positively and negatively?

Malaysia: Well, I actually feel it's given people an opportunity to see different sides as opposed to one particular genre. You know old school drag, we call it old school drag, was more disco versus R&B depression.

Darius: That's R&B what?

Malaysia: Depression. You know, my man done left me, don't want to be alone, don't want to be by myself or strictly blues, strictly blues. You know, the man cheating on me with another woman, we finna be best friends. That's all we really had. Now the implosion/explosion of hip-hop has opened up many doors for us to venture out and do things we wouldn't normally do. Say for instance, Lil Kim, hard core rap or whatnot. Whereas most entertainers wouldn't consider hard core rap. It gives them an opportunity to look at it and say 'oh this is an art form. let me try this'.

Darius: Have you performed any hardcore rap in your repertoire?

Malaysia: I do. I do have a little bit. You know that's when Malaysia wants to step out and cater (laughs) to a different scene. I try to challenge myself to do different things so you won't get used to one particular look or one particular fashion. I keep re-inventing myself which is why I feel I've stayed around for so long.

Darius: What is your boy name or birth name?

Malaysia: My birth name is Purvis Lee Walker, Jr.

Darius: What is the fundamental difference between Purvis Lee Walker, Jr. and Miss Malaysia Andrews Ravore? Are they two different personas?

Malaysia: I consider them to be different now. I guess because I've grown. Malaysia has grown into herself. She's more refined. Not that PJ or Purvis is amiss or anything but Malaysia is [more] aware of her surroundings. She knows there's a proper way to be at different times. She adheres to this. She's extremely professional. Especially now being a national title holder. Once again, she's extremely professional. She's extremely in the art of being a people person or getting to know people or meeting people. You never know what different settings will get you through particular doors. I think as far as being a drag queen, female impersonator, female illusionist or whatever the case may be, it gives you an opportunity to be a role model or icon in gay society. People look up to you so you have to be aware of what you're doing at all times.

Darius: You just mentioned that you are a national title holder. What is your national title to date?

Malaysia: My title is Miss International, Inc. 2009.

Darius: Can you provide us some history on Miss International, Inc.?

Malaysia: Miss International, Inc. was founded by Dr. Mark Colomb of My Brother's Keeper because a few of us, including myself, traveled to Delaware back in June to compete for Mr. and Miss International. Upon getting second runner up this year like I did last year, they found that there was a discrepancy with the owner's outlook on the pageant, which means the owner actually rigged the pageant for who she wanted to win. Upon being exposed of this, she sold the pageant Miss International to someone else and Dr. Colomb decided that he would go on and get his own national pageant started and by me winning the pageant, I was then a national queen.

Darius: For those who are interested in drag, what advice would you offer a young, aspiring drag artist living in the south particularly someone in a small rural community?

Malaysia: The only advice I can offer honestly is to continue to be yourself. You go much further and you get more done by being yourself and not catering to the standard. You understand what I'm saying. You know, for some people the standard is pre-op transexualism, getting breasts, bodywork or whatever the case may be. And if that's not what you want to do, you don't have to in order to have a career. A lot of the young girls feel as if that is what they need to be accepted in the drag world or the female impersonation world but once you make those kinds of decisions there's no turning back. As long as you're pleasing yourself, you're going to exude that wave on stage and people are going to understand who you are.

Darius: I'm interested in you telling me more about the community known as drag in terms of 'the girls' that entertain on the club circuit. Are you guys' one big happy family? What's really the tea especially for those of us on the outside looking in?

Malaysia: Well, you know, the girls they have a close bond. Don't get me wrong. It is what it is. It's just like a job. Everyone wants to do their best at their job. You know, whether we're the best of friends or the worst of enemies, drag is a competition. You know, you're competing for bragging rights. You're competing to be that top girl always in competition with newcomers that come out. One, you have to try to make your name. Two, try to keep your fan base. So we're not [always] catty with one another. Cause we're all cool. We're all friends. But there is that realization that you do have to do what you have to do to stay on top. As long as you're not willing to let someone else steal your glory and you'll continue to do that. You don't have to be brownnose or kiss butt to make your name, but you really have to pattern yourself to be somebody better than anybody else for certain.

Darius: Is there a class system? For instance, do you feel that same amount of support from someone like a Bebe Zahara Benet. I mean, does that type of bonding exist as well with very talented performers in their own right who may reach out to those who've achieved 'mainstream' success like Bebe. In other words, is it possible to forge relationships with drag performers who've achieved more success than others?

Malaysia: I think it's extremely possible. Of course you have people, other entertainers that you know we call 'feeling themselves' or kind of have a big head or whatever and kind of shun people when they go to them to try to figure out career objectives. We do have a lot of entertainers in the drag industry that feel like they are above the rest of us, but there is that occasional person that says 'hey, I like what you do. If you have any questions, comments or concerns about anything. I'll give you advice or I'll advise or help in any possible way that I can.' As far as those who are young and have been shunned, I really think that's what's hurting the drag or entertaining career of a lot of people is because the kids these days that are coming out are searching for people they can look up to.

Darius: Have you mentored or taken an aspiring drag queen under your wings? And are they're still Houses? Do we still have House Mothers? I

Interviews

just asked you three questions back to back (laugh). Basically have you taken on the role of House Mother or once again mentored a young drag queen in any way?

Malaysia: Yeah I am a House Mother. My stage name is Malaysia Andrews Ravore. Ravore is not the official name by marriage but by statue of doing everything for myself, my own clothes, hair and make-up. Being my own stylist, my own promoter. I felt I needed a name to distinguish me from the rest of my family. It's not saying anything bad about my family. That's just saying everything is a growth process. Like I said, I am a House Mother. My kids, the ones that do entertain, I'm their mentor. Which I feel as a person with status, your kids should look up to you, your craft. They should want to learn your craft whereas I do everything for them. But, it's understanding that you have to learn to eventually do something on your own. Not telling them to go out sewing or start doing makeup or whatever, but if you make the effort to learn how to, that's much better. When they make their own mistakes in drag it helps better them in their everyday lives. But I work toward molding them into being positive role models in the community, not just on stage.

Darius: You mentioned earlier breaking out on your own to pursue some of your own personal goals. But, in the early days, during the beginning of your career, how did you officially choose the name Malaysia Andrews? Is Andrews an extension of another house? Can you give me some history on the origin of the name Andrews?

Malaysia: At first I was on my own. I was a part of a smaller family with several of my best friends and my name was Mahogany Monae. It was just a start out , just us two in that little grouping or whatnot. Then I was recruited by The House of Andrews of Jackson, Mississippi to be a child of theirs. When it was one of the leading houses in the city, I found myself privileged to even being thought of or considered as being a child of that family. I accepted it and my best friend stopped entertaining. So I went from being on my own into a family thinking I could learn a few things. That they could teach me how to entertain or how to drag or make-up or whatever the case may be. I got involved in it and it was wonderful. A lot of different experiences taught me about the real world versus where everybody pretends to be real. There's a difference in the way a lot of gay families are presented in public. Behind closed doors, it was extremely different. It was a real family which has patterned me to treat my family in a certain way. We are entertainers. We do the shows. Go to the clubs but that is not what gay life is completely about. There are consequences and repercussions for things that you do and different choices you make. It's not all about drugs, alcoholism or sexual innuendos or anything like that. My family now is made up to be a more respectable family rather than just a group of pretty individuals to look at during a show.

Darius: So, is your house, The House of Ravore?

Malaysia: The Home of Andrews, The House of Ravore.

Darius: Who are some of the female illusionists, drag-queens and impersonators who have influenced your work?

Malaysia: Oh wow. It's so many. I'd like to say first and foremost my mother Senetria Andrews due to the fact when I saw her, I fell in love with the art form. She also invested in the role as my father as someone who molded or created me to be the person I am. Other influences include Sasha Sanchez, Tommie Ross, for different reasons. It ranges from the old entertainers to the newcomers that are coming out. A lot of the newcomers coming out are making the old heads step up their game.

Darius: So tell me more about your performance aesthetic: song choices, costume, wigs, make-up etc.? How do you decide on any given night 'which song am I going to do, what hair am I going to wear' etc.?

Malaysia: Anything that's appealing to the ear. I like to listen to songs to get the most out of them not just what I think people want to see or hear. Anything that has a thought-process to it. What I mean by thought process, the look has to mean something. The lyrics have to mean something. I try to put my audience into the world of what I'm thinking. I try to exude that in my performances or my make-up artistry or my hair. I just don't get on stage in a plain dress and do a song. My dress is going to depict what my song is conveying. For example, when I performed "Dangerously In Love" by Beyonce in a tangerine orange dress. It was a tangerine orange ribbed tank top with a tangerine orange bottom, pumps, fishtails. The belt was handcuffed earrings, the jewelry was handcuffed with stone. Big hair. Then with "Out On The Limb" by Teena Marie. I did the whole Cher affect that had the glittered rib pieces to it, the glittered waist, the sheer bottom, hair pulled in a pony tail with a bun and a tree limb on top with leaves hanging off of it.

Darius: Did you let the children have it on both occasions?

Malaysia: I hope so. They talked about it a lot.

Darius: How do you respond to the stereotype that all drag queens are funny and will read you in a heartbeat as opposed to those who are truly using their craft as a legitimate art form?

Malaysia: Wow. It's true to a certain degree. I think a lot of entertainers feel like they have to be like that because of the so-called stereotypes. A lot of them feel like they have to be assholes, be stuck-up cause that's what is supposedly called for. That's what the stereotype is. Again, many in the drag world feel they have to live up to those myths such as snapping the finger, reading. They're not comfortable living outside of the stereotype. I don't like to be labeled. I like for people to gain an awareness of me by interacting with me.

Darius: If Malaysia had to choose a social cause, what would it be?

Malaysia: My cause would be working on the relationship barriers between male on male as well as female on female committed relationships. Of course, HIV/AIDS is a cause I fight for everyday.

Darius: What's the difference between spirituality and sexuality and is it possible for the two to co-exist?

Malaysia: I think it is possible for spirituality and sexuality to co-exist. The difference between the two: spirituality is an attraction toward your higher power. I can be spiritual in one way and another person could be spiritual in a totally different way. But it's not totally different cause you're reaching for the same goal. I know who my God is and I know who I serve is my God. I have an understanding I can't do anything without him. I can honestly say I have been more spiritual than I've been sexual. I guess for me, it's because of how I am in my personal life. I grew up in the church. I go to church, not as frequently as I need to, but I got to church to get the word and a better understanding of what I need to be dong in my life. In my private life, I have instances where I can blend both of the two together.

Darius: What's the next chapter for Miss Malaysia Andrews Ravore?

Malaysia: Marriage, working toward gaining more national recognition. Hopefully win a few more national titles, become a national symbol of excellence. Do more in the community as far as with up and coming stars, newcomers, people that are looking to get into the art form. Chile, just be real. Just live one day at a time. Continue to do what I do. Make myself happy. Make my home happy and then I can work toward bringing happiness to other people cause I have to live by what I'm preaching. Practice what you preach.

Darius: Lastly, what is the next chapter for Purvis Lee Walker, Jr.?

Malaysia: My main goal is to open a bakery of edible art, doing three-dimensional edible art pieces. I have a passion for the kitchen and I'm doing what I need to do to actually make that happen.

~ Lisa C. Moore ~
Publisher

Company Owned:
RedBone Press, 1997

As one of the first African American GLBT publishers, how do you feel that your contribution has aided in the explosion of same gender loving writing?
RedBone Press isn't one of the first black GLBT publishers. Kitchen Table Women of Color Press, co-founded by Audre Lorde, Cherríe Moraga and Barbara Smith; Sister Vision Press, co-founded by Makeda Silvera in Canada; Vega Press, still run by Vega; Galiens Press, founded by Assotto Saint; these are the ones that immediately come to mind as my forebears. Most of those came about in the 1980s; RedBone Press stands on their shoulders. Founded in 1997, RedBone Press continues to publish literature that celebrates the culture of black lesbians and gay men, and facilitates discussion between the black mainstream and black lesbians and gay men. We have 15 titles currently in print. I believe that RedBone Press has fostered a few writers' careers, and served as an example of how to publish work that looks good and reads well. I hope I've given the right kinds of advice to those who've asked about editing and production of books.

What first prompted you to start RedBone Press?
In 1995, I met a classmate of my younger sister in junior college; this young woman was just coming out, had seen the pink triangle bumper sticker on my car when I picked my sister up from school, and began asking me for coming out literature. I realized there was no book of black lesbian coming out stories, and I set about collecting for *does your mama know?*, which became the first RedBone Press book. In doing the research necessary to self-publish *does your mama know?*, I learned that most of the publishers I interviewed didn't think there was a market for the book. I knew better; what they meant was they didn't know how *they* would market the book. Keep in mind that all of those publishers were white-owned. That knowledge, combined with my growing passion for the politics of publishing, helped me go out on a limb and start RedBone Press.

What results have you seen after the organization of RedBone Press (whether positive or negative)?

RedBone Press has, since publishing its first book in 1997, published an average of 1-3 books a year (minus a house fire in 2002 which stopped me from publishing for a couple of years). I've pushed to have RedBone Press books in independent bookstores, black bookstores, gay bookstores, women's bookstores; as well as coordinating readings with black lesbian and gay community groups. I've also pushed to have RedBone Press books taught in academia, which helps to ensure the longevity of a book. We print small runs (500 to 1,000 books at a time), and keep tight watch on inventory. For my small efforts, I'm grateful to see that RedBone Press is a recognizable name for quality black gay and lesbian writing, and that I continue to receive community support for the work we publish. I wish I could publish more; with more financial resources, I would.

Upon editing the book *Spirited*, in your opinion, what are the tensions found in spirituality versus sexuality?

I believe there aren't any tensions between spirituality and sexuality; it's only when religion is involved that things become fractious. Its man's teachings via the church of what spirituality is about that provide the friction. Hence it's the church and its teachings that become the problem, setting church followers up to believe that there's an inherent tension between sexuality and spirituality. Religion is not spirituality. People often confuse the two.

Do you think that spirituality and sexuality coexist in terms of African American SGL Christians?

Spirituality and sexuality co-exist in everybody; there's no question about that. Organized religion has a tendency to separate the body from its soul, which I think is a mistake. We need both body and soul, integrated, in order to survive and move forward in the world. Realize that a person somewhere wrote down the Christian Bible, and King James (himself reportedly a closeted gay man) revised it, and you'll see that the interjection of that human element means the Bible contains flaws. To err is human. I think the Bible can be used as a guide for Christians to interpret their lives, but realize that no one and no thing can come between you and your God. Not even a good book.

How do you negate or respond to the elitism found in the African American SGL community in terms of divisions created based on social status and/or approved aesthetic?
Me personally? I don't buy into it. Divisions that we create mirror the divisions in society. Come to terms with who you are as a person, and what you are put here on earth to do, then go about doing it, and you'll be OK.

In the age of HIV/AIDS within the African American SGL-GLBT community how have we as a community failed or progressed?
I'm not really equipped to answer that question. My sense is that black people in general (keeping in mind there is no monolithic black community, as there is no monolithic black LGBT community, but rather many communities) need to be reintroduced to the idea that body and soul should be integrated. When you separate the body, people begin to believe that physical behavior can be treated separately from the soul, and that's just not so. The sooner that black people get away from demonizing our sexuality and sexual behaviors, whether it's hetero or homo or somewhere in between, the better.

In what specific ways has your work changed in the past ten years?
When I started RedBone Press, I thought I would only be publishing black lesbian literature. I began publishing men's literature in 2004; I mistakenly thought that black gay men still had their own avenues for publication, but learned that the advent of AIDS in the 1980s destroyed the fledgling presses that existed. There's nearly a whole generation of black gay men who died that could have become mentors to the young ones coming out now. The few who survived that time are tired, and grief-weary. As a result of this knowledge, I put the seminal works, *In the Life* (edited by Joseph Beam) and *Brother to Brother* (edited by Essex Hemphill) back in print in order to facilitate the mentorship that needs to happen. Also, in the past ten years I've become more selective about what I read and what I publish. I've realized that I don't have to be the be-all and end-all for black gays and lesbians who want to be published; that there are other publishers waiting in the wings to do their work, just as I am doing mine.

Can you discuss any writers from the past that you personally connect with?
Unfortunately, I never met Audre Lorde, nor Joseph Beam, nor Pat Parker, nor Essex Hemphill, so I don't have personal connections with them, and I so wish I had. I have met and had many conversations with

Barbara Smith, a co-founder of Kitchen Table Women of Color Press; she is a wonderful essayist and concise critic. (Everyone should read her collection, *The Truth That Never Hurts*.) I greatly admire the writing of Zora Neale Hurston, Langston Hughes, Wallace Thurman from the 1920s and 1930s... there really are too many from the past to single out.

Can you elaborate on your childhood and how it shaped the person you are today?
I'm the oldest of my mother's five children, which makes me the one to clear the path for the ones following. (Eldest children know what I'm talking about.) My mother was, at different times in my youth, a teacher and a librarian; and both my grandmothers were teachers, so education was highly valued in all their houses. My father is a musician, and most of his 12 brothers and sisters, plus his mother, played instruments or sang; music and the arts were also highly valued. And my father has always been self-employed, still is; he is a role model for me. He has always encouraged me, saying I can do anything I put my mind to; I just have to read and research all about whatever the topic is, interview other people that do what I want to do, then do it. As a child, I took care of my younger sisters, and on Sundays my father would take me to his mother's house to visit, where I would see up to 50 first cousins, depending on who was there. I became the child who was always curled up in a corner with a book, and my grandmother made sure that everybody left me alone to read. My father would also take me and my brother to my other grandmother's house, my mother's mother, and she took such pride in our grades. I'm a product of old-school beliefs that education is the great equalizer, and that each one should teach one and lift others up. I also seem to have inherited an ability to connect people with information, and with each other. My father likes to say that on his tombstone, he wants printed: "He tried to help somebody." I identify with that to a great extent.

What is the purpose of Fire & Ink?
Fire & Ink, Incorporated is a nonprofit devoted to increasing the understanding, visibility and awareness of the works of gay, lesbian, bisexual and transgender writers of African descent and heritage. We're an advocacy organization; I am currently the board president, and was one of seven co-founders back in 2002, when we organized our first writers festival, also called "Fire & Ink." Since then, Fire & Ink has had two more festivals, most recently Cotillion in October 2009, and was incorporated as a nonprofit in 2005. We also work with black gay Prides across the United States, Prides that want our collaboration on their literary events. We have other events planned in the near future; details to be announced

soon. Visit www.fireandink.org for more information about the organization; http://2009.fireandink.org for information about the most recent festival, Cotillion.

Would you say that the past three writers' festivals have satisfied your mission?
I would say that we've approached satisfaction, but we have a ways to go. I still encounter people that don't know that, for example, *Brother to Brother* was a book long before it was a movie of the same title but a different topic produced by Rodney Evans in 2004. There are black LGBT writers that need community, to know that their words are needed. Books created and continue to create gay culture, which affects our identity, so books matter. We need to make sure the public knows that our books matter, that the libraries know, community organizations know, bookstores know, academics know.

Could you tell us more about the documentary you are working on?
The video documentary is called *sassy b. gonn: Searching for Black Lesbian Elders*. It stems from my master's research, recording oral histories of black lesbian elders. After my house fire in 2002, I had to put it away for a bit while I rebuilt RedBone Press and the rest of my life from the ground up. I'm almost ready to take it back out and resume work on it.

What is the next chapter for Lisa C. Moore?
That's a very good question! I'm at the age when I am helping to care for older relatives, so that's slowing me down just a bit. But the future is bright: I've just gotten an intern for RedBone Press; I'm working with the Fire & Ink board to research grants and plan fundraisers for our next writers festival; I'm copy editing for *SWERV* magazine, as well as doing other freelance copy editing; I'm researching archival opportunities for my father's collection of his life's work; and am reviewing manuscripts for possible RedBone Press publication in 2010 and 2011. The next RedBone Press book—*Our Name Be Witness*, amazing prose by Marvin K. White—is due out in the spring of 2010. I'm also pursuing speaking engagements on college campuses about the work that I do. I can honestly say I'm never bored!

Archiving Black Queer History: An Interview with Steven G. Fullwood, Founder and Project Director of The Black Gay and Lesbian Archive Project

Conducted by Doug Cooper Spencer

(I first met Steven G. Fullwood in 2005 when he graciously showed Greg and me around the Schomburg Center for Research in Black Culture in Harlem, specifically the Black Gay and Lesbian Archive project. I had been following his work since I first heard of the project in 2000. Steven is not only an archivist, but a first rate essayist, editor and poet. If you're ever in the New York City, contact him at sfullwood@nypl.org to make an appointment to show you the archive ~ Doug Cooper Spencer)

When was the Black Gay and Lesbian Archive Project started?

In 1999, I approached Gay Men of African Descent (GMAD), one of the oldest black gay social services organizations in New York City, about depositing their archives at the Schomburg Center. Kevin McGruder, the executive director at the time, was interested in archiving the organization's records, and helped to develop and execute the project. I was awarded a documentary heritage grant, a program sponsored by the New York State Archives, which essentially provided a modest stipend to process the papers. The records were moved to the Schomburg, processed, and are now available to the public.

While researching for the grant, I searched for Black queer collections in other repositories, in order to know the territory of queer archives, and to develop my grant proposal. The majority of libraries and archival institutions whose stated missions were to collect and preserve Black or queer cultural or historical materials were sadly lacking.

What was available in 1999 at many of these institutions were books by mainstream authors like James Baldwin, Audre Lorde or Samuel Delany, but less than a handful had Black queer archival records. The Schomburg had (and continues to have) the largest collection of Black queer materials to date.

While I don't recall the exact moment I decided to start an archival initiative to collect the universe of Black queer materials, I do remember feeling like I was in the right place and time to do this work.

I spent about ten years collecting materials before formerly instituting the BGLA in 2000. The collection was initially housed at my apartment.

Inspired by the lack of documentation of non-heterosexual black life in libraries and repositories nationally, the genesis of the project began with my collection of books, magazines, flyers, programs, conference materials and other ephemera.

For five years I traveled extensively in the United States and abroad, attending readings, conferences and other cultural events seeking and collecting materials created by and about activists, writers, filmmakers, organizations, businesses and other artists in the United States, Europe and Africa. Materials in the collection, as well, as photographic collections and artifacts, reflect those efforts.

Currently the BGLA contains information dating from the mid-1950s to the present, documenting the experiences of non-heterosexual men and women of African descent primarily in the United States, London and several countries in Africa. Consisting of dozens of small collections of one to five folders, these miscellaneous collections form the bulk of the paper-based, non-photographic materials that I acquired through donation or purchase in an effort to bring to light the culture and history of Black lesbian, gay, bisexual, transgender, same gender loving, queer, questioning, and in the life people.

Subject areas in the collections will be familiar to members and students of Black queer culture and history including files for writers such as Audre Lorde and Essex Hemphill, but there is also information on lesser known individuals and organizations such as information about filmmaker Michelle Parkerson, the Los Angeles-based Association of Black Gays, and IRUWA!, Minnesota Coalition of Black Gays. The span of the collection is the mid-20th Century to the present including a focus on information about under-documented individuals, organizations and subjects in the 1980s when many organizations formed in response to the HIV/AIDS crisis.

Types of materials in the collection include printed matter (reviews and feature articles, programs, flyers and broadsides, newsletters), letters, including correspondence generated by me with donors and individuals documented in the collection, resumes and other biographical information, scripts, academic papers, and speeches. In some cases, files contain scant information. Additionally, the administrative files contain information about the structure and development of the project and its deposit to the Schomburg Center.

How large is the collection and what are some of the items?

The BGLA is about 30 linear feet, and it includes dozens of books, magazines, journals, newsletters, newspapers, flyers, hand cards, posters, photographs, t-shirts, films, music CDs, and a number of other items. There are papers for writers Cheryl Clarke, Donna Allegra, Ira Jeffries and Ron Simmons, along with one to three folder collections for individuals, organizations, pride events, subjects, and house/ballroom scenes. There is more collection materials mentioned below.

How accessible is it to the public?

Currently the archive is open to the public by appointment. Interested researchers should contact me directly at sfullwood@nypl.org. My complete contact information is listed below.

What got you interested in the idea of a black gay and lesbian archive?

As I previously mentioned, I was researching a grant to process the records of the Gay Men of African Descent. What I found was that there were virtually no libraries or archival institutions actively collecting black queer materials. At the time I was working as an archivist at the Schomburg Center for Research in Black Culture, New York Public Library.

The Schomburg had (and continues to have) the largest collection of black queer materials including the papers of Joseph Beam, editor of the first black gay anthology, *In the Life: A Black Gay Anthology*; Melvin Dixon, poet, translator, and author of *Vanishing Rooms*; Assotto Saint, author, activist and publisher of Galiens Press; as well as books and magazines and journals. I was in the best possible position to start the archive because 1) I was at the Schomburg, 2) I has a sense of the history and geography of black queer history, 3) I knew artists, activists, and regular folk personally who were interested in reaching as many people as possible with their work, and 4) the archive project itself was an extension of what I believe might be useful to not just one segment of the black queer community or even the black community, but everyone.

Redefining community so that everyone is valued is a dream of mine. By acknowledging the presence of non-heterosexual people I believe helps develop healthy community dialogue about perceived differences to diffuse and eradicate the stereotypes, distrust and lies that to this day go largely unchallenged.

W.E.B. DuBois, Carter G. Woodson, and others chronicled the lives of black folks, but they totally overlooked black gay history. Who are our historians? Who is out there chronicling our lives?

This is a good question because it makes me think primarily about the role of the artist in Black queer communities. The poets, fictionists, essayists, critics, playwrights, and short story writers, photographers, filmmakers, performing artists (actors, singers, dancers) are archivists in a sense who leave footprints that are invaluable in considering our various historical moments.

There are academics such as Herukhuti's (*Conjuring Black Funk*, contributor to *Think Again*) E. Patrick Johnson (*Sweet Tea*, who is also coeditor of *Black Queer Studies: A Critical Anthology* with Mae G. Henderson), and Thomas Glave (*Words to Our Now*) publishers like Lisa C. Moore (*Does Your Mama Know: Coming Out Stories by Black Lesbians*) poets Marvin K. White, Samiya Bashir, Reginald Harris, and many more writers interested in putting down the stories of various same gender loving people of African descent. I also think of activists like Imani Henry who is at the forefront of Trans rights, and people like Larry D. Lyons II who founded the Rashawn Brazell Memorial Fund in order to honor Brazell, a young black gay male who was murdered in 2005.

How extensive are the submissions to the collection? Is it mostly from the United States or international?

Although the collection is international in scope, most of the donations in the archive are largely from North America, and the largest part from the East Coast (New York, Washington DC, Philadelphia) and then the West Coast (California) and then various parts of the South (Atlanta, Houston, Florida).

How far back in time does the collection go?

There is a chilling special-edition monograph titled "Rape," which dates to the 1950s. The sexually graphic comic was created by an unknown artist, and explores what I call "white gay desire for black male bodies." The brief narrative follows the exploits of two black males and a white rapist by the name of Frank Sinatra. The action is brief and brutal but poignant, and offers scholars ways to image how power, desire and race intersected prior to Stonewall.

I've mentioned to you before that you should do a coffee table edition of the archive. Are there any plans to do that?

At this time I have no plans to do one, but maybe in the future. What I will do is continue developing the archive, doing publicity for it (like this interview) and helping other people start similar archival initiatives. If someone else wants to create that type of publication, I would be glad to assist.

What type of items are you looking for?

Not so much specific items, but materials that describe the earlier presence of black queer people, perhaps in diaries and letters.

Are there any rare items you're looking for?

If I could get a copy of Adrian Stanford's *Black and Gay*, published in 1977 by Gay Sunshine Press, I would be pleased. However, there is a microfilm copy of the book at the Schomburg library. And it would be great to obtain the records of earlier organizations like Salsa Soul Sisters or the Association of Black Gays, or the records of the publishers of B&G, or other early black queer magazines as well as all the issues of MOJA = Black and Gay, and other early publications like Blacklight and Blackheart. I wouldn't mind doing an oral history project with black queer elders in New York City.

Is there a movement towards including black gay history into general historical writings?

I think there is, however slowly. The more professors and teachers use black queer writers and history in their classrooms; I'd like to think that it would have a ripple effect. Well-known figures like James Baldwin, Lorraine Hansberry, Angela Davis, Rustin Bayard, and others whose sexual identity informed their work in some respects might become more evident, and it is certainly a way to rethink and reconsider their creative and political work as well.

But I think the movement to include black queer history into general history is the least of most people's interest. Frankly, there are not enough people pushing for this type of history in the classroom at most levels. Face it, most people do not even want to deal with the Transatlantic Slave Trade.

Some would say sexual orientation should be irrelevant in recording history. What do you think?

Answering questions like this, and I get them a lot, presupposes that there is a position to defend, and thus fuels ignorance about power structures that require you to agree with them or, like most of us, be in conflict with their biases and stupidity.

That said, my belief is that everyone deserves to have their history recorded, for a variety of reasons. Can you imagine for a moment if the world accepted sexuality as it is, not as they want to be? If history is going to be anything useful to people, it cannot continue to be a record of the so-called winners. It needs to expand. This work is a part of that necessary expansion.

So, someone comes up and says 'I want to start archiving black gay and lesbian historical data, artifacts… what would be your initial response?

My gut response is why. What is your interest? And be honest. If you want to make money, just say so, but don't cloak it under some artificial notion that people should know about black queer history blah blah blah. So be clear about your intentions.

Then I would say start from where you are – location. I would also ask why and what is the expected outcome (what does it *look* like, where would it live, who and what would the archive focus on, etc.) I might also mention that this work takes a minute and requires lots of patience, time and vision. Then I would offer my support and experience.

How has the overall experience been?

Tremendous. It's been a revelation to learn about black queer people, how they interact and have interacted with the larger black and gay communities, and the world; how they see and demonstrate their responsibilities to each other, to the communities they live in, and to the political repression of others, the environment, their health, nationalism, global warming and other issues. Mostly I am delighted to be useful in this manner.

For a visit to the Black Gay and Lesbian Archive or to make a donation, you can contact Steven at:

Steven G. Fullwood, Project Director, Black Gay & Lesbian Archive
Schomburg Center for Research in Black Culture
515 Malcolm X Boulevard
New York, New York 10037
sfullwood@nypl.org
schomburgcenter.org
212.491.2226 Tel

Plays

Plays

~ Lo She Comes ~
A Play in Two Acts by Renita L. Martin

O i will purchase my brother's whisper
O i will reward my brother's tongue

>   - Sonia Sanchez
>   <u>Does your house have lions</u>

                    ****

...our love is ancient as blk dirt
is a holy temple, a circular clearing in the trees

though how we love is mighty
i am not deceived by its danger
since we have been here before
have died doing our work before now
i remember you were christ's left palm,
harriet's stamina, hawk's wings

i remember the work we
do is still everlasting;
keep your fingertips
in my memory as reminder

>   - Letta Neely

Plays

Set in the Grove Hill neighborhood of Mississippi, the play opens Sunday night following the murder-suicide of Sweetboy and Halbert Wade the week before. QUEEN ESTER WADE, their mother, has declared that Halbert have a formal funeral in Grove Hill Church and Sweetboy (who is gay) be cremated.

It is important to know that both brothers had AIDS. Halbert - who contracted the disease while active in his heroin addiction - blamed Sweetboy for his illness, he held gays responsible for the existence of AIDS. As a result, he killed his twin brother, Sweetboy, and then killed himself.

Characters:

MAMA ALICE — Aka Muh Dea, in her late sixties, ROSE and SHORTCAKE'S grandmother

ROSE BUCKNER — MAMA ALICE'S granddaughter, SOOT'S lover

SHORTCAKE BUCKNER — ROSE'S brother

SOOT WADE — QUEEN ESTER'S daughter, has come from Chicago after her brothers' deaths

QUEEN ESTER WADE — Mother of church and town. Mother of SOOT, Halbert, Sweetboy and HATTIE.

HATTIE — A crack addict, sister of SOOT, Halbert, and Sweetboy. Mother of CANDY.

TANK — Sweetboy's partner

BIGBOY — Town griot, timekeeper, & church janitor

TOWNFOLK/CHORUS

Set

The stage should always have day-to-day workings and rhythms of the tiny town in which it is set. TANK and Sweetboy's house is upstage right. Hattie's house is down stage left. In HATTIE'S house are a telephone, a watch, a small television, and a cradle full of baby's things. She does not have electricity, her phone is – or is about to be -- disconnected. Aint Lillie Bell's is offstage. The church hovers in the back; QUEEN ESTER'S house sits almost adjacent to the church. MAMA ALICE'S house is down stage center. Most of SOOT and ROSE'S scenes in Act I take place in the yard in back of MAMA ALICE'S. There is a fig tree and an oak in the back yard. Near the oak tree is a black pot (used for boiling crackling, washing clothes, or sitting on). On the front porch is a swing. There is a road that crosses down stage.

Playwright's Note: Humor weighs heavily in many of these character's lines. However, it is important for players to remember that - unless contextually appropriate - lines should be delivered with little or no regard to their comedic value. Also, music should be used only when noted.

SCENE 1

HATTIE *is seen in her house seated next to an object representing a crack pipe. She has run out, and goes through a ritual of searching for money. Finding some change, she quickly exits her house and walks down the street to buy crack. In the church,* ***BIGBOY*** *is cleaning and singing. He sings through the activity. By the time he finishes,* ***HATTIE*** *is home with her package, the lights in* ***MAMA ALICE'S*** *house have gone out, and* ***BIGBOY****, himself, has locked up the church and is walking home.*

BIGBOY

THE DAY IS PAST AND GONE

THE EVENING SHADES APPEAR

OH MAY WE ALL REMEMBER WHEN

THE NIGHT OF DEATH DRAWS NEAR

WE LAY OUR GARMENTS BY

UPON OUR BEDS TO REST

SO DEATH WILL SOON

DISROBE US ALL

OF WHAT WE NOW POSSESS

(may hum this part)

OH LORD KEEP US SAFE THIS NIGHT

SECURE FROM ALL OUR FEARS OH LORD

MAY ANGELS GUARD US WHILE WE SLEEP

TIL MORNING LIGHT APPEARS

SCENE 2

Monday morning at sunrise, **SOOT** *is knocking on* **HATTIE'S** *door.*
HATTIE *sits in a corner next to her "pipe". At first, she doesn't plan to answer.*
SOOT *persists.* **HATTIE** *searches for several places to hide the crack pipe before hiding it in the bathroom.*
The knocking continues. She checks the window, upon seeing **SOOT** *she goes back to the bathroom to fix herself up. Finally lets* **SOOT** *in.*

HATTIE
I knew you would come.

SOOT
Hey, big sis, what chu doin in here you cain't answer the door?

HATTIE
I thought you was Mama.

SOOT
You hidin from Mama?

HATTIE
Jes ain't feel like hearin huh mouth bout how dirty this house is.

SOOT
(referring to Hattie's relationship with crack)
How you doin, Hattie?

HATTIE
This a hard one. Who woulda thought this shit?

SOOT
You seent what happened?

HATTIE
I was there.

SOOT
What happened?

HATTIE

Soot, I cain't talk about it no more. Candy! Candy, come in here and get ready to go to the babysittter's.

SOOT

Who you talkin to?

HATTIE

You ain't been gone so long you don't remember yo niece?

SOOT

Candy? Hattie...

HATTIE

Candy! I ain't gon call you no more.

SOOT

Hattie, you remember what happened to Sweetboy and Halbert?

HATTIE

Soot, I said I cain't talk about it.

SOOT

How you don't remember what happened to Candy?

HATTIE

Soot, what you talkin bout?

SOOT

Nuthin. *(quite shaken, near tears)*

HATTIE

Why you didn't come in time for the funeral?

SOOT

I ain't goin to nobody's funeral who kilt my brother.

HATTIE

Soot, you had two brothers.

SOOT

You had two brothers.

HATTIE

You always have had to 'spute everythang.

SOOT

You thank it's right how Mama doing thangs?

HATTIE

I know it ain't right.

SOOT

That's what I'm sayin.

HATTIE

Mama generelly wrong, that ain't nuthin new.

SOOT

I'm bout to put a stop to it this time.

HATTIE

How you gon put a stop to it?

SOOT

It shoulda been two funerals.

HATTIE

Shoulda been.

SOOT

And it's gon be two.

HATTIE

Mama ain't gon 'low no funeral.

SOOT

Mama ain't got no choice in the matter.

HATTIE

Soot, what is you talkin bout?

SOOT

Let me use yo car to run down ta Jackson.

HATTIE

Soot, you ain't talkin wit no sense.

SOOT

I'ma make sho Sweetboy have a proper burial.

HATTIE

Candy, sit down in that chair right now. Soot, you losing me...

SOOT

Hattie, Candy ain't... *(pause)* Let me use the car. I'ma tell you bout it later.

HATTIE

Tell me bout it now.

SOOT

I cain't. Just let me use yo car.

HATTIE

For what, Soot?

SOOT

I'ma run down ta Jackson, get Sweetboy.

HATTIE

What?

SOOT

I'ma brang him back home, and we gon bury him like he ought ta be.

HATTIE

Soot, I can have no part a nuthin like what you talkin bout.

SOOT

You said yo self that Mama ain't right.

HATTIE

That don't give you the right to 'spute huh.

SOOT

Hattie, why you so scared of Mama?

HATTIE

I ain't scared. I jes ain't letting you mix my car up in this.

SOOT

I won't say nuthin to Mama.

HATTIE

Cain't do it.

SOOT

Hattie, Sweetboy was yo brother, too.

HATTIE

Naw, Soot.

SOOT

Hattie, you a weak...

HATTIE

Naw, Soot, you weak. You wanna come back here and shake everythan all up... Where you gon be when everythang come falling down?

SOOT

Hattie, you ain't...

HATTIE

I'm the one's got to be here...

SOOT

It wadn't my choice to leave.

HATTIE

I done tole you "no". Now, go on. What you doin at somebody's house this early in the mornin anyway?

SOOT

I'm is gon leave cause if I stay here I might be inclined ta... **(HATTIE slams door)**

SOOT *exits, walks down the road.*

HATTIE *begins smoking.*

Lights fade on **HATTIE** *(who's talking to Candy).*

SCENE 3

Lights rise on **MAMA ALICE, ROSE,** *and* **SHORTCAKE** *sitting on the front porch.* **SHORTCAKE** *is putting on his shoes preparing to mow the lawn.* **MAMA ALICE** *is greasing* **ROSE'S** *scalp.* **SOOT** *passes, she waves. The family waves back.*

MAMA ALICE

She wadn't even supposed to be here.

ROSE

But she is. She sho here...

MAMA ALICE

Pretty body, but the flesh part all messed up. You know what they say...

ROSE

(has heard this too many times)

"body all outa wack with the wantings."

SHORTCAKE

(lacing his shoes)

You know, she loves women. But,

MAMA ALICE

her body all outa wack with the wanting.

ROSE

So what? She love women.

MAMA ALICE

But what do she got to put in a woman?

SHORTCAKE

It ain't what you put in em, Muh Dea, it's what you put on em.

ROSE

It's what you put with em, accordin to her. Like tithings...the Lord lay the collection plate down everybody bring a little bit to it and the po goes home wit they belly full.

MAMA ALICE

Hmmph.

SHORTCAKE

The Lord don't lay down no collection plate, niggahs lays down the collection plate.

ROSE

I caint stand nobody to use the word niggah in my conversation...

SHORTCAKE

(Ignoring Rose) MuhDea, when has you seen the po go home wit they bellies full?

ROSE

(Louder) I said I cain't stand that word in my conversation.

SHORTCAKE

This ain't singly yo conversation, this our conversation...

ROSE

Well I cain't stand it when y'all throws that word round like this a dodgeball game.

SHORTCAKE

Po chillen gets they eyes knocked out playing dodgeball. When the air go outa them little plastic grocery store balls--

ROSE

that's when the game really start...

SHORTCAKE

Ain't no telling what a niggah might put in them balls to make it so you can, least, still throw it. I seent niggahs--

MAMA ALICE

Didn't yo sister tell you she cain't stand it when you use that word in her conversation? You needa hurry up cut that grass fore the sun gi ya a heat stroke.

SHORTCAKE

Ain't nobody tryin to put nobody's eyes out. I'm jus tryin to say I got use for the word "niggah" in this conversation.

MAMA ALICE

Well, you better mumble it to yo self cause the girl done said she cain't stand it.

(BIGBOY can be heard singing from down the road)

BIGBOY

WHEN I ROSE THIS MORNING
I SAID "THANK YOU LORD"
WHEN I ROSE THIS MORNING
I SAID "THANK YOU LORD"
WHEN I ROSE THIS MORNING...

SHORTCAKE

Here come crazy Bigboy.

ROSE

You all the time talkin bout somebody. Bigboy ain't crazy.

SHORTCAKE

How many mo people you know walks around sangin all day?

ROSE

Maybe he got somethin to sang about.

SHORTCAKE

All day long?

MAMA ALICE

(as BIGBOY gets closer) Shhh...

BIGBOY

(passing them waving)
Hey, Miss Alice, how y'all. *(everybody waves)*

MAMA ALICE

Hey, Bigboy, how you this mornin?

BIGBOY

Cain't complain, Miss Alice. *(resumes singing)*

SHORTCAKE

I ain't never met somebody so happy bout cleanin up a church.

ROSE

Hush up, boy. Mama Alice, how was the funeral?

MAMA ALICE

Sad, won't but a handful of peoples there. That boy been runnin so much town folks don't member who he is.

SHORTCAKE

Townfolks don't forgit nuthin. Folks don't care who he is.

ROSE

Sides it ain't right.

MAMA ALICE

Hmmph! That boy's mama the muthah o the church. Got mo rights just about than the preacher.

SHORTCAKE

And got mo money than fo' preachers put together.

ROSE

I ain't never met nobody got mo money than the preacher.

SHORTCAKE

That's why they calls huh Queen Ester.

ROSE

Did Soot go?

SHORTCAKE

Soot say she love both huh brothahs evenly. You know she went.

MAMA ALICE

Hmmph. If she went, yo po granddaddy -- God rest his soul -- got up outa Grove Hill Cemetery, come by the house, put on his Sunday suit an met huh at the do'.

ROSE

Mama, hush yo mouth!

MAMA ALICE

They held up the funeral 45 minutes waitin. Til somebody look out the window and saw huh in that very same overall suit pickin gardenias out Judge McGee's lot next do.

ROSE

Mama, she wadn't pickin gardenias whilst they burin her brothah?

MAMA ALICE

Pickin em with one hand and holdin one a them funny cigarettes in the other.

ROSE

Mama, she don't smoke no funny cigarettes.

SHORTCAKE

How you know? You don't go out the house enough to know what nobody doin.

ROSE

Hush. Mama, did they have the casket open?

SHORTCAKE

Now you know they ain't had no casket open.

ROSE

Hush, boy. Mama, did they?

MAMA ALICE

Naw, everybody scared.

ROSE

You cain't catch it from nobody dead.

MAMA ALICE

Everybody scared from when he wadn't dead.

ROSE

He wadn't even here when he was alive.

MAMA ALICE

But his mama was and so was Sweetboy. Lillie Bell say the whole town bout need to get tested, least this family.

ROSE

This family? For what?

MAMA ALICE

Remember when Beatrice died? Queen Ester made the goin home supper: dressin, collard greens...

SHORTCAKE

Them collard greens was good...

MAMA ALICE

...sweet potato pie. She made nelly bout all the someteat we had after the funeral. Ain't nobody know then. But tween Halbert and Sweetboy... and now Soot back... ain't no tellin what Queen Ester done caught in the takin care of them chillen.

ROSE

Mama, you cain't catch AIDS from collard greens.

MAMA ALICE

Sssh!

SHORTCAKE

MuhDea, you got to have relations to get that. You cain't get it takin care o nobody.

MAMA ALICE

Hmmph.

ROSE

Sides, Miss Queen Ester wadn't takin care o nobody but huhself.

SHORTCAKE

That's right. Sweetboy woulda still be layin up half dead...

ROSE

...if Halbert hadn't come along and kilt him.

MAMA ALICE

Don't nobody know that's what happened.

ROSE

Don't take no genius to reckon it. Why you thank Soot wadn't tryna go to that funeral?

MAMA ALICE

Soot done lost the ways of the country since nelly bout fo she was born. Huh mama name huh Princess, she gon name huhself Soot.

SHORTCAKE

Well she look mo like a Soot than a Princess, that's the gospel.

ROSE

Ain't no tellin why she didn't go to that funeral.

MAMA ALICE

Me, myself, I'm suprised to see huh here. Thought she wadn't "never comin back here." An, here, she ain't been gone nelly a year.

SHORTCAKE

Them's huh brothers. She had ta come back, somethin like dat happen ta huh brothers..

MAMA ALICE

Well, she ain't dotted the door a Grove Hill Church fa that funeral. I ont know what she come back fa.

ROSE

Still, Soot ain't the one wit shame on huh head.

MAMA ALICE

Huh mama the head o the church, nelly bout. What she do wit huh God ain't none of folks business.

SHORTCAKE

Might not be folks' business. But folks is mad.

ROSE

Mad wit a right. How Miss Queen Ester look? Buryin one twin in a gold casket on the Lord's very day, wit all his proper rights... then to leave the other one at People's Funeral home, thirty miles from Grove Hill where folks cain't even go see him. And at that, buryin the twin that did the killin, not the one who got the killin.

SHORTCAKE

Both of em dead.

MAMA ALICE

We don't know who kilt who... I'm sure both of em will have a equally proper service.

SHORTCAKE

Ain't nuthin proper bout crematin nobody. If I leave here fore any a y'all, bury me. I don't care if you ain't got nuthin but a cardboard box, bury me. Niggah stand a better chance in the next life if he don't come back in ashes.

MAMA ALICE

You gon say that word one mo time and Ima just go to boppin you upside the head. Course we gon bury you...

ROSE

Mama done paid that burial insurance man enough over the years to bury the lot of Grove Hill. Plus, the Bible say you returns to ashes anyway.

MAMA ALICE

Now, I don't wanna hear no mo bout Queen Ester Wade. What she do wit huh chillen is huh right. Sides, I cain't even start to figgah what it must be like... tween Halbert, Sweetboy, and Soot; she ain't got but one child left. If it wadn't for Hattie, I'm sho she'd be dead by now.

ROSE

Mama, she got two chillen left. Soot still livin.

MAMA ALICE

But, how she livin?

ROSE

I'm goin out back. Y'all is to unphistacated for me.

Lights fade on **MAMA ALICE** *and* **SHORTCAKE** *as they rise on* ROSE *in the backyard sitting under the fig tree. Action continues on the front porch.*

SOOT

Psst...psst...psst

ROSE *looks around hearing something, but unable to locate it.*

SOOT *jumps from behind the fig tree.*

She hands **ROSE** *gardenias.*

SOOT

If yo ass lived in Chicago you'd get robbed on the daily.

ROSE

*(cold, but inwardly happy to see **SOOT**)*

If I lived in Chicago wouldn't be no big fig trees for fools like you to be jumpin out of.

SOOT

Where yo grandma nem?

ROSE

On the front porch gossiping.

SOOT

Must be talkin bout my mama, my brothers and me.

ROSE

Only topic of conversation in Grove Hill this week.

SOOT

Bout to be some mo talk.

ROSE

I know. Everybody thought you wadn't comin-.

SOOT

I gotta tak care of somethin.

ROSE

What?

SOOT

I need yo help. But cain't tell you bout it til you promise to hold it.

ROSE

That's you cain't hold water.

SOOT

I can hold thangs need holdin. I ain't tryna hold nuthin ain't right. My daddy went outa here wit ulcers.

ROSE

So, you tellin everybody you know bout how yo brothah kilt his own twin and how yo mama ain't right.

SOOT

Everybody ((who) is understood) wanna know the truth bout the matter.

ROSE

How you thank that make y'all's family look?

SOOT

As unholy as that big ole hat Mama wear to church every Sunday. As unholy as the Bible she carry round like it's a whip. As unholy as we is-- and the truth be known -- as unholy as everybody else in Grove Hill.

ROSE

You crazy. What you want wit me?

SOOT

What time you gota be a work today?

ROSE

I ain't workin this week.

SOOT

You got laid off?

ROSE

I took off. Now, what you want me to do?

SOOT

Yo Uncle Punce got a car, right?

ROSE

Yeah, but I still cain't drive. He don't let nobody drive it but Shortcake and I'm older than Shortcake. I cain't wait to get outa this town, go somewhere where bein a girl mean somethin more than "you cain't do nuthin what you wanna do."

SOOT

(trying to get to the point)
He'll let you have the keys if you tell him it's for Shortcake, right?

ROSE

Uncle Punce ain't here. Shortcake already got the keys. Who it's gon be for?

SOOT

(leaning over to kiss her)

I'ma get to that. Just answer the question. Shortcake'll let you have the car if you need it, right?

ROSE

Yeah. *(pulling back)* Now, who it's gon be for?

SOOT

I need to use it. But I need you to hold this thang I'm bout to tell you.

ROSE

What you need a car for, Soot?

SOOT

(trying to kiss her again)

You gon hold it?

ROSE

You know my grandma got eyes reach clear round back a this house, why you doing this out here. Plus...

SOOT

(looking back toward Aint Lillie Bell's house)

I know, all Aint Lillie Bell do is look off huh back porch tryna see what we is doin.

ROSE

Tell me that secret; you know she bout to call Mama Alice any minute.

SOOT

Good thang them cataracts turns me into a boy every time.

ROSE

She probably know who you is. Just cain't get the idea to meet wit the tongue.

SOOT

All right. Ima hurry up. First, I gotta know I got yo promise.

ROSE

Oh, we suddenly in the business of keepin promises?

SOOT

What that sposed to mean?

ROSE

Nuthin... hurry up. She done gone in the house to call Mama Alice already.

SOOT

Alright. *(whispering)* My plan is to give Sweetboy a proper buryin.

ROSE

How you gon do that? Yo mama done declared she ain't bringing Sweetboy and his ways up in Grove Hill church.

SOOT

Sweetboy played the piano for Grove Hill and he is gon be buried proper... if for nuthin else, least for his work.

ROSE

How you gon get him from People's? Jackson most thirty miles from here.

SOOT

That's why I need the car.

ROSE

Why don't you ask Hattie to use huh car.

SOOT

I talked to Hattie bout the whole thang. She say she won't have no part.

ROSE

What you gon do when you get the body?

SOOT

I'ma dress him up in one a them miniskirts he liked to wear and hold a funeral at Grove Hill Church.

ROSE

How you gon hold a funeral? You got to schedule to use the church through yo mama and the preacher. How you gon do that?

SOOT

I ain't got to schedule nuthin. The keys in Mama's house, ain't they?

ROSE

Who gon preach a funeral on a Monday mornin? specially after Grove Hill just had a big funeral. You cain't even git no jackleg preacher to preach a funeral for a man wearin a mini skirt. And who gon come? Folks been to one funeral. *(SOOT doesn't respond)* How you gon hold a funeral in broad daylight up in Grove Hill?

SOOT

Ain't nobody gon be at the church on no Monday mornin. Most peoples workin and the ones that ain't ain't tryna go up in Grove Hill. They know that's when Big Boy clean up the church and ain't nobody tryna help him. Folks' laziness gon help me gi my brotha a proper buryin.

ROSE

What you gon do wit Big Boy?

SOOT

We done already made a deal. I give him a bottle of Jack Daniels and a joint fa his troubles. We gon sneak in the church for the funeral, take Sweetboy out back and bury him fore anybody know what happen.

ROSE

Soot, you don't smoke them funny cigarettes, do ya?

SOOT

Naw. Now is you gon help me do this? I gotta go.

ROSE

Soot, grief done stole yo mind.

SOOT

I know xactly what I'm doin. If anybody stealin -- hate done stole Mama's mind.

ROSE

Ain't the cremation sposed to be tomorrow?

SOOT

Yep. How much time we got? *(looking back towards Aint Lillie Bell's)*

ROSE

Bout five minutes, she got to find huh telephone diallin glasses fore she call down here. How they gon account for the body?

SOOT

Don't know. Maybe they'll thank he rose up like Jesus.

ROSE

Ain't nobody gon thank Sweetboy was Jesus.

SOOT

Ain't that much difference tween the two.

ROSE

'cordin to yo mama it is. And yo mama and the Lord got bout equal footin in these parts. She say she hear any talk a them queens having any kinda thang for Sweetboy, she got somethin for em.

SOOT

Yeah, say she gon lock em up huhself.

ROSE

You cain't go through nuthin like what they put you through the last time.

SOOT

I didn't do nuthin else Sweetboy needed me to do... didn't come home so's I could see bout him, didn't have nuthin tosend him, I was so caught up in my dreamin and carryin on, I thought he was gon still be here when the money caught upto the dreamin. Now, this the least I can do. He loved to play that piano for Grove Hill Church and if they cain't honor him for it, I'm gon do it.

ROSE

Guess who playin for Grove Hill now.

SOOT

Don't tell me they got --

ROSE

Lena Smith. She couldn't wait for Sweetboy to get cold fore she calt the preacher talkin bout she still available. You know, she tried to play yesterday, folks say Sweetboy wouldn't even let huh play that thang.

SOOT

That wadn't no Sweetboy. Sweetboy ain't have nuthin to do wit what happened in that church. Everbody wanna blame some'in on Sweetboy. Lena Smith ain't been able to play no piano since I knowed huh.

ROSE

She might not a been able to play before. But she ain't never got huh wrist sprung in the tryin. She say Sweetboy was holdin huh hands everytime she try to hit a new note.

SOOT

Lena Smith ain't hit a new note in twenty years. Probly the devil holdin huh hands. If anything up in Grove Hill Church, it's the devil.

ROSE

Sides if Sweetboy was goin somewhere, he'd probly go on down to Lynch Street wit the rest o the punks.

SOOT

Now, Rose, you cain't go up to the city callin nobody no punk. These sissies'll jack yo ass up you come callin em punk. Sides, if Sweetboy a punk, what that make you? *(kissing Rose. the phone rings)*

ROSE

That's Aint Lillie Bell.

SOOT

Rose, you gon help me out wit this?

ROSE

Is you gon take me way wit you like you promised last time?

SOOT

I woulda took ya then. But, you know how I left here.

ROSE

(Shaking her head) Halbert come all the way from up Detroit...

SOOT

Halbert'd come up from the grave, Mama ask him to. He was all huh evil come to life. Now, Hattie, she at Mama's beck an call, too. But, she tryin not to lose that li'l bit a money Mama give huh. Hattie tryna keep huh some'in to stay high. But, Halbert. Halbert plum evil.

ROSE

I know how you had to leave here. But, that don't explain why you ain't write but three times, you ain't called...

SOOT

Rose, you know yo grandma wouldn't let me through.

ROSE

It was other ways. You coulda wrote mo.

SOOT

This the first time I seen you since –

ROSE

Last year. And the first thang you do is come here astin me for somethin.

SOOT

Rose, that ain't the only reason I come to see you.

ROSE

How I know that? How I know what you been doin way up there in Chicago?

SOOT

Rose, I cain't even believe what you sayin. You know what? don't even worry bout the car.

ROSE

I ain't said all that. *(pause)* I just don't know. Soot, you asts a lot.

SOOT

This my brother, Rose.

ROSE

Come back round here in a hour. See how I feel.

SOOT

Shit.

*(**ROSE** rolls her eyes at **SOOT**)*

SOOT

I ain't got time to be runnin back an forth here for you to see how you feel.

ROSE

Well, if you wait all day, it won't be but a drop in the bucket next to the time I put in waitin fa you.

SOOT

Come by Tank's house. I'ma look suspicious runnin back an forth over here.

ROSE

I ain't gon look suspicious walkin round ta Tank's?

SOOT

Why I always gotta be the one to take the chances?

ROSE

You want the keys, you take the chance... sides, I ain't noticed no chance you took yet.

SOOT

Rose...

ROSE

I got ta get in the house fore Mama Alice come callin back here.

SOOT

Yo grandma always callin, ain't she.

ROSE

I gotta go, Soot.

***ROSE** exits, **SOOT** sits on the pot for a while before leaving.*
*Lights up on **HATTIE**'s.*

SCENE 4

QUEEN ESTER *(who wears a black veil for the duration of the show) stands at* **HATTIE**'s *door.* **HATTIE** *checks the window before finally opening the door.*

QUEEN ESTER
What she say?

HATTIE
Who?

QUEEN ESTER
I know she here. What she want?

HATTIE
I ont know.

QUEEN ESTER
What you tell huh?

HATTIE
Shhhh. The baby sleepin.

QUEEN ESTER
What you tell huh?

HATTIE
Nuthin, mama.

QUEEN ESTER
You remember what I tole you? You didn't see nuthin, no matter who asts.

HATTIE
It don't matter... both of em gone.

QUEEN ESTER
This house is a mess. What's that smell?

HATTIE
Incense.

QUEEN ESTER
Keep this place clean won't have no need fa incense.

HATTIE

I was jes bout ta run out.

QUEEN ESTER

You the one calt me.

HATTIE

Mama, that was yesterday.

QUEEN ESTER

You still need that package don't ya? Or did you git you a job between yesterday and this mornin?

HATTIE

Thank you, mama.

QUEEN ESTER

Not so fas. We ain't had Bible study in two days.

HATTIE

I been studyin on my own.

QUEEN ESTER

The Bible say, "where two or three are gathered in My name". The Lord ain't said nuthin bout readin to yo'self... specially durin times like these. Read me one a the verses you been studyin.

HATTIE

Come on, Mama, I gota take dat down ta Mr. Bozeman's, pay on my grocery bill.

QUEEN ESTER

You'll take it after we reads our scripture and pray. Maxi Bozeman know you buried your brothah yesterday.

HATTIE

Candy ain't gon sleep through --

QUEEN ESTER

Read.

HATTIE

"Yea though I walk through the valley of the shadow of death...

QUEEN ESTER

Here, read this scripture...

HATTIE

"And if thy right eye offend thee, pluck it out, and cast it from thee: for it is profitable for thee that one of thy members should perish, and not that thy whole body should be cast into hell.

And if thy right hand offend thee, cut it off, and cast it from thee: for it is profitable for thee that one of thy members should perish, and not that thy whole body should be cast into hell..." Matthew 5, verses 29 through 30...

QUEEN ESTER

May the Lord add a blessing to the hearing and reading of His word. Now, pray, Hattie.

HATTIE

Heavenly Father, we come again thanking you for your many blessings...

QUEEN ESTER

Yes, Lord...

HATTIE

Lord, you know it's been a hard week. Please help Mama, she got a lot on huh. Bless my baby, and Halbert...

QUEEN ESTER

Yes, Sweet Jesus...

HATTIE

and Sweetboy. Lord, all these things we ask in your darling son, Jesus name. And for His sake, we pray.

QUEEN ESTER

Thank you, Lord. *(fumbling through her purse she goes to hand **HATTIE** the money)* You know she ain't gon come by the house... I'ma need somebody ta tell me what she up to.

HATTIE

I believe the baby up. Mama, thank you fa comin by.

QUEEN ESTER

Remember what I tole you... Everythang God do, He do fa a reason. Sometimes His reasons and His doings is never to be discussed again. You understand me, Hattie?

HATTIE

I understands.

SCENE 5

*Lights up on **TANK'S***

SOOT
Couldn't leave no doors open like this in Chi-Town. *(entering the house)*

TANK
Where you comin from 'fo day in the mornin?

SOOT
I done took to walkin early mornins.

TANK
Chile, please, you was walkin early mornins fore you left here tryna get a glimpse of Miss Rose Buckner. Did you see huh fore she went to work?

SOOT
She ain't goin to work this week. *(pouring two glasses of orange juice)*

TANK
Ummm, say she ain't? Hope she have a job when she get back.

SOOT
I was wonderin how she got off... say she jes took off.

TANK
Who you know ever took a day off from the shirt factory? Bae Mae's nem son got blowed up on the job when they had that explosion the other year. And they fired him cause he had too many sick days.

SOOT
Somebody need to blow up the whole shirt factory while all the niggahs off and the white folks is down in the basement countin the money they saved payin three twenty-five a hour.

TANK
Niggahs don't get no day off. Sides, whole town be outa work... *(handing **SOOT** the juice)* So, Miss Rose has taken the week off? My, my, my...

SOOT
Forget you, Tank. What you doin up so early?

Plays

TANK

Habit. This what time I useta give Sweetboy his medicine.

SOOT

Had he got real bad off?

TANK

He wadn't doin so good. But he ain't want nobody to know it. He was still goin down to Grove Hill playin the piano til they tole him not to come back.

SOOT

When they tell him that?

TANK

Bout two weeks ago. Miss drunk ass Thomasina come marchin over here after church talkin bout it best he stay home an rest. He had this rash all over his face and they couldn't stand to look at him.

SOOT

Them niggahs at Grove Hill makes me sick.

TANK

Church sposed ta be where you get healin.

SOOT

It's gon come back on em.

TANK

Sooner than they thank. Little as this town is, don't nobody know who got it. Folks droppin like flies. You heard bout Leroy, didn't you?

SOOT

Yeah, that's what was wrong wit him?

TANK

His mama tried to say it was cancer. When you ever had to wear a mask to go see somebody wit cancer? Chile, please. Now his wife sick.

SOOT

Rena sick?

TANK

J.B.... Tombstone Jackson...

SOOT

Tombstone Jackson?

TANK

And Reverend Terry.

SOOT

How you doin, Tank?

TANK

Missin my baby. Woulda been ten years come February. I 'ont even know how to start over. I'm too tired for that club shit.

SOOT

I hear you.

TANK

I knowed it was comin specially after they tole him he couldn't play for church no more. He had pneumonia when Halbert come up in here. I had just went to the store to get a can a soup. I could hear Hattie screamin all the way down to Maxi's store. Halbert coulda let him go on his on time.

SOOT

Well, we gon give Sweetboy the homecomin he woulda wanted.

TANK

You get the car?

SOOT

Hattie said "naw".

TANK

I tole you that.

SOOT

How long she been talkin to Candy like that?

TANK

Ever since she died. Most people jes let huh. Shit, you tell huh Candy dead, she go to beatin on you.

SOOT

What Mama say about it?

TANK

You know how your mama is. Long as she can keep Hattie in the house where don't nobody have to see huh, she ain't tryna deal.

SOOT

Hattie need some help. Why ain't nobody call me?

TANK

Wadn't nuthin could be done. You know Queen Ester ain't gon let nobody put that girl in the hospital -- Halbert was in Detroit and Sweetboy wasn't puting up wit huh mess. She had to have somebody to run... Plus Sweetboy was scared if you come down here she might lock you back up. *(pause)* What we gon do bout the car?

SOOT

Well, I asked Rose.

TANK

Rose? Chile, Rose cain't go out the house, let alone drive.

SOOT

I asked huh to get me the keys.

TANK

How she gon do that?

SOOT

Huh Uncle Punce outa town.

TANK

The Lawd works in mysterious ways.

SOOT

She ain't give me the car either.

TANK

Rose wouldn't give it to you?

SOOT

Come talkin bout I wadn't in touch wit huh while I was gone...

TANK

Was you?

SOOT

Best I could be.

TANK

I know what that mean.

SOOT

You know I ain't have no money. I couldna even call Sweetboy like I wanted to.

TANK

Love ain't concerned wit how often you call. Love is a diva, she want you to speak huh name loud and often while muhfuckahs is around to hear it.

SOOT

Rose know I love huh.

TANK

Did you tell huh?

SOOT

I ain't got time to be playing wit Rose. I'm tryna give my brother --

TANK

Rose ain't like you, Soot. She was here by huhself, scared to walk down the aisle to the collection plait -- she give Shortcake huh money. It ain't like everybody don't know she yo woman...

SOOT

I was tryna save up. I wanted huh there.

TANK

Soot, I seen you when you want somethin. And if you hada wanted Rose there. You woulda had huh there. You can tell that shit ta somebody else. You was shackin up wit Big Rachelle and you didn't want Rose ta know bout it.

SOOT

Big Rachelle an me was roommates.

TANK

Yeah, honey. An me an Sweetboy was roommates. Chile, Big Rachelle been tryna get wit you since she was comin down here for summer vacation.

SOOT

I cain't do nuthin wit Big Rachelle.

TANK

Then, what objection you got to takin Miss Rose ta Chicago?

SOOT

Rose ain't ready fa Chicago. Rose scared ta walk down here ta bring me the keys. What I'ma do wit huh in Chicago?

TANK

What you scared of? You been foolin round wit Rose fa years. You know she'll come wit you if you asked huh.

SOOT

She ain't even comin to Sweetboy's funeral.

TANK

Did you ask huh?

SOOT

I ain't feel like hearin huh say she scared huh grandma might find out.

TANK

You oughta ask huh.

SOOT

I got enough goin on. She oughta know I would want huh there... Rose know I love huh.

TANK

Did you tell huh that?

SOOT

She act like I was layin up wit every woman in Chi-town.

TANK

And you wasn't?

SOOT

I'ma tell you jes like I tole huh, I was saving for Rose.

TANK

But what was you savin for Rose? Chile, take yo bull-headed ass on over there and tell huh all that shit so we can get my baby and get him dressed up.

SOOT

You done called everybody?

TANK

Yeah, I took care a that.

SOOT

(after stalling) Well, I'ma go out for a while. I'ma see you in a little bit.

TANK

Tell Rose I said "hey".

SCENE 6

Lights up on **ROSE** *on the front porch alone.*
SOOT *is in the back yard trying to get her attention.*
ROSE *blatantly ignores* **SOOT.**

SOOT

Psst....

MAMA ALICE *enters the porch and sits with* **ROSE**.
SOOT *continues to try to get her attention while* **ROSE** *tries to keep* **MAMA ALICE'S** *attention away from the back yard.*

SOOT

Miss Rose...

MAMA ALICE

You hear som'em?

ROSE

No mam.

ROSE *signals to* **SOOT** *to stop.*
SOOT *continues.*

SOOT

Miss Rose.

MAMA ALICE

Now, I know I heard somethin.

ROSE

Probly Big Boy down the road sangin. I'll go round the back, see if I see some'em.

MAMA ALICE

(to herself) That ain't no Big Boy. Big Boy sangs cordin to the clock. It ain't time fa Big Boy ta be sangin.

ROSE

You is trespassin.

SOOT *moves towards* **ROSE**, *who abruptly hands her the keys.*

ROSE

I'ma let you have these keys, but it don't mean nuthin.

SOOT

Don't mean nuthin like what?

ROSE

When all this is over, you can drop the car off down Rosemary Road. If I don't see you no mo after that, it be fine wit me.

SOOT

Rose, what in the worl is you talkin bout?

ROSE

Go on up Chicago wit yo big, grown, citified girls. I'll be jes fine down here.

SOOT

I ain't tryna go to Chicago without seein you fo' I leave.

ROSE

Yeah, cause I might not never see you no mo. *(sarcastically)* Ain't no way I can fine big o Cbicago by myself.

SOOT

Rose, you misunderstanding...

ROSE

Was you ever gon send for me?

SOOT

Rose...

Plays

ROSE

You wasn't never gonna ask me to come be wit you in Chicago!

SOOT

It ain't that I didn't want you there. I jes wadn't in no position to take care a you. I couldn't give you...

ROSE

I ain't said I needed nobody to take care a me! And I ain't asked you to send fa me. *(pause)* After all we been through... I walked down this road wit you, snuck round the back yard to see you. And while the whole town was mad at me bout it, you was off in Chicago. You wadn't round them ole nasty boys trippin me in the cafeteria cause I want you, not them. The only thing that kept me from feelin all by myself was knowin that if we could, we would be together... *(phone rings)* Then you leave fa Chicago an don't even tell me you leavin... Send me a note two months later talkin bout sendin fa me...

SOOT

It ain't that I didn't wanna be wit you. I was shame. I thought I was jes gon bus up in Chicago an be makin bank. I didn't want nobody ta see how I was livin.

ROSE

I ain't care how you was livin. I thought I had a place to be wit you.

SOOT

Rose, I didn't have no place. You don't understand--

ROSE

I understands mo than you give me credit fa.

SOOT

Then meet me at the church fa Sweetboy's funerall. Eleven o'clock...

ROSE

Soot...

MAMA ALICE

Rose!

ROSE

You know ain't no way--

MAMA ALICE

Rose, is you out there wit some good-fa-nuthin hoodlum? Lillie Bell done called and tolt me...

ROSE

I'm riskin everything to get you that car. Baby --

SOOT

That's what I thought.

MAMA ALICE

Make ace. Rose!

ROSE

I'm comin, Muh Dea!

Plays

SCENE 7

Time and light change. It is shortly after noon.
ROSE *and* **SHORTCAKE** *are on the porch.*
SHORTCAKE *is enjoying peach cobbler.*
BIGBOY *can be heard singing as lights rise. The singing overlaps the dialogue.*

BIGBOY

(passes and waves)
I SEE THE SIGN
HEAH
I SEE THE SIGN
HEAH
I SEE THE SIGN
HEAH!
LORD TIME'S DRAWIN NIGH
THIS SIGN OF THE JUDGMENT
HEAH
THIS SIGN OF THE JUDGMENT
HEAH
THIS SIGN OF THE JUDGMENT
HEAH1
LORD TIME'S DRAWIN NIGH

(The following verses continue as the first two)

HIDIN IN THE FIG TREE...
LOOSE HORSE IN THE VALLEY...
TELL ME WHO GONNA RIDE HIM...
KING JESUS GONNA RIDE HIM...
SINNER, COME OUT THE CORNER

ROSE *is anxious. There is an urgency to her pace.*

SHORTCAKE

Umm, Umm. Baby, you put yo foot in this.

ROSE

If you don't shut up Ima put my foot in somethin else. You makes me sick. Anytime I ast you to do me a favor you wants somethin big in return.

SHORTCAKE

I wouldna ask you for nuthin if you had tole me the truth bout what you need it for. But since you so secretive, could a brothah get a lil icecream to go on top this nice cobbler?

ROSE

That's yo problem. You got to control everythang. You don't tell me nuthin when you wants a favor.

SHORTCAKE

I don't ask for no big two thousand dollar car. That car got my name on it til whoever got it brang it back here today. I got a right to know who riding round on my name.

ROSE

The car in Uncle Punce's name. You ain't got nuthin wit cho name on it but a library card, if you got that.

SHORTCAKE

You oughta fix me this pie for not tellin MuhDea.

ROSE

You ain't got nuthin to tell huh.

SHORTCAKE

I will by the time I finish peakin round Uncle Punce's garage ta see who brang that car back.

ROSE

Show how much you know. The car ain't goin ta Uncle Punce's. It's goin down the street and you gon go pick it up near where you left it and drive it on back.

SHORTCAKE

Look like I'ma need mo icecream than this.

ROSE

Sides, if thangs was right, I could get the car my own self. *(grumbling)* Anywhere else in the world the oldest git the car don't matter if she is a girl.

SHORTCAKE

When you been anywhere else in the world?

MAMA ALICE

(from the front of the house walking to the porch)

Who that fixin peach cobbler?... Rose, you and Shortcake gamblin again? I done tole y'all I don't 'low no gamblin and card playin in this house. Anytime I smell peach cobbler on a Monday afternoon that mean y'all been gamblin and Rose done lost the bet. I ain't no fool.

ROSE

Mama Alice, ain't nobody gamblin. *(snatching the cobbler from in front of Shortcake)* I just thought you might like some nice peach cobbler after yo long walk round to cuzin Floyd and Aint Lillie Bell's.

SHORTCAKE

Naw, MuhDea, Rose don't always make peach cobbler just cause she lose a card game. *(pause)* Sometime she make it for other reasons.

ROSE

(rolls her eyes at SHORTCAKE)

That's right, Shortcake, you want some mo cobbler? Want some icecream to go top a it?

SHORTCAKE *(smiling)*

Sometime she make it just cause she love us. She been talkin bout makin you somethin nice all day, what wit chu doin all that cookin for the funeral yesterday. She say you probly right tired, say you sho look it, say --

ROSE

... Mama Alice, you want some icecream on top a yo cobbler?

MAMA ALICE

Don't mind if I do. *(the phone rings as she is sitting down.)*

ROSE

(looking at her watch)

MuhDea, I'll get it!

MAMA ALICE

What's wrong wit that gal? First, she don't wanna be treated like no slave, don't wanna cook no more than a man, don't wanna be waitin on nobody, don't wanna say "MuhDea" no mo' cause it "too country". Hmmph. Now, she cookin up everythang in the house, done took the day off from work so she can stay home an clean, answerin the phone an everythang, talkin bout, "I'll get it, MuhDea."

SHORTCAKE

Maybe she finely got huh a boyfriend. Be bout time, don't you reckon?

MAMA ALICE

Hush yo mouth, yo sistah fass enough. Liketa got pregnant out there by the fig tree today had not been for Lillie Bell...

ROSE

Mama, Aint Lillie Bell on the phone!

MAMA ALICE

What Lillie Bell want now? I jus left huh house.

ROSE

(returning to kitchen) I ont know, Mama Alice, she say she got somethin to tell ya. **(MAMA ALICE** *exits.* **ROSE** *kicks* **SHORTCAKE.** *)* You gon stop playin wit me, boy, we got a deal.

MAMA ALICE

Lillie Bell, you lyin... I ain't playin. I wadn't Naw... hush... sho nuff?... gon tell huh nuthin. who you thank done it?... Sides you need to tell me hush... blasphemies... hmmmph... what's goin on. You umph... you know she is.

SHORTCAKE

borrow the car all mysterious like, cain't Nobody know what it's for.

MAMA ALICE

Umph umph umph, Lawd ha mercy.

ROSE

Mama Alice, what's wrong.

MAMA ALICE

Somebody done stole that boy's body from People's Funeral Home.

ROSE

What?

MAMA ALICE

Sweetboy. Somebody done stole Sweetboy out the funeral home.

ROSE

How you gon steal a body out a funeral home broad daylight?

MAMA ALICE

Say they musta come in a car, musta been a couple of em.

SHORTCAKE

Could a been just one. They say Sweetboy ain't weighed hardly nuthin.

MAMA ALICE

Folks say it had to be mo than one, dead folks is a lot heavier than live ones.

ROSE

Do they know who stolt it? Anybody see the car?

MAMA ALICE

They say ain't nobody seed nuthin. Say the fire alarm went off all ova the buildin say everybody runt out to the front parkin lot tryin not to get burnt up. They must a took it then.

SHORTCAKE

Somebody seent somethin, jes ain't talkin.

ROSE

How long its been?..... Since they took the body, I mean.

MAMA ALICE

Don't know, Queen Ester jes got the call. Been callin everybody she know see if anybody seent anythang, hear anythang.

ROSE

What she find out?

MAMA ALICE

I done told you, nuthin. That's why she still callin round. She say she gon send the police round them sissies' way. Say if Tank got that body she gon have him in Parchman on a life sentence.

ROSE

You cain't give nobody a life sentence for stealin a dead body.

SHORTCAKE

One night in jail is a life sentence for Tank's sweet behind. He cain't do no hard time. And you better believe he ain't lifted nobody out no funeral home. The only reason they call him Tank is cause his head so big. Somebody bigger than Tank responsible for this. Sides, ain't none a them punks got a car.

ROSE

You oughta be glad you ain't up North. Punks up there will jack you up for callin em punks.

MAMA ALICE

Rose, hush up and run my bath water. All this talk o the dead done got me tired. I believe Ima go on take me a nap.

SHORTCAKE

Mama Alice, you gon take a bath in the middle o the day?

ROSE

(looking at her watch again)

Hush up, boy, it's hot out there, she say she tired. Alright, Mama Alice, I'm runnin that water now. *(**ROSE** exits into the house, **MAMA ALICE** follows. **ROSE** returns, tries to sneak out the back door. **SHORTCAKE** grabs her arm.*

SHORTCAKE

Who got the body?

ROSE

What you talkin bout? How I know who got the body?

SHORTCAKE

You ain't never borrowed the car the whole time I been using it. Now, you wanna borrow it for a "friend".

ROSE

I ain't never asked cause you ain't never had it long enough. Since Uncle Punce gone to Memphis, I thought I'd ask.

SHORTCAKE

Now ya lyin. Uncle Punce go to Memphis all the time.

ROSE

I asked my friend to go to the Metro Center for me so's I could by me some thangs for my trip. That's the secret. I'm bout to go on a trip. That's what you wanna know?

SHORTCAKE

Sho is a coincidence yo trip and Sweetboy's trip out the funeral home scheduled on the same day.

ROSE

I didn't say I was leavin today. Jus gettin my thangs today. Now be quiet fore Mama Alice start wonderin what's goin on.

SHORTCAKE

Queen Ester is lockin folks up. Baby Rose, if you is mixed up in this I can help you. But you gotta tell me what's goin on.

ROSE

Shortcake, you holdin me up. Let me go find out what's goin on and I promise I'll let you know. *(looks at her watch)* Everythang bout over anyway.

SHORTCAKE

Ima be right here.

SCENE 8

Lights rise in the church.
Music is heard.
SOOT *and* **TANK** *sit stiffly.*

BIGBOY

(singing continues through the middle of Scene)
THERE IS A FOUNTAIN
FILLED WITH BLOOD
DRAWN FROM EMANUEL'S VEINS
AND SINNERS PLUNGE
BENEATH THAT FLOOD
LOSE ALL THEIR GUILTY STAINS
LOSE ALL THEIR GUILTY STAINS
LOSE ALL THEIR GUILTY STAINS
AND SINNERS PLUNGE BENEATH THAT FLOOD
LOSE ALL THEIR GUILTY STAINS

TANK
I knew this would be hard. But I ain't got words for how this shit feel.

SOOT
He woulda been so proud of you. This just the way he woulda wanted it.

TANK
Up in Grove Hill Church.

SOOT
Up in Grove Hill Church. *(**ROSE** enters from the back)*

TANK
Honey, look back... *(**ROSE** sits with **SOOT** who slowly begins to melt. **ROSE** holds her hand)*

SOOT

He so little... (**ROSE** *holds her, pause*)

ROSE

Baby, yo mama know.

SOOT

What I care bout what mama know! Mama knowed that boy was layin up in that house, layin up in his own shit, and she ain't done nuthin. I don't give a damn what mama know.

ROSE

She done sent the police over Tank's. Say she gon send him to Parchman fo life.

SOOT

Mama fancy herself mo powerful than she is sinful.

ROSE

She don't fancy herself sinful.

SOOT

The ugly don't fancy theyself ugly. Everybody else jes know bout it.

ROSE

They gon search the church sometime tonight.

SOOT

Ain't this the sweetest funeral you ever wanted to see? I used ta worry all the time bout Sweetboy not gettin enough love in this town, but Tank got so much love. Baby, Tank gave Sweetboy mo love than Mama ever give us put together.

ROSE

I want you to lean on me, take yo rightful place in the grieving.

SOOT

I love....

ROSE

Hush up, baby, I know --

SOOT

I did wanna take you wit me... been wantna take you way since we was pickin blackberries in Bay Mae's patch. Member that day you saw that racin snake and ran clear bout to Jackson?

ROSE

What you want wit some lil girl scared of a snake?

SOOT

Love turn fear right side up. Come up Chicago wit me. Fore you know it, you'll be kissin me smack on the lips no matter if Aint Lillie Bell is watchin, don't matter if yo po pretty mama come back from the grave askin bout what you doin. If you had a been lovin me then, you probly woulda turn around an ask that snake do he wanna be a belt or some new shoes?

ROSE

Just go to show how much you know... *(kisses* **SOOT***)*

BIGBOY

THE DYING THIEF REJOICED TO SEE

THAT FOUNTAIN IN HIS DAY

AND THERE MAY I, THOUGH VILE AS HE

WASH ALL MY SINS AWAY

WASH ALL MY SINS AWAY...

SCENE 9

Lights rise on **QUEEN ESTER WADE.** *She wears a black dress with a black veil, her face is never seen. She is seated in a reclining chair talking on the phone. Beside the chair is a nightstand on which the King James Version of the Bible sits.*

QUEEN ESTER WADE

I don't care if yall ain't got enough evidence. You got the car, ain't ya? *(pause)* Umph, umph, umph, Shortcake Buckner. No wonder his mama made all that goin home supper after Halbert's funeral. *(pause)* Shortcake what usedta cut my yard. I guess he had his own reasons fa bein over here. Well, I don't care what you got ta charge him on, I want him in Parchman Penitentiary fore the sun go down!

Lights fade/cross to **ROSE.** *Shortly after 1pm.* **ROSE** *is trying to sneak onto the porch.*

SHORTCAKE

How was the funeral?

ROSE

Shortcake, what funeral? What is you astin me...

SHORTCAKE

Rosie, I ain't never been no fool bout you an Soot. If I can hold that all these years least you can do is tell me how was the funeral.

ROSE

How did you know?

SHORTCAKE

I been knowin since you took off runnin way from that snake in Bay Mae's field. Soot liketa been broke huh neck tryna kill that snake. Niggahs was yellin, Soot, the snake dead. Soot, the snake dead already!

ROSE

She kilt that snake?

SHORTCAKE

Where they bury the body?

ROSE

Cain't tell nobody.

SHORTCAKE

Who I'ma tell?

ROSE

Right by they daddy. Tank and BigBoy n'em stayed to cover him up.

SHORTCAKE

Where the car?

ROSE

Down Rosemary Road. Want me ta go with you?

(They exit)

SCENE 10

Later that day, **MAMA ALICE** *sits on porch with her head in her hands.*
ROSE is running up into the yard.

ROSE

Mama Alice, they...

MAMA ALICE

I know. Lillie Bell just calt me, tole me they got my boy down at that jail. The whole town talkin bout it.

ROSE

Mama Alice, he...

MAMA ALICE

I know, baby, the whole town talkin bout it. Everybody thought Tank was Sweetboy's boyfriend or whatever they calls each other. All the time it was Shortcake. Lord, why it gotta be Shortcake.

ROSE

Mama, he--

MAMA ALICE

I know the boy ain't have too many mens round. But Uncle Punce tried to teach him somethin...

ROSE

MuhDea, he...

MAMA ALICE

I guess it was too little too late, guess Punce stay in Memphis too much to teach a boy how ta be a man. Lord, don't let it be. Please, Lord, don't let my boy be...

ROSE

MuhDea, what if he is! What if either of us is? You gon write us off like Queen Ester! Take us round People's Funeral Home an burn us up when we die? You loves to sit up on this porch like you so holy, talkin bout peoples passin by, makin judgments on other peoples' children. But too holy to tell Miss Queen Ester she is dead wrong on this, dead wrong.

MAMA ALICE

Rose! Queen Ester and huh peoples done chose they life from years back. Queen Ester's grandmama stood right there in Grove Hill Church and tole the Lawd ta go on and take huh son, Bubbah, say he wouldn't listen to huh. Say she rather pray fa mo stable thangs: money, plenty food in the garden... Say she rather spend the time prayin fo them thangs rather than pray fa chillen who ain't thankin like she want em to thank. Stood right there in Grove Hill Church and cussed the generations to come, say Queen Ester's mama didn't know how ta listen! Say anybody come after huh gon have chillen and grief, chillen and grief. So, here come Queen Ester an all huh crazy chillen: Soot, sittin out there wit them ole men round Maxy Bozeman's storefront whistlin at womens like she got somethin fa em; Sweetboy struttin round here, Miss America, huhself; Halbert, got mo chillen than Father Abraham, and no love fa nobody. Up there in Detroit shootin that mess up his arms then blamin Sweetboy cause he been plagued; Hattie, suckin so hard on that pipe she done let huh own sweet lil baby chile run out in the road and get hit by that car -- po Bud Mack still in jail fa that and he wodn't even drunk that day. Hmmph... That's between Queen Ester and huh legacy. Now, mines ain't the same. My mama 'lowed me to say what need be sayin long as I had some respect bout myself. And I taught my chillen the same way. And yo sweet mama died wit huh mouf wide open fore the sun could get a chance to throw huh some shade. Now when you see ways that coulda kept the ones you love most here, you try ta pass em on. You thank I don't know Halbert kilt Sweetboy jus as show as you standin there lookin at me like I ain't equipped ya to know what to do when ya mouth get too big fa ya hand to keep it covered?

ROSE

Soot say huh daddy died holdin too many thangs in. Say ulcers turnt to cancer ate up his intestines kilt him fo he knowed what happened.

MAMA ALICE

Hmmph. Ain't no ulcer kilt Solomon Wade, 'less the ulcer turnt into a 38 revolver... Solomon Wade kilt hisself. And as for his intestines, MadDog 20/20 took care o that long fore anything else could get to it. Solomon Wade kilt hisself, and Halbert Wade kilt Sweetboy. That's what I'm tryna tell ya, a niggah growin up in Grove Hill got bout much chance o makin it as a snapbean come harvest time, less chance if you ain't rich like them Wades. And they cain't even stay alive cause they great-grandmama done put blood on they heads. *(pause)* Now, I know what you is. I jus wanna keep you alive. Halbert Wade wadn't the only one in this town that blames Sweetboy -- and the lot of his associates -- fa this plague. Now, if

Halbert can jump up behavin like Cain fore the New Testament was wrote, kill up his only brothah outa hate, what chance is you got? Queen Ester Wade's legacy ain't bout keepin huh chillen alive, it's bout keepin huh legacy alive. I'm tryna keep my chillen alive!

ROSE

Mama, what we gon do bout Shortcake?

MAMA ALICE

We gon go get him and somebody gon tell the police what really happened. Now go back Punce's and get the keys to the car.

ROSE

MuhDea, we ain't got the keys to the car. *(stumbling for a reason)* Shortcake got em wit him.

MAMA ALICE

Then call one a ya uncles see cain't they drive us round there to get him. *(they start to exit)*

ACT II

SCENE 1

*ROSE and **MUHDEA** are where they were at the close of Act 1.*
***SHORTCAKE** enters.*

SHORTCAKE
Looks like I still gets to keep my title -- the only Black man in Terry ain't never been to jail.

MAMA ALICE
Boy, you all right? What in the world happened?

ROSE
How ya feelin, Shortcake.

SHORTCAKE
Drylongso, Rosie, drylongso.

MAMA ALICE
We was finna come get you. What happened?

SHORTCAKE
Well, they led me down nere to the courthouse, Queen Ester Wade and a whole lot of nosy niggahs -- felt like Jesus goin down the crucifix...

MAMA ALICE
Don't blaspheme the Lord's name...

SHORTCAKE
Anyway, Queen Ester Wade followin behind me wit a bottle a holy water splashin it all down my back, up on top my head -- and Popeye jes gi me this haircut -- she jes splashin and talkin bout how I led huh son astray wit my lawn mower...

MAMA ALICE and ROSE

Lawn mower?

SHORTCAKE

Yeah, say ole Sweetboy wanted to be a firefighter fore I got to him wit my lawn mower turnt him Sissy.... Awe, she talkin, jes talkin, and the nosy folks behind huh shoutin, "yes, Lord... do, Jesus... Satan is a liar... put him 'way"

MAMA ALICE

Awe naw they ain't....

SHORTCAKE

Let me tell you the rest, MuhDea. So, they takes me inside. Never in my life thought I'd be so happy to be inside a courthouse. They give me them jailhouse clothes and I was ready to go on down that basement and serve my time. Then, here come Soot.

ROSE

Soot come up to the courthouse?

SHORTCAKE

Come up there wearin one a them zook suits outa Chicago.

ROSE

Boy, she wadn't wearin no zook suit, them thangs outa style.

SHORTCAKE

Well it was a man's suit, jes show as I'm tellin you this story. She step up in the courtroom hollerin "hold up" *(to* **MAMA ALICE***)* xcuse me MuhDea "wait jes one gotdamnt minute!"

MAMA ALICE

Lawd, she wadn't cussin in the courthouse?

SHORTCAKE

Jes show as I'm tellin you this story... Then she say, "Shortcake ain't done nuthin. Mama, let Shortcake go on home." Then Miss Queen Ester say,

QUEEN ESTER

Shortcake done led my child to the ways of the beast wit his lawn mower.

SHORTCAKE

Then Soot say, "Mama, Shortcake ain't have nuthin to do wit this.

SOOT

You knowed who both a us was long fore Shortcake could even push a lawn mow.

MAMA ALICE

Hmmph

SOOT

I took the car, Mama. I buried Sweetboy. I did it, Mama.

QUEEN ESTER

Princess Denise Wade, you not standin there tellin me you dilibretly sputed my word.

SOOT

You was wrong, Mama. Look at us, Mama.

QUEEN ESTER

How y'all living is wrong. I ain't brangin that sin up in the church house, don't care whose chile it is.

SOOT

It was alright when he was bustin his ass playin the piano fa free.

QUEEN ESTER

If it was left to me, he wouldna been playin.

SOOT

Well, it ain't left to you! Now, you done kilt Daddy,

Sweetboy and Halbert gone, Hattie suckin on that crack pipe like it's the devil's dick..."

MAMA ALICE

Naw, she didn't tell bout her sistah and that pipe fore them white folk.

ROSE

Huh mama tole everythang else fore them whitefolks. Miss Queen Ester responsible fa brangin mo business o Black folks down ta the court-house than anybody in the history o Terry...

MAMA ALICE

Hmmph

SHORTCAKE

...white or black, better believe that. Anyway, Miss Queen Ester go to cryin an throwin holy water all up in Soot's face. Then, what happened next I sho wouldn't be tellin you bout less I had seent it wit my own disbelievin eyes.

MAMA ALICE

Hush, boy

ROSE

What happened?

SHORTCAKE

Soot had been holdin all that holy water Miss Queen Ester been splashin... jes holdin it tight up in huh mouf...

SOOT

Mama, stop splashin that holy water on me. You ain't qualified to be splashin no holy water.

QUEEN ESTER

(following Soot)

I rebuke you, Satan. In the name of Jesus. I rebuke you...

SHORTCAKE

didn't swallow it or nuthin... jes holding it. When she got huh a mouf ful, she spit it dead in Miss Queen Ester's face, show as I'm tellin you this story. Then she say...

SOOT

Splash that holy water where it need to be, Queen Ester Wade.

MAMA ALICE

Naw she didn't call huh mama by huh birth name.

SOOT and SHORTCAKE

Turn that damn bottle up and drank it.

SOOT

Drank it for Daddy, drank it for Sweetboy, drank it for Hattie. Mama, turn that damn bottle to yo mouth....

QUEEN ESTER

You ungrateful beast. *(**QUEEN ESTER** exits)* Take huh away.

SOOT

...drank it for Hattie. Mama, turn that damn bottle to yo mouth...

ROSE

*(running towards **SOOT**, **SHORTCAKE** grabs her)*
Leave huh be!

MAMA ALICE

Rose, hush!

SOOT

*(to **HATTIE**,)* Hattie, don't let em do this again... Hattie!...*(whispering)* Get wit Rose... come get me...

ROSE

She ain't done nuthin wrong!

MAMA ALICE

Rose, git back on this porch!

HATTIE

Come on, Candy.

ROSE

Let huh go!

MAMA ALICE

Rose!

ROSE

I'm through hushin, MuhDea... *(the two women have a stare-down)*

SHORTCAKE

*(pulling **ROSE** aside)*
Rose, she just don't want you to get hurt.

ROSE

I'm already hurt. *(**MAMA ALICE** begins to walk away)*

SHORTCAKE

MuhDea, where you goin?

MAMA ALICE

I'm bout ta give Queen Ester Wade a piece a my mind. She ain't gon lock my chillens up and embarrass em fore the general public.

ROSE

Ima go witchu.

MAMA ALICE

You gon stay right chere and have my bath runt when I gets back.

ROSE

Mama, I don't wanna spute you but this my business jes much as it's yours.

MAMA ALICE

I won't hear no mo bout it. If she put Shortcake up in that jail, what you thank she gon try ta do to you?

SHORTCAKE

*(pulling **ROSE's** arm)* MuhDea, right. We gon stay here. We'll have yo bathwater runt when you get back.

***MAMA ALICE** exits*

ROSE

Shortcake, what's wrong witchu? If you know all bout me and Soot then you know I gots ta know where they takin huh. You know I gots ta go.

SHORTCAKE

Rose, I been knowing you got ta go since Soot come back. Fore she got here you was lookin like a fried chitlin -- all wrankled up and greasy. Soot come back, you fix yo hair, found some clothes look half decent, and day by day them wrinkles starts to press theyselves out. Course I know you got to go. But you got ta do it right. Now, Miss Queen Ester ain't gon tell MuhDea where Soot is long as you standin up there using yo eyes for razor blades. But, she is gon tell Aint Lillie Bell. Matter fact, she on the phone right now tellin huh. "Lawd, I sho hopes Sistah Alice can forgive me fa what I done done. It's jes they calt and say it was Punce's car what picked up Sweetboy and I know Punce off in Memphis and everybody know when Punce in Memphis he leave the car wit Shortcake. Lawd knows I ain't mean no harm." She gon tell huh what happen down at the courthouse and you know Aint Lillie Bell gon ast, "Well, Queen Ester, what you do with huh embarrassin yall family name all in front a the church folks and them white folks at the courthouse? What you gon do wit huh?" Then Miss Queen Ester gon tell huh.

ROSE

Then Miss Queen Ester gon hafta git off the phone cause somebody at the do'.

SHORTCAKE

And that somebody gon be MuhDea. But Aint Lillie Bell ain't gon know that.

ROSE

So, Aint Lillie Bell gon call MuhDea to tell huh bout what happened.

SHORTCAKE

Matter fact she oughta be done found huh telephone dialin glasses and be callin right now. (phone rings) Now Aint Lillie Bell can hear bout well as she can see, and you been talkin on that phone to them bill collectors like you was MuhDea fa years. So this oughta work.

SHORTCAKE is smiling as he hears ROSE on the telephone

ROSE

Umph, umph, umph.... Sho 'nuff... Hush, Lillie Bell... Queen Ester cain't do nuthin wit that girl... Hush... Now, where ya say they took huh?... Alright, sugar... uh, uh. (Rose enters the porch she is in tears.) They took huh to Whitfield.

SHORTCAKE

Lord, that's worse than Parchman.

ROSE

Aint Lillie Bell say Miss Queen Ester tole em ta give her as many shock treatments as it take to make huh mouth clean.

SHORTCAKE

Rosie, it's gon be alright.

ROSE

Shortcake, it ain't gon be alright! Ain't nuthin alright bout none a this. Queen Ester Wade breeds huh chillen to die and I jes happen to be in love wit the one she tryna kill right now. Soot cain't live through this again.

SHORTCAKE

Soot lived the first time. Run all the way up ta Chicago. Soot can live through this.

ROSE

What Ima do wit a curse? Queen Ester Wade grandmama done cussed the family. Anybody cain't do like Queen Ester want dies, Shortcake, they dies. Soot done said huhself, right out there under that fig tree that if they takes huh back to Whitfield tryna fry the bulldagga outa huh she gon kill huhself right there in Whitfield, she gon kill huhself. And, you know, they gives you the rope ta hang yoself wit at Whitfield.

SHORTCAKE

Well yall is in the breakin out business. Let's go bust huh out.

SCENE 3

Lights rise on **SHORTCAKE** *and* **ROSE** *knocking on* **HATTIE's** *door.*

HATTIE *is crouched in the corner smoking crack.*

SHORTCAKE and ROSE *are persistent; Hattie goes through her ritual of putting away the pipe, checking the door, and fixing herself up...*

SHORTCAKE

Hattie, open up, it's Shortcake.

HATTIE *opens the door wearing a bathrobe.*

HATTIE

Hey, Shortcake. *(pulling her robe tighter)* Oh, I ain't know you had somebody wit chu. How you, Rose?

ROSE

Alright, Hattie, how you?

HATTIE

Candy, get up so our company can sit down.

ROSE *looks at* **SHORTCAKE,** *who gives her a signal to ignore this.*

SHORTCAKE

Look, Hattie, Rose had some'in she wanted to ask you.

HATTIE

What you got ta ask me, Rose?

ROSE

Well, you was out there today...

There is a knock at the door.

HATTIE

Damn niggahs beatin on my door like this the welfare office. Hold on, Rose.

TANK *enters, he is sweaty and still covered with dirt.*

TANK

Hey Miss Rose, hey Shortcake. *(They speak)* Y'all heard bout Soot?

ROSE

Yeah, we come over here to talk to Hattie. You know they got Soot up there at Whitfield?

HATTIE

Yeah, Mama tole me.

TANK

Draggin huh off like a damn animal.

ROSE

You know what they did to huh the last time.

HATTIE

Soot brangs a lot on huhself. I keep tellin huh to jes be quiet sometime. Always have been like that...

TANK

Everybody cain't sit in they house wit the shades drawn scared to stand up for theyself.

ROSE

She don't deserve to be put way like that. She cain't live like that.

HATTIE

Soot strong, she'll get outa there. Probly be out fore the weekend.

ROSE

The weekend too long.

SHORTCAKE

Hattie, come up to Jackson wit us now so we can sign huh out.

HATTIE

I cain't do that.

ROSE

You huh sister, they'll let you take huh out. Ain't nobody got to know.

TANK

You done set up there and let Sweetboy die. Least you can do is get Soot outa there.

HATTIE

Y'all get on outa here. I got to bathe my baby.

ROSE

Hattie, this a matter of life and death.

HATTIE

Cain't do it.

ROSE

Soot trusted you... you the only one...

HATTIE

I ain't able. Soot'a be jes fine. Candy, come back here, let me put your hair up so you can git in the tub.

SHORTCAKE

Look, Hattie --

HATTIE

Candy, sit down!

SHORTCAKE

We can drive you down there, ain't nobody got ta even know...

HATTIE

Hand me that brush over there... *(**SHORTCAKE** gives her the brush. She combs Candy's hair and fades more into her own world)*

SHORTCAKE

She ain't listening. Come on y'all...

ROSE

Soot your sister --

HATTIE

If you don't be still, I'ma bop you dead upside the head with this brush.

ROSE, TANK, *and* ***SHORTCAKE*** *exit.*

Plays

TANK

I didn't mean to say that. I jes don't understand Hattie.

SHORTCAKE

She sick.

TANK

She been walking round here talking to Candy. Candy been dead four months. Now that's who Queen Ester need to be takin to the hospital.

SHORTCAKE

Well, Rosie, we tried.

ROSE

I'ma get huh out.

SHORTCAKE

How you gone do that?

ROSE

Jes git the car.

TANK

Rose, you want me to go with you?

ROSE

Naw, but we gon need somewhere ta hide.

TANK

You got that, Miss Rose Buckner.

TANK walks down the road.
SHORTCAKE and ROSE exit.
BIGBOY walks down the road singing.
HATTIE, having waited for them to leave, runs down the road.

SCENE 4

BIGBOY
IT'S GETTIN LATE OVER IN THE EVENIN
AND THE SUN'S GOING DOWN
IT'S GETTIN LATE OVER IN THE EVENIN
AND THE SUN'S GOING DOWN

*Lights rise on **HATTIE** in the corner of the room smoking and **SOOT** in a small room, her arms are strapped in a straight jacket.*

HATTIE
They're never gonna unstrap you if you don't cooperate. You got ta eat, Princess.

*Lights remain focused on Soot and **HATTIE** as they silently negotiate their individual spaces of imprisonment.*

SCENE 5

SHORTCAKE and ROSE walk down the hallway of the hospital.

SHORTCAKE

I got somethin I been savin. Want you ta have it.

ROSE

What is it? A dodgeball filt up wit rocks?

SHORTCAKE

Naw. I done saved up a pretty penny cuttin up people's yard this summer. I was gon take that money down Jackson State see cain't I get me some University classes, but some thangs is mo pressin than learning how ta speak French through a mouf ful a collard greens.

ROSE

Yo mouf ful a a lot mo thangs than collard greens. I thank college a right fine idea fa you.

SHORTCAKE

Anyway, I wanna gi ya this (hands her an envelope) seven hundred fourteen dollars and eighty fo' cents. It ain't much fa the trip you bout ta make, but I seent nigg... I mean peoples leave here wit three dollars and a bus ticket an make it. Country folks so used to makin it in the country anywhere else they be be like a vacation.

ROSE

Shortcake, how you raise all that money from cuttin yards?

SHORTCAKE

I cuts bout two, three yards a day fore Thursday. Thursday come, I cuts bout six or eight. Charges people ten dollars, xcept Miss Queen Ester, I charges huh twenty. Don't do nuthin wit the money xcept save it fa school an buy MuhDea somethin nice she like. She don't likes too many fancy clothes -- a robe an a gown case she hafta go in the hospital say she don't wanna go in lookin po and country. But, she got nuff robes and gowns by now ta spend a monf in the hospital should she need to. Now, I jes buys huh some orange sherbet icecream and she be happy.

ROSE

Shortcake, you charge Miss Queen Ester twenty dollars?

SHORTCAKE

Sho do. Fa all my troubles. She cain't jes let you cut the yard, she got ta be yellin out the window: Careful fa my rose bush! Watch my turnip patch! Them bushes ain't sposed ta be cut down! Here come somebody walkin by, turn off the lawn mow, I ain't payin fa nobody ta git they eyes put out! She figgah she got that much right ta tell me how ta cut some grass I been cuttin since me and the grass was the same size, I got jes much right ta charge huh fa huh mouf. Sides, one thang bout Miss Queen Ester, she takes a lot a liberties but she pay fa em every time.

ROSE

I caint take all yo money.

SHORTCAKE

The summer ain't quite over, I can make some mo. Sides, I ain't tryna go ta school til next year no way.

ROSE

Still, Shortcake...

SHORTCAKE

(Holding up the money)

This the onliest thang you got. You gits hungry, you cain't make no sammich outa love.

ROSE

I got a little money under MuhDea's bed, right side. It ain't no seven hundred dollars, but you take it... Ima pay you back the rest jes soon as I gits settled.

SHORTCAKE

We got ta git huh outa here first. You thank this gon work?

ROSE

We done made it this far. Jes remember ta call me Hattie. *(pause)* Shortcake, how come Hattie act like she used to you comin over there?

SHORTCAKE

I goes over there from time to time to check on huh. I cuts huh yard on Saturdays.

ROSE

Y'all got some'em goin on?

SHORTCAKE

Naw. It ain't nuthin like that. I jes felt so bad for huh after what happened to Candy.

ROSE

Yeah. That was so sad.

SHORTCAKE

I was out there when she got hit. Me and Catfish nem, out there hangin out by Maxi Bozeman's storefront. I seent Candy run out there and I ran but I couldn't get to huh in time. That pretty l'il girl died right here in my arms. *(pause)* Y'all didn't get there in time to see Hattie beatin on me.

ROSE

She was beating on you?

SHORTCAKE

Askin me to brang huh back. She jes pounding a valley in my shoulder. At first, I was mad, I was thankin, "If she left that crack alone that l'il baby wouldna been out there like that." Then, I looked in huh eyes and all I wanted in life was to brang that baby back. That's why I 'ont say nuthin to huh when she be talkin to Candy. If she need to believe she livin, I lets huh.

ROSE

What y'all talk about when you go see huh?

SHORTCAKE

Mostly nuthin. I jes sits wit huh. Sometime I 'on't even think she know I'm there.

ROSE

Shortcake, you a good man.

SHORTCAKE

You keep that to yourself.

***ROSE** and **SHORTCAKE** enter **SOOT**'s hospital room.*

***SOOT** is strapped and unconscious.*

***ROSE** and **SHORTCAKE** are silent for a while.*

SHORTCAKE

(Helping her) Rosie, what's wrong wit huh? What they done done to huh?

ROSE

I 'ont know. Jes see she don't know who I am.

SHORTCAKE

Is she gon come back?

ROSE

I ain't no docta. Jes know I cain't see huh behind all the glaze.

SHORTCAKE

Maybe we oughta leave huh here. What you gon do wit huh if she don't come back?

ROSE

I'ma love huh, Shortcake. I'ma love huh til she do come back.

SHORTCAKE

MuhDea right bout some thangs. She been round here long time, ain't never seent one a them chillens Queen Ester nem done wrote off live. She done been cussed, Rosie. You the very one say what you gon do wit a cuss.

ROSE

(trying to unstrap **SOOT***)*

You tell Miss Queen Ester when she go ta lookin that you heard somebody took huh down Louisiana.

SHORTCAKE

Rosie! We cain't git huh outa here. This whole plan depended on huh bein able ta walk outa here. How you gon git huh on the bus?

ROSE

Shortcake, I cain't go back. Soot! Soot! Soot, look at me! *(lights fade)*

SCENE 6

Friday evening. **SHORTCAKE** *knocks on* **HATTIE'S** *door.* **HATTIE** *conducts her ritual before cracking the door.*

BIGBOY

(his song continues through their dialogue)
WE LAY OUR GARMENTS DOWN
UPON OUR BED TO REST
OH DEATH WILL SOON DISROBE US ALL
OF WHAT WE NOW POSSESS

HATTIE

Shortcake, that you?

SHORTCAKE

Yeah.

HATTIE

You by yourself?

SHORTCAKE

Yeah. (**HATTIE** *begins kissing* **SHORTCAKE**, *who gently pushes her away.*) Come on, Hattie...

HATTIE

You come on... *(climbing on him)*

SHORTCAKE

I done tole you we cain't be doin this. You got a "boyfriend."

HATTIE

You wouldn't even want me if I straightened up.

SHORTCAKE

I wanted you then.

HATTIE

Candy, sit down. I'ma put my foot dead in...

SHORTCAKE

Hattie, don't holler at huh like that.

HATTIE

Why you even come here? Huh? *(trying again to seduce* **SHORTCAKE***)* Why you come here?

SHORTCAKE

You need ta go see yo sistah.

HATTIE

Baby, let me hold some money.

SHORTCAKE

I ain't givin you no mo money. Hattie, you ain't doin good.

HATTIE

Shortcake, I don't need ta hear that. Candy! Shortcake, it feel so good...Candy be hollerin sounding like Mama and Daddy and that gun and me and Soot and Sweetboy and Halbert didn't make a sound we was under the porch and we was all hollering but Halbert Halbert didn't make a sound... I wanna be like Halbert. I smoke this shit everythang stand still for jes one minute I don't feel no pain everything feel good like rain on a hot ass night... that's why I ain't hear it, Shortcake... that's why I ain't know til I ran out I... was basin and I ran out. I opened the door to get some mo shit... I seent you holding my baby blood runnin that's why I ain't know *(begins to beat* **SHORTCAKE***)* you holdin my baby. *(***SHORTCAKE***, after a bit of wrestling, holds her).* Baby, it ain't no goin back from here *(****Hattie*** *breaks away and heads for her pipe)*

SHORTCAKE

Come on, don't do that tonight. Let me be enough... *(holding her)* come on. Put that down...

HATTIE

You gon be here all night? in the mornin... when i wake up?

SHORTCAKE

I'ma be here. You gon be here?

SCENE 7

Saturday morning, Tank sit in hospital waiting room waiting for Rose. Mama Alice enters.

TANK
(nervous)

Miss Alice... How you?

MAMA ALICE

(making her way into the house) I'm lookin fa my grandbaby.

TANK

Who? Miss Rose? I see huh at church on Sundays. But, m'am, I wouldn't know where she is.

MAMA ALICE

Look, boy. I done had to get somebody ta drive me all the way up here. *(Waiting for a response FROM TANK)* Well, when you see huh tell huh since she sposed ta be grown she can act like a grown woman, come by the house... least have the decency ta tell me how she doin.

TANK

(ROSE enters) I sho will if I see huh.

ROSE

Hey, Muh Dea.

TANK

Lord ha mercy, Miss Rose. What you doin here? *(there is silence, TANK excuses himself)*

MAMA ALICE

If ya gon run away like dat least you could do...

ROSE

I'm sorry.

MAMA ALICE

We done had the police over to the house all week... jes like wit yo mama... I been worried ta death.

ROSE

Muh Dea, I didn't want it ta be like this.

MAMA ALICE

This how you choose to live. This how it gon be.

ROSE

It ain't like this everywhere.

MAMA ALICE

So, you jes gon keep runnin...

ROSE

I ain't runnin, Muh Dea. I love Soot.

MAMA ALICE

(rising and taking some bottles and powders from her purse) I hear she pretty bad off. *(handing her the things)*

ROSE

Cain't talk, ain't said a word since...

MAMA ALICE

You can clean huh system out wit this Golden Seal and it's some mint in there for tea. I been had this powder fa years, stir it up in a big glass a water, make sho it's cold... *(**QUEEN ESTER** bursts into the waiting room followed by **BIGBOY**)*

QUEEN ESTER

They tole me you was coming up here. She ain't spose ta have no visitors. I can have you arrested for trespassing. *(**TANK**, having heard the commotion runs into the room)*

BIGBOY

Rose, I ain't said nuthin.

MAMA ALICE

Queen Ester Wade, what is you talkin bout? You ain't lockin up ...

QUEEN ESTER

And you up here supportin huh! Lawd, Jesus-

BIG BOY

Miss Queen Ester, I seent yo grandmama last night...

QUEEN ESTER

Big Boy, hush up that crazy talk... *(to **MAMA ALICE**)* I ain't never had nuthin against you, Alice, but your chile got the devil in huh jes like mine and she done gone too far this time... I got a warrant fa Tank and if I finds out she involved in this buryin, I'll get one fa huh. (to **ROSE**) And if you don't stay way from this hospital--

ROSE

You ain't got ta do no investigatin. Yes, m'am I was involved and I'm involved wit yo daughter, too. *(MAMA ALICE and QUEEN ESTER simultaneously become acutely aware of the people surrounding them in the hospital— particularly the white people)*

MAMA ALICE

Rose!

BIG BOY

SATAN WE GONNA TEAR YO KINGDOM DOWN
SATAN WE GONNA TEAR YO KINGDOM DO....

QUEEN ESTER

Hush up!

BIG BOY

YOU BEEN BUILDIN YO KINGDOM ALL OVER THIS LAND
SATAN WE GONNA TEAR YO KINGDOM DOWN...

MAMA ALICE

Queen Ester, you need ta leave these chillen alone. This wouldna been my way neither. But, ain't nuthin --

QUEEN ESTER

That don't mean we gota fall into they ways. The Lord said, "Children, obey your...."

MAMA ALICE

I know the Bible, Ester! Time done outgrowed us and we got ta git some clothes to fit, lest we ain't gonna have nuthin ta wear come judgment day...

QUEEN ESTER

Take care a your house, Alice. You ain't done things so right yo self. If you hada taught huh mama some respect...

ROSE

Don't you never say nuthin bout my mama!

QUEEN ESTER

*(to **MAMA ALICE**, who has betrayed her)* Everybody know if she hadn't went off ta school, come back here stirrin up...

MAMA ALICE

Now, that's enough right there, Ester. I declare that's enough.

QUEEN ESTER

*(To **TANK**)* I got some mens coming ta dig up that body. Your trips ta the graveyard is cancelled...

ROSE

You got no right!

QUEEN ESTER

You ain't got no right. You is a walkin abomination

BIGBOY

SAY YOU BEEN BUILDIN YO KINGDOM....

ROSE

If yo grandma got the power ta cuss a whole mass a generations look like I got the power to start turnin some a that cussin round... I ain't no abomination -- matter fact I believe the Lord might look down and smile on me every once in a while. Y'all tole me I gots power in the blood. I reckon that's true, I reckon the livin got jes bout as much power as the dead specially if the dead won't livin right in the first place.

QUEEN ESTER

Big Boy, you can git back ta town and get diggin, or git locked up.

BIGBOY

SATAN WE GONNA TEAR YO KINGDOM DOWN

QUEEN ESTER

I'm goin ta git that body. *(exits)*

TANK

See if I don't git there before you. Y'all feel like diggin over me?

*(**TANK** starts to exit)*

Plays

ROSE

Tank?

TANK

This some'em I gotta go on do, Miss Rose. Ride back wit yo grandma n'em. *(exits)* If they comin fa my baby, they gon hafta take me, too.

MAMA ALICE

*(**ROSE** slowly walks to **MAMA ALICE** and hugs her.)* Come on, now... I got ta git back fore Shortcake burn the house down tryna cook... You know, cain't nobody make yo peach cobbler.

SCENE 8

Later that evening.

HATTIE *and* **SHORTCAKE** *are in bed.*

HATTIE, *who is fiending, sneaks out of bed and searches the house for money. She spends some time doing this and fighting her urge. After losing the battle, she goes into Shortcake's pants, takes his wallet and sneaks from the house.*

After some time, **SHORTCAKE** *realizes* **HATTIE** *is not in bed. In a panic, he yells for her.*

An ambulance and fire truck are heard in the distance.

SCENE 8A

Lights up on **TANK** *at Sweetboy's gravesite. He is laughing hysterically as he covers the grave and talks to Sweetboy. The laugh becomes a cry at some point in his monologue.*

TANK

Hey, baby. Yo mama bout to have a fit. Even been down ta the courthouse raisin hell. They say they coming for you. I'm takin a chance bein out here. Even in death we takin chances tryna get to each other... *(Pulls out Sweetboy's purse and lays it on the grave)* I know you been cussin me out. Honey, I forgot all about it. Me an Soot was tryna get you dressed and tryna plan the funeral and I jes forgot. I know you don't go nowhere without yo pocketbook. *(pause)* But, I keep tellin you the Lord work in mysterious ways. Cause chile! Could you see who all showed up at yo funeral? Honey, Miss Thomasina had huh big ass in a skin-tight leopard suit. Come steppin in late talkin bout didn't nobody call huh personally, but she made it. Soot say, "It ain't but three peoples here, and they all got calt. Look like if we wanted you to make it we woulda calt you. But, since you here, go on, have a seat." Thomasina eyes oughta be permanately rolled up in the corners of huh eyelids. But, she ain't had enough yet. Come askin me can she sang "Amazin Grace" whilst the folks view the body. I tried to tell huh the program was full. But she kept pushin, so, chile, I had to tell huh the truth. "Thomasina," I said, "Sweetboy left specific instructions in case you showed up at his services: one - 'hold on to your purses and wallets cause you might not see em no mo,' and two - 'do not let huh sang.' Now, this Sweetboy's day, jes have a seat." And Soot say, "And sit on them sticky ass fingers." Chile, maybe the Lord made me forget yo purse fo a reason; Thomasina woulda probly snatched it right on out the casket.

Mama calt over to the house the other day. Can you believe that? After all these years she gon finally admit she know where I stay. She know how long we been together an she ain't said shit bout being sorry you gone. Come talkin bout, "See where this lifestyle lead you?" Talkin bout I can come on back home if I leaves my associates alone. You woulda been proud of me, I hung up the phone. Dead in huh ear. She ain't calt me in eight years an she live right roun the corner, an she gon call for that?

Did you like the casket? Bigboy made it. I got the wood and he made it and painted it gold. Made Halbert's casket look like a matchbox...

You woulda found all this shit so funny. You woulda helped me see inside this. You always do that.

Baby, I forgot to call Annie to tell huh. She showed up to give you your vitals and brang yo medication and had a fit, fainted cross the railin of the front porch, draws all up in my face. Shit, I almost fainted....

MAMA ALICE runs up on the porch.

*There is a shift in time and space in that what has happened (the story **MAMA ALICE** is telling) is happening. Individual spaces merge, each player is witness and participant in the action.*

MAMA ALICE

*(Thinking **SHORTCAKE** is in the house)*

Shortcake! Git up. You ain't gonna believe what I'm bout ta tell ya xcept I'm yo grandmama what's tellin ya an I ain't never lied ta ya yet. Now, I was on my way back from Rose's -- I have ta tell you bout that later... Anyway, Lois Funchess come runnin up in the hill talkin bout the pastor hisself done called a special meetin. Hmmph. I show couldn't magine what that might be fa -- everybody know the pastor come from Jackson two days a week: Sunday fa church and Wednesday fa prayer meetin. Hmmph. Couldn't magine nuthin bout this special meetin, but jes show as the Lord sittin on high shakin his head ova Grove Hill, couldn't nobody magine what we seent in that church house.

BIG BOY

*JESUS THE MAN I LONG TO SEE
OH, TELL ME WHERE IS HE?

MAMA ALICE

Now, Queen Ester had decided since she couldn't git BigBoy to dig that boy back up and burn the body like she wanted, she gon send for some big mens from Jackson to do the diggin. Well, they out there diggin – Tank hollahin, laid all out on Sweetboy's plot – and the big menz just diggin, diggin up the dead in the middle of the night. While all this goin on, everybody havin trouble wit they nightly scripture readin, peoples tried to open the Holy book, the verses is stained wit blood. Peoples tried to git on they knees fa prayer an theys feelin nails bustin through they kneecaps.

BIG BOY

GO DOWN AND SEARCH AMONG THE POOR

PERHAPS YOU'LL FIND HIM THERE

MAMA ALICE

So, Queen Ester send Big Boy round ta the church - him bein the janitor an all - ta git the Holy book out the church ...Lois say since she the treasure she give him a lilt extra this week if he take the Holy book from house ta house let peoples read theyselves a scripture fore they rest they eyes. Big Boy say okay.

BIG BOY

IF I SHOULD SEE HIM HOW WILL I KNOW HIM

FROM ANY OTHER MAN?

HE WEARS SALVATION ON HIS BROW

AND CARRIES A WOUNDED HAND

---

*This is a line hymn/Dr.Watts hymn (call and response). So, when **MAMA ALICE** is speaking, **BIGBOY** should be humming the line he just sang.

MAMA ALICE

But fore he git in the church good he come out stumblin shakin like he done seent the very Lawd hisself.

BIGBOY *turns on the lights and backs out of the church.*

MAMA ALICE

Big Boy runt ta git Lois, Lois runt ta git the preacher, preacha say "call a meetin", have the peoples wait til he git there, say make sho Queen Ester be there cause all this done gone on long enough. Big Boy git everybody and when we got ta that church we like ta been livin wit the saints... I know I did... liketa fell flat on this o hip.

BIGBOY

SHOULD I BE CARRIED TO THE SKY

OF FLOWER BEDS OF EASE?

MAMA ALICE

The piano bleedin! I ain't lyin, the piano bleedin. The wood carvin Mike Sibs put up wit Jesus on the cross is burnin... but it ain't burnin but in one place -- right at the foots of Jesus... the foots a Jesus burnin up in the very house a the Lord.

BIGBOY

WHILE OTHERS FIGHT TO WIN THE PRIZE

AND SAIL THROUGH BLOODY SEAS?

MAMA ALICE

The Bible is got sores on it, puss runnin out the Bible! The Bible got the dropsy. Then fore we could magine anythang more could happen, Jesus git the dropsy, start drippin puss an blood right on in the fire. Jesus, our very Lord and savior sittin up in the church house wit the dropsy. Hmmph.

BIGBOY

SHOULD **EARTH AGAINST MY SOUL ENGAGE

AND FIREY DOTS BE HURLED

** The devil

MAMA ALICE

Preacher say it ain't right decent ta try ta pray ta the Lord without no Bible specially wit the pulpit fillin up wit enough blood an puss fa a baptism. The peoples say "we know how ta stop it" say if Queen Ester Wade lives up ta huh title as the mothah a the church say everythang be alright. Everybody say if Queen Ester don't git them mens out the graveyard disturbin the dead, they gon do it theyselves. Preacher say that bout the finest idea he done heard all day.

MAMA ALICE	**BIGBOY**
Say if he hada knowed all this	THEN I CAN SMILE AT
was goin on why he'da been	SATAN'S RAGE
up Grove Hill fore now	AND FACE A FROWNING WORLD
when he cain't even say no	
holy prayer in the church cause	
the church ain't clean. Somebody	
say "We betta git Miss Adaline	
what live down the road on the	
Pearl River." Somebody else say,	
"We ain't brangin no root woman	
up in our holy tabernacle." Say	
"Queen Ester can stop it!"	
But Queen Ester stubborn. Say	
the thangs she do wit huh chillen	
is tween huh and huh god.	
Then, we heard it...	

Lights up on **HATTIE** *returning home*

HATTIE

Candy every time I look around you gone. Don't make me come after you. *(pause)* Candy! *(running into the street.)*

SHORTCAKE

Hattie!

MAMA ALICE

Seem like Hattie -- the onliest one Queen Ester thank she got left-- done went crazy. Say she seent huh baby run in the street. Hmmph, po lil Candy been dead. Hattie run out in the street ta save a child already dead, screamin...

HATTIE

Candy, Candy, baby come ta Mama...

A screech is heard, a thud, then silence. Lights fade on **HATTIE**.

MAMA ALICE

Everybody took off runnin like Republicans at the Armageddon. When they gets there, Hattie dead.

Lights up in **MISS QUEEN ESTER**. *She rocks and cries.*

MAMA ALICE

(emerging from crowd, to **QUEEN ESTER***)*

Queen Ester, you got ta let huh go.

QUEEN ESTER

No!

TANK

Po thang...

MAMA ALICE

She gone, Ester... let huh go...

QUEEN ESTER

No, Lord... not this...

Men take **HATTIE'S** *body away.* **SHORTCAKE** *rushes to her.*

MAMA ALICE

I guess they still waitin ta take Hattie away, I come on home. Pastor say much as he hate consortin wit the devil, he gon git Miss Adaline from down the Pearl River ta least bring some a that root powder over ta the church fore it burn flat down ta the ground. Hmmph. We gon stay in the house and hope it ain't too late. One thang my mama always tole me-- God rest huh soul -- is you ain't got ta have no fancy fixins ta pray. I'ma pray, you can pray wit me if you wants.

QUEEN ESTER
She my only livin baby. I'll git huh out firs thang in the mornin.
MAMA ALICE
The mornin a be too late, Queen Ester. We gotta go now.
ROSE
(ROSE to SOOT) Soot. Soot, baby... *(holding her face up to look into her eyes)* Soot, look that snake in the eye, ast him do he wanna be a belt or some new shoes?

BIGBOY
RUN, MARY, RUN

RUN, MARTHA, RUN

RUN, MARY, RUN, I SAY

YOU GOT A RIGHT TO THE TREE OF LIFE.

YOU GOT A RIGHT YOU GOT A RIGHT

YOU GOT A RIGHT TO THE TREE OF LIFE

finis

Plays

~ Cruising In The Name Of Love ~
(A Monologue)
Charles W. Harvey

Location: Any Mall or any place where an abundance of men are passin
Time: 1980's

AT RISE: (Music Optional) Tina Turner's song "Addicted to Love" can be heard in the background. Donny dressed in a suit and tie with hair curled and slick cruises a variety of men. His movements are very exaggerated and dancelike. He talks to any audience he has.

DONNY

Ooh baby, that is one hot piece of trade. Yes indeed, honey. That one's a man's man with his square face. I like a square face on a man. Means he's solid--all man. Now look at the buns on Mr. Smooth Chocolate there. Chile, if I get my hands on them, I'd be his little *Miss Sunbeam*. Uh oh, here comes a chest of a chest. Even his muscles got muscles. I'd give two lifetimes to be that leather vest he's wearing. Ohh now look at that. Hey you! Excuse me. Did you drop a mayonnaise jar down your crotch before you zipped up your jeans? I'd better shut myself up. I'm running all the men away actin' like a slut. I love men too much to chase them away. I love 'em so much they chase *me* away.

"You drowning me! You drowning me," a guy screamed at me. Shoot all I was doin' was calling his ass fifty-four times a day. Yes I love my men.

... Get outta here! Why you act so surprised? Just because I got on a suit don't mean I'm some stuffed up boardroom girl. I work at Penny's here in the mall--in cookery. I'm tryin' to get into men's underwear--*for real*. That's where I want to do my cooking. So don't let this suit fool you, honey. I love men. Ain't nothin' no woman can do for me, except have my baby.

... Yeah girl, I want a baby--a boy baby. I wish I could get one by a white girl. I want me a pretty baby, yellow just like my first boyfriend Robert

Ray. Well really Robert Ray wasn't *my* first boyfriend. He was my *sister's* boyfriend.

. . . Oh stop actin' so shocked like you ain't never lusted after your sister's man, or even your Mama's. Don't make me go there. I been knowin' some of you girls for years. Shit. Anyway it was Billy who was my first boyfriend--not the first man I had, but the first one I could call a boyfriend instead of a blurry memory.

. . . I'm so silly, talkin to some of you like I been knowin you for years. My name is Donny. And you are? I know--just some nosy girls tryin' to get in my business.

(Sees another fine guy)

. . . Ooh girl, look over there at Mr. Honey Roasted. Hey you! Are you Tyson's twin brother? Well fuck you too and double fuck that fish you're with. I tell you, fish can sure put a ring in a Brother's nose. A piece of fish is what spoiled me and Billy. This is how I found out about the tuna. At first when spent the night with me, we'd lay there all cuddled up like a pair of spoons and fall asleep after doing the nasty.

. . . The nasty, baby. You know what the nasty is. Don't get all innocent and shit on me. I saw you at the *Tree Trunk*. And you was not on your knees studying leafology either. Anyhow Billy started having to leave after he got his rocks off. He gave me the excuse about having to work the next day. I told him--I said, "Baby, you always been a working man, but you used to let me fix breakfast for you." He said, "Yeah but I need time to dress for work." I said, "Why can't you bring your suit over here like you been doin?" He'd lie and say, "Oh I don't want to wrinkle it in the car."

He'd leave and I'd call his house later that night, but no Billy boy. He then started tellin' me he couldn't get in the bed at all. He wanted me to give him a blow job while he sat in the chair with his pants down. I said no way! I ain't no street walker. If me and a man is going to do the do, then I want it to feel like love. I want cuddlin' and huggin'. Billy stopped bothering me about the blow job. But I could feel him rushin' things like when we made love--expecting me to satisfy him real quick like I'm some kind of fast food meal. I didn't like that at all, girl. I want to be loved. I want love to be a warm quilt around my shoulders. I want low lights. I want the rhythm from your breath on my neck to make my toes curl. Say poems in my ears. Strum my back softly like it's a bass violin, nigguh. Love is not standin' up in a bathroom with your dick in a hole lettin' a pair of lips smack on you. Love is not sitting up in Club Boyland buying every stanky breath line being blown in your face. *"Hey, baby, you so fine. Just let me kiss your little toe. I swear that's all I want to do."* That ain't nothin but dick and bourbon talkin' to you.

One dreary morning I was lying in bed thinking about all of the changes Billy was putting me through and wondering what little queen Billy was sleeping with. Everytime I caught up with one of Billy's dilly dallies, he'd make it up to me with a sofa or lamp, or some other trinket. Sometimes I wanted to catch him so I could pretend to be mad and get him to buy me something. But then again a whole lot of times I wished there hadn't been nothing to catch. A lamp or a dining table is a poor substitute for honesty.

I got up and called my friend Michael. Michael ain't nothin' but an ol' messy slut. I says to Michael, "I want you to do me a favor. When Billy leaves here, I want you to follow him and tell me where he's goin'." That huzzy tells me he ain't got no gas. I had to promise to buy him some gas. I tell you, that boy don't do nothin' for nobody unless they give him somethin. That's how he got his apartment furnished. Although everything looks mismatched--a purple chair, a green couch--blue cups, orange saucers. Nothin' in that "Gimme Queen's" house matches. But don't tell him I said so.

Anyhow, Billy comes over that night and we mess around. We lay there for a few minutes afterwards. Sure enough at nine o'clock he has to go. I walk him to the door and give him a peck on the cheek. He just says "bye" and walks on. I saw him pull out of the parking lot and I saw Michael pull out behind him. I said to myself I'm goin' to get the lowdown on this shit. I laid awake with thoughts about the sweetness and pain of love. The sweetness of love when your ass is floatin' up there with the clouds and the wind on your neck reminds you of lips kissing you. The rain takes you back to all them times you took showers together. And the sun reminds you of those hot nights of passion. Love--the stuff that can alter the history and civilizations of moons far away. A man's love is the reason I exist. At least I hope it was love and not hate disguised as love that made my Daddy come home one cool sensuous September night and pour himself into my Mama. Love and a little whiskey to get the fire going. Love, love, loooove . . . A man's love is the reason why I'm one-eyed today. Yes it is.

[Donny mimics "FORMER LOVER"]

FORMER LOVER

(Sweet and Sensuous)

But, baby, I hit you because I saw you talking to *him* and I *love* you!

DONNY

But my eye!

FORMER LOVER

But I *love* you.

DONNY

There is a dark hole where my eye used to be.

FORMER LOVER

If you leave me, I'll have a dark hole in my heart.

DONNY

But my eye. My eye, man!

FORMER LOVER

But I *love* you. Please come back to me.

DONNY

(Covers good eye)

How can I come back to you? I can't see you.

FORMER LOVER

Baby, don't play games with me. I *love* you.

DONNY

My eye that you carry in your coat pocket loves you.

FORMER LOVER

Baby, please stop torturing me.

DONNY

I'm tortured.

FORMER LOVER

If you don't come back to me, I'll kill myself.

DONNY

Go ahead.

FORMER LOVER

I love you. Please forgive me.

DONNY

(Pause)

I don't know.

FORMER LOVER

Listen, if you come back to me, I'll pluck my own eye out.

DONNY

Why?

FORMER LOVER

To prove I love you. I love you with all my heart.

DONNY

I don't know.

(Donny returns to character)

DONNY

And I don't know. I even wonder today if he really loved me; if he's walking around with two eyes in his coat pocket--mine and his own. I wonder if he's looking for me so he can show me that he really loved me. Then I close my good eye and really hate that man. I hate him and his *love* with all the bitterness I can find in my heart.

Oh shit! I've gotten away from my story. My brain is just like a vegetable strainer. Don't know what you gonna find trapped in the bottom. Michael calls me later that night and he's laughing. I say, "What you laughing about, bitch?" He say, "Girl, you ain't goin to believe this shit." "Tell me. Tell me," I scream. Michael says, "Honey your trade is at fish's house."

"Fish? You a lyin' bitch," I say to Michael. "You don't believe me? Donny girl come and see for yourself," Michael tells me.

I go bangin' on the fish's door at two a.m. and calling Billy's name. She leans out the window--tits hanging over the window sill like they're full of rocks. "What the fuck do you want?" she screams. I say, "I want my man, Bitch." The door never opened.

I cried for weeks. I played Natalie Cole over and over on my stereo. Everytime she sang *"Cry Baby"* I cried right along with her. It was me singing to Billy--telling him *welcome back home, Daddy*. But Billy never came back. He just disappeared. I still love him. I imagine in a way he still loves me--in a man's way, cool and distant.

I heard she had a baby for Billy. I understand she's kind of mean to it. Goes off and leaves him by himself. I thought about calling the Child Welfare Office on her and seeing if I could get that baby. I know how to love a child. You have to hug it a lot, make it go to school, and make it go to church. You have to put God in its soul or else it won't be nothin' but a rotten apple. That's what my Mama did. She gave me a whole lot of love and a whole lot of church.

(Sings a short medley of Gospel songs)

DONNY

Ooh I was hot. Honey, let me tell you about them Sunday mornings. The church was always packed. Fine young men strutted like birds in their blue, red, black, or green suits with the shoes to match. We greeted each other, adjusting our ties or pulling at a sleeve cuff to show we had on something new. The women paraded in hats unlike anything you can imagine. One Sister wore a hat as round and brown as one of Mama's cakes. Everytime she sat in front of me, my mouth started watering. Sister Hocklight's hat reminded me of something George Washington might of wore. Her hat was shaped like a triangle and had a big ol' black rooster feather on the front of it. In whatever direction she snapped her face, that tail feather snapped too.

When we weren't pouring tea about how much our suits cost, we carried on over the new Deacon's cute high yellow son. "Girl, did you see him staring at me?" . . . "That boy ain't stuttin' your boney butt" . . . "He likes the meat on these bones." . . . "I think he had a hard on when he spoke to me." . . . "You know he wears a size thirteen shoe" . . ."When he goes to the restroom I'm goin' to follow him." . . . Now you wouldn't do that in the church house would you?" . . . "Honey, I'd do it on the altar". . .

All of this went on in the "Rec Room" behind the church. In the sanctuary we were the "angels of sanctomonium" That's what Sister Hocklight called us. We'd march into the Church in front of the Senior Choir dressed in our red robes and with heads held so high, we was almost too good to be touched by God. After Service everybody went over to Wyatt's Cafeteria and sit up in that big dining room like we was the last queens. My mama laughing, the choir voices ringing in my ears, the tinkling of silverware against plates--all of those sounds were heaven for me. There was no silent dad to make me gloomy--no fussin' and fightin' with my brothers.

I think Sunday mornings would have lasted forever if Harry and Paul hadn't been caught in the tool shed behind the Church. They weren't doing no harm. Just kissin' on one another. No more of a sin than what men and women folks do.

"Excuse me, Pastor Booker, I caught these two young <u>men</u> in acts of ungodliness and unmanliness. And I don't think the 'Chutch' ought to stand for that." Reverend Booker couldn't do nothing but stand there like a stuffed bear. *"And furthermore, Pastor, I believe this 'Chutch' has been catering to and encouraging sin by having this Youth Choir. I'm a fourth generation Hocklight. I serve on the Usher Board, The Mission Board, The Charity Committee, and if you remember, the Pastor's Anniversary Committee. Why that tool shed was the very first Burning Bush Baptist Church Sanctuary . . ."*

Next Sunday there wasn't no youth choir, and no Harry and Paul. I sat next to my Mama 'cause nobody would look at me funny. She'd ask them what in the hell was they looking at. Pastor Booker preached a long sermon about *"Homosexuuaalitity."* His whole speech was about Sodom and Gomorrah and how the angels of the lord had to fight off the funny men and how God destroyed those cities because of the funny men, and so on and so on he droned. Sister Hocklight sat in the front pew in a new red feathered hat looking as puffed up as a frog. I stopped going to Church soon after that. I decided I'd rather stay home with silent dad and cook Sunday dinner.

I love my Mama though. She's probably the only woman I'll ever love. I used to help her beat her cakes. *"Donny, put more sugar in that batter . . . Beat that some more, you see all of them lumps . . . and you know I don't sell no lumpy cakes . . ."*

Mama didn't believe in no electric mixer either. Didn't like mechanical things touching her works of art. A cake made with sweat is the best kind she said. When all of the beating and mixing quieted down, Mama would get on the telephone and chat about her "Soap Operas." I'd sit on the back steps and listen to the flies buzz. Way off in the distance I'd see the stick arms of my Brothers waving in the air. Their voices sounded like birds chirping. I never did play with them. They didn't want me to. They'd call me a little sissy and throw pebbles at my back. So I stayed close to Mama's cakes rising with sweetness through the glass oven door.

You know you got to love something. Grandma say if you don't love anything, God will make sure you become dust mighty quick. "Can't live without loving," she'd say. Sometimes you can't live with loving. But I guess you're better off spending a lifetime trying to love. If you can't love a people person, maybe a plant will do. But I'd rather love a person. A man person.

(Slightly ashamed)

Well sometimes I did what I thought was love. I messed around in the back of bookstores and upstairs in the dark at the Mens Club. It was so dark in there, you didn't know who was who. You might have been messin' with your Brother and never knowed it. Maybe some of them times in the dark it was Robert Ray. I did smell the perfume my Sister wears on some guy's body. I felt his face and it was square . . .

What do you mean by "My Fantasy?" You queens need to quit judging people--talking about I ain't got no scruples. I'm just telling the truth. My Robert Ray did play football, did have a dimple on his cheek, a cute sixty-three red GTO and he did pat my ass when nobody was lookin'. So why couldn't it been him in the dark at the Men's Club? I don't have to lie. I've had some good things in my fucked up life! And love is one of those things. And if I make it to heaven, I'm going to love God like a man ought to. Thank you very much.

(Music starts. Donny resumes cruising. Fade to black)

~ blue's song ~
Keelyn Bradley

Characters

Billie Holiday — a murdered woman

Bishop Abraham Hunger — a preacher

I-Be — a lawn jockey

Ishmael Benjamin Israel — a writer/director

Young Mary — an actress/ witness

A workshop production of ***blue's song*** was presented at the 1999 Philadelphia Fringe Festival, as part of its BYOV (Bring Your Own Venue) series of independent productions. Keelyn Bradley, Director/Videographer. Takeshi Hatori, Videographer/Lighting/Sound. Amadi Braxton, Costumes/Props. Gail Lloyd, Videographer/Editor. Video Production: Colleen Bartley, Inja Coates, Chetana Jois. Lorenza Collins, Publicity. Cast: Linda Waters, Hasan Andrews, Samuel F. Reynolds, Valentine King. Very special thanks to Artistic Directors Am Weaver (The Art Sanctuary) and Michael LeLand (Theatre Double) for allowing the use of their theater spaces for rehearsals and performances.

The Set

A Church in Philadelphia. Cloth like that which might be draped over a catafalque, covered in soot, suspended from behind an altar. This is where the memories and dreams of the congregation are projected. Next to the altar, an empty chair. This is where Young Mary will sit to take the 'witness stand'. A gaudy royal blue, velvet banner with shiny gold letters hangs from a gold post to the right of the altar. The altar is slightly askew, appearing as if it might topple over at any moment. The banner reads "All Saints Church/ Defenders of the Spirit." This is the sanctuary. On the other side of the stage (far right, upstage) a fragmented corner of a wall indicates another room. A bedroom. It too appears to have been damaged by fire. It is empty except for an iron-cast bed, resembling one that might be found in a hospital in the late nineteenth, early twentieth century. To the right of the bed there is a window suspended in mid-air that looks out onto nothing. There is a chair directly in front of the window. This is where Bishop will sit. In the middle of the stage, between the sanctuary and the bedroom, there is a flight of stairs that lead to nowhere. Yellow "crime scene" tape cordons the parameter of the stage.

There are video cameras placed at different points throughout the set. The church is monitored through closed-circuit television (CCTV). There will be groupings of television monitors to the right and left of the stage. Each monitor will show an image captured by one of the cameras. Ideally, there will also be monitors situated throughout the audience so that each member of the audience can 'act' as a CCTV operator—choosing to 'watch' from different cameras.

Plays

Scene 1: *Somewhere on a journey.*

[The sounds of a storm: wind beating and falling rain. The sound of bells ringing. The sound of a train in the distance, tracks shaking].

A form enters the dark theater from the back of the audience. A strikingly beautiful, middle-aged black woman appears. She is dressed in a tattered, Victorian-lace wedding gown of high collar and long-sleeves. She walks down through the center aisle of the audience as you might expect at a wedding. A long, endless veil of white tulle, knotted the entire distance of its length, enwraps her body, binding her arms and legs. Her every step is stilted and belabored. She slowly steps onto the stage, dragging the veil behind her. As she steps into the strangely unreal, dim light, we notice her frightening appearance. She is partly bald with burnt patches of short, kinky matted hair. She is Billie Holiday. She stops and looks around for a moment.

Billie:
>before you share
>
>your table
>
>know you don't need
>
>too much
>
>before you give your heart
>
>know his love
>
>won't be enough

(She steps completely into the light.)

>before you sale
>
>your ticket
>
>give back the luggage
>
>buy a piece of land
>
>before you settle down
>
>swear your right hand
>
>know truth
>
>won't fill
>
>the judge's courtroom

won't keep the house
from disrepair
won't keep emptiness
from hurting
when no one's there to share

been too long in solitude
too long in solitude
been too long in solitude

(She walks up the set of stairs that lead to nowhere. The sound of wind beating and rain falling. The sound of the train, further away in the distance.)

[Blackout]

Plays

Scene 2: *Remembrances.*

[Silent video/film projection appears on the catafalque-like cloth that hangs behind the altar and continues until the final scene.]

These are dreams...memories...history and herstory...critical points of absence...geography that has been lost or forgotten...tiny bits of paper once written on...reminders   grocery   lists   things   to   do   i   love yous...someone's obsession...scraps of cloth leftover...from a quilt...sewn together between job hunting lovemaking   having babies   arguments   homework   church   holidays   birthdays anniversaries family reunions civil rights meetings   freedom marches deadlines and funerals...These are invisible rool/outes returning in the middle of a thought...caught in a daydream...broken by a word glance figure of speech   time   system...that reminds you of when you first learned skin had another name...somehow became associated with your obscured reflection...and intense loneliness...could be the cause of your disappearance and death...when you first discovered that that funny looking little thing...your parents had a nickname for...grew hard when you touched it...felt like...you wanted to save it for the next day...hide it in your hands like a secret you didn't want to get out...had the ability to make women and men stupid...give birth to violent fantasies...chase you from home with disseminations of Christian suffering ... train dogs to track diagrams of your flesh...as strangers gossip about recent castrations...carve fallacies of you in walls...as if you were responsible for the destruction of their fathers...This is speech failing...alienated space left by abandoned dreams...secant caves...mysteries multiplying in metaphors...that converge in God's poetry...dawn opening her eyes...to crisis cresting in marble footprints...unmarked plots...once...a man or woman...who loved   cried   laughed   cussed...the strain...hoped   for   tomorrows...horizons...stolen   by   lynch   mobs...fragile maniacs...who captured a cacophony of mangled echoes...coveting all that was left of mutilated lives...with mechanical precision...mementos in a theater of death...30 frames per second...

A short 30min, silent video-film (shot on hi-8 video and super-8 film) was produced for the 1999 workshop production. A video graphic rendering of dream sequences, memories, imagined scenarios, and historical photographs was created from staged improvisations with the actors.

Scene 3: *Bishop's bedroom.*

A tall, strong-looking, handsome black man lies in bed, looking up at the ceiling. He is stiff as a corpse. He is naked, except for a white sheet covering his body. His naked arms and feet are exposed. He is Bishop Abraham Hunger. There is only silence and sick, yellow light that fills the room.

Bishop: (lying in bed) When I was a boy, I spoke the dreams of dead men. I was a sleepwalker among the devastation of shadows, bending light in trees of rotting flowers. I roamed the hallways and attic of the house in chaos, opening doors to rooms filled with men shouting at their blood stained reflections. At first, I was afraid of their naked and dismembered bodies. They cradled their genitals in their hands like treasures stolen from them, masses of mutilated flesh. Their faces hung from their skulls, eyes swollen with painful memory. The dead men spoke of others like them. Men whose curses bore annihilated suns. To forget the dead men of my dreams, I drank from the jars of liquor my mother sold out the back of the house to keep us from starving. I never met my father. My mother said he was lynched while I was still in her womb. He was a decorated veteran of World War I. Awarded the Purple Heart and Bronze Star. But to me he was the dignified man in the picture on the wall. A Black Jesus we waited to return. My mother thought the dreams were a message from my dead father. She'd ask, "Bishop, remember the words of the dead men I hear you mouth in your sleep? Have they seen your father? He is lost among the men you grieve. You must wait with the murdered men at night so they are not lost to the legend of our songs. Don't allow their stories to be buried beneath the haunted trees where their loved ones gather to mourn." For years, I dreamt of their mutilated bodies, lamented their exile. I used to speak of their murders to the Harlem pimps and racketeers, who gave me a nickel to run errands for them up and down Lennox Avenue. "Hey little boy," they'd holler, "come here." I'd come running, as if I had heard my dead father calling to me. "Tell me about those ghosts you always dreamin' about?" they would ask. They cried for the men and women they'd left behind in the south. I had never seen grown men cry. The tears softened their mean faces. I saw memory eclipse their rage; their rowdy, gold-toothed grins turn to anguish. I was no longer just their storyteller but a messenger of shame and sorrow. I hid in every dark corner of the city to avoid being asked to midwife another diseased birth. I drank to forget. When drinking no longer quieted the voices, I smoked reefers and anything else I could get my hands on. One night, to escape the strangers, who by now were approaching me as if I had the ability to keep grief from visiting their doorstep with my recollections of the dead men, I entered a church. A choir of tongues lured me from the glittering humiliation of the streets. All my extravagant ruins collapsed in devout praise, when The Reverend said, "God is a black sun in the morning!" I wanted to be a star in the sky. I wanted to fall into the ocean like rain, stir ancient sand into a celebration of noise, struggle against the deep, underwater currents of my people. I thought that if I became a preacher I could expose the paradox of blackness, repute its cataclysmic cross. I thought that I could remove one more stone from the invincible mouth of that tormented tomb. I have never believed God could rescue me from the purulent landscapes of all those lynched men. I have never been a true believer. Still, I wait for Black Jesus. I wait by the window that looks out into nowhere and watch dead men pace the night, searching barren trees for their remains. I am no longer haunted by dreams. They have been swept away with the ashes of Billie. They are the dead men of her song.

Scene 4: *The sanctuary.*

I-Be enters the sanctuary. He is a dwarf. He wears a lawn jockey's uniform and carries a lantern.

I-Be: (laughing) Bishop was a drug addict and career criminal by the time he was twenty-one. His mother ran a bootleg and a whorehouse out of her home. Bishop definitely never knew his father. He might have been a war hero. Who would know the truth? By the time Bishop was eighteen, his mother, Ms. Doris, had married three husbands younger than she, and they all mysteriously died before she did. When she finally died, not one church in the city would give her a funeral. Billie knew about Bishop's sordid past. Everybody knew about him. She was desperately in love with him. She could forgive him for being a man, for wanting to fuck every woman who had something between her legs for him to conquer. He had slept with half the women in the church. Billie's father, The Reverend, despised him because he reminded him of his own limitations. Billie's mother left The Reverend because he was a liar and a cheat. Billie was just three years old. After The Reverend died, Bishop became the pastor of the church. He spent hours looking out the window praying to "Black Jesus" and calling out to "the dead men in his dreams." She thought her love would heal his suffering. Every bit of the church's money was spent on his heroin addiction and gambling debts. Billie was always giving a concert somewhere to pay for his sins. She toured the country singing about the dead men in Bishop's dreams. The dead men haunted her. By the end of her life, Billie was shooting up four or five times a day.

(He sets the lantern down and replaces it with a serving tray. He enters Bishop's bedroom. He walks with quick, abrupt gesticulations.)

I-Be: I brought your clothes and some coffee. (Puts a black suit on the foot of the bed.)

Bishop: (Sits on the edge of the bed, takes the hot coffee, blows on it a few times, and then sips it. Irritated.) Look at the cynical black characters we have become. I feel like I am being pecked to death by crows. We are nothing more than what people expect to see at a crime scene. (He stands up, holding the sheet loosely around his waist, and walks downstage. He stares out into the audience, as if trying to make out their faces. After a long moment, he walks back to the bed and begins dressing.)

I-Be: (Studying a list he pulls from his back pocket.) Do you plan to say a few words of remembrance for Our Lady? I think you should. Her death was a tragic loss. Her body was nearly burnt to ashes. (A long pause.) You are final about your plans to leave the church, I presume.

(Bishop stands up half-dressed and barefoot. His shirt is unbuttoned; his head appears to have sunk down, between his shoulders. He stares out the window that looks out onto nothing, almost catatonic. I-Be turns Bishop around to face him, straightens up his slouching body and buttons his shirt.)

Bishop: (His back to the audience, facing the window, occasionally looking back.)

[There is a camera above the window. The cameras allow the audience to see him from every possible point of view. What they cannot see with the unaided eye they will see in the television monitors. Projection of remembrances (from scene 2) continues.]

Have they come to glamorize this decay? Are they expecting profound speeches on The State of Black Life? Or hoping to get a glimpse at the inner-workings of the criminal, black mind? Maybe they're hoping to hear the silent world of dead men.

I-Be: (Buttoning Bishop's shirt.) Have I ever told you the story of how Polyphemus, the Cyclops, regained his sight? This was long after Odysseus and his men left him on the shore, mocking his blindness.

Bishop: (Staring out the window.) I have seen more visions of Black Jesus. He is returning with Young Mary. They are walking amid hyacinths that bloom for eternity. She is pregnant with my child. We are a family. We are idealistic and in love.

I-Be: (Begins tying Bishop's necktie.) The Cyclops lived as a blind man for a hundred years before his father, Poseidon, returned his sight, giving him two good eyes. He had fallen in love with a beautiful sea nymph, Galatea. The Cyclops chased the sea nymph all around the island, but blind and clumsy he did not catch her. She laughed at his grotesque appearance as he sang mournful love songs to her, at the shore of thrashing sea.

Bishop: Young Mary is with Black Jesus who braids lilac and Queen Anne's lace in her beautiful, long hair while she recites my letters. They are hiding in a town where people have abandoned their memories for dreams. They are safe because no one can remember a time when they did not live there, and so there is nothing to fear.

I-Be: Where are you going to go? Everywhere you go the dead men will follow.

(I-Be begins strangling Bishop with the necktie. Bishop struggles to his knees. He manages to release himself from I-Be's grip.)

Bishop: (shocked) You are teetering on the brink of full-fledged insanity! Have you settled for your cramped humiliation? (He rises to his feet.)

I-Be: (outraged, with clinched fists and crying) I want things to be as they were!

[Blackout]

[Projection of remembrances are seen]

Scene 5: *The Church.*

[The sound of the train is further in the distance.]
Billie appears, bound by her veil.

Billie: (singing)
love is a sorrow song
make a woman forget
about her sins
love is a sorrow song
make a woman
throw commonsense out the door
take a cheatin man in

love make a woman
want a man so much
she forget to sleep
forget to wash
her clothes
can't hardly eat

love make a woman
want a man so much
she forget to breathe
keep her down
cryin on her knees
she'd rather die
than see him leave

love is a sorrow song
make a woman wear flowers
in her hair
love is a sorrow song
make a woman lonely
to herself
and her man don't even care

(She stands alone on stage for a moment.)

[Blackout]

[Projection of remembrances are seen]

Scene 6: *Somewhere outside the church.*

Bishop is in his bedroom—sitting in a chair in front of the window that looks out onto nothing. His back is to the audience. He is fully dressed, now, in a black suit. His necktie in the same disarray in which I-Be left it. [The audience can see his expressionless face in the television monitor.]

A young man enters from the audience. He is an average looking, elegant man. He is dressed as one of the "Founding Fathers," George Washington perhaps. He wears a powdered wig and men's clothing of the late 1700's, American Federalist period. He is carrying a brown leather suitcase that he places on the stage. He is Ishmael Benjamin Israel.

Young Mary enters from the stage. The same actress who plays Billie plays her. She is wearing a black leotard and jazz skirt. She opens the suitcase and takes out a wig of long, straight black hair and cellophane mask with big, painted on eyes and pronounced smile—a costume. She puts on the costume.

I-Be enters. (He looks at Young Mary in recognition.) Young Mary, once more goes in the suitcase, pulls out two cellophane masks like hers and gives them to Ishmael and I-Be to wear. She closes the suitcase, carrying it as if she is prepared to take a trip.

[All this action takes place far downstage, between the Sanctuary and Bishop's Room. Ishmael and I-Be act out the voices of Young Mary's parents. They wear the cellophane masks for the entire scene.]

Young Mary: When I got pregnant, my father said to my mother, "Kitty no daughter of mine is going to have a bastard child by some nigger preacher!" My father was a graduate of Fisk University, where he studied the Greek Classics. He was the first black man to earn a Ph.D. from Harvard University. "Your father thinks that all preachers are poverty pimps," my mother said. "He says that 'if Negroes are going to take their place at the table it will be through education and the opportunity that education and perseverance affords,'" she imitated. She, however, was not quite sold on his black manifesto. While he spent long evenings poring over his papers, dictating the science of dreams to his secretary, she was at some speakeasy way uptown, her skin light enough to sit in the front row with white people at the Cotton Club. During the day, she lived marvelous clichés, moonlight and ambrosia, sweeping vistas and rambunctious conversations with friends, but at night she lived the blues, hummed the songs of black women singers, disheartened by the failings of the world. My parents took me out of Barnard College and sent me down south. I lived with my aunt and uncle until I had the baby. He was a beautiful child. His face looked like an angel had kissed it; chubby, dimple cheeks as soft as summer dew. I called him my "little blossom" for the two weeks I nursed him. I couldn't give him a name. I was not going to be his mother. I wanted a life on the stage. I dreamed of being in the movies and on Broadway, dancing like Cyd Charisse in Ziegfeld Follies. When I returned to New York, my father said, "Now that you've got that nigger out of your system you can resume your studies and become a teacher. Marry a good husband and have a respectable life." I wanted to be a dancer and an actress, but there were no parts for black female ingénues. I had to be either a mammy or a wench, or an exotic bird caught in some incomprehensible tragic circumstance. I was never going to dance the lead in Sleeping Beauty or exchange love verses from my balcony. Most conditions of black women are lost to imagination.

[The light changes. All the characters seem frozen in time, as though reality has been paused. Projection of remembrances continues. Ishmael steps out in front of the scene to address the audience. He removes the cellophane mask.]

Ishmael: My mother always wears black, as is if she is mourning her life. Yes, I said my mother. Well, that is who she is, you know. She acts as if she doesn't know. She only cares about her next role and her aging beauty. After all these years, she discovers that her "little bastard" is a writer and director in the theatre and can give her what she most desires—adoration that she mistakes as love. What I am is a liar. I lie about everything and take great pleasure in doing so. I lie because nothing should be sacred in life, with the exception of life itself and all things that make life worth living. The theatre should be a laboratory of lies or else it is dead religion. I know, you're probably thinking, "how does he feel to know his mother doesn't love him, may not have ever loved him?" Well, love is a question of lies. Lies are the secret ingredient of any great love affair. I see this in the face of every aging actress or dancer, for that matter, who was once idolized for their grace and beauty. She has had years of hearing nothing but how perfect her hair and makeup is under those artificial lights that distort any resemblance of reality; and how impeccable she wears her clothes. She is merely a celebrity acting-out her public's fantasies. It is only by the time she realizes that her beauty is her ugliness that she becomes a true artist. It is only when she no longer cares about the inferiorities of time showing on her face that the audience can truly see their dreams reflected in her performance.

[The light changes again. Ishmael puts on the cellophane mask and steps back into the scene with the other characters. All the characters seem to resume their place in time.]

(Young Mary notices her image in the television monitor and looks around for the camera.)

Young Mary: (to Ishmael, while fixing the image of herself in the television monitor—fixing her hair, touching-up her makeup. This is all while wearing the mask.) Why are the lights so bright? What is my character?

Ishmael: You will be playing the role of Billie Holiday.

Young Mary: But I don't sing?

Ishmael: You are returning from the groundless ground of death to confront your husband who has murdered you in your sleep.

Young Mary: Don't make me a victim of their dreams (pointing to the audience). I am an actress and a black woman. I know all too well the difficulties of trying to please an audience. Did you know I played Nina in an Orson Welles production of Chekhov's The Sea Gull?

I-Be: (Intercedes.) What Ishmael is trying to say is that the role will allow you to go so far inward until you have reached a point where you have found another reason for dying—that is your own.

Young Mary: A tragedy?

Ishmael: (To I-Be.) What I am saying is that as the guardian of this myth you have surrendered to violence and misery, which threatens the mere idea of dreaming.

I-Be: (growing defensive) I've always questioned the peace of these ruins.

Ishmael: Questions are not enough to assuage the insanity that crowds this church. Look at him (pointing to an image of Bishop on the television monitor). Waiting for Black Jesus. All those years he roamed the north Atlantic shore carrying his head in hands, spouting those empty, profane testimonies of dead men. He thinks he is fighting for black liberation. He is just another poor, down trodden nigger preaching with clinched fists.
(He reaches in his waistcoat and pulls out a piece of paper. He hands the paper to I-Be.)

I-Be: What? A plan? (Carefully looks over the paper.) Twenty-four hours isn't nearly enough time to stage a production of this magnitude. You can't be serious (looking at Ishmael). (Hysterically laughing.)

[Young Mary is still fixing the image of herself in the television monitor]

[Blackout]

[Projection of remembrances are seen]

Scene 7: *Bishop's bedroom.*

Billie enters Bishop's bedroom. She is still wearing the wedding gown, but her veil no longer binds her arms and legs. She walks up behind Bishop, who is still sitting in the chair in front of the window. [We still see his image from multiple points of view on the television monitors. In the other monitors, we see various shots of Billie and Bishop captured on camera, as if we are watching a film of the scene].

Billie: (Moving her hands across his shoulder, massaging him in a sexual way.)
Bishop Abraham Hunger. My man…my husband…my lover. You once laid your head on my naked thighs and promised devotion. Oh, how I collapsed under your handsome beauty. (Caressing his face.)

Bishop: (startled) She is nothing more than memory, the ashes of dreams.

Billie: No, Bishop. Living and breathing. I am witness to the gains of light, its reflection and shadow. Did you think that you could just make me disappear into the rage of another militant fire? Did you think that you could escape your misery by killing me? (She steps away from him.)

Bishop: (Turns back to face the window; the camera still on his face.) As a child, I was fascinated by how sunlight reflected the slightest movement. A butterfly I managed to seduce into the uncertainty of my hands.

(He stands and moves toward her; reaches out to stroke her face. She turns her head and recoils)

Billie: There is no air in the city for butterflies. Longing for the lover is as immeasurable as the years before life and as certain as its death. Can you be stronger than your vanity, or is pride all the strength you have?

Bishop: (exhausted, a whirlwind of apology and defense) All those years I believed, or wanted to believe. You reminded me of the sorrow I tried to forget. Billie, I tried to love you. I tried to love you more than you needed me. I was as haunted by your need to be loved as you were by the dead men of my dreams. It became unbearable. There is shame in belonging to absence.

Billie: The dream is a ghost. Me…a murdered woman. Breath in place of fear. Breath that nourishes blood and bones, silence swollen with the memory of history. Murdered by my husband's hands.

Bishop:
I saw you burn.
I saw you die.
I murdered you in your sleep.
I choked the last breath out of you
and watched the house burn to ashes.

Billie: I joined the record of others who had tried to overcome the inertia of sun. I am the wife that mourned her husband Bishop who prayed for the love of Black Jesus. I am the woman who was murdered in her sleep by her husband who sat in the car watching the house burn to ashes.

Bishop:
I saw you burn!
I saw you die!
I murdered you in your sleep!
I choked the last breath out of you
and watched the house burn to ashes!

[Blackout]

[Projection of remembrances disappear]

Scene 8: *The sanctuary.*

[*All the action of the stage has replaced the projection of remembrances. On the television monitors, there is only the image of Bishop's expressionless face as he sits in his bedroom with his back to the audience, looking out the window.*] *Ishmael and I-Be enter. Ishmael coaxes I-Be onto the altar. Young Mary enters, dancing as if to the rhythm and beat of drums. Ishmael stands over I-Be as he lies on the altar. I-Be looks like a limp corpse, splayed out on the altar. I-Be is laughing as Ishmael manipulates his twitching body.*

Ishmael: Stay still and open your mouth I-Be. (Pushes down on I-Be's head and chest and yanks open his jaw.) It is very important that the corpse remain stiff and opens his mouth for the purpose of releasing all his excretions and making his organs serviceable, and so vitalizing the image. (Folds I-Be's hands on his chest, like a body in a casket being prepared for public viewing.) We cannot be satisfied with just fashioning an image with the creation of a work of art in mind, but must make the work of human hands come alive.

I-Be: What difference does it make? Nothing will remain of me after I am dead. My weathered parts will fall to the ground like ruins and this ritual will only be reminiscent of them.

Ishmael: Seeing is to eyes and hearing is to ears among the dead as well as the living.

I-Be: (angrily) I will not lie down and allow you to distort me into some violent visualization of Black Nationalism! (Jumps up, off the altar.) I am an estranged African taken from the blood and bones and dust of her birth, and thrust into the lethargy of wandering shadows. I am the embodiment of the viciously grotesque hold of the slave ship and shallow shores of stigmatized light—heaving, barely conscious. I am the seventh son of the free American new world order. I exist in a perpetual time of forgetfulness, that demeaning indifference to my perpetual cruelty and suffering.

Ishmael: (Standing behind the altar.) It's the excerpts of your performance that we want to preserve. The circumstances surrounding the extremes of your desperate condition. Young Mary, perform your dance for us.

Young Mary: (Dancing.) You can watch, but it's not for your entertainment. I will not be your black bitch condemned to a life of shak'n big ass and grinning seductive smiles to cure the way down misery of ghetto strife.

(Dancing more pronounced, as she quotes from the bible. I –Be begins dancing with her, gyrating behind her.)

Young Mary: "So God made the man fall into a deep sleep. And while he slept, he took one of his ribs and enclosed it in flesh. God built the rib he had taken from the man into a woman, and brought her to the man. The man exclaimed: 'This atlas is bone from my bones, and flesh from my flesh! This is to be called woman, for this was taken from man.' This is why man leaves his father and mother and joins himself to his wife, and they become one body." (Genesis: 1:21-6).

I-Be: (Offering his arm to Young Mary.) Venus, Hera, goddess of War. Helen! Daughter of Eve...bone of my bones, flesh of my flesh.

Young Mary: (Stops abruptly.) Don't mock me you little monkey! Do I look like an evil, barbaric Roman or tragic, Greek whore to you? (pushing him in the head). I am beautiful, lavender and coral stone...

I-Be: (Laughing.) Isis, goddess of life, keeper of creation, celestial partner to Ra...

Young Mary: (Dramatically loud, as if she is greeting him through a large crowd, she opens her arms wide and walks toward him.) Why, my dear Caesar! My God! My Caesar...

(She violently stabs him. I-Be falls to the ground, and plays dead until every limb of his body dies. A moment passes. They laugh uproariously, as he rises to his feet)

Ishmael: You damn simpletons. You're not Caesar and she's no Cleopatra. Alexandria is under the sea. This is all self-deprecating minstrelsy. Let's get down to the matters at hand.

I-Be: The matters at hand! The matters at hand! You speak about it as if it were an episode of Crime Stories or Unsolved Mysteries. Let us be clear, here. We are speaking of an execution. A good ol' fashion murder. (Takes white gloves from his pocket and shoves his hands into them.) Nothing more, nothing less...in a reasonable amount of time.

Ishmael: (affected) Time is never reasonable. That jaundice worn over, ages upon ages, incarcerated in the past. Attempts to touch, caress ambivalence, protect memory, determine odds and ends—fit back together the barely visible. Time is cemented in loneliness. (He begins setting out objects on the altar: artifacts, sacraments and symbols for the ceremony to redeem their souls.)

I-Be: (Suddenly at attention, like a soldier, running around waving a sword and shield.)
Ha! The enemy! The enemy! The enemy!...

Young Mary: (Dancing, nonchalantly.) He can be a fearless leader when he's provoked.

I-Be: (Holding up a gun.) The enemy! The enemy! Bang! Bang! (Looking around, on the defense—as if at war.) Bang! Bang!...

Young Mary: No guns! For Heaven's sake, no guns! Guns and crack have stripped Blacks of all their pride and morality. Niggas aren't just murdering each other for tally marks on their thug belts. The condition has become a matter of spiritual survival.

Ishmael: Young Mary, your language is so degenerative.

Young Mary: Nigga Please! (She begins gyrating in front of I-Be.)

Ishmael: Damn you Young Mary! This is the problem. This is exactly the reason why we can't overcome this tragic suffering anthem. Tragedy is dead subject matter. We must choose our instruments for this production wisely. If it is not guns, then what shall it be, the sword or the rope? (He holds up a noose.)

I-Be: (chiding) Oh, will you please shut up Nigga.

Ishmael: (Stiffens and in a breath is about to erupt.) Now you look here...

I-Be: (sweet, coy manner) Pretty, please. I know how you revolutionary niggas are concerned about making appearances between semi-permanent dwellings in other countries. Oh, invisibility is just about the cruelest manifestation of white racist fantasy. (He begins singing and shuffling).

America, America, God shed his grace on thee…And crown thy good with brotherhood, from sea to shining sea…

Ishmael: (lashing out) You status quo chumps are so clever in clarifying the colored man's grief.

Young Mary: Will you crusaders step-off your pulpits long enough to stay on the subject: the poetics of our existence and the disputable problem of our progress.

Ishmael: There you go again, looking for an explanation where there isn't one. Now, if you would just answer the question, we wouldn't keep getting caught-up in this vapid nomenclature—the semantics of critics.

Young Mary: Do you think you can turn your blues into just anything? Pick-away at the inevitable until blackness becomes something more permanent than it really is. I have a vivid imagination but I could never write the expressions of so many desperate voices. Like many of the witnesses who testified, I too have fed on the deadly speeches of soothsayers whose prophesies cursed the people for trusting their instincts and watched the crowds repeatedly offer their nakedness with the hope that they might be saved. You all don't have the courage to confront these wounds. To say, 'yes we hate you for your asinine ways and what you are doing to us, and this hate is killing us as quickly as your oppression, and something has got to be done about it!'

Ishmael: Bravo! Bravo! You dancers can be quite the orators when your positions are threatened. You make a lovely ingénue. (Drawing nearer to Young Mary.) However, you've missed the point again, Miss. We are assassins, not the girl who dreams of riots in exclusive colored spots. We fear for our lives, and rather than plunge the depths of psychological terror we take on the wicked protections and assaulting alienation that is now absorbing a century into a millennium of drudge. We dull our imaginations. So, while the question remains conclusively intact, titillating every quizzical fantasy, there is only bereft fear. Nothing that alludes a bitter act…no evidence of pain.

[Blackout]

[The lights come up on Bishop's lifeless body. He is standing atop the stairs, where we first see Billie. He has a noose around his neck. It is the noose that we saw Ishmael hold up.]

Young Mary: (Staring at Bishops' body. mortified) Murderers… (Coming to full realization, she walks towards them to get up closer on their faces. she jumps back in terror, frantically screaming.) Murderers! Murderers! Murderers! Murderers! (She removes her mask and wig and drops them to the floor.)
[Blackout]
[When the lights come up, Young Mary is sitting in a chair next to the altar. Bishop's lifeless body is still hanging from the noose.]

I-Be: I keep telling you that those depressing French feminist philosophies cannot replace the subtlety of hate. You need to take a lover. (He tries to kiss her. Grabbing her face, he pulls her toward him, forcing himself on her.) You need a brother who can share something sweet with you and still make you feel secure.
(He grabs her waist and pulls her toward himself. She slaps him and turns away. She returns to her seat. I-Be presents her with a bouquet of artificial flowers—yellow tulips. Scared, she reluctantly takes the tulips.)

I-Be: A disgusting pain burns with so much fervor in me right now. If I was to be cut open and pulled apart to the last layers, there would be a heat so hot and a light so bright the world would fizzle, like the tiny dab of sulfur at the end of a match. (Falls to his knees, takes her feet in his hands and begins massaging them.)

Ishmael: (Simpering.) Flowers are hell to pay for the woman who dares hope that after her family is fed and her bills are paid there will be anything left to spend on a pretty bouquet.

Young Mary: (Terrified, she smells the fake flowers.) Quoting from the bible: "God said, 'you must not eat it, nor touch it, under death.' Then the serpent said to the woman, 'No! you will not die! God knows in fact that on the day you eat it your eyes will be opened and you will be like gods, knowing good and evil.'"

Ishmael: Now look, you don't need to burden us with conversation about your travails. There is no need to implicate us in your sexual relations, get us involved in your sick shit!

I-Be: (Kneeling in front of Young Mary.) I am an estranged African taken from the blood and bones and dust of her birth, and thrust into the lethargy of wandering shadows. (Strokes her feet, flicks his tongue out at her like a snake.)

Ishmael: You perverted bitch! You're ruining the entire subtlety of his performance. You manipulative, irrational bitch! (Pauses for a moment and then speaks as if motivated by emotion and thought.) I am your bastard child! I was with your father, Dubois, before he died. I placed the crown on his head, as he proclaimed himself Emperor of Alexandria, "the only free black empire in the world." I watched him become obsessed with the black power struggle, trying to explain the unintelligible matters of race, until he slipped into a maddening depression.

Young Mary: (Rises from the chair and stands.) You pigs! Murdering pigs! Is there nothing you wouldn't do to release your sorrow? Is this how you intend to reclaim our gift of sight? Is this great plan to save our souls? What you call progress? The ability to baptize blackness in castrated devotions to violated dreams. You want to give holy meaning to the bitter life on your lips while I disappear in ceremony, singing circulatory migrations of a misery you glorify. I heard the dead men of Bishop's dreams shouting at their blood stained reflections. I watched the dead men pace the night, searching barren trees for their remains. I sing the prosecutions that perish in your mouths.
  I sing the prosecutions that perish in your mouths...
  I sing the prosecutions that perish in your mouths...
  I sing the prosecutions that perish in your mouths...

(I-Be and Ishmael watch as Young Mary evolves into Billie.)

[The entire stage goes black except for a single spotlight on Billie and the vague impression of Bishop's dead body in the background. I-Be and Ishmael disappear in the blackness.]
  Billie/Young Mary: I joined the record of others who had tried to overcome the inertia of sun. I am the women you've heard your fathers and uncles and their friends speak about as danger zones: the whore flaunting mockery between her thighs, having the ability to birth death from her womb; the celluloid mammy stomping-out demands, interrogating her mistress' lovers until every persecution feels like sex. I am the girl who dreams of riots and revolutions against the tyrannical principles of 'blind justice'. I am the wife that mourned her husband Bishop who prayed for the love of Black Jesus. I am the woman who was murdered in her sleep by her husband who sat in the car watching the house burn to ashes.
[Blackout]

The End

~Chocolate Cocoa On A Winter Night~
Part One: Akel Dama
Darius Omar Williams

CHARACTERS:

TRIUMPHAL ROSS: *a self-published poet and Professor of African American Studies*
JONAH LOCKHART: *Triumphal's life-partner, Business Manager for Yeah Boy Records*
SEAN HUNTER: *Triumphal's best friend, Director of a Civil Rights Museum in Louisiana*
TONY WALKER: *President and CEO of Yeah Boy Records*
MALAYSIA ANDREWS: *a female impersonator, formerly Miss Black Gay America*
JOHN ROSS: *Triumphal's father*
THE BLACK GAY TRINITY: *Spirit of Essex Hemphill, Joseph Beam and Marlon Riggs*

Other Characters in Part One

PASTOR HOSEA HIMES, *a Baptist minister played by the actor playing John Ross*

MRS. POETICS, *the apparition of a white academic creative writing teacher, played by the actor playing Marlon Riggs*

THE CRACKHEAD AT THE BUSSTOP, *played by the actor playing Marlon Riggs*

MISTRESS OF CEREMONIES, *voice-over*

DOCTOR FANAMI OSADEBE, *Sean's primary care doctor, played by the actor playing Joseph Beam*

PHIL BANKS, *Executive Director of The Black Gay and Lesbian Coalition, played by the actor playing Essex Hemphill*

DEE DEE LABELLE, *the spirit of a dead drag queen, played by the actor playing Essex Hemphill*

ANGELICA LABELLE, *the spirit of another dead drag queen, played by the actor playing Malaysia*

DESIREE DAMORIA, *a drag queen, played by the actor playing Joseph Beam*

TRADEBOY, *played by the actor playing Tony*
BAYARD RUSTIN, played by the actor playing Malaysia
ASSOTTO SAINT, *played by the actor playing Sean*
PEPPER LABEIJA, *played by the actor playing Sean*

Special Note: Triumphal, Jonah, Tony, Malaysia and Desiree are from Mississippi.

ACT ONE
Akhona

September 2005

Scene 1

Club City Lights. Philadelphia, Pennsylvania. Miss Malaysia Andrews is on stage with a large clear plastic bucket sitting beside her. She's holding a hand held microphone. Her head is adorned with an elaborate crown. Neon lights in various colors illuminate the club and there is a tight spotlight shining directly on her.

MALAYSIA: Can I get you to shut the fuck up so I can say something! Can you shut the fuck up please! Thank you. (pause). Before we get started with tonight's show...you bitches know I gotta read some of ya'll out there. Ya'll round here sucking dick, picking up trade at the bookstore or laying up with one of your sisters bumping pocket books and some of ya'll don't even know how to spell the word condom. That's right I said it, now learn it bitch, Con-dom! That's C-O-N-D-O-M okay. Wear it! Listen, I really need ya'll to listen to me. DJ can you fade the music please. For those of you who can hear the sound of my voice...Malaysia is here to let you know: gay folks, punks, sissies, faggots, whatever you want to call yourselves. We are the underdogs...yes the underdogs darling. Some of us ain't got no family, some of us ain't hardly got no friends all because of our sexual orientation good people. And quite frankly some of you crazy bitches just make us look bad. Love yourself...love your goddamn self and not that 12" piece of the dick down your throat and you know some of ya'll use teeth. Any way....like I said we the underdogs see and it ain't nothing for the rest of the world to watch our asses drop like flies over some shit man created. Yeah I said it, you heard it from me ladies and gentleman. HIV is a man made disease and some of our irresponsible asses is getting it every day. I ain't judging nobody. But all I got to say, is play safe. (pause) Miss E.T., come over here you anorexic worm. I just spilled my cocktail girl. Come mop this shit up. (a slim deshelved dragqueen, Miss E.T. approaches Malaysia carrying a mop) Bitch, you so goddamn ugly there ought to be a law. Ladies and Gentlemen please remember next Friday is our 2nd Annual Miss Continental pageant with special guests Miss Tommie Ross, Miss Kitty Litter and Mr. Adarius Black. On another note, a sad note....no, for real, for real ya'll. We lost one of our own to this awful epidemic this past week. Without further adieu, coming to the stage, she's a former Miss Club City Lights and current reigning Miss Black Gay Philadelphia, paying tribute to one of our very own legends, Miss Blade Monroe, ladies and gentleman put your hands together for the very talented , the very beautiful Miss Sanetria Andrews! Applause please!   *The opening bars of Patti Labelle's You Are My Friend begins to play as lights fade.*

Scene 2

Two days later. A Monday afternoon. Yeah Boy Records. Jonah and Tony in Tony's office.

TONY: I'm trying to get Yeah Boy records on some global shit. You hear me Jonah. Like Berry Gordy back in the day. We don't have time to play politics with our music man.

JONAH: But Tony man can you let me explain

TONY: There's nothing to explain brother. You want our music here to be less homophobic and more embracing of the black gay community....that is what you said, right?

JONAH: I'm not asking you to produce any tracks with gay themes or anything like that...I just feel since we do seem to have a diverse audience we can afford to tone down some of our heterosexist lyrics...

TONY: Man we can't afford to do that shit. Do you want my fucking ship to sink?

JONAH: Tony, I don't think you're hearing me clearly man...

TONY: Oh I hear you loud and clear brother...you're trying to create some type of black gay hip-hop movement at Yeah Boy records. And I am not having that shit. Hell no.

JONAH: Well, I am a black gay man...and quite frankly you—

TONY: Don't!

(silence)

JONAH: The truth hurts sometimes doesn't it?

TONY: (spilling coffee on his shirt) Damn. Now see what you made me do. (He rips his shirt off clearly taunting Jonah in a subtle display of seduction) You're a bright man Jonah. I give you that. But you're too damn soft sometime. Toughen up. You don't owe your sissy ass community a damn thing. It's all about that paper baby.

JONAH: See that's exactly what's wrong with you Tony. You're greedy, manipulative and self-serving.

TONY: Hey, watch yourself Prophet Jonah before I end up serving your ass to the unemployment line. Which reminds me, I need a favor.

JONAH: You're asking me for a favor?

TONY: Yes you, the best account and business manager a man can asks for.

JONAH: Don't patronize me.

TONY: Calm down dawg, calm down. One of my former artists, Genesis is threatening to sue my black ass over some back time royalties. Can you believe that shit? The bitch only had a few hits. And you know I don't take kindly to threats especially from a country ass back woods bitch like Genesis.

JONAH: Genesis was holding it down for a minute Tony.

TONY: Which is what I need you for man. You know them books that you keep in order for me. All accurate and neat and shit.

JONAH: Yeah, but I'm not sure where you going with this.

TONY: Well, I need you to switch some numbers around, make a few figures disappear here and there so when they subpoena my ass to court Tony Walker will be prepared to bring 'em down.

JONAH: So basically you're asking me to be dishonest.

TONY: I'm asking you to do what's in the best interest of Yeah Boy Records.
I'm the man, you hear me. I'm not about to give up what I have busted my ass for all these years over some greedy ass has been artist who ain't about shit! (goes over to him and gently rubs head) I need for you to be a good boy, okay and do what daddy asks you.

JONAH: I am not your good boy.

TONY: Look man you're like a brother to me. Sometimes you got to learn to separate business from your own personal ethics and right now Jonah man you are allowing your own personal ethics to interfere with how I do things around here.

JONAH: Wasn't it you Tony who used to say that speaking the truth to the people is the most important thing in music.

TONY: Truth my man is this 10 story building that we're standing in right now that I happen to own. Truth is three of my artists on the top ten hip hop singles charts in Billboard magazine this week. Truth is when I walk into a room and every motherfucker up in that joint including your black ass caters to me, Tony Walker, President and CEO of Yeah Boy records. And as far as I'm concerned, no matter what, that's the only truth I need.

Scene 3

Later that evening. Triumphal at home alone at his desk. He is editing a poem and reciting it as he writes. Eventually he delivers the rest of the poem by memory to the audience.

TRIUMPHAL: *(to himself)* Should I, a Black man, gay speak of black manhood. Whites, Asians , Puerto Ricans, Mexicans, Japanese, others disown us, would never intone us. And our flesh: Skinned, burned alive, strung up, left to hang for several days compels me to speak for us. *(to the audience)* If I could speak of Black manhood in all its propensity. If I could hold it up like a flag. Let it impede upon our psyche. Let it rise to the occasion of a turbulent past. No longer entrapped by the memory of a corpse, castrated and beaten by lynch mob's hands; then and only then will I be free. *(pause)* Black manhood is essential must not be superficial like inarticulate speech. It has been questioned, sequestered, pounced on and objectified in academic institutions. It remains foisted, second-rate, conspicuously lynched by other means. I must speak of its terrible beauty.

It is irregular like a gangster rolling a blunt.

(Mrs. Poetics , a creative writing teacher appears)

MRS. POETICS: Emotionally, intellectually and viscerally!

TRIUMPHAL: What?

MRS. POETICS: Does your poem resonate emotionally, intellectually and viscerally?

TRIUMPHAL: You mean is it academically appealing?

MRS. POETICS: Right, do you read?

TRIUMPHAL: What kind of silly ass questions are these? I am Professor of African American Studies at one of the most prestigious institutions in the country.

MRS. POETICS: My point exactly.

TRIUMPHAL: Who the hell are you?

MRS. POETICS: Mrs. Poetics, the crème del a crème of American Literature. The Emancipator of Truth. The Creative Controller of every poet's pen. I push all writers, regardless of race, sex, gender or class, far and beyond the scope of limited literary practice.

TRIUMPHAL: Oh please. So now you're going to tell me Miss Emily and Miss Sylvia and Miss Sexton are the only bitches who know how to write.

MRS. POETICS: Miss Sexton, she was quite a romantic you know. Have you read any of her love poems?

TRIUMPHAL: I have the complete collection.

MRS. POETICS: Good for you. Have you ever written a sestina my poor child?

TRIUMPHAL: Yes I have. What is your point and why the hell are you here?

MRS. POETICS: To ascribe upon your delicate psyche the complexities of structure, form and mechanical technique.

TRIUMPHAL: Oh, I got some mechanical technique for your ass. And it ain't on this piece of paper.

MRS. POETIC: That is exactly my point.

TRIUMPHAL: Look, I do not need your approval in order to write. I'm thirty-five years old okay. I have a Ph.D. from one of the finest institutions in the country. My man makes a six-figure salary and he still kisses my feet. We are moving on up in the world. I read Essex Hemphill, Assoto Saint and even Audre Lord from time to time. I've written my poetry in almost every existing form. I make sure I go see The Bill T. Jones Dance Company once, maybe even twice a year. I'm okay. I'm really okay. We got books. Black gay people finally got some books. Books that rethink our culture in provocative ways. There is renewed hope for my community and personally I am ecstatic about it. Black Gay Prides aren't limited to D.C. and New York anymore. We are starting to come out of the woodworks honey. At least I hope so. I hope black men loving black men will become an absolute fact. I hope white gay Americans we'll realize it's not all about them. We exist too. We do. We really do. We are not this group of well-hung erotic beasts. All of us don't vogue and snap our fingers you know. I want to smash all these damn stereotypes. When Bill Clinton was elected President I wanted him to invite us to The White House and throw a hellified party. And I really wanted somebody, anybody, to speak for us, about us at the first Black Million Man March. These are the issues I write about.

MRS. POETICS: Carry on!

(Mrs. Poetics disappears as the phone rings.)

TRIUMPHAL: Hello. Hey baby. Is everything alright. Oh pookie no! That bastard. You need to leave that fucking place. Wait a minute…if you decide to quit now does that mean our trip to Morocco is off? Just kidding, baby. Alright, alright we'll talk about it later night. See you soon. I love you too.

Scene 4

Same night. Sean and Triumphal inside Triumphal's apartment.

SEAN: My grandmother used to plant flowers in her front yard. Daisies, gardenias, petunias. She was a crazy woman. But she loved me though. I was her favorite. She used to always say to me, "Baby, don't ever get caught up in other people cause people will stab you in the back, all the time." I sure did love that woman. My uncle Willy would get on Bea's last nerve, he'd say, Mama loan me twenty dollars....

TRIUMPHAL: Your uncle Willy. Where is he? I wanted to marry his fine ass.

SEAN: He still in Mississippi. Living in Bea's house. She left him everything before she died.

TRIUMPHAL: Well I need to carry my black ass back to Mississippi. He still looks good?

SEAN: Huh Hmm. Creole men. We got something special in our genes. Good looks run in my family.

TRIUMPHAL: You are one vain bitch.

SEAN: My great grand mama was Creole, Bea's mother-in-law, and she couldn't stand Bea just because she was dark. Bea took care of her though when she got sick. Fed her. Bathed her. Helped her get dressed every day. For five long years she cared for my great grand mama and not once did she complain.

TRIUMPHAL: Old Bea. I miss her too.

SEAN: Before she died I brought Dennis home to meet the family. I know she knew. She just smiled and asked him, "baby can I fix you something to eat?"

TRIUMPHAL: Of course she knew, as fish as you are. Bitch please! I can't take your ass nowhere without you falling out over some man, "Girl he is p-h-i-n-e, phine!" Pussy just dripping.

SEAN: I love a good-looking man.

TRIUMPHAL: Chile I do too. Especially the ones that look you straight in the eye when they walk into a room and greet you with that rough deep bass, "Wassup".

SEAN: See now you talking about trade.

TRIUMPHAL: Okay!

SEAN: I don't do trade. No ma'am. Too dysfunctional.

TRIUMPHAL: Hmph. I bet you'd do trade if he threw your ass down and said, "Bitch give me some pussy!"

(They laugh)

TRIUMPHAL: And the pinky finger! Chile, you know you extend the pinky finger whenever you drink some coffee or tea. (mimicking him drink tea). And that my dear is a tell-tell sign of a bonafide punk!

SEAN: You might be right about that.

TRIUMPHAL: Bitch I know I'm right.

SEAN: Baby boom. Chile please. At least I never did drag.

TRIUMPHAL: That was for a play, okay. Don't even try it.

SEAN: Well you looked a hot mess! *You* didn't do drag, *drag* did you.

TRIUMPHAL: Fuck you bitch.

SEAN: Speaking of drag, how's Malaysia?

TRIUMPHAL: She's alright. I haven't spoken to her in a minute. Whatever you do, don't call her a drag queen to her face.

SEAN: Well shit, she is a drag queen!

TRIUMPHAL: She's not a drag queen darling. She's a female illusionist.

SEAN: Same thing. (beat) Do you have any wine?

TRIUMPHAL: Yeah, I got some. What kind you want, red or white?

SEAN: It doesn't matter. Whatever kind you'd like.

TRIUMPHAL: You know I don't drink any more. I keep this around for company.

SEAN: Since when did you stop?

TRIUMPHAL: Since about a year ago before I met Jonah. Remember when I had syphilis and went into depression for six months. Doctor gave me some pills. Antidepressants. I've been taking them ever since.

SEAN: So whatever happened with the syphilis?

TRIUMPHAL: I got a shot in my ass for three weeks.

SEAN: Are you serious?

TRIUMPHAL: Yes I am bitch and it hurt like hell too. Anyway, I lost weight; I broke out in my face. Did you hear what I said? I said I broke out in my face.

SEAN: And?

TRIUMPHAL: This fabulous mug, I was devastated.

SEAN: Well you definitely gained the weight back.

TRIUMPHAL: Fuck you. Have you been tested yet?

SEAN: Have you spoken to your daddy yet?

TRIUMPHAL: My father or lack thereof ain't got a damn thing to do with the uncertainty of your health.

SEAN: I just can't bring myself to do it. I hate it. You hear me. I hate that shit. Shit! I hate that shit! I hate that shit! I hate that shit!

TRIUMPHAL: Sean calm down. You're scaring a bitch, okay. Let's talk about something else. I'm glad you came up to visit.

SEAN: Thanks for having me. I'm sorry for being so emotional.

TRIUMPHAL: It's okay.

SEAN: I miss Bea.

TRIUMPHAL: Yeah, I do too. I miss Bea too.

"The Reflections" by The Supremes softly play as lights fade out.

Scene 5

Late that night. Split scene: Triumphal and Jonah home in bed. Tony and Malaysia in her apartment.

TRIUMPHAL: Rise to the level of Motown? Honey, he has lost his fucking mind.

JONAH: Well, you got to give him credit. He definitely has ambition.

TRIUMPHAL: Baby, Yeah Boy Records is an enormous revolving door of uneducated rappers trying to make some quick money. That ain't got shit to do with Motown.

JONAH: Look at Suge Knight and what he did with Death Row.

TRIUMPHAL: And Tupac and Biggie are dead. Don't ever forget that shit. So what are you going to do?

JONAH: We have plenty of money in our savings, Triumphal.

TRIUMPHAL: And you're reminding me of that fact to say what.

JONAH: Yeah Boy Records is a dead end road. We both know that. Tony will always be the asshole he is. I want more for myself baby. I'm thirty-five years old and I have yet to pursue some of my dreams. When I used to run around with my frat brothers I had so many dreams man. Like starting my own restaurant. Baby you know how much I love to cook.

TRIUMPHAL: In the beginning Motown was a two-story shack with background singers harmonizing in an attic. Berry Gordy designed his business strategy after the car manufacturing industry. All you need is a model to follow.

TONY: (zipping up his pants) Why do you keep wasting your time preaching to them damn faggots anyway. They are not going to listen to you.

MALAYSIA: (in the mirror putting on make-up) I happen to care!

TONY: The great transgender activist! Blade was an evil bitch anyway.

MALAYSIA: That doesn't mean he deserved to die like that.

TONY: Like I said, the motherfucker was evil. I'm surprised he lasted as long as he did. I fucking hated his black ass.

MALAYSIA: Voulez-vous coucher avec moi (ce soir)?

TONY: Are you speaking to me in Japanese?

MALAYSIA: It's French. It means, "do you want to sleep with me tonight?".

TONY: Why do you do what you do?

MALAYSIA: It's the only thing that makes sense. It's the only thing that gives me a real reason to get up everyday with purpose and meaning. Because most of the shit we go through is just so damn meaningless. Like me and you and what we do. What the fuck do we mean to each other? You don't even know who the hell you are. Impure. That's what I've been called from time to time. Theorized by academicians as some gender-bending 'other'. My children call me first lady, martyr, saint. That's the only real thing human beings need. Someone to look up to. Someone to make them feel like they matter in the big scheme of thing.

TONY: The Bible says we are an abomination in the eyes of God.

MALAYSIA: I am the Lord God Almighty's finest creation.

TONY: Oh please. You are a man too afraid to stay on course. A drag queen. You want to make yourself feel better about who you really are so you mouth words to songs and blaspheme God.

MALAYSIA: I am a female illusionist, not a drag queen. Never a drag queen. There's a difference.

TONY: Well hallelujah praise the lord Miss Malaysia. And I'm a man. You hear me. A man. A God-fearing, bible-toting, scripture-quoting believer.

MALAYSIA: Well you tell God come and see me sometime.

(They begin to kiss passionately. Malaysia removes his shirt and they continue to kiss as lights cross fade back to Triumphal and Jonah)

TRIUMPHAL: You'll open your restaurant. We'll call it The Lion's Den. And grow old together like George and Louise. I'll still collect old vinyl and listen to Diana Ross . Two queens in love.

JONAH: I am not a queen and neither are you.

TRIUMPHAL: I'm just fucking with you cause I know that works your nerves.

JONAH: And why would you want to work my nerves. Didn't I just tell you about my day you silly old queen.

TRIUMPHAL: Yes you did. And what did I say. I said go for your dreams baby now didn't I. Dreams are the unrealized totality of all American people. Black Americans have been searching for their dreams long before Martin Luther King told us about his. Long before Walter's dream in Miss Lorraine's *A Raisin in the Sun*. Baby, black folks know they love to dream. Especially black gay folks. I think our dreams tend to always come in sequin or silk. Our dreams are accompanied by DJ's playing some House. In the sixties and seventies, black folks in Mississippi walked all the way to Chicago only to find out it was just a windy city after all with nothing but houses stacked on top of each other and more dreams to find. Did you know that Bayard Rustin said, "The only weapons we have is our bodies and we have to tuck them in places where wheels don't turn" Isn't that something. He said something so profound during a time when blacks were still trying to mobilize themselves talking about a new nation. And The Panthers were still carrying their guns. Black men beat down by the war. Women and children trying hard to lift them up. And in the midst of all that madness, all that chaos a black gay man reminded us to preserve our flesh.

JONAH: Yeah, that is something.

TRIUMPHAL: Dreams. Humph. I have a few of my own.

JONAH: Tell me about them?

TRIUMPHAL: We'll for starters your damn socks and underwear that have been clinging to the bathroom floor for the past two weeks...

JONAH: Two weeks?

TRIUMPHAL: Two weeks. I'm not picking up after you anymore. I meant what I said.

JONAH: Tell me more about your dreams baby (kissing his feet)

TRIUMPHAL: Stop it. (laughing loud)

JONAH: Triumphal, tell me.

TRIUMPHAL: Stop. You'll wake Sean.

JONAH: Sean? When did he get here?

TRIUMPHAL: Earlier tonight. And be nice. You guys are like watching a showdown on *America's Next Top Model*.

JONAH: Be nice? You're telling me to be nice? You need to be telling that old hag to be nice to me. He's such a bitch.

TRIUMPHAL: You two are not gonna work my nerves this weekend. I have an article that I have to finish before Monday.

JONAH: Whatever you say Professor Ross. You never did finish telling me about your dreams.

TRIUMPHAL: Well, there's an antique armoire that I've been dreaming about and that a certain someone will help make some special room for in a special bedroom that he so happens to share with a very special person.

JONAH: Oh really.

TRIUMPHAL: And a child. I want a child. A little boy. I think I'll name him Jesus. And to visit at least thirty countries with my pookie.

JONAH: Thirty!

TRIUMPHAL: Yes thirty.

JONAH: Why thirty?

TRIUMPHAL: Because it's the closest number rounded off with 28.

JONAH: Anything else?

TRIUMPHAL: No, I think that's it for now. I'll let you know if there's anything else.

JONAH: I'm sure you will.

TRIUMPHAL: I love you.

JONAH: I love you too boy.

(They kiss. Lights fade.)

Scene 6

Donny Hathaway's "Someday We'll All Be Free" softly plays as lights come up. Two weeks later. Sean sitting on a doctor's examination bed softly crying to himself.

SEAN: Men who feel pain, Men who know pain, go home alone, humming a fractured hum, reading books at night, memorizing history and art, ignoring their swollen cries...

Whenever I examine art, when I look at it closely from a historical perspective, I am able to see which artists are relevant. It's so broad, for example Georgia O'Keefe painted the skulls of dead animals to the dismay of so many people. Risks, it's all about risks. I admire artists who take risks. And she was definitely a risk taker. Which reminds me about the importance of aesthetics: the nature, creation and appreciation of beauty. What is beauty? How does it inform or does it only conform us to the frugality of our sinister minds? What if America was a sexless nation? What if we were to move toward a humanism not limited to human flesh? What if inferior subjects were no longer inferior subjects in a colonized world? What if our standards of excellence were no longer limited to what is deemed to be ideal?

Aesthetics, aesthetics, aesthetics, aesthetics, aesthetics. I am all about aesthetics and technique. Any artist worth their salt works to master technique. African American painters like Conrad Obrezio did these amazing murals that depicted Louisiana's history. Paul Collins' work highlights human emotion through the technique of light and shading. And Henry Tanner's *Banjo* at the Hampton is simply amazing.

The human body is also a glorious work of art: curvaceous butts, pristine bone structure, wide broad shoulders, make some men look strong, Boris Kodjoe in string bikini underwear, now that is definitely art. Lately, my body has been confusing me. My immune system is taunting my brain. My face is dry. The tip of my fingers tingle. My eyes explode into inarticulate waves. My muscles move. My hemorrhoids bleed. My unconsciousness taunts my flesh . My liver hurts. My mind is caught in a ridiculous rush tethered by the nuances of my soul. I don't want to die young. I want to live to be honorable, old, esteemed and respected. I want to live, live, live, live, live, live.....

Doctor Osadebe enters the private office with folder in hand.

DOCTOR OSADEBE: Mr. Hunter?

SEAN: Yes.

DOCTOR OSADEBE: I have your results.

SEAN: Okay. Tell me so I can get this over with.

DOCTOR OSADEBE: You can rest your nerves good sir. You are HIV negative. You have no other diseases and you're healthy as a horse.

SEAN: Thank God.

DOCTOR OSADEBE: Yes, thank god. You are one lucky man especially since you told me you've had unprotected sex before.

SEAN: I know. Never again.

DOCTOR OSADEBE: Do you know how many brothers come through here. Professional brothers like your self and I have to tell them that their newly diagnosed disease will drastically change their lives. Yet there is hope, there will always be hope I tell them. You can live for twenty more years, thirty years and there is the remote possibility you might be dead in five. Things have gotten a little better but it's still rough on us man.

SEAN: Thank you, thank you Doc.

DOCTOR OSADEBE: No, thank God. I'm just one of his humble little servants.

SEAN: I'm Buddhist.

DOCTOR OSADEBE: Wow! A Black Gay Buddhist. Interesting.

SEAN: Actually I'm Creole. So I guess that makes me A Creole Gay Buddhist.

DOCTOR OSADEBE: Even more interesting. Well, I'm sure you've figured out after all this time that I also reside on your side of the fence.

SEAN: No shit.

DOCTOR OSADEBE: Yes I do.

SEAN: Even Ray Charles can see that. Sorry.

DOCTOR OSADEBE: It's okay. I get that all the time. It comes with being a man who is not ashamed of his heritage.

SEAN: Well I'm definitely not ashamed of mine.

DOCTOR OSADEBE: Well you be safe Mr. Hunter. Stay healthy.

SEAN: Don't worry Doc, I will. Trust.

DOCTOR OSADEBE: And remember, *Niga Bori Dankaona.*

SEAN: Wait a minute Dr. O, are you trying to call me a nigger or something?

DOCTOR OSADEBE: No, not at all. Of course not. It's from my native language. It's Zelma and Hausa. It means, "You are beautiful. You are loved".

SEAN: Thank you Dr. O. That is so sweet.

DOCTOR OSADEBE: Feel free to call me Funami. It's a West African name. My family is from Nigel. I was named after my great-great grandfather.

Scene 7

Early evening. Phil and Jonah sitting in a lavish bar.

PHIL: Black people in Philadelphia are not paying enough attention to this epidemic. We really need to shift our focus this year. We got masculine gays against effeminate gays, transgender men are pushed into a category by themselves. And let's not even start talking HIV prevention. Shit. Most of these young hot in the ass mother-fuckers don't wanna hear about that shit. I've been thinking about creating workshops this year about specific issues such as: same sex marriage, monogamy, financial stability, lucrative ways in which we can work toward a more vibrant black gay culture. We need to organize a Million Black Gay and Lesbian March in Washington. We need to let America know that we mean business now. No more sexual imprisonment. A new day for Black Gay America.

JONAH: I don't know about all that Phil. Let's just focus on this year's Black Pride before we start trying to speak before congress.

PHIL: That's exactly what I'm talking about Jonah. You got to broaden your horizons man. You have the potential and ability to be one of our most competent leaders.

JONAH: I don't want to be a leader.

PHIL: Too late, my friend, you already are. Or have you forgotten that you're the chair of the committee this year? Look, I think we should also plan a special memorial fund for J. Arthur Warren, the black gay man in Virginia who was brutally murdered around the same time as Matthew Shepard? What do you think?

JONAH: Sounds great. *(pause)*

PHIL: Jonah?

JONAH: What?

PHIL: My assistant Miguel tested positive last month?

JONAH: No, you're kidding me, right? What the hell happened?

PHIL: What do you mean what happened?

JONAH: Exactly.

PHIL: His partner of twelve years cheated and now they're both sick.

JONAH: Man, I'm sorry to hear that.

PHIL: Don't be. He'll be fine. You know how strong Miguel is.

JONAH: And what about his partner?

PHIL: He left. They don't talk.

JONAH: We'll I'll be damned. Any more suggestions?

PHIL: Yes, in fact I do have one more. I need for you to stop overanalyzing everything and order us another drink. Go tell that hot waiter to get his fine ass over here.

JONAH: You are so crazy.

PHIL: I'm not crazy Jonah. I'm just real. I'm just keeping it real.

Scene 8

Late at Night. The Black Gay Trinity Dream. Triumphal and Jonah's bedroom. Jonah is wrapped in the sheets in a deep relaxing sleep. Triumphal is dressed in silk pajamas standing in front of a mirror. He is applying an avocado and oatmeal clay masque on his face. He reaches for a fashionable shirt on the edge of the bed places it against his chest.

TRIUMPHAL: I am trying to find a connection. A space inside this moment to escape unnamed pain. (looking at Jonah sleeping in bed) I am trying too hard, although my body has adjusted to your touch like a swimmer who has found his clotted breath. Weeping with my hands, I want to be open again. I want to know the appropriate questions because my voice cannot find its organic flow. My need for uncrowded spaces, which we both yearn for, is no less a fact than your swollen solid sex. I want to travel inside the damp spaces where my arms cannot climb and my feet cannot land like a horn player that opens and releases sound in the intensity of real time. I want to dangle with you in this incense filled air and touch and feel and know love again, more than the unnoticed clarity of my adult life.

My life. My exasperated life. I'm having a mid-life crisis. Look at my stomach. A damn shame. I used to be so fit. Fat bitch. You fat insecure bitch! Even your own man doesn't want to touch you anymore.

(Essex Hemphill appears)

ESSEX: Have you ever made fierce love?

TRIUMPHAL: Who are you? What are you doing in my bedroom?

ESSEX: Relax child. I'm Essex. An intricate part of your muse.

TRIUMPHAL: Essex, Essex Hemphill?

ESSEX: That's what my mama named me.

TRIUMPHAL: Essex Hemphill of Philadelphia?

ESSEX: Stop stalling and answer my question child.

TRIUMPHAL: What question?

ESSEX: Have you ever made fierce love with that fine man over there?

TRIUMPHAL: Yes. We used to make fierce love all the time then I started going through this thing.

ESSEX: What thing?

TRIUMPHAL: The change of life.

ESSEX: Honey please, you are a drama queen. I can tell you a thing or two about the change of life. Have you ever had sores on your feet? Have you ever been in so much pain all your lover, sister, or good-judy could do was rub your head?

TRIUMPHAL: No, I guess I haven't.

ESSEX: You are blessed child. At least you don't have this dreadful disease. Stop moping and groping and do something about this pitiful funk you're in.

TRIUMPHAL: I'm not in a funk.

ESSEX: Denial is a motherfucker, ain't it?

TRIUMPHAL: I'm not in denial.

ESSEX: Meet my good friend Joseph. He can tell you a thing or too about black men and denial.

(Joseph Beam appears)

JOSEPH: Triumphal. What seems to be the essence of your plight?

TRIUMPHAL: The essence of my plight?

ESSEX: She's in denial.

JOSEPH: I can clearly see that but what is *he* in denial about may I ask?

(Marlon Riggs appears)

MARLON: He's in denial about that fine man over there.

ESSEX: *(beaming with absolute joy)* Marlon, darling!

TRIUMPHAL: Marlon, Marlon Riggs? Where did you come from?

MARLON: I just left a dreadful watering hole in a useless attempt to revisit some old friends of mine. After three long hours of a tired ass DJ playing some tired ass songs, plus a dead beat drag show, I figured I'm better off on the other side.

TRIUMPHAL: The other side? You mean all of you are dead.

MARLON: What part of "as a door nail" do you not understand?

JOSEPH: Right now, however, we are all apparitions of that fruitful imagination of yours?

MARLON: Did you know that your husband wants to fuck his boss?

ESSEX: Marlon, you can't hold nothing Miss Thing! We we're getting to that part!

MARLON: Oops, sorry. I didn't mean to spill the tea.

Plays

TRIUMPHAL: Oh no, you bitches got me real fucked up. My man is perfectly fine with me and only me.

MARLON: Acceptance is the first step.

TRIUMPHAL: If you don't get out my face your head will be accepting my fist!

JOSPEH: Calm down, Triumphal calm down. I hear you are a writer of sorts.

TRIUMPHAL: Yes, I am.

JOSEPH: Exactly what do you write about?

TRIUMPHAL: Oh you know the typical: love, relationships, pain, loss, community empowerment, tired ass punks…you know gay shit.

MARLON: See I told ya'll he was a dizzy one.

JOSEPH: Marlon please, pull yourself together. I am trying to educate the child on issues of family, identity and the true meaning of home.

TRIUMPHAL: Home. What about my home? Frankly, I don't appreciate your dead asses all up in it.

JOSEPH: Triumphal, when I said home I meant the larger perspective of things including the church, the workplace, political environments, community organizations.

ESSEX: To elaborate on what my good brother here is trying to explain, I ask, have you Mr. Triumphal figured out how you fit, meaning your black gay self, into the overall scheme of things.

MARLON: In other words, what legacy are you trying to leave for the children?

JOSEPH: How do you want to be remembered?

ESSEX: Or do you even want to be remembered at all?

MARLON: And baby beware: your man is getting ready to creep.

(they all disappear)

TRIUMPHAL: Wait! Stop! What do you mean how do I want to be remembered and what do you mean by my man is getting ready to creep. He loves me. He loves me!

(Lights shift. Underscore of a bumping house beat)

MISTRESS OF CEREMONIES: Ladies and Gentlemen…

TRIUMPHAL: Huh?

MISTRESS OF CEREMONIES: Ladies and Gentlemen…

TRIUMPHAL: What the fuck?

MISTRESS OF CEREMONIES: Put your hands together.

TRIUMPHAL: For who?

MISTRESS OF CEREMONIES:

Pepper LaBeija

Pepper LaBeija

Pepper LaBeija

Pepper LaBeija

TRIUMPHAL: Oh noooo! I want this to stop! (voices and music abruptly stop). How do I want to be remembered? How *do* I want to be remembered? (pause) Jonah. Please don't do it. Baby please don't do it.

Scene 9

The next day. Early evening. The sounds of Diana Krall's "S'Wonderful" gently strolls across the room from an upstage stereo system. Triumphal enters from an offstage kitchen dressed in khakis and the shirt from the night before. He is holding a pair of wine glasses. He continues setting the table for two. He's in what appears to be an upbeat mood, but on the inside he is lethargic. Eventually Jonah enters as Triumphal turns down the volume on the stereo.

TRIUMPHAL: Hey baby, you're home. How was your day?

JONAH: A fucking mess. Phil is driving me insane with this year's Black Pride talking about a Million Black Gay and Lesbian March. Can you believe that shit? And he wants me to be the one to organize it. Tony keeps hounding my ass to rearrange some figures in my books. I've had it with him.

TRIUMPHAL: Well let me take your coat. And you have seat. Forget about Tony for now. Dinner's almost done. We're having lamb chops.

JONAH: Lamb chops. My favorite.

TRIUMPHAL: I know. Sit down honey let me take off your shoes.

JONAH: Thanks babe. It looks nice in here. Why are you in such a good mood?

TRIUMPHAL: I'm just catering to my man right now.

JONAH: You know that's why I love you. You know exactly what to do when I'm feeling like shit.

TRIUMPHAL: Well stop feeling like shit and kiss me you sexy devil.

(They begin kissing passionately, They both remove their shirts and Jonah eventually rips off Triumphal's pants and underwear. Triumphal begins gently biting Jonah's nipples.)

JONAH: You better stop. If we keep this up we might not get to eat.

TRIUMPHAL: Who cares.

(Jonah throws Triumphal on the couch and lands on top of him. They continue to kiss. Jonah tickles Triumphal. Triumphal jumps up and runs across the room. Jonah rushes after him.)

TRIUMPHAL: Baby, stop. You know I'm ticklish.

JONAH: *(clearly having fun)* Where you going boy? I thought you wanted to skip dinner.

TRIUMPHAL: I was just kidding. You better stop tickling me. You need to eat anyway. You've had a long day.

JONAH: Don't you try to get away from me.

(Jonah grabs him from behind. Tickles him some more. Eventually he stops. They hold each other in silence, for dear life.)

JONAH: Baby, let's eat.

TRIUMPHAL: Wait. *(Triumphal puts on his underwear and crosses to the stereo system. He places Ella Fitzgerald's and Louis Armstrong's "Don't Be That Way" in the CD player. They lip synch the song in a playful familiar routine. Eventually there's a loud knock on the door. Jonah stops the CD. Triumphal rushes to put on his pants and shirt)*

JONAH: Who the hell is that? You expecting company?

TRIUMPHAL: No, are you?

JONAH: Hell no! Who is it? And stop beating on my door like that!

TONY: *(from behind the door)* It's me, Tony, man.

TRIUMPHAL: Tony? What in the hell does he want?

JONAH: I don't know. *(Jonah opens the door)*

TONY: Hey man, sorry to drop by like this but it's kind of urgent. Can I talk to you for a minute?

JONAH: Tony, we were just about to have dinner.

TONY: This will only take a few minutes. I need you right now. *(silence)*

JONAH: Sure, come on in. What's up?

TRIUMPHAL: We were getting ready to eat!

TONY: Hey, how's it going T?

TRIUMPHAL: My name is *Triumphal*. Only Jonah calls me T.

JONAH: Baby, come on now.

TRIUMPHAL: What do you mean come on? I don't appreciate this shit.

JONAH: *(trying to break the tension)* Hey, Tony man you want something to eat?

TONY: Naw man. I'm cool. I need to talk to you. I really need to talk to you. Alone.

(Tony makes eye contact with Triumphal)

TRIUMPHAL: I'm not going anywhere. This is me and Jonah's house. Does this look like Yeah Boy records to you?

TONY: This really can't wait. Seriously. Can you meet me in my office later, say half an hour?

Plays

JONAH: I can come meet with you now if it's that urgent.

TRIUMPHAL: What?

JONAH: Baby, I'll be back okay

TRIUMPHAL: But what about dinner? What about your fucking dinner?

JONAH: Look, calm the fuck down. This is my job we're talking about.

TRIUMPHAL: Your job! You don't even care about your goddamn job! And Tony, who do you think I am, stupid, like all the rest of your gold-tooth artists!

JONAH: Triumphal. Enough okay!

TONY: Look man I ain't trying to cause no problems between you two.

TRIUMPHAL: Oh really. Then why the hell are you here? That man standing over there is with me you hear me Mr. Tony Raphael Walker. Mr. CEO! You can't have everything you want and definitely not this one you dysfunctional piece of shit!

TONY: Man what the fucking is he talking about! You better calm his ass down.

JONAH: I have no idea. Let's go. T, I'll be back in a minute.

TRIUMPHAL: This is bullshit!

(Tony and Jonah exits. Triumphal crosses downstage falling softly on the sofa in despair.)

Scene 10

Same night. Split scene: Malaysia, Desiree and Trade in the park/ Sean and Triumphal on the telephone.

MALAYSIA: (smoking a cigarette) I was a freshman in college and it was my third time going out to the club. Miss Lena, Miss Brian and Miss Kareem took me there. I remember walking inside and seeing so many sissies. We drove from Birmingham, all the way to Jackson and nobody couldn't tell us we weren't the fiercest punks in the south. And of course we had Miss Martha blasting on the car stereo: *to you gonna give it, gonna give it to you*. I was a contestant in the Miss Newcomer pageant and decided to fly the bitches back to Oz for talent prior to slaying the girls in presentation: "Good evening Ladies and Gentlemen, I am your contestant number one, Miss Malaysia Andrews proudly sponsored and motivated by the illustrious House of Andrews. And for those of you who are into catty ass musicals, I have one thing to say, *"the hills are alive with the sound of Miss Andrews"*. We stole all the costumes at the school from our production of The Wiz. Miss Lena was The Tinman, Miss Kareem was The Lion, Miss Brian was The Scarecrow and I of course was Dorothy, okay!

TRIUMPHAL: Can you believe he walked out on me like that!

SEAN: Your husband is crazy and you crazy for letting him do that shit.

TRIUMPHAL: Well what was I supposed to do, fight him? You know I'm not into violence.

SEAN: What you need to do is start living for Triumphal.

TRIUMPHAL: I know that but I love him so much.

SEAN: I know you do but you need to love you more.

TRIUMPHAL: Did you ever get tested like I asked you to?

SEAN: Yes, I did. And did you finally call your father?

TRIUMPHAL: No I did not and don't ask me that shit again.

SEAN: He's your father Triumphal. You need to forgive him at some point.

TRIUMPHAL: I'm a grown ass man. There is no goddamn point.

SEAN: I'm negative.

TRIUMPHAL: Thank god.

SEAN: That's exactly what Funami said.

TRIUMPHAL: Who's Funami?

SEAN: My primary care doctor. He's from West Africa. He's p-h-i-n-e, phine!

MALAYSIA: I smoked so much weed after I lost. Shit so I went and sucked this motherfucker's dick in the back of Miss Lena's car. A blue nineteen ninety-one Hyundai Excel. The dick was love. Black, long and fat. He got pissed off cause I was using teeth, jumped out, told me I couldn't suck dick, called me a bitch and stole my pager. So, I went back in the club and told them bitches I was ready to go. But Miss Lena was busy trying to push up on this piece of Trade named Eric and he was fine. Now Eric was Blade Monroe's husband, Mother of The House of Elegance and everybody from her house was looking like they wanted to whip Miss Lena's ass. I went outside and sat on top of the car. Lady Ashtray was busy working Mill Street, that crack head ho. Miss Kareem was getting his cakes beat in the alley around the corner and I just sat there. Before I knew what was going on and before my high came down good, everybody ran out that club before I even realized there was a gunshot. I was so damn high. Two gunshots. Them bitches flew out that bar. Lady Ashley almost got trampled on and her piece of a wig fell off. Miss Brian started yelling, "they killed my sister, they killed my sister!" A fight broke out and my head was bleeding. Miss Brian was crying in the middle of the street. We was some bleeding sissies that night. (pause) Me, my good judies and the kids from The House of Elegance are enemies for life. Miss Lena died two days later.

SEAN: Should I go out with him?

TRIIUMPHAL: You are not asking something so ridiculous right now. I just know you aren't.

SEAN: Just answer the question.

TRIUMPHAL: No, have you lost your damn mind. He's your primary care doctor.

SEAN: But he's good.

TRIUMPHAL: I bet you're wondering how good he is.

SEAN: You know I am.

TRIUMPHAL: Slut!

SEAN: Whore!

TRIUMPHAL: Drag queen!

SEAN: I am not a drag queen you Miss Ross wannabe. Don't get it twisted.

DESIREE: They killed your sister over a piece of dick?

MALAYSIA: Yep.

DESIREE: That's real fucked up.

MALAYSIA: Tell me about it.

DESIREE: See, that's how come I don't go out no more. These bitches are crazy. It is not that serious. (pause) My first real boyfriend was this guy named Bobby and he said he would never date a drag queen. Well let me you something honey, me and Bobby were together for three and a half years. He left his wife for me. My baby was one of dem dark skinned Wesley Snipes looking motherfuckers. Oooo, and Bobby could sang. He could sang with his black country ass. He was from ahh, Tupelo and had the most beautiful voice. Well, everything was alright until he started knocking me upside my head. Finally I just told him as lady like as I could: "Naw motherfucker you gots to get the hell up on outta here cause you ain't gon be hitting me!" He wouldn't stop. So I started hitting him back. And we didn't dance no more. And we didn't go out that much no more. And he didn't sing no mo. And we didn't make fierce love on the couch no mo. Then he started back on the pipe. I started smoking it too, especially before a show. Honey, I was worse off than Whitney Houston so you know I was fucked up. Finally, he got sick of me fighting him back. So he left. Took my car. Took my color T.V. Took my brand new VCR. Took my jewelry including my class ring. He would've taking my wood floors and the enclose screen porch if that weren't attached to the house. That sorry motherfucker took everything, except me.

(Trade appears from upstage and crosses to Malaysia and Desiree.)

TRADE: You wanna smoke some weed baby. You wanna suck my dick. You wanna fuck. Now, I don't kiss but I'm a freak.

DESIREE: Little boy, go home.

TRADE: Now why you gonna play me like that, besides I wasn't talking to you. I was talking to the pretty lady over there.

DESIREE: No she don't wanna suck your little three-inch dick either. Now go on to your mama and play Nintendo or something.

TRADE: You got me fucked up player.

DESIREE: Let me tell you something little boy. I am not your player. The name is Desiree Domoria. You hear me chile! You better learn how to speak to a lady.

TRADE: You fucking faggots!

DESIREE: Oh so now you want me to take off my shoes. Somebody please pass me the Vaseline cause I'm about stick my twelve-inch heel up Trade boy's ass!

TRADE: I'm outta here.

DESIREE: And don't let me catch you on my block again either! You hear me little boy! Bitch ass. Malaysia girl are you alright?

MALAYSIA: I need Jesus.

DESIREE: And I'm sure he needs *you* cause you wearing them pumps. Now get up. Are those mine by the way?

MALAYSIA: I'm serious Desiree. I need him. Now. I need you right now lord!

DESIREE: Girl, you cracking up? Are you trying to run me out of business? We are not having a revival meeting tonight. Now get off that sidewalk so we can make us some money. Now, Miss Thing!

MALAYSIA: Renew a new spirit in me! Give me a clean heart lord, clean heart, clean heart. I don't wanna do this no more. Jesus! Praise you! Praise you! Hallelujah! Hallelujah. I need you Jesus.

(Desiree puts her arms around Malaysia and slowly helps her up)

DESIREE: Yes. Just relax baby. Just relax. Everything is gonna be alright. Relax. There you go. It's about to rain out here. Let's go home and take off these shoes. I'm beat.

MALAYSIA: I need Jesus.

DESIREE: I know you do honey. I know you do.

Scene 11

Late that night. Yeah Boy Records. Tony and Jonah are in Tony's office.

JONAH: Now what was so important you had to drag me out my house?

TONY: Thanks for coming.

JONAH: For sure. What's going on Tony?

TONY: See, it's hard to explain man.

JONAH: Well just start from the beginning.

TONY: It's not that simple. Oh, and by the way. I owe you one dawg. The judge threw out the case. After they saw those books of yours Genesis' fat ass was history.

JONAH: Look, my lover is livid Tony. He'll be calling my cell in exactly five minutes screaming like a madman through the phone. He went out of his way to prepare a special dinner for me tonight. I'm supposed to be at home right now, making love to him, thanking him for having my back….instead, I'm here, in this office with you at almost ten o'clock at night and it's raining outside so if you don't start talking soon I'm going home.

TONY: Home. You know Triumphal is blessed. You are one hell of a man.

JONAH: My parents raised me well.

TONY: Well? Humph. Mr. Southern Baptist CEO is not doing so well kid.

JONAH: Tony please…

TONY: I am not well out all man! They say I have that fucking shit! Me, one of Hip Hop's finest. They said," Mr. Walker, you have been sick for a very long time." Not well? Me? Only sissies and faggots are not well man. When one of the leading doctors in this country tells you the blood in your veins is eating you alive, you better fucking pay attention Jonah. For nearly eight years, *eight years* I have not been paying attention. I've been riding it out. Pumping iron at the gym five days a week. I refuse to take their pills. Their toxic poison. Cause if I do I am saying to everybody else, to the rest of the world, including myself that I'm another statistic. Mr. Tony Raphael Walker, a statistic. And you. You. Who supposed to be my road dog, my main man You of all people tell me it's raining outside and you have to go home. You ungrateful son of a bitch. Well take your punk ass home Miss Foxy Brown. Get the hell out of my office! Now! I don't need none of ya'll. I'm like Muhammad Ali baby. Float like a butterfly, sting like a bee. I'm going out like a champ.

JONAH: Tony, I'm....

TONY: Sorry? I brought you into this company when you didn't have shit. And this is how you repay me. Yeah your black ass is sorry alright!

JONAH: Tony. Everything used to be so good between us. I remember when we were down home growing up together. I remember how much we used to dream about moving to the city and making it to the top. I remember the first time you said you loved me and I was too young to understand. I remember all the times you protected me when the boys in the neighborhood would try to beat me up....you said anybody that messes with Jonah answers to me. And now. After all this time I still love you. I feel like Jonah in the belly of the whale. Swallowed up. Swallowed up whole. There's something that's come between us man and it can't be undone. I've been knowing you since I was a little boy. Now you're like a stranger me. Perhaps you're right. Perhaps my personal ethics do get in the way of business. Perhaps I'm too smart for my own good.

TONY: Your own good? You are in love with another man. You have blasphemed god. An abomination Jonah! That's exactly what you are. I don't care how much you march, how many civil rights you get or how many speeches you recite. In the eyes of god you mean absolutely nothing. Nothing man. An abomination. The lowest of all animals. You get up, you put on your fancy drawers and your fancy suit and you jump into your fancy car with absolutely no respect for your creator.

And you want to know why, do you really want to know why. Cause you and that deranged professor friend of yours are like the blind leading the blind. Two high-class faggots in a bottomless pit. And you know what man. It's not just me who feels this way. The Producers and all the other Record execs in Philadelphia, Atlanta, Los Angeles, New York don't give a fuck about your undying love for Black Gay America. And that my friend, is the gospel.

JONAH: I should go.

TONY: No, don't leave me. Don't leave me like this. (long silence)

JONAH: Poet Amiri Baraka once wrote in his poem called *Notes for a Speech*, "African blues does not know me. Their steps in sands of their own land. A country in black and white, newspapers blown down pavements of the world. Does not feel what I am". Tony. My brother. You are an empty man. Your speech is hollow. Your heart is made of steel. Your eyes are red with delirium. You are inhumane. You are an empty American.

TONY: I don't want to die alone.

JONAH: You don't have to die alone Tony.

TONY: Hold me Jonah. Please, hold me. I'm so scared. I'm so scared. I'm scared.

(Tony begins to cry. They embrace and eventually begin to kiss. It is a soft, sensual kiss. Jonah eventually pulls away)

JONAH: Tony, my man, I got to go. I really got to go.

(Jonah leaves. Tony falls to his knees crying ferociously.)

TONY: God, Oh my God! Oh my God! My God!

Assotto Saint appears

Scene 12

Early the next morning. Stevie Wonder's "Lately" softly plays and fades as Triumphal stands alone in the apartment. Jonah enters. Split Scene: Jonah and Triumphal at home/ Tony and Assotto in Tony's office.

TRIUMPHAL: Where the hell have you been?

JONAH: Get out my face.

TRIUMPHAL: It's three o'clock in the fucking morning.

JONAH: I know what time it is.

TRIUMPHAL: Where were you? Answer me Jonah?

JONAH: I went and had a drink at Woody's Bar.

TRIUMPHAL: With who?

JONAH: What do you mean with who? I went by my damn self.

TRIUMPHAL: Did you go with Tony? You hear me talking to you. Did you drag your black ass to Woody's with Tony!

JONAH: Look you need to calm your ass down.

TRIUMPHAL: Did you fuck him?

JONAH: Get out my face?

TRIUMPHAL: Get out your face? Get out your fucking face? You asshole!

JONAH: Whatever?

TRIUMPHAL: Did you fuck him?

JONAH: What?

TRIUMPHAL: You heard me, DID YOU FUCK HIM?

JONAH: You're crazy!

TRIUMPHAL: Oh so now I'm crazy. I'm crazy! I spent half the night preparing a special dinner for your ungrateful trifling ass only for you to rush out of here with that goddamn Tony Walker as if his shit don't stank! As if our relationship means absolutely nothing to you and I'm fucking crazy!

JONAH: Fine. Do you really want to know what's going on? I'll tell you.

ASSOTTO: "There's a grave in your heart".

TONY: Who the hell are you?

ASSOTTO: I've been a good fuck to some, a lover to others, a healer, a friend, a poetic sage. I am the Heterosexist Westernized Symbol of, should I say, morally degenerative existentialism: in short, a proactive black faggot. And right about now, my boundless energy is spinning through the universe like nobody's business.

TONY: My head hurts.

ASSOTO: Would you like some aspirin doll?

TONY: Have you lost your fucking mind? Get the hell away from me. I can't believe it. My throat has been sore for months. I can barely hold my shit. My neck is starting to swell.

ASSOTO: You are definitely on your way.

TONY: What do you mean I'm on way? HELL TONY RAPHEAL WALKER IS THE WAY! THE TRUTH AND THE FUCKING LIGHT! A Black American success! I made the cover of Black Enterprise and VIBE magazine all in the same month. I CAN WALK ON WATER BABY. ON MY WAY? MY DICK IS SO GOOD THEY CALL IT JOHN HENRY. Come put your mouth on these nuts baby. Let Tony Walker redeem your soul and set you free!

JONAH: The man is sick okay. He has AIDS. He's been sick for a long time. There. Are you satisfied Triumphal? Are you happy now?

TRIUMPHAL: Baby, I'm sorry. I didn't know. How? When did you find out?

JONAH: He told me tonight.

TRIUMPHAL: That's why he wanted to talk.

JONAH: He's not taking any meds. He's trying to act like he's invincible or something.

TRIUMPHAL: He is so damn stubborn. *(pause)* So?

JONAH: So what?

TRIUMPHAL: What are you gonna do?

JONAH: I'm gonna be there for him. What do you think I'm gonna do?

TRIUMPHAL: Good. Are you in love with him?

JONAH: Huh? How can you ask me something like that?

TRIUMPHAL: Answer the question.

JONAH: Look, baby, I'm gonna take a shower. It's been a long night.

TRIUMPHAL: Don't you walk away from me. Be honest. Please!

JONAH: I can't believe you're asking me this shit especially after what I just told you.

TRIUMPHAL: I saw how you looked at him when he walked through that door tonight. Anybody in their right mind would recognize that look. I'm not sure if he has it too but with you, it's different. Something happens to your face when you're in his presence. You get all nervous and fidgety inside especially if I'm in the room. Sometimes it's as if you're afraid of him and other times it's as if you worship him. Are you in love with him?

JONAH: Yes. I mean no. I was.

TRIUMPHAL: You *were* in love with him. Wow. I can't believe this. I mean I hate he's sick. That's real fucked up and I hate that. But I've been blind this whole time. I try so hard to create this sanctuary of fantasy with you. This utopian paradise. And maybe it's my fault I 'm such a hopeless romantic. Maybe I'm mentally deranged like all my students say. Maybe we don't need each other at all. Maybe I just thought we did. I was dreaming. I've just been dreaming Jonah. Reconstructing our lives through poems. Trying to run our relationship like it's a fucking marathon. If we could only get to the tenth year we would be an ideal role model for black same gender loving couples. And you know what baby. That's some bulls shit. Some egotistical, unrealistic bullshit.

JONAH: You're depressed baby. You're talking nonsense. You don't trust me anymore. And *that's* bullshit. I have been faithful to you. What we have, for the most part, is damn good. It really is. What more do you want from me T?

TRIUMPHAL: All I want is the truth.

JONAH: I kissed him tonight. It was a short kiss.

TRIUMPHAL: So basically what you're saying is that you were unfaithful to me?

JONAH: No, there's a difference T. He needed me tonight and I had to be there for him.

TRIUMPHAL: I *needed* you tonight. I cooked lamb chops.

JONAH: You know what. You are so damn selfish sometimes. I just told you the man could very well die in less than a year because he is not taking care of himself and all you can think about is some goddamn lamb chops.

TRIUMPHAL: When, when, when! When did this happen? When did you fall in love with him?

JONAH: I can't remember.

TRIUMPHAL: Well try thinking about it.

JONAH: I'm here with you. That's all that matters.

TRIUMPHAL: It's not enough.

JONAH: Maybe I should leave.

TRIUMPHAL: Maybe you should.

JONAH: I've given you all I can. I have no more to give T. I am all dried up baby. When I was fourteen years old living in the hood, I used to watch these five boys outside play basketball. That was before I started shooting hoops. There was a rundown court across from my house. There they would play basketball and shoot dice, and talk shit and smoke weed and run game on young girls. And you know what I would do. I would stay inside the house every day watching The Flintstones or some shit like Good Times or something. Sometimes I'd hide behind a curtain staring at those boys. The sweat dripping down their fine bodies. Their bulging chests. Their immaculate thighs. One day one of them boys saw me and he knew what was up and I think he was gay too plus everybody knew I was. He gestured for me to come down all seductive like. His name was Quincy. Quincy Brown. Man, I was in heaven. I was gonna go down there and get busy with him. Like a damn fool, I went into that courtyard and they beat the living shit out of me. One of them had a knife. He pulled it out and slit it across my face. I was screaming, screaming begging for them to stop, "No, no please don't kill me man, please don't kill me!" They dragged me around this alley down the street, they gang raped me, every single one of them. Stuck a pipe up my behind. Just before the last one was about to shoot me in the head, Tony came running around the corner yelling, "Stop, man don't do it! Please don't do it! He's only a kid! He's only a kid!" They spared my life. Me and Tony became best friends shortly after that. There's nothing I wouldn't do for him. I would've been dead if it wasn't for Tony Walker.

TRIUMPHAL: You were raped. You never told me that.

JONAH: I never wanted to remember. (pause) I slept with him. Once. Almost a year ago.

TRIUMPHAL: What?

JONAH: I'm sorry baby. (reaches for him)

TRIUMPHAL: Don't! (pause) I knew it. I fucking knew it. Did you use protection?

JONAH: It happened so fast. We were on this business trip see....

TRIUMPHAL: Did you use protection?

JONAH: He came to my room that night and he was drunk and baby I was kinda tipsy too and things just kinda got carried away…

TRIUMPHAL: Did you sleep with that man without a condom?

JONAH: I don't even remember. We was so goddamn wasted.

TRIUMPHAL: You fucked him without a condom?

JONAH: Yes.

(Triumphal rises walks away in silence. Jonah rushes to Triumphal)

JONAH: Baby don't shut down on me now. I need you. We got to think through this.

TRIUMPHAL: Think through this? There's nothing to think through. You had unprotected sex with Tony during our relationship. He has AIDS! Do you realize you may have killed our children. My children! How many times have you done this? Huh? Tell me Jonah. How many times? Oh I been a fool, a goddamn fool! Walking around this apartment with a blinder on my face, writing poetry, taking antidepressants twice a day trying to remain sane for you, for myself while you're off bare backing with Tony Walker, doing it raw putting both of our lives at risk. why Jonah, why? Cause it feels good. It feel so goddamn good. You are wrong for this Jonah! You wrong for this! You wrong for this!

JONAH: I haven't been with anyone else besides Tony. I swear. And it was one time. I know words don't mean shit right now but for the life me Triumphal, baby I apologize. I didn't mean to put all we have worked so hard for at risk. But you had to know. After tonight, I had to let you know. (pause) We both need to get tested. That's the only way to definitely find out. That's what we gonna have to do T.

TRIUMPHAL: Okay. Will you please not sleep here tonight?

TONY: "Though I walk through the valley of the shadow of death, I will fear no evil".

ASSOTO: And by the way hun, you are going to die.

TONY: Jesus.

ASSOTO: He's vacationing in The Key West. Try calling him next week. You will die very soon, my friend.

TONY: Lord help me.

ASSOTO: Call on him baby. Say a special prayer for me while you're at it.

TONY: Who are you?

(He leaps across the room toward Tony. He is bursting with energy and life. His movements are specific, yet impulsive.)

ASSOTTO: My name is Assotto Saint but I was born Yves Lubin. I was raised in Haiti and eventually moved to Brooklyn. I was an edgy playwright and a flamboyant poet.

TONY: You were one of those loud mouth activists!

(Tony slowly rises)

ASSOTTO: The Haitian Revolution didn't have nothing on me.

TONY: Let me tell you something. I am like Miles Davis and his horn. I'm gonna run this voodoo down man. There's a hellhound on my trail Miss Poetic Queer Delight. You know what I'm gonna do? I'm gonna choke that bastard with the palm of my hands.

ASSOTTO: Brothers loving brothers don't diminish your light! Brothers loving brothers keep your head on tight. Brothers loving brothers try to honor what is right. Brothers loving brothers choose life, choose life cause this sick mother fucker is about to anoint your brow with oil and lay his hands on you. CALLING ALL SAME GENDER LOVING BROTHERS! CALLING ALL SAME GENDER LOVING BROTHERS! COME AND BE BLESSED BY THE SPIRIT OF THIS POEM. COME AND BE BLESSED BY THE FIRE OF THIS POEM! CALLING ALL SAME GENDER LOVING BROTHERS! CALLING ALL SAME GENDER LOVING BROTHERS!

It's our 25th Anniversary children and we are still running, running, running, running through a *Field of Blood*

Eva Cassidy's "Wade in the Water" softly plays.
Tony and Assotto stand in tableaux as lights fade.

END OF ACT ONE

ACT TWO

Sankofa

Scene 1

John Coltrane's "Spiritual" softly plays and fades as lights come up. Two days later. Triumphal is in the apartment sitting at his desk typing a poem. He pours a glass of wine. He eventually recites his poem into the morbid atmosphere of the living room.

Incognito

I WANTED YOU TO LOVE ME IN SPITE OF
SEXUAL QUESTIONS
I WANTED YOU TO LOVE ME IN SPITE OF CULTURAL
FRICTION AND ADDICTION
I WANTED YOU TO LOVE ME IN SPITE OF
MEMORIES SUFFERING AND DISEASE
I WANTED YOU TO LOVE ME IN SPITE OF HEAT
INSIDE THE KITCHEN
WANTED YOU TO LOVE TO LOVE ME
WITHOUT BARRIERS TO CRUSH
WITHOUT BAGGAGE AT THE DOOR
I WANTED YOU TO LOVE ME IN SPITE OF
WORDS

I WANTED TO FEEL
YOUR WARMTH AT THE BOTTOM OF MY SHOES
LIKE CHOCOLATE COCOA ON A WINTER NIGHT

(Triumphal stretches on his couch and begins to fall asleep. A disco light is lowered from the ceiling. First Choice's "Let No Man Put Asunder" begins pulsing through the room. Triumphal slowly awaken as the room begins to fill with smoke.)

TRIUMPHAL: Oh my goodness. Where am I? Where the fuck am I?

(Dee Dee LaBelle appears. Underscore of music.)

DEE DEE LABELLE: Welcome to the Land of the 70's honey. Good evening. Greetings and salutations. I am your special tour guide Miss Dee Dee Labelle, but you can just call me Dee Dee. Come on in doll, join the party!

TRIUMPHAL: 70's? Party? What? Where's my apartment in south Philly. Where's Jonah?

DEE DEE: Jonah doll? Who's Jonah?

TRIUMPHAL: My boyfriend. We had a terrible fight cause he had unprotected sex outside our relationship. I asked him to leave. I tested negative yesterday. He won't answer his phone. I haven't spoken to him in almost a week.

ANGELICA: Have some? (she offers what appears to be cheese on the tip of her finger)

TRIUMPHAL: No thank you. Who are you?

DEE DEE: Oh, forgive my manners. This is my daughter, Angelica.

TRIUMPHAL: Your daughter. Aren't you a, you know....

DEE DEE: She's my *daughter* dammit. In a very spiritual sense. We are from the same house. The Infamous House of Labelle. Where legends are made and drag queens are born. And me! I am a Griot of sorts. You see I teach the children. I teach them how to survive, how to avoid getting their asses beat or their brains blown out, how to be real. I'm a mother in a very spiritual sense.

TRIUMPHAL: Okay, you're a mother. Are you alive? Now!

DEE DEE: Baby, I've been pushing daises since 1986. I died of Alicia Inez Domoria Sinclair.

TRIUMPHAL: Alicia Inez Domoria Sinclair?

DEE DEE: AIDS sweetie, I died of AIDS. That evil bitch. And I was just starting to live when I got the gift.

TRIUMPHAL: And what about you? *(referring to Angelica)* Were you blessed with the almighty gift too?

ANGELICA: Oh she got me real good. I went blind and I couldn't walk. Can you imagine a queen not being able to walk?

TRIUMPHAL: Of course, I can't.

ANGELICA: I died two years after my mama.

TRIUMPHAL: Well I'm negative okay...I don't plan to die that way. I want to grow old very old. I want children too, my own biological children.

ANGELICA: You don't have to rub it in. Do you think we wanted to go out like that.

TRIUMPHAL: How old were you when you died?

DEE DEE: I was thirty-eight years old and absolutely fabulous.

ANGELICA: I was nineteen.

DEE DEE: I was a crazy woman, a very crazy woman and I died a wounded soul.

TRIUMPHAL: It didn't have to end that way. You could have lived a very meaningful life.

DEE DEE: I did have a meaningful life. I raised all of my children. Alone.

TRIUMPHAL: I'm not talking about that sanctuary of fantasy of yours. That self-made paradise that makes you feel safe.

ANGELICA: Who said anything about a fantasy? Our lives were as real as your jacked up haircut.

TRIUMPHAL: My hair. What's wrong with my hair?

ANGELICA: Never mind.

(Music rises)

DEE DEE: Honey let's dance! Forget about all your trouble's sweetie?

TRIUMPHAL: I don't want to dance with you. I want my boyfriend back.

ANGELICA: Baby, what is your sign?

TRIUMPHAL: I'm a Gemini. Why?

ANGELICA: Oops, should've known, crazy bitch.

TRIUMPHAL: I am not crazy, okay. I'm in love.

(Music abruptly stops.)

DEE DEE: Sure you are honey, sure you are. And my vagina is a natural gift from the universe. (she laughs)

TRIUMPHAL: Go ahead and laugh if you want. It doesn't matter. That is what's wrong with all of us anyway. We need to learn to commit, to do something, to do something other than party and smoke blunts and fuck. We need to love ourselves better.

ANGELICA: Speak for yourself, darling, speak for yourself. (smoking a blunt)

TRIUMPHAL: Forgive me. I apologize. I don't mean to marginalize to clump us all into one group. I have a problem doing that from time to time.

ANGELICA: Your problem is not us, it's you, my sister. Stop projecting!

TRIUMPHAL: You know what. You're right. You are absolutely right. I should go.

DEE DEE: Honey is this husband of yours as fine as Billy Dee Williams.

TRIUMPHAL: What?

DEE DEE: Is he as fine as Billy baby. *(she mimics Billy extended her arm to Jonah)* "Are you gonna let my arm fall off?"

TRIUMPHAL: Don't tell me, *Lady Sings The Blues*, right?

DEE DEE: Right. Bitch how you'd know?

TRIUMPHAL: I've seen it twenty times.

ANGELICA: Have some? *(She again offers what appears to be cheese on the tip of her finger)*

TRIUMPHAL: For the last time no! I don't want any cheese off of your damn finger?

ANGELICA: It's not cheese?

TRIUMPHAL: I don't even want to know. I just want to go home okay! I want to go home.

DEE DEE: Well just click your heels three times Miss Dorothy girl!

TRIUMPHAL: These are not heels. I don't wear heels. For your information, these are Steve Madden shoes.

DEE DEE: Same thing.

ANGELICA: Triumphal, honey, what's the matter?

TRIUMPHAL: The matter, what's the matter, the matter. When I was a little boy I used watch these television shows starring none other than the infamous Miss Diana Ross. She would strut her ass on stage wearing some of the baddest gowns and didn't give a shit whether you liked it or not. I mean she was something, she was really something. Then after cracking a couple jokes with the audience, she'd toss that wig of hers back and forth, back and forth and then flash those shiny white teeth and before you knew it the bitch was singing her heart out and every motherfucker in the room was reaching out holding somebody's hand. It didn't matter what color you were, whether you were old or fat. People would bond in that space, in that moment for one woman, one woman. And I always said I wanted to be like that. To be able to touch human beings, to matter, to dig into their armpits with my words.(pause) My boyfriend and I have been together for almost ten years and half the time he just doesn't get me, he doesn't get me.

DEE DEE: Well what is there to get?

TRIUMPHAL: He doesn't know how to handle me. I, I'm an artist you see....

DEE DEE: Oh really. No shit. Could you do me one of those oil on canvas things, of me and my baby Andre. I have a picture of him. We were together for twenty-five years.

TRIUMPHAL: I'm not a painter, I'm a poet.

DEE DEE: Honey, we're all poets.

TRIUMPHAL: No really, I'm a poet. I write poems.

ANGELICA: Whoopdeedoo!

TRIUMPHAL: You know what forget it. Why am I talking to you guys. Besides, you're all just a bunch of has beens anyway. A bunch of throw back queens from the 70's.

DEE DEE: For your information Miss Triumphant....

TRIUMPHAL: It's Triumphal

DEE DEE: Whatever. We are beings of convenience, of your convenience that is. The poetry you write, the music that inspires your art, the way you dress, the history you teach is all a product of our existence. So in order for you to salvage that seven year relationship with that poor little man of yours Jonah you're gonna have to go back...go back chile....deep within yourself....beyond this room and these balloons...beyond all them souped up poems you write....beyond Gloria's disco and Coltrane's jazz down into the pit of your soul....and find your heart. Triumphal, find your heart!

TRIUMPHAL: Find my heart. Find my heart. Find my heart.

(Dee Dee and Angelica disappear)

Sonia Sanchez's poem Catch the Fire *can be heard as lights fade*

Scene 2

Later that night. A Park. Jonah and Bayard Rustin sitting on a bench.

JONAH: You're not really Bayard Rustin, are you?

BAYARD: Yes, I am. Really. And you are Jonah Lockhart.

JONAH: Yes. Why are you here? I thought you were dead.

BAYARD: I am. I mean technically I am. I am a by-product of an industrious Black Quaker family. We never die.

JONAH: You're a Quaker?

BAYARD: The last time I checked I was.

JONAH: Sorry, I didn't know that. I just knew you were black and gay and somehow involved with the March On Washington.

BAYARD: The March on Washington. What a glorious march. I shall never forget it. The profundity of 1963. Teeth and fist gleamed for the righteous redeemed. Martin spoke and the mutter of the crowd swallowed in warfare wounds stopped in their calamity.

JONAH: I had unprotected sex outside of a six year committed relationship.

BAYARD: Sex. The pure joy of unrequited desire. I've been called a tyrant and a sexual nonconformist.

JONAH: A sexual nonconformist?

BAYARD: The attitude about sex in the sixties was far more heterosexist than it is now. Men were jailed for merely holding hands in public. You couldn't even ask another man for a date without the possibility of being beaten. I was jailed for having sex.

JONAH: You went to jail for having consensual sex?

BAYARD: Those inhumane conservatives. I fell in love with a few straight men myself.

JONAH: I am not in love with a straight man.

BAYARD: You are a good man. Your heart is genuine. You want to live a noble life.

JONAH: I'm in a committed relationship with a sweet neurotic poet.

BAYARD: You do love him deeply. The fervor of your relationship is quite apparent. But that doesn't eliminate the fact your heart bleeds for a very troubled man.

JONAH: My heart does bleed for Tony. We literally grew up together. I think I'm the only person that understands him.

BAYARD: I saw many men just like him. When I was on a chain gang. In my political circles as well. Microscopic masculinity. It wrestles with us from time to time.

JONAH: He saved my life once.

BAYARD: Jonah. You must stop doing this to yourself.

JONAH: Doing what? What am I doing?

BAYARD: Trying to save someone who doesn't want to be saved. I fought for the humanity of mankind for a very long time. I argued for world peace and racial solidarity to the dismay of many black nationalists. And yes I did sway a few of the militant activists. I am sure of that. And at other times there were those who simply refused to listen to me. Who attacked my homosexuality to simply diminish my credibility as an agitator for Justice. You cannot transform everyone.

JONAH: Human Transformation.

BAYARD: It should be the ultimate purpose of self-actualization. Unfortunately, there are those who will never stop rebelling against the remaking of themselves. His life is practically over. Yours has only just begun.

JONAH: An Urban Hip Hop Prince who was poisoned by a lethal virus prior to his falling from grace. Unbelievable. (pause) I tested negative today.

BAYARD: Congratulations but remember the struggle in your community is far from over. You must continue to love in spite of all the porous hatred you face and fight to preserve yourself.

JONAH: Preserve myself.

BAYARD: You should be at home making love to your man. That sweet neurotic poet.

JONAH: He's gonna kill me. I haven't been home in days.

BAYARD: But your address is still the same. Go home and fight hard for him. Your personal happiness is just as significant as the social injustices you fight against. Go home and fight to win him back. He's waiting for you.

JONAH: I should go clean myself up first. I haven't showered in days.

BAYARD: No. Go to him as you are. Bruised. Scarred. Full of bitterness and rage. Go to him like a poet and speak from your unconscious mind. You smell of sex and he will definitely be aware of that. You smell of Truth. It will be rough in the beginning. The two of you will work to get through it together. Soon you will taste like sweet Freedom to him.

JONAH: But what if there is nothing but silence between us. A cold empty silence.

BAYARD: You must break the silence no matter what.

Bayard sings Just As I Am and Jonah stands collecting his thoughts as lights fade.

Scene 3

Same Night. A bus stop in a rundown neighborhood. A crack head is standing on the sidewalk singing a blues song holding a cup to collect change. John Ross is sitting with a suitcase beside him.

CRACKHEAD:
i was born in mississippi with two strikes against my name.
said i was born in mississippi with two strikes against my name.
all the boys called me sissy, my daddy was ashamed.

CRACKHEAD: Excuse me, sir. Can you spare a dollar? I need to get something to eat man. I've been standing on this corner all day.

JOHN: Sorry. I don't give away dollars to strangers. I never give dollars to strangers.

CRACKHEAD: Stranger? I ain't no mother-fucking stranger. I'm black just like you or have you forgot?

JOHN: I have a quarter. Would you like that?

CRACKHEAD: I don't want no quarter. What the hell can I do with a fucking quarter?

JOHN: Do you want it or not?

CRACKHEAD: Yeah, give it to me.

JOHN: I can take you to get something to eat.

CRACKHEAD: Aw, now there you go. You think I'm trying to get some crack. I don't want no crack. I didn't *ask* you for no mother-fucking crack. Man I'm trying to eat. You goddamn church folk. You think you better than me. Huh? You think you better than me man? I ought to slice your fucking throat.

JOHN: Please, please. Calm down, sir. I am on my way to see my son. He's in a lot of trouble and I have to get to him. I took a cab from the airport and for some strange reason he dropped me off here.

CRACKHEAD: You're in the heart of Philadelphia man. West Philly. Even better than Center City.

JOHN: When is the next bus? I'm trying to get to Vine Street. I have to get to my son.

CRACKHEAD: Have you ever almost spit your guts out?

JOHN: Excuse me?

CRACKHEAD: I need to cop some more stuff. For five dollars, I'll suck your dick.

JOHN: You're sick man.

CRACKHEAD: Come on man. Just five dollars.

JOHN: You know what man. I'll just give you the five dollars and I'll pray for you.

CRACKHEAD: Pray for me? Pray for me? I don't need nobody to pray for me. I gotta a direct line to Jesus through this mother-fucking pipe. I have visions. You ever have visions? One time a serpent stood on top of my chest. One time a dragon blew fire through my nose. My eyes are red. See. See. They're red. It's because of that dragon. He has a name too. I call him Wallace Thurman! Isn't that fucking crazy dude. A dragon called Wallace. This dragon is white. He loves black pussy. We're all dragons. I got so much fucking smoke coming out of my ears. You ever had smoke coming out your ears? I read this book once by Frantz Fanon called *Black Skin, White Masks*.

JOHN: What's the name of it again?

CRACKHEAD: Hold up. I just forgot. It talks about the meaning of dreams and shit like that. Why black men like me feel small sometimes. What it means to be black in the fucking Immunity States of America.

JOHN: Stop blaming everybody for all your problems man. You overgrown crybaby. Look at you. You're absolutely pathetic. You smoke that mess and blaspheme god. You talk to white dragons that lust after black women. You need help. Let me get you some help. Let me take you to a hospital.

CRACKHEAD: I don't need fucking hospital man. No rehab. I can lay hands on myself. I fly above buildings at night. Me, David and Matthew talk all the time. One night we all went flying over the Franklin Bridge.

JOHN: None of us are perfect. I'm definitely not perfect. I haven't spoken to my son in almost five years.

CRACKHEAD: Why?

JOHN: Because he's a homosexual.

CRACKHEAD: Oh man. That ain't shit. Try being me for a day. A homosexual? They're some of the best people in the world. I haven't seen my pops since I was ten years old. I hope that bastard is dead. You better be grateful you can at least get to your son. I'll be trying to get to my dad for the rest of my life.

JOHN: I love him but I hate the sin.

CRACKHEAD: Sounds like an oxymoron to me. Sounds like your son is not the one with all the problems. Sounds like it's you and not him who's struggling with their immortality. Sounds like your brain has been programmed by all the garbage that other human beings feed us in the name of Jesus, Allah, Yowey, Jehovah. Sounds like you're not of god at all.

JOHN: I need to see him. We need to talk.

CRACKHEAD: Here comes your bus. The #22. Stay on it until you get to Penn's Landing. Vine Street is not too far from there. You did say Vine Street, right?

JOHN: Yes I did.

JOHN: Thank you man.

CRACKHEAD: Anytime my brother. Good luck with your son.

JOHN: Thank you. Thank you very much.

Scene 4

Same Night. Malaysia's Apartment. Tony is standing near her front door. He is extremely intoxicated.

TONY: Miss Malaysia Andrews.

MALAYSIA: That's what the children call me.

TONY: Well I'll be damned. But what did your mama name you?

MALAYSIA: Cordell. I hate it with a passion. (beat) You know what, you're drunk. I think you should leave.

TONY: I love you girl.

MALAYSIA: What? Man, what did you just say? You don't love me. You don't even know what love is. You love this black pussy that's what you love.

TONY: I have full-blown AIDS.

MALAYSIA: I know. And I'm still negative.

TONY: My life is over.

MALAYSIA: Child, please. You are just starting to live.

TONY: Eight years. I'm gonna fucking die Malaysia. You hear me. Tony Walker is signing out. Avoir. The shit ain't fair. It ain't fair man. Fuck! Fuck! Fuck!

MALAYSIA: Calm down. You're getting too worked up. Come here.

(Malaysia rests Tony's head against her chest and begins to softly rub it)

TONY: God spoke to me again last night.

MALAYSIA: What did he say?

TONY: He said, "Tony, I'm ready for you". There was all this music. It sounded like Motown music. The Lord was wearing a purple suit and smoking a pipe.

MALAYSIA: Jesus came to you in a purple suit?

TONY: Yeah. And it didn't look cheap either. I was like, man even the Savior himself got some class. He was surrounded by three beautiful angels. They was singing a popular show tune or something. They reminded of the Supremes.

MALAYSIA: Were they wearing lavish gowns?

TONY: You know it. (pause) My mama used to tell me I ain't never gon be shit. She was a trip. She'd say, " Your daddy ain't shit and you ain't shit". And just look at me now. I am a diseased beast. I feel like Daniel in The Lion's Den.

MALAYSIA: You'll be up and about again before you know it.

TONY: I can't think straight no more. I feel like shit. *(Tony begins to cry)*

MALAYSIA: You just rest your head against my breasts.

TONY: I wish we could really be together.

MALAYSIA: Malaysia is here for you. I'm here for you baby.

TONY: Thank you.

MALAYSIA: Go on sugar. Let it out. Let it all come out.

Scene 5

Jonah stumbles into the apartment obviously drunk as Triumphal sits on the sofa cleared consumed in his own thought process before being interrupted by Jonah's off-key voice.

JONAH: "Don't you remember when you told me you love me baby. You said you'd be coming back again". Do you remember that song?

TRIUMPHAL: Of course I do. Luther Vandross. Superstar.

JONAH: Do you remember how I used to play it all the time?

TRIUMPHAL: I remember.

JONAH: "Baby. Baby. Oowee baby".

TRIUMPHAL: Jonah. Baby why do you keep singing that. We need to talk.

JONAH: "I really love you. I really do". Damn I love that song?

TRIUMPHAL: Did you hear what I just said?

JONAH: The best song Luther ever recorded is *A House Is Not Home*. An all time classic. Even Dionne had to take a back seat on that one. "A chair is still a chair even when there's no one sitting there." Yeah that damn Luther.

TRIUMPHAL: We really need to talk.

JONAH: We are talking. (pause) I can't believe a lot of blacks don't know a thing about Bayard Rustin.

TRIUMPHAL: Is that surprising to you?

JONAH: Do they even remember him or do they choose not to remember. I bet they remember Strom Thurmond. Now he was really a nut. They remember his hatred for blacks.

JONAH: I think Phil's idea of a Million Black Gay and Lesbian March is absolutely brilliant. At first I was resisting because I was afraid to politicize my life like that. But you know what baby. Our lives have already been politicized by those fundamentalists bastards out there. The same ones who'd rather have their children blown up in this stupid ass war as opposed to learning how to love people like you and me.

TRIUMPHAL: Jonah.

JONAH: I tested negative today. But I still felt like shit when I walked out of that office. Because we still can't find a fucking cure for a twenty five year old disease. Now that really makes me sick.. The need for oil is more important. Motor oil allows our lives to run smooth. Like water based lubricant. What would good old North America do without its goddamn oil? Oil has made people inhumane. Oil kills. Oil that is smart knows how to give power and take it away. Power! (pause)

TRIUMPHAL: Baby calm down. You're getting too worked up.

JONAH: Them powerful motherfuckers can't even control the flow of water in New Orleans. I laughed my ass off when Kanye West got on live T.V. and said that George W. Bush don't give a damn about black people. Shit, he was right too. And folks talking about that was inappropriate. Hell, the whole goddamn Bush Administration is inappropriate if you asks me. Even Condalezza Rice, Miss Topsy Washingtom herself. She don't give a damn about us. We're nothing but a bunch black faggots to her. Bayard Rustin said that we are viewed as an unstable element in society. Fundamentalists feel that we don't deserve our human rights cause we can't produce children. Ain't that some backwards bullshit. We got bonafide black homosexuals in the church preaching the same hate. Fuck fundamentalists. Hell, fuck Bush. Fuck Condalezza too. Fuck spiritual soothsayers! Fuck antigay propagandists! Moral behavior my ass! They want to amend the constitution in order to ban gay marriage and at the same time drop nuclear bombs on women and children! That's some bullshit. You hear me George W. Bush! Some motherfucking bullshit!

TRIUMPHAL: I'm negative too. (long silence)

JONAH: Do you forgive me?

TRIUMPHAL: Don't you ever hurt me like that again? You hear me. The shit you pulled was dangerous, okay. I don't care if you were drunk or not. I trusted you and you betrayed that trust....

JONAH: You're right. What do you want me to do?

TRIUMPHAL: Just be honest with yourself and be honest with me too. At least try to be. We both got to do that. I know it ain't easy all the time. But we got to keep on working at it Jonah. If there someone out there you feel you need to be with instead of me, let me know about that shit so I can make some decisions for myself.

JONAH: You're the only man I want in my life.

TRIUMPHAL: Okay. Alright. I hear you and I forgive you.

JONAH: Baby thank you. Thank you. Oh, I love you. I love you so much

TRIUMPHAL: Get up. Boy get off of that floor.

JONAH: Will you shower with me. Please.

TRIUMPHAL: Oh you ain't getting none of this that damn quick. You gon have to work to get some more of this. Shit.

JONAH: Oh come on. Don't do me like that?

TRIUMPHAL: Do you like what? Negro please. Don't play with me.

JONAH: I ain't playing with you. *(Jonah rises. The two men are now standing face to face. They kiss and exit to the bedroom.)*

Scene 6

The same night. Triumphal and Jonah's apartment. Malaysia can be seen sleeping on their couch. Suddenly there is a loud knock on the door that awakens her.

MALAYSIA: Who the hell is knocking on the door this time of night. Triumphal somebody's knocking on your door! Will you answer it please! A bitch is trying to sleep! (pause. There is an even louder knock) Who is it?

JOHN: It' Tony, Miss. Tony Ross.

MALAYSIA: Who the hell is Tony Ross. I'm sorry sir, I think you have the wrong apartment!

JOHN: Is this 450 Vine Street?

MALAYSIA: Yes it is.

JOHN: I have the right place. *(she opens the door)* Hi, my name is…

MALAYSIA: I know your name honey. It's Tony, Tony Ross. I heard you before I opened the door. How can I help you?

JOHN: I'm looking for my son, Triumphal. He lives here, right?

MALAYSIA: You're Triumphal's daddy? Well I'll be damned. Excuse my manners. Come on in?

JOHN: Thank you Mrs.

MALAYSIA: It's Miss, Miss Malaysia Andrews. Good evening.

JOHN: Is my son home?

MALAYSIA: Yes, he is. But he's asleep at the moment. I'll tell him you're here.

JOHN: I would appreciate it.

MALAYSIA: Put your bags down papi. I don't bite.

JOHN: Thanks for assuring me of that.

MALAYSIA: Now I see where he gets his good looks. You are one handsome man.

JOHN: I beg your pardon.

MALAYSIA: You look fierce to be somebody's daddy. Are you married?

JOHN: No. Actually, I'm not. I've been divorced for over twenty years.

MALAYSIA: I'll go get your son.

JOHN: Thank you.

MALAYSIA: *(goes up the stairs into Triumphal's bedroom. Jonah is sleeping beside him)* Triumphal, wake up. Wake up. You have company.

TRIUMPHAL: Huh? What? Company? What time is it?

MALAYSIA: It's one o'clock in the morning. Wake up. Someone's here to see you Miss Thing.

TRIUMPHAL: Who is it?

MALAYSIA: It's your daddy!

TRIUMPHAL: (fully coming back to life) My daddy? What? (Triumphal grabs a robe and rushes down the stairs. Malaysia rushes down behind him) Dad, what are you doing here?

JOHN: Hello son.

TRIUMPHAL: Answer my question. Why are you here?

JOHN: I need to talk to you son.

MALAYSIA: I should leave. *(As she starts to exit, she addresses John in a deep bass voice.)* Nice to meet you sir.

JOHN: Nice to meet you too Mr., I mean Miss Malaysia.

TRIUMPHAL: I'll talk to you later Malaysia.

MALAYSIA: Thanks for letting me crash baby.

TRIUMPHAL: Anytime. Call me if you need anything.

MALAYSIA: Don't worry, I will. Bye big poppa.

(Malaysia exits)

JOHN: So I take it, that's your boyfriend, girlfriend or whatever.

TRIUMPHAL: Actually, she's just a friend. My *partner* is upstairs asleep. Why didn't you call to tell me you were coming?

JOHN: Cause I knew you would tell me not to come.

TRIUMPHAL: You damn right.

JOHN: Son, I didn't come here to argue.

TRIUMPHAL: Don't call me that.

JOHN: Call you what?

TRIUMPHAL: Your son.

JOHN: You are my son.

TRIUMPHAL: We never had a relationship.

JOHN: Is that my fault?

TRIUMPHAL: Well, it's certainly not all mine. I'll never forgive you for how you treated mom.

JOHN: Your mother and I were very young when we got married. I was young, wild and immature.

TRIUMPHAL: Some things never change, now do they?

JOHN: Look Triumphal. I'm not perfect. I'll admit that. I have made some mistakes over the years. Sure your mother and I had a few problems while you were growing up.

TRIUMPHAL: A few?

JOHN: You were too young to understand.

TRIUMPHAL: Oh don't give me that. You used to beat the shit out of her. How hard is it to understand that?

JOHN: I think we should try to put the past behind us.

TRIUMPHAL: I think you should leave.

JOHN: I just stopped by to see you man cause I miss you. How are you son?

TRIUMPHAL: Well let me see. I'm still tenure track last time I checked. Me and my lover of seven years just made up. I take Seroquel so I can sleep at night. I write poems everyday and I don't have AIDS. Anymore questions?

JOHN: Well thank god you're not sick.

TRIUMPAL: What else you would like to know?

JOHN: Triumphal, I know we never had the best relationship in the world. When me and your mama got divorced, I thought maybe, just maybe we could try to build something. Son, you don't owe me a goddamn thing. I know that. I'm not asking you to spend the rest of your life learning how to love me. I came all the way up here to make sure you were alright and to remind myself the road you have chosen is completely out of my hands. It's out of my hands Triumphal. You are thirty-five years old. I'm almost sixty-five. We're too old for this. We got to mend this thing before it's too late.

TRIUMPHAL: What the fuck do you mean before it's too late? You walked out on us. I had to listen to my mama tell me over and over again," Triumphal, you know your daddy loves you." But where the hell were you? Huh? Where were you dad? You talk about going down a road less traveled. Do you think I chose to be who I am? Do you think I wake up everyday for people like you to throw stones in my face and say boy you are wasting your life. If I got anything from you at all, it's this stubborn will of mine. Don't you tell me shit about mending things before it's too late!

JOHN: I just wanted to say I'm sorry. I'm sorry for not being there for you more. I'm sorry it's got to be this way and not the opposite. Son, I know I made a lot of mistakes. I know most of them can never be undone. But I want to give you something. I want to give something that's a part of me, something to pass down to you before I die.

TRIUMPHAL: Every time I begged you to take me to a baseball or football game you told me you were busy. I watched you board airplanes with other women even when you and mom were still together. You were no example of a man. You fucked up dad. I had to learn to be proud of myself cause you were too busy messing around. You're old and you're sick and now you wanna be my dad. You're all washed up. You're already dead man. You're dead and don't even know it.

JOHN: Son. Yes I am old. And I may be a bit washed up like you say. But I am still your father. I am alive. I am here.

TRIUMPHAL: You're a pathetic, self-righteous whore!

JOHN: And what are you son? What are you? You're thirty five years old and you're depressed. You claim to be black and proud and gay! You're a middle-aged professor who acts like a bitch!

TRIUMPHAL: I'm a middle age professor alright. And you damn right I'm a bitch. I'm also a poet and I'm proud of that too. I have a man upstairs who loves me. He loves me dad. I got my man. I got my poems. I got some blues to put on when it gets hard sometime. And I got myself. That's right daddy. Me. Triumphal Ross. Poet Sonia Sanchez once said, "We are all passing through, let us touch". Everyday of my life I am touched by that man up there. I am touched by the aggressive and over-sized thoughts of my students. I am touched by the memory of my grandfather who loved me like I was his own. He used to always say, "Alright now little papa. Don't ever stop working for what you want because once you stop working, your life is over."

JOHN: I was the best husband and father I knew how to be.

TRIUMPHAL: You were the best you knew how to be by slapping mama to the floor and grabbing her by the throat? You were the best you knew how to be by storming into my room at night and calling me a worthless faggot? You were the best you knew how to be?

You was a drunkard. Those low life whores came to the house for you whether mama was there or not. You almost made her lose her mind.

Whenever we did spend time together, it was with one of your female sluts who could never stop laughing at your jokes.

JOHN: Son, I did a lot of things that I regret. When you were five years old I remember being at home one day watching you, your brothers and your little sister. Your mother was at work. It was 1979. My mama had just had a stroke.

You was something. People used to always tell me how zealous you were. I used to drive you to all the small towns in Mississippi and everywhere we went, both the whites and the blacks would gloat all over you and pinch your dimples. You used to walk in those old furniture stores and start singing your heart out. I used to tell you to stop singing like a girl and work from your lower register. Sing from your gut son. Faces of old women would beam. Some of them would even cry sometimes cause you sounded like an angel. At times I cried too but you never knew it. I used to play my horn at all those clubs on Saturday night. I wanted to be angelic like you. But the rich, savory sound I strived for never came. So I started courting women cause they treated me like a king. Women gave me ambition. They gave me drive. I could go anywhere, like a gas station or a department store and women would swoon all over me.

Your baby sister died the day your mama went to work. I was in the driveway outside arguing with this old lady friend of mine. She kept threatening to leave me cause at the time I refused to divorce your mama. I kept yelling for her to calm down and barely noticed when your sister Carla walked outside. I told that loose woman of mine to go home and I would call her later that night. Carla started playing in the street. You were standing near the screen door yelling girl come back in the house. I might of said something like Carla get out the street! The next thing you knew it, that crazy woman slapped me. I was holding my face for what seemed like days and before I could look up she stormed into her car and slammed on the brakes. Carla was running up the driveway when she went into reverse. I whispered instead of yelling, "Carla get back". That woman killed my baby girl. I know she didn't mean to it. But it was because of me and my slothful ways that she was dead. My baby girl was dead and you was standing at the screen door staring at me.

TRIUMPHAL: It's because of you my baby sister is dead?

JOHN: Yes, son.

TRIUMPHAL: I never could remember what happened. I guess I blocked it in the back of my mind.

JOHN: I miss her so much.

TRIUMPHAL: I know you do dad. She was your favorite.

JOHN: How long you gonna keep punishing me son? I'm trying so hard to pay back my debt to you.

TRIUMPHAL: Dad, look let's just take it one day at a time okay. I can't establish a relationship with you over night.

JOHN: I'm proud of you for standing up for who you are.

TRIUMPHAL: Don't say that if you don't mean it.

JOHN: I'm proud that you're my son. I'm proud that you found somebody in this world that's worthy for you to love. I'm proud that your life amounted to more than mine would ever be.

(John picks up his suitcase and walks toward the door. He stops and turns to look back at Triumphal.)

JOHN: Son, I am proud of you. *(He exits.)*

Scene 7

Six months later. Tony in his hospital bed. Assotto is standing nearby.

TONY: Will you fucking leave me alone! I'm begging you. Please. Let me die in peace!

ASSOTTO: I am here to redeem your soul.

TONY: I'm already redeemed. I read *The Souls of Black Folk* six times.

ASSOTTO: Soon you will die my dear friend. *The Souls of Black Folk* won't help you tonight.

TONY: Make yourself useful and come remove these goddamn sheets. I'm drowning in my own sweat.

(Assotto helps him up and leads him to a chair.)

ASSOTO: Hold on. Be careful. There you go. Just sit there while I push a button for the nurse. You look like shit.

TONY: You don't look so fucking great your damn self you red bone Haitian faggot.

ASSOTTO: You better watch yourself Mr. CEO before I come lay my hands on you and I'm not talking about giving you the Holy Ghost neither.

(Nurse enters.)

NURSE: Is everything okay? Mr. Walker how did you get over there?

TONY: I sweated out my sheets.

NURSE: Oh my. Well give me one second and I'll change these sheets. Soon we'll have you all nice and comfy in your bed again.

TONY: Can she see you too?

ASSOTTO: Not unless she's a queen like you.

NURSE: Excuse me Mr. Walker? Did you say something?

TONY: Forgive me. Forgive me. I'm just thinking aloud.

ASSOTTO: He's que queuing with the spirits darling!

TONY: Will you shut the fuck up before she thinks I'm crazy.

ASSOTTO: Your mind *is* slipping doll. You have dementia dear.

TONY: Dementia?

NURSE: Mr. Walker?

TONY: I'm fine. I'm fine! Just do the fucking bed and get the hell out of here.

NURSE: Here you go. Let me help you.

TONY: I can handle it myself. Just get lost man! Beat it, okay!

(Nurse exits)

NURSE: Oh my.

MALAYSIA: *(enters holding flowers. Rushes to help him.)* Hey baby. You shouldn't be up.

TONY: I just got back from a jog. What's up with you?

MALAYSIA: I brought you some flowers. Honey, they're your favorite. Red tulips.

TONY: Gee thanks. Did you bring along some fresh blood too? Or how about a magic pill for my infested brain. No, I got it. Did you bring a pump so I can suck out my liver, my kidneys and my lungs? You know what, just bring me a knife so I can cut off my dick and give it to you for safekeeping. Bring me my fucking life back!

MALAYSIA: Look man, I came to see your black ass and this is the appreciation I get.

(Triumphal and Jonah enter. Jonah is holding a plant)

JONAH: Hey Tony. What's up?

TRIUMPHAL: Hey.

TONY: Well ain't this some shit. We got a nice little reunion party going on up in here. All we need now is to start singing, "We are family. I got all my sisters and me".

You know what we should do? We should all break bread together in the name of Black Gay American fellowship. My great-great granddaddy was a slave. When he was finally free he walked all the way to Toledo, Ohio to find his new life. He did whatever he had to do along the way, carpentry, railroads, sharecropping, maybe sucked a good dick or two.

Now me, I don't suck no dick and I ain't never picked cotton a day in my life. You know what I love about Black Gays, Transgender and Bisexuals. They will sit down and pray and let the preacher preach and then *out* his self-righteous ass in a minute. You see, I'm a born again Democrat. I don't fuck with none of that Republican bullshit. I admire mother fuckers like Bill Clinton who really knew how to get down.

Plays

MALAYSIA: Oh my God baby. You need to stop.

TRIUMPHAL: Well, well, well, Mr. Walker. I must say you are still your old self, in spirit at least. It appears you will never lose your drive. It appears even in your hour of need, that mouth of yours still goes on and on. It appears. It appears. It appears we should reach out to you man. Keep your head up Tony. We're rooting for you.

TONY: I appreciate that Triumphal. I really do. Hey, recite one of them poems for me man. Lift a brother up. Set my soul on fire tonight.

JONAH: Yeah baby. Let's hear a poem.

TRIUMPHAL:

A Poem Written On World AIDS Day
i am here in the presence of unchained feet
men and women still suffering at the hands
of American dreams fashionably anointed in silence
as they crouch to their knees in prayer;

i am here brown skin one who in the quiet memory
of genital insanity have come to mark my birth
in a self-righteous town of colorless sol
in the presence of skeletal faces who chant my demise;

i am here in affirmative strength cause once when I was
young little black boys startled me with hate, unbroken,
baptized in southern speech, in ripened sexual peace;

i am here moving on the altar of spiritual freedom
in a country where millions perish in vain voices wailing
like oversized hallelujahs, their abandoned prayers rising
out of the incessant suffering of incurable disease;

because of j.r. warrens blood, essex hemphill's rage,
james baldwin's profundity, because of bayard rustin's
common sense I am here, because of state decisions and race
decisions, church decisions and fate decisions, because of anti-hate
and supreme court decisions;

i am here, a southern black poet, a messenger for those
crippled by 21st century rage in the presence of inhumane
fundamentalists and their red-eyed delirium

in a city throwing stones from divided pulpits
in a city of bible-stunned conservatives, preachers,
congressmen, legal analysts, self- proclaim prophets
who deconstruct family, salvation, gender, morality, justice;

i am here to unequivocally profess the legality, spirituality
and principality of my existence is not a political agenda
but a human agenda;

i am here chanting peace for pimps, whores, crack-heads, thugs
homeless unpatriotic bodies straining their brains for life

i am here in masculine strength
i am here in feminine strength
not darting my eyes at you
not covering my desires with poems
praying for the sanity of a disenchanted earth;

OVERCOME
OVERCOME
OVERCOME

brotha overcome/sista overcome for your FREEDOM.

(Tony is in bed in an upright position. His eyes are open but he is clearly dead. Jonah eases his back flat against the mattress, then closes Tony's eyes with his hands. Malaysia and Triumphal embrace. Jonah stares at Tony. There is nothing but silence.)

Scene 8

Mid November. The funeral of Tony Walker. Pastor Hosea Himes standing behind a pulpit dressed in an elaborate purple robe.

PASTOR HOSEA HIMES:

This morning we would like to acknowledge the life and work of Mr. Tony Darnell Walker, President and CEO of Yeah Boy Records. Now I'm not going to stand here this morning and drown your hearts with superfluous and eclectic thoughts on Mr. Walker's life. I refuse to ignore the human flaws and errors of this man in his hour of bereavement. Mr. Walker was known to some as a relentless contemptible tyrant. But to others he was also a selfless servant particularly in the ever changing commodity of Hip Hop Music. Although, Mr. Walker may have been at times physically and verbally abusive in some of his ways, although he may have shunned some of the family, thus only embracing a chosen few, regardless of whatever his spiritual struggles and imperfection were, most importantly we have to acknowledge, whether we are willing or not willing to do so that Tony Darnell Walker was indeed a same gender loving brother. Whether this was a matter of public fact or whether Mr. Walker chose to remain in the crippling crevices of a revolving closet door, he was a man who was victimized by his own internal conflicts.

Unfortunately the Holy Ghost gatekeepers and spiritual soothsayers of this world forced a man like Mr. Walker to remain in limbo with his sexual and spiritual self. The right wing conservatives and illustrious agitators of traditional family have pushed many of us and not just Tony into a crippling darkness that continues to cripple the individual construction of our identity. Biblical misinformation, scriptures taken out of their historical context have afforded black people the opportunity to imprison their own kinfolk. Brothers and sisters, mothers and daughters, fathers and sons left astray because nobody wants to be *of* God, everybody wants to *be* God.

I don't care what conservative Christians have to say. I don't care how they choose to interpret language in the Bible. I don't care about their hate. I refuse to allow their hate to become my hate. I refuse to allow their sinister stones to pull, bend and break my soul. Somebody call the White House; tell the Supreme Court that my sexual liberty and spiritual freedom is not a political agenda but a human agenda!

The God I serves says the children are free. I said the God I serve says the children are free indeed.

Scene 9

Night. Early January. Triumphal and Jonah in bed. Triumphal is wide awake struggling to breathe.

TRIUMPHAL: Jonah! Jonah! Baby help me! I'm having a panic attack. Help me!

(Jonah quickly rises from a deep sleep.)

TRIUMPHAL: My heart is pounding. My chest hurts. It hurts so bad.

JONAH: Breathe, baby. Come on Triumphal. Breathe!

TRIUMPHAL: I can't.

JONAH: The hell you can't. Breathe. Come on goddammit!

TRIUMPHAL: I'm okay, I'm okay, I'm okay.

JONAH: No, you are not okay! I'm going to the bathroom to get your medicine.

TRIUMPHAL: No, I don't want it. I'm not taking those anxiety pills anymore. I'll be alright. Just give me a minute Jonah, okay. I just need to get myself together.

JONAH: This is not the time to be stubborn T.

TRIUMPHAL: I AM NOT TAKING ANYMORE SEROQUEL!

JONAH: Baby, you got to calm down.

TRIUMPHAL: I'm calm. I'm calm. I'm calm

(Jonah rushes into the bathroom and back with a bottle of Seroquel and a cup of water).

TRIUMPHAL: Jonah. No. No. No. I'm not taking it. I refuse. *(he takes the medicine)* Dammit Jonah. I'm trying to do this my way. I could get diabetes if I keep taking this shit!

JONAH: And I could die of a heart attack if I keep watching you go through this.

TRIUMPHAL: Baby, just hold me. Please. Don't let go. Whatever you do. Don't let go.

JONAH: Triumphal. There is no way you're teaching tomorrow. Not like this. You'll have to cancel your classes. You need to rest.

TRIUMPHAL: I dreamt we were being eaten alive by hellhounds. It made me think of Robert Johnson standing at the crossroads. Robert made a deal with the devil. He sold his soul so he could play the guitar. Johnson was tall, dark and lovely like you. The devil was a white man with a redneck voice. I hate it whenever I have that dream. Sometimes I'm the only one in it. Struggling through this spiritual warfare alone. Old poems sung to the sound of the blues.

JONAH: We should move.

TRIUMPHAL: Why.

JONAH: I'm tired of Philly.

TRIUMPHAL: You are not by yourself. Where you wanna go?

JONAH: I don't know. Atlanta maybe.

TRIUMPHAL: Oh please. Too many queens for me.

JONAH: Well what about Chicago? It's not that bad. Where do you wanna go.

TRIUMPHAL: I don't know baby. To the moon.

JONAH: I'm there. Just let me know when.

TRIUMPHAL: Are you serious?

JONAH: You damn right I am.

Phyllis Hyman's "Meet Me On The Moon" softly plays and fades as the two men embrace.

Scene 10

inal Dream Sequence. The Penthouse: A fabulous Black Gay Heaven featuring Miss Pepper LaBeija. Triumphal is standing center stage

MISTRESS OF CEREMONIES:
Ladies and Gentlemen
Club Escuelita's is proud to present
Miss Pepper LaBeija

TRIUMPHAL: I can't believe this happening again.

MISTRESS OF CEREMONIES:
Pepper LaBeija
Pepper LaBeija
Pepper LaBeija
Pepper LaBeija   *(Pepper LaBeija appears)*

TRIUMPHAL: She's wearing a white mink coat, feathers and jewelry and PUMPS!

(She walks to the beat of pulsating music. It is a keen, precise, stupendous strut. She stops center stage as music fades.)

PEPPER LABEIJA:
Good Evening
I am the Queen Mother darling,
Miss Pepper LaBeija
Straight from the heart of New York,
MY ARMS ARE WRAPPED AROUND THE CITY
I walk to the beat of Disco and House
I just had brunch with Princess Diana
And I am here to congratulate you:
TRIUMPHAL ROSS

TRIUMPHAL: Congratulate me? I haven't done anything. I'm just a middle age professor with a loud ass mouth.

PEPPER LABEIJA: You are

The Soul of Black Gay America
The Soul Emancipator of Truth
The crème del a crème of inarticulate fierceness
The most captivating strut on a Ballroom floor
Chocolate Cocoa On A Winter Night because of your ennoble heart the
Children are running honey, running to the edge of their lives

TRIUMPHAL: Wait a minute. I was born in Mississippi. I'm a lanky black poet from the south. I got bills coming out my ass. My student loans are overdue. And I don't know a damn thing about working a ballroom floor. You're crazy.

PEPPER LABEIJA: The Black Gay Trinity has spoken.

TRIUMPHAL: The Black Gay Trinity?

PEPPER LABEIJA: Right! Essex, Marlon and Joseph. Those three fine ass prophets who barged into your room a few months ago.

TRIUMPHAL: You mean the journey toward the remaking of myself was motivated and encouraged by those beautiful black men.

PEPPER LABEIJA: Yes. Hold up. Prepare yourself. Wait one second. I can hear my lovely children getting ready to walk!

TRIUMPHAL: You mean them bitches will be voguing and stomping on my brand new floor! I don't think so!

PEPPER LABEIEJA: Listen. Listen. Listen closely Triumphal. They are walking from afar inside that enormous penthouse in the sky!

TRIUMPHAL: This is unbelievable.

PEPPER LABEIJA: And so the children walked into a land called Escuelita. They all wore the color purple and the fiercest pairs of pumps. Their bodies were restored and House music played on and on throughout the night. All the red ribbons were burned and their faces were young and alive again. Langston Hughes blessed them with his psalms. Alvin Ailey burned their eyes with a deliberate and Revised Revelation. James Baldwin set their tongues afire and Miss Lorraine melted their hearts with blue dreams.

TRIUMPHAL: James Baldwin. Alvin Ailey. Lorraine Hansberry. You've got to be kidding.

PEPPER LABEIJA: Listen. Listen. Your life. Your exasperated life will be remembered in the poems you write, in the lives you save, in the wicked wisdom you pass down to the children.

TRIUMPHAL: I'm just trying to do me.

PEPPER LABEIJA: In doing so, you have left an indelible mark, one hell of a legacy child.

TRIUMPHAL: I think I'm beginning to understand.

PEPPER LABEIJA: Good. Now then, have a seat.

TRIUMPHAL: For what?

PEPPER LABEIJA: The show is about to begin.

MISTRESS OF CEREMONIES: Ladies and gentlemen, Club Escuelita is proud to present, the legendary, the very beautiful, the most fearless diva of them all, Miss Pepper LaBeija!!!

(Pepper LaBeija lip synchs to Patti Labelle's "Come What May" as colored winged men and women surround her, their faces painted in various colors. The stage should be surrounded by smoke with an immaculate sunset, an oversized sun peering in the background. Pepper LaBeija disappears as song fades.)

MISTRESS OF CEREMONIES:

Walk together children.
Don't you get weary.
Walk together children.

BLACKOUT

Plays

PERMISSIONS

Thanks to the following authors and publishers who granted permission to reprint the following work:

"Teenage Drag-Queen" and "Kinfolks" copyright © 2010 by Shane Allison previously published in *SlutMachine* (Rebel Satori Press). Reprinted with author's permission.

"For the Chil'ren" copyright © 2010 by Uriah Bell published in *Epiphany: Poems in the Key of Love*. (Rising Voices Press) Reprinted with author's permission. "For those Newly Diagnosed" copyright © 2010 by Uriah Bell previously published in *Epiphany: Poems in the Key of Love* (Rising Voices Press). Reprinted with author's permission. "Four to Seven Hundred Fourteen" copyright © 2008 by Uriah Bell previously published in *Mood Swings* (Rising Voices Press). Reprinted with author's permission.

"Pussy Was My Drug Dealer" copyright © 2010 by Laurinda D. Brown published in *LM Lesbian Memoirs*. Reprinted with author's permission.

Excerpt from *Captain Swing* copyright © 1993 by Larry Duplechan previously published by Alyson Publications. Reprinted with author's permission.

"Another 100 People" copyright © 2005 by L. Michael Gipson previously published in *Clik Magazine*. Reprinted with author's permission. "Conviction" copyright © 2010 by L. Michael Gipson previously published in *Collisions: A Collection of Intersections*, Red Dirt Publishing. Reprinted with author's permission.

"The Fan" copyright © 2000 by Charles W. Harvey previously published in *New Verse News*. Reprinted with author's permission. "Hypocrisy" copyright © 2000 by Charles W. Harvey previously published in *When Dogs Bark*. Reprinted with author's permission. "The Needy" copyright © 2000 by Charles W. Harvey previously published in *When Dogs Bark*. Reprinted with author's permission.

"Church" copyright © 1996 by G. Winston James published in *Shade: an Anthology of Short Fiction by Gay Men of African Descent*, Avon books, 1996; *Adult Learning and Development: Multi-Cultural Stories*, Krieger Publishing, 1999; and *Shaming the Devil: Collected Short Stories*, Top Pen Press, 2009. Reprinted with author's permission.

"Question and Answers" copyright © 2007 by Alan Miller previously published in *Voices Rising*, Redbone Press, 2007. Reprinted with author's permission.

"Brown Eyes and Unavailable" copyright © 2009 by Travis Montez previously published in *MONTEZ WAS HERE*. Reprinted with author's permission. "Before Iraq Comes" copyright © 2005 by Travis Montez previously published in *Bullets & Butterflies: Queer Spoken Word Poetry* edited by Emanuel Xavier. Reprinted with author's permission. "Sudda" copyright © 2009 by Travis Montez previously published in *MONTEZ WAS HERE*. Reprinted with author's permission.

"Dream # 6", "gawd and alluh huh sistahs", "8 ways of looking at pussy", "blksestina" copyright © 1998 by Letta Neely previously published in *juba* (Wildheart Press). Reprinted with author's permission. "Singer, sing" copyright © 2001 by Letta Neely previously published in *here* (Wildheart Press). Reprinted with author's permission.

"Another Direction" copyright © 2009 by Richard Peacock previously published in an earlier version entitled "Him" as part of a Master's Thesis by Florida Atlantic University. Reprinted with author's permission.

"Liberation Theology Affirms All Who Are Oppressed, Including LGBT Community" copyright © 2008 by Buster Spiller published in *Windy City Times*. Reprinted with author's permission.

"The Worm" copyright © 2010 by Talyor Siluwé previously published in *Cheesy Porn... And Other Fairytales*. Reprinted with author's permission. "Over Me" copyright © 2005 by Travis Montez previously published in *Bullets & Butterflies: Queer Spoken Word Poetry* edited by Emanuel Xavier. Reprinted with author's permission.

CONTRIBUTORS' BIOGRAPHIES

Shane Allison is the author of six books of poetry including *Ceiling of Mirrors*, *Slut Machine* and *Black Fag*. His poems have been published in the *New York Quarterly*, *Mississippi Review*, *New Delta Review* and others. He is editor of over five anthologies.

Uriah Bell a native of Detroit is author of two poetry collections: *Mood Swings* and *epiphany: poems in the key of love*.

Badilisho is a freelance writer & a newbie to proper commentary.

Bobby Blake is a retired African-American porn star. In 2007, Blake appeared on the CD by rap artist Trudog titled *Booty Ain't Got No Face*. His book, *My Life in Porn*, was released in 2008.

Keelyn Bradley holds an M.A. in Philosophy from Cleveland State University. He worked on several video and feature-length film productions, including Cheryl Dunye's *Watermelon Woman*. His poetry has been included in the anthology *In Defense Of Mumia*. He is currently writing his first novel, *the origin of clouds*, as well as *hunger*, his first collection of poems.

Djola Branner, an original member of Pomo Afro Homos, is an artist whose interdisciplinary work combines music, movement, and text as language. Associate Professor of Theatre at Hampshire College, his work has appeared in *Voices Rising*, *Colored Contradictions*, and *Staging Gay Lives*.

Laurinda D. Brown a native Memphian published the novels: *Fire & Brimstone*, *The Highest Price for Passion*, *Walk Like A Man* and *Undercover*. Brown's *Walk Like A Man*, has evolved into the first African-American lesbian play to be performed Off-Broadway.

W. Jeffrey Campbell is Program Director for St. Hope's Fusion Program, designed to provide HIV prevention services to young men of color who have sex with men. Nationally, Jeffrey serves as the Minister of Health and Wholeness for The Fellowship, a conglomeration of affirming /radically inclusive churches.

C.C. Carter is a writer, poet, and performer who helped to develop audiences for poetry, music by women of color, writing by women in prison, African American literature and art, and women's health awareness. Her first book, *Body Language*, a collection of poetry, was a 2003 Lambda Award nominee.

Stanley Bennett Clay, an international journalist and publisher, editor-in-chief of SBC magazine (the nation's oldest black gay and lesbian periodical), Clay is also author of the novels *Looker* and *In Search of Pretty Young Black Men*.

Christopher David, born and raised in Bedford-Stuyvesant in the borough of Brooklyn, writer and poet David, is author of the novel *I'm On My Way*.

Senoj David is a 32 year old musician and aspiring writer. David enjoys jazz, family, cooking and just enjoying life.

Larry Duplechan is the author of numerous novels, including *Captain Swing* and *Tangled Up in Blue*. He lives in his hometown of Los Angeles.

MacArthur Flourney has been in ministry for twenty years, starting as a missionary in Lagos, Nigeria, West Africa in 1989. His life work is committed to access to health care for marginalized communities, human rights, public policy and justice for all humanity, particularly in the area of HIV/AIDS/substance use.

Steven G. Fullwood, author of the book of essays *FUNNY*, serves as founder/archivist for the Black Gay and Lesbian Archive at the Schomburg Center for Research in Black Culture, New York Public Library in New York City.

Sanford E. Gaylord is an actor, creative activist and award-wining writer. He's performed at the Randolph Street Gallery, Black Ensemble Theatre and in the Jeff nominated musical, *Being Beautiful*, at the Bailiwick Repertory. His film/T.V. credits include *Leaving the Shadows Behind*, *Living with Pride* and *Kevin's Room*.

L. Michael Gipson author of *Collisions: A Collection of Intersections* has worked in journalism, public health, and youth development for 15 years. He is also co-founder of the *Beyond Identities Community Center*, a multi-focused youth drop-in center that has served the needs of over 1500 youth since 2004.

John-Martin Green is Co-founder and Director of Programs for The Black Men's Xchange-New York (BMXNY), an empowerment organization of same gender loving (SGL) and bisexual African descended men which work to bridge gaps and build dialogue and community with the larger Black community.

Timothy Hampton a native of Columbia, TN, is the author and producer of the play *"You Shall Live!"* His organization Thunder Kellie Productions seeks to assist those that are affected with HIV/AIDS.

Reginald Harris is a recipient of the Individual Artist Awards for both poetry and fiction from the Maryland State Arts Council. Harris authors *10 Tongues* and is a co-compiler of *Carry the Word: A Bibliography of Black LGBTQ*.

Charles W. Harvey is an award-winning writer of fiction, poetry and drama. His story *Cheeseburger* won the 1987 PEN/Southwest Award. His work has appeared in *Shade*, *Soulfires*, the *James White Review* and other publications.

Jair- The Literary Masturbator is a poet, spoken word artist, vocalist and activist living in Oakland, CA. He is the author of *Touch Poems & Other Writings of Love, Erotica, and Sensuality*

G. Winston James, a Jamaican-born poet, short fiction writer, essayist and editor, James authors two poetry collections: *The Damaged Good* and *Lyric*. James is also co-editor of *Voices Rising* and *Spirited*. His first collection of short fiction is *Shaming the Devil*.

Dwayne Jenkins is the coordinator of Brothers United Network of Tennessee, Inc. a collective of African American Gay/SGL Men that seek to provide community empowerment and self actualization through its individual BU Chapters in Nashville, Chattanooga, Memphis, Knoxville, and West TN.

Cornelius Jones is an actor, writer, activist, arts educator, motivator, and storyteller. In 2001, he landed his first Broadway show, *Thou Shalt Not*. Currently he serves as a resident artist educator for Opening Act New York.

Rickey Laurentiis is a Cave Canem Fellow and student at Sarah Lawrence College, N.Y. His work is published or forthcoming in *Indiana Review, Knockout Literary Magazine, Nashville Review* and *jubilat*.

Renita Martin is a playwright, performer and poet whose one woman shows include Five Bottle in a Six Pack performed at Cherry Lane Theatre in New York City. She is Artistic Director of *Rhythm Visions Productions*.

Greg McNeal is a photographer based in Southern California who specializes in creating artistic, empowering images of African-American men. McNeal's work has toured with the Smithsonian Institute. He has shot political events, HIV Campaigns, celebrity and political field galas.

Tommie V. McNeil is an HIV/AIDS Activist and Educator. He has guest lectured at various civic organizations and churches including Webster University Counseling/University of Minnesota Divinity Program and John's Hopkins Bloomberg School of Public Health Center.

Alan Miller is the author of the chapbook *At the Club*. He appeared reading/performing some of his poems in Marlon Riggs's documentary *Tongues Untied*. His appeared in numerous publications including *Brother to Brother*, *The Road Before Us* and *Sojourner: Black Gay Voices in the Age of AIDS*.

Travis Montez is a native Tennessee poet whose poetry collections include *Reluctant Poet* and *Montez was Here*.

Lisa C. Moore is the founder and editor of RedBone Press, which publishes work celebrating the culture of black lesbians and gay men that promotes understanding between black gays and lesbians and the black mainstream.

Letta Neely is a Boston based poet and playwright whose poetry collections include *juba* and *here*. Her plays include the powerful drama *Hamartia Blues: Stuck in the Game*.

Durell Owens is the author of the novel *The Song of a Manchild*. His short story, *Unfinished Business* has appeared in *Rebel Yell 2 More Stories of Contemporary Southern Gay Men*.

Richard Peacock is a graduate of Morehouse College and Florida Atlantic University. His work has been recognized by the Hurston Wright Foundation and he has received writing fellowships including one from the Vermont Studio Center.

Donald Peebles is a writer whose poems and short stories have been published in *Writes of Passage USA*, *SBC*, *Shoutout!* and *Urban Dialogue*. Peebles' short story *Social Studies* was included in the anthology *Flesh to Flesh*. He authors the novel *Hidden Fires*.

Poet On Watch is the founder & director for the Media Arts & Literacy Institute, in Austin, Texas. P.O.W. is traditional in the Diaspora sense of a poet as historian, storyteller, Spiritual Griot/ sacred Word keeper/ traditional like the poets of the 60's who used blood memories to create a context for revolution.

Malaysia Andrews-Ravore is a nationally known female impersonator, seamstress, make-up artist and gifted cook. Her coveted titles include Miss International, Inc.

Benjamin L. Reynolds lives in Chicago, and is a PhD student at the Chicago Theological Seminary focusing on Theology, Ethics and Human Sciences. He also directs the LBTQ Religious Studies Center at CTS and serves as a Transitional Pastor at the Pilgrim Congregational Church in Oak Park, Illinois.

Stewart Shaw writes poetry, fiction and essays. He is affiliated with several organizations including Cave Canem and B/GLAM (Black Gay Letters and Arts Movement).

Lucy Shumbert is an artist, poet, writer who has two collections of poetry entitled, *Shades of Gray and Other Rainbow Colors* and *My Bible Memory Book*. Her one-woman show, *"The Butterfly Collection"*, was performed by the Theatre Department of Tuskegee Institute, Tuskegee, AL.

Taylor Siluwe, after studying creative writing at New York University, his first erotically charged short story, *"A Taste for Cherries"* appeared in the anthology, *Tough Guys*. His work has since appeared in the anthologies, *Law of Desire* and *Best Gay Erotica 2008*.

Charles Michael Smith is a freelance journalist and book reviewer in New York City. He has written for several newspapers and magazines. His work was included in *In the Life: A Black Gay Anthology*. He is also the editor of *Fighting Words: Essays by Black Gay Men*

Justin B. Terry-Smith has been an HIV and Gay Civil Rights activist in the Washington DC area since 1998. Justin writes for many publications including *GBMNews.com*, *Baltimore Gay Life*, *POZIAM Radio* and *Swerve Magazine*.

R. Bryant Smith is author of two novels: *When The Children Get Together* and *Let It Be Real*. Smith is also the author of a short story collection entitled *Blessed and Highly Favored*.

Max Smith is a long time activist and African America's 3rd Rail who resides in Chicago, IL. His essays have appeared in many publications including *In the Life: A Black Gay Anthology*.

Doug Cooper Spencer is a writer, lecturer and commentator living in Cincinnati. He writes commentary for various publications. His novels include *This Place of Men* and *People Like Us*.

Buster Spiller is a freelance writer, government sub-contractor, performing artist and founder/owner of a Dallas-based theater company. Buster is an occasional *Viewpoints* columnist for a number of publications, including the *Dallas Morning News*, *Dallas Voice*, and *Windy City Times*.

H.L. Sudler has been a publisher, editor, essayist, and novelist. He served as a book critic for the LGBT publication *Lambda Book Report*. His essays and columns have appeared in numerous newspapers and magazines, including the recent anthology *Spirited*. He recently completed a new book of essays *Patriarch*.

Jonathan "Jona Bryant" Thomason is a Cincinnati, OH native. His poetry is a mesh of raw complex thoughts and emotions in free flowing form.

Clay Turner has written on a broad range of topics for local newspapers, e-journals and poetry magazine. He resides in Washington, D.C. with his partner of 22 years.

Tim'm T. West is a teacher, performance artist, author, and cultural producer, has become an exemplar among contemporary Renaissance personalities of the early 21st Century as he brings others to voice through education for critical consciousness.

LaCelle N. White is an aspiring writer who currently resides in Augusta, GA where she works in health care administration.

Marvin K. White is author of two poetry collections: *last rights* and *nothin' ugly fly*. He is a poet, performer, playwright, visual artist and community arts organizer.

Darius Omar Williams is the author of two poetry collections: *Silk Electric* and *Akhona*. His first novel, *Blue Light 'Til Dawn* will be released in 2011.

Phillip B. Williams is a Cave Canem Fellow and Chicago, IL native. His poetry has appeared or is forthcoming in *The Drunken Boat, Reverie, Mythium, Tidal Basin, Gertrude* and others. Phillip works as an HIV tester/counselor.

L. Lamar Wilson, a Cave Canem Fellow, is published or forthcoming in journals and anthologies, including *Rattle, Crab Orchard Review* and *100 Best African-American Poems*, edited by Nikki Giovanni. His essays have appeared in the *Milwaukee Journal Sentinel, Atlanta Journal-Constitution* and *Washington Post*.

Larry Wilson (aka Dapharoah69, The King of Erotica) is co-editor of the anthology *Voices From Within*. His first book, *The King of Erotica: The Throne* is a collection of erotic short stories that touches on taboo topics.

Vince Wilson is a Black, gay social observer, writer & musician. Vince is currently based in Philadelphia, PA.

Mystalic Writing is a native Philadelphian poet. His first poetry collection, *Chronicles Of A Gay Man's Pen* is the first of a mass collection of "Alternative Poetry".

ABOUT THE EDITORS

R. BRYANT SMITH is author of two novels: *When The Children Get Together* and *Let It Be Real* and a collection of short stories entitled *Blessed & Highly Favored*. Smith matriculated and graduated magna cum laude from Lane College, Jackson, Tennessee. He is also a UNCF Andrew F. Mellon/Benjamin Mays Fellow.

DARIUS OMAR WILLIAMS is the author of two poetry collections: *Silk Electric* and *Akhona*. His first novel, *Blue Light 'Til Dawn* will be released in 2011. He holds a M.A. in Theatre from Bowling Green State University and an M.F.A. in Creative Writing from Antioch University Los Angeles. Currently, Darius is a Ph.D. candidate in Theatre at The Ohio State University.